HANDBOOK OF RADIO COMMUNICATIONS AND ENGINEERING

HANDBOOK OF RADIO COMMUNICATIONS AND ENGINEERING

Volume 1

James Stewart
Addison Grant

Kruger Brentt
Publishers
2026

Kruger Brentt Publishers UK. LTD.
Company Number 9728962

Regd. Office: 68 St Margarets Road, Edgware, Middlesex HA8 9UU

ISBN: 978-1-78715-642-5 (Vol. 1)

Disclaimer:

Every possible effort has been made to ensure that the information contained in this book is accurate at the time of going to press, and the publisher and author cannot accept responsibility for any errors or omissions, however caused. No responsibility for loss or damage occasioned to any person acting, or refraining from action, as a result of the material in this publication can be accepted by the editor, the publisher or the author. The Publisher is not associated with any product or vendor mentioned in the book. The contents of this work are intended to further general scientific research, understanding and discussion only. Readers should consult with a specialist where appropriate.

Every effort has been made to trace the owners of copyright material used in this book, if any. The author and the publisher will be grateful for any omission brought to their notice for acknowledgement in the future editions of the book.

For information on all our publications visit our website at http://krugerbrentt.com/

PREFACE

Radio communications form the backbone of modern telecommunication systems, enabling wireless connectivity across vast distances and supporting applications ranging from mobile networks and satellite communications to emergency services and defense systems. As technology advances, the field of radio communications continues to evolve rapidly, integrating new methodologies, devices, and signal processing techniques.

Handbook of Radio Communications and Engineering provides a comprehensive reference for students, engineers, and researchers in the field of wireless communications and radio engineering. The book covers fundamental principles, modern technologies, system design, and practical applications, offering a detailed exploration of both theoretical and applied aspects. Topics such as modulation techniques, antennas, wave propagation, RF circuits, signal processing, and emerging technologies are addressed in depth to provide a well-rounded understanding of the field.

The text aims to bridge the gap between foundational knowledge and practical engineering solutions, making it a valuable resource for academic study, research, and professional practice. It emphasizes problem-solving, design considerations, and real-world applications to equip readers with the tools required for effective communication system development and analysis.

James Stewart

Addison Grant

CONTENTS

VOLUME 2

Chapter 1 RADIO COMMUNICATION ARCHITECTURES

1. INTRODUCTION: AN OVERVIEW

Wireless communications, including radio communications, are extensively utilized for many daily requirements. Numerous examples exist, with standard designations such as BLUETOOTH, WiFi, WiMAX, UMTS, GSM, and, more recently, LTE being widely recognized [Baudoin et al. 2007]. Numerous publications address general applications within the domains of RFID and UWB. This chapter delineates the architecture of radio-frequency (RF) communication systems for mobile wireless local area networks (WLAN) and connectivity terminals. A significant facet of contemporary applications is the escalation of data rates, particularly in connectivity protocols such as WiFi and WiMAX, due to user demands for high Quality of Service (QoS). To enhance the data rate, we typically employ wideband or multi-standard architectures. The notion of software radio encompasses a self-reconfigurable radio link, which is delineated below about its RF characteristics. The phrase "multi-radio" is favored. This chapter concentrates on the transmitter, while also addressing certain aspects of the receiver. A crucial element of the architecture is that a transceiver is constructed in accordance with radio-communication signals. In section 2, we categorize them by distinguishing between Continuous Wave (CW) and Impulse Radio (IR) systems. Section 3 provides the technical background necessary for practical applications. Section 4 encapsulates cutting-edge high data rate architectures and the most recent advancements in multi-radio systems. Section 5 presents IR architectures for Ultra Wide Band (UWB) systems, highlighting the coexistence and compatibility problems between Continuous Wave (CW) and IR systems.

2. TRANSCEIVER ASPECTS FOR RADIO-COMMUNICATIONS

2.1 Radio communications signals

Radio-communications applications deal with communicating and non-communicating links with their different parameters. People expect high quality from their different services (QoS) whatever the telecommunications system used. For example, voice (low data rate) or visio-phone and multimedia download (high data rate) are assumed to be present on the new generation mobile phone. This reveals the co-existence and interaction goals between mobile communication systems (GSM, GSM EDGE, UMTS...) and connectivity standards (BLUETOOTH, WiFI, WiMAX...) [Baudoin et al., 2007]. Thanks to Impulse Radio

Ultra Wide Band (IR-UWB), other fields of interest such as Radio Frequency Identification (RFID) and localization systems are examples of where radio-communications transceivers are currently being designed. Each kind of application can be classified by the resulting radio signals emitted/received. Determining factors are (i) the use of power efficient or spectrum efficient modulation schemes, (ii) the frequency and type of carrier signal used: Continuous Wave (CW) or Impulse Radio (IR) based signals and (iii) the data rate needed (defining a major subdivision of CW based systems). Depending on the choice of the factors involved, the design faced by the RF architect can be varied and challenging. We differentiate three types of cases in this chapter, as illustrated in Fig. 1.

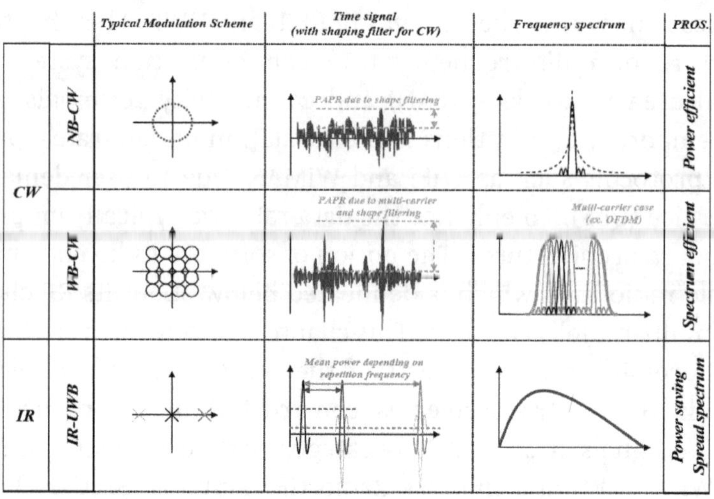

Fig. 1. Main types of radio-communications signals

NarrowBand CW (NB-CW) systems, like GSM (GMSK), EDGE (D-QPSK), BLUETOOTH, RFID tags, etc... These systems are often power efficient modulation schemes (EDGE is an exception) because these applications use a low data rate transfer. Major problems of the NB-CW architecture involve with the coexistence and the signal protection against interferers or blocking signals. Some spread-spectrum techniques are often added to improve the communication range (frequency-hopping in the case of BLUETOOTH). The NB-CW case is also considered to be the classic radio communications link and reference system because it corresponds to the popular AM/FM radio broadcasts. NB-CW systems are often considered as using constant envelope signals. This could be true only if FSK modulation schemes are performed, but it is also possible to use x-QAM low symbol rate modulations (EDGE). Additionally, the shaping filter (root raised cosine filter) implies amplitude variations (non-constant envelope) even on FSK modulated signals (GSM).

WideBand CW (WB-CW) systems, like: UMTS (W-CDMA), WiMAX (OFDM enhanced), LTE (OFDM based), WiFI (OFDM), UWB (OFDM version)... These systems correspond to high data rate transfer, often for multimedia applications. We can see an increasing need in this field of interest due to the large number of new standards which can be found. Due to the bandwidth limitations for each standard, the modulation scheme is often spectrum efficient (x-QAM) and the use of multi-carrier transmission is usually performed, e.g., OFDM or MC-CDMA. Since there are high amplitude variations of such signals, the transceiver architecture is designed in function with the unavoidable non-linear effects (NL) caused by the power amplification block. Emitting a high PAPR (Peak to Average Power Ratio) has always been a well-known transmitter challenge. The linearization of such a transmitter is mandatory and will be discussed in part 3. WB-CW transceivers also need a wideband design for all of its key elements: antennas, LNA (Low Noise amplifier), HPA (High Power Amplifier) and mixers. This often results in lower performance of the abovementioned blocks than for NB-CW systems.

IR-UWB systems such as UWB localization systems, RFID-UWB... These systems are special because they are based on (one of the) spread spectrum techniques in order to protect the information. The idea is to spread the information in frequency while lowering the emitted power. The use of UWB (3.1-10.6 GHz in the USA) was highly discussed in order to evaluate its co-existence with NB-CW and WB-CW. What is important here is how the power amplification is processed differently for this type of communication. An average power is defined in function of the Pulse Repetition Frequency (PRF), given by the specifications of the IR-UWB standard. For a fixed emitted power: the shorter the pulse, the higher the instantaneous power and bandwidth. Transceivers for these signals are based on impulse generators and energy detectors or correlation receivers, see section 5.

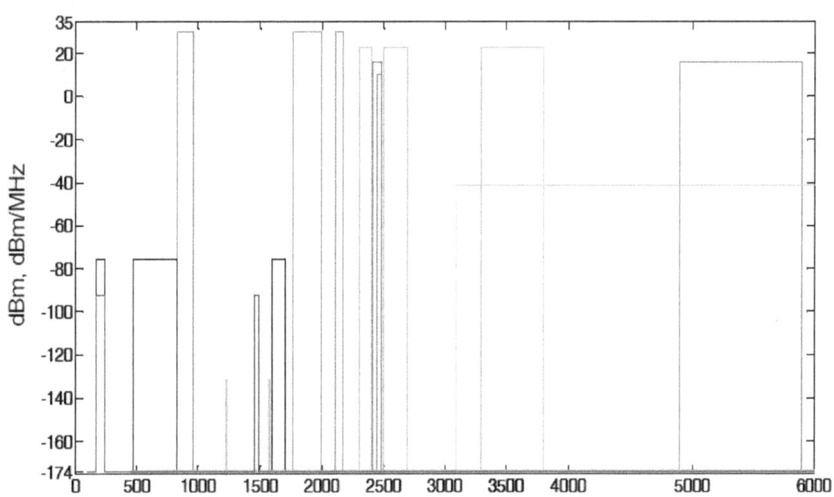

Fig. 2. Telecommunications spectrum sharing and power limitations up to 6 GHz

The three types described can represent every kind of radio-communications signal. The characteristics which have an impact on the architecture are mainly the centre frequency (choice of the technology) and bandwidth (circuits' topologies and performance limitations), and also the PAPR for CW signals. Fig. 2 qualitatively summarizes the power limitations and frequency specifications for some telecommunications standards up to 6 GHz: cellular, WiMAX, WiFI, Bluetooth, UWB and DVB-H. The goal of RF architecture is to emit and receive such signals with no alteration of the information (no constellation distortion for CW). Designing the architecture implies other considerations such as noise, linearity, efficiency and systems co-existence and immunity. The receiver part of a transceiver has to correctly identify information without adding too much noise, even when high power unwanted signals are close (in the frequency domain). The transmitter part has to linearly amplify the signal in order to emit as far as possible, respecting the standard power limitations (spectrum mask) for co-existence. Architectures for NB-CW, WB-CW and IR-UWB use some basic elements (blocks) that will be described in the next sub-section. Multi-radio is interpreted as a possible reconfigurable architecture for most of the signals presented (mainly NB-CW and WB-CW). This helps drive improvements on classic structures.

2.2 Basic elements and their imperfections

Transceiver architectures for radio-communications signals is defined from the Digital to Analog Converter (DACs, in the baseband section) to the transmitter (Tx) antenna and, respectively, from the receiving (Rx) antenna to the Analog to Digital Converter (ADCs). Each of the Tx and Rx sections deal with unavoidable tradeoffs such as linearity/efficiency (Tx), noise/gain (Rx). Other transceivers in the spectrum vicinity are supposed to correctly receive (co-existence) and/or emit their signals (immunity) without lowering QoS. The basic functions (blocks) in radio-communications are conversion (digital/analog), high frequency transposition and modulation, filtering, power or low noise amplification and radiation/sensing (Tx/Rx antenna).

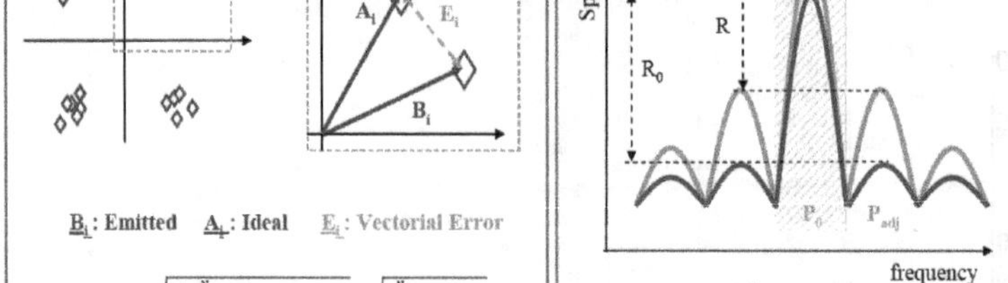

$$EVM_{rms} = \sqrt{\frac{\frac{1}{N}\sum_{i=1}^{N}|A_i - C_1B_i - C_0|^2}{\frac{1}{N}\sum_{i=1}^{N}|A_i|^2}} = \sqrt{\frac{\sum_{i=1}^{N}|A_i - S_i|^2}{\sum_{i=1}^{N}|A_i|^2}}$$

$$ACPR = \frac{P_0}{P_{adj}} = \frac{\int_{P_0} DSP(f)\,df}{\int_{P_{adj}} DSP(f)\,df}$$

Fig. 3. EVM and ACPR definitions

Here, we are describing a system and how it relates to these blocks in radio-communications architecture. We will focus on their imperfections and their impact on the system performance (noise, spectrum distortion...). Sometimes, for CW standards, the influence of noise or spectral re-growths is quantified by certain criteria such as the EVM and/or the ACPR as defined in Fig. 3 [Baudoin et al., 2007] [Villegas et al., 2007].

DACs and ADCs will not be presented in details because their performance in terms of bandwidth (up to 100 MHz) and resolution (up to 16 bits) is almost sufficient for today's radio-communications signals. The main limitations are the current consumption of fast converters and the difficulty in designing near-GHz Sigma Delta ($\Sigma\Delta$) encoders, often in the context of polar transmitters as is presented in section 4. It should be noticed that for WBCW signals, the bandwidth limitation is the criterion of choice and a source of important spectrum degradation (approximated qualitatively by a windowing effect).

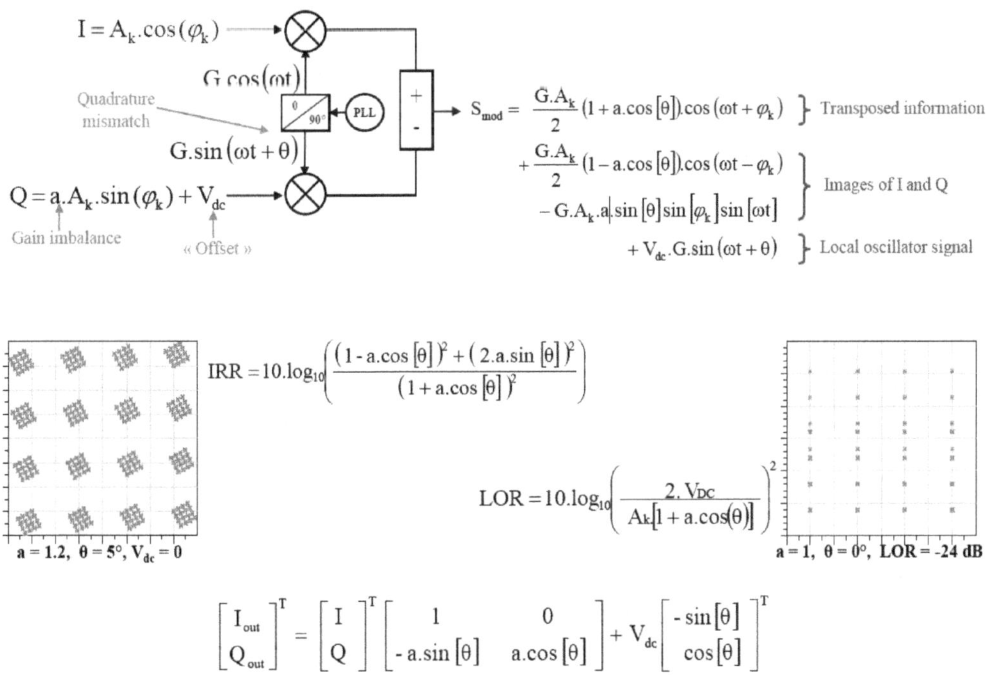

Fig. 4. IQ modulator equations and the effects of its imperfections

The IQ modulator is the block providing the transposition of the information at high frequency (up-converter) or at baseband/intermediate frequency (down-converter). We describe the case of the up-converter for simplicity. It needs the baseband information components I and Q (I and Q channels) and a carrier frequency signal, provided by a frequency synthesizer. Key components are the non-linear multipliers provided thanks to passive (PIN diodes...) or active circuits

(Gilbert cell...). Every component should be carefully designed with regards to the synthesizer frequency value. Moreover, the noise added by the multipliers will be impossible to filter. The main difficulty for the modulator is the perfect matching between I and Q paths. As is reported in Fig. 4 (at one fixed frequency), gain and phase imbalances (a and θ) create unwanted images of the information. Also the presence of an offset VDC can create the emission of the synthesized carrier frequency (called Local Oscillator, LO). All of these imperfections result in the distortion of the information and are quantified by the IRR and LOR power ratio (the actual performance is in the range of -50 dB). These imperfections are not seen on the spectrum because their equivalent added noise is inside the main lobe. The biggest challenge concerns the modulation of wideband signals because it is hard for the modulator to perform and to be frequency independent (over the entire bandwidth). An example of this can be seen in the conversion gain (ratio between the RF output power and the baseband input power). A variation of this gain produces an unwanted AM on the emitted signal and can distort the information. Another problem is the image frequency. This effect is due to the multiplication of signals in a modulator. A multiplication of harmonic signals results in two signals whose frequencies are, respectively, the sum and the difference of the input frequencies. This duality is mathematically illustrated and discussed for the case of the receiver in Fig. 16, section 3. At the outgoing emission, an image is created at RF and increases the EVM. At the reception (only for heterodyne architectures), an image frequency different from RF can be sensed and interpreted as unwanted information which increases the EVM, too. This is illustrated in section 3.3 with the presentation of the Hartley and Weaver image rejection receiver architectures for NB-CW. To conclude, the effects of the IQ modulator imperfections are: non-linearities, noise and the possibility of image frequencies. Selective filtering and stable reference signals are needed to improve the system (easier for NB-CW than for WB-CW).

Frequency synthesizers are blocks which produce a stable reference signal for transposition. RF architectures need flexibility and stability in the choice of their reference frequency. It is usually not possible to provide this simultaneously with a simple oscillator circuit such as Quartz (stable), SAWR... The stabilization and synthesis by a Phase Lock Loop (PLL) is usually necessary. The PLL is a looped system whose different designs will not be discussed here, only its system's characteristics, which are reported in Fig. 5. The worst imperfection of the PLL is its phase noise. An example of the resulting phase noise profile of a synthesizer is illustrated in Fig. 5 (N=1). The different transfer functions of each noise of the sub-blocks are reported in the same figure. The great challenge of the PLL is to keep the stability performance of the synthesized signals for different values of N. It is also possible to modulate the signal in frequency by directly adding the baseband information on the Voltage Controlled Oscillator (VCO) input. This is called an "over the loop" modulation. For CW systems, synthesizers are used to produce the different Local Oscillators (LOs) needed for transposition(s) and for channel selection (fine tuning of the LO value). PLL can be used to transpose the information, but only for angular modulations schemes: PM, PSK, FSK or FM. This is not usually used for constant envelope WB-CW signals for noise and stability reasons.

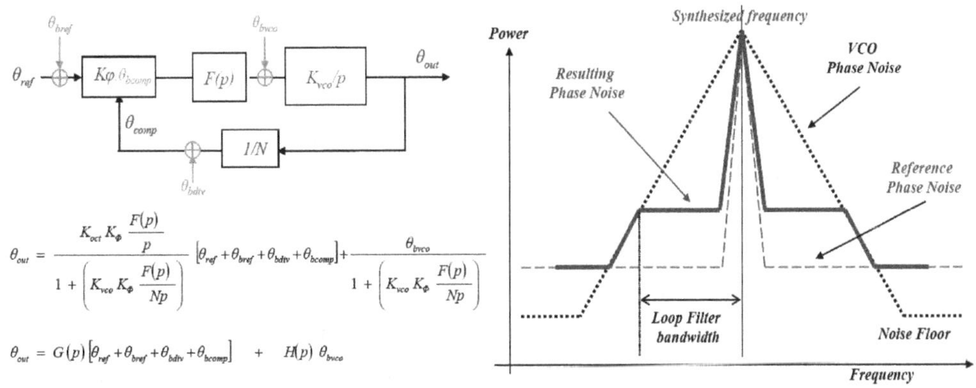

Fig. 5. PLL functional blocks and frequency synthesizer phase noise

RF filters are essential in communications chains for information selectivity (interferences, noise, image-filtering for example). They are used at emission (limiting spectral re-growths), reception (rejecting unwanted signals) and for channel selection (high selectivity for discrimination and for image rejection). Their system characteristics are well-known: attenuation/rejection, selectivity, ripple, group delay... Different technologies are used depending on the frequency, implying different sources of imperfections.

At GHz frequencies, LC filtering is preferred for its low noise property but the components' sensitivity (especially for integrated technology) implies low order filters. For higher selectivity, active or high speed digital filters can be used, but often need a frequency transposition section due to the circuit bandwidth and the sampling rate limitations. Moreover, these filters consume power and add much noise (circuit or quantification).

Whatever the technology used, the wider the bandwidth the higher the ripple (oscillation of the transfer function). This ripple problem introduces an unwanted amplitude variation. In order to reduce this, the order is increased as much as possible and some prototype functions like Butterworth or Cauer are chosen for the design. Attenuation in the rejection band is worst in these cases. Additionally, the group delay of the filter is mandatory for non-distortion of the information. For NB-CW, it is usually not a problem but the phase response has to be linear for WB-CW and IR-UWB systems. In the case of a multi-band system, being linear in each sub-band is sufficient. These remarks point out that filters for WB-CW are more difficult to design than filters for NB-CW due to the performance limitations over the bandwidth.

To conclude, the RF filters imperfections are modeled by their noise factors (noise added, distortions and non constant group delays), insertion losses (due to the ripples and mismatches) and selectivity (finite attenuation of unwanted frequencies).

Power Amplifiers (PA) in RF architectures are designed to linearly amplify radiocommunication signals with the highest efficiency possible and with the lowest spectrum re-growths or added noise (see spectrum mask/ACPR and EVM criteria to respect). Since the active components of the amplifier are operating at maximum power, non-linear (NL) compression/conversion and memory effects are unavoidable (Fig. 6). The PA design, identified as "class of operation", impacts the performances [Villegas et al., 2007][Diet et al., 2004-2007]. Efficiency and linearity of the PA are mandatory for NB-CW and WB-CW architecture because the signal is transmitting information continuously. Low efficiency reduces battery lifetime and increases the dissipated power and the temperature of the circuit. Low linearity affects the quality of the signal. For IR-UWB systems, only peak performances in time are needed (see section 5). We are focusing upon the PA impact on the architecture in the case of the CW system. The most difficult case is for WB-CW due to the bandwidth, and the usual high PAPR of chosen modulation schemes (high data rate). A PA class of operation is determined by the hypothesis of transistor saturation (current source or switch). There are two families of PA classes: the switched mode (SW) and the continuous wave (CW) or biased mode. The different load-lines are illustrated in Fig. 6 (right).

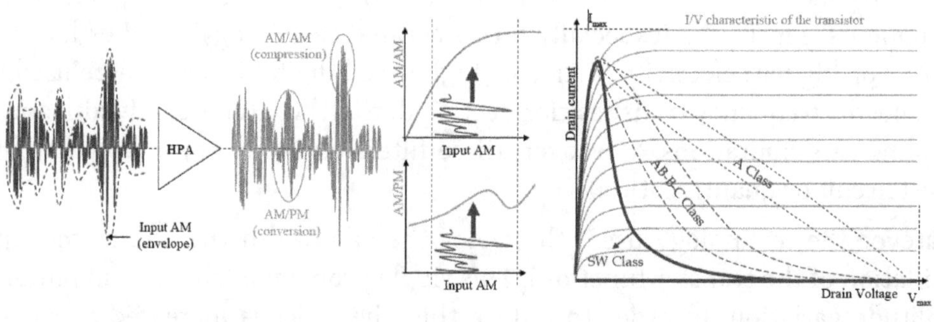

Fig. 6. AM/AM, AM/PM effects (without memory effects) and PA class load-lines

Due to the need of polarization, CW classes (namely A, B, AB and C) present lower efficiency than SW classes (D, S, E and F). SW classes need a switching of the transistor and cannot reproduce an amplitude modulation for that reason. Their linearity is also worse than in CW classes because of this switching operation. Moreover, it is possible to restore the amplitude information by adjusting the voltage supply. This is theoretically linear in the case of SW classes and there is a tracking effect for CW classes. For AM signals the average efficiency will rely on the statistical properties of the signal itself. Additionally, it is important to consider that efficiency is given as a peak value for CW classes. An improvement in efficiency is gained if saturation/clipping on the peak values is introduced in order to increase the average power of the output signal for the same power dissipated by the amplifier. WB-CW signals for high data rate applications present such a high PAPR that the amplification by a CW class PA requires a power back off (very low efficiency) or a linearization technique to reduce the NL effects of compression (AM/AM) and conversion (AM/PM), see Fig. 6. Techniques which are interesting for the designer in the case of wideband and high PAPR signal are those providing the highest efficiency of the entire architecture including the PA (see section 3). Polynomial modeling of the AM/AM can be done by the PA response to 1 or 2 frequency signals, called 1 or 2 tons. These indicators are the 1 dB compression point (P1dB) and the 3rd order Interception Point (IP3), as defined in Fig. 7.

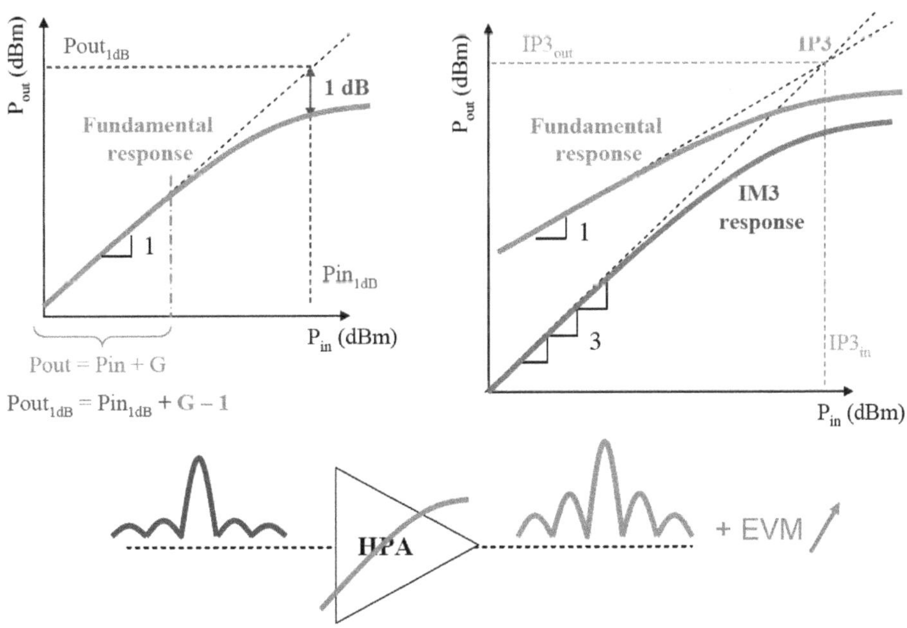

Fig. 7. Compression effect modeling for 1 ton (P1dB) and 2 tons (IP3)

These are considered to illustrate the main PA imperfections. AM/AM and AM/PM measurements, when it is possible to take them, can be the best way of characterizing the effects of the PA on the architecture: EVM and noise factor increase and spectral re-growths (ACPR, spectrum mask). In CW systems, the PA has to amplify modulated signals (a sum of several tons). For NB-CW signals, the PA behavior is well-characterized by the P1dB and the input power is usually set at this value for the linearity/efficiency trade-off (if the PAPR is not too high). In the case of WB-CW, the IP3 is a good representation of NL effects on the spectrum if the frequency separation of the two tons is coherent with the modulated bandwidth (symbol rate frequency). Moreover, the conversion effects are, by far, more complex to analyze. It is almost impossible to determine an equivalent of the P1dB or the IP3 for AM/PM. This relies upon the influence of transistor technology. For wideband and high PAPR signals, the conversion effect increases the EVM significantly and often destroys the information.

SW classes are based on the hypothesis that the transistor switches perfectly (no power dissipated). The filtering is mandatory in RF applications, except if the SW PA is dedicated to the amplification of a square signal (class D). The load-line of every SW PA class tends to be that of an ideal switch, which is impossible in practice due to the physical realities of the transistor (resistive and capacitive output effects). Although the switching cannot be perfect, SW classes present higher efficiency than CW classes, see the 100% efficiency class E PA [Sokal & Sokal, 1975][Raab et al., 2003][Diet et al., 2008]. Moreover, they are used for AM signals only with a recombination process: supply modulation or amplification of an envelope coded signal (PWM, ΣΔ) [Robert et al., 2009][Suarez et al., 2008]. Using supply modulation creates NL effects of compression and conversion on the output signal. These effects are named Vdd/AM and Vdd/PM [Diet et al., 2004]. For new RF architectures, high efficiency (SW) classes are preferred due to their high efficiency, but the challenge then shifts to the linearity of the amplified signals. Whatever the CW system is, NL effects of the PA are unavoidable and are sources of important imperfections (i.e., loss of linearity). In the case of high PAPR signals, a correction or a modification of the architecture is needed, as is presented in the following section.

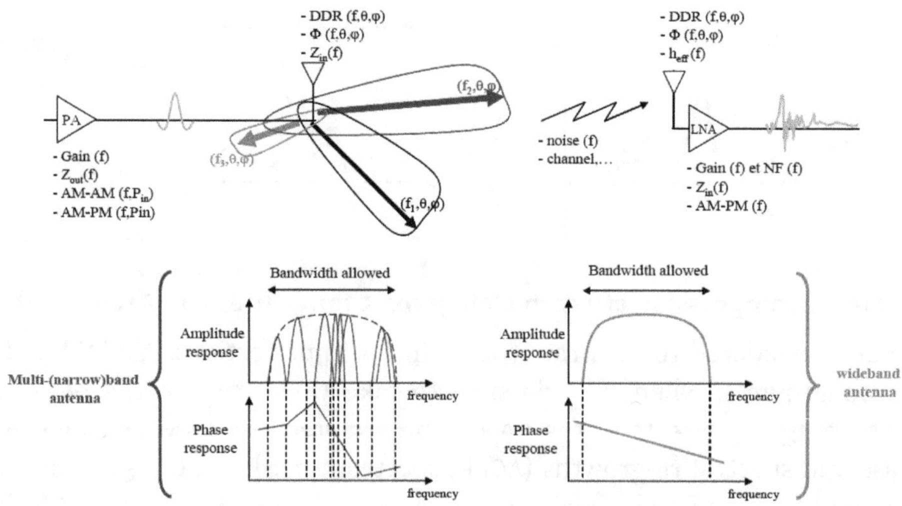

Fig. 8. Antenna system characteristics in radio-communications

Antenna characteristics from a "system" point of view are reciprocal interfaces between electrical and radiated signals. Depending on the application, antennas have to be adapted to their environment (omni-directivity of their radiation pattern, polarization...). Fig. 8 summarizes the different system parameters of an antenna that can influence the performance of the radio-communications link: spatial and frequency variations of the radiation pattern, bandwidth limitations and phase distortion. Some of the imperfections are equivalent to those of the filter, but they depend on the signal direction and the channel. For wideband systems, i.e. WB-CW and IR-UWB, the use of a UWB antenna is mandatory for keeping the phase information unaltered [Schantz, 2005]. For NB-CW and separated multi-band signals using a wide bandwidth (see Fig. 8), the use of a multi-band antenna is sufficient. The latter can present phase linearity only for used sub-bands [Diet et al., 2006]. To conclude, the communications channel composed of the emitting and receiving antennas and the propagation channel is the source of amplitude and phase distortion, with a statistical dependence on time and space. Noise is added and the techniques of signal protection and antenna diversity (e.g., MIMO) are exploited as much as possible to improve the system's range.

3. ARCHITECTURE BASICS

RF architectures are adapted to radio-communications signals and provide emission and reception. Linearity improvements are needed when power amplification NLs can destroy the information. This section first focuses on the transmitter section where different major modifications are described. We especially focus on CW systems because of their important challenges about efficiency and linearity.

3.1 Classic architectures for RF transmitters

Radio-communications architecture is composed of the above-mentioned blocks in section 2 and provides the emission and reception of the signal. There exist three kinds of basic architectures, the classic ones, designed for NB-CW systems (the oldest application of which is radio broadcasting): homodyne, heterodyne and PLL modulated.

The homodyne architecture means that the I and Q signals (the information after DACs) is transposed directly from baseband to RF see Fig. 9. If the modulation scheme is not x-QAM, there is only one frequency transposition in the transmitter. This type of architecture is the simplest combination of function blocks and theoretically requires the minimum number of components.

If the signal is transposed directly to RF, the frequency synthesizer output is at the same frequency value, and so is the HPA and the antenna. In a compact system (mobile phones for example), the spatial proximity is the cause of unavoidable coupling between the synthesizer, the HPA and the antenna. This problem of electromagnetic coupling (EMC, EM Compatibility) is that it highly distorts the signal (EVM increase). EMC effects can be reduced by circuit spatial optimization, when possible, and more efficiently with a shielding of the considered block (LO, HPA). Additionally, a ground plane acting as a reflector can be added between the antenna and these elements (HPA and/or LO synthesizer) to reduce the amount of radiated waves toward the circuit. Choosing the homodyne structure results from multiple trade-offs concerning the EVM, the simplicity and the size of the system.

The heterodyne architecture, as represented in Fig. 9, means that the frequency transposition is achieved in two or more steps. In fact, heterodyne means that the frequency synthesizers are not at RF values. Any combination is possible, but for a minimum use of components only two transpositions are usually performed. As the frequencies are different, the coupling effect is highly reduced in this architecture. In heterodyne structures, there are more components than in homodyne ones (with at least one filter and one additional mixer) and imperfection sources are added. For example, the phase noise is a function of the number of synthesizers. An additional mixer also means the possibility of an image frequency that can distort the emitted information if the intermediate frequency (IF) filter is not selective enough. This IF filter is traditionally an external SAW one (because of its selectivity). This increases the cost and complexity of building this system. An advantage of the heterodyne architecture is that the need of frequency flexibility for channel selection can be more easily achieved with two synthesizers than with one (homodyne case).

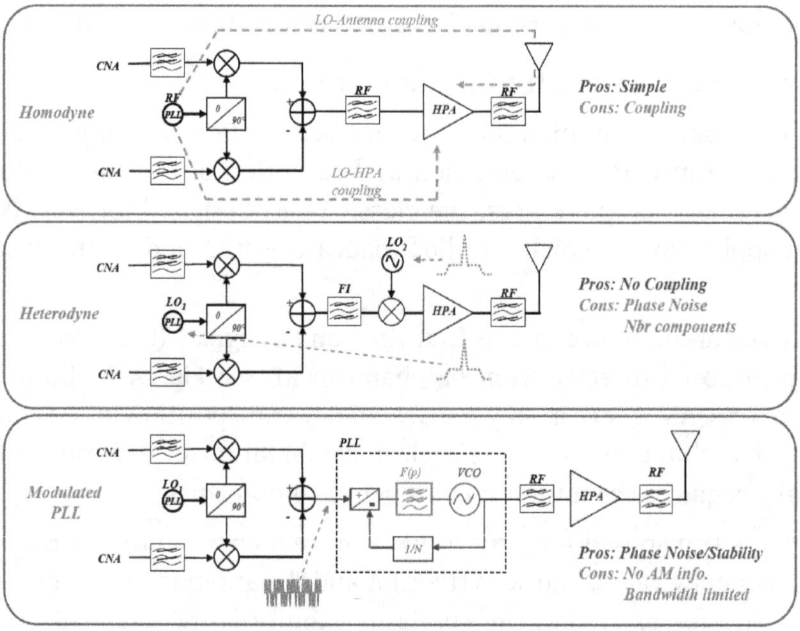

Fig. 9. Classic architectures for RF transmitters

Architectures using modulated PLL can benefit from PLL advantages. This corresponds to the direct modulation of a synthesizer (with N=1). The signal of a PLL is stable and its noise profile depends on the loop filter bandwidth. It is possible to modulate the PLL by introducing small variations of the reference frequency which will be stabilised by the loop reaction. This is called a modulation "in the loop" and is used for narrow-bandwidth modulations (low symbol rate). On the contrary, the input voltage of the VCO can be directly modulated to produce a wider bandwidth modulation (modulation "over the loop") but this could affect the stability of the PLL. As is understood here, only angular modulations are possible with modulated PLL architectures. If the signal to transmit has AM information, this latter should be reintroduced after the PLL. To conclude, architectures using modulated PLL are very interesting with regards to their noise property (less noise than an IQ modulator) and their design for non-constant envelope signals implies some important modifications of the architecture.

The classic architectures presented are widely used for NB-CW signals. While the efficiency and linearity of the transmitter is not significantly affected, these well-known structures are preferred for their simplicity. In the case of WB-CW systems, the bandwidth and the probable increase of the PAPR (due to high data rate) lower the performance of such architectures. For power amplification in particular, high PAPR values of OFDM and other multi-carrier signals cause such compression and distortion/conversion effects that the information cannot be interpreted at reception. Additionally, standard limitations are, by far, not respected. The first choice is to perform a PA back-off, but this drives it to unacceptably low values for the architecture efficiency. To achieve a linear transmitter, linearization techniques are provided. The next sub-section is dedicated to their descriptions.

3.2 Linearization techniques for the transmitter

Wireless communications require highly efficient and compact transceivers, whatever the signal characteristics are. Transmitter architecture, at worst, must meet design constraints of: providing high efficiency and linearity for a wideband and high PAPR signal (or high dynamic). Power amplification of WB-CW multi-carrier signals (WiFI, WiMAX, LTE...) introduces crippling Non-Linearities (NLs) in amplitude and in phase in the communication system. The linearization of such this kind of transmitter is mandatory. Identifying a type of architecture for such signals requires a careful study of linearization techniques and their performance. A linearization technique is beneficial only if it provides linearity with the maximum efficiency possible. There are several linearization techniques, depending on the PAPR of the signal, the added complexity and the increase in size and consumption of the system that can be accepted by the RF designers [Villegas et al., 2007]. Many criteria characterize the technique used: static/dynamic processing, adaptability, frequency (digital, baseband, IF or RF), correction of memory effects, complexity, stability, resulting efficiency, size increase... Herein, we basically classify these techniques in three types: (i) correction techniques, (ii) anticipation of NLs and (iii) those based on a decomposition and recombination of the signal, often dedicated to wideband signals.

Examples of correction techniques are (A) feed-back, (B) feed-forward and the anticipated technique of (C) pre-distortion, illustrated in Fig. 10. Their point in common is to modify the modulated signal as close as possible to the PA (before or after). The architecture considerations here, do not include the modulator nor the baseband signal processing. To linearize, we need a carefully selected NL model of the PA (Volterra series, Wiener or Saleh model...). Adaptability to the signal amplitude can be introduced in order to compensate for the model's lack of accuracy and the PA memory effects (a temperature influence can be considered) [Baudoin et al., 2007]. Each structure contains a major defect. (A) Feed-back reduces the gain of the amplification and introduces a bandwidth limitation due to the transfer function of the loop (stability and dynamic response). The feed-back can be performed on the amplitude (Polar feed-back) or on I and Q quadrature components of the signal (Cartesian feed-back) and both are dedicated to narrowband signals. (B) Feedforward requires a significant increase in signal processing and RF blocks in the transmitter, with the hypothesis of a precise matching between NLs and reconstructed transfer functions. The improvement in linearity will be costly in terms of consumption and size (integration criterion). The advantages are stability and the possibility to process wideband signals. The most interesting of the three techniques is (C) pre-distortion because of its flexibility: the anticipation can be done in the digital part and, by doing so, can provide adaptability of the technique if using a feed-back loop (with an additional DAC). The digital pre-distortion represents an additional and non-negligible consumption of a Digital Signal Processor (DSP) and often requires a look-up table [Jardin & Baudoin, 2007]. The signal is widened in frequency because of the non-linear law of the pre-distorter (as for NL effects of compression on the spectrum), requiring baseband and RF parts to be wideband designed. Interesting improvements of pre-distortion have been made with OFDM WB-CW signals in [Baudoin et al., 2007] [Jardin & Baudoin, 2007].

Other techniques presented are based on a vectorial decomposition of the signal. The goal is to drive high efficiency switched mode RF PAs with constant envelope (constant power) signals, avoiding AM/AM and AM/PM [Raab et al., 2003] [Diet et al., 2003-2004].

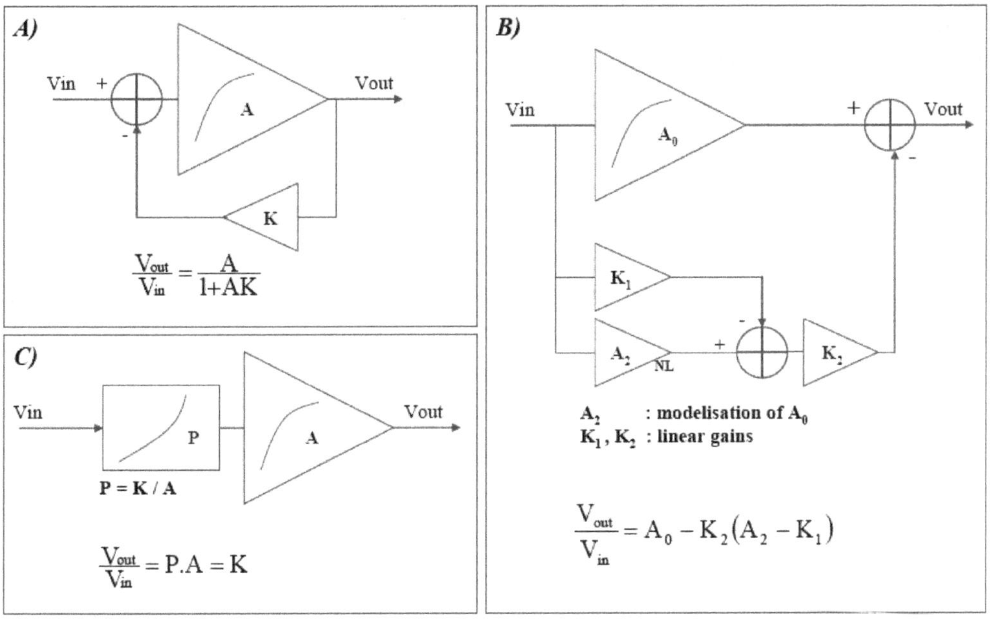

Fig. 10. Correction (A and B) and anticipation (C) linearization techniques

These techniques are used when NL effects are so great that feed-back or pre-distortion cannot sufficiently improve the linearity. We can consider the problem of linearization in the communication chain from the digital part to the antenna (front end). This drives one to completely modify the architecture and its elements' specifications in baseband, IF/RF and power RF. After the amplification of constant envelope parts of the signals, the challenge is to reintroduce the variable envelope information with lower NLs than in a direct amplification case, keeping high efficiency of the architecture. Basic examples of these techniques are the LINC (LInearization with Non-linear Components) and the EER (Envelope Elimination and Restoration) methods (and their recent evolutions) [Cox, 1974] [Kahn, 1952] [Baudoin et al., 2003-2007] [Diet et al., 2004] [Suarez et al., 2008].

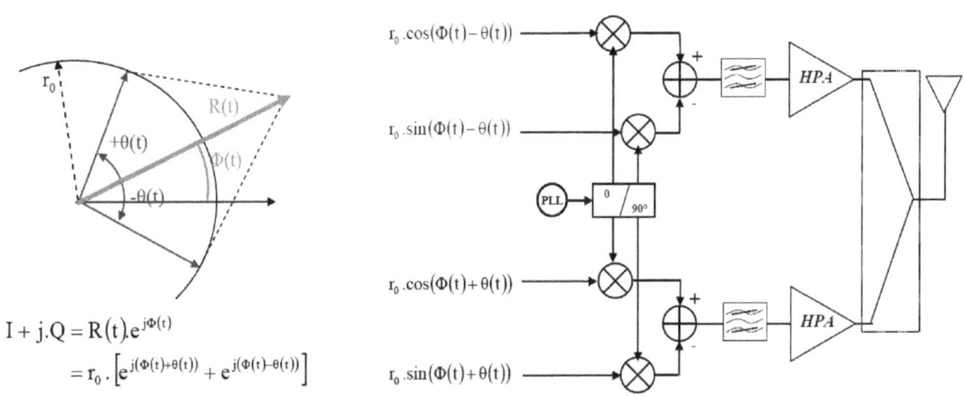

Fig. 11. LINC decomposition and recombination at RF power amplification

The LINC principle relies on a decomposition of the modulated signal into two constant envelope signals as is shown in Fig. 11. The decomposition can be computed by a Digital Signal Processor (DSP) or by combining two VCOs in quadrature PLL configuration: CALLUM. This latter configuration is an interesting architecture but presents the possibility of instability and additional manufacturing costs. The amplification of the two constant envelope signals implies the design of two identical HPAs at RF frequency, and this often causes signal distortion due to imbalance mismatches. Also the HPA must be wideband because the signal decomposition is a non-linear process (widening of the spectrum), and the phase modulation index is increased. Whatever the decomposition technique is (LINC/CALLUM), the problem is that the efficiency is directly determined by the recombination step: a sum of the powers. It is very difficult to avoid losses at RF while designing a RF power combiner.

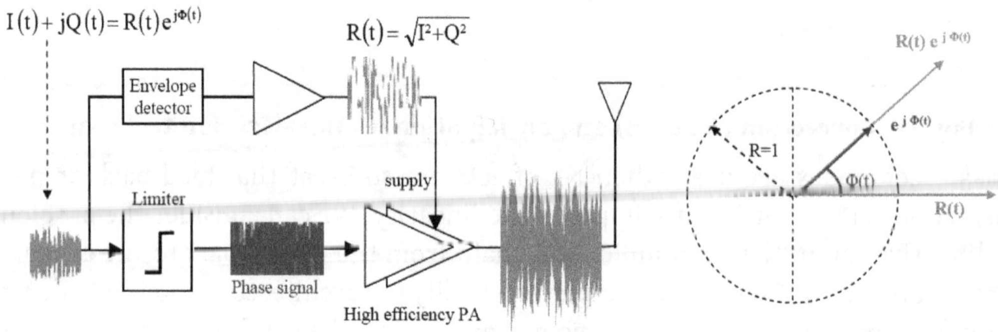

Fig. 12. Principle of the EER technique [Kahn, 1952]

Another decomposition technique was proposed by Kahn in 1952 and this is basically an amplitude and phase separation technique (polar): Envelope Elimination and Restoration (EER). This method was first proposed for AM signals as represented in Fig. 12. The advantage of EER is that it drives the RF PA with a constant envelope modulated signal (carrying the phase information), enabling the use of a SW high efficiency amplifier [Raab et al. 2003] [Sokal & Sokal, 1975] [Diet et al., 2005-2008]. The difficulty is to reintroduce the amplitude information linearly using the variations of the PA voltage supply. This implies a power amplification of the envelope signal at a frequency equal to the symbol rate (lower than RF). The recombination can be done with a SW class PA because the output voltage is linearly dependant on the voltage supply for this PA mode. Two difficulties are to be considered in such a linearization technique: (i) synchronization between the phase and the amplitude information and (ii) linear and efficient amplification of the amplitude before the recombination (directly impacting the overall efficiency), as reported in [Diet, 2003-2005].

Recently, a lot of work has been done on the EER based architectures, often named as "polar" ones [Nielsen & Larsen, 2007] [Choi et al., 2007] [Suarez et al., 2008] [Diet et al., 2008-2009]. The generation of the amplitude and phase components can be expected to be done digitally thanks to the power of DSPs, as is shown in Fig. 13. As was previously discussed in [Diet et al., 2003], the bandwidths of the envelope and phase signals are widened due to NL processing and make it necessary to design the circuit for three to four times the symbol rate (as for LINC or any other NL decomposition). Fortunately, a clipping in frequency and on the envelope is possible, increasing the EVM and ACPR under acceptable levels. These polar architectures are suited for new high data rate standards where efficiency of the emitter and linearization are mandatory. Also, the multi-standard and multi-radio concepts have helped polar architectures to evolve in multiple ways. For example, recombination on the PA's input signal is possible because the amplitude information can modulate the phase signal (RF) and can be restored by the band-pass shape function of the following blocks: PA + emission filter + antenna. The emitted spectrum is the criterion of quality to be considered carefully, because the PWM or ΣΔ envelope coding are the source of useless and crippling spectral re-growths. The efficiency is also penalized by the power amplification of such frequency components, but this is counter-balanced by the advantages of high flexibility of this architecture [Robert et al. 2009]. The digitally controlled PA and the mixed-mode digital to RF converter are key parameters in the evolution of these polar architectures [Suarez et al., 2008] [Robert et al., 2009] [Diet et al., 2008].

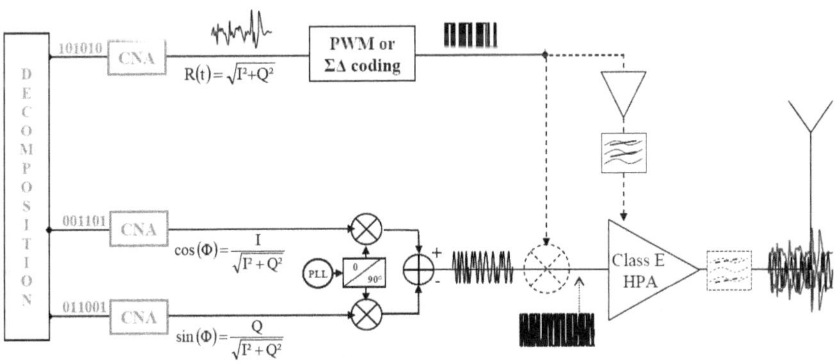

Fig. 13. Recent improvements of EER/polar architectures for wideband OFDM signals

We have presented the main linearization techniques. Actual needs, in terms of transmitter linearity and efficiency for high data rate applications, have caused the RF designer to consider RF architectures based on combined techniques. For example, digital pre-distortion is an improvement on polar based architectures, as is shown in section 4. Another example is described in [Diet et al., 2008] where a combination of cascaded EER and LINC techniques can theoretically provide an architecture which cancels the PAPR influence, see Fig. 14.

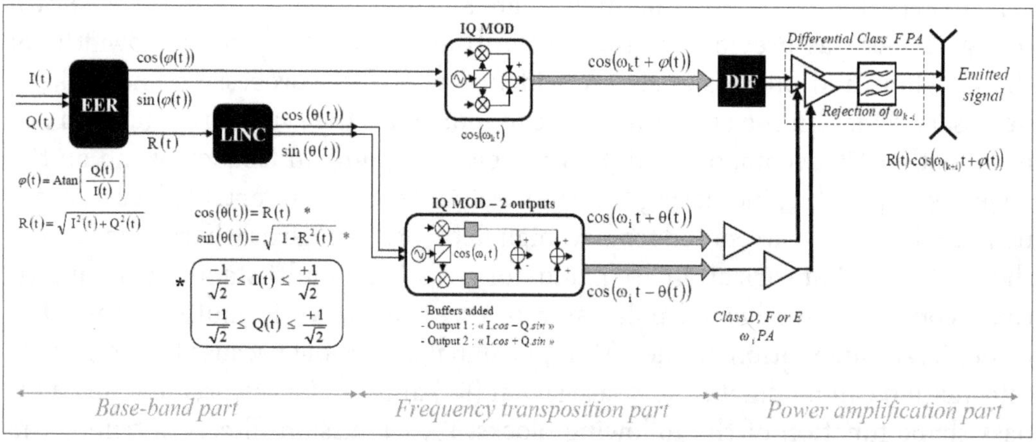

Fig. 14. EER-LINC method for high PAPR signals

This architecture needs some new components (e.g., a balanced switched PA with frequency transposition). This also represents an increase in complexity, but proposes new ways to improve WB-CW signals transmitters. In EER-LINC, the envelope information is converted to two angular modulated signals. The RF balanced PA (also called differential PA) is in SW class and is supply-modulated with the two above-mentioned signals. The fact that the PA is differentially supplied allows for the combining operation and a transposition at the same time (due to the multiplication). As the antenna is supposed to be differential, there is no balun after the PA.

This review of linearization techniques reveals that the different parts of an efficient and linear transmitter cannot be designed separately: baseband, frequency transposition and power amplification (and antenna for wideband systems). The modification of the architecture for global performance improvements must be done, considering each block's impact, digital or analog (and their imperfections). To conclude this theoretical sub-section, linearized architectures are mandatory for the major part of actual and future CW systems, which are WB-CW (high data rate). The highest performance can be reached if a combination of different techniques is exploited: pre-distortion and EER seem to be the most popular.

3.3 Receiver architectures

The challenges of the receiver architectures are the noise level, the presence of other channels and blocking/interference signals. This is summarized by the immunity and the coexistence of the standards, illustrated in Fig. 15.

The information received is at such a low level that other RF emissions can mask it. It is easily possible to saturate the receiver if a signal is too strong in the vicinity of the spectrum. Other characteristics of the receiver are its sensitivity and selectivity. The sensitivity is the lowest level of power that can be received and demodulated correctly (providing a Bit Error Rate sufficient for interpretation). This latter, is altered by the total amount of noise added by the receiver itself. The noise factor (F) expresses an equivalent of a white Gaussian noise addition, for each block. It is possible to compute the global noise factor for the receiver thanks to Friis formula, see Fig. 15. This formula shows that amplifying the signal as close as possible to the antenna, at the front–end, is better for minimizing the total added noise. This is the goal of the Low Noise Amplifier (LNA) whose design is optimized for noise and not for gain or output power performance. Unfortunately, the presence of high power signals (blocking) often implies starting the reception chain with a selective band-pass filter, as is reported for the Rx architectures in Fig. 15. At this point, the signal bandwidth is another limiting factor for the design of the receiver because it directly impacts the reception filter design and the LNA. The selectivity and sensitivity performance are also affected. At reception, the decrease in the signal quality is expressed by the EVM and the BER. This degradation results from the noise in the system (noise factor) but other imperfections are due to the architecture design: block interactions, CEM, image frequency and so on. In digital radio-communications, the channel coding (block and convolution types) improves the robustness of the system against the noise, but this point will not be developed here.

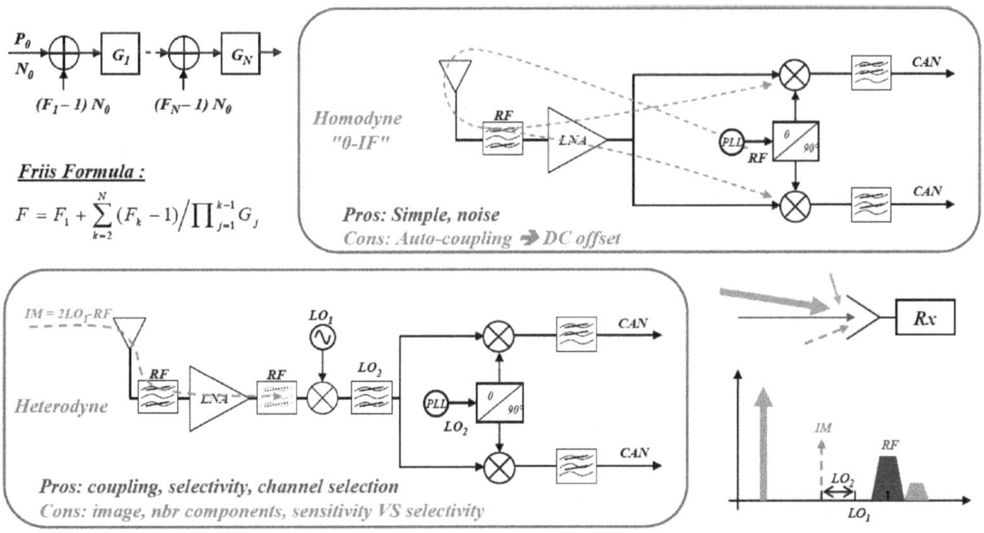

Fig. 15. Considerations for receiver architectures

The topic of this sub-section is to present the main types of receiver architectures. As there is no PA NL effects (Tx architecture), there is no need for linearization techniques. If the receiver is saturated, it suffices to reduce the gain of the LNA (if possible) or to attenuate the signal (back-off). The basic receiver structures are similar to that of the classic transmitter structures, that is to say homodyne and heterodyne types as represented in Fig. 15.

Homodyne receivers are composed of a direct IQ demodulator which comes after the LNA. RF filters, before and after the LNA, tend to avoid a masking effect by other signals received. The filter technology for RF is subject to a trade-off between the selectivity and the losses, which increase the noise factor of the filter. Swapping the LNA and the RF filter in the receiver chain creates a limitation of the received band. This is set in function with disturbing signals and the resulting noise factor (sensitivity). This architecture is simple, as it requires few components, and theoretically limits the total amount of noise added. The transposition needs a Local Oscillator (LO) signal that is stronger than the received signal. The coupling effects between the Rx antenna and the frequency synthesizer is very important and a shielding is mandatory to reduce CEM effects. Moreover, if a part of the LO signal is sensed by the antenna, it creates an offset (DC) by auto-mixing of the RF signal. This DC component may saturate the ADCs and is added to the baseband signal. The sensitivity of the homodyne receiver is not as low as expected due to this coupling effect whose impact is greater than that for Tx architecture.

To summarize, homodyne architecture is very attractive for its simplicity if the integration of the synthesizer is not causing crippling CEM effects. The addition of RF filtering can reduce the offset but reduces the receiver sensitivity (noise factor increased).

Heterodyne receivers need two (or more) transpositions of the signal. The number of components is important and represents an additional current consumption compared to the homodyne structure (simpler). The coupling effect due to the strong LO1 and LO2 signals, see Fig. 15, is minimized due to the different frequency values. This architecture needs more filters than the homodyne one but this can be useful for improving the receiver selectivity: Intermediate Frequency (IF) filters can reach higher selectivity than in RF. Moreover, additional filters inevitably decrease the signal-to-noise ratio, as well as the receiver performance. Sensitivity and selectivity are the sources of the challenges faced by the receiver designer. Additionally, the mixers' operation frequency and the IF filters enable different manufacturing technologies. A great challenge of the heterodyne structure is the possibility of receiving unwanted image information. An image is a signal producing an IF signal after the first mixer (IF = LO2 = LO1 RF, as reported in Fig. 15). A signal whose frequency is "IM = 2LO1 RF" produces, after mixing, an output signal whose frequency is "LO1 – RF = IF". The receiver should reject this IM component in order to protect the receiver from this perturbation. Without selectivity, the receiver cannot attenuate IM components. If the addition of a filter after the antenna is not sufficient to do this, an improvement is possible with "image-rejection" architectures. The principle here is to eliminate the image signal by an addition of 180° phase shifted copy. The considered improvements were proposed by Hartley and Weaver. This is possible if the total power level of received signals (information at RF and image at IM) are not saturating the receiver. An RF filter is mandatory even if these architectures are used.

Hartley and Weaver improvements are called "image-rejection" (heterodyne) receiver architectures. The different structures are summarized in Fig. 16.

As is reported, these structures are supposed to cancel the received signal whose frequency value is IM. The Hartley structure uses an all-pass filter with a phase shift of 90°. For NBCW systems, this filter can be realized by R-C structures. For WB-CW systems, a filter with such frequency independent characteristics is called a Hilbert filter. The realization of this filter is a source of imperfections which directly impact the image rejection property. In order to avoid filter design difficulties, Weaver proposed a structure in which the 90° phase shift is achieved by a second frequency transposition. This heterodyne structure can directly output the baseband signal (information), as expressed in Fig. 16. The cost of this improvement is the number of added components, which is almost twice as much when compared to a classic heterodyne structure. If the signal is IQ modulated, it is possible to create quadrature image rejection architecture by using two more mixers, as is illustrated by the IQ Weaver schematic in Fig. 16.

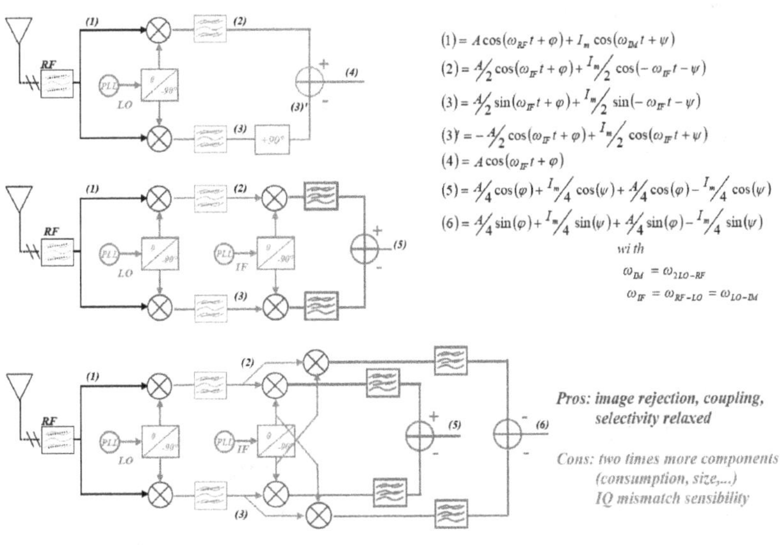

Fig. 16. Hartley (top), Weaver (middle) and IQ Weaver (bottom) architectures.

The increase in size, complexity and consumption is balanced by the image rejection property, if IQ mismatches are low enough. Hartley, Weaver and IQ Weaver were first designed for NB-CW systems. Their use for WB-CW can be discussed if IQ modulator performance and filters enables it. The bandwidth of the filter implies the choice of LO values. Some receivers, whose required bandwidths are too wide, are not possible to design. "Image-rejection" architectures are an interesting alternative to reduce selectivity constraints in the receiver design, at the cost of additional components and additional noise (lower sensitivity).

Another interesting improvement of heterodyne architecture is a group of LowIntermediate Frequency (low-IF) receivers whose goal is to use ADCs at IF and not in baseband. There are two main possibilities for signal processing at IF frequencies: (i) using a poly-phase filter in a modified IQ Weaver architecture or (ii) using fast ADCs with digital signal processing on the baseband information. These ADCs imply a large increase in current consumption in function with the IF value. Nowadays, solution (ii) is more popular due to the state-of-the-art ADC performance (resolution versus sampling rate) and the high improvement possibilities provided by digital algorithms. Low-IF architectures with bandpass ADCs represent a sub-group of heterodyne architectures and are popular for its potential flexibility.

To conclude this section in the case of CW systems, there are two approaches for receiver architectures: (i) homodyne (also called "zero-IF") with limitations of LO coupling effects and (ii) low-IF heterodyne structures, with a growing interest in IF ADCs.

4. HIGH DATA RATE STATE-OF-THE-ART TRANSMITTERS

4.1 Front-end considerations

Many new standards for high data rate communications have appeared recently or are under development whether in the frequency range below 6 GHz or in the millimeter wave range (60 GHz radio in particular). In the first case, the data rates are in the range of several tens to several hundreds of Mbps and in the second case they can be in the range of several Gbps. There are many challenges for the design of high data rate RF Transceivers. Among the most critical are:

- Designing power transmitters with a good linearity and efficiency for wideband, high PAPR signals with a large range of necessary transmit power control.
- Designing mobile transceivers using OFDM and multi-antenna MIMO and smart antenna techniques in order to achieve very high performance (throughput and BER) in mobile channels with large delay spreads while maintaining low power consumption and reduced size and cost.

- Designing flexible and scalable devices able to accommodate for many standards, frequency bands and modes

Multi-carrier (OFDM and OFDMA for multiple user access) and multiple-antenna (MIMO) techniques have emerged as enabling technologies for beyond 3G and 4G high data rate communication systems. Many new standards use OFDM and MIMO approaches. Examples include: IEEE 802.11n for wireless local area networks, IEEE 802.16d and IEEE 802.16e fixed and mobile WIMAX or IEEE 802.20 for wireless metropolitan area networks, IEEE 802.22 for wireless regional networks, 3GPP LTE (Long Term Evolution) for beyond 3G cellular networks. OFDM and MIMO have also generated new challenges in term of transmitter architectures with good efficiency and linearity, and in term of integration of MIMO transceiver and antennas in mobile user terminals. One of the main advantages of OFDM in mobile wireless channels is the simplification of the channel equalization in comparison with single carrier modulation. Indeed, for an OFDM modulation with N carriers, the original high data rate M-QAM data stream with a rate R is split into N parallel lower speed streams with a rate R/N that modulate one of the N carriers with a M-QAM modulation. In practice, the N parallel single carrier modulation is achieved thanks to a baseband IFFT. For a given data rate R, the bandwidth of the M-QAM/OFDM signal is similar to that of a single carrier M-QAM signal. An OFDM symbol comprises N QAM original symbols. A guard interval (GI) is introduced between successive OFDM symbols in order to prevent inter-symbol interference. The duration of the GI is of the order of the delay spread of the impulse response of the channel. Therefore, the larger the number of carriers, the more efficient the system. Unfortunately, the PAPR value of the modulated signal also depends on the number of carriers. The larger the number of carriers, the larger the PAPR value, and the more difficult it is to design a power transmitter with a high efficiency and a high linearity. In order to accommodate for multiple users, a set of carriers can be allocated to each user resulting in the OFDMA principle. The LTE standard proposes an uplink (mobile emitter) variant called single-carrier FDMA (SC-FDMA) which has a smaller PAPR value. In a SC-FDMA emitter, the OFDM modulator is preceded by a DFT, which increases the baseband complexity.

MIMO technology uses multiple antennas at the transmitter and the receiver. The obtained diversity and spatial multiplexing allow for better BER performance and increased data rate or link range without increasing the bandwidth or the transmitted power. In comparison with a SISO system (Single antenna at the emitter and at the receiver) the maximal achievable increase of the data rate depends on the minimum number of antennas in the transmitter and the receiver. For example, for 2 Tx and 2 RX antennas, the data rate can be multiplied by 2 at the maximum. There is a compromise between the diversity gain and the multiplexing gain. In the WiMAX standard, different modes are defined depending on whether one wants to increase the diversity (Space time bloc code STBC approach referred to as MIMO matrix A) or the spatial multiplexing (referred to as MIMO matrix B). It is possible to use MISO approach (multiple Tx and single Rx antennas) and use transmit diversity with space time coding (called MIMO matrix A). WiMAX also includes possibility for uplink collaborative MIMO technique. This is intended to allow for 2 separate user devices, each with a single transmit antenna, to communicate on the same frequency with a base station using 2 antennas. The MIMO approach can be associated with beam-forming to control the direction and shape of the radiation pattern.

MIMO techniques allow for tremendous improvements in throughput performances. But it is a challenge to integrate many antennas and transceivers in a small mobile user device. With a multiple antenna base station and a single antenna user device it is possible to achieve some improvement but a multiple antenna user device is necessary to really take advantage of MIMO technique. In the "WiMAX Wave 2" device certification, 2 receive antenna systems are mandatory. Another kind of challenge for high data rate front-end transmitters is the case of millimeter wave (mmWave) mobile communications. At 60 GHz, the available unlicensed bandwidth is very large and the mmWave technology is a good candidate for indoor very high data rate (several Gbits/sec) communication systems. The high data path loss allows for high frequency re-use. The small wave-length allows for the use of very small antennas and integrating multiple antennas for MIMO or beam-forming approaches can be easily achieved. The standard IEEE 802.15.3c is intended to provide Gbits data rate at distance of the order of a few meters. For fixed equipments, the situation at mmWave is quite similar to the preceding one (at frequency below 6 GHz) and OFDM technique is widely used. But the design of mobile devices with low power consumption constraint is still very challenging. The OFDM approach with high speed DAC/ADC and baseband processors has generally crippling power consumption. Among the challenges are: design of PAs with a sufficient output power, efficiency and linearity; power consumption of DAC and ADC with Gigahertz sampling frequencies; design of a physical layer with a low complexity and sufficient performance. Two approaches are commonly proposed: single carrier QPSK and UWB techniques.

4.2 Polar architectures

One of the main challenges for OFDM based mobile transmitters is to design power transmitters with a good linearity and efficiency for wideband, high PAPR signals with a large range of transmit power control. For example, for the WiMAX mobile standard:

- The signal bandwidth is scalable up to 10 MHz.

- For a full OFDM WIMAX signal with a 1024 FFT and a 16-QAM mapping, the PAPR (or effective power ratio with a probability of 10-3) is approximately 12 dB.
- The Peak transmit power is typically 23 dBm for subscriber terminals.
- The power control of the transmitted signal (TPC) that compensates for variations in signal strength (e.g., distance variation) must be monotonic and able to cover a range of at least 45 dB by steps of 1 dB with a relative accuracy of 0.5 dB.

For common PAs operating in CW classes (A, AB, B or C), the power efficiency is better for high power output values (close to the P1dB) than for low output values while the linearity is usually better for small power values. In order to transmit a modulated signal with a good linearity, the maximum instantaneous power of the signal must be kept smaller than the P1dB. Therefore, for a given PAPR, the average input power is PAPR dB below P1dB. The amplifier is operated with a back-off depending on the value of the PAPR and for large PAPR values; the efficiency can be very small. The common efficiency obtained with class AB PA for WiMAX signal is typically smaller than 20% while it would be at least twice bigger for constant envelope signals such as GSM signals.

Another parameter to take into account is the average output power. For the same PAPR, the power amplifier efficiency also depends on the average output power. The power supply of the PA should be adjusted in order to take into account the desired average output power and keep a constant efficiency on a large range of average output power.

Different kinds of polar architectures have been proposed as candidate solutions for high PAPR management or for adjustment of power supply to the average power. The terminology is not very stable. But, one can distinguish:

- Polar lite architectures.
- Polar feedback loop.
- Dynamic power supply and amplifier gain control with dynamic biasing, envelope or power tracking for linear PA, drain (collector) modulation for non-linear PA.
- EER and Sampled-EER architectures.

Whatever the modulation, the complex envelope z of the modulated signals can be expressed by its cartesian coordinates: real and imaginary parts usually called quadrature or I and Q components or by its polar coordinates: amplitude ρ and phase Φ, see (1). As the amplitude ρ and phase Φ are obtained by very non-linear operation from I and Q, their bandwidth is much higher than that of I and Q, as discussed in section 3.

$$z(t) = I(t) + jQ(t) = \rho(t)\exp(j\phi(t)), \quad \rho(t) = \sqrt{I(t)^2 + Q(t)^2}, \quad \tan(\phi(t)) = \frac{Q(t)}{I(t)}. \tag{1}$$

When the amplitude ρ(t) is constant, the polar decomposition is interesting since only one signal (Φ(t), or its time derivative) has to be digital to analog converted. GSM Transmitters can take advantage of this characteristic. As seen in section 3.1, the modulation of the frequency synthesis loop is a common GSM architecture that benefits of the good noise floor of the VCO and suppresses the need for external filtering. Since the envelope of the modulated signal is constant, the PA can operate in saturated CW or SW class (high efficiency). An average power controller must be added. This architecture is also called translational (or tracking offset) loop. The modulation of the PLL becomes very difficult for large bandwidth signals such as WCDMA. Therefore this approach is mostly used for GSM/EDGE signals. The name "polar transmitter" is sometimes limited to architectures in which the phase/frequency modulation is applied directly to the RF carrier by a modified PLL, using different techniques such as a "2-point modulation" [Durdodt 2001]. But we will use the adjective "polar" whenever the signal is decomposed in polar coordinates

The translational loop technique was extended for EDGE-GSM signals using the so-called polar lite architecture. The 8-PSK EDGE-GSM modulated signal is decomposed in polar coordinates. The idea is to keep the benefits of the translational loop architecture but to introduce an AM capability. In such architecture, the signal is decomposed in polar coordinates. The phase modulates the loop and the amplitude multiplies the output of the modulated loop by controlling the gain of a high dynamic range variable-gain amplifier (VGA). Since the signal at the input of the PA is envelope-varying, this architecture does not support a saturated PA. It uses a linear PA and has no particular efficiency advantage. It is sometimes associated with some dynamic power supply technique in order to increase the efficiency. An example is given in [Staszewski et al 2005].

The polar feedback loop architecture is a derivation of the polar lite architecture with the advantage of using a saturated PA. In the polar feedback loop, the PA is fed with a constant envelope signal and is modulated in amplitude. A feedback path takes a portion of the PA output signal (with a coupler) and an error signal is calculated between the ideal and actual output. The phase of the error drives the input of the PA and the error magnitude is used for the amplitude modulation of the PA. The feedback loops provides some linearization to the transmitter. But as in any feedback loop, the stability constraint limits the possible bandwidth. An example of a polar feedback loop architecture for GSM and EDGE is given in [Sowlati et al, 2004]. In that example, the PA efficiency is 54% in GSM mode at 33dBm output power and 37% in EDGE mode at 27dBm output power.

Many techniques are possible for dynamic power supply: dynamic biasing (at gate or drain), envelope or power tracking for linear PA, drain (collector) modulation for non-linear PA. Dynamic power supply using DC-DC switching regulators are interesting in terms of efficiency but they are still limited in term of signal bandwidth to a few tens of MHz. For envelope tracking (ET), the DC-DC is fed with the amplitude of the modulated signal (Fig. 17). ET was not presented in section 3 because it is not strictly a decomposition technique of linearization, but an improvement of the PA output power (and consequently the efficiency). This optimisation of PA biasing can increase of more than 40% the efficiency of a class A PA. In some standards the power-control dynamic range must be very wide (i.e., 80 dB for WCDMA). The amplitude modulation (envelope restoration) can be applied on a VGA or directly on the PA which leads to a better efficiency.

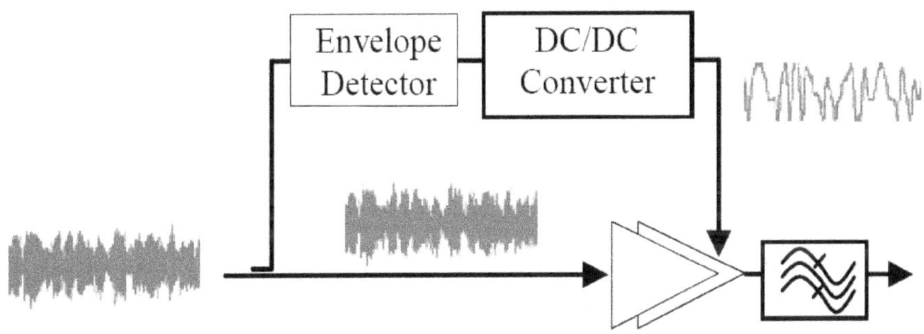

Fig. 17. Envelope tracking

The principle and interest of EER architectures and their variants under different names such as polar architectures were explained in section 3.2. The critical points for this architecture are: (i) the time mismatch between the envelope and the RF phase signals, (ii) the NL of the envelope restoration, (iii) the distortion caused by difficulty of biasing the PA when the amplitude of the envelope signal is very small, (iv) the leakage of the RF PA input to the output, (v) the influence of the necessary limitation of the frequency bandwidth of the envelope and phase signals. It can be shown [Baudoin et al., 2003] that the signal to noise ratio due to a time mismatch T between these two paths is in a first approximation inversely proportional to T and to the bandwidth of the envelope signal. Therefore, the wider the signal bandwidth, the smaller should be the time mismatch. For an OFDM signal, such as in WiFI, the time mismatch T must be kept smaller than typically 2 ns (which is a small percentage of the QAM symbol duration) in order to fulfil the specifications of the standard. The time mismatch can be corrected by adaptive techniques and the NL of the envelope restoration can be compensated by adaptive pre-distortion techniques. But, as already stated for dynamic power supply, it is difficult to design DC-DC converters with a bandwidth superior to a few tens of MHz. This is all the more critical as the envelope signal bandwidth is wider than the original modulated signal bandwidth. For example, an OFDM modulated WiFI signal has a frequency bandwidth close to 20 MHz. But the bandwidths of its envelope and phase signals cannot be filtered to a bandwidth smaller than respectively 40 MHz and 100 MHz if one wants to meet the specifications of the standard. The polar EER approach can be illustrated by Tropian's Timestar (TM) RF IC supporting GSM/GPRS, EDGE and WCDMA signals [Wendell et al., 2003] [McCune et al., 2005] or Sequoia Communications Inc. SEQ7400 chip that supports HSDPA, GSM and EDGE and WCDMA [Groe et al., 2007-2008].

In polar architectures, the recombination of amplitude and phase signals can be done whether by PA amplitude modulation (EER architecture) or before the PA input. We will now consider the second approach, and we will focus on architectures using sampled signals and switched RF amplifiers (typically class D, E, F and their variants) [Jeong et al., 2007] [Hibon et al., 2005] [Berland et al., 2006] [Nielsen et al., 2007]. We will call these architectures "polar sampled architectures". The major motivations for using sampled signals and switched amplifiers are the ease of integration of digital circuits and the very high theoretical efficiency of switched PA. In polar sampled architectures, the envelope signal is "sampled" (converted/coded) by a pulse width modulation (PWM) or a 1-bit Sigma-Delta (ΣΔ) modulator with bipolar output ±A [Murmann et al., 2007]. This two level signal multiplies the RF phase modulated signal before the switched PA. The result is a constant envelope signal. The switched RF PA is fed with this constant envelope signal that controls the switching of the PA. The output of the PA must be filtered in order to suppress the PWM or ΣΔ noise and to recover the modulated signal. Fig. 18 illustrates this principle.

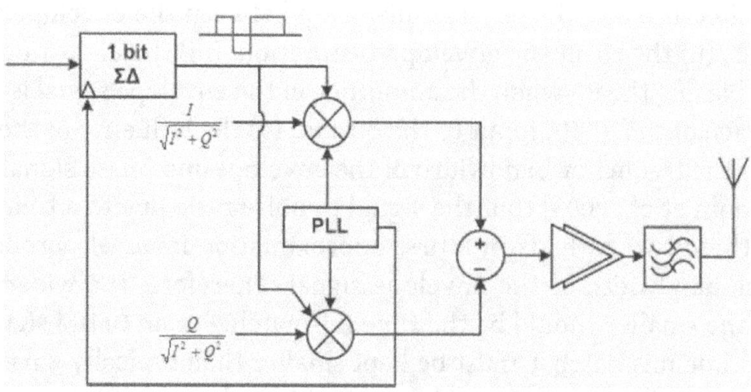

Fig. 18. Polar sampled architecture with envelope-phase recombination before the PA

In comparison with direct ΣΔ architectures [Rode et al 2003] in which the modulated RF signal is directly covered by a 1-bit ΣΔ coder before the switched amplifier, the coding of the envelope signal is interesting because it allows using smaller clock rates for the ΣΔ coder. One difference with EER architecture is the position and type of the filter used to eliminate the noise of the ΣΔ or PWM modulator. As illustrated in Fig. 13, EER architectures use a low-pass filter at the output of the envelope BF amplifier to recover the envelope signal. But when the recombination of envelope and phase signals is done before the RF PA, the noise must be eliminated after the RF PA with a band-pass RF filter (Fig. 18). For a given standard, this RF band-pass filter should be unique and correspond to the full uplink bandwidth. It should not be specific to a given channel. Therefore the over-sampling ratio of the ΣΔ modulator must be calculated in reference to the full uplink bandwidth and not to channel bandwidth (bandwidth of the modulated signal). In [Andia et al., 2008] the possibility of using BW filters for WiMAX standard has been studied.

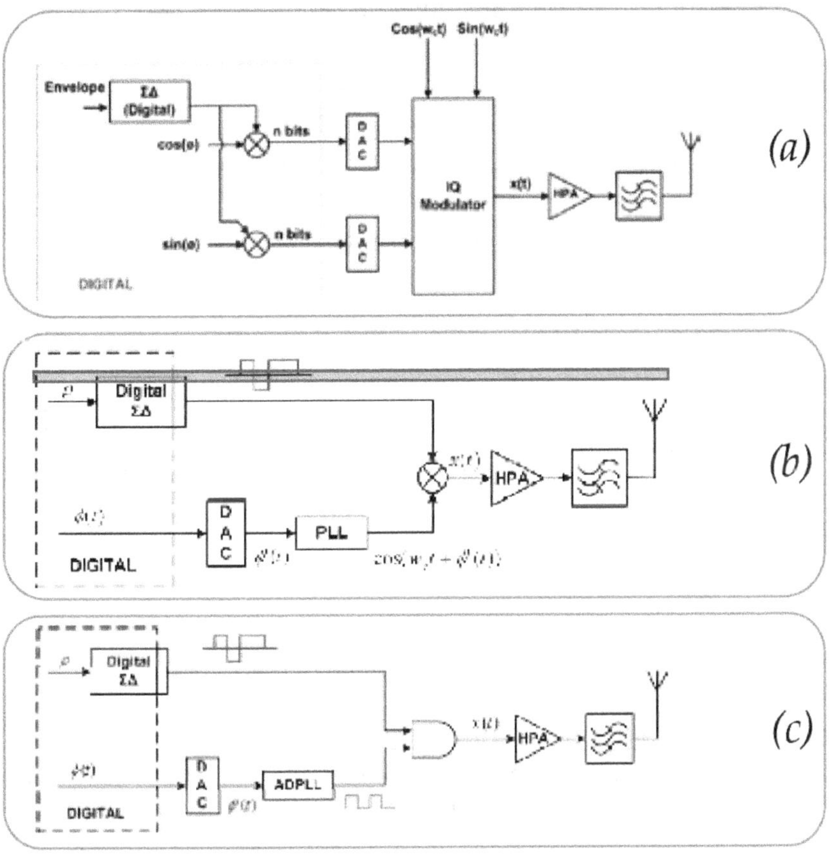

Fig. 19. (a) Polar Sampled Architecture, PSA, with 2 DACs. (b) PSA with a single DAC and an analog mixer. (c) PSA with a single DAC and with digital mixing.

Different structures have been proposed for polar sampled architectures [Suarez et al., 2008], see Fig. 19. In the structure (a) of this figure, ΣΔ modulator output is digital, as well as I(t) and Q(t) (ρ cos(Φ) and ρsin(Φ)). Therefore, two DACs are necessary before the IQ modulator. DACs sampling frequency is chosen according to the ΣΔ frequency. It has to be high enough to avoid ΣΔ noise overlapping. Targeted communication standards require high Sigma-Delta frequencies and therefore significant sampling frequency for DACs. In the structure (b), envelope and phase signals (ρ(t) and Φ (t)) are calculated and processed independently. The output of the low-pass sigma-delta modulator is analog. The digital phase signal is converted by a DAC and then modulated to the carrier frequency (fc). Finally constant envelope and phase signals are recombined.

The advantage of this approach compared to the first one is that it only requires one DAC. Furthermore, DAC frequency requirements are mitigated. In the first architecture, modulation to the carrier frequency is performed by the IQ modulator bloc with help of an analog mixer. Similarly, this second architecture makes use of an analog multiplier to recombine envelope and phase. The third architecture, structure (c), uses a digital carrier and replaces the analog mixer by a digital one, like an AND gate for example. In this case, an All-Digital Phase Locked Loop (ADPLL) whose input is the phase signal is used. The digital mixing is advantageous because it offers all the typical advantages of a digital signal treatment and digital IC integration but it introduces harmonics of the carrier frequency in the output spectrum with replication of the spectrum every 3*fc (Fig. 20). If digital mixing is implemented in a polar ΣΔ architecture, frequency ratio between carrier frequency and sigma-delta frequency has to be carefully chosen to avoid ΣΔ noise overlapping.

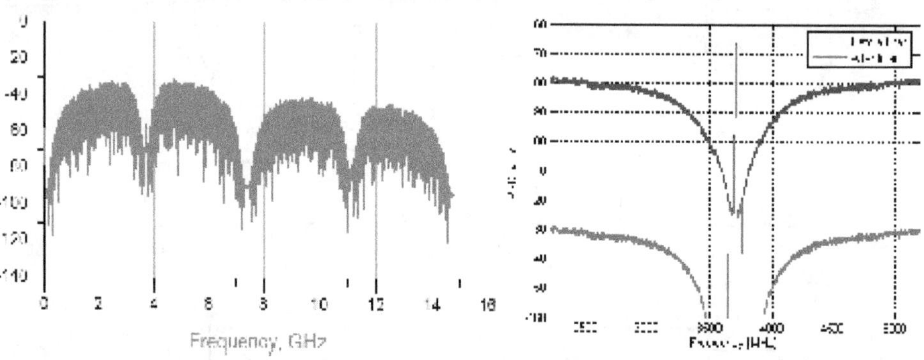

Fig. 20. Power spectral density of the signal at the PA input for a PSA with digital mixing (right), WiMAX case. Zoom on the power spectral density before and after the RF filter (left)

Fig. 20 corresponds to the third architecture, (c) in Fig. 19, and gives the power spectral density (PSD) of the signal at the input of the PA in the case of a WiMAX signal with a 3.7 GHz carrier and for a second order ΣΔ modulator, using a clock equal to 3.7 GHz. Fig. 20 also shows a zoom on the PSD before and after the RF filter. In that case the considered filter bandwidth is 100 MHz (while the channel bandwidth is 10 MHz) and the over-sampling ratio is equal to (3.7 GHz)/(200 MHz)=18.

4.3 Digital architectures

The performance of ADCs and processors, and research activities on RF-DACs (e.g., Sigma Delta) argue for integrating more and more functions in the digital part of a transmitter. Based on the software radio concept, the actual idea is to "digitalize" the design of some basic blocks such as the modulator, DACs RF and PA (D-PAs). Brand new cellular devices lead to the use of two or three different standards in the same mobile platform. As explained in a previous part, it requires constringent spectrum performance under very high speed data treatments. Each element of the transmitter must be designed with regards with several parameters: (high) frequency, dynamic power control and consumption (leading to high efficiency). Due to the use of Sigma Delta modulators, WB-CW standards such as WiMAX 3.5 and 5.8 GHz need an over-sampling frequency in the range of 15 GHz (more than four times the carrier frequency).

Using CMOS 90 nm technology is a current solution to address this challenge, while reducing the number of analog blocks. In this sub part we present two digital architectures, representing the digitalization trend.

The first architecture presented is based on a classic direct conversion architecture using only one frequency transposition. The "Direct Digital to RF Modulator" (DDRM) architecture [Eloranta et al] was developed as a basis toward further architecture digitization. In this architecture the system is digitalized the closest possible to the amplifier, which is still an analog part of the transmitter, see Fig. 21.

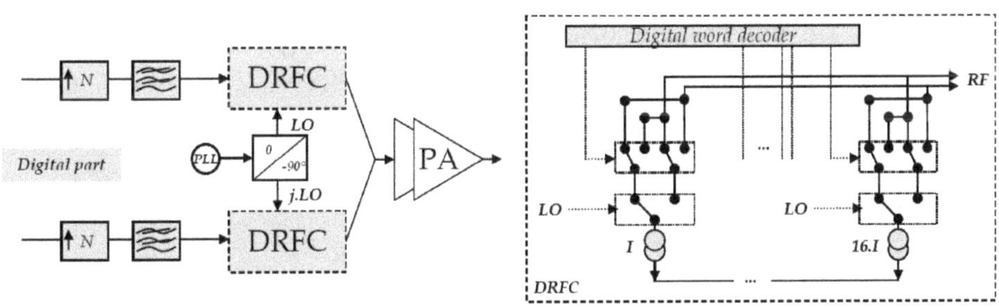

Fig. 21. DDRM architecture (left) and DRFC (right) [Eloranta et al]

The advantage of being digital is that it limits the imperfections due to variations in the process. In analog architectures, the multiple filtering blocks see their basic characteristics varying, and so the architecture performance varies as well. This leads to the use of a calibration loop. Digitization provides size optimization and good stability of the circuit. As the first stage is an over-sampling stage, there is no baseband signal and no need to filter with high selectivity before the DACs. In this architecture, mixing and D/A conversion are performed by a single block: "Digital to RF converter" (DRFC), a kind of RF-DAC. Weighted Gilbert cells are parallelized. No baseband signal in the architecture implies a very low LO leakage

(DC offset). The principle is that the data is over-sampled at the carrier frequency by switches. The signal amplitude is coded into a digital word (MSB to LSB). At the output of Gilbert cells, the current is proportional to the code word. The linearity performance and the signal resolution increase with the number of parallel cells. Due to this parallelization, IQ imbalance is limited and can only result from the average cell imbalances. Power control can be achieved by a bias current variation, which reduces the output current from each unit cell. As it uses no filter, the choice of the converter frequency is paramount. Indeed, the only filtering applied (SINC) is the zero-order hold. The frequency must be chosen so that baseband harmonics are cancelled thanks to the zeros of the filter response.

Thanks to CMOS evolutions, this architecture was optimized to address spectrum cohabitation issues [Pozsgay et al] under the name of "Sigma Delta – RFDAC" architecture, illustrated in Fig. 22. In this architecture, the gain control can take place throughout the transmitter. The first power control appears after the first up-sampling filter. It is then a low speed dynamic control, resulting from multiplying IQ signals with a binary word. This word size depends on the control resolution. A second power control stage is achieved, by deleting successive LSBs of the signal (6 dB steps). Several Delta-Sigma modulators in MASH structures are then used and I and Q channels are duplicated (I and I', Q and Q'). I and Q signals go through a modulator, and signals I' and Q' are first delayed before a second modulator. This will result in the recombination of mixed signals around the carrier, and the creation of notches in desired frequency bands (certainly used by other standards). An additional 6 dB power control can be done by by-passing I' and Q', and the corresponding RF-DAC, losing the advantage of notches as a result.

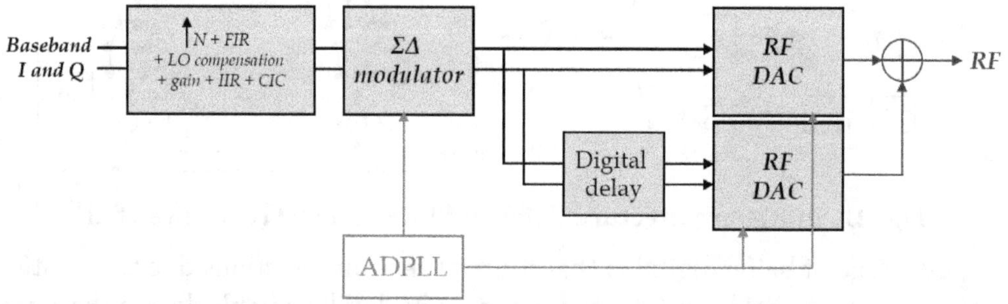

Fig. 22. Sigma Delta – RF-DAC architecture [Pozsgay et al]

The second architecture presented is based on an EER-like architecture. As will be explained, there is no complete separation between phase and amplitude in the transmitted signal processing. The architecture was developed by [Parikh et al], see Fig. 23. IQ signals are over-sampled and filtered in order to place the spectral re-growths far enough (zero order hold) and setting notches at multiples of the over-sampling frequency.

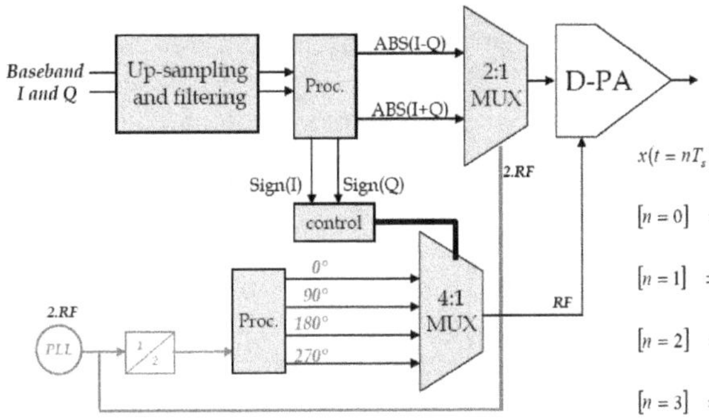

$$x(t) = I(t)\cos(\omega t) - Q(t)\sin(\omega t)$$

$$x(t = nT_s) = I\left(\frac{(2n+1)\pi}{4}\right)\cos\left(\frac{(2n+1)\pi}{4}\right) - Q\left(\frac{(2n+1)\pi}{4}\right)\sin\left(\frac{(2n+1)\pi}{4}\right)$$

$$[n=0] \Rightarrow x(0) = \frac{1}{\sqrt{2}}\left(I\left(\frac{\pi}{4}\right) - Q\left(\frac{\pi}{4}\right)\right)$$

$$[n=1] \Rightarrow x(1) = \frac{1}{\sqrt{2}}\left(I\left(\frac{3\pi}{4}\right) - Q\left(\frac{3\pi}{4}\right)\right) = \frac{1}{\sqrt{2}}\left(-I\left(\frac{\pi}{4}\right) - Q\left(\frac{\pi}{4}\right)\right)$$

$$[n=2] \Rightarrow x(2) = \frac{1}{\sqrt{2}}\left(I\left(\frac{5\pi}{4}\right) - Q\left(\frac{5\pi}{4}\right)\right) = \frac{1}{\sqrt{2}}\left(-I\left(\frac{\pi}{4}\right) + Q\left(\frac{\pi}{4}\right)\right)$$

$$[n=3] \Rightarrow x(3) = \frac{1}{\sqrt{2}}\left(I\left(\frac{7\pi}{4}\right) - Q\left(\frac{7\pi}{4}\right)\right) = \frac{1}{\sqrt{2}}\left(I\left(\frac{\pi}{4}\right) + Q\left(\frac{\pi}{4}\right)\right)$$

Fig. 23. Digital Quadrature Modulator [Parikh et al]

Two signals are created: "abs(I + Q)" and "abs(I-Q)". Moreover, we determine phase control signals (2 bits) with the signs of I and Q (complex quadrant). Amplitude signals are alternately sent to a digital differential amplifier (DDPA) at a rate of twice the carrier frequency. Thus we get a higher resolution of the variation of the original signal envelope. This can be seen as an over sampling by four of the IQ symbols leading to a better estimation of the amplitude, see Fig. 23. In Fig. 24, we can look at what would happen if I and Q take the value 4 and 3 respectively. This coded amplitude signal feeds a Digital Power Amplifier (DPA). This block will mix the signal around a carrier depending on the instantaneous sign of both I and Q. Knowing I and Q signs, gives us information on the phase (linked to the quadrant position). A part of the phase information can be taken from "abs(I+Q)" and "abs(I-Q)" signals.

This amplitude-coded signal can then be modulated by an RF carrier with an estimated phase. As seen in Fig. 23 and Fig. 24, four carrier signals with four different phases (0° 90° 180° and 270°) feed the DDPA depending on I and Q signs (2-bit control signals). As we obtain a NZR signal, the filtering condition after the DDPA will be less constringent than when using I and Q directly. One of the carrier frequency signals and the coded amplitude are fed to the DDPA. The carrier frequency signal is logical ("0" or "1" values) and activates one or another of the two differential pairs in the DDPA, in function with the sign signals. If the carrier is set to "0", "1", respectively, the output is alternately "–abs(I-Q)" and "– abs(I+Q)", or "abs(I+Q)" and "abs(I-Q)" (see Fig. 24). The output network of the DDPA is a band-pass filter around the carrier frequency, to reconstruct the original signal. Looking at the spectrum, performance is well suited to multi-standard applications. This is not due to flexibility in changing the operating frequency. In [Parikh et al] an example is given at 5.8 GHz for a 64QAM modulation scheme and 10 MHz bandwidth WiMAX signal, which is very constringent. The resulting spectrum re-growths are less than -50 dBc/Hz.

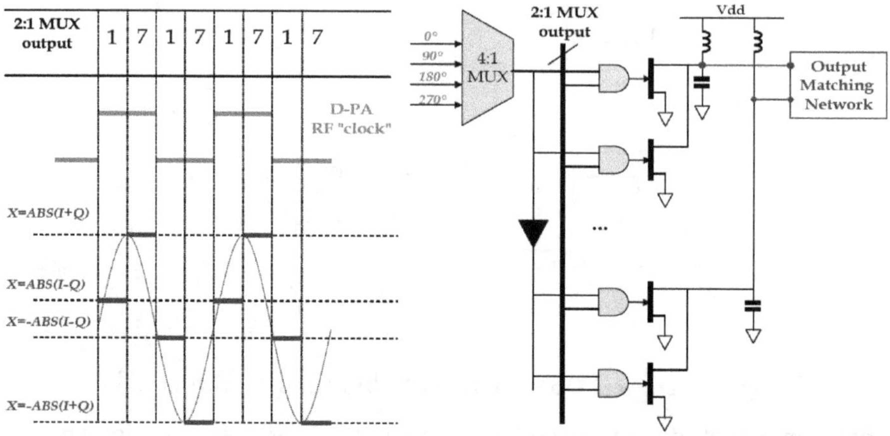

Fig. 24. Signal amplitude and phase estimation (left), DDPA (right). [Parikh et al]

To conclude, digital RF architectures for WB-CW are providing several advantages such as flexibility and size optimization. Their design is subject to the improvement in power consumption of RF blocks. This research topic is currently popular for mobile and connectivity high data rate standards.

5. IR-UWB ARCHITECTURES

This section is dedicated to IR based and all the UWB systems. Why to consider the UWB systems in addition to already existing technologies? Currently, interfaces have different characteristics in terms of throughput, coverage, access efficiency, quality of service (QoS) and energy consumption. Some of these interfaces offer a QoS for multimedia applications, particularly through a given performance of transmission in a period of time. Other technologies offer specific services such as distance measuring (ranging) like the some UWB systems. UWB technologies are not made for metropolitan networks. The potential of UWB lies in the use of interconnections of a wireless pico-network.

5.1 UWB communications, goals and aspects

There are systems that transmit and receive waves whose relative bandwidth (BW) is greater than or equal to 0.25, see the definition in Fig. 25. The first definition has been amended and replaced by a new one proposed by the FCC. Under this new definition, a UWB signal is a signal whose "-10dB bandwidth" exceed 500 MHz and 20% of center frequency. The main UWB frequency band is between 3.1 and 10.6 GHz. This bandwidth of about 7 GHz could be divided into 14 sub-bands of 500 MHz. A system using the full bandwidth or a set of sub-bands will be considered a UWB system. Today, we can classify UWB into two main categories of applications: UWB Low Data Rate (UWB LDR) and UWB High Data Rate (UWB HDR). They are attached to the IEEE 802.15.4a and 802.15.3a.

Low data rate systems are generally characterized by data rates lower than to 2 Mbps, by ranges of up to 300 meters and finally by a low consumption. They may allow positioning and location functionalities. The high data rate systems are characterized by data rates exceeding 100 Mbps with short ranges (up to a few tens of meters). Their fields of application are the computer data transmission and multimedia systems. Fig. 25 shows the frequency masks used in the USA.

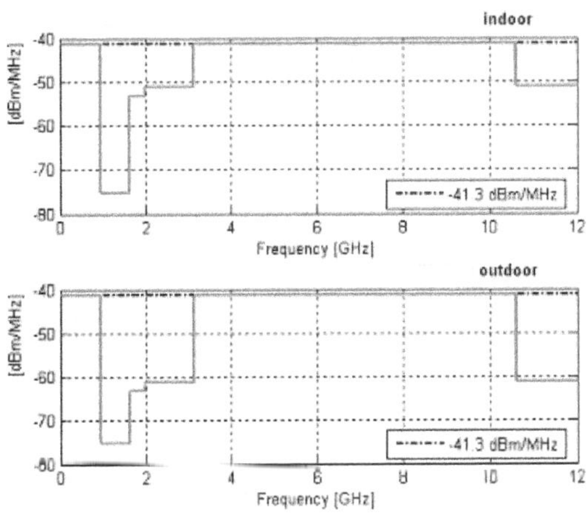

$$BW = \frac{f_h - f_l}{f_c}$$

$$f_c = \frac{f_h + f_l}{2}$$

$$P_{pic}^{\lim}(RBW) = 20\log_{10}\left(\frac{RBW}{50}\right)$$

Fig. 25. Frequency masks, relative bandwidth and peak radiated power (RBW in MHz).

The -41.3dBm/MHz limit correspond to a measurement of electromagnetic field equal to 500mVm-1, in any sub-band of 1 MHz, at a distance of 3 meters from the antenna. This level is also named the "Part 15 limit". In the FCC report, the peak power is also limited. It is measured around the frequency for which the radiation is at its maximum, and is defined in Fig. 25. For RBW = 50 MHz, the peak power must not exceed 0 dBm (1 mW). Several transmission techniques approaches have been studied and can be divided into:

- UWB mono-band: impulse approach (IR-UWB, or "classic UWB")
- UWB Multi-bands: MB-OFDM approach and MB-OOK approach. These systems presents high similarities with WB-CW ones.

5.2 IR-UWB transceiver architectures

The communication is based on short pulses transmission (a few hundred picoseconds), occupying all or part of the UWB spectrum, and repeated with a period of a few `nanoseconds. The signal is transmitted at the baseband frequency. It is interesting even in presence of multi-paths channel. By using a pulsed mode, it allows the measurement of the propagation delay time between the transmitter and the receiver and, consequently, the location. Informations are encoded in the shape of the impulse (amplitude or phase), by the position in time of the pulse or by random sequences of pulses.

Possibilities for modes transmission of the UWB pulses are: coherent, differentially coherent, and non coherent. In the case of coherent transmission, the modulations used are PSK, PAM, and PPM. The receiver will be of a correlator type, e.g. Rake. In the case of differentially coherent transmission, the modulation used is DPSK. Moreover, synchronization becomes un-necessary. For the last case of non coherent transmission, modulations used are OOK or PPM. The receiver will be based on energy detection. The transceiver architectures for IR-UWB are simpler than those for the MB-OFDM or any other WB-CW. The functional blocks of the architecture are given in Fig. 26.

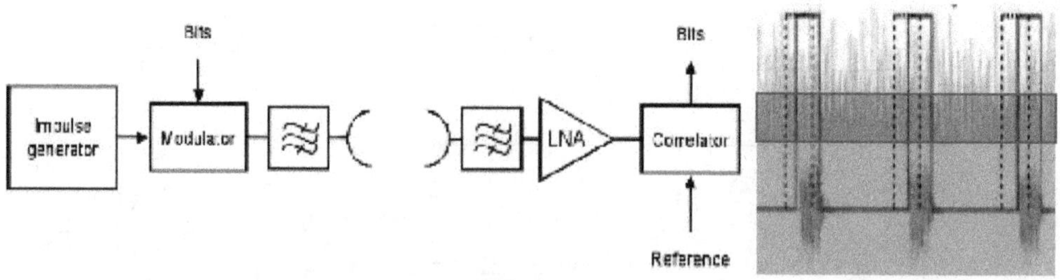

Fig. 26. Functional blocks of IR-UWB transceivers and receiver windowing.

Demodulation should be made on windows slots containing a pulse, as illustrated in Fig. 26. Architectures for impulse radio are divided into two types: Coherent Reception (Co-Rx), requiring knowledge of the phase of the received signal, and Non-Coherent Reception (NCo-Rx), based on detection of energy when pulses are transmitted. In the case of Co-Rx, the receiver uses the recognition of the phase signal. It is generally based on a sliding correlation scheme which produces almost the optimal performance. Therefore the complexity leads to a limitation on the implementation in low consumption equipment. Care should be taken to the synchronization at the acquisition that requires a very fine time to get the precision needed for coherent demodulation.

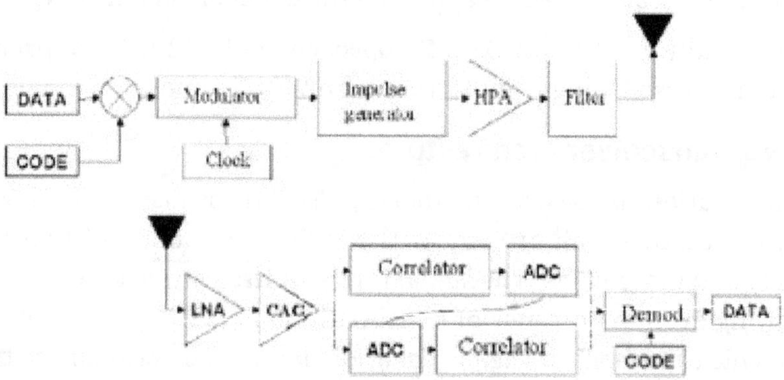

Fig. 27. Examples of Co-Rx transmitter and receiver

The two diagrams in Fig. 27 show the blocks of the transmitter and receiver of a coherent system. Two configurations are possible, the first is mixed analog/digital circuits, the second one is all-digital. Key points of the architecture are: the co-design antenna/LNA, ADC converter performance and the design of the correlator.

For the NCo-Rx, several architectures are possible but the principle is still based on energy detection. This technique is less complex than the previous one but its performance is not as good. The problem is related to the difficulty in designing a receiver able to detect the pulse, when the signal to noise ratio is very poor.

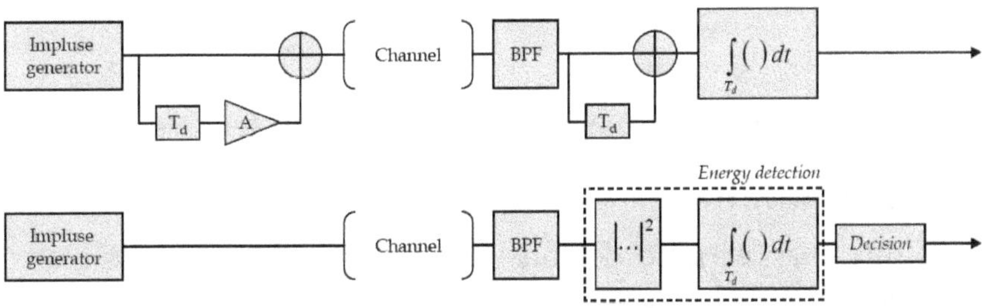

Fig. 28. Examples of NCo-Rx transmitter and receiver

In the case of a non-coherent system, architectures are based on energy detection whose principles are given in Fig. 28. Different types of pulses are used to perform the IR-UWB link: the Gaussian monocycle and its derivatives, the Hermite pulse (Hermite polynomials) or a sinusoid signal windowed by a Gaussian shape. Only the Gaussian pulse or the sinusoid signal windowed by a Gaussian shape are interesting because they can be implanted easily in practice [Marchaland et al., 2007].

5.3 MB-OFDM UWB transceiver architectures

As for CW systems, the MB-OFDM is characterized by a continuous transmission. It uses frequency hopping on at least three bands, 128 sub-carrier band of 528 GHz (in the case of 3.1 10.6 GHz band), and the QPSK modulation scheme. It allows a great flexibility in shaping the spectrum. This parallel multi-carrier operation minimizes inter-symbol interference, and the recovery of the energy available can be optimized. The MB-OFDM approach is based on an IFFT at emission and FFT at reception as shown in Fig. 29.

The overall topology of the receiver is very complex. The MB-OFDM technique is well suited to high speeds data transfer in indoor environments. It has good resistance to multipaths channel, and, allows flexible shaping of the spectrum. Modulation is complex to implement and requires circuitry to perform an FFT in real time, so the digital part of the architecture is quite complex. It needs synchronization. This technique requires front-end with high linearity and low noise (RF elements). Additionally, the consumption of the analog area may be important.

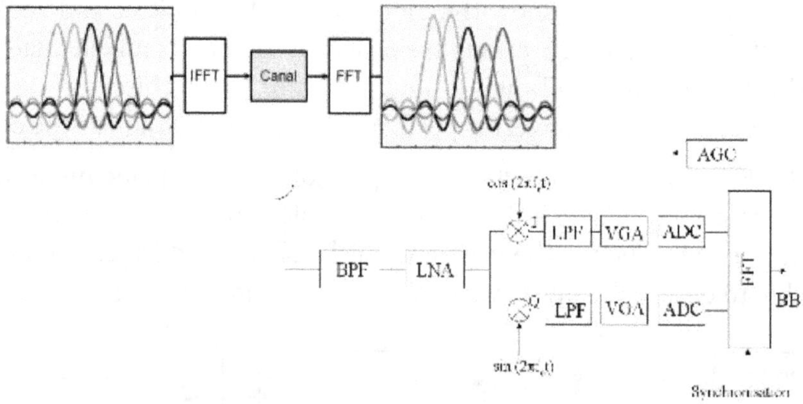

Fig. 29. Considerations for MB-OFDM UWB transceivers

6. CONCISE SUMMARY

The goal of this chapter is to demonstrate the absolute need of matching the architecture design and the signal carrying the information.

In this, considerations about current users' needs helped to identify three types of carrier signals in the context of radio-communications: NB-CW, WB-CW and IR. A separation between CW and IR signals is unavoidable because it drives us to a different technological design. Whatever the system is, the design of the transceiver architecture has to fulfill challenges such as co-existence (for the transmitter part) and immunity (for the receiver part). This implies a careful reduction of the spectral emission (spectral re-growths) for a transmitter. It also implies a high selectivity for the receiver and, of course, with the lowest sensitivity possible. RF architectures are becoming more and more complex. Especially, in the cases of RF transmitters, high efficient power amplification often results in a combination of different linearization techniques. The ever-increasing performance of the digital part gives us the opportunity to provide more flexibility in the architecture when the dynamic control and the power delivered to the load are satisfying standard requirements. This can be done thanks to the digitalization of some functions such as constant amplitude envelope coding, RF converters and/or PA (D-PA). The concept of multi-radio points out that the future of RF standards lies in favoring cooperation and flexibility in the managing of the system resources (bandwidths, power and time partitioning). Actual state-of-the-art results are that architectures are merging to reconfigurable RF blocks and when possible RF-digital blocks.

REFERENCES

1. Andia, L. et al. Specification of a Polar Sigma Delta Architecture for Mobile Multi-Radio Transmitter Validation on IEEE 802.16e. Proc. of IEEE Radio and Wireless Symposium, pp. 159-162, Orlando, USA. Jan. 2008.

2. Baudoin, G. et al. Radiocommunications Numériques : Principes, Modélisation et Simulation. Dunod, EEA/Electronique, 672 pages, 2ème édition 2007.

3. Baudoin, G. et al. Influence of time and processing mismatches between phase and envelope signals in linearization systems using EER, application to hiperlan 2. Proc. Conf. IEEE MTT'2003 Microwave Theory and Technique, Philadelphia USA, June 2003.

4. Berland, C. et al. A transmitter architecture for Non-constant Envelope Modulation. IEEE Trans. Circuits and Systems II: Express Briefs, vol. 53, no. 1, pp. 13-17, January 2006

5. Choi, J. et al. A ΣΔ digitized polar RF transmitter. IEEE Trans. on Microwave Theory and Techniques, Vol. 52, n°12, 2007, pp 2679-2690.

6. Cox, D. Linear amplification with non-linear components, LINC method. IEEE transactions on Communications, Vol COM-23, pp 1942-1945, December 1974.

7. Diet, A. et al. EER architecture specifications for OFDM transmitter using a class E power amplifier. IEEE Microwave and Wireless Components Letters (MTT-S), ISSN 1531-1309, V-14 I-8, August 2004, pp 389-391.

8. Diet, A. et al. Flexibility of Class E HPA for Cognitive Radio. IEEE 19th symposium on Personal Indoor and Mobile Radio Communications, PIMRC 2008, 15-18 september, Cannes, France. CD-ROM ISBN 978-1-4244-2644-7.

9. Diet, A., Baudoin, G., Villegas, M. Influence of the EER/polar Transmitter Architecture on IQ Impairments for an OFDM Signal. International Review of Electrical Engineering, IREE Praise Worthy Prize, ISSN 1827-6660, V-3 N-2, March-April 2008, pp 410-417.

10. Diet, A., Villegas, M., Baudoin, G. EER-LINC RF transmitter architecture for high PAPR signals using switched Power Amplifiers. Physical Communication, ELSEVIER, ISSN: 1874-4907, V-1 I-4, December 2008, pp. 248-254.

11. Dürdodt, D. et al. A low-IF Rx two-point ΣΔ-modulation Tx CMOS single-chip bluetooth solution. IEEE Trans. Microw. Theory Tech., vol. 51, no. 9, pp. 1531–1537, Sep. 2001.

12. Eloranta, P., Seppinen, P., Parssinen, A. Direct-digital RF-modulator: a multi-function architecture for a system-independent radio transmitter. Com. Magazine, IEEE V46, I4, 2008, pp 144-151.

13. Groe, J. A Multimode Cellular Radio. IEEE Trans. On circuits and systems—II: Express briefs, Vol. 55, No. 3, March 2008, pp. 269-273.

14. Groe, J. Polar Transmitters for Wireless Communications. IEEE Communications Magazine September 2007, pp. 58-63.

15. Hibon, I. et al. Linear transmitter architecture using a 1-bit ΔΣ. European Microwave Week 2005, Proc. Conf. ECWT, pp. 321-324, Octobre 2005.

16. Jardin, P., Baudoin, G. Filter Lookup Table Method for Power Amplifier Linearization. IEEE Trans. on Vehicular Technology, N° 3, Vol. 56, pp. 1076-1087, IEEE, Mai 2007.

17. Jeong, J., Wang, Y. A Polar Delta-Sigma Modulation (PSDM) Scheme for High Efficiency Wireless Transmitters. IEEE MTT-S Int. Microwave Symp. Dig. June 2007.

18. Kahn, L. Single Sideband Transmission by Envelope Elimination and Restoration. Proc. of the I.R.E., 1952, pp. 803-806.

19. Marchaland, D., Badets, F. Générateur d'impulsions ULB doté d'une fonction intégrée d'émulation numérique. FR0700683, le 31 Janvier 2007.

20. McCune, E. Polar Modulation and Bipolar RF Power Devices. IEEE Bipolar/BiCMOS Circuits and Technology Meeting (BCTM), October 2005.

21. McCune, E. High efficiency, multimode, multiband terminal power amplifiers. IEEE Microwave Magazine, March 2005, Volume: 6, Issue: 1, pp: 4455.

22. Murmann, B, Digitally Assisted Analog Circuits – A Motivational Overview. IEEE International Solid-State Circuits Conf.: Special Topic Evening Session, February 2007.

23. Nielsen, M., Larsen, T. Transmitter Architecture Based on ΔΣ Modulation and SW Power Amplification. IEEE Trans. on Circuits and Syst. II, 2007, vol. 54, no. 8, pp. 735-739.

24. Parikh, V., Balsara, P., Eliezer, O. A fully digital architecture for wideband wireless transmitters. IEEE RWS, Radio and Wireless Symposium, 2008.

25. Pozsgay, A. et al. A Fully Digital 65nm CMOS Transmitter for the 2.4-to-2.7GHz WiFi/WiMAX Bands using 5.4GHz RF DACs. IEEE ISSCC 2008, pp 360-619.

26. Raab, F. et al. RF and Microwave PA and Transmitter Technologies. High Frequency Electronics, May-November 2003, pp 22-49.

27. Robert, F. et al. Study of a polar ΔΣ transmitter associated to a high efficiency switched mode amplifier for mobile Wimax. 10th annual IEEE Wireless and Microwave Technology Conference, WAMICON, april 2009, Clearwater, FL, USA.

28. Rode, J., Hinrichs, J., Asbeck, P. Transmitter architecture using digital generation of RF signals. IEEE Radio and Wireless Conf., pp. 245-248, August 2003.

29. Schantz, H. Art and Science of UWB Antennas. Artech House, 2005.

30. Sokal, N., Sokal, A. Class E, A new Class of high efficiency Tuned single ended switching PAs. IEEE journal of Solid State Circuits, Vol. 10, No. 3, Juin 1975, pp 168-176.

31. Sowlati, T. et al. Quad band GSM/GSM/GPRS polar loop transmitter. IEEE Journal of SolidState Circuits, Volume 39, Issue 12, Dec. 2004 Page(s): 2179 – 2189.

32. Staszewski, R et al. All digital PLL and transmitter for mobile phones. IEEE Journal of SolidState Circuits, Volume 40, Issue 12, Dec. 2005 Page(s): 2469 – 2482.

33. Suarez Penaloza, M. et al. "Study of a Modified Polar Sigma-Delta Transmitter Architecture for Multi-Radio Applications", EuMW, 27-31 Octobre 2008, Amsterdam.

34. Villegas, M. et al. Radiocommunications Numériques : Conception de circuits intégrés RF et micro-ondes. Dunod, EEA/Electronique, 464 pages, 2ème édition 2007.

35. Wendell, B. et al. Polar modulator for multi-mode cell phones. Proceedings of the IEEE 2003 Custom Integrated Circuits Conference, Sept. 2003, pp: 439 – 44.

2 Chapter | ANALYTICAL SIR FOR CROSS LAYER CHANNEL MODEL

1. INTRODUCTION: AN OVERVIEW

In a wireless communication environment characterized by dynamically-varying channels, high influence of interference, bandwidth shortage and strong demand for quality of service (QoS) support, the challenge for achieving optimum spectral efficiency and high data rate is unprecedented. One of the bottlenecks in achieving these goals is modeling of the propagation environments Yun & Iskander (2004).

The commonly used radio propagation models only account for the large scale path loss Rappaport (2001) or only multipath propagations Alouini & Goldsmith (1997), which are incomplete for studying realistic system deployment scenarios. The authors in Alouini & Goldsmith (1997) calculate the capacity of Nakagami multipath fading (NMF) channels assuming that the carrier-to-noise ratio (CNR) is gamma distributed. This assumption neglects the effects of shadowing and large scale path loss. This chapter presents an "exact" pdf derived from a model which is more closely related to a realistic deployment scenario. With the results provided here, it is possible to calculate more precise capacity figures. Moreover since the new path loss model takes into consideration the interaction of the system or data link layer with the physical layer (PHY), it is particularly important in studying the cross-layer interaction between MAC and PHY layer.

The general approach of cross-layer design is to maintain the already established layered architecture, capture the important information that influences other layers, exchange the information between layers and implement adaptive protocols and algorithms at each layer to optimize the system performance Xia & Liang (2005).

Adhering to the idea of cross-layer solutions, many researchers are working towards finding viable cross layer designs spanning the different layers of the OSI model. Yeh and Cohen proposed a generalized analytical framework for cross-layer design focusing on resource allocation in the presence of multi-access fading channels Yeh & Cohen (2003). Ahn Ahn et al. (2002) uses the information from the medium access control (MAC) layer to do rate control at the network layer.

Cross-layer design relies on channel quality information. The channel quality can be captured by a single parameter, namely the received SIR. The SIR between two communicating nodes will typically decrease as the distance between the nodes increases, and will also depend on the signal propagation and interference environment. Moreover, the SIR varies randomly over time due to the propagation environment and interference characteristics. Therefore modeling the SIR on the assumption of the cellular structure and the well known path loss model that ignores the small scale fading would not be applicable to self-configuring cross-layer design. Therefore analytical derivation of the pdf of SIR is a crucial step in constructing efficient crosslayer design.

Tellambura in Tellambura (1999) uses a characteristic function method to calculate the probability that the SIR drops below some predefined threshold (probability of outage) under the assumption of Nakagami fading. Zhan Zhang (1996) also uses a similar characteristic function approach to derive outage probability for multiple interference scenario. These papers give a significant advantage in reducing the computational complexity involved in solving multiple integrals in SIR computation. But, a major shortcoming of these and other similar papers Zorzi (1997) is that, only the small scale fading (physical layer) or large scale fading (data link layer) is considered in analytically deriving the SIR statistics.

The rest of this chapter is organized as follows. In Section II the system model considered is presented and in Section III the analytical derivation is described in detail. Section IV provides the numerical and the simulation results. Section V concludes the chapter.

2. SYSTEM MODEL AND PROBLEM FORMULATION

For simplicity the cell layout used to derive the pdf of the SIR assumes circular cells, as shown in Fig. 1, with maximum cell radius Rc instead of hexagonal cells. The cells are randomly positioned resulting in potentially overlapping cells. Randomly positioned cells model an important network scenario, which lacks any frequency planning as a result of self-configuring and self-organising networks, cognitive radio, multihop ad hoc communication and cross layer system design. A receiver experiences interference from transmitters within its accessibility radius, Rac. Due to propagation path loss, a transmitter outside the accessibility region incurs only a negligible interference. Since the aim is to model a realistic interference limited environment, the receiver accessibility radius is taken to be much greater than the cell radius i.e Rac»Rc. The dashed line in Fig. 1 represents the interference link between transmitter, Tx y, and receiver, Rx z while the solid line shows the desired link between transmitter Tx x and receiver Rx z and vise versa. Throughout the derivation omni-directional antennas with unity gains are considered. The pdf is calculated assuming one interfering user. The results obtained can be extended to multiple interfering users by using laguerre polynomials to approximate the multiple integration resulting from the multiple interfering users. The analytical derivation of SIR for multiple interference is under study.

3. ANALYTICAL DERIVATION OF THE PDF OF THE SIR

In an interference limited environment, the received signal quality at a receiver is typically measured by means of achieved SIR, which is the ratio of the power of the wanted signal to the total residue power of the unwanted signals. let Pt and Pr denote the transmit and received power respectively. Let G denote the path gain and Gyz is the link gain between the interfering transmitter y and the receiver z. For the purpose of clarity, unless otherwise stated, a single subscript x, y or z specifies the node, and a double subscript such as xz specifies the link between node x and node z. A node is any entity, mobile station(MS) or base station(BS) that is capable of communicating. For a single interfering user y depicted in Fig. 1:

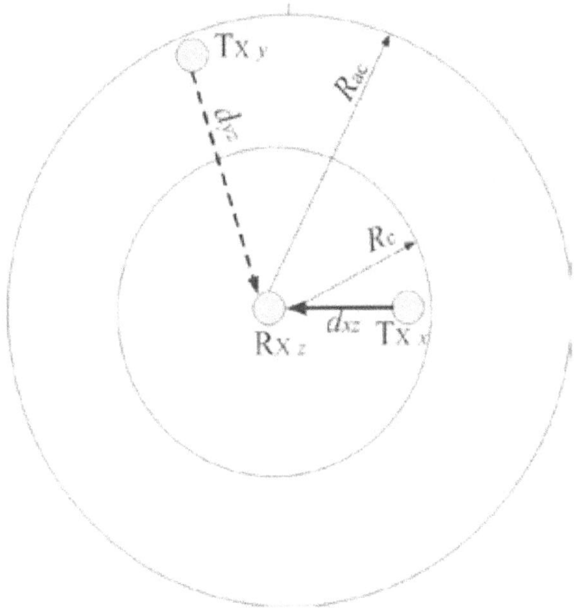

Fig. 1. Model to drive the pdf of the SIR from a single neighboring cell

$$\mathrm{SIR}_z = \frac{P_{tx} G_{xz}}{P_{ty} G_{yz}} \tag{1}$$

Assuming fixed and constant transmit powers, Ptx = Pty = const, (1) simplifies to:

$$\mathrm{SIR}_z = \frac{G_{xz}}{G_{yz}} \tag{2}$$

$$L = \frac{1}{G} \Rightarrow \mathrm{SIR}_z = \frac{L_{yz}}{L_{xz}} \tag{3}$$

where Lxz, Lyz are the path losses between transmitter Tx x and receiver Rx z and Tx y and Rx z respectively.

Like the gain parameter G, the loss parameter th fading.

The generalized path loss model for the cross layer environment is given by:

$$L = \underbrace{C\left(\frac{d}{d_0}\right)^{\gamma} e^{(\beta\xi)}}_{\text{large scale path loss}} \cdot \underbrace{\frac{1}{|H(f)|^2}}_{\text{small scale path loss}} \tag{4}$$

Where C $\frac{\hat{C}}{\tilde{C}}$ is an environment specific constant, C^ the constant corresponding to the desired C link while C˜ corresponds to the interference link. The distance d0 is a constant and d is a random variable, Γ is the path-loss exponent, Ξ is the random component due to shadowing, β = ln(10)/10 and |H(f)| is a random variable modeling the channel envelop.

The commonly used path loss equation Rappaport (2001) only accounts for the large scale path loss with regular cell deployment scenarios, which is incomplete for studying self-organizing networks. The new path loss model proposed here takes into consideration the interaction of the large scale path loss as well as the small scale fading. This model is particularly important in studying the performance of self-organizing self-configuring networks.

For the interference scenario described in the system model, the path loss for the desired path and the path loss between the interfering transmitter y and the receiver z (interfering link) are:

$$L_{xz} = \tilde{C} d_{xz}^{\gamma_{xz}} e^{(\beta\xi_{xz})} \frac{1}{|H_{xz}|^2} \tag{5}$$

$$L_{yz} = \hat{C} d_{yz}^{\gamma_{yz}} e^{(\beta\xi_{yz})} \frac{1}{|H_{yz}|^2} \tag{6}$$

where Lxz is the path loss model for the desired link and Lyz is the path loss model for the interfering link. dyz models the distance between the interference causing transmitter, x, and the victim receiver y. Γyz and Γxz are the path loss exponents, Ξxz and Ξyz are Gaussian distributed random variables modeling the shadow fading with each zero mean and variances v^2_{xz} and v^2_{yz} respectively, and |Hxz |and |Hyz|are the channel envelope modeling the channel fading. For the purpose of clarity, the time and frequency dependencies are not shown. The channel envelope is assumed to follow the Nakagami-m distribution. Nakagami distribution is a general statistical model which encompasses Rayleigh distribution as a special case, when the fading parameter m = 1, and also approximates the Rician distribution very well. In addition, Nakagami-m distribution will also provide the flexibility of choosing different distributions for the desired link and interfering link, such as the Rayleigh for the channel envelope of the desired link, and Rician for the interfering link, or vice versa.

Using equations (3) and (5), the SIR can be given as:

$$\mathrm{SIR} = \frac{Cd_{yz}^{\gamma_{yz}} \mathrm{e}^{(\beta\xi_{yz})} |H_{xz}|^2}{d_{xz}^{\gamma_{xz}} \mathrm{e}^{(\beta\xi_{xz})} |H_{yz}|^2} \tag{7}$$

From (7), the SIR has six random variable components, $\Phi_{xz} = d_{xz}^{\gamma_{xz}}$, $\Phi_{yz} = d_{yz}^{\gamma_{yz}}$, $\Lambda_{xz} = \mathrm{e}^{(\beta\xi_{xz})}$, $\Lambda_{yz} = \mathrm{e}^{(\beta\xi_{yz})}$, $|H_{xz}|^2$ and $|H_{yz}|^2$. In order to analytically derive the pdf of the SIR, the pdf of the individual components and also their ratios and products need to be determined first.

The following two formulas provide the basic framework for the analysis and will be used throughout the derivation. Given two independent random variables X and Y the pdf of their product fZ (z) where Z = XY is

$$f_Z(z) = \int f_X(z/x) f_Y(x)(1/|x|)dx \tag{8}$$

Given two independent random variables Y and X the pdf of their ratio fZ (z) where Z = $\frac{Y}{X}$ is

$$f_Z(z) = \int f_X(x) f_Y(zx)|x|dx \tag{9}$$

3.1 Pdf of the ratio of the propagation loss

It is assumed that the distance between the interfering transmitter and the receiver, dyz, is uniformly distributed up to a maximum distance of Rac, and that the distance between an interfering transmitter and intended receiver, dxz, is uniformly distributed up to a maximum distance of Rc . Therefore Φxz and Φyz are both functions of random variables, and their pdfs can be derived using the following random variable transformation Papoulis (1991).

$$p(\theta) = \left. \frac{p(\delta)}{\left|\frac{d(\theta)}{d(\delta)}\right|} \right|_{\delta = \mathrm{F}^{-1}(\theta)} \tag{10}$$

Where θ and δ are random variables with pdfs p(θ) and p(δ) respectivly, and where θ is a function of F(ffi), d(θ) and d(δ) are the first derivatives of θ and δ respectively. The mathematical representation of the pdfs of dxz and dyz are

$$f_{D_{xz}}(d_{xz}) = \frac{2d_{xz}}{R_c^2} \quad 0 < d_{xz} \leq R_c \tag{11}$$

$$f_{D_{yz}}(d_{yz}) = \frac{2d_{yz}}{R_{ac}^2} \quad 0 < d_{yz} \leq R_{ac} \tag{12}$$

Let fΦxz (Φxz) and fΦyz (Φyz) denote the pdfs of Φxzand Φyz. Then employing the transformation (10), fΦxz (Φxz) and fΦyz (Φyz) are derived as

$$f_{\Phi_{xz}}(\phi_{xz}) = \frac{2\phi_{xz}^{2/\gamma_{xz}-1}}{R_c^2\gamma_{xz}} \quad 0 < \phi_{xz} \leq R_c^{\gamma_{xz}} \tag{13}$$

$$f_{\Phi_{yz}}(\phi_{yz}) = \frac{2\phi_{yz}^{2/\gamma_{yz}-1}}{R_{ac}^2\gamma_{yz}} \quad 0 < \phi_{yz} \leq R_{ac}^{\gamma_{yz}} \tag{14}$$

Using (9), the pdf of the ratio of the propagation loss, $\Phi = \frac{\Phi_{yz}}{\Phi_{xz}}$ is found to be,

$$f_\Phi(\phi) = \begin{cases} Y\phi^{2/\gamma_{yz}-1} & \text{for } 0 < \phi \leq \varsigma \\ \tilde{Y}\phi^{-2/\gamma_{xz}-1} & \text{for } \varsigma < \phi < \infty \end{cases} \tag{15}$$

where $\varsigma = \frac{R_{ac}^{\gamma_{yz}}}{R_c^{\gamma_{xz}}}$, $Y = \frac{2R_c^{2\frac{\gamma_{xz}}{\gamma_{yz}}}}{R_{ac}^2(\gamma_{yz}+\gamma_{xz})}$ and $\tilde{Y} = \frac{2R_{ac}^{2\frac{\gamma_{yz}}{\gamma_{xz}}}}{R_c^2(\gamma_{yz}+\gamma_{xz})}$

The next step to derive the pdf of the SIR is find the pdf of the ratio of the lognormal shadowing.

3.2 Pdf of the ratio of the lognormal shadowing

Given a normally distributed random variable X with mean μ and variance Σ2, and a real constant c, the product cX is known to follow a normal distribution with mean cμ and a variance c2 Σ2 and eX has a log-normal distribution. Since Ξxz is normally distributed with mean μ and variance Σ2, Λxz = e(βΞxz) is a lognormal distributed random variable with mean μxz and variance v2 = β2Σxz2 expressed in terms of the normally distributed Ξxz, while the mean and variance of Λyz = e(βΞyz) are μyz and v2 = β2 Σyz2 respectively.

$$f_{\Lambda_{xz}}(\lambda_{xz}) = \frac{e^{-1/2\frac{(\ln(\lambda_{xz})-\mu_{xz})^2}{v_{xz}^2}}}{\lambda_{xz}v_{xz}\sqrt{2\pi}}, \quad 0 \leq \lambda_{xz} < \infty \tag{16}$$

$$f_{\Lambda_{yz}}(\lambda_{yz}) = \frac{e^{-1/2\frac{(\ln(\lambda_{yz})-\mu_{yz})^2}{v_{yz}^2}}}{\lambda_{yz}v_{yz}\sqrt{2\pi}}, \quad 0 \leq \lambda_{yz} < \infty \tag{17}$$

Since the ratio of two independent lognormal random variables is itself a lognormal distributed random variable. Therefore the pdf of $\Lambda = \frac{\Lambda_{yz}}{\Lambda_{xz}}$ is:

$$f_\Lambda(\lambda) = \frac{e^{-1/2\frac{(\ln(\lambda)-\mu)^2}{\sigma^2}}}{\lambda\sigma\sqrt{2\pi}}, \quad 0 \le \lambda < \infty \tag{18}$$

where

$$\sigma = \beta\sqrt{v_{xz} + v_{yz}}, \; \mu = 0;$$

The last components remaining from (7) are the random variables modeling the channel envelop and their ratios.

3.3 Pdf of the ratio of the channel envelope

In order to accommodate different channel fading distributions, Nakagami-m distribution was used to model the channel envelope. Nakagami-m distribution is the most general of all distribution known until now Nakagami (1960).

The Nakagami-m pdf is given by:

$$f_{|H_{xz}|}(h_{xz}) = \frac{2}{\Gamma(m_{xz})}\left(\frac{m_{xz}}{\Omega_{xz}}\right)^{m_{xz}} h_{xz}^{2m_{xz}-1} e^{-\frac{m_{xz}h_{xz}^2}{\Omega_{xz}}}, \quad 0 \le h_{xz} < \infty \tag{19}$$

$$f_{|H_{yz}|}(h_{yz}) = \frac{2}{\Gamma(m_{yz})}\left(\frac{m_{yz}}{\Omega_{yz}}\right)^{m_{yz}} h_{yz}^{2m_{yz}-1} e^{-\frac{m_{yz}h_{yz}^2}{\Omega_{yz}}}, \quad 0 \le h_{yz} < \infty \tag{20}$$

where m ≥ 1/2 represents the fading figure, Ω = E(x2) is the average received power and Γ(.) is the gamma function given as

$$\Gamma(m) = \int_0^\infty x^{m-1}e^{-x}dx.$$

The pdfs of the received instantaneous power, Hxz = |Hxz|2 are modeled by a gamma distribution. For the desired user the pdf of the receive signal power, fHxz (hxz), is given as

$$f_{H_{xz}}(h_{xz}) = \frac{h_{xz}^{m_{xz}-1}}{\Gamma(m_{xz})}\left(\frac{m_{xz}}{\Omega_{xz}}\right)^{m_{xz}} e^{-\frac{m_{xz}h_{xz}}{\Omega_{xz}}}, \quad 0 \le h_{xz} < \infty \tag{21}$$

and for the interfering user the PDF, f|Hyz|(hyz), is

$$f_{H_{yz}}(h_{yz}) = \frac{h_{yz}^{m_{yz}-1}}{\Gamma(m_{yz})}\left(\frac{m_{yz}}{\Omega_{yz}}\right)^{m_{yz}} e^{-\frac{m_{yz}h_{yz}}{\Omega_{yz}}}, \quad 0 \le h_{yz} < \infty \tag{22}$$

Using (8) and (9) the pdf of the ratio of gamma distribution, Ψ = is:

$$f_\Psi(\psi) = M\frac{\psi^{m_{xz}-1}}{\left(\frac{m_{yz}}{\Omega_{yz}} + \frac{m_{xz}}{\Omega_{xz}}\psi\right)^{(m_{yz}+m_{xz})}} \quad 0 \le \psi < \infty \tag{23}$$

where

$$M = \frac{\Gamma(m_{yz})\Gamma(m_{xz})}{\Gamma(m_{yz}+m_{xz})}\left(\frac{m_{yz}}{\Omega_{yz}}\right)^{m_{yz}}\left(\frac{m_{xz}}{\Omega_{xz}}\right)^{m_{xz}}. \tag{24}$$

Using the beta function, also called the Euler integral of the first kind, M can be re-written as

$$M = \frac{\left(\frac{m_{yz}}{\Omega_{yz}}\right)^{m_{yz}} \left(\frac{m_{xz}}{\Omega_{xz}}\right)^{m_{xz}}}{\mathrm{B}(m_{xz}, m_{yz})}, \tag{25}$$

where

$$\mathrm{B}(m_{xz}, m_{yz}) = \int_0^1 t^{m_{xz}-1}(1-t)^{m_{yz}-1} dt = \frac{\Gamma(m_{yz}+m_{xz})}{\Gamma(m_{yz})\Gamma(m_{xz})}.$$

The final step in the derivation of the pdf of the SIR is deriving the product of the above obtained pdfs.

3.4 Pdf of the SIR

As shown in (7) the pdf of the SIR is the product of the three individual random variables, Φ, Λ and Ψ. Using the equations presented so far, the final pdf of the SIR is presented in (26)

$$f_{\mathrm{SIR}}(\zeta) = M\zeta^{2m_{xz}-1} \times \tag{26}$$

$$\int_0^\infty \frac{A_1\chi^{q_1}\left(\mathrm{erf}\left(\frac{\frac{2}{\gamma_{yz}}\sigma^2 + \ln\left(\frac{\chi}{\left(\frac{R_{ac}^{\gamma_{yz}}}{R_c^{\gamma_{xz}}}\right)}\right)}{\sqrt{2}\sigma}\right) - 1\right) + B_1\chi^{q_2}\left(-1 - \mathrm{erf}\left(\frac{\frac{-2}{\gamma_{xz}}\sigma^2 + \ln\left(\frac{\chi}{\left(\frac{R_{ac}^{\gamma_{yz}}}{R_c^{\gamma_{xz}}}\right)}\right)}{\sqrt{2}\sigma}\right)\right)}{\left(\frac{m_{yz}}{\Omega_{xz}} + \frac{m_{xz}}{\Omega_{yz}}\left(\frac{\zeta}{\chi}\right)^2\right)^{(m_{yz}+m_{xz})}} d\chi$$

where $q_1 = \frac{2}{\gamma_{yz}} - 2m_{yz} - 1$, $q_2 = \frac{-2}{\gamma_{xz}} - 2m_{yz} - 1$,

$$A_1 = \frac{-\frac{2R_c^{2\frac{\gamma_{xz}}{\gamma_{yz}}}}{R_{ac}^2(\gamma_{yz}+\gamma_{xz})}}{2} e^{\left(\frac{2}{\gamma_{yz}^2}\right)\sigma^2}$$

and

$$B_1 = \frac{-\frac{2R_{ac}^{2\frac{\gamma_{yz}}{\gamma_{xz}}}}{R_c^2(\gamma_{yz}+\gamma_{xz})}}{2} e^{\left(\frac{2}{\gamma_{xz}^2}\right)\sigma^2}$$

The final equation does not have a closed form solution but it is possible to solve the integration using numerical methods.

4. SIGNAL TO INTERFERENCE AND NOISE RATIO

In case of an environment that is is not interference limited, the SINR (signal to interference and noise ratio) is required to fully describe the communication channel. SINR can easily be found by modifying the SIR equation given in (1):

$$\mathrm{SINR}_z = \frac{G_{xz}}{G_{yz} + N} \tag{27}$$

where N is the random variable modeling the Gaussian noise with mean mN = 0 and a standard deviation of ΣN . By applying the generalized path loss equation in (4), SINR at the receiver Rx z is given by:

$$\mathrm{SINR_z} = \frac{\frac{|H_{xz}|^2}{d_{xz}^{\gamma_{xz}} \mathrm{e}^{(\beta\xi_{xz})}}}{\frac{|H_{yz}|^2}{d_{yz}^{\gamma_{yz}} \mathrm{e}^{(\beta\xi_{yz})}} + N} \tag{28}$$

where the pdfs of the individual random variables are given in the previous section. let Θxz = ΦxzΛxz = dxzΓxz e(βΞxz) which are derived in the previous section. The pdf of Θxz, fΘ (θxz), is given as:

$$f_\Theta(\theta_{xz}) = \int f_\Phi(\theta_{xz}/\lambda_{xz}) f_{\Lambda_{xz}}(\lambda_{xz})(1/|\lambda_{xz}|) d\lambda_{xz} \tag{29}$$

$$f_\Theta(\theta_{xz}) = \int_{\frac{\theta_{xz}}{R_c^2}}^{\infty} \frac{2(\frac{\theta_{xz}}{\lambda_{xz}})^{2/\gamma_{xz}-1}}{R_c^2 \gamma_{xz}} \frac{\mathrm{e}^{-1/2 \frac{\beta(\ln(\lambda_{xz})-\mu)^2}{v_{xz}^2}}}{\lambda_{xz} v_{xz} \sqrt{2\pi}} \frac{1}{\lambda_{xz}} d\lambda_{xz} \tag{30}$$

$$f_\Theta(\theta_{xz}) = D \left(1 - \frac{\mathrm{erf}(2v_{xz}{}^2 - \gamma_{xz} m_{xz} + \gamma_{xz} \log \frac{\theta_{xz}}{R_c^{\gamma_{xz}}})}{\sqrt(2) \gamma_{xz} v_{xz}} \right) \tag{31}$$

$$\text{where } D = \frac{\mathrm{e}^{\frac{2v_{xz}{}^2 - 2\gamma_{xz} m_{xz}}{\gamma_{xz}{}^2}}}{R_c^2 \gamma_{xz}} \theta_{xz}{}^{\frac{2}{\gamma_{xz}-1}}$$

The next step in the derivation is to find the pdf of the path loss of the desired link by utilizing (9) and (19). Let S = $\frac{H_{xz}}{d_{xz}^{\gamma_{xz}} \mathrm{e}^{(\beta\xi_{xz})}}$ be the random variable denoting the path loss of the desired link. The pdf of S is given as:

$$f_S(s) = \mathrm{K} \int_0^\infty h_{xz}{}^{2m_{xz}} \mathrm{e}^{-\frac{m_{xz} h_{xz}{}^2}{\Omega_{xz}}} \left(1 - \frac{\mathrm{erf}(2v_{xz}{}^2 - \gamma_{xz} m_{xz} + \gamma_{xz} \log \frac{s h_{xz}}{R_c^{\gamma_{xz}}})}{\sqrt(2) \gamma_{xz} v_{xz}} \right) dh_{xz} \tag{32}$$

$$\text{where } \mathrm{K} = \frac{2}{\Gamma(m_{xz})} \frac{m_{xz}{}^2}{\Omega_{xz}} D$$

The pdf of the path loss of the interference path denoted by the random variable I = $\frac{|H_{yz}|}{d_{yz}^{\gamma_{yz}} \mathrm{e}^{(\beta\xi_{yz})}}$ is give as:

$$f_I(i) = \hat{\mathrm{K}} \int_0^\infty h_{yz}{}^{2m_{yz}} \mathrm{e}^{-\frac{m_{yz} h_{yz}{}^2}{\Omega_{yz}}} \left(1 - \frac{\mathrm{erf}(2v_{yz}{}^2 - \gamma_{yz} m_{yz} + \gamma_{yz} \log \frac{i h_{yz}}{R_{\hat{c}}^{\gamma_{yz}}})}{\sqrt(2) \gamma_{yz} v_{yz}} \right) dh_{yz} \tag{33}$$

$$\text{where } \hat{\mathrm{K}} = \frac{2}{\Gamma(m_{yz})} \frac{m_{yz}{}^2}{\Omega_{yz}} D$$

In order to find the pdf of the interference plus noise, I + N, it is assumed that interference is independent of noise. The pdf of the sum of two independent random variables U and V, each of which has a probability density function, is the convolution of their individual density functions:

fU+V (z)= fU (z - x) fV (x)dx (34)

therefore the pdf of I + N, f I+N (z) is given by:

$$f_{I+N}(z) = \int_0^\infty f_I(z-x) f_N(x) dx \tag{35}$$

where $f_N(x) = \frac{e^{-\frac{1}{2}(\frac{x}{\sigma_N})^2}}{\sqrt{2\pi}\sigma_N}$. Utilizing (9), the pdf of the SINR is given by :

$$f_{\mathrm{SINR}}(\nu) = \int_0^\infty f_{I+N}(z) f_S(\nu z) z dz \tag{36}$$

For the special case where the noise approaches zero, the pdf of the noise is represented as delta function or also known as, a unit impulse function, around zero. Therefore (35) can be rewritten as:

$$f_{I+N}(z) = \int_0^\infty f_I(z-x) f_N(x) dx = \int_0^\infty f_I(z-x)\delta(x) dx = f_I(z) \tag{37}$$

Thus

$$f_{\mathrm{SINR}}(\nu) = \int_0^\infty f_{I+N}(z) f_S(\nu z) z dz = \int_0^\infty f_I(z) f_S(\nu z) z dz \tag{38}$$

by the definition given in (9), the fSINR(v) given in (38) is the pdf of the SIR S . Therefore, when the noise approaches to zero, the pdf of the SINR given in (36) reduces to the pdf of SIR given in (26).

This sub-section has presented the pdf of the SINR as an extension to the pdf of the SIR. To validate the analytically derived SINR pdf, it is important to show that the core derivation, SIR derivation, is valid. The next sub-section validates the derivation through comparative numerical simulations of the SIR. The results presented were obtained using the adaptive Simpson quadrature numerical integration of the SIR.

5. RESULTS AND DISCUSSION

Monte Carlo simulations are carried out in order to validate the analytically derived pdf results. Fig. 2 and 3 show plots of the pdf of the SIR fSIR(ζ) for different scenarios. The results presented in Figs. 2 4 show that the analytical pdf is in good agreement with the Monte Carlo simulation. The parameters used for the shadow fading, channel standard deviation and path loss exponents reflect a realistic deployment scenario for users moving at a speed of 25 to 40 km/h Eltahir (2007). All simulations assume a channel envelope with a Nakagamim distribution with different m parameter, which corresponds to different fading scenario.

Fig. 2 depicts three different plots depending on the $\frac{R_{ac}}{R_c}$. As the cell radius Rc increases there is a significant cell overlap leading to high mean value of interference which in turn leads to lower SIR mean value. Therefore, as the ratio of the cell radius to the accessibility radius approaches to one, the pdf is skewed towards smaller SIR. These plots show that the node with the lowest cell radius, Rc = 100 m, has the highest SIR mean.

Fig. 3 shows the effect of different environments on the pdf of the SIR. The figure presents plots from an ad hoc free space outdoor deployment with line of sight scenario on the desired link, $\Gamma = 2$ and $m = 3$, to the most severe non-line-of-sight scenario of obstructed indoor (in building) environment, $\Gamma = 4$ and $m = 0.5$. The radius of the cell, Rc, has been set to 100 m, which is considered a good configuration example for ad hoc networks. The accessability radius, Rac is assumed to be 500 m. The results illustrate that the node with the best line-ofsight (LOS) link, $\Gamma xz = 2$ and $\Gamma yz = 4$, has the highes mean SIR value and the biggest variance or spread. While the node with the most obstructed inbuilding environment, exhibits the lowest mean and the smallest variance or spread of all. These can be attributed to the higher interference contribution of interfering node in NLOS link than those in LOS condition.

Fig. 4 present the cumulative density function of the SIR. The simulation parameters are summarized in table 3. From Fig. 4 it can be observed that for a target SIR of 25 dB, being a reasonable assumption for 64-QAM modulation, the probability that the SIR exceeds the target SIR in the most severe non-line-of-sight scenario of obstructed indoor (in building) environment is about 10% resulting in a high outage probability enforcing the use of lower order modulation schemes. On the other hand, for the link with best LOS condition of outdoor free space environment the the probability that the SIR exceeds the target SIR is 85% allowing the use of higher order modulation. Therefore from the results in Fig. 4, it can be deducted that the analytical work presented in this chapter can be used in determining the boundaries for varying the modulation order. A similar work of determining the boundaries for adaptive modulation was presented by Goldsmith et al. Alouini & Goldsmith (2000) assuming Nakagami distribution thus ignoring the shadowing effect, the pdf presented here can be used to extend the results presented in Alouini & Goldsmith (2000).

6. CONCISE SUMMARY

This chapter primarily contributes by deriving the probability density function of the SIR for cross-layer design without utilizing Monte Carlo simulations. The derivation utilized a generalized path loss model that incorporates both large-scale and small-scale path loss. The application of Nakagami-m distribution for fading channels provides the versatility to employ Rayleigh or alternative channel fading models for both desired and interfering links. The results obtained demonstrate remarkable concordance with the Monte Carlo-based findings. The SIR derivation was then employed to calculate the probability density function of the SINR. The derivation of SINR is crucial in non-interference constrained environments. These derivations can be utilized in situations where an understanding of SIR is essential, such link adaptation algorithms and cognitive radio design. This chapter's analytical derivation of the probability density function from a single interferer establishes a robust basis for calculating statistics from many interferers.

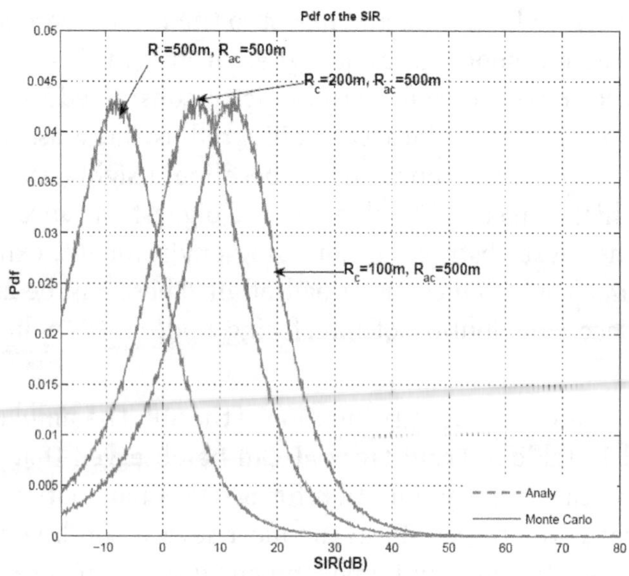

Fig. 2. Plots of the pdf of the SIR for different values of cell radius

Table 1. System parameters for Fig. 2(varying cell and accessability radius)

Parameter	Values
Rc	100 m
Rac	500 m
vxz	6 dB
vyz	10 dB
Γxz	2
Γyz	4
mxz	5
myz	0.5
Ωxz	4 dB
Ωyz	6 dB

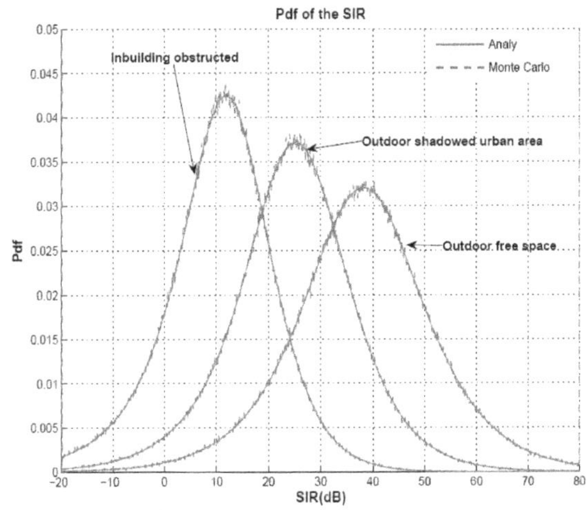

Fig. 3. Plots of the pdf of the SIR for different environments

Table 2. System parameters for Fig. 3

Parameter	Inbuilding obstructed	Outdoor shadowed urban	Outdoor free space
Rc	100 m	100 m	100 m
Rac	500 m	500 m	500 m
vxz	10 dB	8 dB	10 dB
vyz	10 dB	10 dB	10dB
Γxz	4	3	4
Γyz	4	4	4
mxz	3	1	0.5
myz	0.5	0.5	0.5
Ωxz	4 dB	4 dB	4 dB
Ωyz	6 dB	4 dB	6 dB

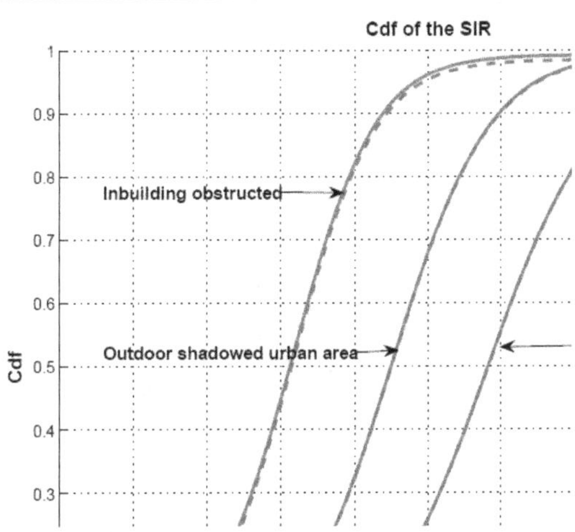

Fig. 4. Plots of the pdf of the SIR for different environments

Table 3. System parameters for Fig. 4

Parameter	Inbuilding obstructed	Outdoor shadowed urban	Outdoor free space
Rc	100 m	100 m	100 m
Rac	500 m	500 m	500 m
vxz	10 dB	8 dB	10 dB
vyz	10 dB	10 dB	10 dB
Γxz	4	3	4
Γyz	4	4	4
mxz	3	1	0.5
myz	0.5	0.5	0.5
Ωxz	4 dB	4 dB	4 dB
Ωyz	6 dB	4 dB	6 dB

REFERENCES

1. Ahn, G.-S., Campbell, A., Veres, A. & Sun, L.-H. (2002). Support Service Differentiation for Real-Time and Best-Effort Traffic in Stateless Wireless Ad Hoc Networks (SWAN), IEEE Trans. Mobile Comput. 1(3): 192–207.
2. Alouini, M.-S. & Goldsmith, A. (1997). Capacity of Nakagami Multipath Fading Channels, Proc. of the IEEE Vehicular Technology Conference(VTC), Vol. 1, Arizona, USA, pp. 358– 362.
3. Alouini, M.-S. & Goldsmith, A. (2000). Adaptive Modulation over Nakagami Fading Channels, Kluwer Journal on Wireless Commun. 13(1–2): 119–143.
4. Eltahir, I. (2007). The Impact of Different Radio Propagation Models for Mobile Ad hoc NETworks (MANET) in Urban Area Environment, Proc. of the International Conference on Wireless Broadband and Ultra Wideband Communications (AusWireless), Sydney, Australia, pp. 30–30.
5. Nakagami, M. (1960). The m-distribution: A General Formula of Intensity Distribution, Statistical Methods of Radio Wave Propagation, W. C. Hoffman, Ed., New York, Pergamon pp. 3–36.
6. Papoulis, A. (1991). Probability, Random Variables, and Stochastic Processes, 3 edn, McGraw–Hill. Rappaport, T. S. (2001). Wireless Communications: Principles and Practice, 2 edn, Prentice Hall PTR.
7. Tellambura, C. (1999). Cochannel Interference Computation for Arbitrary Nakagami Fading, IEEE Trans. Veh. Technol. 48(2): 487–489.
8. Xia, X. & Liang, Q. (2005). Bottom-up Cross-layer Optimization for Mobile ad hoc Networks, Proc. of the IEEE Military Communications Conference (MILCOM), Vol. 4, Atlantic City, USA, pp. 2624–2630.

9. Yeh, E. & Cohen, A. (2003). A Fundamental Cross-layer Approach to Uplink Resource Allocation, Proc. of the IEEE Military Communications Conference (MILCOM), Vol. 1, Monterey, CA, pp. 699–704.
10. Yun, Z. & Iskander, M. (2004). Progress in Modeling Challenging Propagation Environments, Proc. of the IEEE Antennas and Propagation Society International Symposium, Vol. 4, California, USA, pp. 3637–3640.
11. Zhang, Q. (1996). Outage Probability in Cellular Mobile Radio Due to Nakagami Signal and Interferers With Arbitrary Parameters, IEEE Trans. Veh. Technol. 45(2): 364–372.
12. Zorzi, M. (1997). On the Analytical Computation of the Interference Statistics with Applications to the Performance Evaluation of Mobile Radio Systems, IEEE Trans. Commun. 45(1): 103–109.

3 Chapter

THE INFLUENCE OF STATIC AND DYNAMIC SCATTERERS ON THE STATISTICAL PROPERTIES OF MIMO VEHICLE-TO-VEHICLE CHANNELS

1. INTRODUCTION: AN OVERVIEW

In numerous nations, the mitigation of road fatalities is a paramount objective. The Intelligent Transportation System (ITS) is a national initiative in the United States designed to enhance roadway safety. To implement the ITS, vehicle-to-vehicle (V2V) communication systems are required. The Dedicated Short Range Communication (DSRC) standard (ASTM, 2003) is intended for vehicle-to-vehicle (V2V) communications. Multiple task groups are engaged in developing this standard, including IEEE 802.11p (2006) and IEEE 1609.4 (WAVE, 2005).

The statistical characteristics of V2V channels differ from those of traditional fixed-to-mobile connections. Consequently, novel channel models are requisite for vehicle-to-vehicle communications. The geometrical two-ring model (Patel et al., 2003; Pätzold et al., 2005) has been proposed for vehicle-to-vehicle communications. This channel model is unsuitable for characterizing propagation conditions along streets for V2V channels. Indeed, in such a setting, wave-guiding along the street exerts a predominant influence. Molisch et al. (1999) proposed that wave-guiding can be realized by geometry-based channel models, wherein the scatterers are positioned along straight lines. The geometric street model presented in (Chelli & Pätzold, 2007) encapsulates the propagation effects when communicative cars traverse a straight street. The street model has been augmented to account for various clusters of scatterers and frequency selectivity (Chelli & Pätzold, 2008). A 3D channel model for vehicle-to-vehicle communications was proposed by Zajic´ et al. (2008). Measurement data from (Zajic et al., 2008) indicate that for vehicles operating in the central lanes of roads or in metropolitan settings, double-bounce rays produced by stationary scatterers are predominant. Unlike our model given in (Chelli & Pätzold, 2007) and (Chelli & Pätzold, 2008), which assumes single-bounce scattering, we posit double-bounce scattering for stationary scatterers. Double-bounce models fundamentally vary from single-bounce ones. In double-bounce models, the angles of departure (AoD) and angles of arrival (AoA) are independent of each other. This contrasts with single-bounce models, where the Angle of Departure (AoD) and the Angle of Arrival (AoA) are tightly correlated. The statistical features of double-bounce models and single-bounce models differ due to this dissimilarity. Consequently, double-bounce models warrant meticulous examination.

Moreover, the existence of dynamic scatterers in a roadway setting significantly influences channel behavior. Consequently, we examine the impact of passing cars on the statistical features of the channel. Measurement data in Millott (1994) indicate that the amplitude of waves dispersed from several vehicles is minimal, and the practical effect of vehicular scattering is limited to single-bounce rays. Consequently, double-bounce scattering from dynamic scatterers has been excluded from our model. When scatterers move at high speeds relative to the transmitter (receiver), the Angle of Departure (AoD) and Angle of Arrival (AoA) become time-variant, leading to a non-stationary channel model. However, during road congestion, the relative speed of vehicles near the transmitter or receiver is diminished. Under these conditions, we can still regard the AoD and AoA as non-time-variant for a sufficiently extended duration. This assumption is valid, particularly when the scatterers are moving in the same direction as both the transmitter and the receiver.

2. THE GEOMETRICAL STREET MODEL

A typical highway propagation environment for V2V communication is presented in Fig. 1. The highway encompasses three lanes used for traffic in the same direction. We can distin- guish between two types of scatterers namely fixed scatterers and moving scatterers. The fixed scatterers are represented by the buildings located on both sides of the street, while the moving scatterers are the vehicles in the vicinity of the transmitter MST and the receiver MSR. In order to be able to develop an appropriate channel model for the propagation scenario presented in Fig. 1, we first need to produce a representative geometrical model for such an environment. Towards this aim, we model each building by a cluster of scatterers located on a straight line on the left or right hand side of the street. A vehicle can be modeled by a cluster of scatterers located on a line as well. The fixed clusters are represented by solid lines while the moving clusters are represented by dashed lines. The geometrical street model encompassing fixed and moving scatterers is illustrated in Fig. 2. The fixed scatterers around the transmitter (receiver) are denoted by STm (SRn). The moving scatterers are designated by SMp. The propagation environment encompasses CT (CR) fixed clusters around the transmitter (receiver) and CM moving clusters. For fixed clusters, the AoD is referred to as αTm, whereas the AoA is denoted by βRn. For moving clusters, the symbols αMp and βMp stand for the AoD and the AoA, respectively. It has to be noted that for fixed clusters the AoD and the AoA are independent since double-bounce scattering is assumed. For moving clusters, the AoD and the AoA are closely related due to the single-bounce scattering assumption. All scatterers belonging to a given moving cluster have the same velocity vS and the same direction of motion ΦS. The transmitter and the receiver are moving with velocity vT and vR, respectively. The angle of motion of the transmitter and the receiver w.r.t the x-axis is referred to as ΦT and ΦR, respectively. Moreover, the transmitter (receiver) is equipped with MT (MR) antenna elements. The antenna element spacing at the transmitter and the receiver antenna are denoted by δT and δR, respectively. The angle ΓT (ΓR) describes the tilt angle of the transmit (receive) antenna array.

3. THE REFERENCE MODEL

Starting from the geometrical model shown in Fig. 2, we derive a reference model for the MIMO V2V channel. First, we consider the case where we have one moving cluster and two fixed clusters: one cluster is near to the transmitter and the other cluster is close to the

receiver. The total number of fixed scatterers around the transmitter (receiver) is denoted by M (N), while the number of moving scatterers is referred to as P. The complex channel gain $g_{kl}(t)$ describing the link between the lth transmit antenna element A_l^T ($l = 1,2,\ldots,M_T$) and the kth receive antenna element $A_k^R(k - 1,2,\ldots,M_R)$ of the underlying $M_T \times M_R$ MIMO V2V channel model can be expressed as $g_{kl}(t) = g_{kl}^{\mathrm{F}}(t) + g_{kl}^{\mathrm{M}}(t)$. The term $g_{kl}^{\mathrm{F}}(t)$ stands for the channel gain due to double-scattering from the fixed clusters. The channel gain caused by the moving cluster is denoted by $g_{kl}^{\mathrm{M}}(t)$. We assume that the line-of-sight component is obstructed. Next, we derive analytical expressions of the channel gains $g_{kl}^{\mathrm{F}}(t)$ and $g_{kl}^{\mathrm{M}}(t)$.

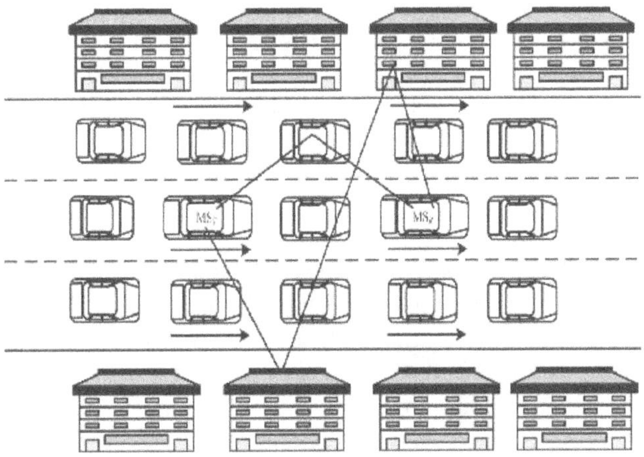

Fig. 1. A highway propagation environment for vehicle-to-vehicle communications under congestion conditions.

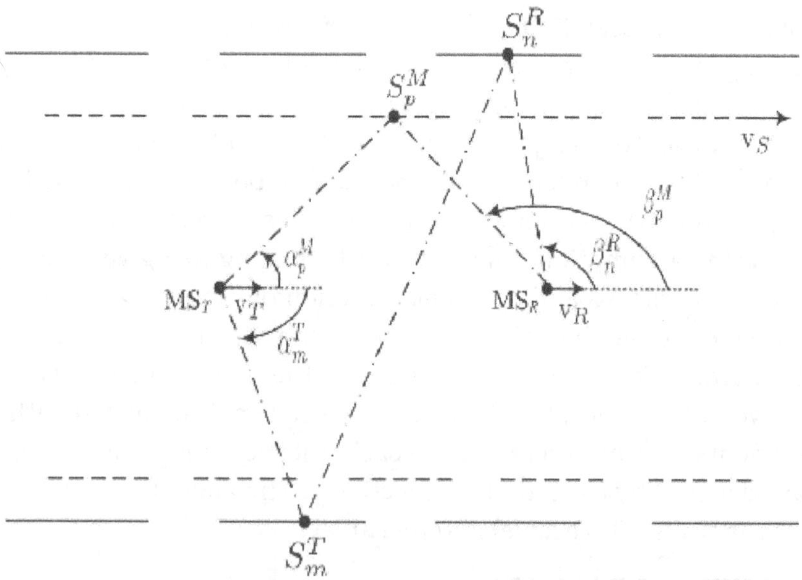

Fig. 2. The geometrical street model encompassing moving and fixed scatterers.

3.1 The Channel Gain Due to Fixed Scatterers

The plane wave emitted from the lth transmi antonna element ATl travels over the scatterers STm and SRn before impinging on the kth rcceive antenna element ARk . Based on the geometrical model in Fig. 2, the channel gain, due to double-scattering from fixed clusters, gFkl(t) can be written as

$$g_{kl}^{F}(\vec{r}_T, \vec{r}_R) = \sum_{m,n=1}^{M,N} c_{mn}\, e^{j\left(\theta_{mn} + \vec{k}_m^T \cdot \vec{r}_T - \vec{k}_n^R \cdot \vec{r}_R - k_0 d_{mn}\right)} \tag{1}$$

where c_{mn} and θ_{mn} stand for the joint gain and the joint phase shift resulting from the interaction with the fixed scatterers S_m^T and S_n^R. The joint channel gain can be written as $c_{mn} = 1/\sqrt{MN}$, while the joint phase shift can be expressed as $\theta_{mn} = (\theta_m + \theta_n) \mod 2\pi$, where mod stands for the modulo operation. The terms θ_m and θ_n are the phase shifts associated with the scatterers S_m^T and S_n^R, respectively. It has to be noted that θ_m, θ_n, and $\theta_{m,n}$ are independent identically distributed (i.i.d.) random variables uniformly distributed over $[0, 2\pi)$.

$$\vec{k}_m^T \cdot \vec{r}_T \quad = \quad 2\pi f_{\max}^T \cos(\alpha_m^T - \phi^T)t \tag{2}$$

where $f_{\max}^T = v_T/\lambda$ stands for the maximum Doppler frequency associated with the mobility of the transmitter. The symbol λ denotes the wavelength.

The third phase term in (1), $\vec{k}_n^R \cdot \vec{r}_R$, is caused by the receiver movement. The symbol $\vec{k}_n^R$ denotes the wave vector pointing in the propagation direction of the nth received plane wave, and $\vec{r}_R$ is the spatial translation vector of the receiver. The scalar product $\vec{k}_n^R \cdot \vec{r}_R$ can be written as

$$\vec{k}_n^R \cdot \vec{r}_R = -2\pi f_{\max}^R \cos(\beta_n^R - \phi^R)t \tag{3}$$

where $f_{\max}^R = v_R/\lambda$ stands for the maximum Doppler frequency due to the receiver movement.

The term $k_0 d_{mn}$ in (1) is associated with the total travelled distance and can be expressed as

$$k_0 d_{mn} = \frac{2\pi}{\lambda}(D_{lm} + D_{mn} + D_{nk}) \tag{4}$$

where D_{lm} denotes the distance from the lth transmit antenna element A_l^T to the scatterer S_m^T. The symbol D_{mn} stands for the distance between the scatterers S_m^T and S_n^R. The term D_{nk} denotes the distance from the scatterer S_n^R to the kth receive antenna element A_k^R. The distances D_{lm} and D_{nk} can be approximated as

$$D_{lm} \approx D_m^T - (M_T - 2l + 1)\frac{\delta_T}{2}\cos(\alpha_m^T - \gamma_T) \tag{5}$$

$$D_{nk} \approx D_n^R - (M_R - 2k + 1)\frac{\delta_R}{2}\cos(\beta_n^R - \gamma_R) \tag{6}$$

where D_m^T denotes the distance from the transmitter to the scatterer S_m^T and D_n^R corresponds to the distance from the receiver to the scatterer S_n^R. After substituting (2)–(6) in (1) the channel gain caused by double-scattering from fixed clusters can be expressed as

$$g_{kl}^F(t) = \sum_{m,n=1}^{M,N} \frac{a_m^T b_n^R c_{mn}^{TR}}{\sqrt{MN}} e^{j\left(2\pi(f_m^T + f_n^R)t + \theta_{mn}\right)} \tag{7}$$

where

$$a_m^T = e^{j\pi\frac{\delta_T}{\lambda}(M_T - 2l + 1)\cos(\alpha_m^T - \gamma_T)} \tag{8}$$

$$b_n^R = e^{j\pi\frac{\delta_R}{\lambda}(M_R - 2k + 1)\cos(\beta_n^R - \gamma_R)} \tag{9}$$

$$c_{mn}^{TR} = e^{-j\frac{2\pi}{\lambda}\left(D_m^T + D_{mn} + D_n^R\right)} \tag{10}$$

$$f_m^T = f_{\max}^T \cos(\alpha_m^T - \phi^T) \tag{11}$$

$$f_n^R = f_{\max}^R \cos(\beta_n^R - \phi^R). \tag{12}$$

It has to be mentioned that the envelope |gklF (t)| follows a double Rayleigh distribution since double-bounce scattering is assumed (Salo et al., 2006).

3.2 The Channel Gain Due to Moving Scatterers

The plane wave emitted from the lth transmit antenna element ATl travels over the scatterer SMP before impinging on the kth receive antenna element ARk . Based on the geometrical model in Fig. 2, the channel gain gMkl (t) of the moving cluster can be expressed as

$$g_{kl}^M(\vec{r}_T, \vec{r}_R, \vec{r}_S) = \sum_{p=1}^{P} c_p\, e^{j\left(\theta_p + \vec{k}_p^T\cdot\vec{r}_T - \vec{k}_p^R\cdot\vec{r}_R - \vec{k}_p^T\cdot\vec{r}_S + \vec{k}_p^R\cdot\vec{r}_S - k_0 d_p\right)} \tag{13}$$

where cp and Θp represent the gain and the phase shift resulting from the interaction with the moving scatterer SMp , respectively. The channel gain is given by cp = 1 / $\sqrt{P}$ while the phase shifts Θp are i.i.d. random variables uniformly distributed over [0, 2π). The phase changes $\vec{k}_p^T \cdot \vec{r}_T$ and $\vec{k}_p^R \cdot \vec{r}_R$ associated with the movement of the receiver and the transmitter, respectively, and can be written as

$$\vec{k}_p^T \cdot \vec{r}_T = 2\pi f_{\max}^T \cos(\alpha_p^M - \phi^T)t \quad (14)$$

$$\vec{k}_p^R \cdot \vec{r}_R = -2\pi f_{\max}^R \cos(\beta_p^M - \phi^R)t. \quad (15)$$

The spatial translation $\vec{r}_S$ of the moving scatterer S_p^M influences the wave emitted from the transmitter resulting in a phase change $\vec{k}_p^T \cdot \vec{r}_S$. Moreover, the scatterer S_p^M interacts with the wave reflected to the receiver resulting in a phase change $\vec{k}_p^R \cdot \vec{r}_S$. These phase changes can be expressed as

$$\vec{k}_p^T \cdot \vec{r}_S = 2\pi f_{\max}^S \cos(\alpha_p^M - \phi^S)t \quad (16)$$

$$\vec{k}_p^R \cdot \vec{r}_S = -2\pi f_{\max}^S \cos(\beta_p^M - \phi^S)t \quad (17)$$

where f S =vS /Λ is referred to as the maximum Doppler frequency caused by the moving cluster. Recall that all scatterers SPM belonging to the moving cluster have the same speed vS. The phase change resulting from the total travelled distance dp can be expressed as

$$k_0 d_p = \frac{2\pi}{\lambda}(D_{lp} + D_{pk}) \quad (18)$$

with

$$D_{lp} \approx D_p^T - (M_T - 2l + 1)\frac{\delta_T}{2}\cos(\alpha_p^M - \gamma_T) \quad (19)$$

$$D_{pk} \approx D_p^R - (M_R - 2k + 1)\frac{\delta_R}{2}\cos(\beta_p^M - \gamma_R) \quad (20)$$

where D^T_P and D^R_P denote the distances from the scatterer SM to the transmitter and the receiver, respectively. After substituting (14)–(20) in (13) the channel gain due to the moving cluster can be written as

$$g_{kl}^M(t) = \sum_{p=1}^{P} \frac{a_p^M b_p^M c_p^M}{\sqrt{P}} e^{j\left(2\pi(f_p^{TM} + f_p^{RM} - f_p^{TS} - f_p^{RS})t + \theta_p\right)} \quad (21)$$

where

$$a_p^M = e^{j\pi\frac{\delta_T}{\lambda}(M_T-2l+1)\cos(\alpha_p^M-\gamma_T)} \tag{22}$$

$$b_p^M = e^{j\pi\frac{\delta_R}{\lambda}(M_R-2k+1)\cos(\beta_p^M-\gamma_R)} \tag{23}$$

$$c_p^M = e^{-j\frac{2\pi}{\lambda}(D_p^T+D_p^R)} \tag{24}$$

$$f_p^{TM} = f_{\max}^T\cos(\alpha_p^M-\phi^T) \tag{25}$$

$$f_p^{RM} = f_{\max}^R\cos(\beta_p^M-\phi^R) \tag{26}$$

$$f_p^{TS} = f_{\max}^S\cos(\alpha_p^M-\phi^S) \tag{27}$$

$$f_p^{RS} = f_{\max}^S\cos(\beta_p^M-\phi^S). \tag{28}$$

It has to be noted that the AoD αpM and the AoA βpM are dependent since single-bounce scattering is assumed. The exact relationship between the AoD and the AoA can be found in (Chelli & Pätzold, 2007). The envelope |gM(t)| follows a Rayleigh distribution due to the single-bounce scattering assumption.

3.3 The Multiple-Cluster Channel Gain

The channel gain gkl (t) has been derived assuming a scattering environment with two fixed clusters and one moving cluster. However, in real environment, one can find several buildings and several vehicles near to the mobile transmitter and receiver. Therefore, it is of interest to derive an expression for the channel gain in a multiple-cluster case zkl (t). The environment encompasses CT (CR) fixed clusters around the transmitter (receiver) and CM moving clusters. We added the subscripts (·)cT , (·)cR , and (·)cM to all affected symbols to distinguish between the fixed clusters around the transmitter, the fixed clusters around receiver, and the moving clusters, respectively. The fixed cluster cT has a limited length LcT , it follows that the AoDs

α^T_{m,c^T} are restricted to the interval $[\alpha^T_{\min,c^T}, \alpha^T_{\max,c^T}]$. Analogously, the AoDs β^R_{n,c^R}, α^M_{p,c^M}, and β^M_{p,c^M} are confined to the intervals $[\beta^R_{\min,c^R}, \beta^R_{\max,c^R}]$, $[\alpha^M_{\min,c^M}, \alpha^M_{\max,c^M}]$, and $[\beta^M_{\min,c^M}, \beta^M_{\max,c^M}]$, respectively. Moreover, all the AoDs α^T_{m,c^T} $(m = 1, 2, \ldots)$ have the same distribution and will be noted henceforth by $\alpha^T_{c^T}$. The same statement holds for the angles β^R_{n,c^R}, α^M_{p,c^M}, and β^M_{p,c^M} which will be denoted by $\beta^R_{c^R}$, $\alpha^M_{c^M}$, and $\beta^M_{c^M}$, respectively.

In a multiple-cluster scenario the channel gain describing the link ATl –ARk can be expressed as

zkl (t) = zF kl (t)+ zM kl (t) (29)

where zklF (t) is the received diffuse component due to double-scattering from all fixed clusters. The term zklM(t) is the received diffuse component caused by single-scattering from all moving clusters. The channel gains zFkl (t) and zkl M(t) can be written as

$$z_{kl}^{\mathrm{F}}(t) \;=\; \sum_{c^T,c^R=1}^{C^T,C^R} w_{c^T}\, w_{c^R}\, g_{kl,c^T,c^R}^{\mathrm{F}}(t) \tag{30}$$

$$z_{kl}^{\mathrm{M}}(t) \;=\; \sum_{c^M=1}^{C^M} w_{c^M}\, g_{kl,c^M}^{\mathrm{M}}(t) \tag{31}$$

where wcT , wcR , and wcM are positive constants representing the weighting factors of the clusters cT , cR, and cM , respectively. We impose the boundary $\sum_{c^T,c^R=1}^{C^T,C^R} w_{c^T}^2 w_{c^R}^2 + \sum_{c^M=1}^{C^M} w_{c^M}^2 = 1$ condition , to normalize the mean power of zkl (t) to unity.

4. CORRELATION PROPERTIES

In this section, we derive analytical expressions for the correlation functions of the proposed MIMO V2V channel model, such as the 3D space-time CCF, the temporal ACF, and the 2D space CCF. The 3D space-time CCF ρkl,k l (δT , δR, T) can be expressed as

ρkl,k l (δT , δR, T) := E z∗kl (t) zk l (t + T)

$$\begin{aligned} &= \sum_{c^T,c^R=1}^{C^T,C^R} w_{c^T}^2\, w_{c^R}^2\, \rho_{kl,k'l',c^T,c^R}^{\mathrm{F}}(\delta_T,\delta_R,\tau) \\ &\quad + \sum_{c^M=1}^{C^M} w_{c^M}^2\, \rho_{kl,k'l',c^M}^{\mathrm{M}}(\delta_T,\delta_R,\tau) \end{aligned} \tag{32}$$

where (·)* denotes the complex conjugation and E{·} stands for the expectation operator. The term ρFkl,k_l_,cT,cR (δT, δR, T) represents the 3D space-time CCF due to double-scattering from the clusters cT and cR. This correlation function can be written as

$$\begin{aligned} \rho_{kl,k'l',c^T,c^R}^{\mathrm{F}}(\delta_T,\delta_R,\tau) &:= E\left\{ (g_{kl,c^T,c^R}^{\mathrm{F}}(t))^* \, g_{k'l',c^T,c^R}^{\mathrm{F}}(t+\tau) \right\} \\ &= \rho_{c^T}^{\mathrm{F}}(\delta_T,\tau) \cdot \rho_{c^R}^{\mathrm{F}}(\delta_R,\tau) \end{aligned} \tag{33}$$

where

$$\rho_{c^T}^{\mathrm{F}}(\delta_T,\tau) \;=\; \int_{\alpha_{\min,c^T}^T}^{\alpha_{\max,c^T}^T} c_{ll'}^{\mathrm{F}}(\delta_T,\alpha_{c^T}^T)\, e^{j2\pi f^T(\alpha_{c^T}^T)\tau}\, p_{\alpha_{c^T}^T}(\alpha_{c^T}^T)\, d\alpha_{c^T}^T \tag{34}$$

and

$$\rho_{c^R}^{\mathrm{F}}(\delta_R,\tau) \;=\; \int_{\beta_{\min,c^R}^R}^{\beta_{\max,c^R}^R} d_{kk'}^{\mathrm{F}}(\delta_R,\beta_{c^R}^R)\, e^{j2\pi f^R(\beta_{c^R}^R)\tau}\, p_{\beta_{c^R}^R}(\beta_{c^R}^R)\, d\beta_{c^R}^R \tag{35}$$

are the transmit and the receive correlation functions, respectively, and

$$c^F_{ll'}(\delta_T, \alpha^T_{c^T}) = e^{j2\pi\frac{\delta_T}{\lambda}(l-l')\cos(\alpha^T_{c^T}-\gamma_T)} \quad (36)$$

$$d^F_{kk'}(\delta_R, \beta^R_{c^R}) = e^{j2\pi\frac{\delta_R}{\lambda}(k-k')\cos(\beta^R_{c^R}-\gamma_R)} \quad (37)$$

$$f^T(\alpha^T_{c^T}) = f^T_{\max}\cos(\alpha^T_{c^T} - \phi^T) \quad (38)$$

$$f^R(\beta^R_{c^R}) = f^R_{\max}\cos(\beta^R_{c^R} - \phi^R). \quad (39)$$

The distributions of the AoD $\alpha^T_{c^T}$ and the AoA $\beta^R_{c^R}$ are denoted by $p_{\alpha^T_{c^T}}(\alpha^T_{c^T})$ and $p_{\beta^R_{c^R}}(\beta^R_{c^R})$, respectively.

In (32), the term $\rho^M_{kl,k'l',c^M}(\delta_T, \delta_R, \tau)$, which represents the 3D space-time CCF of the moving cluster c^M, can be expressed as

$$\rho^M_{kl,k'l',c^M}(\delta_T, \delta_R, \tau) := E\left\{(g^M_{kl,c^M}(t))^* g^M_{k'l',c^M}(t)(t+\tau)\right\}$$

$$= \int_{\alpha^M_{\min,c^M}}^{\alpha^M_{\max,c^M}} c^M_{ll'}(\delta_T, \alpha^M_{c^M})\, d^M_{kk'}(\delta_R, g(\alpha^M_{c^M}))\, e^{j2\pi\left(f^{TM}(\alpha^M_{c^M})+f^{RM}(g(\alpha^M_{c^M}))-f^{TS}(\alpha^M_{c^M})\right)\tau}\, e^{-j2\pi f^{RS}(g(\alpha^M_{c^M}))\tau}\, p_{\alpha^M_{c^M}}(\alpha^M_{c^M})\, d\alpha^M_{c^M} \quad (40)$$

where

$$c^M_{ll'}(\delta_T, \alpha^M_{c^M}) = e^{j2\pi\frac{\delta_T}{\lambda}(l-l')\cos(\alpha^M_{c^M}-\gamma_T)} \quad (41)$$

$$d^M_{kk'}(\delta_R, g(\alpha^M_{c^M})) = e^{j2\pi\frac{\delta_R}{\lambda}(k-k')\cos(g(\alpha^M_{c^M})-\gamma_R)} \quad (42)$$

$$f^{TM}(\alpha^M_{c^M}) = f^T_{\max}\cos(\alpha^M_{c^M} - \phi^T) \quad (43)$$

$$f^{RM}(g(\alpha^M_{c^M})) = f^R_{\max}\cos(g(\alpha^M_{c^M}) - \phi^R) \quad (44)$$

$$f^{TS}(\alpha^M_{c^M}) = f^S_{\max}\cos(\alpha^M_{c^M} - \phi^S) \quad (45)$$

$$f^{RS}(g(\alpha^M_{c^M})) = f^S_{\max}\cos(g(\alpha^M_{c^M}) - \phi^S). \quad (46)$$

The function g(·) in (40) expresses the exact relationship between the AoD aMcM and the AoA βM $_{c^M}$. An expression for g(·) can be found in (Chelli & Pätzold, 2007).

The temporal ACF rzkl (T) of the channel gain zkl (t) is defined as rzkl (T) := E {z*kl (t)zkl (t + T)}(Papoulis & Pillai, 2002). The temporal ACF rzkl (T) can be deduced from the 3D space-time CCF ρkl,k l (δT , δR, T) by setting the antenna element spacings δT and δR to zero, i.e.,

rzkl (T)= ρkl,k l (0, 0, T)

$$= \sum_{c^T,c^R=1}^{C^T,C^R} w_{c^T}^2 w_{c^R}^2 \rho^{\mathrm{F}}_{kl,k'l',c^T,c^R}(0,0,\tau)$$

$$+ \sum_{c^M=1}^{C^M} w_{c^M}^2 \rho^{\mathrm{M}}_{kl,k'l',c^M}(0,0,\tau). \quad (47)$$

The 2D space CCF ρkl,k l (δT , δR) is defined as ρkl,k l (δT , δR) := E{z∗kl (t)zk l (t)}. Alternatively, the 2D space CCF ρkl,k l (δT , δR) can be derived from the 3D space-time CCF ρkl,k l (δT , δR, T) by setting T to zero, i.e.,

$$\rho_{kl,k'l'}(\delta_T,\delta_R) = \rho_{kl,k'l'}(\delta_T,\delta_R,0)$$

$$= \sum_{c^T,c^R=1}^{C^T,C^R} w_{c^T}^2 w_{c^R}^2 \rho^{\mathrm{F}}_{kl,k'l',c^T,c^R}(\delta_T,\delta_R,0)$$

$$+ \sum_{c^M=1}^{C^M} w_{c^M}^2 \rho^{\mathrm{M}}_{kl,k'l',c^M}(\delta_T,\delta_R,0). \quad (48)$$

5. NUMERICAL RESULTS

In this section, we confirm the validity of the analytical expressions presented in the previous section by simulations making use of the sum-of-cisoids method. The simulation models for moving and fixed scatterers are designed using the modified method of equal area (MMEA) proposed in (Gutiérrez & Pätzold, 2007). In order to model all fixed clusters, 50 cisoids are used for the simulation model. The same number of cisoids is used to model all moving clus- ters. The propagation environment contains six moving clusters: three clusters are located on the right side of the transmitter and the receiver, while the remaining clusters lie on the left side. Each moving cluster has a length of 5 m and is separated by a distance of 45 m from its neighbour clusters. The distance between the transmitter and the moving scatterers located on the left and the right side is set to 3 m. For the fixed clusters, we consider a propagation environment encompassing three clusters on each side of the transmitter. Each cluster has a length of 2 m and is separated by a distance of 34 m from its neighbour clusters. The same number of fixed clusters is considered around the receiver. The distance between the trans- mitter and the fixed scatterers on the left and right side is set to 300 m. The distance between the transmitter and the receiver is equal to 100 m. The transmitter and the receiver have a speed of 50 km/h and equal angles of motion ΦT = ΦR = 0. The transmitter and the receiver antenna tilts ΓT and ΓR are set to π/2. We consider the case of non-isotropic scattering conditions. The AoDs αT and αM are uniformly distributed over the intervals [αT T T max,c and [αMM M max,c], respectively. The uniform distribution is also assumed for the AoAs βRcR over the interval [βR min,c max,cR ,β R].

We present some illustrative examples for the temporal ACF rM (T) of the moving clusters in Fig. 3. We study the influence of the speed of the vehicles in the vicinity of the transmitter andthe receiver on the channel behaviour. The term vS in Fig. 3 denotes the speed of the vehicles on the left and right side. From Fig. 3, we can notice that as the speed vS decreases, the coher- ence time of the channel increases. It is well known that the coherence time indicates whether we are facing a fast or a slow fading. As the speed of the vehicles relatively to the transmit- ter and the receiver decreases the channel results can be observed in Fig. 3. In Fig. 4, we show the numerical results obtained for the 2D space CCF ρM11,22 (δT , δR) caused by moving scatterers. It could be seen from Fig. 4 that the cross-correlation function decreases as we increase the antenna spacings δT and δR.

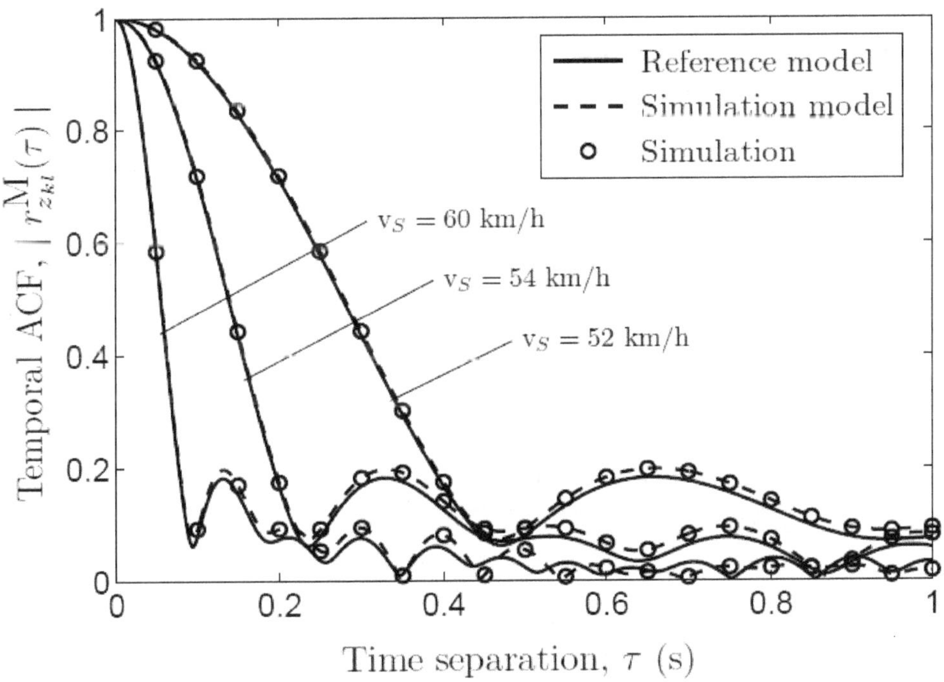

Fig. 3. The absolute value of the temporal ACF rMzkl (T) associated with moving scatterers for various values of the velocity vS of the surrounding vehicles.

However, the decay of the 2D space CCF ρM11,22 (δT , δR) is faster along the δR direction. Hence, a small antenna spacing at the receiver side guarantees a diversity gain, but at the receiver side, we need a larger spacing to get non-correlated channels.

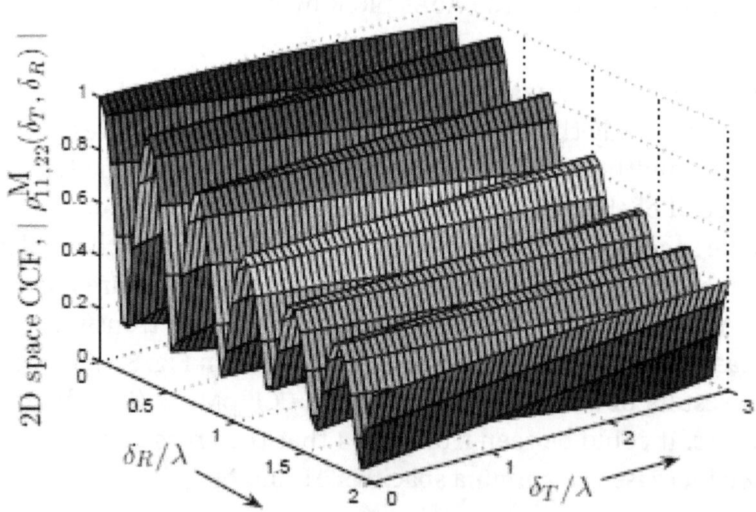

Fig. 4. The absolute value of the 2D space CCF $\rho M_{11,22}$ (δT , δR) of the reference model caused by moving scatterers.

In Fig. 5, we illustrate the numerical results for the transmit correlation function ρF (δT , T) of the reference model resulting from fixed scatterers. The obtained results are confirmed by simu- lation in Fig. 6. Similar results have been found for the receive correlation function ρF (δR, T) associated with fixed scatterers since the same setting for the scatterers is considered around the transmitter and the receiver. Limited space prevents us from including these results.

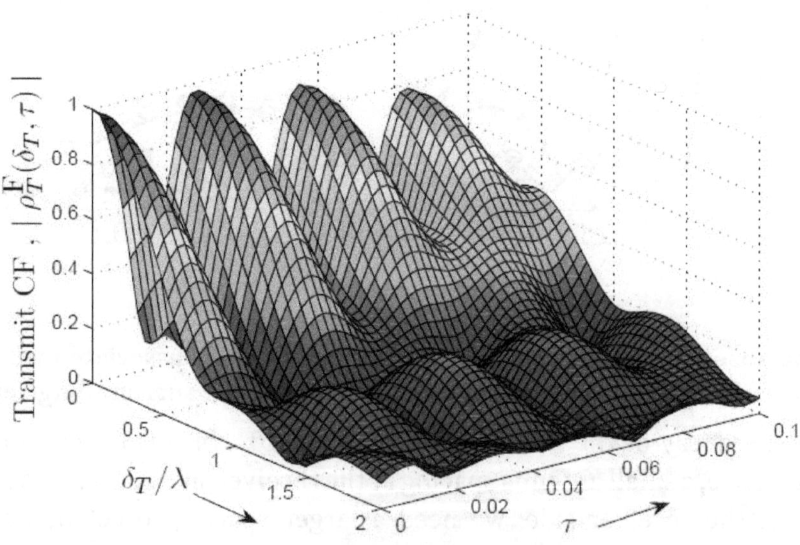

Fig. 5. The transmit correlation function ρTF (δT , T) of the reference model due to fixed scatterers.

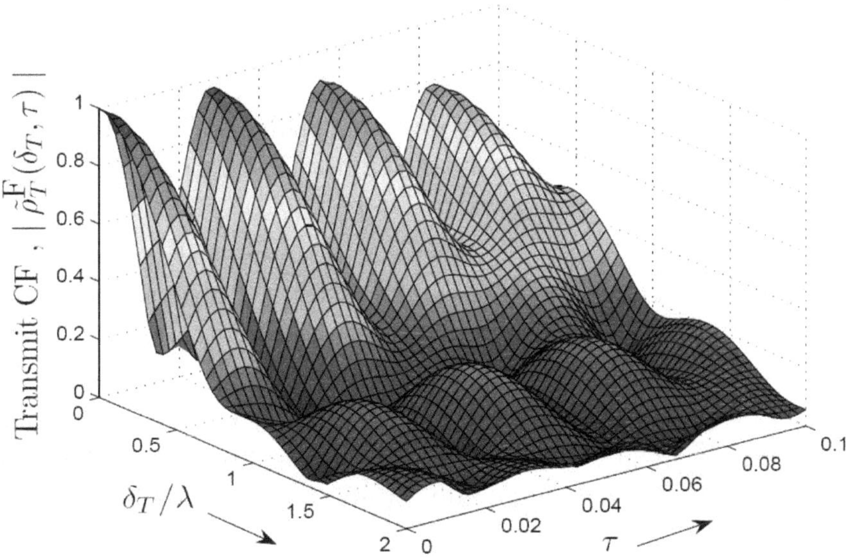

Fig. 6. The transmit correlation function of the simulation model related to fixed scatterers.

6. CONCISE SUMMARY

This chapter presents a narrowband MIMO V2V channel model that considers the effects of both stationary and mobile scatterers. Double-bounce scattering is presumed for stationary scatterers, but single-bounce scattering is regarded for mobile scatterers. To maintain brevity, we have limited our investigations to non-line-of-sight scenarios. A reference model has been developed based on the geometrical street model. The statistical characteristics of the suggested channel model have been analyzed. We have supplied analytical formulations for the three-dimensional space-time cross-correlation function, the temporal autocorrelation function, and the two-dimensional space cross-correlation function. Our investigation substantiates that the influence of mobile scatterers on the statistics of V2V MIMO channels is significant and cannot be overlooked. The examination of the effects of mobile scatterers has demonstrated that a reduction in the speed of vehicles near the transmitter and receiver results in an increase in channel coherence time. The suggested channel model is appropriate for a highway setting during congested situations. Under these circumstances, the minimal relative velocity of the vehicles near the transmitter and receiver permits the assumption that the Angle of Departure (AoD) and Angle of Arrival (AoA) observed from moving clusters remain constant over an adequately extended duration. If the Angle of Departure (AoD) and Angle of Arrival (AoA) are time-variant, the channel model is non-stationary. The latter feature will be examined in subsequent research.

REFERENCES

1. 802.11p (2006). Wireless access in vehicular environment (WAVE) in standard 802.11 infor- mation technology telecommunications and information exchange between systems, local and metropolitan area networks, specific requirements, part 11: Wireless lan medium access control (MAC) and physical layer (PHY) specifications, Technical Re- port p/D1.0, IEEE 802.11.
2. ASTM (2003). Standard specification for telecommunications and information exchange be- tween roadside and vehicle systems - 5 ghz band dedicated short range communica- tions (DSRC) medium access control (MAC) and physical layer (PHY) specifications. ASTM E2213-03.
3. Chelli, A. & Pätzold, M. (2007). A MIMO mobile-to-mobile channel model derived from a geometric street scattering model, Proc. 4th IEEE International Symposium on Wireless Communication Systems, ISWCS'07, Trondheim, Norway, pp. 792–797.
4. Chelli, A. & Pätzold, M. (2008). A wideband multiple-cluster MIMO mobile-to-mobile channel model based on the geometrical street model, Proc. 19th IEEE Int. Symp. on Personal, Indoor and Mobile Radio Communications, IEEE PIMRC 2008, Cannes, France.
5. Gutiérrez, C. A. & Pätzold, M. (2007). Sum-of-sinusoids-based simulation of flat fading wireless propagation channels under non-isotropic scattering conditions, Proc. 50th IEEE Global Telecommunications Conference, GLOBECOM 2007, Washington, DC, USA, pp. 3842–3846.
6. Millott, L. (1994). The impact of vehicular scattering on mobile communications, Proc. 44th IEEE Veh. Technol. Conf., VTC'1994, Stockholm, Sweden, pp. 1733–1736.
7. Molisch, A., Kuchar, A., Laurila, J., Hugl, K. & Bonek, E. (1999). Efficient implementation of a geometry-based directional model for mobile radio channels, Proc. 50th IEEE Veh. Technol. Conf., VTC'1999-Fall, Amsterdam, Netherlands, pp. 1449–1453.
8. Papoulis, A. & Pillai, S. U. (2002). Probability, Random Variables and Stochastic Processes, McGraw-Hill, New York.
9. Patel, C. S., Stüber, G. L. & Pratt, T. G. (2003). Simulation of Rayleigh faded mobile-to-mobile communication channels, Proc. 58th IEEE Veh. Technol. Conf., VTC'03, Orlando, FL, USA, pp. 163–167.
10. Pätzold, M., Hogstad, B. O., Youssef, N. & Kim, D. (2005). A MIMO mobile-to-mobile channel model: Part I - The reference model, Proc. 16th IEEE Int. Symp. on Personal, Indoor and Mobile Radio Communications, PIMRC 2005, Berlin, Germany, pp. 573–578.

11. Salo, J., El-Sallabi, H. & Vainikainen, P. (2006). Impact of double-Rayleigh fading on system performance, Proc. 1st IEEE Int. Symp. on Wireless Pervasive Computing, ISWPC 2006, Phuket, Thailand.
12. WAVE (2005). Wireless access in vehicular environments (WAVE) channel coordination. IEEE P1609.4/D05.
13. Zajic´, A. G., Stüber, G. L., Pratt, T. G. & Nguyen, S. (2008). Statistical modeling and experi- mental verification of wideband MIMO mobile-to-mobile channels in highway envi- ronments, Proc. 44th IEEE Veh. Technol. Conf., VTC'1994, Cannes, France.

Chapter 4 HYBRID BEAMFORMING OF PLANAR ANTENNA ARRAYS FOR SDMA IN MILLIMETER WAVE WPAN

1. INTRODUCTION: AN OVERVIEW

The escalating bandwidth requirements for personal and indoor wireless multimedia applications have propelled research and development towards a new generation of broadband wireless personal area networks (WPAN), as well as advancements in IEEE 802.11 WLAN Very High Throughput at 60GHz, IEEE 802.15 WPAN Millimeter Wave Alternative PHY Task Group (TG3c), and WirelessHD. This new WPAN aims to provide data rates of up to 5Gbps or higher and enables wireless connectivity across devices, including laptops, camcorders, monitors, DVD players, and cable boxes. Furthermore, it may function as a wireless substitute for the High-Definition Multimedia Interface (HDMI).

The new WPAN requires not just extensive bandwidth but also short-range and secure wireless communications. The attributes of extensive unlicensed bandwidth (FCC, 2004), elevated penetration loss (Smulders, 1995; 2002), and considerable oxygen absorption (Anderson & Rappaport, 2004) at 60GHz render it an optimal wireless interface for the forthcoming generation of WPAN. Moreover, the 60GHz millimeter wavelength enables the utilization of several small antennas to direct radio signals with high precision towards the designated receivers. The high-directivity beam pattern enhances wireless link quality (Balanis & Ioannides, 2007) and raises the spatial reuse factor, enabling several users to access the wireless channel simultaneously at the same frequency. This paper examines a straightforward hybrid beamforming (HBF) technique for spatial division multiple access (SDMA) utilizing planar antenna arrays (PAAs), considering the significant potential of 60GHz radio in WPAN and the benefits of beamforming (BF) for millimeter wave (mmWave) applications. Digital beamforming has been employed to mitigate the relatively rigid radiation patterns of switch-beam or beam-selection antennas, thereby generating more adaptable hybrid beam patterns. Celik et al. (2006); Rezk et al. (2005); Zhang et al. (2003). Smolders & Kant (2000) propose a hybrid type of beamforming (BF) that leverages the benefits of BF in both the baseband

and radio-frequency (RF) regimes, in conjunction with the phase shifters of the element antennas of phased array antennas (PAAs). Driven by the aforementioned results and considering the practical constraints and implementation costs of the complete digital beamforming (BF), we examine a specific variant of baseband and RF hybrid beamforming (HBF) for spatial division multiple access (SDMA) that necessitates only four digital processing pathways to facilitate HBF on an 8 × 8 phased array antenna (PAA) as depicted in Fig. 1. The complete PAA seen in Fig. 1 is divided into four segments of patch antennas. Each block is driven by a digital BF weight, while each element patch antenna in a block is equipped with

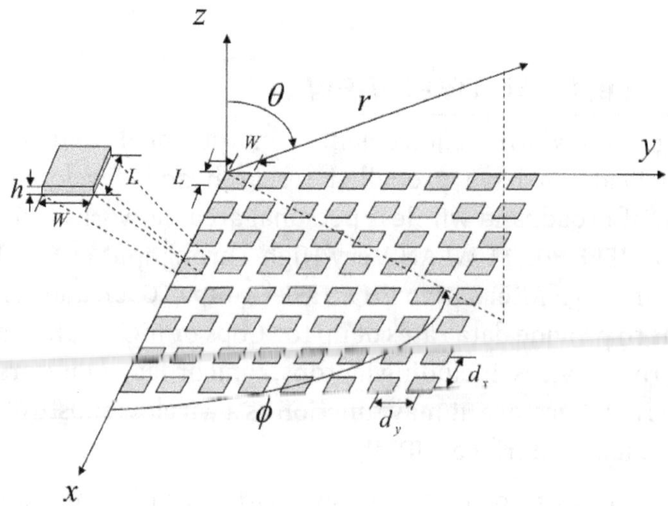

Fig. 1. Antenna arrays of 8 × 8 planar antennas.

an individual phase shifter. With this configuration, we study the design of HBF for two-user SDMA and compare its performance with that of RF BF only.

2. THE CONFIGURATIONS OF PLANAR ANTENNA ARRAYS

We specify in this section the configurations of planar antenna arrays (PAA) for hybrid BF. Sixty-four identical patch antennas are aligned to form an 8 8 antenna matrix as shown in Fig. 1. Each element antenna is equipped with a phase shifter to maneuver the phase of the signal radiating through it. Given the large number of antennas available for 60GHz applica- tions, it is beneficial to use the antennas to serve multiple users in addition to increasing the received signal to noise ratio (SNR) of a single user. Taking into account the practical limitations of circuit implementations, the arrays of antennas are partitioned into blocks, and each of which is driven by a baseband signal processing path. In other words, the baseband BF weights are applied to the antennas on a block basis. Antennas within the same block are applied the same baseband BF weight. In this section, we characterize the beam pattern of this hybrid type of radio-frequency (RF) and baseband (BB) BF.

To facilitate the analysis and highlight the performance of hybrid BF (HBF), the coupling effects among element antennas are neglected in the sequel. As a result, the total beam pattern of a block of a partition can be expressed as the product of the electric field of a single antenna and the array factor corresponding to the block Balanis (1997).

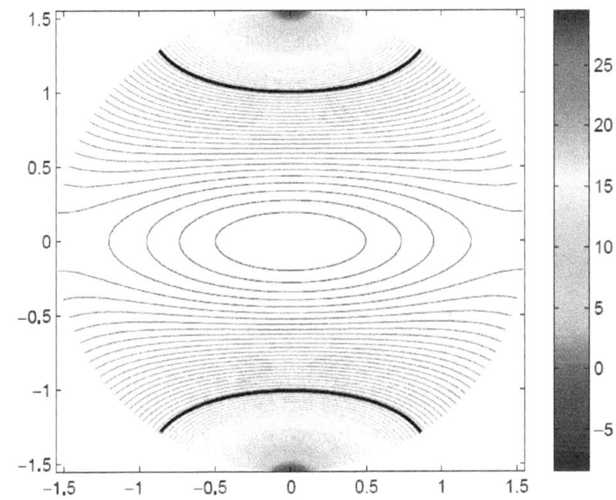

Fig. 2. The contour plot of the antenna pattern when P=30dB.

The far-zone electric field of a single element antenna is given by

$$E(\phi,\theta) = E_\theta \vec{a_\theta} + E_\phi \vec{a_\phi} + E_r \vec{a_r} \tag{1}$$

where

$$E_\theta = j\frac{hWkE_0e^{-jkr}}{\pi r}\left[\cos\phi\cos X\left(\frac{\sin Y}{Y}\right)\left(\frac{\sin Z}{Z}\right)\right] \tag{2}$$

$$E_\phi = j\frac{hWkE_0e^{-jkr}}{\pi r}\left[\cos\theta\sin\phi\cos X\left(\frac{\sin Y}{Y}\right)\left(\frac{\sin Z}{Z}\right)\right] \tag{3}$$

and $E_r \cong 0$ as $r \gg \frac{2LW}{\lambda}$ (see Balanis (1997) for the far field definition). The physical meaning of some of the parameters are illustrated in Fig. 1, and E_0 is a constant. For convenience of expression, we also define $X \triangleq \frac{kL}{2}\sin\theta\cos\phi$, $Y \triangleq \frac{kW}{2}\sin\theta\sin\phi$, $Z \triangleq \frac{kh}{2}\cos\theta$ and $k \triangleq \frac{2\pi}{\lambda}$ with λ being the radio wavelength.

The contour plot of the electric field is shown in Fig. 2 as P|E(Φ, Θ)|2 in dB in the cylindrical coordinate, with P = 30dB. The dimensions of the element patch antenna used in the simula- tion are L = W = 1mm, h = 0.1mm and the distances between adjacent antennas are set to dx = dy = 2.5mm. The radial coordinate is mapped to the elevation angle Θ and the angular coordinate is to the azimuth angle Φ of the antenna pattern. The vertical coordinate displays the antenna gain in decibel. We note that the antenna pattern is not symmetric with respect to the azimuth angle, Φ. The pattern is narrower in the direction of Φ ± π/2.

The array factor of each block depends on its relative position in the PAA. For the partition shown in Fig. 3, we define an index pair, (p, q) ∈ {0, 1}2, for each block of the PAA. Given the index pair (p, q) of a block, the corresponding array factor follows

$$A_{(p,q)}(\phi,\theta) = e^{jpN(\Psi_x+\beta_{x,(p,q)})}\sum_{n=1}^{N} e^{j(n-1)(\Psi_x+(-1)^p\beta_{x,(p,q)})} \times e^{jqM(\Psi_y+\beta_{y,(p,q)})}\sum_{m=1}^{M} e^{j(m-1)(\Psi_y+(-1)^q\beta_{y,(p,q)})} \quad (4)$$

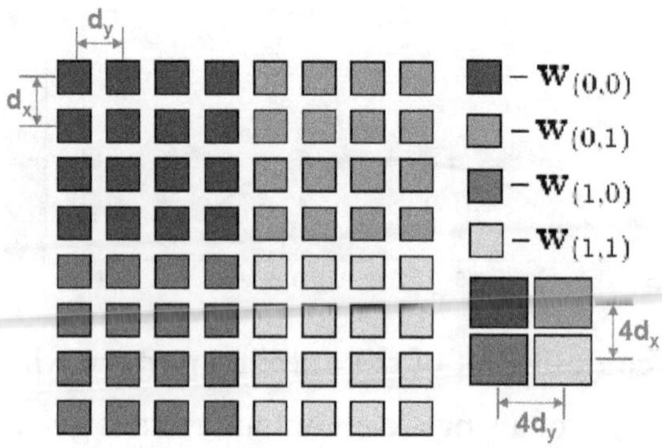

Fig. 3. Partitions of the planar antenna Patch antennas in different color belong to arrays. different block.

where Ψx ≜ , kdx cos Φ sin Θ and Ψy ≜ kdy sin Φ sin Θ. The distances in the x and y directions between adjacent patch antennas are denoted by dx and dy, respectively. And βx,(p,q) and βy,(p,q) are the corresponding phase differences in the x and y directions between adjacent patch antennas. The number of antennas in the x direction of a block is M and the number of antennas in the y direction is N. Given the desired direction (Φd,(p,q), Θd,(p,q)) set for the block (p, q), βx,(p,q) and βy,(p,q) are equal to

βx,(p,q) = (-1)p+1 kdx sin Θd,(p,q) cos Φd,(p,q) ± 2c1 π (5)

βy,(p,q) = (-1)q+1 kdy sin Θd,(p,q) sin Φd,(p,q) ± 2c2 π (6)

where c1 and c2 are any integers. It is noted that the array factor (4) is a periodic function with a period of 2π and is zero whenever (Φ, Θ) satisfy either one of the following two conditions

Ψx + (-1)pβx,(p,q) = 2c3 π/N (7)

Ψy + (-1)qβy,(p,q) = 2c4 π/M (8)

when c3 and c4 are integers not equal to the multiples of N and M, respectively.

2.1 SDMA using reconfigurable PAA

Adjusting the antenna phases of a block based on (4) ~ (8), the main beams of different blocks can be tuned towards the directions of different users, offering spatial division to support multiple access (SDMA) of users. Despite the array gain provided by (4), the SINR of SDMA also depends on the antenna pattern of (1) and the beam patterns of adjacent users.

Suppose that all patch antennas in Fig. 3 are used to support a single user. The maximum achievable array gain in this case is 20 log10(64)= 36 dB when

$$\Psi x + (-1)p\beta x,(p,q) = 2c5\ \pi \tag{9}$$

$$\Psi y + (-1)q\beta y,(p,q) = 2c6\ \pi,\ \{c5,\ c6\} \in Z \tag{10}$$

where Z stands for the integer number. Fig. 4 shows the contour plot of the corresponding array pattern when $\theta d,(0,0) = 0$. It is clear that the maximum array gain of 36 dB is achieved at $\theta = \theta d,(0,0) = 0$. Scaling the power by 1/MN for each element antenna of the M × N PAA, the maximum effective array gain is 10 log10(64) = 18 dB.

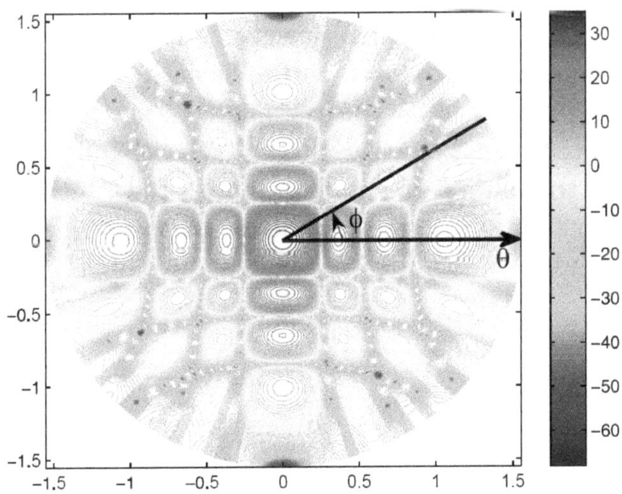

Fig. 4. Contour plot of the array pattern for one-user case when $\theta d,(0,0) = 0$.

On the other hand, if each block in Fig. 3 serves a user with an 4×4 antenna array, the maximal array gain now reduces to a smaller value of $20\log_{10}(16) \doteq 24$ dB. Except for the smaller array gain, each user's signal is also interfered by the signals of adjacent users. Fig. 5 shows the array factors for the 4-user SDMA based on the partition in Fig. 3. The four beams are pointed toward the elevation angle of $\frac{\pi}{4}$ and the azimuth angles of $\frac{i\pi}{4}$, $i = 1, \ldots, 4$, respectively. As can be seen from the figures, the side beams of adjacent users overlap with the main beam of the user of interest, making it difficult to maintain the SINR in practice. To provide a better control for the SINRs of users supported with PAA, a hybrid approach of BF (HBF) is introduced in the next section to take the advantage of baseband BF techniques.

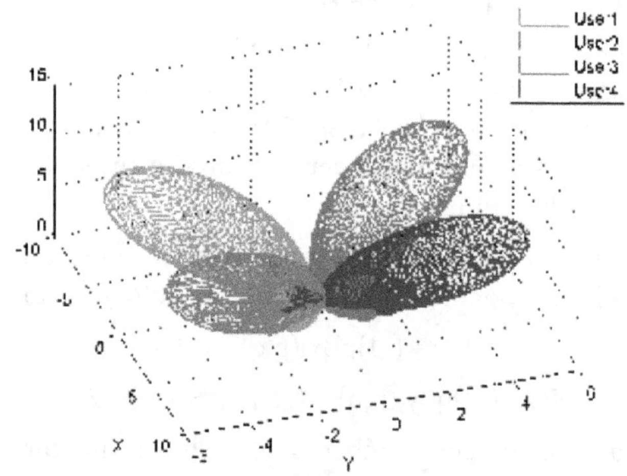

Fig. 5. The array factors of the 4-user SDMA based on the partition in Fig. 3.

3. SDMA USING HYBRID BEAMFORMING

The SDMA method introduced in Section 2.1 is based on phase adjustment with the phase shifter of each element antenna. However, adjusting only the phases of the radio signals sometimes may not be able to achieve the desired SINR for the user of interest, as the beam direction of the user might be severely jammed by the side beams of other users. To overcome this difficulty, baseband BF techniques can be used to jointly steer the beam patterns and suppress the interference for all users. More specifically, in addition to steering the main beam towards the direction of interest, the baseband array factor can be nulled as well in the directions of other users' main beams.

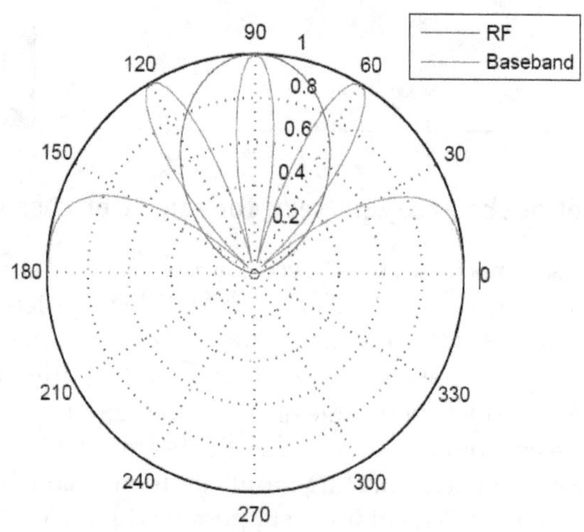

Fig. 6. The polar plot of the HBF pattern with the partition in Fig. 3 when θd = π/2.

However, it is impractical to apply a baseband BF weight for each element antenna of the 8 × 8 PAA. Taking into account the implementation cost, each partition of PAA is driven by a common baseband BF weight, while each antenna is still equipped with an individual phase shifter. To distinguish the array factor B(Φ, θ) formed with the baseband BF weights of a user from the array factor A(Φ, θ) obtained by tuning the phase of the radiated wave of each antenna, we refer to B(Φ, θ) as the baseband array factor (BAF) in contrast to the array factor A(Φ, θ) tuned in the radio-frequency (RF) band.

Now we consider this hybrid type of baseband and RF BF for the simple partition shown in Fig. 3. Suppose that the RF array factor (RAF) for different blocks of a user are the same and pointed to the desired direction of interest, the composite beam pattern of HBF is given by

$$H(\Phi, \theta) \doteq B(\Phi, \theta)A(\Phi, \theta)E(\Phi, \theta) \tag{11}$$

where A(Φ, θ) is the array factor of the 4 ×4 antenna arrays. In the extreme case of Fig. 3 that the entire PAA is used to support a single user, the BAF is given by

$$B(\phi,\theta) = \sum_{r=0}^{1}\sum_{s=0}^{1} w_{(r,s)} e^{j4r\Psi_x} e^{j4s\Psi_y}. \tag{12}$$

where $\Psi x \triangleq kdx \cos \Phi \sin \theta$ and $\Psi y \triangleq kdy \sin \Phi \sin \theta$. The enlarged distances between the ad- jacent effective antennas make 4kdx = 4kdy = 4π in (12) as dx = dy = Λ/2, which in turn results in the periodic baseband beam pattern of B(Φ, θ) shown in Fig. 6. The angular coordi- nate corresponds to the elevation angle θ and the radial coordinate represents the normalized BF gain. Due to the periodic pattern, the product of B(Φ, θ) and A(Φ, θ) will yield significant sidelobes on both sides of the main beam. For clarity, the RAF A(Φ, θ) of the 4 ×4 block is also shown in Fig. 6. Since the patch antenna has a fixed radiation pattern, its pattern is not shown in the figure.

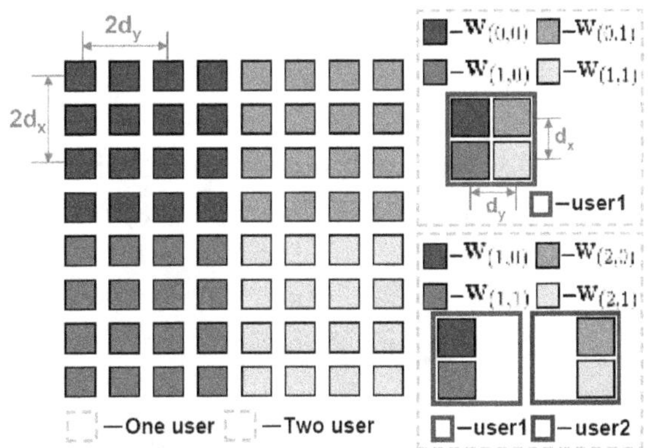

Fig. 7. The partition of the PAA for two-user SDMA, where patch antennas of the same color belong to the same block.

3.1 HBF based on the MD beamforming

According to the configuration of Fig. 3, we now implement HBF for two-user SDMA based on the partition in Fig. 7. The antennas in blue and green colors of Fig. 7 belong to user one, and the antennas in orange and yellow belong to user two. Namely, two BF weights are employed for each user. The resultant BAF for user one and two are given by

$$B_1(\phi,\theta) = w_{(1,0)} + w_{(1,1)}e^{j\Psi_x} \tag{13}$$
$$B_2(\phi,\theta) = w_{(2,0)}e^{j\Psi_y} + w_{(2,1)}e^{j\Psi_x+j\Psi_y}. \tag{14}$$

Now to steer the main beam towards the direction of the user of interest and, in the mean time, to suppress the interference in the direction of the other user, a typical method is the so-called maximum directivity (MD) BF Kuhwald & Boche (1999).

The MD BF basically constructs the baseband BF weights by superposition of the steering vectors

$$\mathbf{s}_1(\phi,\theta) \triangleq [1 \; e^{j\Psi_x}]^T \tag{15}$$
$$\mathbf{s}_2(\phi,\theta) \triangleq [e^{j\Psi_y} \; e^{j(\Psi_x+\Psi_y)}]^T \tag{16}$$

of user one and two in (13) and (14), respectively. Specifically, the BAFs are expressed as

$$B_1(\phi,\theta) \triangleq \sum_{i=1}^{2} b_i[1 \; e^{-j\Psi_{xi}}]\mathbf{s}_1. \tag{17}$$
$$B_2(\phi,\theta) \triangleq \sum_{i=1}^{2} c_i[e^{-j\Psi_{yi}} \; e^{-j(\Psi_{xi}+\Psi_{yi})}]^H\mathbf{s}_2 \tag{18}$$

where $\Psi xi \triangleq 4kdx \cos \Phi i \sin \Theta i$ and $\Psi yi \triangleq 4kdy \sin \Phi i \sin \Theta i$, and $\{\Phi i, \Theta i\}$ is the desired beam direction of user i. Substituting the constraints of

$$B_m(\phi_i,\theta_i) = \begin{Bmatrix} 1, & i=m \\ 0, & i \neq m \end{Bmatrix}, \; i,m \in \{1,2\}. \tag{19}$$

back into (17) and (18) yields the coefficients bi and ci . Furthermore, equating the Bm (Φ, Θ) respectively for m $\in \{1, 2\}$ in (13) ~ (18) results in the baseband BF weights

$$w_{(1,r)} = \sum_{i=1}^{2} b_i e^{-jr\Psi_{xi}}, \tag{20}$$
$$w_{(2,r)} = \sum_{i=1}^{2} c_i e^{-j\Psi_{xi}}e^{-jr\Psi_{yi}} \; r \in \{0,1\}. \tag{21}$$

3.2 HBF based on the linear constrained minimization of power

Though simple and straightforward, the MD BF does not take into account the power con- sumption in HBF design. A widely used approach for power minimization is the linear con- strained minimum power (LCMP) method Trees (2002). To minimize the power consumption of BF and, in the mean time, null the interference in the beam direction of the user of interest, we apply the LCMP subject to (s.t.) constraints similar to that of the MD BF in (19).

Let ui (t), I ∈ {1, 2} be the transmitted signal of user i, with E [|ui(t)|2] = 1. The baseband transmitted signal for the two-user SDMA can be modeled as

$$x(t)= s1\ u1(t)+ s2\ u2(t). \quad (22)$$

where the steering vectors s1 and s2 are defined in (15) and (16), respectively. To design the BF weight vector wi for user i such that the output power and the interference to the beam direction of the other user are both minimized, the LCMP is formulated as

$$\arg\min_{\mathbf{w}_i} \mathbf{w}_i^H \mathbf{S}_x \mathbf{w}_i \quad (23)$$

$$\text{s.t.} \quad \mathbf{w}_i^H \mathbf{C} = \mathbf{e}_i \quad (24)$$

where $\mathbf{S}_x \triangleq E\{\mathbf{x}^2(t)\}$, $\mathbf{C} \triangleq [\mathbf{s}_i(\phi_1, \theta_1), \mathbf{s}_i(\phi_2, \theta_2)]$ with $\{\phi_i, \theta_i\}$ being the desired beam direction of user i, and $\mathbf{e}_i$ is a 1×2 basis vector with 1 in the ith position and the others zero.

The above optimization problem can be easily solved by making use of the Lagrange multiplier as below

$$J = \mathbf{w}_i^H \mathbf{S}_x \mathbf{w}_i + \left[\mathbf{w}_i^H \mathbf{C} - \mathbf{e}_i^H\right] \lambda + \lambda^H \left[\mathbf{C}^H \mathbf{w}_i - \mathbf{e}_i\right] \quad (25)$$

with the Lagrange multiplier $\lambda \triangleq [\lambda_1, \lambda_2]^T$. Taking the complex gradient of J respect to $\mathbf{w}_i^H$ and setting it to zero yields

$$\mathbf{S}_x \mathbf{w} + \mathbf{C}\lambda = 0 \Longrightarrow \mathbf{w} = -\mathbf{S}_x^{-1} \mathbf{C}\lambda. \quad (26)$$

Substituting (26) into (24) gives

$$-\lambda^H \mathbf{C}^H \mathbf{S}_x^{-1} \mathbf{C} = \mathbf{e}_i^H \Longrightarrow \lambda^H = -\mathbf{e}_i^H [\mathbf{C}^H \mathbf{S}_x^{-1} \mathbf{C}]. \quad (27)$$

Furthermore, substituting (27) back into (26), the resultant optimal BF weight vector for user i is given by

$$\mathbf{w}_i^H = \mathbf{e}_i^H [\mathbf{C}^H \mathbf{S}_x^{-1} \mathbf{C}]^{-1} \mathbf{C}^H \mathbf{S}_x^{-1}. \quad (28)$$

4. COMPUTER SIMULATIONS

We demonstrate simulation results for the HBF schemes studied in the previous section for SDMA. The transmit SNR in the following simulations is set to 30 dB for each user if no specific description.

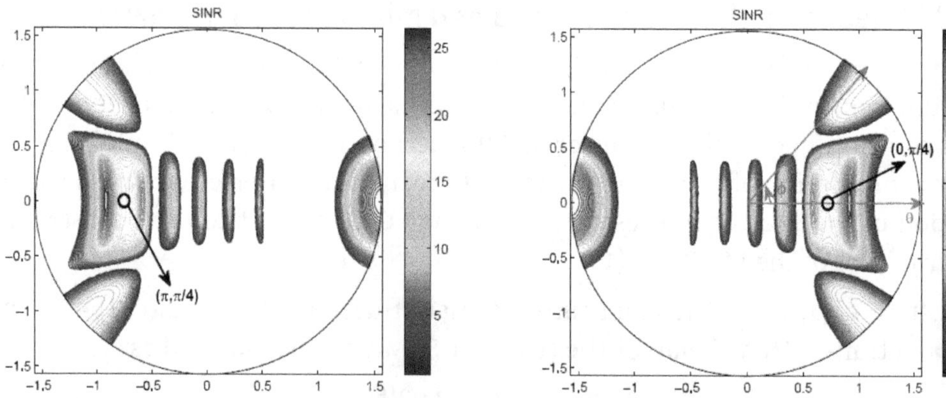

Fig. 8. The contour plots of SINR for user 1 and 2 using the RF BF. The left plot corresponds to user 2 and the right plot to user 1, with the desired directions of user one and two set at (Φ1, θ1)=(0, π/4) and (Φ2, θ2)=(π, π/4), respectively.

Fig. 8 presents the contour plots of the SINRs of user one and two when using the RF BF method of (4). The contour plots are shown in the cylindrical coordinate. The radial coordi- nate maps to the elevation angle θ and the angular coordinate maps to the azimuth angle Φ. The desired directions of user one and two are set at (Φ1, θ1)=(0, π/4) and (Φ2, θ2)=(π, π/4), respectively. The resultant SINR in the desired direction of each user is equal to 16.18dB.

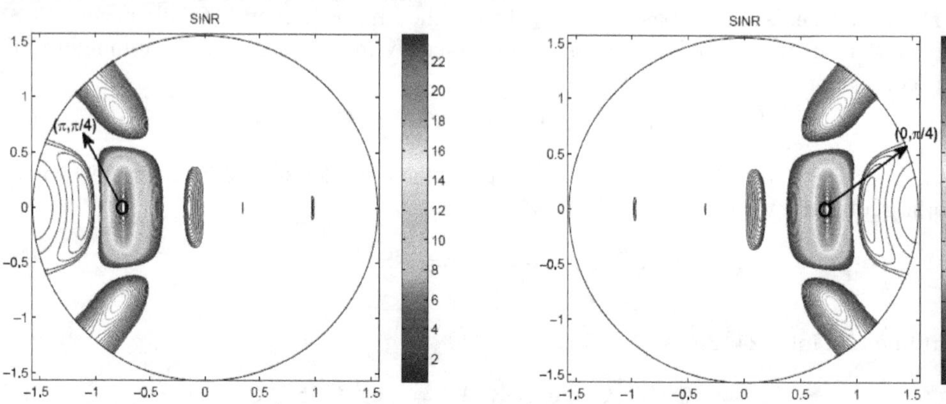

Fig. 9. The contour plots of SINR for user 1 and 2 using the HBF of LCMP. The left plot corresponds to user 2 and the right plot to user 1, with the desired directions of user one and two set at (Φ1, θ1)=(0, π/4) and (Φ2, θ2)=(π, π/4), respectively.

With the same simulation setting for RF BF, the contour plots of SINRs with HBF of LCMP are shown in Fig. 9. In comparison with the results in Fig. 8, we can see that the main beam here for each user is much more stronger and narrower, while the side beams are relative fewer and weaker. In addition, the resultant SINR in the desired direction of each user is now increased to 24.09dB in Fig. 9 as oppose to the 16.18dB in Fig. 8 for the RF BF. This demonstrates that the interference can be suppressed effectively in the desired directions of users with the HBF of LCMP method. Besides, the results of HBF with MD BF are also similar to those of LCMP and, hence, are not shown here.

In addition to SINR, directivity is also an important performance measure to characterize the effectiveness of BF. To reflect the interference due to the multiple access in SDMA, the original definition for directivity in Balanis (1997) is modified into

$$\frac{4\pi\mathrm{SINR}_i(\phi_i,\theta_i)}{\int_0^{2\pi}\int_0^{\frac{\pi}{2}}\mathrm{SINR}_i(\phi,\theta)\sin(\theta)d\theta d\phi}. \tag{29}$$

This new definition for directivity automatically refers to the traditional notion of directivity in the single-user system.

According to this definition of directivity, Table 1 summarizes the results of SINRs, directiv- ities and radiation powers for the RF BF and HBF schemes of MD and LCMP, respectively, when the desired directions of users are set at (Φ1, θ1) = (0, π/4) and (Φ2, θ2) = (π, π/4). The radiation power for each user is evaluated withand is denoted by PT in the table.

$$\int_0^{2\pi}\int_0^{\frac{\pi}{2}}|H_i(\phi,\theta)|^2\sin(\theta)d\theta d\phi \tag{30}$$

It is clear from the table that HBF not only achieves higher SINRs and directivities in this case, but also uses less power for BF. This demonstrates its great potential for SDMA in mmWave applications.

Table 1. The SINRs, directivities and the radiation power of the RF BF and the HBF schemes of MD and LCMP.

User1 User2 (ϕ ,θ)	User1 (0, π /4)			User2 (π, π /4)		
	RF	MD	LCMP	RF	MD	LCMP
SINR (dB)	16.18	24.09	24.09	16.18	24.09	24.09
Directivity	13.33	156.3	156.3	13.55	159.4	159.4
PT	0.1388	0.0775	0.0775	0.1358	0.0764	0.0764

In addition to typical measures for the evaluation of a BF scheme, we also investigate the effectiveness of HBF from the perspective of wireless communications systems. To this end, we study the performance of a two-user SDMA with PAA in orthogonal frequency division multiplexing (OFDM) wireless communications systems. The OFDM system simulates the physical layer proposal of IEEE802.11 task group AD for very high throughput in 60GHz Channel Models for 60 GHz WLAN Systems (n.d.). Specifically, we consider an indoor simu- lation setting as shown in Fig. 10 for a two-user SDMA system operating in the 60GHz wire- less channel model proposed for IEEE802.11ad Channel Models for 60 GHz WLAN Systems (n.d.). The system bandwidth is assumed to be 1GHz and the length of fast fourier transform (FFT) is 1024.

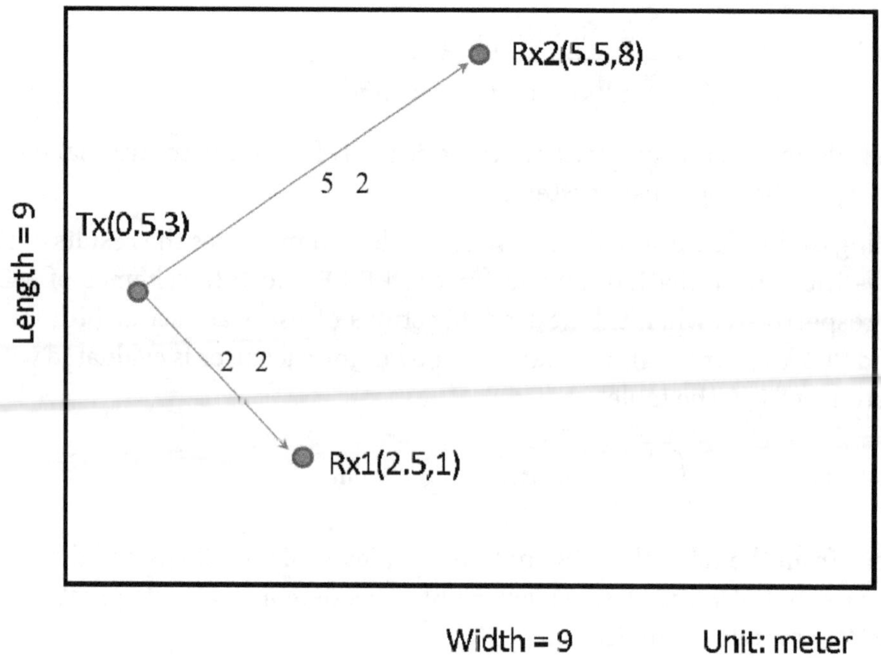

Fig. 10. The indoor simulation setting for a two-user SDMA system.

The simulated transmitter is placed at the position of (0.5, 3) from the lower left corner of the room and transmits signals simultaneously to the two users locating at (2.5, 1) and (5.5, 8), respectively, using either the RF BF setting shown in Fig. 8 or the HBF setting of LCMP in Fig. 9. The users' data are first modulated with QPSK and then transformed with the 1024-point inverse fast fourier transform (IFFT). The transformed OFDM symbol is added with a cyclic prefix of 1/8 of the OFDM symbol and then transmitted with the corresponding BF techniques to the intended users simultaneously. The transmitted signals propagate through the 60GHz channel modeled according to Channel Models for 60 GHz WLAN Systems (n.d.) to come to the two receivers of Fig. 10. At the receivers, we assume that the same RF BF with a 8 × 4 PAA is used by each receiver to enhance the signal qualities, supposing that the beam pattern of each user is pointed to its desired angle of arrival.

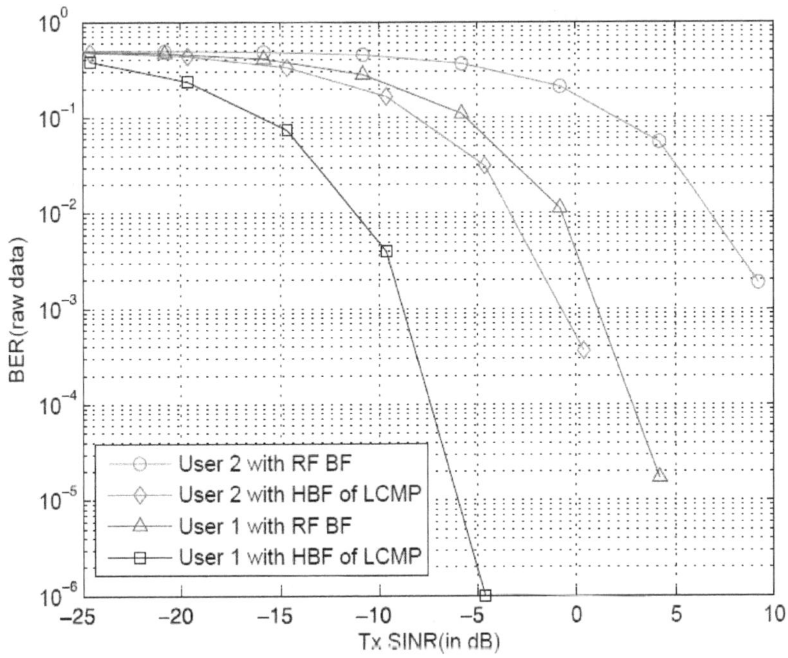

Fig. 11. The BERs for a two-user SDMA system in an indoor environment of Fig. 10.

To recover the data, the receivers first remove the cyclic prefixes of each and then perform FFT followed by channel equalization for symbol detection. The bit error rate (BER) for each user is shown in Fig. 11 with respect to the transmitted SINR. As can be seen from the figure, the SNR advantages for users using the HBF of LCMP are around 10dB against the users using the RF BF only, even though the HBF gain of LCMP is only 7.91dB higher than that of RF BF.

5. CONCSE SUMMARY

We introduced HBF methodologies for SDMA in 60GHz radio utilizing reconfigurable PAA. Our modeling tests indicate that the BF gain of HBF can exceed that of RF BF by as much as 7.9 dB. Moreover, the Bit Error Rate (BER) associated with employing Hybrid Beamforming (HBF) in a simulated Orthogonal Frequency Division Multiplexing (OFDM) environment can exhibit a superior Signal-to-Noise Ratio (SNR) advantage of 10 dB compared to utilizing simply Radio Frequency Beamforming (RF BF). These findings illustrate the capability of HBF with PAA for SDMA in millimeter-wave applications..

REFERENCES

1. Alliance, W. (n.d.). http://www.wimedia.org/.
2. Anderson, C. R. & Rappaport, T. S. (2004). In-building wideband partition loss measurements at 2.5 and 60 GHz, IEEE Trans. on Communications 3(3): 922–928.

3. Balanis, C. A. (1997). Antenna Theory, 2 edn, John Wiley & Sons.
4. Balanis, C. A. & Ioannides, P. I. (2007). Introduction to Smart Antennas, Morgan and Claypool. Celik, N., Kim, W., Demirkol, M., Iskander, M. & Emrick, R. (2006). Implementation and experimental verification of hybrid smart-antenna beamforming algorithm, IEEE Antennas and Wireless Propagation Letters 5: 280–283.
5. Channel Models for 60 GHz WLAN Systems (n.d.). 11-09-0334-02-00ad-channel-models-for-60-ghz-wlan-systems.doc. available at http://www.ieee802.org/11/Reports/tgad_update.htm.
6. FCC (2004). Code of federal regulation, title 47 telecommunication, chapter 1, part 15.255.
7. IEEE 802.11 WLAN Very High Throughput in 60GHz (n.d.). available at http://www.ieee802.org/11/.
8. IEEE 802.15 WPAN Millimeter Wave Alternative PHY Task Group (TG3c) (n.d.). available at http://www.ieee802.org/15/pub/TG3c.html.
9. Kuhwald, T. & Boche, H. (1999). A constrained beam forming algorithm for 2D planar antenna arrays, Proc. IEEE VTC-Fall, Amsterdam, The Netherlands.
10. Rezk, M., Kim, W., Yun, Z. & Iskander, M. (2005). Performance comparison of a novel hybrid smart antenna system versus the fully adaptive and switched beam antenna arrays, IEEE Antennas and Wireless Propagation Letters 4: 285–288.
11. Smolders, A. B. & Kant, G. W. (2000). THousand Element Array (THEA), Proc. IEEE Antennas and Propagation Society International Symposium, Salt Lake City, UT.
12. Smulders, P. (1995). Broadband wireless LANs: a feasibility study, Ph. D. thesis, Eindhoven, Univ. of Tech., The Netherlands, ISBN 90-386-0100-X . available at http://alexandria.tue.nl/extra3/proefschrift/PRF11B/9505571.pdf.
13. Smulders, P. (2002). Exploiting the 60 GHZ band for local wireless multimedia access: prospects and future directions, IEEE Communications Magazine 2(1): 140–147.
14. Trees, H. L. V. (2002). Optimum array processing. Part. IV of detection, estimation and modulation theory., John Wiley & Sons.
15. WirelessHD (n.d.). http://www.wirelesshd.org/index.html.
16. Zhang, Z., Iskander, M., Yun, Z. & Host-Madsen, A. (2003). Hybrid smart antenna system using directional elements - performance analysis in flat Rayleigh fading, IEEE Trans. on Antennas and Propagation 51(10): 2926–2935

5 Chapter

A MULTILAYER SOFTWARE ARCHITECTURE THAT IS SPREAD OUT FOR MIMO TESTBEDS

1. INTRODUCTION: AN OVERVIEW

The implementation of multiple antennas for both transmission and reception, referred to as Multiple Input Multiple Output (MIMO) systems, has garnered significant attention from the wireless communications sector in recent years. Wireless communication with MIMO technology demonstrates enhanced performance regarding spectrum efficiency, reliability, and data rate in contrast to traditional single antenna systems (Foschini & Gans, 1998; Telatar, 1999). Current and developing protocols for wireless communications, including IEEE 802.11 (WiFi), IEEE 802.16 (WiMAX), and Long Term Evolution (LTE), facilitate multi-antenna transmission in their optimal performance configurations.

Despite their promise to enhance performance, the majority of research on MIMO technologies to yet is grounded in theoretical studies. The anticipated benefits of MIMO technology are generally demonstrated solely under optimal conditions, as most analyses depend on simulations. Hardware implementations in real-world circumstances are essential for assessing the true performance of multi-antenna transmission techniques. Hardware implementations consider both the actual multipath propagation in wireless channels and the implementation defects sometimes overlooked in simulations. Hardware implementations can be categorized into three classes (Rupp et al., 2006). The first category comprises demonstrators that are often created with a certain standard or specification in mind. Demonstrators typically provide commendable technological attributes for real-time applications; yet, they are prohibitively costly and lack flexibility and adaptability. The second group consists of prototypes of a final product. A prototype is a real-time implementation of a system designed to address a specific industrial requirement. Prototypes frequently represent an initial phase in which the system is developed and refined before being launched as a consumer product. The third category comprises testbeds that provide real-time transmission capabilities while data is generated and then processed offline.

Moreover, hybrid solutions can be formulated. A testbed can perform some operations in real-time to expedite the measurement process. Typically, candidate signal processing procedures suitable for real-time implementation are those that function at the sample level and/or perform common duties throughout all trials, such as I/Q modulation, up-sampling, and pulse-shaped filtering. This chapter will concentrate on testbeds due to their open designs and prevalence in public research institutions and academics.

Numerous MIMO testbeds have been documented in the literature (Borkowski et al., 2006; Caban et al., 2006; Fabregas et al., 2006; Haustein et al., 2006; Nieto et al., 2006; Ramírez et al., 2008;) Rao et al. (2004), Wilzeck et al. (2006), Zhu and Fitz (2005). Some have been developed to assess a certain standard or specification, while others have been designed for general use. Flexibility, development time, throughput, and costs are critical factors when evaluating existing testbeds. Furthermore, the educational potential of testbeds should be acknowledged, as they provide numerous teaching possibilities. Nevertheless, the literature reveals a deficiency of contemporary instructions and tutorials pertinent to the building of a new testbed from the ground up. There are indeed limited contributions (Caban et al., 2006; García-Naya et al., 2008a; Rao et al., 2004; Rupp et al., 2007) that provide a comprehensive description of the developed MIMO testbed, and with the exception of (García-Naya et al., 2008a; Rupp et al., 2007), the information presented is largely obsolete.

Drawing from the prior expertise of the authors' research group in constructing and establishing MIMO testbeds, alongside conducting indoor measurements (Pe´rez-Iglesias et al., 2008; Ram´ırez et al., 2008), we assert that once the testbed hardware is accessible and correctly configured, the primary concern, often overlooked, is the accessibility of the testbed. When a research team initiates the acquisition or construction of a new testbed, they must consider various factors pertaining to both the hardware and its technical specifications, as well as future extensibility options (García-Naya et al., 2008a; Rupp et al., 2007). Typically, the majority of resources are allocated to the testbed configuration, resulting in equipment that is scarcely operable by individuals not engaged in its design and subsequent setup. This renders access to the testbed exceedingly difficult.

The transition of an algorithm from a simulation environment to a testbed necessitates intricate low-level programming to interface with the hardware, along with comprehensive knowledge of the hardware itself. Moreover, hardware implementation issues often overlooked by simulations emerge, including time and frequency synchronization, I/Q imbalances, and nonlinear distortions induced by power amplifiers, among others. These concerns complicate the evaluation of novel MIMO transmission techniques in a testbed. Consequently, it is advantageous to render the testbed available to end users at an appropriate level of abstraction. This objective is a significant difficulty because to the extensive array of heterogeneous technologies and development environments that must be merged. Nonetheless, if this barrier is surmounted, the ultimate outcome is a highly appealing product for the user, who may concentrate on the advancement of novel transmission strategies that can be readily implemented in the testbed and subsequently assessed in genuine contexts.

This chapter outlines the resolution of all previously identified restrictions through the implementation of a distributed multilayer software architecture. This architecture facilitates easy accessibility of the testbed for researchers and its integration into their development environment. While all designs and results presented are specific to our MIMO testbed (García-Naya et al., 2008b; Ramírez et al., 2008), they can be readily adapted to most existing testbeds, facilitating the integration of heterogeneous testbed nodes to create a multi-terminal testbed..

The proposed software architecture consists of three different layers:

1. **The middleware layer (MWL)** is the lowest-level layer that interacts with the testbed hardware. It makes the testbed accessible through standard TCP socket connections.
2. **The signal processing layer (SPL)** performs the necessary operations required to con- vert the discrete-time sequences provided by the final user into discrete-time signals suitable to be transmitted by the hardware. At the receiver, it is usual to perform signal processing operations like time and frequency synchronization in case they are not car- ried out by the testbed hardware. The tasks compounding the signal processing layer can also be executed in real-time by the testbed hardware. For example, digital up and down converters are frequently available in the libraries of programmable hardware modules.
3. **The testbed interface layer (TIL)** is the highest-level layer and presents the testbed to the user at an adequate abstraction level. The TIL has to be designed and implemented for a specific development environment. For example, if the final user makes use of Matlab, then a specific implementation of the TIL for Matlab has to be developed. The main purpose of the TIL is to provide a simplified interface to access the testbed. This does not prevent from providing mechanisms to control the hardware in detail from the TIL. It is very important to emphasize that there is no logic in the TIL except that necessary for adapting the data format from the specific environment used by the SPL and vice versa. The only requirement for the TIL to be implemented is the availability of a standard TCP socket library.

The whole design and implementation of the proposed software architecture is done under the following premises:

1. **Layers have to be as decoupled as possible.** This is a fundamental idea in modern software design and structured programming. The key idea is not to replicate function- alities that are already present in another layer, which would be a symptom of a bad design. The basic premise is to design everything to be fully decoupled and reusable; and later on introduce some small violations of this principle only if they are strictly needed to increase the overall system performance.
2. **Each layer can be extended and/or customized** to be able to adapt them to future spec- ifications and/or heterogeneous hardware environments. It is important that this layer upgrade be done without needing a complete remake of the software, which is fre- quently the only solution in case of monolithic non-layered systems.
3. Finally, **layers should be distributed,** which means that they use remote connections to interact among them. On the one hand, this helps to ensure the decoupling and independence principles whereas, on the other hand, allows the testbed to be remotely accessible from the user Personal Computer (PC).

2. BASIC TESTBED HARDWARE

Testbeds are often used to verify if a new signalling technique (or even a complete standard system) that has been proven useful by simulations is also valid in realistic wireless scenar- ios. Testbeds allow the dimensioning of the hardware needs for real-time implementations, not only for the digital signal processing modules (mainly, DSP and FPGA) but also for the analogue Radio Frequency (RF) front-ends. Testbeds allow capturing the requisites for the hardware used in the final real-time implementation. Consequently, evaluating performance with testbeds allows knowing whether a given technique is feasible from the real-time hard- ware and implementation requirements.

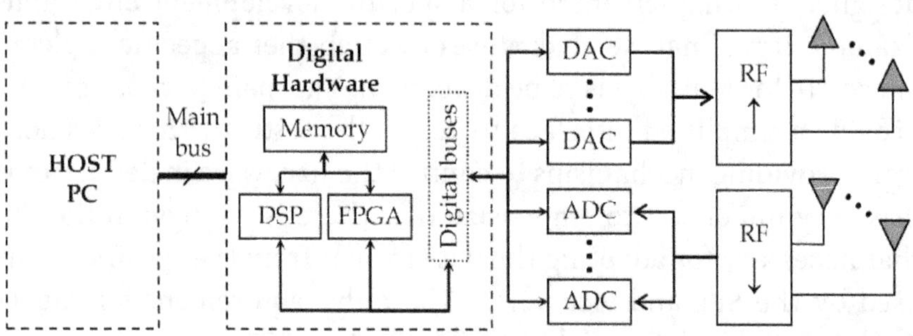

Fig. 1. Block diagram of the basic hardware configuration of a testbed.

Among the three different types of hardware implementations described above (demonstrators, prototypes and testbeds), testbeds present the following advantages:

- **Flexibility:** Testbed hardware is meant to be used for off-line processing. Only the signals are sent and acquired in real-time. This implies that testbed hardware is not subject to the real-time restrictions even though the hardware can include some sort of real-time capabilities.
- **Modularity:** Usually, the minimum modularity found in a testbed is given by the separation between the digital hardware (up to the D/A and A/D converters) and the RF hardware. Sometimes, the digital hardware can be split in different modules performing specific operations: D/A and A/D conversion, digital up and down conversion, signal buffering, etc. For the RF section it is possible to find self-made solutions or commercial products. Lastly, commercial RF front-ends also permit some degree of flexibility, for example allowing dual-band operation, RF carrier selection for each band or adjusting the gains at the transmitter and receiver amplifiers.
- **High-level language development:** Having in mind that most of the processing tasks are carried out off-line, general-purpose processors are the most adequate for processing the generated/acquired signals. This allows the utilization of high level programming environments (e.g. Matlab, C/C++, Java) and the simplification of the implementation stages both in time and complexity. This feature also provides an additional flexibility degree, because it is easy to change the implementation on the fly.
- **Floating-point versus fixed-point precision:** As a consequence of the off-line processing and the usage of high-level programming environments, the operations are carried out in the floating-point domain instead of using fixed-point operations available for real-time devices. This permits the researcher to focus on the implementation rather than considering some other problems like arithmetic precision of the operations.

Testbed hardware components can be classified into three groups according to their functionality, as shown in Fig. 1. The first one is the host system, usually a PC and consequently referred to as host PC. It is the equipment that allocates one or more boards containing the digital section of the hardware testbed (including D/A and A/D converters). The second group is constituted by the digital hardware components and, finally, the third one is formed by the RF front-ends. The D/A and A/D converters generally constitute the frontier between the digital and analogue hardware. In the digital section, a bus termed main bus allows trans- ferring the data from the host to the testbed hardware and the other way around. Next, a set or just one digital bus interconnects the digital hardware (DSPs, FPGA, memory buffers, etc.) with the D/A and A/D. Finally, for the interconnection among the D/A and A/D converters and the RF front-ends coaxial cables are used.

With this basic configuration, it is possible to send samples directly coming from the main bus, convert them into the analog domain using the D/A converters and up convert them to the desired carrier RF using the front-ends. At the receiver side, the signals are down converted by the RF front-ends, digitally converted by the A/D converters and then sent to the host through the main bus. Note that the main bottleneck in this scheme is the maximum data rate provided by the main bus, especially if there are no digital up and down converters available. In the most recent boards, by using PCI express or similar solutions is possible to use the host memory as a buffer while samples are transferred in real-time through the main bus.

A first improvement of this basic scheme consists in incorporating a digital up converter (DUC) before each D/A converter at the transmitter and a digital down converter (DDC) after each A/D converter at the receiver. These devices can be dedicated elements or can be implemented in a FPGA. Incorporating DUC and DDC into the MIMO testbed design allows transferring complex signals from/to the host, reducing both the transfer rate at the main bus and the software complexity. For MIMO operation, DDCs and DUCs must be fully synchronized. Additionally, another improvement consists in implementing some of the time-consuming sample-level tasks in FPGAs (e.g. time and frequency synchronization).

2.1 Baseband Components

Baseband components are the hardware elements necessary to deal with baseband and/or Intermediate Frequency (IF) signals. Frequently, such baseband components are allocated on carrier boards installed on conventional PCs. Current testbeds use carrier boards equipped with standardized buses to access testbed hardware such as USB, PCI, cPCI, PCI express or similar. A manufacturer compliant with the PXI alliance (PXI, 2009) produces carrier elements that are compatible with the most typical buses present in host equipments. When available, important hardware components in a testbed are the storage buffers, especially when the main bus does not support the necessary rate demanded by the D/A and A/D converters. Such buffers allow performing signal operations off-line while data is sent and acquired in real- time.

2.2 RF Front-Ends

RF front-ends constitute one of the major hindrances in the testbed building process. They are responsible of up converting IF or baseband signals to RF. The most common RF bands are the unlicensed ISM located at 2.4 and 5.8 GHz. It is easier to find components for such bands but also unpredictable interference is present in such spectrum portions. High linearity and flexibility in terms of supported carried frequencies and bandwidths are desirable features for the RF front-ends. However, the most advanced front-ends commercially available are only dual-band and have fixed maximum bandwidth. A fundamental feature needed to be able to carry out experiments is the possibility of modifying the transmit power. Also, the majority of the front-ends are designed for SISO operation, making difficult to adapt them to a MIMO system. Moreover, once the front-end has been acquired, extensive test on it is needed and expensive measurement equipment is required.

It is important to emphasize that RF hardware is expensive compared to the cost of the digital hardware and does not follow Moore's law (Moore, 1998).

3. BASIC TESTBED SOFTWARE

Methodologies that cover the entire development process, from source code suitable for sim- ulations and executed off-line, to real-time implementation in the testbed, as well as software tools according to these methodologies, are extremely scarce. The most popular methodology for testbed development is rapid prototyping (Kaiser et al., 2004; Rupp et al., 2003; 2006). A typical approach used to develop real-time algorithms to be run in a testbed consists in start- ing with a simulation implementation. Next, the simulation is migrated to the testbed and, finally, a real-time implementation is obtained. It is also convenient to split the real-time implementation into several steps: firstly, a fixed-point code is produced; next a DSP implementation is obtained; and, afterwards, the software modules that do not meet time requirements are migrated to FPGA, making use of high level tools when possible. Nowadays, except for the Mathworks tool suite (Mathworks, 2009) combined with some VHDL code generators, there is a lack of high level tools and development environments suitable to fit the previous steps.

Also, some standardisation efforts have just started in order to make compatible hardware components and software modules from different manufactures and developers. The PXI alliance (PXI, 2009) plus the Software Defined Radio (SDR) Forum (SDR Forum, 2009) and initiatives such as the Software Communications Architecture (SCA) (SCA, 2009) constitute the starting point of a new generation of modular, flexible and standard radio interfaces suit- able for research. Nowadays, however, the previously mentioned initiatives have not already produced as a result the availability of high level tools allowing final users and researchers not involved in the hardware development to access the testbed hardware at a reasonable abstraction level.

All above reasons serve as a motivation for our work, which aims at bridging the existing gap among the hardware, the software elements provided by the manufacturers and the abstraction level required by the final users. Moreover, the proposed solution allows embedding real-time modules in the processing chain, as if they were part of the testbed hardware. For example, real-time frequency and time synchronization algorithms can be run at the receiver side and integrated into the digital hardware. Additionally, given that the proposed solution is designed to be easily and quickly integrated in any other kind of system, it becomes a very useful tool to help in testing real-time applications, especially during the first stages of the development. A good example is the ability to develop in parallel different parts of the transmitter and the receiver in real-time. While the real-time transmitter is still under development, the team developing the real-time receiver can make use of the testbed to generate the transmit signals and feed the real-time receiver with them.

4.SOFTWARETECHNOLOGYBEHINDTHEDISTRIBUTEDMULTILAYER ARCHITECTURE

The field of computer science has come across problems associated with complexity since its constitution. The software architecture discipline is centred on the idea of reducing complex- ity through abstraction and separation. There are different kinds of software architectures. Among them, the most interesting for our work are: the client-server architecture, which serves as the basis for most of the available architectures; the three-tier model; and finally, the most recent and advanced model-view-controller architecture.

4.1 Client-Server Software Architecture (Two-Tier Software Architecture)

Client-server describes the relationship between two computer processes in which one process (the client) makes a service request to another process (the server). Applications following the client-server architecture represent an evolution with respect to those called "monolithic".

The basic operation mode for client-server applications consists in that each instance of the client process sends requests to one or more connected servers. In turn, servers accept these requests, process them, and return the requested information to the client. The basic client- server architecture considers only two types of hosts: clients and servers. Consequently, it is also known as two-tier model. A special case of the two-tier software architecture arises when an instance simultaneously acts as a client or as a server, resulting in the peer-to-peer architecture.

The two-tier software architecture presents the following advantages with respect to monolithic systems:

- The responsibilities of the whole system are now split between the client and the server, which brings the opportunity to decouple them.

- Servers can control the access to the resources to guarantee that only those clients with appropriate permissions access and change the data.
- Different client/server types can work with different kinds of servers/ clients, which helps in the integration of heterogeneous systems.

As a main disadvantage, the mechanism used to interconnect clients and servers (frequently standard socket connections) may become both a bottleneck and a weak point of the system, because a failure in the interconnection mechanism will stop the whole system.

4.2 Multi-Tier Software Architecture

The multi-tier software architecture represents a natural evolution of the client-server model towards a higher number of levels. That is the reason why it is also known as the n-tier software architecture. Basically, the multi-tier software architecture is a client-server architecture consisting of more than two tiers, and where the inner tiers act simultaneously as client for one tier and as server for the other. The main difference with respect to the peer-to-peer model is that the tier order (its position or level in the multi-tier structure) does matter. An inner layer is also termed middleware because acts as an intermediary between two adjacent tiers.

Note that the multi-tier software architecture, as well as the two-tier one, is a mechanism to design the physical structure of the system. Given one of the models, several degrees of freedom are still possible to get the logic structure of the system.

4.3 Tier Interconnection Mechanisms

Up to now, we were using a certain abstraction level to define the previous architectures. Usually, each tier is mapped to a set of processes obtained from the same master process. This can be easily understood with an example. Imagine a two-tier system. One tier is the client while the other is the server and they are mapped into two different processes interconnected by means of sockets. It does not matter if both processes are in the same physical machine or not. What is important is how they interact with each other. The server will be waiting for a request from one of the clients. As soon as the request arrives, the server starts to serve the petition and, simultaneously, starts waiting for another request. When the server process is going to serve a new request, it clones itself to serve the petition. Frequently, this process cloning mechanism is omitted and it is considered as an implementation detail. Therefore, to describe the interaction between different tiers, it is assumed that each tier is mapped into a process that interchanges messages with other processes (tiers). Although this approach is not completely rigorous, it is enough for our purposes. In the literature such interactions are described my means of sequence diagrams as we will do.

But there is still one open question: How are messages sent from one tier to another? In principle, data transfer between two tiers is part of the architecture design, but in practice only the message types and the data are defined by using sequence diagrams, which drives to the definition of a part of the system termed protocol. A protocol defines the interaction among all tiers, specifying the type of messages to be sent from one tier to another or to several other tiers, as well as the type of data sent in each message. Messages are transferred using plain socket connections or more elaborated mechanisms (e.g. SNMP, CORBA, Java RMI or even Web Services). The different approaches have their own advantages and disadvantages and there is still no perfect system for message interchange. However, what is really important is to use standardized mechanisms for message interchanging, thus guaranteeing independence among tiers.

4.4 The Model-View-Controller Architectural Pattern

The Model-View-Controller (MVC) is a pattern used in software engineering derived from the multi-tier software architecture. Successful use of the pattern drives to the isolation of the business logic from the user interface, allowing one to be freely modified without affecting the other. The controller collects user inputs, the model manipulates (and usually stores) application data, and the view presents results to the user. The MVC was first described in (Trygve, 1978) and can be used as an architectural or design pattern. As an architectural pattern, it splits an application into three independent layers that can be run in different computers: the presentation or user interface layer, termed the view; the business logic, called the model; and the controller, an intermediate layer adapting the view to the model and vice versa.

4.5 Applying Software Engineering to MIMO Testbeds

In the first sections of this chapter we present the typical hardware architecture available in MIMO testbeds as well as the typical abstraction level offered by the software included with the hardware. We stressed that such abstraction level is by far not enough and, consequently, a final user or a researcher not involved in the testbed development and later setup cannot directly access it. Along this Section, we introduced architectural software models, starting with the well-known client-server model and ending with the recently proposed model-view- controller, widely used in web applications as well as distributed applications. These architectural models serve as an inspiration to propose a novel software architecture useful to bridge the existing gap between the abstraction level offered by testbeds and the one demanded by researchers and final users. This new architecture is explained in the following Section.

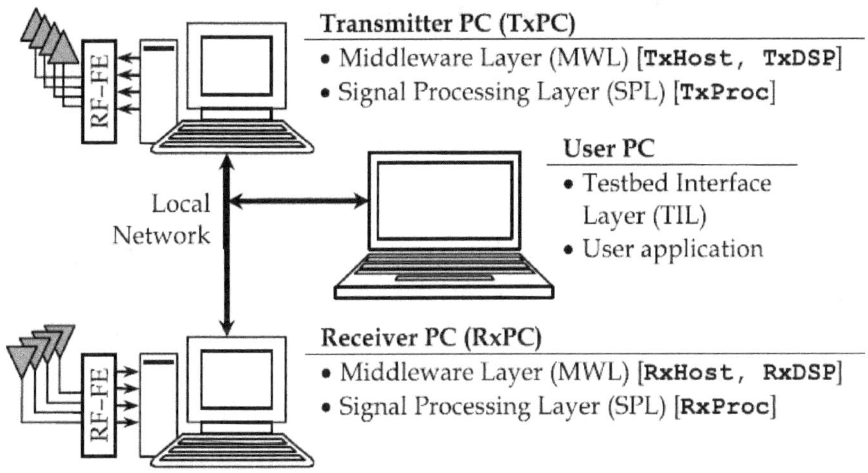

Fig. 2. General scheme of the MIMO Testbed showing the three different layers: middleware (MWL), signal processing (SPL) and testbed interface (TIL). The corresponding process name for each layer and each PC is shown between brackets.

5. DISTRIBUTED MULTILAYER SOFTWARE ARCHITECTURE FOR MIMO TESTBEDS

Fig. 2 shows the proposed testbed hardware organization, which can be extrapolated to most of the testbeds. It is constituted by two ordinary PCs hosting the testbed hardware, one for the transmitter (referred to as TxPC) and other for the receiver (named RxPC). The digital section of the testbed hardware is installed inside the PCs while the RF front-ends (RF-FE) remain outside the PC case. The two PCs are attached to the network, something that is very useful because this way the PC desktops can be remotely accessed. The remote user PC is also attached to the network. In the rest of the Section we are assuming the following:

1. The testbed consists of the transmitter and the receiver, i.e., two nodes. Although our designs can be easily extended to an arbitrary number of nodes, it is better to start with the simplest case of two nodes to keep things simple.
2. It does not matter whether the testbed operates outdoor, indoor, outdoor to indoor or vice versa. We assume that a network connection can always be established among the testbed nodes and the user PCs.
3. The testbed PCs will use a standard operating system supporting remote desktop or remote operation from a PC attached to the network. This is a fundamental feature because it enormously simplifies software deployment as well as day-to-day maintenance of the systems. Otherwise, a replacement for such tools should be provided.

5.1 From the MIMO Testbed to the Multilayer Software Architecture

Fig. 2 shows, close to the PC drawings, the names of the corresponding three layers of the proposed architecture that are, from the lowest to the highest level: the middleware layer (MWL), the signal processing layer (SPL) and the testbed interface layer (TIL). The MWL and the SPL are split into transmit and receive parts, while the TIL has just one instance running on the user PC. Actually, the TIL is just an Application Program Interface (API) that has to be included with the user application. In our standard deployment, the MWL and the SPL are allocated in the same PCs containing the rest of the testbed hardware. Although the MWL is the only layer required to be installed in the hardware PCs, the rest of the software can be deployed in any machine attached to the network.

This is not an arbitrary proposal but a design inspired on the multi-tier and the model-view- controller software architectures. First of all, let us identify the use cases of our application. Basically, there is just one use case or action carried out by the final user: transmitting a set of discrete-time sequences through the testbed and, consequently, through the wireless channel. Therefore, the layer corresponding to the view is the interface that allows accessing the testbed, sending the sequences and getting back the acquired signals. This is what we term testbed interface layer, and is the topmost layer of our software architecture.

The controller plays a very important role in a system. It is responsible of getting the service requests from the view, adapting and sending them to the model where the business logic resides. The gathered results are then sent back to the view to be presented to the user. The controller plays the role of the middleware concept presented in the multi-tier software architecture. In the testbed system the controller is called middleware and its functionality is clear: to configure and control the hardware in order to be able to take the requests (discrete-time sequences) from the TIL; to adapt and send them to the hardware to be transmitted by the antennas; and, finally, to carry out the reciprocal operations at the receiver side. At the end of the process the TIL returns the acquired discrete-time signals.

However, our architecture presents three strong differences with respect to the model-view- controller and the multi-tier architecture:

- Adaptation of the discrete-time sequences provided by the TIL in the requests, both at the transmitter and the receiver, consists in performing different signal processing operations that sometimes can even be executed using different kind of processors. For instance, a general-purpose processor (GPP), a graphic processor unit (GPU) or real- time devices like an FPGA or a DSP. It is thus necessary to put all these operations together and, consequently, the SPL concept comes out. Therefore, the SPL is in charge of carrying out most of the signal processing operations needed between the MWL and the TIL.

- One of the reasons to use a multi-tier architecture jointly with the model-view-controller is the ability of the resulting application to be distributed among different machines. Thus, different instances of the tiers run on different machines. However, in the testbed system there are two kinds of nodes: the transmitter and the receiver. If a multi-node testbed is available, different transmitter and receiver pairs will be distributed among different nodes. As a result, the MWL (and consequently the SPL) is split into two sides: the transmitter side and the receiver side. They will be referred to as Tx MWL, Rx MWL, Tx SPL and Rx SPL, respectively. Additionally, they are also identified because the processes mapping the architecture design are also split into two sets, one for the transmitter and the other for the receiver.
- Finally, another particularity present when adapting the model-view-controller and the multi-tier software architectures to testbed software architecture is that the hardware is required to be attached to the host system by means of a bus (e.g. PCI, PCIX, PCI Express, etc.). Consequently, it is not possible to sustain standard network connections through such buses, and the standard tools and techniques available for interconnecting layers are not applicable (except when a custom implementation is provided or when the hardware is attached through a network connection).

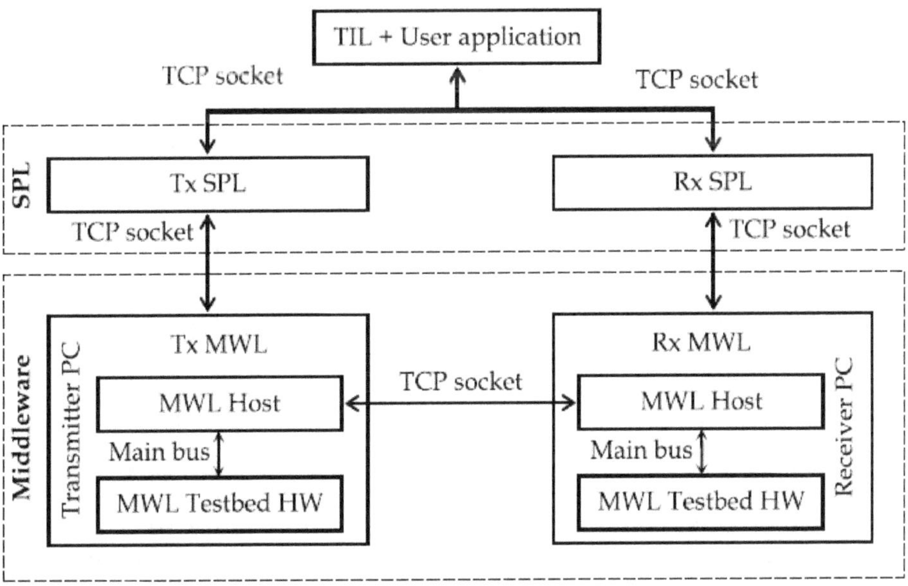

Fig. 3. Basic structure of the distributed multilayer software architecture for MIMO testbeds. The three layers are shown: MWL, SPL and TIL. Additionally, the testbed-hardware sub-layer in the middleware and the different interconnection mechanisms are included.

These reasons motivate an- other division in the MWL, generating a Testbed-hardware sub-layer (with its respective parts for the transmitter and the receiver sides) responsible of dealing with hardware aspects as well as solving the bus connection issues with the host part of the MWL. Having in mind that in our testbed this sub-layer runs on the DSPs available at the transmitter and the receiver, the corresponding processes are referred to as TxDSP and RxDSP.

5.2 Logical and Physical Designs of the Distributed Software Architecture

In Fig. 3, the basic structure of the proposed architecture is shown. There are two sides, transmitter and receiver, joined at the TIL, which has to hold connections with both sides of the SPL. All links between the different layer elements are implemented by using standard socket connections. The exceptions are the links between the sub-layers of the MWL that use a proprietary protocol over the existing main bus interconnecting the hardware and the host. There are strong reasons for using standard socket connections instead of any other higher- level mechanism like, for example, web services. However, this does not imply that in some situations other connection types can better solve some problems. It is also possible to use different link types among different layers.

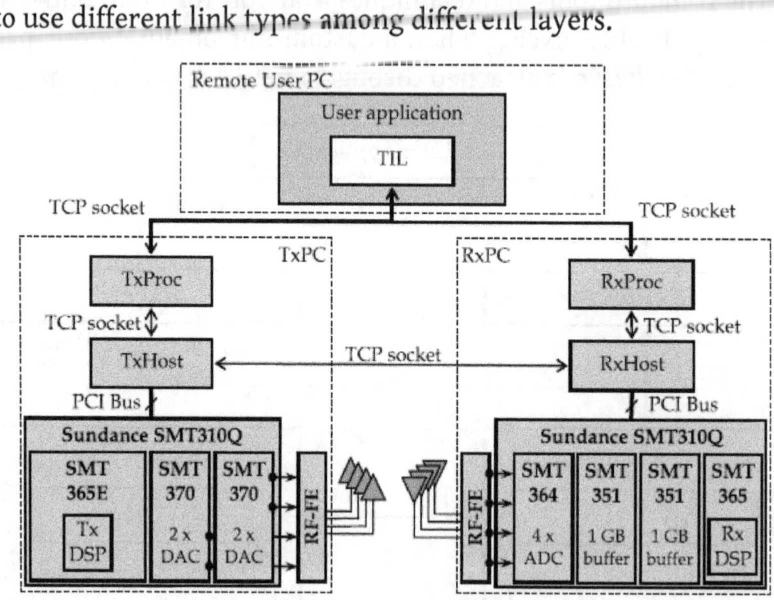

Fig. 4. Testbed scheme containing the hardware and the software architecture deployment as well as the links among the components. The different processes are shown in blue, and are located in the usual place for a typical architecture deployment. The digital hardware sections of the testbed, as well as the RF front-ends, are shown in gray. Finally, the user application is in dark green, containing the TIL in white. Note that TIL appears in white and not in blue because it is not a process but an user application.

For example, the TIL and the SPL can be connected using web services, thus allowing total independence of the platform and full remote access. However, the ability of such high level techniques to sustain high data rates and low latency connections is not the best. For these reasons, sockets offer enough flexibility while providing fast connections. In the case of bus connections the bus type obviously limits the latency and the data rates.

While in Fig. 2 the general structure of the testbed is depicted, showing the correspondence between the hardware elements and the software layers, Fig. 4 illustrates the block diagram of the entire system. Three main parts can be distinguished: the testbed hardware that allows us to transmit discrete-time signals over multiple antennas; the multilayer software architec- ture that makes the hardware accessible to end researchers at a high abstraction level; and, finally, the user application implemented using the testbed capabilities and the architecture facilities. The lowest software level (i.e. the MWL) is required to be installed in the same PCs as the testbed hardware because it uses the system buses to communicate with the hardware. Otherwise, this restriction would not be applicable. The other two layers can be installed in any other available PC. However, in the standard deployment, the SPL is included with the MWL in the testbed PCs. Finally, the TIL is installed in the remote user PC.

5.3 Short Description of the MIMO Testbed Hardware

At the bottom of Fig. 4 a very basic diagram of our testbed hardware is shown. A first release of the testbed hardware was presented in (Ram´ırez et al., 2008), where the baseband modules were from Sundance Multiprocessor Ltd. and the RF front-ends were developed at the University of Cantabria. This hardware has been updated and new RF front-end modules from Lyrtech have been included. Also, minor module reorganisations have been done.

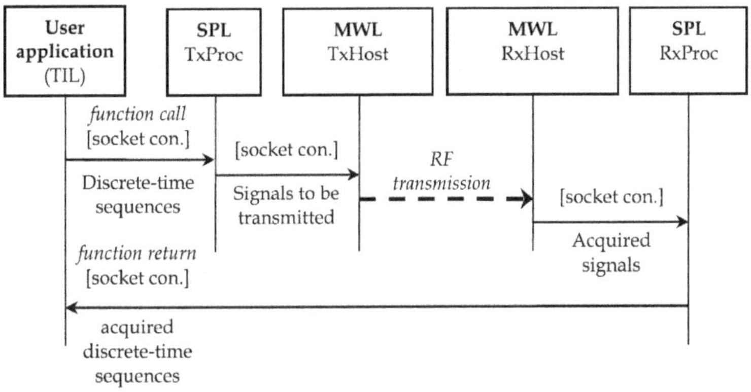

Fig. 5. Frame transmission example. It shows how a single frame transmission is carried out from the discrete-time sequences. For the sake of simplicity, the MWL is considered as a whole, even when it is actually split in two sub-layers.

Currently, the hardware of the testbed is based on a Sundance Multiprocessor (Sundance, 2009) SMT310Q PCI carrier board and a basic processing module: the Sundance SMT365 equipped with a Xilinx Virtex-II FPGA and a Texas Instruments C6416 DSP at 600 MHz. The processing module has two buses that can transfer 32-bit words up to 400 MB/s, allowing the connection with the Sundance SMT370 module, which contains a dual AD9777 D/A converter and two AD6645 A/D converters. The SMT370 module also has a 2 Msamples per- channel memory that is used to load the frames to be transmitted. At the receiver side, the data acquired by the A/D converters is stored in real-time in two SMT351G memory modules offering 256 Msamples per A/D converter. Finally, in an off-line task, data is passed to the middleware through the PCI bus. At the transmitter side the Sundance SMT365E is used in- stead of the SMT365. It contains a larger FPGA as well as a larger amount of memory but the remaining features are the same.

5.4 Simple Transmission Example

In order to shed more light into the system architecture, let us explain, step by step, the trans- mission of a single frame (see Fig. 5). After the discrete-time sequences to be transmitted have been generated at the user application, a function from the TIL is called passing to it the corresponding symbol vectors (one vector per transmitting antenna). These symbols are then sent to the SPL (TxProc) where they are converted (if necessary) to discrete-time signals ready to be transmitted by the hardware. Finally, such signals are subsequently sent to the middleware (TxHost). When both the Tx and Rx PCs are ready to complete a transmission, the signals are passed to the testbed hardware through the corresponding TxDSP process to be transmitted by the antennas. At the receiver side, the MWL (RxHost) acquire the signals stored into the hardware buffers by RxDSP. Next, they are forwarded to the receiver SPL (RxProc). At this moment, the Tx-Rx PCs are ready to process another frame while the acquired signals are converted to discrete-time sequences in the same format required by the end user. Finally, the discrete-time sequences are forwarded to the user application through the TIL, completing the entire process.

The previous example clearly shows the advantages derived from the use of a multilayer architecture instead of a monolithic system: the hardware is better exploited and each layer can be customized or extended according to specific capabilities of the hardware or particular needs demanded by users, all without developing a completely new monolithic system each time the specifications change. The last advantage turns especially valuable in a research environment where specifications change very fast.

5.5 Testbed Interface Layer

After describing the complete system architecture in the previous sections, this and the fol- lowing sub-sections focus on the layers that compound the architecture designed for our MIMO testbed (Ram´ırez et al., 2008). In this subsection we deal with the topmost testbed interface layer (TIL), leaving the description of the other two lower-level layers for the next sub-sections.

The TIL interacts with the researcher or the final user by calling a simple function implemented and specifically adapted to the development environment under consideration, with the only requirement of supporting standard TCP socket connections. At the transmitter side, its main task consists in sending to the SPL the discrete-time sequences to be transmitted plus the necessary parameters. In the same way, the TIL receives the acquired signals, being noticed if any error occurs.

The main goal of the TIL is making the rest of the layers accessible to the final users by taking into account the type of development environment they use. For this reason, the user layer is jointly executed with the user application (see Fig. 3 and Fig. 4), being also integrated in the same process (or set of processes) forming the user application (i.e. a simulation or a demonstration software showing the rest of the testbed capabilities). Therefore, a different TIL implementation satisfying the particular user development environment requirements can be made available (Matlab, Simulink, C/C++, Java, etc).

5.6 Signal Processing Layer

The signal processing layer (SPL) is network-connected to both the TIL and the MWL (see Fig. 3 and Fig. 4). It provides remote access and makes the other two layers platform-independent with respect to each other. This fact permits the SPL to be run in a PC cluster, allowing inten- sive computing to generate the data to be transmitted and to process the acquired sequences. This layer consists of two different processes that carry out the signal processing operations needed to link the TIL and the MWL. The first process (TxProc) receives the discrete sequences to be transmitted from the TIL and performs all necessary operations such as up sampling, pulse-shape filtering, I/Q modulation and frame assembly, in order to generate the discrete time signals that will be sent to the middleware (TxHost). Similarly, the second process (Rx- Proc) waits for the acquired signals from the MWL and performs the time and frequency synchronization operations followed by the demodulation, filtering and down sampling. The resulting vectors are sent to the TIL. It is important to emphasize that the SPL is designed and implemented by clearly separating its two main tasks: interconnection with the adjacent layers (TIL and MWL) and execution of the required signal processing tasks. Depending on the type of sequences given to TxProc, not all operations will be required either at the transmitter or the receiver side.

The SPL can also incorporate advanced features such as a limited feedback channel for the evaluation of precoded MIMO systems. This feedback channel is easily implemented using the network connection available between the transmitter and the receiver.

A SPL detached from the other architecture layers is fundamental to deploy multiuser MIMO scenarios. After extending the current TxProc and RxProc implementations in order to support multiuser MIMO techniques, the set of TxProc processes run at the transmitter users while the RxProc processes do at the receiver users.

In some cases, the researchers may wish to implement most or even all operations present in the SPL. It is still possible to configure the layer as a bypass, making only use of the interconnection capabilities and not performing any signal processing operation at all.

5.7 Middleware Layer

The middleware layer (MWL) fills the gap between the testbed hardware and the signal pro- cessing layer, allowing discrete-time signals to be transferred through the system bus and making possible the synchronization between the TxPC and the RxPC using standard TCP network connections. The MWL is split into two different sub-layers (see Fig. 3 and Fig. 4). The topmost sub-layer is responsible of establishing the network connections between the transmitter and the receiver, and with the higher layer (the SPL). The bottom sub-layer corresponds to the testbed hardware configuration and control software. Fig. 3 and Fig. 4 shows the MWL with its two sub-layers plus the connections with adjacent layers.

Four different processes constitute the middleware. The first two, termed TxHost and RxHost, run respectively on the TxPC and RxPC. They are implemented in standard C++ language and use sockets to establish the necessary network connections:

- One connection between the TxHost and RxHost processes. It is used to synchronize the transmitter and the receiver, so the receiver knows when the signal acquisition process has to start.
- Another connection is established between the TxHost and the TxProc processes and it is used to link the transmitter side of both the middleware and the signal processing layers.
- Finally, there is also a connection between the RxHost and the RxProc processes.

The remaining two processes are the transmitter and the receiver processes that run on their respective Digital Signal Processors (DSPs) available in the testbed hardware. Thus, the trans- mitter DSP process (TxDSP) performs data transfers through the PCI bus jointly with the Tx- Host process and configures and controls the hardware components at the TxPC. In the same way, the RxHost process and the DSP receiver process (RxDSP) are responsible of transferring the data through the

PCI bus and, from the DSP side, controlling and configuring the testbed hardware components.

The MWL serves the maximum number of requests that the hardware supports. It serves a request while the data for the next frame is still being generated by any computer in the network and, when the first frame is passed to the SPL, the MWL is ready to accept a new frame. With this architecture scheme, the MWL simultaneously serves requests from other SPL instances running in different PCs.

For the specific case of our MIMO testbed, in order to release the MWL implementation from dealing with the lowest level hardware details, the Sundance SMT6025 software development kit and the Sundance SMT6300 operating system driver are used in the TxHost and the Rx- Host implementations.

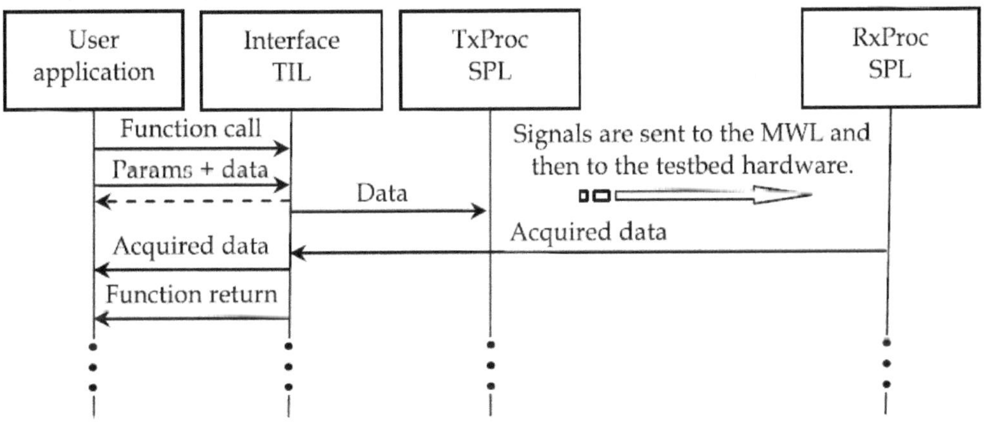

Fig. 6. Sequence diagram describing the interaction among the user application, the testbed interface layer (TIL) and the signal processing layer (SPL).

The Texas Instruments Code Composer (Texas Instruments, 2009), as well as the 3L Diamond DSP+FPGA (3L Ltd., 2009), are utilized for the TxDSP and RxDSP implementations. If a different hardware type is considered, there should exist different tools avoiding dealing with the lowest-level hardware details.

The middleware concept constitutes a great leap forward in MIMO testbed technology, allowing access to hardware using ordinary network connections and allowing synchronization between the transmitter and the receiver. It also permits to incorporate a wired feedback channel. The MWL design supports extensibility in many senses. For instance, many transmitter and receivers can be used through broadcast network connections. Also, although the DSP processes are hardware dependent, the control logic between the transmitter and the receiver, as well as with the higher layers, is valid for different hardware testbeds. Finally, since the hardware interfaces from the host side and the software related to DSPs are developed as separated software modules, they can be replaced by implementations suitable for any other testbed.

6. INTERACTION BETWEEN TIL, SPL AND THE USER APPLICATION

Fig. 6 shows a simplified version of the interaction among the user application, the TIL and the SPL. When the user application has generated the discrete-time sequences to be transmitted, the testbed calls some function in the TIL. Both sequences, as well as their type, are included as input parameters. Then, depending on the specified additional input parameters, the TIL offers the possibility to return the control to the user application in order to carry on doing other tasks while the signals are being transmitted and acquired. The TIL establishes a connection with the TxProc at the SPL and sends the transmit data. Next, the interaction described in Fig. 7 takes place and, as a result, the signals are properly transmitted and after- wards acquired by the MWL and sent to the RxProc at the SPL. Finally, the acquired data is transferred to the TIL and sent to the user application. If the user application got the control after calling the TIL, then the acquired sequences are not transferred to the TIL until the user application calls again the TIL.

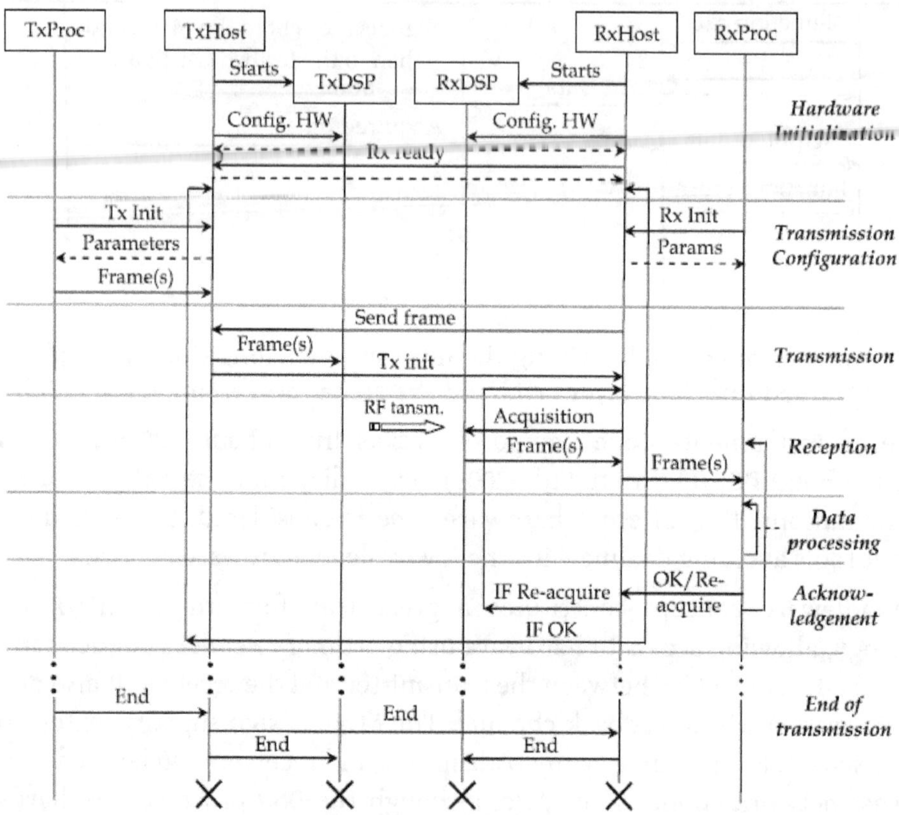

Fig. 7. Basic sequence diagram of one of the variety of protocols implemented in our testbed. It is termed basic operation mode. Dashed arrows represent acknowledgements (ACK). Regular arrows represent messages sent from a source to a destination.

7. INTERACTION BETWEEN SPL, MWL AND THE HARDWARE

In this section we will explain some functioning modes of the testbed architecture. All of them have been implemented in our MIMO testbed and they allow us different operational modes.

7.1 Basic Mode Operation

Fig. 7 shows the sequence diagram of the "basic operation mode protocol". The protocol fully specifies the behaviour of the six processes of the software architecture. Thus, different protocols allow using the testbed and the software architecture in different scenarios and for distinct purposes. The basic operation protocol consists of the following seven stages:

1. **Hardware initialization:** Both transmitter and receiver hardware must be set up before beginning the actual operation. At the operating system level, two ordinary processes are started: TxHost and RxHost, which then load the TxDSP and RxDSP binaries into the respective DSPs. Once loaded, these processes initialize the baseband hardware modules. Additionally, they allocate the memory buffer needed for communication through the PCI bus. In this stage, the "Starts" message ensures that the communication between the host and the DSP can be successfully established. Afterwards, the "Config. HW" messages are sent to the DSP and the TxDSP and RxDSP proceed to properly configure the hardware. They reply with an acknowledgement (ACK) represented in Fig. 7 by a dashed arrow.

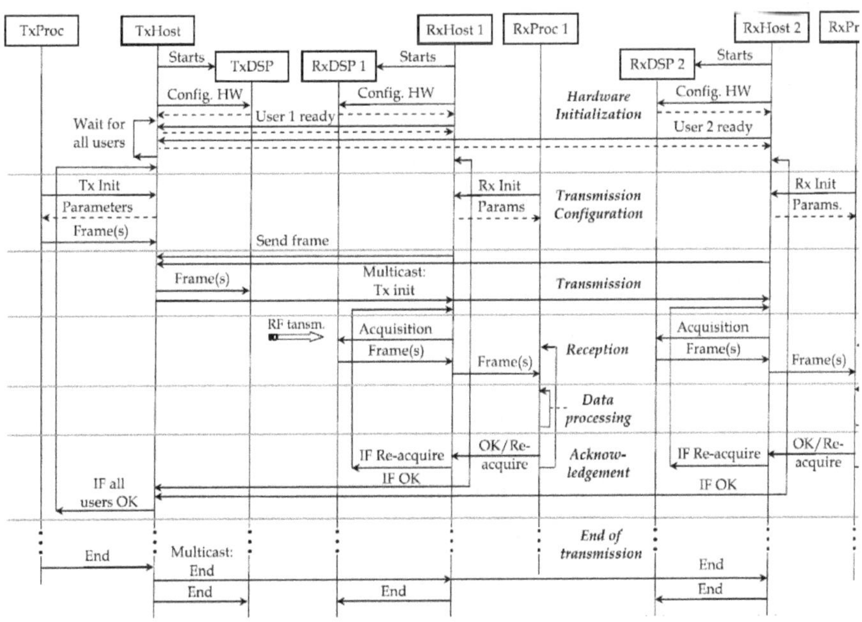

Fig. 8. Sequence diagram of the multiuser testbed protocol particularized for the case when just two receive users are considered.

2. **Transmission configuration:** At this stage an instance of the SPL accesses the MWL to configure a transmission. The process starts when a user application that makes use of the TIL transmits a set of discrete-time sequences. After receiving the sequences to be sent, TxProc sends the "Tx Init." message to the TxHost, which returns the parame- ters needed by the TxProc. Control parameters such as the frame size or the number of frames to be transmitted are configured. Moreover, other parameters such as the signal power strength, can be sent to TxHost during this stage. Also, the frame or set of frames to be transmitted is sent to TxHost. Finally, at the receiver side, a communication between RxHost and RxProc is established to ensure that the transmission can be carried out.
3. **Transmission:** Once TxHost has received all parameters, the transmission process can begin. First, RxHost must notify that it is able to receive frames by using the message "Send Frame". Then, TxHost sends to TxDSP the parameters and the frames acquired in the previous step and TxDSP communicates the inminent cyclic transmission of the current frame. Finally, TxHost sends the message "Tx init" to RxHost notifying the availability of the frame; TxHost sends an "Acquisition"message to TxDSP; and the frame is acquired and transferred to the TxHost through the PCI bus. Later on, the signals are sent to the RxProc and, finally, they are transferred to the user application through the TIL. The transmitter side will continuously send the frame until a new message "Send Frame" is received from RxHost.
4. **Reception:** After receiving the "Tx init" message from TxHost, RxHost sends the "Acquisition" message to RxDSP. Then, RxDSP captures the signals and sends them back to RxHost through the PCI bus. Then, signals are sent to RxProc, properly processed in this layer, and finally they are sent to the TIL, making them available to the user application.
5. **Data processing:** In our testbed data processing is completely carried out off-line, even though hardware permits real-time processing by means of, for instance, available FP- GAs. Basically, during this stage the received data are properly adapted and processed.
6. **Acknowledgement:** After processing the data, the receiver must tell the transmitter what to do next. The receiver can ask for retransmission of the last frame or for a new frame. In the first case, the receiver moves on the transmission stage. In the latter, the receiver needs to prepare a new transmission, so it must go back to the transmission configuration stage.
7. **End of transmission:** TxProc receives a finalization message, which is properly propagated to the rest of the testbed processes with the objective of adequately closing all opened resources and to finish all testbed processes.

7.2 Burst Transmission

This case involves the transmission of a number of data frames with the goal of testing a given transmission system. The sequence diagram is the same as the one depicted in Fig. 7 with the following two exceptions:

- At the beginning of the transmission configuration stage, TxProc notifies the number of frames to be transmitted and sends them to TxHost.
- After finishing each single-frame transmission (probably with a certain number of re- acquisitions carried out by the receiver side) TxHost automatically moves on the next frame to be transmitted.

This mode can be exploited to emulate a real wireless communication system. For instance, a video can be sent in real-time and the users can watch it at the receiver side.

7.3 Performance Measurements

Another case of use is the automation of performance measurements corresponding to a particular algorithm or a specific transmission system. In this case, the protocol works in a quite similar way as in burst transmission: during the data processing stage the measurements are performed and the receiver decides whether it has to keep on doing measurements or it has already collected enough data. This functioning mode was used while doing performance measurements in (Pe´rez-Iglesias et al., 2008; Ram´ırez et al., 2008), where different STBC techniques were tested in real environments. The data processing stage can be modified in order to just store the acquired signals at the receiver side to be later on processed off-line.

7.4 Using a Feedback Channel

MIMO systems performance can be improved if the receiver feeds back Channel State Information (CSI) from the receiver to the transmitter, so it can adapt its transmssion scheme to the actual channel characteristics. It is straightforward to implement a feedback channel with in the protocol: the CSI information must be sent during the acknowledgement stage to notify the transmitter whether it has to re-configure the transmission parameters or not. To do so, in the sequence diagram shown in Fig. 7 there should be added two "Send CSI" messages: one from the RxHost to the TxHost and another from the TxHost to the TxProc.

If the signal adaptation at the transmitter side takes place at the user application, then no feedback messages are needed in the protocol because everything is available at the user application. It is necessary to call the testbed interface layer twice: one to be able to estimate the channel and the following with the adapted signals.

7.5 Deployment of a Multiuser Environment

The last given case of study describes the functioning of the designed protocol when working in a multiuser environment where several nodes receive information from a central node (broadcast channel). The protocol just needs to be generalized to support the synchronization of several receiver nodes.

Fig. 8 presents the use case for two receiver users. In order to implement this scenario it is necessary to incorporate some modifications:

- After configuring the testbed hardware, TxHost waits for the "ready" message from all receive users.
- TxHost waits for the "Send Frame" message from all users before starting the transmis- sion.
- The frame is cyclically transmitted and each individual user can carry out as many acquisitions as desired. Once all users have acquired all necessary data, they send an "OK" message to the TxHost. When TxHost has received all "OK" messages from all users, the current frame transmission is finished.
- When TxProc receives an end message, it passes it to TxHost which launches a multicast message to all receive users in order to properly finish.

7.6 Using a Simpler Protocol

In some cases it is interesting to provide a simpler protocol in order to delegate most of the control mechanisms to the user application. Now the TIL has two different functions allowing the control of the transmitter and the receiver separately. After the hardware initialization step (see Fig. 7), the user application decides to send a set of discrete-time sequences and then uses the TIL to send them to the SPL. Afterwards, the SPL sends them to the MWL to be transmitted, but RxHost is waiting for RxProc in order to carry out the acquisition. When the user application decides to acquire the data, it calls again the TIL which asks RxProc to acquire the data. Immediately, RxProc asks RxHost to acquire the data and returns it to the user application through the RxProc and the TIL.

The main difference of this functioning mode with respect to the basic operation mode is the lack of messages between TxHost and RxHost, which are now completely autonomous. This presents the advantage of easier integration of the testbed nodes with other nodes and, at the same time, all nodes can be directly controlled from the user application. However, as a disadvantage, the testbed control is moved to the user application. Consequently, the user application has now to deal with some hardware details (e.g. the size of buffers) but properly encapsulated in the TIL. In addition, performance losses arise as a consequence of the testbed being controlled from the user application.

8. CONCISE SUMMARY

This chapter presents a novel distributed multilayer software architecture for user access in a MIMO testbed. The architecture bridges the gap between commercial hardware components and the prevalent abstraction level utilized by researchers. The architecture transcends the constraints of directly implementing new algorithms from the testbed. The architecture offers high-level interface access for testbeds, rather than relying on the low-level interfaces commonly given by manufacturers. It liberates researchers from the obligation of understanding the specifics of the testbed hardware. For example, they can efficiently evaluate new algorithms without the necessity of creating an entirely new source code release for the testbed, hence accelerating the development and testing processes.

The fundamental aspect of multilayer architecture design is the utilization of standard network connections to interconnect software modules and hardware components. These connections are also advantageous for decoupling the software layers. The layered software architecture yields numerous advantages. Additionally, multiuser situations and feedback channels can be developed by extending the proposed architecture. Ultimately, the described architectural protocols might be streamlined to facilitate integration with heterogeneous nodes. The testbed control has been transferred to the user application rather than remaining within the inner layers.

REFERENCES

1. 3L Ltd (2009), http://www.3l.com/
2. Borkowski, D.; Brhl, L.; Degen, C.; Keusgen, W.; Alirezaei, G.; Geschewski, F.; Oikonomopou- los, C. & Rembold, B. (2006). SABA: A testbed for real-time MIMO systems. EURASIP Journal on Applied Signal Processing, Vol. 2006, 2006.
3. Caban, S.; Mehlfu¨ hrer, C.; Langwieser, R.; Scholtz, A.L. & Rupp, M. (2005), Vienna MIMO Testbed, EURASIP Journal on Applied Signal Processing, Vol. 2006, 2006.
4. Fabregas, A.G.; Guillaud, M.; Slock, D.T.M.; Caire, G.; Gosse, G.; Rouquette, S.; Ribeiro Dias, A.; Bernardin, P.; Miet, X.; Conrat, J.M; Toutain, Y.; Peden, A. & Li, Z. (2005), A MIMO-OFDM Testbed for Wireless Local Area Networks, EURASIP Journal on Ap- plied Signal Processing, Vol. 2006, 2006.
5. Foschini, G. & Gans, M. (1998), On Limits of Wireless Communications in a Fading Environ- ment when Using Multiple Antennas, Wireless Personal Communications, Vol. 6, 1998, pp. 311-335.
6. Garc´ıa-Naya, Jose´ A.; Gonza´lez-Lo´pez, M. & Castedo, L. (2008), An Overview of MIMO Testbed Technology, Proceedings of 4th International Symposium

on Image/Video Com- munications over Fixed and Mobile Networks (ISIVC 2008), July, 2008, Bilbao

7. Garc´ıa-Naya, Jose´ A.; Pe´rez-Iglesias, He´ctor J.; Ferna´ndez-Carame´s, T. M.; Gonza´lez-Lo´pez, M. & Castedo, L. (2008), A distributed multilayer architecture enabling end-user access to MIMO testbeds, Proceedings of IEEE 19th International Symposium on Per- sonal, Indoor and Mobile Radio Communications, 2008 (PIMRC 2008), September, 2008, Cannes.
8. Haustein, T.; Forck, A.; Ga¨ber, H.; Jungnickel, V. & Schiffermu¨ ller, S. (2005), Real-Time Signal Processing for Multiantenna Systems: Algorithms, Optimization, and Implementa- tion on an Experimental Test-Bed, EURASIP Journal on Applied Signal Processing, Vol. 2006, 2006.
9. Kaiser, T.; Wilzeck, A.; Berentsen, M. & Rupp, M. (2004). Prototyping for MIMO Systems An Overview, Proceedings of the XII European Signal Processing Conference (EUSIPCO 2004), September, 2004, Vienna.
10. The Mathworks (2009), http://www.mathworks.com/
11. Moore, G. (1998), Cramming more components onto integrated circuits, Proceedings of the IEEE, Vol. 86, No. 1, 1998, pp. 82–85.
12. Nieto, X.; Ventura, L.M. & Mollfulleda, A. (2006), GEDOMIS: a broadband wireless MIMO- OFDM testbed, design and implementation, Proceedings of 2nd International Conference on Testbeds and Research Infrastructures for the Development of Networks and Communities (TRIDENTCOM 2006), 2006, Barcelona.
13. PXI: PCI eXtensions for Instrumentation (2009), http://www.pxisa.org
14. Pe´rez-Iglesias, H.J.; Garc´ıa-Naya, J.A.; Dapena, A.; Castedo, L. & Zarzoso, V. (2008), Blind channel identification in Alamouti coded systems: a comparative study of eigende- composition methods in indoor transmissions at 2.4 GHz, European Transactions on Telecomunications, Vol. 19, No. 7, November 2008, pp. 751–759.
15. Ram´ırez, D.; Santamar´ıa, I.; Pe´rez, J.; V´ıa, J.; Garc´ıa-Naya, J.A.; Ferna´ndez-Carame´s, T.M.; Pe´rez-Iglesias, H.J.; Gonza´lez Lo´pez, M.; Castedo, L. & Torres-Royo, J.M. (2008), A comparative study of STBC transmissions at 2.4 GHz over indoor channels using a 2 x 2 MIMO testbed, Wireless Communications and Mobile Computing, Vol. 8, No. 9, November 2008.
16. Rao, R.M.; Wiejun Zhu Lang, S.; Oberli, C.; Browne, D.; Bhatia, J.; Frigon, J.-F.; Jingming Wang Gupta, P.; Heechoon Lee; Liu, D.N.; Wong, S.G.; Fitz, M.; Daneshrad, B. & Takeshita, O. (2004), Multi-antenna testbeds for research and education in wireless communications, Communications Magazine, IEEE, Vol. 42, No. 12, December 2004, pp. 72–81, ISSN: 0163-6804.

17. Rupp, M.; Burg, A. & Beck, E. (2003). Rapid Prototyping for Wireless Designs: the Five-Ones Approach, Signal Processing Europe, Vol. 83, 2003, pp. 1427-1444.

18. Rupp, M.; Mehlfhrer, C. & Caban, S. (2006), Testbeds and Rapid Prototyping in Wireless Sys- tem Design, EURASIP Newsletter, Vol. 17, No. 3, 2006, pp. 32-50.

19. Rupp, M.; Caban, S. & Mehlfhrer, C. (2007), Challenges in Building MIMO Testbeds, Proceed- ings of European Signal Processing Conference (EUSIPCO 2007), 2006, Poznan.

20. SDR Forum: Software Defined Radio Forum (2009), http://www.sdrforum.org SCA: Software Communication Architecture (2009), http://sca.jpeojtrs.mil Sundance Multiprocessor, Ltd. (2009), http://www.sundance.com

21. Telatar, I. E. (1999), Capacity of Multi-Antenna Gaussian Channels, European Transactions on Telecommunications, Vol. 10, No. 6, 1999, pp. 585-595.

22. Texas Instruments (2009), http://www.ti.com

23. Trygve, M. H. (1978), MVC, XEROX PARC, http://heim.ifi.uio.no/˜trygver/themes/mvc/mvc-index.html

24. Wilzeck, A.; El-Hadidy, M.; Cai, Q.; Amelingmeyer, M. & Kaiser, T. (2006). MIMO Prototyping Testbed with off-the-shelf plug-in RF Hardware, IEEE Workshop on Smart Antennas (WSA 2006), 2006 Ulm.

25. Zhu, W.; Browne, D. & Fitz, M. (2005). An Open Access Wideband Multi-Antenna Wireless Testbed with Remote Control Capability, Proceedings of 2nd International Conference on Testbeds and Research Infrastructures for the Development of Networks and Communities (TRIDENTCOM 2005), Trento

Chapter 6

RECENT ADVANCEMENTS IN CHANNEL ESTIMATION AND DETECTION FOR MIMO SYSTEMS

1. INTRODUCTION: AN OVERVIEW

MIMO systems are recognized for their ability to deliver exceptional spectrum efficiency in a richly scattered propagation environment (Telatar, 1999). Consequently, they represent a viable solution for high-speed, spectrally efficient, and stable wireless communication. Raoof et al. (2008). Coherent signal detection at the receiver necessitates channel state information at the receiver (CSIR), which requires a channel estimate step. Channel estimate is pivotal to the efficacy of the receiver. In actual MIMO systems, ensuring high-quality data recovery is a significant challenge, almost as crucial as achieving elevated data throughput.

To acquire the Channel State Information Reference (CSIR), the transmitter typically transmits designated training symbols, enabling the receiver to estimate the channel prior to detecting data symbols. The classical method involves time-multiplexing pilot and data symbols, commonly known as pilot symbol-assisted modulation (PSAM) Cavers (1991). This chapter commences with an introduction to PSAM channel estimation for MIMO systems (Section 2). Rather than relying just on pilot symbols for conventional channel estimation, we can employ semi-blind estimation, which incorporates both pilot and data symbols in the channel estimate process. A significant enhancement in performance can be attained at the cost of augmented receiver complexity. De Carvalho and Slock (1997); Giannakis et al. (2001); Sadough (2008). Typically, these semi-blind methodologies are executed inside an iterative framework during the channel coding process. Channel estimation is executed iteratively in conjunction with signal detection and channel decoding. Sadough, Ichir, Duhamel, and Jaffrot (2009). We will thus proceed with Section 2 by examining semi-blind estimate in the context of time-multiplexed pilots.

The disadvantage of the PSAM scheme is the reduction in spectral efficiency due to the periodic insertion of pilot symbols. Alternatively, overlay pilots (OP) can be utilized, wherein pilot symbols are transmitted concurrently with data symbols.

Hoeher and Tufvesson (1999). In Section 3, we present the OP methodology and specifically elucidate pilot-only-based and semi-blind estimation methodologies. The advantages and disadvantages of OP in relation to PSAM are also examined.

Regardless of the channel estimating method employed, the receiver can ultimately get only an imperfect estimation of the channel. Traditionally, in signal detection, the estimated channel is regarded as an accurate representation. This inefficient method is commonly referred to as the mismatched receiver. The sub-optimality arises from the receiver's failure to consider channel estimation errors. Sadough and Duhamel (2008); Sadough (2008). A more suitable method is to consider channel estimation mistakes in the formulation of the detector.

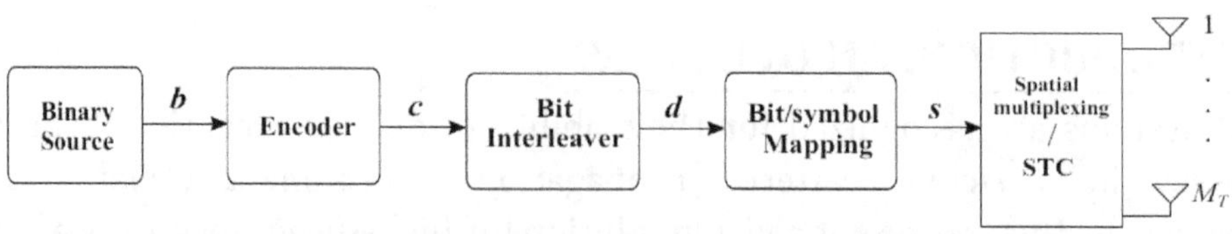

Fig. 1. Transmitter architecture of MIMO-BICM scheme.

1.1 Assumptions and notations

We consider a single-user MIMO system with MT transmit and MR receive antennas, transmitting over a frequency non-selective channel and refer to it as an (MR × MT) MIMO chan- nel. Unless otherwise mentioned, single carrier modulation and block fading channel model is considered where the channel is assumed to remain almost constant over the duration of a block of symbols.

Figure 1 shows the block diagram of the transmitter that employs the bit-interleaved coded modulation (BICM) scheme which is known to be a simple and efficient method for exploiting channel time-selectivity. The binary data sequence b is encoded by a forward error correction (FEC) code before being interleaved by a quasi-random interleaver. The output bits d are mapped to constellation symbols s and then either multiplexed spatially or encoded according to a space-time scheme before being sent through the wireless channel. Let us denote by x and y respectively the (MT × 1) and (MR × 1) vectors of transmit and received symbols at a given time reference. For simplicity, we assume for now the simple spatial multiplexing scheme. We have:

$$y = Hx + z \quad (1)$$

where H denotes the (MR × MT) channel matrix and z is the vector of additive complex white Gaussian noise of zero mean and covariance matrix Σz = Σ2 IM , where In denotes an (n × n) Identity matrix. We assume here that Σ2 is perfectly known at the receiver and focus on the estimation of H.

2. TIME-MULTIPLEXED PILOTS AND DATA

Most current systems use a training-based channel estimation scheme in the form of time- multiplexed pilot symbols. In what follows, we present the PSAM approach for MIMO systems and explain two cases of pilot-only-based and semi-blind estimation; the latter is implemented in an iterative receiver.

2.1 Pilot-only-based PSAM channel estimation

When using the PSAM method, we have a trade-off between the channel estimation quality and the data throughput. With an increased number of pilots, a better channel estimate can be obtained, but at the same time, the spectral efficiency is sacrificed more. There is a minimum number of channel-uses that should be devoted to the transmission of pilots in order that the MIMO channel be identifiable at the receiver. As a general case, if L denotes the maximum length of the underlying subchannels' impulse response, the number of pilot channel-uses Np should satisfy Balakrishnan et al. (2000):

$$(Np - L + 1) \geq MT\ L \tag{2}$$

Under flat fading conditions where L = 1, this implies: Np ≥ MT . Several works have been done on the optimal placement of pilots in a frame of symbols, as well as on the optimal power allocation between pilot and data symbols Hassibi & Hochwald (2003); Dong & Tong (2002); Adireddy et al. (2002); Ma et al. (2003). They consider the criteria of mean-square channel estimation error, channel capacity, or the Crame´r-Rao bounds. In particular, it is shown in Hassibi & Hochwald (2003) that, if power optimization over pilot and data symbols is allowed, the optimum Np is Npopt = MT . In such a case, we should place pilot symbols with lower power at the beginning and the end of the frame, and those with higher power in the middle of the frame Dong & Tong (2002). However, if equal power has to be allocated to pilot and data symbols, then Npopt can be larger than MT Hassibi & Hochwald (2003).

Considering the simple case of flat block-fading MIMO channel, to estimate the channel, corresponding to each fading block, we send Np pilot symbol vectors with the same power as the data symbols. Let xp [k] denote an (MT × 1) pilot symbol vector at the time sample k. We denote the received vector corresponding to xp [k] by yp [k]. We can constitute the (MT × Np) matrix Xp by stacking in its columns the pilot vectors xp [k], k = 0, 1, Np − 1, i.e., Xp = [xp[0], ... , xp [Np − 1]].

According to (1), during a given channel training interval, we have:

$$Yp = HXp + Zp. \tag{3}$$

The definitions of Yp and Zp are similar to that of Xp. We denote by Ep the average power of the training symbols on any subcarrier as

$$\mathbf{E}_p \triangleq \frac{1}{N_p M_T} \operatorname{tr}\left(\mathbf{X}_p \mathbf{X}_p^{\dagger}\right). \tag{4}$$

The maximum likelihood (ML) channel estimate H^ , which is equivalent to the least-squares solution, is Balakrishnan et al. (2000):

$$\hat{\mathrm{H}} = \left(\sum_{k=0}^{N_p-1} \boldsymbol{y}_p[k]\, \boldsymbol{x}_p^{\dagger}[k] \right) \left(\sum_{k=0}^{N_p-1} \boldsymbol{x}_p[k]\, \boldsymbol{x}_p^{\dagger}[k] \right)^{-1}, \tag{5}$$

which can be written in a more compact form as:

H^ = Yp X† (XpX†)-1, (6)

where .† denotes transpose-conjugate.

Let us denote by E the matrix of estimation errors, that is, E = H^ - H. From (3) and (6), it is easy to show that

E = Zp X† (XpX†p)-1. (7)

It is known that the best channel estimate is obtained with mutually orthogonal training se- quences, which result in uncorrelated estimation errors. In other words, we should choose Xp with orthogonal rows such that

$$\mathbf{X}_p \mathbf{X}_p^{\dagger} = N_p E_p \, \mathbb{I}_{M_T}. \tag{8}$$

Then, the j th column E j of E has the covariance matrix Σ given by

$$[\mathcal{E}_j \, \mathcal{E}_j^{\dagger}] = \sigma_e^2 \, \mathbb{I}_{M_R}, \quad \text{where } \sigma_e^2 = \frac{\sigma_z^2}{N_p E_p} \cdot \tag{9}$$

2.1.1 Statistics of the Channel Estimation Errors

We saw that the estimated channel matrix H^ can be viewed as a noisy version of the perfect channel matrix H. In Section 5 we show that for channel estimators having this feature, the detection performance can be improved if the statistics of the channel estimation errors are known.

Let us reconsider the pilot-based ML channel estimator of equation (7). The good feature of this estimator is that the statistics of the channel estimation error matrix are known (see equation (9)). By using these statistics and equation (7), the conditional pdf of H^ given H can be easily expressed as:

p(H^ |H)= CN(H, IMT ⊗ Σe), (10)

where denotes the Kronecker product and denotes the complex Gaussian distribution. Furthermore, we assume that the channel matrix H has a normal prior distribution as:

$$\mathrm{H} \sim \mathcal{CN}(0, \mathbb{I}_{M_T} \otimes \boldsymbol{\Sigma}_H) = \frac{1}{\pi^{M_R M_T} \det\{\boldsymbol{\Sigma}_H\}^{M_T}} \exp\left\{ -\operatorname{tr}\left(\mathrm{H} \boldsymbol{\Sigma}_H^{-1} \mathrm{H}^{\dagger} \right) \right\} \tag{11}$$

where ΣH is

the (MR × MR) covariance matrix of the columns of H, and det{} denotes ma- trix determinant. We assume that the entries of , i.e., the fading coefficients of different subchannels, are i.i.d. Then, ΣH is a diagonal matrix with equal diagonal entries Σ2h.

By using the prior pdf of H from (11) and the pdf of (H^|H) from (10), we can derive the posterior distribution of the perfect channel matrix, conditioned on its ML estimate, as follows (see Sadough & Duhamel (2008) for the details of the derivation):

$$p(\mathbf{H}|\hat{\mathbf{H}}) = \mathcal{CN}\left(\boldsymbol{\Sigma}_\Delta \hat{\mathbf{H}}, \mathbb{I}_{M_T} \otimes \boldsymbol{\Sigma}_\Delta \boldsymbol{\Sigma}_e\right), \tag{12}$$

Where

$$\boldsymbol{\Sigma}_\Delta = \boldsymbol{\Sigma}_H \left(\boldsymbol{\Sigma}_e + \boldsymbol{\Sigma}_H\right)^{-1}. \tag{13}$$

Under the above-mentioned assumptions, we have

$$\Sigma\Delta = \delta IMR \tag{14}$$

where

$$\delta = \frac{\sigma_h^2}{\sigma_h^2 + \sigma_e^2} \cdot \tag{15}$$

In particular, when the number of pilot symbols tends to infinity, it is not difficult to see that δ → 1 and δΣe2 → 0 and consequently p (H|H^) tends to a Dirac delta function. The availability of the estimation error distribution is an interesting feature of pilot-only-based PSAM channel estimation that we used to derive the posterior distribution (12). This distribution constitutes a Bayesian framework which is exploited in Section 5 for the design of detectors by taking into account channel estimation inaccuracies.

2.2 Semi-blind PSAM channel estimation

In order to preserve the spectral efficiency for the transmission of data symbols, we are interested in minimizing the number of pilot symbols in a frame. However, by reducing the number of pilot symbols, the channel may be learned improperly and channel estimation errors may become important. This can result in a considerable performance degradation and in the need to data retransmission. This performance degradation can be compensated by smart signal processing at the receiver. In fact, instead of estimation methods based on pi- lot symbols only, we can use semi-blind approaches that in addition to pilot symbols, make use of data symbols in channel estimation. In this way, a considerable performance improve ment can be achieved at the price of increased receiver complexity de Carvalho & Slock (2001); Sadough, Ichir, Duhamel & Jaffrot (2009). We present here two semi-blind channel estimation schemes that we implement in an iterative receiver. The first semi-blind method that we consider is the thresholded hard-decisions (Th-HD) method and the second one is based on the ex- pectation maximization (EM) algorithm Dempster et al. (1977); Moon (1996). For both methods, at the first iteration, we calculate a primary channel estimate based on the pilot sequences only, which allows the semi-blind estimator, used in the succeeding iterations, to bootstrap. Before describing these methods, we present in the following details on the iterative receiver.

2.2.1 Iterative signal detection

We usually consider in this paper iterative signal detection in the case of using non-orthogonal space-time codes at the transmitter. As shown in Fig. 2, the receiver mainly consists of a combination of two sub-blocks that exchange soft information with each other. The first sub-block, referred to as soft detector or demapper, produces extrinsic soft information from the input symbols and send it to the second sub-block, the soft-input soft-output (SISO) channel decoder. Here, we consider SISO channel decoding based on the well known forward-backward algorithm Bahl et al. (1974). Soft MIMO signal detection and soft-input SISO channel decoding are performed iteratively and the estimates of the channel coefficients are updated at each iteration of the turbo detector Sadough, Ichir, Duhamel & Jaffrot (2009); Berthet et al. (2001). The blocks Π and Π 1 denote bit-level interleaver and de-interleaver, respectively, corresponding to the BICM scheme used at the transmitter.

2.2.2 Th-HD semi-blind estimation

In the Th-HD method, in addition to pilot symbols, we use in channel estimation the symbols detected with high reliability at each iteration Khalighi & Boutros (2006); Sellathurai & Haykin (2002). For instance, consider the a posteriori probability P(m) at the decoder output at iteration m, corresponding to the coded bit ci. We compare it with a threshold 0.5 < PTH < 1. If Pi $^{(m)}$ > PTH, we make the hard decision ci $^{(m+1)}$ = 1 ; otherwise,

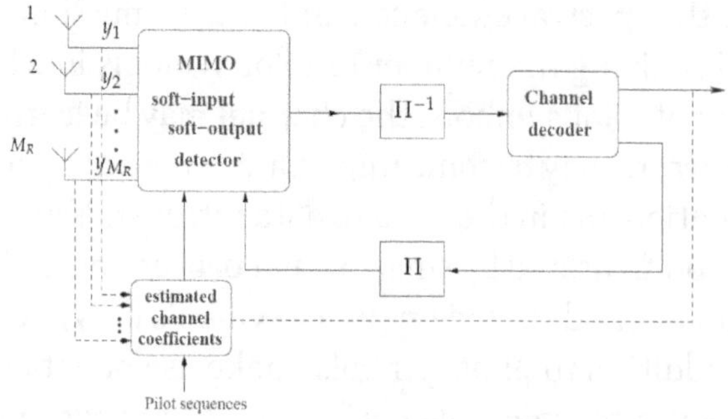

Fig. 2. Iterative channel estimation and data detection, yi denotes the received signal on the ith antenna.

if Pi $^{(m)}$ < (1 - PTH), we make the hard decision c^i $^{(m+1)}$ = 0; and if none of these conditions are verified, we give up the channel-use corresponding to ci and do not consider it in channel estimation. If a hard decision is made on all BMT constituting bits of a channel-use, we use the resulting hard-detected symbol vector in channel estimation, in the same way as pilot symbols. The resulting channel estimate is then used in the next iteration of the detector.

The performance of Th-HD depends highly on the choice of the threshold PTH that determines whether or not the SISO decoder soft-outputs are reliable enough. The practical limitation is that the optimum threshold value depends on the MIMO structure, i.e., the number of trans- mit and receive antennas, as well as on the actual SNR Khalighi & Boutros (2006). Note that, if we take PTH very close to 0.5, we effectively make hard decisions on all detected symbols and use them in channel estimation. This coincides with the so called decision-feedback channel estimation Visoz & Berthet (2003).

2.2.3 EM-based semi-blind estimation

The interest of the EM algorithm is that it is guaranteed to be stable and to converge to an ML estimate Moon & Stirling (2000). We do not present here the details on the formulation of the EM-based estimator and refer the reader to Khalighi & Boutros (2006), for instance. A simple and classical formulation is when data and pilot symbols are used in the same way in channel estimation. By this approach, the estimated channel matrix is given below:

$$\hat{\mathrm{H}} = \overline{\boldsymbol{R}}_{yx}\boldsymbol{R}_{x}^{\ 1}, \tag{16}$$

where

$$\overline{\boldsymbol{R}}_{yx} = \sum_{k=1}^{N_s} \boldsymbol{y}[k]\ \tilde{\boldsymbol{x}}^{+}[k] \tag{17}$$

and

$$\overline{\boldsymbol{R}}_{x,i,j} = \begin{cases} \mathrm{N_s} & ; \quad i = j \\ \sum_{k=1}^{N_s} \tilde{\boldsymbol{x}}_i[k]\ \tilde{\boldsymbol{x}}_j^*[k] & ; \quad i \neq j \end{cases} \tag{18}$$

Here, Ns denotes the number of channel-uses per frame, y[k] is the received symbol vector at the time reference k, and x˜ [k] is the corresponding soft-estimates of the transmitted sym- bol vector, calculated using the SISO channel decoder outputs at the preceding iteration. For k = 1, , Np, we have x˜ [k]= xp [k]. Also, Rx,i,j denotes the (i, j)th entry of matrix Rx. The formulation that we provided for EM can be modified further to improve the receiver performance. Interested reader may refer to Khalighi & Boutros (2006); Khalighi et al. (2006) for details.

2.2.4 Case study

BER curves versus Eb /N0 are shown in Fig. 3 for the case of (8 × 8) and (8 × 6) MIMO structures using the PSAM technique. Rayleigh independent quasi-static fading model is con- sidered with blocks of length Ns = 64 channel-uses. The number of channel-uses devoted to pilot transmission is Np = 10. Three cases of pilot-only-based estimation, and Th-HD and EM-based semi-blind estimations are considered. The case of perfect-CSIR is also provided as reference. The simple spatial multiplexing scheme is used at the transmitter and MIMO signal detection is based on soft parallel interference cancellation (Soft-PIC) Sellathurai & Haykin (2002); Lee et al. (2006). Results shown in Fig. 3 correspond to the eighth iteration of the receiver. We notice that the performance of the semi-blind Th-HD and EM-based estimator are very close to each other and they outperform the pilot-only-based method. Yet, their performance is about 2 dB away from the perfect-CSIR case that is due to the relatively high co-antenna interference, as we have MT = 8. We can approach further the perfect-CSIR case by increasing Np.

3. SUPERIMPOSED PILOTS AND DATA

The main drawback of the PSAM approach is that, for finite-length blocks, if channel estima- tion is to be done on each block of symbols, the periodic insertion of pilot symbols can result in a considerable reduction of the achievable data rate. This loss in the data rate becomes important, specially for large number of transmit antennas, at low SNR, and when the channel undergoes relatively fast variations Hassibi & Hochwald (2003). As an alternative, we can use overlay pilots (OP), also called superimposed or embedded pilots, for channel estimation Hoeher & Tufvesson (1999); Zhu et al. (2003). In this approach, a pilot sequence is superim- posed on the data sequence before transmission, as shown in Fig. 4; thus, no separate time slot is dedicated to pilot transmission.

3.1 Channel estimation using OP

By using OP, we prevent the loss in the data throughput but we experience degradation in the quality of the channel estimate due to the unknown data symbols Hoeher & Tufvesson (1999). As a matter of fact, here also there is a trade-off between high quality channel estimation and the information throughput: To obtain a better channel estimate, we should increase the percentage of the power dedicated to pilot symbols; this, however, reduces the SNR for the detection of data symbols Tapio & Bohlin (2004). In general, OP may be preferred to PSAM for high SNR, not too short channel coherence times, and larger number of receive than transmit antennas Khalighi et al. (2005).

Consider again the block fading channel model. Assuming uncorrelated data and pilot sequences, we can estimate channel coefficients by calculating the cross-correlation between the received sequences on each antenna and the transmitted pilot sequences, known to the receiver. As the pilot sequences transmitted from different antennas are orthogonal, the estimation errors arise from noise and the data sequences. Indeed, the main problem in the estimation of channel coefficients concerns the latter interference component, i.e., the unknown data symbols. In fact, although data and pilot sequences are statistically uncorrelated, the cross-correlation is calculated over a block of symbols of limited length, over which the channel coefficients are supposed to remain unchanged. The smaller is the block length (i.e., the faster the channel fading), the more important this cross-correlation is. This can result in an error floor in the receiver BER performance Jungnickel et al. (2001), especially at high SNR, and make the OP scheme lose its interest.

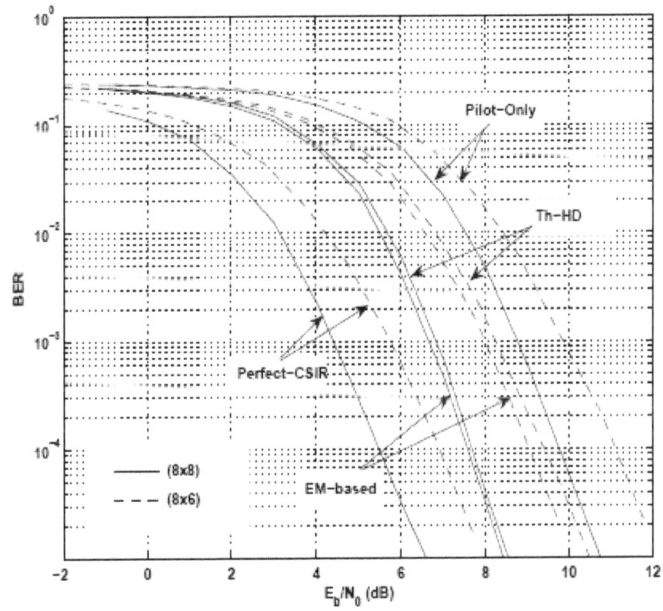

Fig. 3. Comparison of different estimation methods based on PSAM, iterative Soft-PIC de- tection, 8th iteration of the receiver (almost full convergence); (8 × 8) and (8 × 6) systems, i.i.d. Rayleigh quasi-static fading, QPSK modulation, (5, 7)8 NRNSC rate 1/2 channel code, orthogonal pilot sequences with Np = 10, Ns = 64 channel-uses. Eb /N0 takes into account the receiver antenna gain MR.

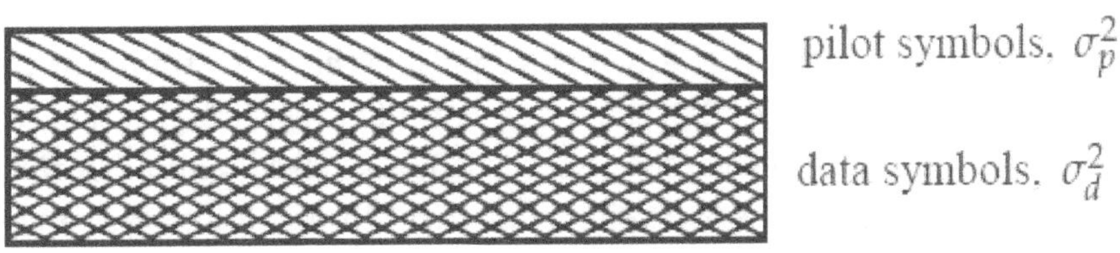

Fig. 4. Overlay pilot scheme

3.2 Iterative channel estimation for OP

Iterative data detection and channel estimation can be a solution to the problem of error floor Zhu et al. (2003); Khalighi et al. (2005); Cui & Tellambura (2005). We consider in the following, two such iterative schemes; a pilot-only-based decision-directed estimator Khalighi et al. (2005) and an EM-based semi-blind estimator Khalighi & Bourennane (2007).

Let us denote by xd and xp the vectors of data and pilot symbols, respectively, corresponding to the transmitted (MT × 1) vector x: x = xd + xp. We denote by Σ2 and Σ2 the power allocated to the entries of xd and x p, respectively.

3.2.1 Pilot-only-based decision-directed estimator

Consider the estimation of the entry Hij of the channel matrix H. As explained above, this estimate can be obtained by calculating the cross-correlation Γij between the sequence received on the antenna #i, yi, and the pilot sequence transmitted on the antenna #j, xp,j. By the decision-directed method that we denote by DD, we use in each iteration, the soft-estimates x˜d of transmitted data symbols using a posteriori LLRs at the SISO decoder output, and cancel their effect in Γij.

3.2.2 EM-based semi-blind estimator

To obtain a better performance, similar to the case of PSAM, we can employ semi-blind estimation methods Khalighi & Bourennane (2008); Bohlin & Tapio (2004); Meng & Tugnait (2004) at the price of increased Rx complexity. For instance, a semi-blind estimator based on the EM algorithm may be used. Its formulation is analogous to the case of PSAM and can be found in Khalighi & Bourennane (2007).

3.2.3 Data-dependent overlay pilots

A solution for getting rid of the interference from data symbols in channel estimation is to use data-dependent overlay pilot sequences such that the corresponding pilot and data sequences are orthogonal Ghogho et al. (2005). The drawback of this method is that it results in nulls in the equivalent channel impulse response (seen by data symbols), and hence, in a performance degradation. This degradation could be reduced by performing iterative channel equalization Lam et al. (2008). On the other hand, such a scheme leads to increased envelope fluctuations of the transmitted signal. We do not consider this scheme here.

3.2.4 Case study

Let us denote by α the ratio of the power of pilot symbols to the total transmit power at a symbol time, i.e., α = Σ2/(Σ2 + Σ2). For a (2 × 4) MIMO system, we have presented in Fig. 5, BER curves versus SNR for DD, EM-based, and perfect channel estimation, and different values of α. Pilot sequences for MT antennas can be QPSK modulated and chosen according to the Walsh-Hadamard series to ensure their orthogonality. Results correspond to the fifth it- eration of the Rx where almost full convergence is attained. SNR in Fig. 5 stands for the actual average received SNR, i.e., MR (Σd2 + Σp2)/Σn2, in contrast to Eb /N0 that takes into account only Σd2. In this way, we can directly see the compromise between the channel estimation quality and the data detection performance, e.g. by increasing α. Again, Soft-PIC MIMO detection is performed. For both estimation methods, we notice an error floor at high SNR for α < 15% which is especially visible for α = 2% and α = 5%. On the other hand, by increasing α, better channel estimates are obtained, but at the same time, less power is dedicated to data symbols. So, increasing α too much, will result in an overall performance degradation. Comparing the performance curves of the EM-based and DD estimators, we see that the performance improvement by semi-blind estimation is quite considerable. This improvement is more im- portant for smaller α values. For increased α, more power is dedicated to pilot symbols, and hence, the performance of the pilot-only-based estimator approaches that of the semi-blind estimator.

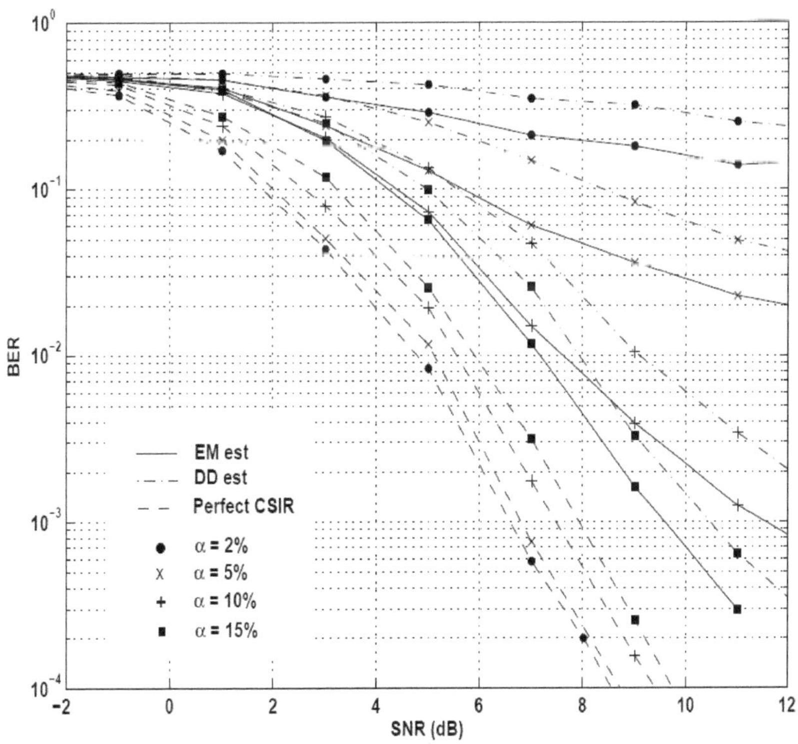

Fig. 5. Overlay Pilot scheme: BER after five receiver iterations for EM-based semi-blind, DD, and perfect channel estimation ; (2 × 4) MIMO system, i.i.d. Rayleigh quasi-static fading, QPSK-modulated pilot and data, (133, 171)8 NRNSC rate 1/2 channel code, Ns = 100. SNR takes into account MR.

4. IMPACT OF SPACE-TIME SCHEME

An important aspect is the the impact of channel estimation errors on the receiver performance for different ST schemes. We would like to compare the two general classes of ST schemes, i.e., orthogonal and non-orthogonal schemes. In the case of perfect channel knowledge, a comparison is made between these two categories in Khalighi et al. (2009), where iterative signal detection based on Soft-PIC is proposed for the case of non-orthogonal schemes. Note that optimal signal detection is too computationally complex for these schemes. Conditioned to the presence of sufficient (time or frequency) diversity, it is shown that a substantial gain is obtained by using the appropriate non-orthogonal schemes for moderate-to-high spectral efficiency MIMO systems, as compared to orthogonal schemes, which justifies the increased complexity of the receiver Khalighi et al. (2009).

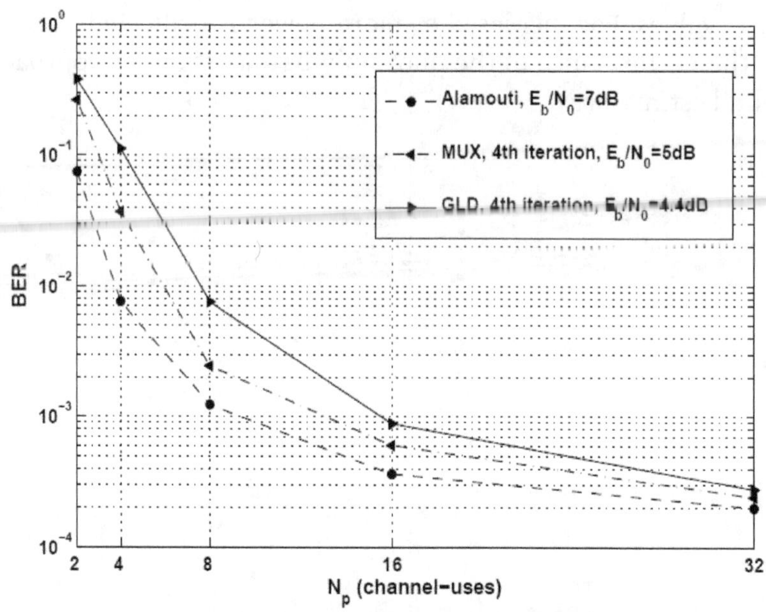

Fig. 6. Sensitivity to channel estimation errors; (2×2) MIMO channel, η = 2 bps/Hz, (133, 171)8 NRNSC rate 1/2 channel code, i.i.d. Rayleigh flat block fading channel with 32 independent fades per frame of 768 channel-uses. Iterative Soft-PIC used for MUX and GLD.

Concerning the practical case of imperfect channel estimate, in fact, lower-rate orthogonal schemes could be more sensitive to channel estimation errors as, in general, they have to use a larger signal constellation to attain a desired spectral efficiency. Concerning non-orthogonal schemes, we need, in general, smaller constellation sizes as compared to orthogonal ones. However, the iterative detector for the non-orthogonal schemes could be more sensitive to channel estimation errors because its convergence, and hence, its performance is affected by these errors.

To study the effect of channel estimation errors, let us consider pilot-only-based channel estimation using time-multiplexed pilots. For each fading block, we devote Np channel-uses to the transmission of power-normalized mutually orthogonal QPSK pilot sequences from MT transmit antennas Khalighi & Boutros (2006). For a (2 × 2) MIMO system, we have shown in Fig. 6 the average BER after four detector iterations versus Np for a spectral efficiency of η = 2 bps/Hz. We have considered the Alamouti code Alamouti (1998) as the orthogonal scheme, and two cases of spatial multiplexing (denoted here by MUX) and Golden coding Belfiore et al. (2005) (denoted by GLD) as non-orthogonal schemes. The Eb /N0 for each ST scheme is set to what results in BER 10-4 in the case of perfect channel knowledge. From Fig. 6 we notice an almost equivalent sensitivity to the channel estimation errors for MUX and GLD schemes. This comparison makes sense as the SNRs for these schemes are close to each other. On the other hand, we see that the Alamouti scheme has the lowest sensitivity. This is due to the orthogonal structure of the code, and the fact that the SNR is higher, compared to those for MUX and GLD schemes, and as a result, the quality of channel estimate is much better.

5. IMPROVED SIGNAL DETECTION IN THE PRESENCE OF CHANNEL ESTIMATION ERRORS

For the case of time-multiplexed pilot and data, as we explained previously, in order to obtain a good channel estimate, we should increase Np, which in turn, results in a larger loss in the spectral efficiency, specially for relatively fast time-varying communication channels Hassibi & Hochwald (2003). One solution is to use semi-blind channel estimation in or- der to reduce the number of channel-uses devoted to pilot transmission, as seen in Section 2.2. The disadvantage of semi-blind approaches is the increased receiver complexity. For a reduced-complexity semi-blind joint channel estimator and data detector the reader is refered to Sadough, Ichir, Duhamel & Jaffrot (2009).

An alternative to this solution is to modify the detector so as to take into account channel estimation errors. As a matter of fact, the classical approach is to use the channel estimate in the detection part in the same way as if it was a perfect estimate, what is known as mismatched signal detection. Obviously, this approach is suboptimal and can degrade considerably the receiver performance in the presence of channel estimation errors.

In this section we provide the general formulation of a detection rule that takes into account the available imperfect CSIR and refer to it as the improved detector. To this end, we consider the model (1) and denote by J(y, x, H) the quantity (cost function) that would let us to decide in favor of a particular x at the receiver if the channel was perfectly known. Note that depending on the detection criteria, the quantity J(y, x, H) can be the posterior pdf p(x|y, H), the logarithm of the likelihood function p(y|H, x), the mean square error (as in Sadough, Khalighi & Duhamel (2009); Sadough & Khalighi (2007)), etc. Assume a channel estimator in which the statistics of the estimation errors are known. Such a scenario occurs for instance in pilot-only-based PSAM channel estimation studied in Subsection 2.1 where we saw that the estimation process can be characterized by the posterior pdf of the channel (12). In this case, we propose a detector based on the minimization of a new cost function defined as

$$\bar{J}(y,x,\hat{\mathbf{H}}) = \int_{\mathbf{H}} J(y,x,\mathbf{H})\, p(\mathbf{H}|\hat{\mathbf{H}})\, d\mathbf{H} = \mathrm{E}_{\mathbf{H}|\hat{\mathbf{H}}}[J(y,x,\mathbf{H})|\hat{\mathbf{H}}] \tag{19}$$

where by using the posterior distribution (12), we have averaged the cost function J over all realizations of the unknown channel H conditioned on its available estimate H^ . Note that the mismatched detector is based on the minimization of the cost function J(y, x, H^). This latter cost function is obtained by using the estimated channel H^in the same metric that would be used if the channel was perfectly known, i.e., J(y, x, H). Using the metric of (19) differs from the mismatched detection on the conditional expectation E H H^ [.] which provides a robust design by averaging the cost function J(y, x, H) over all (true) channel realizations which could correspond to the available estimate.

Consider the problem of detecting symbol vector x from the observation model (1) in the ML sense, i.e., so as to maximize the likelihood function p(y|H, x).

It is well known that under perfect channel knowledge and i.i.d. Gaussian noise, detecting x by maximizing the likelihood p(y|x, H) is equivalent to minimizing the Euclidean distance DML as

$$\hat{x}_{\mathrm{ML}}(\mathbf{H}) = \underset{s_0,\ldots,s_{M-1}\in\mathcal{C}}{\arg\min}\ \{\mathcal{D}_{\mathrm{ML}}(x,y,\mathbf{H})\}, \tag{20}$$

with DML(x, y, H) f',. log p(y H, x) ∝ y H x 2, where ∝ means "is proportional to" and denotes the set of constellation symbols of size M. Assuming B bits per symbol, we have M = 2B .

$$\hat{x}_{\mathrm{MM}}(\hat{\mathbf{H}}) = \underset{s_0,\ldots,s_{M-1}\in\mathcal{C}}{\arg\min}\ \{\mathcal{D}_{\mathrm{MM}}(x,y,\hat{\mathbf{H}})\} = \underset{s_0,\ldots,s_{M-1}\in\mathcal{C}}{\arg\min}\ \{\|y-\hat{\mathbf{H}}x\|^2\},$$

where

$$\mathcal{D}_{\mathrm{MM}}(x,y,\mathbf{H}) \triangleq \mathcal{D}_{\mathrm{ML}}(x,y,\mathbf{H})\big|_{\mathbf{H}=\hat{\mathbf{H}}}, \tag{21}$$

The detection rule (20) requires the knowledge of the perfect channel matrix H. The sub- optimal mismatched ML detector consists in replacing the exact channel by its estimate H^ in the receiver metric as and the subscript .MM denotes mismatched. Obviously, the sub-optimality of this detection technique is due to the mismatch introduced by the channel estimation errors; while the decision metric is derived from the likelihood function p(y H, x) conditioned on the perfect channel H, the receiver uses an estimate H^ different from H in the detection process.

As an alternative to this mismatched detection, an improved ML detection metric is proposed in Tarokh et al. (1999); Taricco & Biglieri (2005). This metric is based on modified likelihood p(y|H^ , x) which is conditioned on the imperfect channel H^ . The pdf p(y|H^ , x) can be derived as follows:

$$p(\boldsymbol{y}|\hat{\mathbf{H}},\boldsymbol{x}) = \int_{\mathbf{H}\in\mathbf{C}} p(\boldsymbol{y},\mathbf{H}|\hat{\mathbf{H}},\boldsymbol{x})\, d\mathbf{H} = \int_{\mathbf{H}\in\mathbf{C}} p(\boldsymbol{y}|\mathbf{H},\boldsymbol{x})\, p(\mathbf{H}|\hat{\mathbf{H}})\, d\mathbf{H} = \mathrm{E}_{\mathbf{H}|\hat{\mathbf{H}}}\left[p(\boldsymbol{y}|\mathbf{H},\boldsymbol{x})|\,\hat{\mathbf{H}}\right], \tag{22}$$

where p(H|H^) is the channel posterior distribution of equation (12) and C denotes the set of complex matrices of size (MR × MT). In fact, equation (22) shows that p(y|H^ , x) can be simply derived from the general formulation in (19). It is shown in Sadough & Duhamel (2008) that the averaged likelihood in (22) is shown to be a complex Gaussian distributed vector given by is referred to as the improved ML decision metric under imperfect CSIR.

p(y|H^ , x)= CN mM , ΣM , (23)

where mM = δ H^ x, and ΣM = Σz + δ Σe /||x/||2. Finally, the estimate of the symbol x is

$$\hat{\boldsymbol{x}}_{\mathcal{M}}(\hat{\mathbf{H}}) = \underset{s_0,\ldots,s_{M-1}\in\mathcal{C}}{\arg\min} \left\{\mathcal{D}_{\mathcal{M}}(\boldsymbol{x},\boldsymbol{y},\hat{\mathbf{H}})\right\}, \tag{24}$$

where

$$\mathcal{D}_{\mathcal{M}}(\boldsymbol{x},\boldsymbol{y},\hat{\mathbf{H}}) \triangleq -\log p(\boldsymbol{y}|\boldsymbol{x},\hat{\mathbf{H}}) = M_R \log \pi(\sigma_z^2 + \delta\sigma_e^2 \|\boldsymbol{x}\|^2) + \frac{\|\boldsymbol{y} - \delta\hat{\mathbf{H}}\boldsymbol{x}\|^2}{\sigma_z^2 + \beta\sigma_e^2 \|\boldsymbol{x}\|^2} \tag{25}$$

Note that when CSIR tends to the exact value, which is obtained when the number of pilot symbols tends to infinity, we have δ → 1, Σ2 → 0, and the improved metric (25) tends to the mismatched metric:

$$\lim_{N\to\infty} \frac{\mathcal{D}_{\mathcal{M}}(\boldsymbol{x},\boldsymbol{y},\hat{\mathbf{H}})}{\mathcal{D}_{\mathrm{MM}}(\boldsymbol{x},\boldsymbol{y},\hat{\mathbf{H}})} = 1. \tag{26}$$

In the following two sections, we apply the proposed receiver design method of equation (19) for improving the performance of two usually-used MIMO receivers working under imperfect channel estimation: one based on the maximum a posteriori (MAP) criterion, and the other on Soft-PIC. For both cases, we consider the simple spatial multiplexing as the space-time scheme at the transmitter, and iterative MIMO detection and channel decoding at the receiver.

6. RECEPTION SCHEME I: ITERATIVE MAP DETECTION

Here, we consider MIMO signal detection based on the MAP algorithm. In the following, we make use of the improved ML metric derived in the previous section to modify the MAP detector part for the case of imperfect CSIR Sadough et al. (2007). Let us denote by x[k] and y[k], the transmitted and received symbol vectors corresponding to the the time slot k, simply by xk and yk , respectively. Also, let dk,j denote the j-th (j = 1, ..., BMT) coded and interleaved bit corresponding to xk . We denote by L(dk,j) the coded log-likelihood ratio (LLR) of the bit dk,j at the output of the detector. Conditioned on the imperfect CSIR H^ k , L(dk,j) is given by:

$$L(d_{k,j}) = \log \frac{P_{\text{dem}}(d_{k,j}=1 | \boldsymbol{y}_k, \hat{\mathbf{H}}_k)}{P_{\text{dem}}(d_{k,j}=0 | \boldsymbol{y}_k, \hat{\mathbf{H}}_k)}, \tag{27}$$

where Pdem(dk,j yk , H^ k) is the probability of transmission of dk,j at the detector output. We partition the set C that contains all possibly-transmitted symbol vectors xk into two sets Cm and Cm, for which the j-th bit of xk equals "0" or "1", respectively. We have:

$$L(d_{k,j}) = \log \frac{\sum_{\boldsymbol{x}_k \in \mathcal{C}_1^{m}} e^{-\mathcal{D}_{\mathcal{M}}(\boldsymbol{x}_k, \boldsymbol{y}_k, \hat{\mathbf{H}}_k)} \prod_{\substack{i=1 \\ i \neq j}}^{BM_T} P_{\text{dec}}^{1}(d_{k,i})}{\sum_{\boldsymbol{x}_k \in \mathcal{C}_0^{m}} e^{-\mathcal{D}_{\mathcal{M}}(\boldsymbol{x}_k, \boldsymbol{y}_k, \hat{\mathbf{H}}_k)} \prod_{\substack{i=1 \\ i \neq j}}^{BM_T} P_{\text{dec}}^{0}(d_{k,j})}, \tag{28}$$

where P1 dec (dk,j) and P0 dec (dk,j) are prior probabilities on the bit dk,j coming from the SISO decoder.

Note that using the metric DM(xk , yk , H^ k) for the evaluation of the LLRs in (28) is an alter- native to using the mismatched ML metric MM(xk , yk, H^ k) which replaces at each iteration, the exact channel Hk by its estimate H^ k in ML(xk, yk , Hk). By doing so, the LLRs are adapted to the imperfect channel knowledge available at the receiver and consequently the impact of channel uncertainty on the SISO decoder performance is reduced. We refer to the latter approach as improved MAP detector Sadough et al. (2007).

The summations in (28) are taken over the product of the likelihood p(yk |xk, H^ k) = e-DM(xk ,yk ,H^ k) given a symbol xk and the estimated channel coefficient H^ k , and of the a priori probability on xk (the term Π Pdec), fed back from the SISO decoder at the previous iteration. In this latter term, the a priori probability of the bit dk,j itself has been excluded, so as to let the exchange of extrinsic informations between the channel decoder and the soft detector. Also, note that this term assumes independent coded bits dk,j, which is a reasonable approximation for random interleaving of large size. At the first iteration, no a priori information is available on bits dk,j, therefore the probabilities P0 dec(dk,j) and P1 dec (dk,j) are set to 1/2. The decoder accepts the LLRs of all coded bits and computes the LLRs of information bits, which are used for decision, at the last iteration.

6.1 Case study

We now present some numerical results. First, the BER performance of the improved and mismatched detectors are compared. Let us first address the case of BICM iterative decoding with 16-QAM and Gray labeling for a 2 × 2 MIMO channel. It can be seen from Fig. 7 that for Np = 2 (the shortest possible training sequence), the improvement in terms of required Eb /N0 in order to attain a BER of 10–5 is about 1 dB, compared to the mismatched solution, while staying still 3 dB away from the perfect channel knowledge case. We also notice that, logically, these quantities are reduced when increasing the length of the training sequence, that is, the performances of mismatched and improved detectors get closer to the case of perfect channel knowledge.

Similar plots are shown in Fig. 8 for the case of 16-QAM and set-partition (SP) labeling on the (2 2) MIMO channel. These show the behavior of the detectors with respect to the type of bit-symbol labeling. At a BER of 2 10–4 with Np = 2, we obtain an SNR gain of about 1.4 dB by using the improved detector. In other words, iterative decoding with SP labeling benefits more from the improved metric than the one with Gray labeling. Otherwise, similar conclusions hold between the SP-labeling curves.

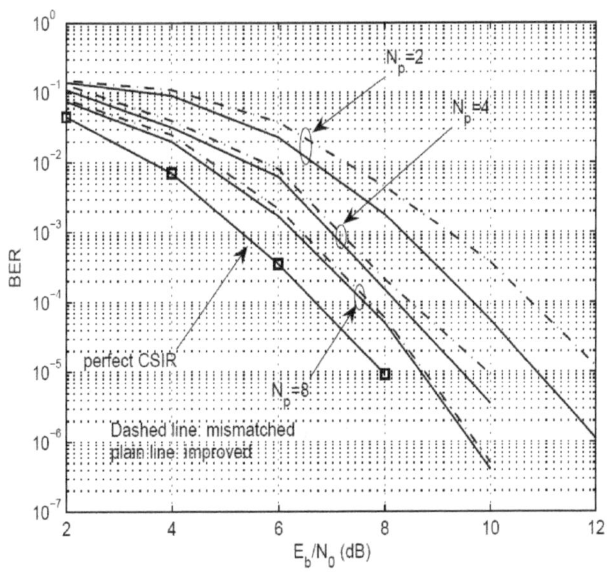

Fig. 7. BER performance improvement over (2 2) MIMO channel with i.i.d. Rayleigh fading for various training sequence lengths. 16-QAM modulation with Gray labeling, iterative MAP detection after four receiver iterations.

7. RECEPTION SCHEME II: ITERATIVE SOFT-PIC DETECTION

MAP detection is the optimal solution under perfect CSIR in the sense of bit error rate but its complexity grows exponentially with the number of transmit antennas and the signal constellation size. For this reason, suboptimal detection techniques are usually preferred. One interesting solution is that based on Soft-PIC and linear minimum mean-square error (MMSE) filtering Wang & Poor (1999); Sellathurai & Haykin (2002); Lee et al. (2006), what we considered in Sections 2 to 4. In fact, in these parts, we considered in the iterative detector a simplified formulation of Soft-PIC, which assumes perfect interference cancellation after the first iteration. In this section, however, we consider the exact formulation of Soft-PIC. In order to better understand the formulation of the improved detector, we present in the following the formulation of (exact) Soft-PIC under perfect channel knowledge at the receiver. Then, we present the improved Soft-PIC detector in the presence of channel estimation errors in Subsection 7.2.

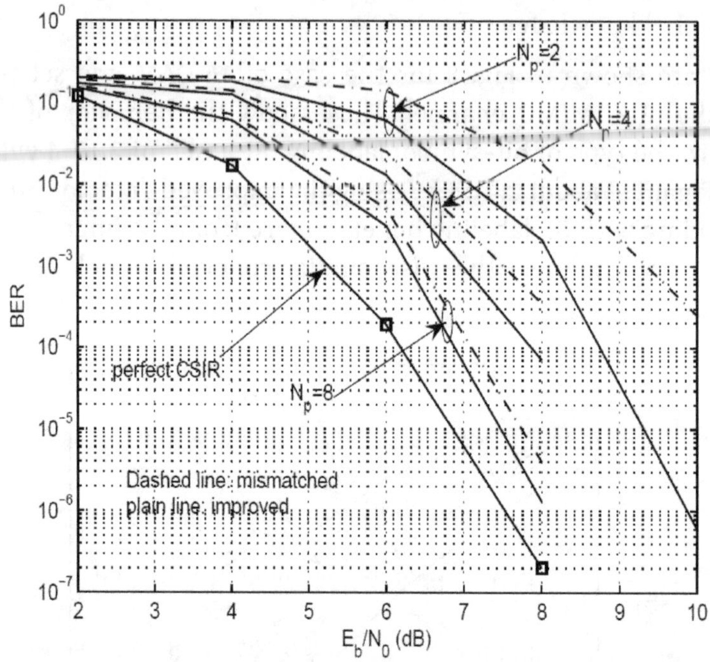

Fig. 8. BER performance improvement over (2 2) MIMO channel with i.i.d. Rayleigh fad- ing for various training sequence lengths. 16-QAM modulation with set-partition labeling, iterative MAP detection after four receiver iterations.

7.1 Soft-PIC detection under perfect channel knowledge

Consider the general block diagram of Fig. 2. Here, to detect a symbol transmitted from a given antenna, we first make use of the soft information available from the SISO channel decoder to reduce and hopefully to cancel the interfering signals arising from other transmit antennas. At the first iteration where this information is not available, we perform a classical MMSE filtering.

Let us consider the transmitted vector xk = [x1k, ..., xMkT]T at time k and assume that we are interested in the detection of its i-th symbol xi . We start by evaluating the parameters x^j and 2 for the interfering symbols xj , j = i, from the SISO decoder as follows:

$$\hat{x}_k^j = \mathbb{E}[x_k^j] = \sum_{j=1}^{2^B} x_k^j P[x_k^j] \tag{29}$$

$$\sigma_{x_k^j}^2 = \mathbb{E}[|x_k^j|^2] = \sum_{j=1}^{2^B} |x_k^j|^2 P[x_k^j] \tag{30}$$

where P[xjk] is the probability of the transmission of xj and is evaluated using the probabilities Pdec k (dj,n) at the decoder output:

$$P[x_k^j] - K \prod_{n=1}^{B} P_{\text{dec}}(d_k^{j,n}),$$

where K is a normalization factor. We further introduce the following definitions. Hi is the (MR × (MT - 1)) matrix constructed from H by discarding its i-th column, namely hi. We also define the ((MT - 1) × 1) vectors

$$\underline{\boldsymbol{x}}_k^i \triangleq [x_k^1, x_k^2, ..., x_k^{i-1}, x_k^{i+1}, ..., x_k^{M_T}]^T$$

and

$$\underline{\hat{\boldsymbol{x}}}_k^i \triangleq [\hat{x}_k^1, \hat{x}_k^2, ..., \hat{x}_k^{i-1}, \hat{x}_k^{i+1}, ..., \hat{x}_k^{M_T}]^T,$$

where x^jk are estimated in (29).

Now, given the received signal vector yk, a soft interference cancellation is performed on yk for detecting the symbol xi by subtracting to yk the estimated signals of the other transmit antennas as Sadough, Khalighi & Duhamel (2009):

yi = yk – Hi x^ ik = hixik + Hi xik – Hi x^ ik + zk, for i = 1, ..., MT. (31)

Except under perfect prior information on the symbols which leads to x^j = xj , there remains a residual interference in yi . In order to reduce further this interference, an instantaneous linear MMSE filter wi is applied to yi to minimize the mean square value of the error ei defined as

$$e_k^i = x_k^i - r_k^i \tag{32}$$

where the filter output ri is equal to

ri = wik yik. (33)

Here, wik is obtained as

$$\mathbf{w}_k^i = \underset{\mathbf{w}_k^i \in \mathbb{C}^{M_R}}{\arg\min}\ \mathbb{E}_{\mathbf{x}_k, \mathbf{z}_k}\left[|x_k^i - \mathbf{w}_k^i \underline{\mathbf{y}}_k^i|^2\right]. \tag{34}$$

By invoking the orthogonality principle Scharf (1991), the coefficients of the MMSE filter *wik* are given by

$$\mathbf{w}_k^i = \mathbf{h}_i^\dagger\left[\mathbf{h}_i\mathbf{h}_i^\dagger + \frac{\underline{\mathbf{H}}_i(\Lambda_{k,i} - \widetilde{\Lambda}_{k,i})\underline{\mathbf{H}}_i^\dagger}{\sigma_{x_k^i}^2} + \frac{\sigma_z^2}{\sigma_{x_k^i}^2}\mathbb{I}_{M_R}\right]^{-1} \tag{35}$$

where

$$\Lambda_{k,i} = \mathbb{E}\left[\underline{\mathbf{x}}_k^i \underline{\mathbf{x}}_k^{i\dagger}\right] \approx \operatorname{diag}\left(\mathbb{E}[|x_k^1|^2], \dots, \mathbb{E}[|x_k^{i-1}|^2], \mathbb{E}[|x_k^{i+1}|^2], \dots, \mathbb{E}[|x_k^{M_T}|^2]\right), \text{ and}$$

$$\widetilde{\Lambda}_{k,i} = \underline{\hat{\mathbf{x}}}_k^i \underline{\hat{\mathbf{x}}}_k^{i\dagger} \approx \operatorname{diag}\left(|\hat{x}_k^1|^2, \dots, |\hat{x}_k^{i-1}|^2, |\hat{x}_k^{i+1}|^2, \dots, |\hat{x}_k^{M_T}|^2\right).$$

Note that the off-diagonal entries in $\Lambda_{k,i}$ and $\Lambda_{k,i}$ have been neglected to reduce the complexity without causing significant performance loss Loc et al. (2006). At the first decoding iteration, we have no prior information available on the transmitted data, i.e., k,l = 2 xik IMT−1 and $\Lambda_{k,i}$ = 0MT−1. Consequently, (35) reduces to

$$\mathbf{w}_k^i = \mathbf{h}_i^\dagger\left[\mathbf{H}\mathbf{H}^\dagger + \frac{\sigma_z^2}{\sigma_{x_k^i}^2}\mathbb{I}_{M_R}\right]^{-1} \tag{36}$$

which is no more than the linear MMSE detector for xi_k.

Before passing the detected symbols rk to the SISO decoder, we convert them to LLR. This is done assuming a Gaussian distribution for the residual interference after Soft-PIC detection (see Wang & Poor (1999) for details on the LLR conversion).

7.2 Improved Soft-PIC Detection Under Imperfect Channel Estimation

As we see from (31) and (35), we need the channel H for both interference canceling and MMSE filtering. As the receiver has only an imperfect channel estimate H^ , the suboptimal mismatched solution consists in replacing Hi and hi in (31) and (35) by their estimates H^ i and h^ i, respectively. As a first step toward a realistic design, we make use of the available channel estimate H^ for interference cancellation. That is, equation (31) is rewritten as

$$\underline{\mathbf{y}}_k^i = \mathbf{y}_k - \underline{\hat{\mathbf{H}}}_i \underline{\hat{\mathbf{x}}}_k^i = \mathbf{h}_i x_k^i + \underline{\mathbf{H}}_i \underline{\mathbf{x}}_k^i - \underline{\hat{\mathbf{H}}}_i \underline{\hat{\mathbf{x}}}_k^i + \mathbf{z}_k, \quad \text{for } i = 1, \dots, M_T \tag{37}$$

where H^ i is the (MR × (MT - 1)) matrix constructed from H^ by discarding its i-th column, namely h^ i. We note that (37) naturally depends on the unknown channel matrix H of which the receiver has only an imperfect estimate available. Instead of replacing the unknown channel by its estimate (i.e., the mismatched approach), we use the posterior distribution and make two modifications to the detector described in Subsection 7.1, as follows (see Sadough, Khalighi & Duhamel (2009) and Sadough & Khalighi (2007) for more details). The first modification concerns the design of the filter wik in (34). Themodified filter wik should minimize the average of the mean square error over all realizations of channel estimation errors. In other words,

$$\widetilde{\mathbf{w}}_k^i = \arg\min_{\widetilde{\mathbf{w}}_k^i \in C^{M_R}} \mathbb{E}_{\mathbf{H},x_k,z_k}\left[|x_k^i - \widetilde{\mathbf{w}}_k^i \underline{\mathbf{y}}_k^i|^2 \,\middle|\, \hat{\mathbf{H}}\right] = \arg\min_{\widetilde{\mathbf{w}} \in C^{M_R}} \mathbb{E}_{\mathbf{H}|\hat{\mathbf{H}}}\left[\mathbb{E}_{x_k,z_k}\left[|x_k^i - \widetilde{\mathbf{w}}_k^i \underline{\mathbf{y}}_k^i|^2\right]\right] \quad (38)$$

where we have assumed the independence between H, xk, and zk . After some simple algebraic manipulations Sadough, Khalighi & Duhamel (2009); Scharf (1991), we obtain:

$$\widetilde{\mathbf{w}}_k^i = \overline{\mathbf{R}}_{x_k^i \underline{\mathbf{y}}_k^i} \overline{\mathbf{R}}_{\underline{\mathbf{y}}_k^i}^{-1} \quad (39)$$

where

$$\overline{\mathbf{R}}_{x_k^i \underline{\mathbf{y}}_k^i} = \delta \sigma^2_{x_k^i} \widehat{\mathbf{h}}_i^\dagger + (\delta - 1)\, \mathbf{m}_{k,i} \underline{\hat{\mathbf{H}}}_i^\dagger \quad (40)$$

with $\mathbf{m}_{k,i} = \hat{x}_k^i \hat{\underline{\mathbf{x}}}_k^{i\dagger}$ and δ is given by (15), and

$$\overline{\mathbf{R}}_{\underline{\mathbf{y}}_k^i} = \delta^2 \sigma^2_{x_k^i} \widehat{\mathbf{h}}_i \widehat{\mathbf{h}}_i^\dagger + \delta^2 \underline{\hat{\mathbf{H}}}_i \Lambda_{k,i} \underline{\hat{\mathbf{H}}}_i^\dagger + (\delta^2 - \delta)\, \widehat{\mathbf{h}}_i \mathbf{m}_{k,i} \underline{\mathbf{H}}_i^\dagger + (\delta^2 - \delta)\, \underline{\hat{\mathbf{H}}}_i \mathbf{m}_{k,i}^\dagger \widehat{\mathbf{h}}_i^\dagger$$
$$+ (1 - 2\delta)\, \underline{\hat{\mathbf{H}}}_i \widetilde{\Lambda}_{k,i} \underline{\hat{\mathbf{H}}}_i^\dagger + \left(\sigma_z^2 + (1-\delta)\sigma^2_{x_k^i} + (1-\delta)\,\mathrm{tr}(\Lambda_{k,i})\right)\mathbb{I}_{M_R}. \quad (41)$$

To get more insight on the proposed detector, let us consider the ideal case where perfect channel knowledge is available at the receiver, i.e., H^ = H and Σ2 = 0. We note that in this case, δ = 1 and the posterior pdf (12) reduces to a Dirac delta function; consequently the two filters wi_k and wi_k coincide. Similarly, under near-perfect CSIR, obtained either when Σe → 0 or when Np we have , and the filter wik gives a similar expression as wi k in (35). However, in the presence of estimation errors, the proposed improved and mismatched detectors become different due to the inherent averaging in (38), which provides a robust design that adapts itself to the channel estimate available at the receiver.

The second modification concerns the application of the derived filter $\widetilde{\mathbf{w}}_k^i$ to the received signal $\underline{\mathbf{y}}_k^i$. As this latter depends on $\mathbf{H}$ (see (37)), we average the filter output r_k^i as follows:

$$\widetilde{r}_k^i = \mathbb{E}_{\mathbf{H}|\hat{\mathbf{H}}}[r_k^i] = \underbrace{\delta\, \widetilde{\mathbf{w}}_k^i \widehat{\mathbf{h}}_i}_{\mu_{k,i}} x_k^i + \underbrace{\delta\, \widetilde{\mathbf{w}}_k^i \underline{\hat{\mathbf{H}}}_i \underline{\mathbf{x}}_k^i - \widetilde{\mathbf{w}}_k^i \underline{\hat{\mathbf{H}}}_i \hat{\underline{\mathbf{x}}}_k^i + \widetilde{\mathbf{w}}_k^i \mathbf{z}_k}_{\eta_{k,i}} = \mu_{k,i} x_k^i + \eta_{k,i}, \quad (42)$$

where ηk,i contains interference and noise. From (42) it is clear that the output of the im- proved MMSE filter can be viewed as an equivalent AWGN channel having xi at its input. The parameters μk,i and Σ2 are calculated at each time-slot by using the symbols statistics.

In order to transform the detected symbols at the output of the MMSE filter to LLRs on the corresponding bits, we approximate ηk,i by a zero-mean Gaussian random variable with variance 2 Σ ηk,i (see Sadough, Khalighi & Duhamel (2009) for details on the calculation of this variance).

Let di,m denote the m-th (m = 1, ..., B) bit corresponding to xi . The LLR on di,m is given by:

$$L(d_k^{i,m}) = \log \frac{P_{\text{dem}}\left(d_k^{i,m}=1 \mid \tilde{r}_k^i, \mu_{k,i}\right)}{P_{\text{dem}}\left(d_k^{i,m}=0 \mid \tilde{r}_k^i, \mu_{k,i}\right)} = \log \frac{\sum\limits_{x_k^i \in \mathcal{S}_1^m} \exp\left\{-\frac{|\tilde{r}_k^i - \mu_{k,i} x_k^i|^2}{\sigma_{\eta_{k,i}}^2}\right\} \prod\limits_{\substack{n=1 \\ n \neq m}}^{B} P_{\text{dec}}^1(d_k^{i,n})}{\sum\limits_{x_k^i \in \mathcal{S}_0^m} \exp\left\{-\frac{|\tilde{r}_k^i - \mu_{k,i} x_k^i|^2}{\sigma_{\eta_{k,i}}^2}\right\} \prod\limits_{\substack{n=1 \\ n \neq m}}^{B} P_{\text{dec}}^0(d_k^{i,n})}. \quad (43)$$

Note that here the cardinality of the sets S m and S m equals 2B−1.

7.2.1 Case study

Figure 9 shows BER curves of the mismatched and improved receivers for the case of QPSK modulation and a (2 × 2) MIMO system. The number of channel uses for pilot transmission is Np ∈ {2, 4, 8}. As a reference, we have also presented the BER curve for the case of perfect CSIR. We observe that the gain in SNR of the improved detector to attain the BER of 10-5 is about 1.4 dB, 0.5 dB, and 0.2 dB, respectively for Np = 2, 4, and 8.

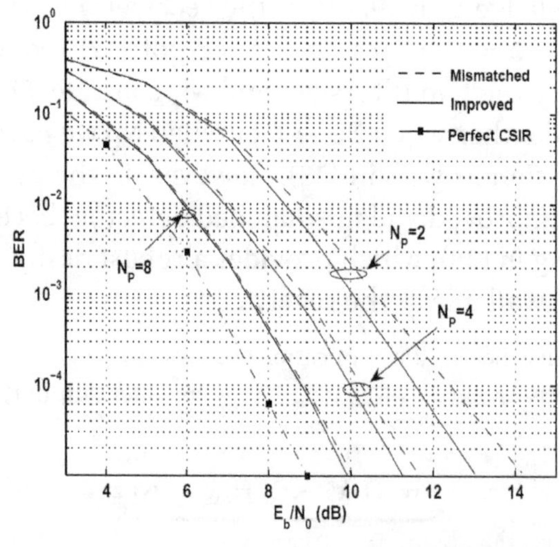

Fig. 9. BER performance of improved and mismatched iterative Soft-PIC; (2 ×2) MIMO with MUX ST scheme, i.i.d. Rayleigh block-fading channel with 4 fades per frame, QPSK modula- tion, training sequence length Np ∈ {2, 4, 8}.

The interesting point is that the two detectors have almost the same convergence trend and the major improvement is obtained after the second iteration for both detectors Sadough, Khalighi & Duhamel (2009). So, if for the reasons of complexity reduction, we only process two receiver iterations, we still have a considerable performance gain by using the improved detector.

8. CONCISE SUMMARY

This chapter examined the interplay between iterative data detection and channel estimation in realistic wireless communication systems, where the receiver possesses only an incomplete estimate of the unknown channel characteristics. To get the CSIR, we evaluated various contemporary and traditionally employed methodologies. Initially, we introduced a channel estimating method reliant solely on pilots and demonstrated that achieving an accurate channel estimate using this approach necessitates a substantial quantity of pilots per frame, potentially leading to a significant reduction in system data throughput. From this perspective, overlay pilots may be favored over time-multiplexed solutions; nevertheless, the quality of channel estimation is generally inferior compared to PSAM. We also introduced semi-blind channel estimation techniques that utilize both pilot symbols and data symbols in the estimate process. While iterative semi-blind channel estimation surpasses pilot-only assisted channel estimation in performance, it entails greater complexity, which could pose significant challenges for practical applications.

Irrespective of the channel estimation method employed, a critical consideration is the influence of estimation inaccuracies on receiver performance. The conventional method involves treating the (imperfect) channel estimate as if it were perfect and employing it for data detection. We designated this as the mismatched method. In this instance, we observed that the effect of estimate errors is somewhat analogous for both orthogonal and non-orthogonal space-time schemes. We subsequently examined the enhanced method that incorporates channel estimation imperfections in data detection. Specifically, by utilizing the statistics of channel estimation errors, we implement a novel detection method in place of the sub-optimal mismatched detector. By using this detection design principle in MAP and Soft-PIC detectors, we demonstrated a substantial enhancement relative to the mismatched detector. Ultimately, it is important to note that implementing the enhanced reception technique does not significantly elevate the complexity. The enhanced detectors necessitate only a minimal increase in matrix additions and multiplications, which does not significantly affect the complexity of the receiver.

REFERENCES

1. Adireddy, S., Tong, L. & Viswanathan, H. (2002). Optimal placement of training for frequency- selective block-fading channels, IEEE Trans. Inf. Theory 48(8): 2338–2353.

2. Alamouti, S. (1998). A simple transmit diversity technique for wireless communications, IEEE J. Sel. Areas Commun. 16(8): 1451–1458.
3. Bahl, L., Cocke, J., Jelinek, F. & Raviv, J. (1974). Optimal decoding of linear codes for minimiz- ing symbol error rate, IEEE Trans. Inform. Theory pp. 284–287.
4. Balakrishnan, J., Rupp, M. & Viswanathan, H. (2000). Optimal channel training for multiple antenna systems, in Proc. MMT . Miami, FL.
5. Belfiore, J.-C., Rekaya, G. & Viterbo, E. (2005). The golden code: a 2 2 full-rate space-time code with nonvanishing determinants, IEEE Trans. Inform. Theory 51(4): 1432–1436.
6. Berthet, A., Unal, B. & Visoz, R. (2001). Iterative decoding of convolutionally encoded signals over multipath Rayleigh fading channels, IEEE J. Sel. Areas Commun. 19(9): 1729–1743.
7. Bohlin, P. & Tapio, M. (2004). Optimized data aided training in MIMO systems, in Proc. VTC pp. 679–683. Milan, Italy.
8. Cavers, J. K. (1991). An analysis of pilot symbol assisted modulation for Rayleigh fading channels, IEEE Trans. Veh. Technol. 40(4): 686–693.
9. Cui, T. & Tellambura, C. (2005). Superimposed pilot symbols for channel estimation in OFDM systems, in Proc. Globecom pp. 2229–2233. St. Louis, MO.
10. de Carvalho, C. & Slock, D. T. M. (2001). Semi-blind Methods for FIR Multichannel Estimation, in Signal Processing Advances in Wireless and Mobile Communications; Vol. I: Trends in Channel Estimation and Equalization, Editors: G. B. Giannakis, Y. Hua, P. Stoica, and L. Tong, Upper Saddle River, NJ: Prentice Hall.
11. Dempster, A., Laird, N. & Rubin, D. (1977). Maximum-likelihood from incomplete data via the EM algorithm, J. Royal Statatistical Society 39(1): 1–38.
12. Dong, M. & Tong, L. (2002). Optimal design and placement of pilot symbols for channel estimation, IEEE Trans. Signal Processing 50(12): 3055–3069.
13. Ghogho, M., McLernon, D., Alameda-Hernandez, E. & Swami, A. (2005). Channel estimation and symbol detection for block transmissionusing data-dependent superimposed training, IEEE Signal Processing Letters 12(3): 226–229.
14. Giannakis, G. B., Hua, Y., Stoica, P. & Tong, L. (2001). Signal Processing Advances in Wireless and Mobile Communications, Vol. 1, Trends in Channel Estimation and Equalization, Prentice Hall PTR, Upper Saddle River, NJ.
15. Hassibi, B. & Hochwald, B. M. (2003). How much training is needed in multiple-antenna wireless links?, IEEE Trans. Inform. Theory 49(4): 951–963.
16. Hoeher, P. & Tufvesson, F. (1999). Channel estimation with superimposed pilot sequence, in Proc. Globecom 4: 2162–2166. Rio de Janeiro, Brazil.

17. Jungnickel, V., Haustein, T., Jorswieck, E., Pohl, V. & von Helmolt, C. (2001). Performance of a MIMO system with overlay pilots, in Proc. Globecom 1: 594–598. San Antonio, TX.

18. Khalighi, M. A., Berriche, L. & He´lard, J.-F. (2005). Overlaid or time-multiplexed pilots for channel estimation in iterative MIMO receivers, in Proc. ISSPA pp. 483–486. Sydney, Australia.

19. Khalighi, M. A. & Bourennane, S. (2007). Semi-blind channel estimation based on superim- posed pilots for single-carrier MIMO systems, in Proc. VTC pp. 1480–1484. Dublin, Ireland.

20. Khalighi, M. A. & Bourennane, S. (2008). Semi-blind single-carrier MIMO channel estimation using overlay pilots, IEEE Trans. Veh. Technol. 57(5): 1951–1956.

21. Khalighi, M. A., Boutros, J. & He´lard, J.-F. (2006). Data-aided channel estimation for Turbo-PIC MIMO detectors, IEEE Commun. Lett. 10(5): 350–352.

22. Khalighi, M. A. & Boutros, J. J. (2006). Semi-blind channel estimation using EM algorithm in iterative MIMO APP detectors, IEEE Trans. Wireless Commun. 5(11): 3165–3173.

23. Khalighi, M. A., He´lard, J.-F., Sadough, S. M. S. & Bourennane, S. (2009). Suitable combination of channel coding and space-time schemes for moderate-to-high spectral efficiency mimo systems, AEU¨ E International Journal of Electronics and Communications . to appear.

24. Lam, C., Falconer, D. & Danilo-Lemoine, F. (2008). Iterative frequency domain channel estima- tion for DFT-precoded OFDMsystems using in-band pilots, IEEE Journal on Selected Areas in Communication 26(2): 348–358.

25. Lee, H., Lee, B. & Lee, I. (2006). Iterative detection and decoding with improved V-BLAST for MIMO-OFDM systems, IEEE J. Selected Areas Commun. 24(3): 504–513.

26. Ma, X., Giannakis, G. & Ohno, S. (2003). Optimal training for block transmission over doubly selective wireless fading channels, IEEE Trans. Signal Processing 51(5): 1351–1366.

27. Meng, X. & Tugnait, J. (2004). MIMO channel estimation using superimposed training, in Proc. ICC pp. 2663–2667. Paris, France.

28. Moon, T. (1996). The expectation-maximization algorithm, IEEE Signal Processing Mag. 13(6): 47–60.

29. Moon, T. K. & Stirling, W. C. (2000). Mathematical Methods and Algorithms for Signal Processing, Upper Saddle River, NJ: Prentice Hall.

30. Raoof, K., Khalighi, M. A. & Prayongpun, N. (2008). "MIMO Systems: Principles, Iterative Tech- niques and Advance Polarization" in ADAPTIVE SIGNAL PROCESSING FOR WIRE- LESS COMMUNICATIONS, CRC Press.

31. De Carvalho, E. & Slock, D. T. M. (1997). Cramer-Rao bounds for semi-blind, blind, and training antenna arrays, a tutorial study, International workshop on Signal Processing Advances in Wireless Communications (SPAWC) pp. 129 –132. Paris, France.

32. Sadough, S. M. S. (2008). Ultra Wideband OFDM Systems: Channel Estimation and Improved Detection Accounting for Estimation Inaccuracies, PhD thesis, Universite´ Paris-Sud 11.

33. Sadough, S. M. S. & Duhamel, P. (2008). Improved iterative detection and achieved through- puts of OFDM systems under imperfect channel estimation, IEEE Trans. Wireless Com- mun. 7(12): 5039 – 5050.

34. Sadough, S. M. S., Ichir, M. M., Duhamel, P. & Jaffrot, E. (2009). Wavelet based semi-blind channel estimation for ultra wideband OFDM systems, IEEE Trans. Veh. Technol. 58(3): 1302–1314.

35. Sadough, S. M. S. & Khalighi, M. A. (2007). Optimal turbo-blast detection of MIMO-OFDM systems with imperfect channel estimation, IEEE International Symposium on Personal, Indoor and Mobile Radio Communications .

36. Sadough, S. M. S., Khalighi, M. A. & Duhamel, P. (2009). Improved iterative MIMO signal de- tection accounting for channel estimation errors, IEEE Trans. Veh. Technol. . to appear. Sadough, S., Piantanida, P. & Duhamel, P. (2007). MIMO-OFDM optimal decoding and achievable information rates under imperfect channel estimation, in Proc. Signal Process. Advances Wireless Commun. (SPAWC) .

37. Scharf, L. (1991). Statistical Signal Processing, Addison-Wesley.

38. Sellathurai, M. & Haykin, S. (2002). Turbo-BLAST for wireless communications: theory and experiments, IEEE Trans. Signal Process. 50(10): 2538– 2546.

39. Tapio, M. & Bohlin, P. (2004). A capacity comparison between time-multiplexed and superim- posed pilots, in Proc. Asilomar Conf. on Signals, Systems and Computers pp. 1049–1053. Pacific Grove, CA.

40. Taricco, G. & Biglieri, E. (2005). Space-time decoding with imperfect channel estimation, IEEE Trans. Wireless Commun. 4(4): 1874–1888.

41. Tarokh, V., Naguib, A., Seshadri, N. & Calderbank, A. R. (1999). Space-time codes for high data rate wireless communication: Performance criteria in the presence of channel estimation errors, mobility, and multiple paths, IEEE Trans. Commun. 47: 199–207.

42. Telatar, E. (1999). Capacity of multi-antenna Gaussian channels, European Trans. Telecommun. 10(6): 585–595.

43. Visoz, R. & Berthet, A. (2003). Iterative decoding and channel estimation for space-time BICM over MIMO block fading multipath AWGN channel, IEEE Trans. Commun. 51(8): 1358– 1367.

44. Wang, X. & Poor, H. V. (1999). Iterative (turbo) soft interference cancellation and deoding for coded CDMA, IEEE Trans. Commun. 47(7): 1046–1061.

45. Zhu, H., Farhang-Boroujeny, B. & Schlegel, C. (2003). Pilot embedding for joint channel estimation and data detection in MIMO communication systems, IEEE Commun. Lett. 7(1): 30–32.

7 Chapter

COOPERATIVE MIMO SYSTEMS INSIDE WIRELESS SENSOR NETWORKS

1. INTRODUCTION: AN OVERVIEW

The term numerous-Input Multiple-Output (MIMO) originally refers to the utilization of numerous antennas or the application of spatial diversity techniques. Initial research introduced the MIMO concept to meet the need for dependable high-speed wireless communication lines in challenging conditions. MIMO technology has been proposed for implementation in wireless local area networks and cellular networks, namely at the base station and access point, to address issues of low transmission rates and dependability without compromising energy economy. Conversely, Wireless Sensor Networks (WSNs) must contend with energy limitations because each sensor node relies on its battery for functionality. In adverse conditions, sensor nodes require dependable communication connectivity. Nonetheless, contemporary WSN design specifications do not necessitate elevated transmission rates.

The notion of cooperative MIMO was used in wireless sensor networks by leveraging the collaborative characteristics of densely packed sensor nodes alongside the broadcast wireless medium to establish dependable communication links, hence minimizing the overall energy consumption of each sensor node. Consequently, rather than employing numerous antennas connected to a single node or device as in the conventional MIMO framework, cooperative MIMO introduces the idea of multiple sensor nodes collaborating to broadcast and/or receive signals. Numerous sensor nodes are physically clustered to collaboratively transmit and/or receive data. Sensor nodes inside a group can communicate with comparatively low power relative to inter-group communication. Moreover, employing this cooperative MIMO idea enables the provision of the benefits of conventional MIMO systems to wireless sensor networks, especially regarding energy-efficient operation.

This chapter presents the ideas of diversity approaches and their association with cooperative MIMO systems, while also examining their feasibility for implementation in wireless sensor networks (WSNs). This chapter will employ a comparative analysis and performance assessment of key diversity strategies and their applications in cooperative MIMO systems. The results may serve as a foundation for additional research to identify the best appropriate cooperative MIMO method for implementation in the WSN environment.

2. COOPERATIVE MIMO CONCEPTS

The MIMO term originally describes the use of the multiple antennas concept or exploitation of spatial diversity techniques. In early research work, the MIMO concept was proposed to fulfil the demand for providing reliable high-speed wireless communication links in harsh environments. Subsequently, MIMO technology has been proposed to be used in wireless local area networks and cellular networks (Proakis, 2001), particularly at the base station and access point sides to tackle the challenges of low transmission rates and low reliability with no constraints on energy efficiency. In contrast, WSNs have to deal with energy constraints due to the fact that each sensor node depends on its battery for its operation. In harsh environments, sensor nodes must be provided with reliable communication links. However, current WSN design requirements do not require high transmission rates.

The concept of cooperative MIMO was introduced in WSNs by utilising the collaborative nature of dense sensor nodes with the broadcast wireless medium to provide reliable communication links in order to reduce the total energy consumption for each sensor node. Therefore, instead of using multiple antennas attached to one node or device such in the traditional MIMO concept, cooperative MIMO presents the concept of multiple sensor nodes cooperating to transmit and/or receive signals. Multiple sensor nodes are physically grouped together to cooperatively transmit and/or receive. Within a group, sensor nodes can communicate with relatively low power as compared to inter-group communication (Singh and Prasanna, 2003; Gupta and Younis, 2003; Yuksel and Erkip, 2004). Furthermore, by using this cooperative MIMO concept, we can provide the advantages of traditional MIMO systems to WSNs, particularly in terms of energy efficient operation.

3. TECHNIQUES OF DIVERSITY

In this section we discuss various diversity techniques to reduce the deep fading problem in WSNs which requires higher retransmission rates. By tackling this problem, we are clearly satisfying two design requirements: energy efficient operation and higher communication link reliability. It is important to observe that deep fading contributes to packet errors (if a portion of the packet is affected) or packet loss (if the whole packet is totally lost which can be common as data packets in WSNs are normally small (Kohvakka et. al., 2006; Karl and Willig, 2007). The basic concept of diversity is to provide the receiver with copies of independently faded transmitted packets with the hope that at least one of these copies will be received correctly. Diversity can be implemented in various ways such as frequency diversity, spatial diversity, time diversity, modulation diversity and polarisation diversity to suit different design requirements.

Frequency diversity is achieved when the same signal is transmitted over different frequency bands. The separation of the frequency bands has to be more than the coherence bandwidth of the channel (Duman and Ghrayeb, 2007). Time diversity is achieved when the same signal is transmitted with redundancy using different time intervals. The separation of the time intervals has to be more than the coherence time of the channel. Also, time diversity can be achieved by means of channel coding. The idea is to transmit the different parts of the codeword corresponding to a particular symbol using different time intervals. The most practical channel codes discussed in the literature include block codes, convolutional codes and trellis-coded modulation (Duman and Ghrayeb, 2007).

Spatial diversity is achieved by the use of multiple antennas or nodes at either end or at both ends of the MIMO communication link. The separation between the antennas or nodes has to be more than half a wavelength in a uniform scattering environment. Systems with multiple antennas are also referred to as MIMO systems (Duman and Ghrayeb, 2007). Therefore we can refer to systems with multiple nodes as cooperative MIMO systems. Spatial diversity gains increase channel capacity which leads to higher data throughputs and significant improvement in data transmission reliability. These advantages are achieved without any expansion of bandwidth or higher transmit power which makes this technique very suitable to be implemented in energy constrained WSNs.

Diversity techniques can be combined to achieve greater improvements in reliability and achievable transmission rates. Perhaps the most popular combination technique is between space diversity and time diversity by using channel coding. The combination yields the space-time coding (STC) scheme. The variants of the STC scheme depend on the channel coding being used. For example, space-time block coding (STBC) schemes are based on block coding and space-time trellis coding scheme (STTC) schemes are based on trellis- coded modulation.

Multiple antennas or nodes can be exploited in different ways at both ends of the MIMO communication link. Early work in this area concerned designs of multiple antennas at the receiver side to achieve receive spatial diversity in order to boost link reliability as the number of receiving antennas grows. Among the earliest users of receive spatial diversity schemes are mobile communications systems to improve uplink performance by implementing multiple receive antennas at the base station (Proakis, 2001). If only a single transmit antenna and multiple receive antennas are used, the resulting system is referred to as a Single-Input Multiple-Output (SIMO) system.

In later work transmit spatial diversity was achieved by exploiting multiple transmit antennas with proper coding or weighting of the transmitted data signals. It is important to note that both spatial diversity schemes achieve improved transmission reliability at the cost of transmission rates comparable to the Single-Input Single-Output (SISO) systems. Clearly the achievement of higher link reliability is a trade-off with transmission rates. When multiple transmit antennas and single receive antenna are used, the resulting system is referred to as a Multiple-Input Single-Output (MISO) system.

Further research to achieve higher transmission rates and higher capacity has been done using multiple antennas at both ends of the communications link. These multiple transmit antennas and multiple receive antenna systems are referred to as MIMO systems. One of the common techniques to boost the transmission rates is to provide the receivers with independent streams of the same data signal from different transmit antennas. In this way, the transmit antennas are exploited to boost the transmission rates at the cost of lower link reliability. However, when operating under certain constraints, the same scheme can achieve full diversity gain leading to higher link reliability.

A comparison between the different spatial diversity schemes discussed above is shown in Table 1 where M and N denote the number of transmit antennas and receive antennas, respectively.

Table 1. Comparison of main spatial diversity schemes

Scheme	M	N	Example	Benefits
SISO	1	1	No transmit or receive diversity	No diversity gain.
SIMO	1	> 1	Receive diversity	Diversity proportional to N.
MISO	> 1	1	Transmit diversity	Diversity proportional to M.
MIMO	> 1	> 1	Use of multiple antennas at both the transmitter and receiver	Diversity proportional to the product of M and N. Array gain (coherent combining assuming prior channel estimation).

4. MULTIPLE NODES IN WIRELESS SENSOR NETWORKS

A major design requirement of WSNs is to reduce the total energy consumption of the sensor nodes. The transmission power can be reduced by providing the highest diversity gain possible which leads to higher link reliability and thus lower the retransmission rates. Therefore the exploitation of multiple nodes in WSNs (referred to as cooperative MIMO) is inevitable in order to provide higher reliability communication link and reduce transmission power.

Most of the previous work in the area of cooperative MIMO has assumed that the cooperating sensor nodes are perfectly synchronised during transmission and reception (Jagannathan et. al., 2004). Recently, the impact of imperfect synchronisation effects on the performance of cooperative MIMO operation in WSNs has gained more attention (Li, 2004; Li et. al., 2004; Li and Hwu, 2006). Imperfect synchronisation could occur due to the lack of carrier synchronisation or because of imperfect timing in frame and bit level synchronisation. In this chapter, we consider the impact of imperfect synchronisation caused by clock jitter alone. Each cooperating transmit node from a set of M cooperative nodes experiences clock jitter with the jitter around a reference clock, To denoted as Tjm where 1≤m≤M. The detailed system model of clock jitter will be explained in Section 5.

The following discussion explains in detail the three major MIMO schemes in both synchronous and asynchronous scenarios and their practicality in WSNs. Synchronous operation assumes perfect synchronisation between cooperating transmitting nodes and asynchronous operation refers to scenarios where imperfect synchronisation occurs. The three MIMO schemes are:

- SIMO System
- MISO System
- Spatial Multiplexing MIMO System

4.1 SIMO System

Perhaps the first technique in diversity particularly related to spatial utilisation is the receive diversity (SIMO) technique. The transmitter can choose to perform frequency, time, or polarisation due to the fact that the source of diversity does not affect the method of combination at the receiver side (with the exception of transmit spatial diversity (Jafarkhani, 2005). At the receiver side, more than one antenna or node must be used, N ≥ 2, to gain spatial diversity which leads to higher reliability by increasing the average signal-to-noise ratio (SNR) and lowering the bit error rate (BER).

There are four popular combining methods that are utilised at the receiver: Maximum Ratio Combining (MRC), Equal Gain Combining (EGC), Selection Combining (SC) and Switched Combining (Simon and Alouini, 2000; Rappaport, 2002; Jafarkhani, 2005; Duman and Ghrayeb, 2007). MRC achieves diversity gain equal to the number of the receive antennas, N, with N Radio Frequency (RF) chains as shown in Figure 1. EGC is a special case of MRC with equal weights' amplitudes where all the received signals are co-phased and then combined together with equal gain. The EGC receiver's circuit is less complex but at the cost of lower diversity gain than for MRC.

Assume that the receiver receives N replicas of the transmitted signal, s through N independent paths. The kth received signal is defined by:

$$rk = hk\ s + \eta\ k \tag{1}$$

where k = 1, 2, ..., N, ηk is the complex white Gaussian noise sample vector added to the kth copy of the signal with zero mean and σ2 variance, ηk ~ Nc(0,σ2) and hk is the complex channel fading gain vector with zero mean and ρ2 variance, hk ~ Nc(0,ρ2). We assume that the receiver is coherent where the channel information is known and perfectly estimated at the receiver. If the average power of the transmitted symbol is E s 2 , the instantaneous SNR of the kth receiver is given by (Jafarkhani, 2005):

$$\gamma_k = |h_k|^2 \cdot \frac{E\left[|s|^2\right]}{\sigma^2}. \tag{2}$$

The attempt to recover s can be given by the following MRC linear combination:

$$\tilde{s} = \sum_{k=1}^{N} h_k^* r_k = \sum_{k=1}^{N} |h_k|^2 s + \sum_{k=1}^{N} \eta_k h_k^* \tag{3}$$

where $\tilde{s}$ is the resulting decision variable with s mean and $\frac{\sigma^2}{\sum_{k=1}^{N}|h_k|^2}$ variance which can be represented as $\tilde{s} \sim \left(s, \frac{\sigma^2}{\sum_{k=1}^{N}|h_k|^2}\right)$. The resulting effective SNR at the output of the MRC block is proportional to $\sum_{k=1}^{N}|h_k|^2$ and given as:

$$\gamma = \sum_{k=1}^{N} |h_k|^2 \cdot \frac{E\left[|s|^2\right]}{\sigma^2} = \sum_{k=1}^{N} \gamma_k. \tag{4}$$

From Equation (4), the effective SNR of the system with a receive diversity scheme is equivalent to the sum of the instantaneous receive SNRs for N different paths. If we assume that all the different paths have the same average SNR, then the average of the effective SNR at the output of the MRC block is:

$$\bar{\gamma} = \sum_{k=1}^{N} E\left[|h_k|^2\right] \cdot \frac{E\left[|s|^2\right]}{\sigma^2} = \sum_{k=1}^{N} E[\gamma_k] = N \cdot \bar{\gamma}_k. \tag{5}$$

By increasing the number of receiving antennas N, the receive average SNR can be increased by N-fold which leads to the lowest possible BER for the system such that at the high SNRs regime, the error probability decays as SNRa-N (Proakis, 2001). On the other hand, when N increases, the receiver becomes more complex and larger in size. It seems that we have to trade off the cost, size and complexity of the devices or nodes for higher link reliability.

Selection combining was introduced to reduce the Nth RF chains complexity with only one RF chain used where the receiver performs signal selection with the highest SNR for decoding as shown in Figure 2. Also, channel state information is not needed which means that selection combining can be used for both coherent and non-coherent receivers (Simon and Alouni, 2000). The average SNR at the output of the selection combiner is given as:

$$\bar{\gamma} = \bar{\gamma}_k \sum_{k=1}^{N} \frac{1}{k}. \tag{6}$$

As can be seen from Equation (6), selection combining does not achieve the full N diversity gain which clearly trades off the diversity gain for lower complexity.

Later, a hybrid selection/MRC technique was proposed to balance the requirements between higher diversity gain and lower complexity (Jafarkhani, 2005).

Switched combining employs scanning and selection operation where the receiver scans all the diversity branches and selects a particular branch with the SNR above a certain predetermined threshold (Jafarkhani, 2005). The signals from the selected branch are selected as the output until its SNR drops below the threshold. Then the receiver starts to scan again and switches to another branch. This scheme is simpler since it does not require any channel knowledge but at the cost of lower achievable diversity gain.

In the context of practicality in WSNs, a SIMO with MRC scheme is more practical and promising for implementation as shown in Figure 3. This is due to the fact that each node in the network represents a single path processing including the RF chain processing. It seems that the complexity issue in the traditional SIMO approach can been reduced with the cooperative SIMO implementation while providing the highest SNR possible. Moreover, the transmission by the transmit node can be done without the need for time synchronisation, thus the cooperative SIMO system is not affected by clock jitter.

On the other hand, there are other issues that we have to consider such as the fact that data signals received by all the receiving nodes must be forwarded to a common destination node in order to combine and decode them successfully. Moreover, the diversity gain does not contribute to the reduction of the total transmission power and the use of N receiving nodes can contribute to the higher circuit power in the network.

4.2 MISO System

The main motivation for using of multiple antennas at the transmitter is to reduce the required processing power and complexity at the receiver which leads to lower power consumption, lower size and lower cost. However, the MISO concept is not easy to exploit and to implement (Naquib and Calderbank, 2000). Additional signal processing is required at both the transmitters and receiver in order to correctly decode the received signals. Also, another challenge is that the transmitter does not know the channel conditions unless channel information is fed back by the receiver to the transmitter (Liu et. al., 2001).

A number of MISO schemes have been proposed in the literature and can be categorised into two major classes:

a. Closed-loop MISO schemes with feedback
b. Open-loop MISO schemes without feedback

The difference between the two types of schemes is that the former relies on channel state information which has to be fed back to the transmitter and the latter eliminate the need for channel state information at the transmitter.

4.2.1 Closed-loop MISO System

The modulated signals are weighted with different weighting factors and transmitted with multiple antennas M at the transmitter. The weighting factors are chosen with the assistance of the channel state information so that the received SNR can be maximised at the receiver. The weighting factors must be optimised in order to achieve full diversity gain. One of the drawbacks of this system is that when the weighting factors are not optimised due to imperfect channel estimation, the received SNR is decreased.

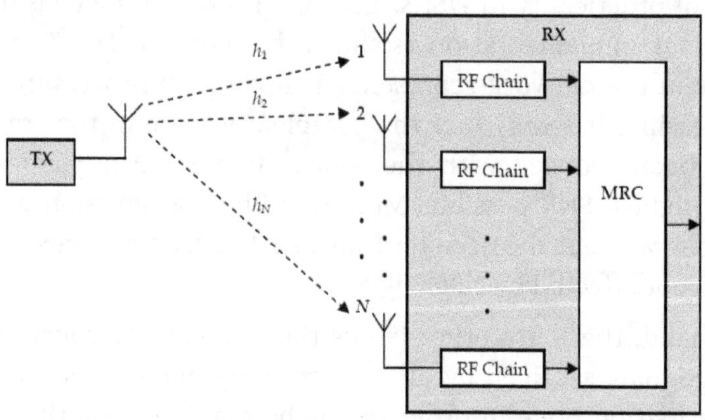

Fig. 1. A system with one transmit antenna and N receive antennas with MRC.

Two of the most popular closed-loop MISO schemes are switched diversity (Winters, 1983) and digital beamforming (Litva and Lo, 1996). Among the two schemes, the best solution, if the transmitter has perfect knowledge of the channel, is the MISO beamforming scheme. The MISO beamforming scheme is less complex and easier to deploy which makes it more practical to implement in WSNs.

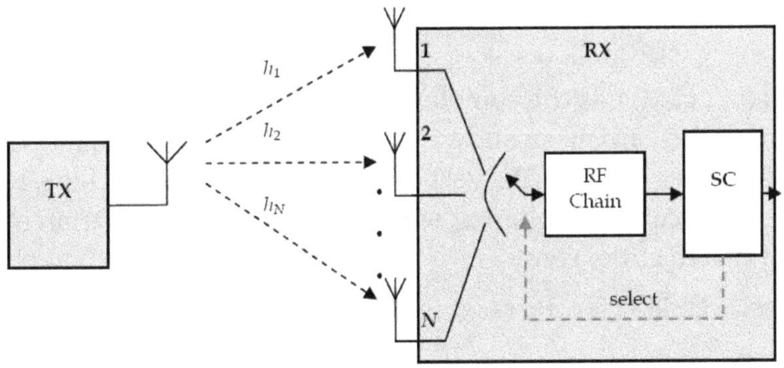

Fig. 2. A system with one transmit antenna and N receive antennas with SC.

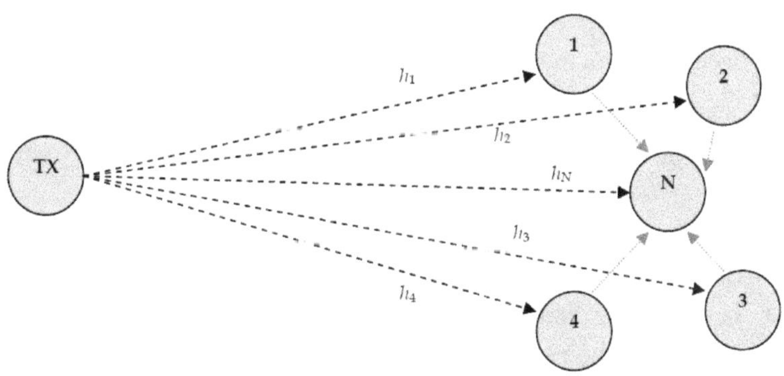

Fig. 3. A cooperative receive diversity system with one transmit node and N receive nodes.

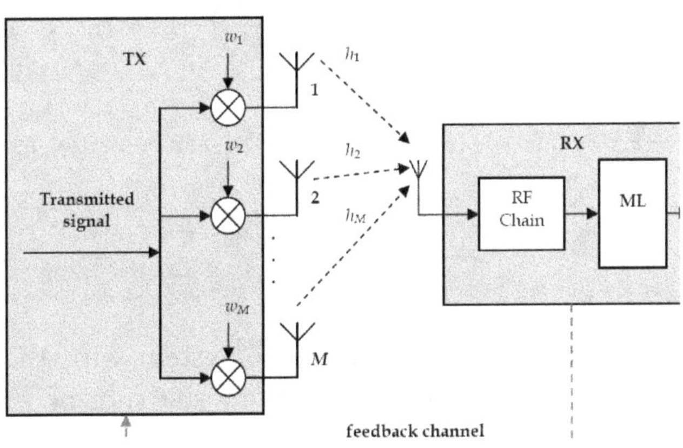

Fig. 4. A beamforming transmit diversity system with M transmit antennas and 1 receive antenna.

Let us consider a digital MISO beamforming system with M antennas at the transmitter and one antenna at the receiver as shown in Figure 4. The transmitter transmits M weighted transmitted signals, wk.s through M independent paths. The received signal is then given as:

$$r = \sum_{k=1}^{M} h_k w_k s + \eta \tag{7}$$

where k = 1, 2, ..., M, η is the complex white Gaussian noise sample added to the received signal with zero mean and σ2 variance, η ~ Nc(0,σ2) and hk is the complex channel fading gain vector with zero mean and ρ2 variance, hk ~ Nc(0,ρ2). We assume that the receiver is coherent where the channel information is known and perfectly estimated at the receiver.

The decision variable ~s for the Maximum Likelihood (ML) detector has s mean and $\frac{\sigma^2}{\sum_{k=1}^{M} h_k w_k}$ variance. If the average power of the transmitted symbol is $E\left[|s|^2\right]$, the instantaneous effective SNR is then given as.

$$\gamma = \sum_{k=1}^{M} h_k w_k \cdot \frac{E\left[|s|^2\right]}{\sigma^2}. \tag{8}$$

Given the transmitter knows the channel perfectly through feedback from the receiver, the weights are scaled and optimised proportionally to hk* so as to maximise the SNR in s^. The resulting instantaneous SNR is proportional to $_M\Sigma$ hk k =1 2 and given as:

$$\gamma = \sum_{k=1}^{M} |h_k|^2 \cdot \frac{E\left[|s|^2\right]}{\sigma^2}. \tag{9}$$

Let $\gamma_k = |h_k|^2 \cdot \frac{E\left[|s|^2\right]}{\sigma^2}$, then the effective receive SNR can be written as:

$$\gamma = \sum_{k=1}^{M} |h_k|^2 \cdot \frac{E\left[|s|^2\right]}{\sigma^2} = \sum_{k=1}^{M} \gamma_k . \tag{10}$$

From Equation (10), the effective SNR of the system with the transmit MISO beamforming diversity scheme is equivalent to the sum of the instantaneous receive SNRs for M different paths. If we assume that all the different paths have the same average SNR, then the average of the effective SNR at the output of the ML block is:

$$\bar{\gamma} = \sum_{k=1}^{M} E\left[|h_k|^2\right] \cdot \frac{E\left[|s|^2\right]}{\sigma^2} = \sum_{k=1}^{M} E[\gamma_k] = M \cdot \bar{\gamma}_k . \quad (11)$$

As M grows, the receive average SNR is increased by M-fold which leads to the lowest possible BER for the system. Furthermore, the total radiated power for all M antennas is the same as the total transmission power of one single transmit antenna, as in the receive diversity cases (Larsson and Stoica, 2003). It is clear that the transmission power Pt has been reduced down to Pt/M as the diversity gain increases up to M.

In the context of practicality in WSNs, the main obstacle for MISO beamforming implementation is the issue of how to provide each transmitting node with the knowledge of the channel. A multi-channel approach can be used where one channel is dedicated for the feedback and the other channel for data transmission. The channel is estimated periodically through training sequences on the feedback channel. However, a multi-channel approach is not practical for WSNs because such an approach increases the hardware and processing complexity at both the transmitter and the receiver. Also, such an approach requires tight frequency synchronisation to maintain the dual channel utilisation which obviously increases the total energy consumption of the network.

A better and practical alternative approach is to exploit the existing control protocols in WSNs such as those utilising RTS-CTS packets to provide the channel state information to the transmitter as shown in Figure 5. Both the control and data communications can be maintained over a single-channel with less complexity and loose synchronisation.

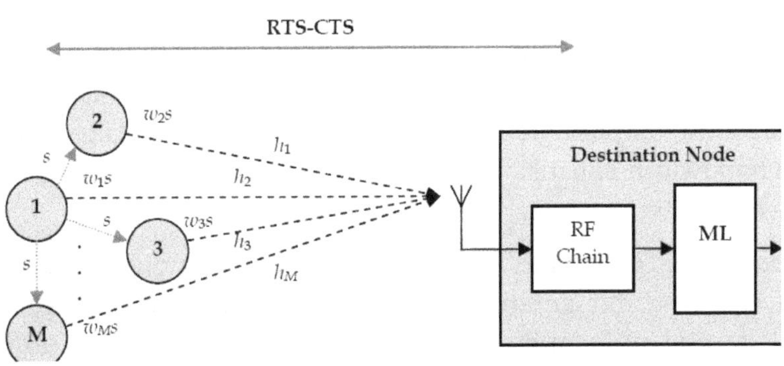

Fig. 5. A cooperative beamforming transmit diversity system with M transmit nodes and 1 destination.

Moreover, the transmission power of each transmitting node is reduced down to Pt/M which leads to the reduction of the total power consumption in the network. In addition, the RTS-CTS implementation can also reduce the hidden node problem in such densely distributed sensor networks.

4.2.2 Open-loop MISO System

The modulated signals must be processed at the transmitter first before being transmitted from multiple antennas M. The main motivation is to reduce the complexity of the feedback schemes in the closed-loop MISO systems. The transmitter design is enhanced with more advanced signal processing and/or a combination of various diversity techniques in order to provide the receiver with the capability to exploit full diversity gain from the received signals.

One of the early proposed open-loop MISO schemes is the antenna hopping scheme (Seshadri and Winters, 1993; Wittneben, 1991). The modulated signals are transmitted from M antennas with different time intervals. At the receiver, the delayed signals introduce a multipath-like distortion for the intended signal.

The multipath-like distortion can be resolved at the receiver by using a ML detector or a Minimum Mean Square Error (MMSE) detector to obtain M diversity gain. The antenna hopping scheme has been shown to achieve fully diversity gain up to M without any bandwidth expansion but at the cost of a lower spatial rate.

In order to gain the full spatial rate, the diversity gain achieved from a multiple antennas implementation is combined with the coding gain achieved from the error control and channel coding schemes. The combination schemes of error control coding and multiple antennas have gained the full spatial rate in addition to the diversity benefit but at the cost of bandwidth losses due to code redundancy (Vucetic and Yuan, 2003). A better and practical approach is a joint design of multiple antennas with channel coding schemes. This approach can be achieved when the multiple antennas and channel coding schemes are designed as a single signal processing module. Coding techniques for multiple antenna communications are called space-time coding (STC). STC schemes provide redundant transmission in both spatial and temporal domains. In addition to the diversity gain, full spatial rate and no bandwidth expansion advantages, STC schemes can be combined with multiple receive antennas to achieve capacity gain.

The most popular STC scheme is due to Alamouti (Alamouti, 1998) who studied the case of two transmit antennas. The Alamouti space-time encoder picks up two symbols s1 and s2 from an arbitrary constellation and the two symbols are transmitted in two consecutive time slots as shown in Figure 6. In the first time slot, s1 is transmitted from the first antenna while s2 is transmitted from the second antenna. Consecutively in the second time slot, -s2* is transmitted from the first antenna while s1* is transmitted from the second antenna. Since both the symbols are transmitted in two time slots, the overall rate is given as one symbol per channel use. The key concept of the Alamouti STC scheme is the orthogonal design of the transmit sequences. The inner product of the sequences x1 and x2 is given as:

$$x1 \,.\, x2 = s1\, s2^* - s1\, s2^* = 0\,. \tag{12}$$

The transmitted code matrix has the following property:

$$X \cdot X^H = \begin{bmatrix} s_1 & -s_2^* \\ s_2 & s_1^* \end{bmatrix} \cdot \begin{bmatrix} s_1^* & s_2^* \\ -s_2 & s_1 \end{bmatrix} = \begin{bmatrix} |s_1|^2 + |s_2|^2 & 0 \\ 0 & |s_1|^2 + |s_2|^2 \end{bmatrix}. \tag{13}$$

Assume that both the paths experience quasi-static fading where the fading coefficients are constant across the two consecutive symbol transmission intervals which can be expressed as:

$$\begin{aligned} h_1(t) = h_1(t+T) = h_1 = |h_1| e^{j\theta 1} \\ h_2(t) = h_2(t+T) = h_2 = |h_2| e^{j\theta 2}. \end{aligned} \tag{14}$$

where hk andθ k , k = 1, 2, are the amplitude gain and phase shift for the path from transmit antenna k to the receiver antenna and T is the symbol duration. The received signal in the first time slot is given as:

$$r(t) = r1 = h1\, s1 + h2\, s2 + \eta 1 \tag{15}$$

and in the second time slot, the received signal is given as:

$$r(t + T) = r = -h\, s^* + h\, s^* + \eta \tag{16}$$

where η1 and η2 are the complex white noise with zero mean and variance σ2 for the first time slot and second time slot, respectively. The received signal vector is defined at the receiver as:

$$r = \begin{bmatrix} r_1 \\ r_2^* \end{bmatrix} \tag{17}$$

which can be written as:

$$r = \begin{bmatrix} h_1 & h_2 \\ h_2^* & -h_1^* \end{bmatrix} \begin{bmatrix} s_1 \\ s_2 \end{bmatrix} + \begin{bmatrix} \eta_1 \\ \eta_2^* \end{bmatrix}. \tag{18}$$

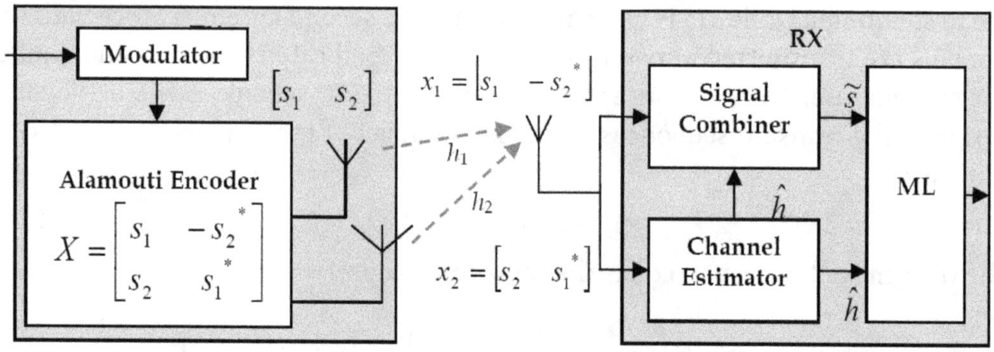

Fig. 6. An alamouti STC transmit diversity system with 2 transmit antennas and 1 receive antenna.

Assume that the receiver is coherent and optimal. Then the attempt to recover s1 and s2 can be given by the following linear combination:

$$\tilde{s} = \begin{bmatrix} h_1 & h_2 \\ h_2^* & -h_1^* \end{bmatrix}^H \begin{bmatrix} r_1 \\ r_2^* \end{bmatrix} = \begin{bmatrix} \sum_{k=1}^{M} |h_k|^2 s_1 + h_1^* \eta_1 + h_2 \eta_2^* \\ \sum_{k=1}^{M} |h_k|^2 s_2 + h_2^* \eta_1 - h_1 \eta_2^* \end{bmatrix}. \tag{19}$$

The resulting decision variables in Equation (19) are equivalent to the one obtained with receive diversity using the MRC scheme. The only difference is the phase rotations on the noise components which do not degrade the effective SNR (Alamouti, 1998).

The decision variable vector $\tilde{s}$ with s mean and $\frac{\sigma^2}{\sum_{k=1}^{M} h_k}$ variance is sent to the ML detector. If the average power of the transmitted symbols is $E\left[|s_n|^2\right]$, the receive SNR in each sub-channel is given as:

$$\gamma = \sum_{k=1}^{M} h_k \cdot \frac{E\left[|s_n|^2\right]}{2\sigma^2}. \tag{20}$$

We can observe from Equation (20) that the linear processing in Equation (19) transforms the space-time channel into two parallel and independent scalar channels. If we assume that the symbols are Phase Shift Keying (PSK) modulated signals with equal energy constellations, the total transmission power is effectively doubled as shown in Equation (20) compared to the SIMO MRC and MISO beamforming schemes. Let $\gamma_i = |h_i|^2 \cdot \frac{E\left[|s_n|^2\right]}{2\sigma^2}$ then the effective receive SNR can be written as: effective receive SNR can be written as:

$$\gamma = \sum_{k=1}^{M} |h_k|^2 \cdot \frac{E\left[|s_n|^2\right]}{2\sigma^2} = \sum_{k=1}^{M} \gamma_k . \tag{21}$$

If we assume that all the different paths have the same average SNR, then the average of the effective SNR at the output of the ML block is:

$$\bar{\gamma} = \sum_{k=1}^{M} E\left[|h_k|^2\right] \cdot \frac{E\left[|s_n|^2\right]}{2\sigma^2} = \sum_{k=1}^{M} E[\gamma_k] = M \cdot \bar{\gamma}_k . \tag{22}$$

As we can observe, the MISO Alamouti STC scheme provides the same diversity gain as the SIMO MRC and MISO beamforming schemes with M equal to two but with 3 dB loss in error performance (Larsson and Stoica, 2003). In addition, the MISO Alamouti STC scheme can be applied for a system with 2 transmitting antennas and N receiving antennas to gain higher capacity. Although such systems are very important for high-speed networks, careful consideration of circuit and processing energies and decoder complexity at the receiver in WSNs keeps our discussion to systems with only one receive antenna which corresponds to one receive node in cooperative MISO transmission.

The Alamouti STC scheme can be generalised from two transmit antennas up to M transmit antennas by using the same theory of orthogonal design (Tarokh et. al., 1999). The generalised scheme is referred to as Orthogonal Space-Time Block Codes (OSTBC). In general, OSTBC can be categorised into two types: real and complex, based on the signal constellation.

The basic operation of OSTBC is shown in Figure 7 where the scheme can achieve full transmit diversity up to M order with M transmit antennas while allowing the use of a very simple ML decoding algorithm and linear combining at the receiver. However, OSTBC trades off full diversity gain for lower spatial rate when M > 2. In order to provide a compromise between full diversity and full rate, a Quasi-Orthogonal STBC (Quasi OSTBC) scheme was proposed in (Jafarkhani, 2005).

Another class of STCs is the Space-Time Trellis Codes (STTC) (Tarokh et. al., 1998). STTC achieves higher coding gain and is comparable to STBC in terms of achieving full transmit diversity gain. However, the encoder design based on trellis-coded modulation leads to a more complex receiver with a Viterbi algorithm decoding implementation. The ML decoder complexity grows exponentially with the number of bits per symbol, thus limiting the achievable data rates.

In the context of practicality in WSNs, the main obstacle of MISO STBCs and STTCs schemes implementation is the issues of how to provide each transmitting node with the transmit sequences knowledge and how different transmit sequences are assigned to each node in order to provide an orthogonal or quasi-orthogonal design.

A better and practical approach as suggested in (Yang et. al., 2007) is when the source node broadcasts the transmit sequences to its particular neighbours in order to provide the transmit sequences knowledge together with the original data signal. Such an approach introduces an increasing packet overhead as M increases, prior data packet transmission. The overhead is a compromise with full diversity gain which achieves higher reliability and lower transmission energy.

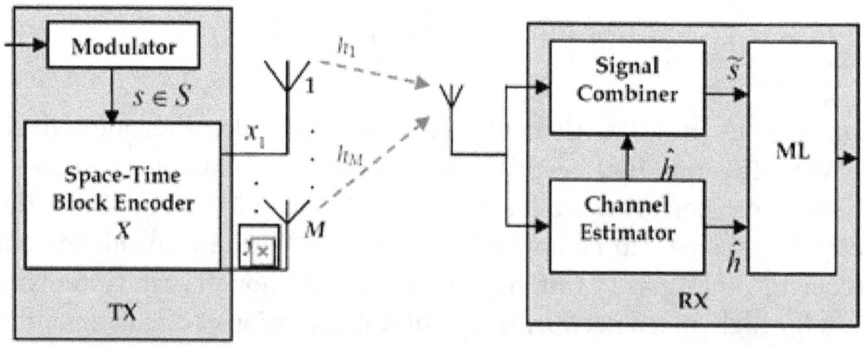

Fig. 7. A STBCs transmit diversity system with M transmit antennas and 1 receive antenna.

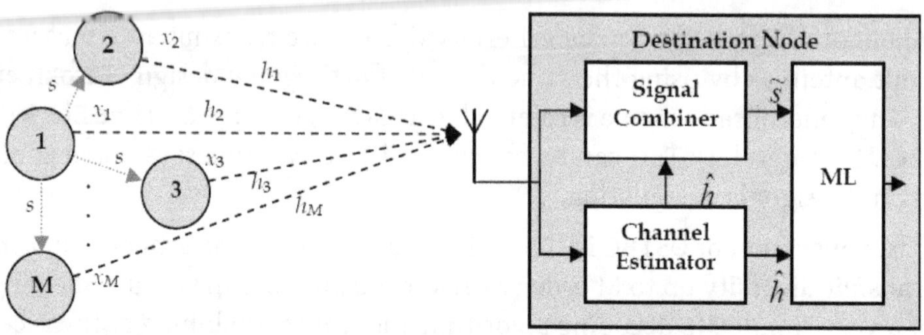

Fig. 8. A cooperative STBC transmit diversity system with M transmit nodes and 1 destination.

As a comparison, MISO STBC is more practical and promising to be implemented in WSNs due to a simpler decoding algorithm which leads to lower processing energy at the receiver. On the other hand, the simpler encoding and decoding algorithms of MISO STBC come at the cost of higher transmission power compared to the MISO beamforming scheme. The pictorial concept of cooperative MISO STBC is shown in Figure 8.

4.2.3 Spatial Multiplexing MIMO System

The main motivation of spatial multiplexing (SM) scheme is to achieve a higher data rate while maintaining the same full diversity gain. Thus the main purpose of SM schemes is basically to complement the lack of spatial rate in MISO STBC and STTC schemes. Therefore SM schemes are designed purposely for high data rate applications such as mobile communications systems and wireless local area networks. Though the current WSNs target only low to medium data rate applications, future generations of WSNs may require to operate with such high data rate applications which makes the investigation of cooperative SM in WSNs relevant and useful.

The main concept of SM (also referred as Layered Space-Time Codes – LSTC (Foschini, 1996)) is to provide simultaneous transmissions of M information streams in the same frequency band from M transmit antennas. However, by using such a transmission method, a constraint is introduced where the number of receive antennas must be equal or greater than the number of transmit antennas ($N \geq M$) in order to separate and detect the M transmitted signals. The separation process involves a combination of interference suppression and cancellation. The achievable spatial rate is given as RcbM where Rc denotes the rate of the channel code whenever channel coding is employed and 2b is the signal constellation size. When full channel code is achieved with Rc = 1 and Binary PSK is used with b = 1, we can show that the spatial rate is increased linearly with M.

Among the simplest SM schemes is Bell Laboratories Layered Space-Time (BLAST) (Golden et. al., 1999). There are various versions of the BLAST schemes in the literature such as Vertical BLAST (VBLAST), Horizontal BLAST (HBLAST) and Diagonal BLAST (DBLAST). The simplest version is VBLAST due to the simplest encoder architecture compared to HBLAST and DBLAST (Vucetic and Yuan, 2003). VBLAST is also referred to as an un-coded LST scheme while HBLAST and DBLAST are classified as coded LST schemes. The simple encoder architecture makes VBLAST the most practical version of SM schemes for implementation in WSNs in order to keep the complexity and power consumption as low as possible. There are other SM schemes such as threaded LSTCs and multilayered LSTCs, with higher spatial rate but they come at the cost of more complex encoding and decoding mechanisms. Obviously these schemes are not practical to be implemented in WSNs and thus are not considered in our work.

A VBLAST encoder is shown in Figure 9. As shown in the figure, the bit stream is de- multiplexed into M sub-streams. Each M sub-stream is then modulated and transmitted from M transmit antennas. The transmitted signal matrix is given as:

$$X = [st_k] \tag{23}$$

where k = 1, 2, ..., M and t = 1, 2, ..., L with L is the transmission block length. At a given time t, the transmitter transmits the tth column from the transmission matrix, one symbol from each kth antenna. The given transmission mechanism represents vertical structuring referring to transmission sequences of the matrix columns in the space-time domains (Vucetic and Yuan, 2003). Given the system constraint of N ≥ M, the achievable spatial rate is bM and the achievable spatial diversity depends on the detection scheme employed at the receiver. When a Zero Forcing (ZF) or a Minimum Mean Square Error (MMSE) decoder is used at the receiver for the separation and detection, the achievable spatial diversity varies between 1 to N (Vucetic and Yuan, 2003). In order to gain full spatial diversity equal to N, a ML decoder must be employed at the receiver at the cost of a more complex decoder compared to ZF and MMSE. The complexity of the ML decoder increases linearly with bN. Thus the use of a modulation scheme with the smallest constellation size (e.g. b = 1) is very helpful to reduce the decoder complexity while achieving higher spatial diversity gain.

In the context of practicality in WSNs, there are three major issues that must be tackled: how to provide the data packet stream to M-1 transmitting nodes, how to transmit each M data packet stream simultaneously from M nodes and how to forward the receive data packets by N-1 receiving nodes to the destination. An example of architecture for cooperative SM which is based on the VBLAST scheme was proposed in (Yang et. al., 2007) and is shown in Figure 10. The cooperative SM scheme has the following operations:

a. Source node broadcasts the original data packet stream to its M-1 neighbour nodes with very low power and all the M transmitting nodes send the same data packet streams simultaneously after the sending timer expires.
b. N receiving nodes receive the data packet streams from M transmitting nodes and each receiving node employs a ML decoder to decode the data packet and forward the data packet to the destination node.

In order to gain both spatial diversity and spatial rate, the constraint of the traditional SM scheme such as N ≥ M also works for the cooperative SM scheme. Consider the transmission route in Figure 10. The error rate in each route is given as:

$$P_e = P_{eM\_1} + P_{e\,pp(dst)} - P_{e\,pp(dst)} P_{eM\_1(recv)} \tag{24}$$

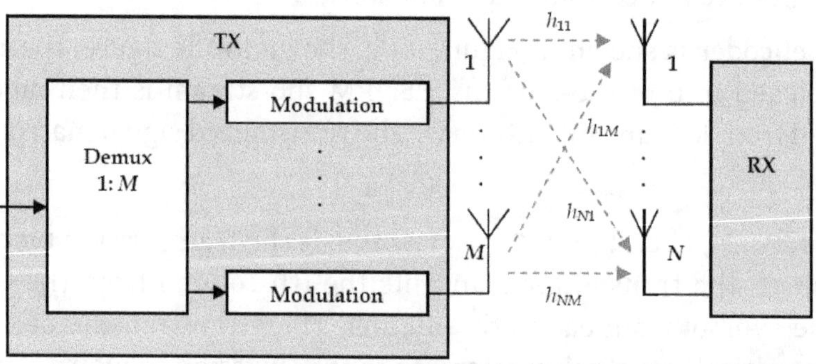

Fig. 9. A VBLAST spatial multiplexing system with M transmit antennas and N receive antennas.

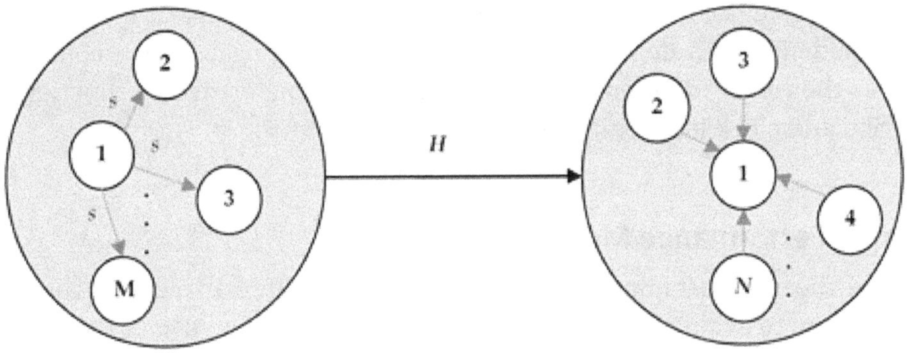

Fig. 10. A cooperative spatial multiplexing system with M transmit nodes and N receive nodes.

where Pe M _1 is the error rate for M nodes cooperatively sending to one receiving node which relates to the power summation from multiple paths M, and different fading characteristics that may occur in different signal transmission paths. Pepp(dst) is the error rate from one receiving node to the destination. A simple majority decision rule is employed at the destination node when multiple packets are received from N-1 nodes (Yang et. al., 2007). The data packet stream with the lowest BER, which means that the SNR is maximised, is selected at the destination node. If each receiving node in the receiving group has the same BER, the BER in the destination node after the reception from the N nodes forming the reception group is given as:

$$P_{eM\_N} = \sum_{k=N/2}^{N} \binom{N}{k} P_e^{\,k} \left(1 - P_e\right)^{N-k} . \tag{25}$$

5. PERFORMANCE ANALYSIS

In this section, we study the performance of cooperative MIMO schemes discussed earlier on, namely cooperative MISO Beamforming (BF), MISO STBC and MIMO SM schemes. The clock jitter impact is modelled as a timing error function in Section 5.1. The error performance for each cooperative scheme is modelled in Section 5.2 while the results are discussed in Section 5.3.

5.1 Timing Error Modeling

We consider the impact of imperfect synchronisation which is caused by clock jitter alone. Each cooperative sending nodes experiences clock jitter with the jitter around a reference clock, T denoted as T m where 1 ≤ m ≤ M . The worst case scenario is considered here with $T_j^1 = -\frac{\Delta T_b}{2}, T_j^2 = +\frac{\Delta T_b}{2}$ only 2 cooperative transmitting nodes where the clock jitters are fixed at the extreme ends, where 0 ≤ ΔTb ≤ Tb and Tb is the bit duration. Thus the clock jitters difference is ΔT = T 1j – T 2j = ΔTb . The effect of imperfect synchronisation can be modelled as a degrading function of the bit period which consequently degrades the received bit energy. Therefore the timing error as a function of the bit period and clock jitters difference is given as:

$$Te = Tb - \Delta Tj \,. \tag{26}$$

5.2 Error Performance Modeling

We derive the two most important performance parameters to measure the channel condition and to evaluate the link reliability: BER and PER. Without Forward Error Correction (FEC), the relationship between Packet Error Rate (PER), Pp and BER, Pb is given by:

$$Pb = 1- (1- Pb)Ndata \tag{27}$$

where Ndata is the packet length in bits. Consider the case of BPSK modulation under quasi- static Rayleigh fading with fading gain h, experiencing a square law path loss without channel codes. In the SISO system, the conditional SNR is given by (Proakis, 2001):

$$\gamma_{bSISO} = \frac{P_t |h|^2 G_t G_r}{N_o M_l \left(\frac{4\pi d}{\lambda} \right)^2} \tag{28}$$

where Pt is the transmission power, d is the distance between the sending and destination node, Gt and Gr are the transmission and reception antenna gain, Λ is the carrier wave length, Mι is the link margin and No is single-sided thermal noise power spectral density (PSD) given as -171 dBm/Hertz.

The probability density function (PDF) of Γ bSISO is given by:

$$p(\gamma_{bSISO}) = \frac{1}{\bar{\gamma}_{bSISO}} \exp^{-\frac{\gamma_{bSISO}}{\bar{\gamma}_{bSISO}}} \tag{29}$$

where Γ bSISO is the average SNR. Assume that E[h 2]= 1 (Larsson and Stoica, 2003), then the value of Γ bSISO is given by:

$$\bar{\gamma}_{bSISO} = \frac{P_t E\left[|h|^2\right] G_t G_r}{N_o M_l \left(\frac{4\pi d}{\lambda} \right)^2} = \frac{P_t G_t G_r}{N_o M_l \left(\frac{4\pi d}{\lambda} \right)^2} \,. \tag{30}$$

The average BER can be expressed as:

$$E_h\left[P_{bSISO}\right] = E_h\left[Q\left(\sqrt{2\gamma_{bSISO}}\right)\right]. \tag{31}$$

The upper bound of the average BER can be derived as (Proakis, 2001):

$$Q\left(\sqrt{2\gamma_{bSISO}}\right) = p\left(x \geq \sqrt{2\gamma_{bSISO}}\right) \leq \exp\left(-\frac{\left(\sqrt{2\gamma_{bSISO}}\right)^2}{2}\right) \tag{32}$$

$$E\left[Q\left(\sqrt{2\gamma_{bSISO}}\right)\right] \leq E\left[\exp\left(-\gamma_{bSISO}\right)\right]. \tag{33}$$

The moment generating function of Γ bSISO is given by (Proakis, 2001):

$$\Phi(S) = E\left[\exp\left(\gamma_{bSISO} S\right)\right] = \frac{1}{S\bar{\gamma}_{bSISO}} \tag{34}$$

$$E_h\left[P_{bSISO}\right] \leq E\left[\exp\left(-\gamma_{bSISO}\right)\right] = \Phi(-1) = \left(1 + \bar{\gamma}_{bSISO}\right)^{-1}. \tag{35}$$

If there are M nodes in the sending group and we are comparing between optimal cooperative BF and STBC schemes, the SNRs for both schemes for perfect synchronisation scenario at the destination node can be given by:

$$\gamma_{bBF} = \sum_{k=1}^{M} \left|h_k\right|^2 \frac{P_t G_t G_r}{N_o M_l \left(\frac{4\pi d}{\lambda}\right)^2} = \sum_{k=1}^{M} \gamma_{BFk} \tag{36}$$

$$\gamma_{bSTBC} = \sum_{k=1}^{M} \left|h_k\right|^2 \frac{P_t G_t G_r}{M \cdot N_o M_l \left(\frac{4\pi d}{\lambda}\right)^2} = \sum_{k=1}^{M} \gamma_{STBCk} \tag{37}$$

and the SNRs for imperfect synchronisation scenario at the destination node can be given by:

$$\gamma_{bBF} = \sum_{k=1}^{M} \left|h_k\right|^2 \frac{P_t G_t G_r}{N_o M_l \left(\frac{4\pi d}{\lambda}\right)^2} \cdot \frac{T_e}{T_b} = \sum_{k=1}^{M} \gamma_{BFk} \tag{38}$$

$$\gamma_{bSTBC} = \sum_{k=1}^{M} \left|h_k\right|^2 \frac{P_t G_t G_r}{M \cdot N_o M_l \left(\frac{4\pi d}{\lambda}\right)^2} \cdot \frac{T_e}{T_b} = \sum_{k=1}^{M} \gamma_{STBCk} \tag{39}$$

where Γ BFk and Γ STBCk are the instantaneous SNR on the kth channel.

The PDF of Γ BFk and Γ STBCk are:

$$p(\gamma_{BFk}) = \frac{1}{\overline{\gamma}_{BFk}} \exp^{-\frac{\gamma_{BFk}}{\overline{\gamma}_{BFk}}} \tag{40}$$

$$p(\gamma_{STBCk}) = \frac{1}{\overline{\gamma}_{STBCk}} \exp^{-\frac{\gamma_{STBCk}}{\overline{\gamma}_{STBCk}}} . \tag{41}$$

Assume that $E\left[\|h_k\|^2\right] = 1$ (Larsson and Stoica, 2003), then the values of $\overline{\gamma}_{BFk}$ and $\overline{\gamma}_{STBCk}$ for perfect synchronisation scenario become:

$$\overline{\gamma}_{BFk} = \frac{P_t E\left[\|h_k\|^2\right] G_t G_r}{N_o M_l \left(\frac{4\pi d}{\lambda}\right)^2} = \frac{P_t G_t G_r}{N_o M_l \left(\frac{4\pi d}{\lambda}\right)^2} \tag{42}$$

$$\overline{\gamma}_{STBCk} = \frac{P_t E\left[\|h_k\|^2\right] G_t G_r}{M \cdot N_o M_l \left(\frac{4\pi d}{\lambda}\right)^2} = \frac{P_t G_t G_r}{M \cdot N_o M_l \left(\frac{4\pi d}{\lambda}\right)^2} \tag{43}$$

and the average SNRs for imperfect synchronisation scenario can be given by:

$$\overline{\gamma}_{BFk} = \frac{P_t E\left[\|h_k\|^2\right] G_t G_r}{N_o M_l \left(\frac{4\pi d}{\lambda}\right)^2} \cdot \frac{T_e}{T_b} = \frac{P_t G_t G_r}{N_o M_l \left(\frac{4\pi d}{\lambda}\right)^2} \cdot \frac{T_e}{T_b} \tag{44}$$

$$\overline{\gamma}_{STBCk} = \frac{P_t E\left[\|h_k\|^2\right] G_t G_r}{M \cdot N_o M_l \left(\frac{4\pi d}{\lambda}\right)^2} \cdot \frac{T_e}{T_b} = \frac{P_t G_t G_r}{M \cdot N_o M_l \left(\frac{4\pi d}{\lambda}\right)^2} \cdot \frac{T_e}{T_b} . \tag{45}$$

The moment generating functions of Γ bBF and Γ bSTBC are (Proakis, 2001):

$$\Phi(S) = E[\exp(\gamma_{bBF} S)] = \prod_{k=1}^{M} \frac{1}{S\overline{\gamma}_{BFk}} \tag{46}$$

$$E_h[P_{bBF}] \le E[\exp(-\gamma_{bBF})] = \Phi(-1) = (1 + \overline{\gamma}_{BFk})^{-M} \tag{47}$$

$$\Phi(S) = E[\exp(\gamma_{bSTBC} S)] = \prod_{k=1}^{M} \frac{1}{S\overline{\gamma}_{STBCk}} \tag{48}$$

$$E_h[P_{bSTBC}] \le E[\exp(-\gamma_{bSTBC})] = \Phi(-1) = (1 + \overline{\gamma}_{STBCk})^{-M} . \tag{49}$$

The average BER for the cooperative SM scheme in (Yang et. al., 2007) is given as:

$$P_{bSM} = \sum_{k=N/2}^{N} \binom{N}{k} P_e^k (1-P_e)^{N-k} \tag{50}$$

$$P_e = E_h[P_{bMISO}] + E_h[P_{bSISO}] - E_h[P_{bSISO}]E_h[P_{bMISO}] \tag{51}$$

where Pe is the error rate in each route and N is the number of nodes forming the reception group. The average SNR of the MISO scheme in Equation (51) is the same as the average SNR of the cooperative MISO BF scheme (Yang et. al., 2007). Thus we assume that the average BER is the same for both schemes. Table 2 lists the system parameters used for evaluating BER performance of the three cooperative MIMO schemes.

5.3 Performance Results and Discussions

Figures 11, 12 and 13 show the corresponding results for perfect synchronisation scenarios. For comparison, those figures also show the BER performance of the corresponding SISO scheme. As we can see, in general, cooperative BF outperforms the other schemes except for the special case below the 10mW transmit power where cooperative SM performs better.

However, this special case may not have a significant impact due to the fact that the operating transmission power for WSNs is in the range between 25mW to 50mW (Kohvakka et. al., 2006). Also, we can observe that the diversity gain of cooperative SM depends on N and not M as shown in Figures 12 and 13. In addition, the cooperative SM achieves spatial rate equal to M.

Figures 14 and 15 show the corresponding results for imperfect synchronisation scenarios. As we can see, in general SISO outperforms other schemes above 0.8Tb and cooperative SM outperforms the other schemes when the diversity gain is getting higher. However, when the diversity gain of all the cooperative schemes is the same, cooperative BF outperforms the other schemes.

Table 2. System parameter for ber and per modeling

Symbol	Quantity
fc	2.4 GHz
GtGr	5 dBi [5]
M	40 dB [5]
d	100 meters
dm	10 meters
Rb	250 Kbps

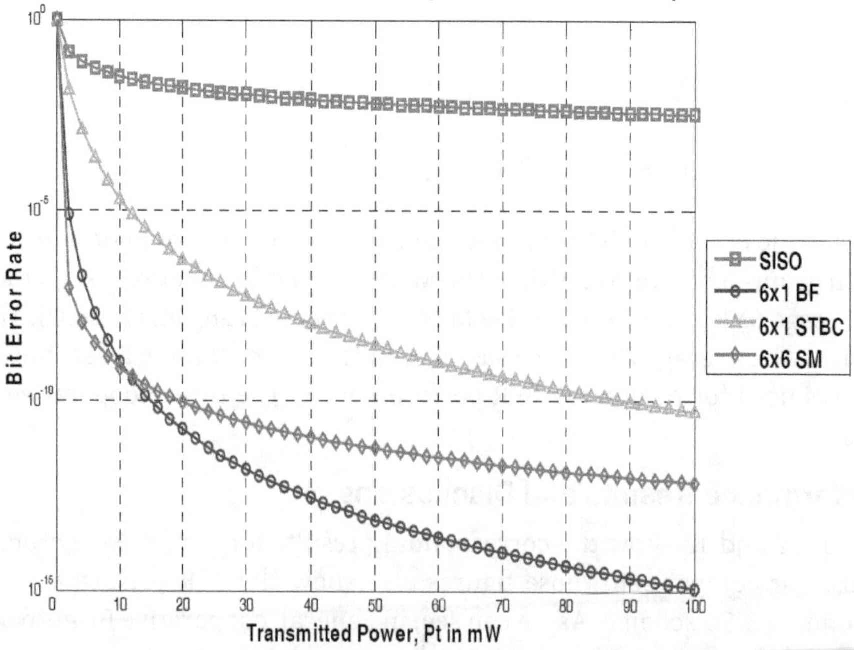

Fig. 11. BER vs. transmission power for various cooperative schemes with M = 6 and N = 1 (Cooperative BF and Cooperative STBC) and M = N = 6 (Cooperative SM).

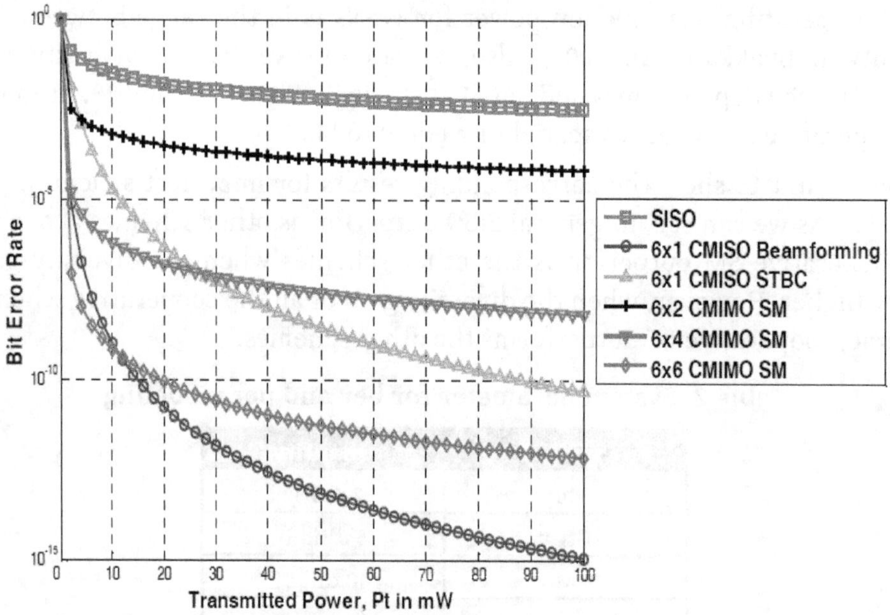

Fig. 12. BER vs. transmission power for various cooperative schemes with M = 6 and N = 1 (Cooperative BF and Cooperative STBC) and various N = 2, 4 and 6 for Cooperative SM with M = 6.

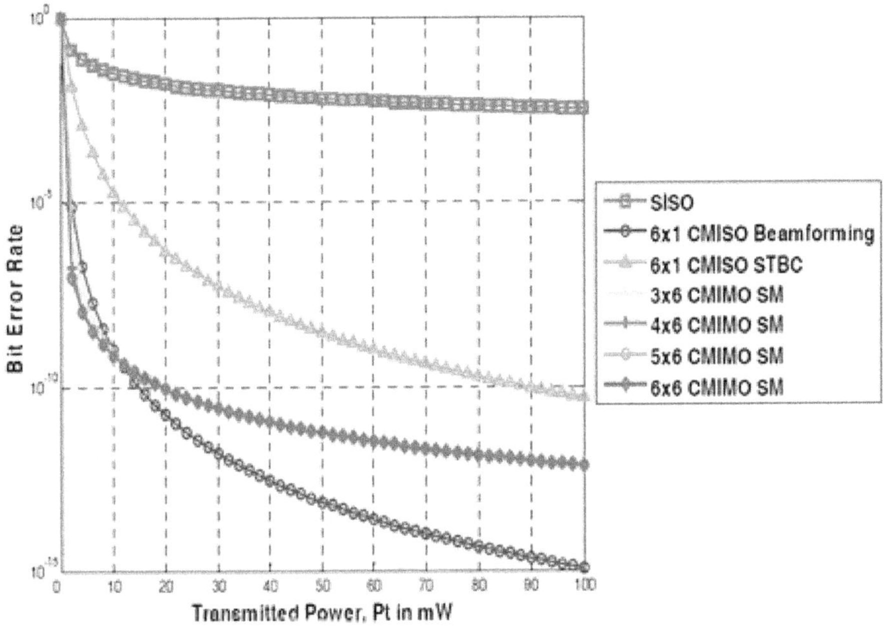

Fig. 13. BER vs. transmission power for various cooperative schemes with M = 6 and N = 1 (Cooperative BF and Cooperative STBC) and various M = 3, 4, 5 and 6 for Cooperative SM with N = 6.

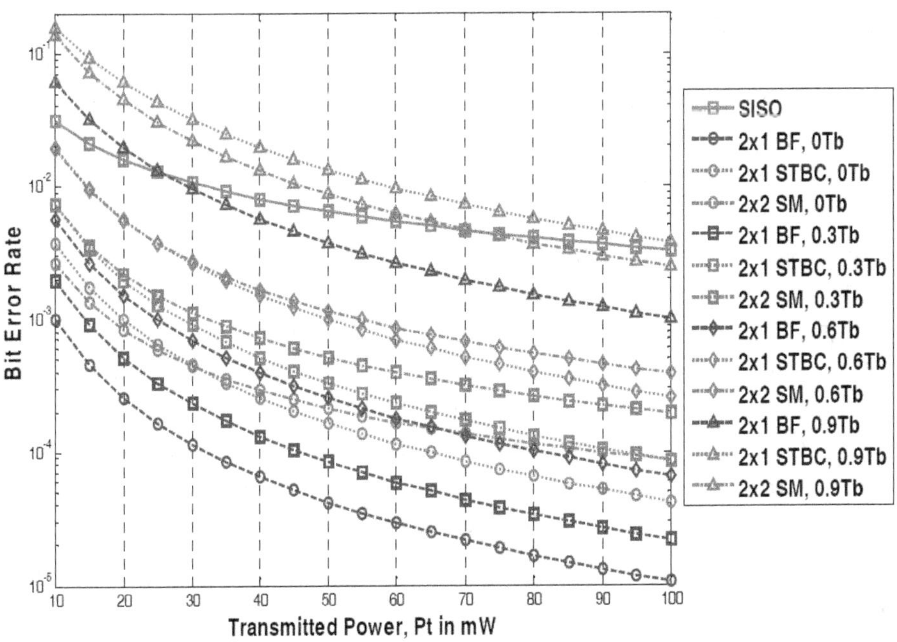

Fig. 14. BER vs. transmission power for various imperfect synchronisation cooperative schemes with M = 2 and N = 1 (Cooperative BF and Cooperative STBC) and M = N = 2 (Cooperative SM).

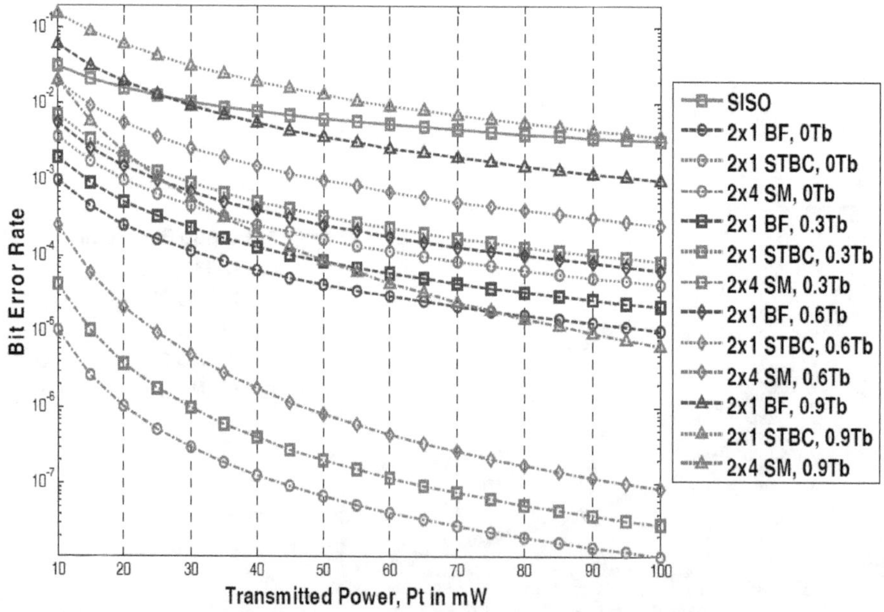

Fig. 15. BER vs. transmission power for various imperfect synchronisation cooperative schemes with M = 2 and N = 1 (Cooperative BF and Cooperative STBC) and N = 4 for Cooperative SM with M = 2.

6. CONCISE SUMMARY

This chapter has analyzed the principal diversity strategies and numerous cooperative configurations, including BF, STBC, and SM schemes, alongside performance evaluation and comparative literature. Both cooperative BF and STBC methods employ the MISO concept, whereas the SM scheme employs the MIMO concept. We have demonstrated that cooperative MISO beamforming is the most advantageous approach for implementation in wireless sensor networks, owing to its superior error performance compared to alternative methods with equivalent diversity gain. Furthermore, cooperative MISO beamforming surpasses alternative cooperative strategies in circumstances with imperfect synchronization. Conversely, cooperative MIMO SM demonstrates greater practicality due to its superior error performance and resilience to clock jitter, provided its diversity gain exceeds that of alternative methods. Furthermore, cooperative MIMO SM yields an increased spatial rate as M expands.

The comparative analysis correlates the enhancement of variety with the decrease in transmission power through the augmentation of communication link reliability. To identify the appropriate strategy for Wireless Sensor Networks (WSNs), it is essential to analyze all three methods based on total energy consumption, encompassing both transmission power and circuit power for each sensor node inside the network. This chapter's discussion establishes a foundation for subsequent research to identify the ideal cooperative MIMO scheme, taking into account both transmission and circuit power for all necessary energy components in cooperative communications within WSNs..

REFERENCES

1. Alamouti, S.M. (1998). A Simple Transmit Diversity Technique for Wireless Communications, IEEE Journal on Selected Areas in Communications, vol. 16, pp. 1451-1458.
2. Duman, T.M. & Ghrayeb, A. (2007). Coding for MIMO Communication Systems, First ed. West Sussex, England: John Wiley & Sons Ltd.
3. Foschini, G.J. (1996). Layered Space-time Architecture for Wireless Communication in A Fading Environment when using Multi-element antennas, Bell Labs Technical Journal, pp. 41-59.
4. Golden, G.D.; Foschini, G.J.; & Valenzuela, R.A. (1999). Detection Algorithm and Initial Laboratory Results using the V-BLAST Space-time Communication Architecture, Electronic Letters, vol. 35, pp. 14-15.
5. Gupta, G. & Younis, M. (2003). Fault-Tolerant Clustering of Wireless Sensor Networks, presented at IEEE Wireless Communications and Networking Conference (WCNC).
6. Jafarkhani, H. (2005). Space-Time Coding: Theory and Practice, First ed: Cambridge University Press.
7. Jagannathan, S.; Aghajan, H.; & Goldsmith, A. (2004). The effect of time synchronization errors on the performance of cooperative MISO systems, presented at IEEE Global Communications Conference (Globecom), Dallas, Texas, USA.
8. Karl, H. & Willig, A. (2007). MAC Protocols, In: Protocols and Architectures for Wireless Sensor Networks, pp. 111-148, John Wiley & Sons, 978-0-470-09510-2, West Sussex, England.
9. Kohvakka, M.; Kuorilehto, M.; Hannikainen, M. & Hamalainen, T.D. (2006). Performance Analysis of IEEE 802.15.4 and Zigbee for Large-scale Wireless Sensor Network Applications, Proceedings of ACM International Workshop on Performance Evaluation of Wireless Ad hoc, Sensor, and Ubiquitous Networks,, pp. 1-6, Malaga, Spain.
10. Kuorilehto, M.; Kohvakka, M.; Suhonen, J.; Hamalainen, P.; Hannikainen, M. & Hamalainen, T.D. (2007). MAC Protocols, In: Ultra-Low Energy Wireless Sensor Networks in Practice, pp. 73-88, John Wiley & Sons, 978-0-470-05786-5, West Sussex, England.

11. Larsson, E.G. & Stoica, P. (2003). Space-Time Block Coding for Wireless Communications, First ed. Cambridge, UK: Cambridge University Press.

12. Li, X. & Hwu, J. (2006). Performance of Cooperative Transmissions in Flat Fading Environment with Asynchronous Transmitters, presented at Military Communications Conference (MILCOM 2006), Washington DC, USA.

13. Li, X. (2004). Space-Time Coded Multi-Transmission Among Distributed Transmitters Without Perfect Synchronization, IEEE Signal Processing Letters, vol. 11, pp. 948- 951.

14. Li, X.; Chen, M.; & Liu, W. (2004). Cooperative Transmissions in Wireless Sensor Networks with Imperfect Synchronization, presented at Conference on Signals, Systems and Computers, Pacific Grove, CA.

15. Litva, J. & Lo, T.K.Y. (1996). Digital Beamforming in Wireless Communications: Artech House Publisher.

16. Liu, Z.; Giannakis, G.B.; Zhuo, S.; & Muquet, B. (2001). Space-time coding for broadband wireless communications, Wireless Communications and Mobile Computing, vol. 1, pp. 35-53.

17. Naquib. A.F. & Calderbank, R. (2000). Space time codes for high data rate wireless communications, in IEEE Signal Processing, vol. 47, pp. 76-92.

18. Proakis, J.G. (2001). Probability and Stochastic Processes, In: Digital Communications, pp. 17- 36, McGraw-Hill, 0-07-232111-3, Singapore, Singapore.

19. Rappaport, T.S. (2002). Wireless Communications: Principles and Practice, second ed. Upper Saddle River, NJ, USA: Pearson Education International.

20. Seshadri, N. & Winters, J.H. (1993). Two Signaling Schemes for Improving the Error Performance of Frequency-division-duplex (FDD) Transmission Systems using Transmitter Antenna Diversity, presented at IEEE Vehicular Technology Conference.

21. Simon, M.K. & Alouini, M.S. (2000). Digital Communication over Fading Channels: A Unified Approach to Performance Analysis: John Wiley & Sons.

22. Singh, M. & Prasanna, V.K. (2003). A Hierarchical Model for Distributed Collaborative Computation in Wireless Sensor Networks, presented at IEEE International Parallel and Distributed Processing Symposium.

23. Tarokh, V.; Jafarkhani, H.; & Calderbank, A.R. (1999). Space-time Block Codes from Orthogonal Designs, IEEE Transactions on Information Theory, vol. 45, pp. 1456- 1467.

24. Tarokh, V.; Seshadri, N.; & Calderbank, A.R. (1998). Space-time Codes for High Data Rate Wireless Communication: Performance Criterion and Code Construction, IEEE Transactions on Information Theory, vol. 44, pp. 744-765.

25. Vucetic, B. & Yuan, J. (2003). Space-Time Coding. West Sussex, England: John Wiley & Sons Ltd.

26. Winters, J.H. (1983). Switched diversity with feedback for DPSK mobile radio systems, IEEE Transactions on Vehicular Technology, vol. 32, pp. 134-150.

27. Wittneben, A. (1991). Base Station Modulation Diversity for Digital SIMULCAST, presented at IEEE Vehicular Technology Conference.

28. Yang, H.; Shen, H.-Y. & Sikdar, B. (2007). A MAC Protocol for Cooperative MIMO Transmissions in Sensor Networks, Proceedings of IEEE Global Telecommunications Conference (GLOBECOM), pp. 636-640, Washington, USA.

29. Yuksel, M. & Erkip, E. (2004). Diversity Gains and Clustering in Wireless Relaying, presented at IEEE International Symposium of Information Theory.

8 Chapter OPTIMAL COOPERATIVE MIMO STRATEGY IN WIRELESS SENSOR NETWORKS

1. INTRODUCTION: AN OVERVIEW

Cooperative Multiple-Input Multiple-Output (MIMO) has been suggested as a transmission approach to mitigate the fading issue in Wireless Sensor Networks (WSNs), thereby decreasing the chance of retransmission and minimizing transmission energy consumption. One of the initial studies on cooperative MIMO in wireless sensor networks (WSNs) is the examination of the Space-Time Block Coding (STBC) method to attain reduced Bit Error Rate (BER) and considerable energy conservation. The project proceeds with the implementation of the Low Energy Adaptive Clustering Hierarchy (LEACH) Medium Access Control (MAC) protocol for cluster-based architectures. The integration of STBC with the LEACH protocol led to a considerable enhancement in transmission energy efficiency relative to the Single-Input Single-Output (SISO) system.

Additional research is undertaken to evaluate the efficacy of Space-Time Block Coding (STBC) against other Spatial Multiplexing (SM) methodologies, including Vertical Bell Labs Layered Space-Time (V-BLAST) and Diagonal BLAST. This study employed LEACH MAC, resulting in reduced transmission energy and latency compared to the SISO method. The centralized architecture results in energy inefficiency and increased latency relative to a distributed system. The implementation of a distributed architecture must address synchronization difficulties. Therefore, a functional cooperative MIMO strategy for distributed asynchronous wireless sensor networks is required.

Furthermore, a functional MAC suitable for cooperative transmission is necessary. The integration of a pragmatic MAC protocol with an effective MIMO scheme for asynchronous cooperative transmission results in a more energy-efficient and lower-latency cooperative MIMO system. A prior work introduced a hybrid MAC protocol and cooperative SM scheme for cooperative MIMO transmission, resulting in enhanced energy efficiency and reduced delay.

Moreover, a transmit Maximum Ratio Combiner (MRC) strategy is proposed to exhibit greater tolerance to jitter discrepancies compared to the Alamouti Space-Time Coding (STC) scheme in networks with inconsistent synchronization among sending nodes. This chapter extends the research to two further cooperative MIMO schemes: Beamforming (BF) and Space-Time Block Coding (STBC), addressing both scenarios of perfect and poor synchronization among transmitting nodes. The ideal cooperative MIMO strategy, coupled with a suitable MAC protocol, should result in minimal energy usage and reduced packet latency.

2. SYSTEM MODEL

The baseline system for cooperative MIMO communication is equipped with a CMACON protocol as proposed and evaluated in (Yang et. al., 2007). Sleep cycles are not implemented in order to ensure that the cooperative nodes are always available to perform cooperative transmission and reception. In order to avoid collision, we assume that during the cooperative transmission and reception, other nodes in the vicinity that are not involved in the transmission are put in the silent mode for the whole transmission duration. The duration to remain silent is obtained from the Network Allocation Vector (NAV).

Also in this chapter we consider the impact of imperfect synchronisation caused by clock jitter alone. Each cooperative transmitting node experiences clock jitter with the jitter around a reference clock, To denoted as m where 1 ≤ m ≤ M . The worst case scenario is considered here with only 2 cooperative transmitting nodes where the clock jitters are fixed at the extreme ends, T 1 = - ΔTb ,T 2 = + ΔTb where 0 ≤ ΔT j2≤ Tj and Tb2 is the bit duration. Thus the clock jitters difference is ΔTj = T 1j - T 2j = ΔTb . The effect of imperfect synchronisation can be modelled as a degrading function of the bit period which consequently degrades the received bit energy.

In this section, we introduce two kinds of network configurations. The first network configuration involves data transmission from M cooperating transmitting nodes to one destination node by utilizing either of the two MIMO schemes: BF or STBC. An RTS-CTS handshaking method is performed as described in (Yang et. al., 2007) and the source node broadcasts the original data packet to its M-1 neighbours.

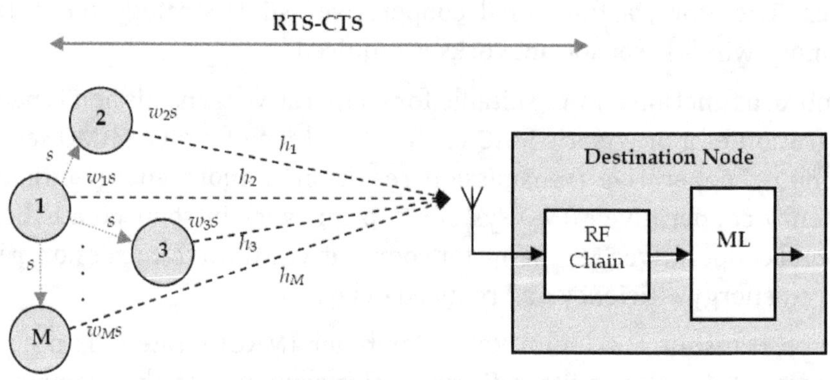

Fig. 1. A cooperative beamforming transmit diversity system with M transmit nodes and 1 destination.

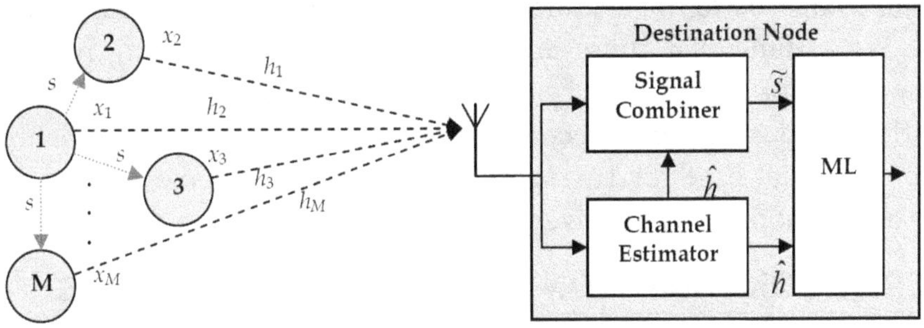

Fig. 2. A cooperative STBC transmit diversity system with M transmit nodes and 1 destination.

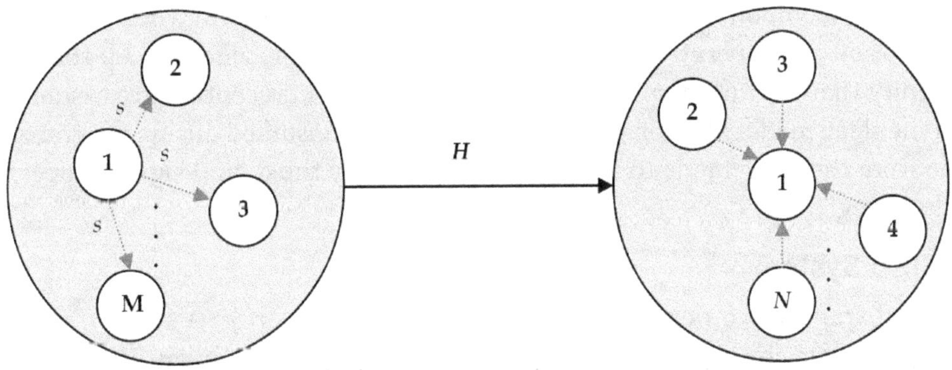

Fig. 3. A cooperative spatial multiplexing system with M transmit nodes and N receive nodes. In the case of the BF scheme, the channel information is estimated and optimized from the CTS packet by all the M nodes in order to weight the data packet. In the case of the STBC scheme, all the M nodes encode the original data packet with the information supplied by the source node in the broadcast packet. Both schemes utilize a Maximum Likelihood (ML) detector and a coherent receiver is used. The second network configuration is the data transmission from M cooperating transmitting nodes to N cooperating receiving nodes by utilizing the concept of SM. The recovered data from N-1 nodes is forwarded to the destination node.

The baseline network configurations for MISO BF and STBC are shown in Figures 1 and 2 while for MIMO SM it is shown in Figure 3. The network is assumed to be distributed without any infrastructure and the nodes are fixed once they are deployed. A new node that wants to join the network should broadcast a packet after powering up to acknowledge its presence in the neighbourhood. A node checks its remaining energy regularly and when its total remaining energy is below the threshold, which indicates that its death is near, it informs the other nodes in the vicinity of the expected death time. Therefore the neighbouring nodes will exclude this node from any future cooperative MIMO transmission. The distance between the cooperating nodes either at the transmitting or receiving side is assumed to be very small compared to the distance between the source node and the destination node, d. We assume that there are M cooperative transmitting nodes and one receiving node for the perfect synchronisation scenario and M = 2 cooperative transmitting nodes and one receiving node for the imperfect synchronisation scenario. A special case for the spatial multiplexing scheme is used where the number of the cooperative receivers is assumed to be N.

3. ENERGY CONSUMPTION PERFORMANCE ANALYSIS

The energy consumed by a sensor node can be categorized into two major parts (Cui et. al, 2004; Nguyen et. al., 2007): energy expended during running the transceiver circuits, Pc and energy expended during packet transmission, Pt. Therefore, both energy components must be considered when comparing the total energy consumption of cooperative MIMO and SISO transmission schemes. All the nodes in vicinity that are not involved in the transmission and reception are assumed to be in the sleep mode. Also for simplicity, the energy consumed during the transient mode from the sleep mode to the active mode and by the digital signal processing blocks is neglected.

3.1 SISO System

To model transmission energy for the non-cooperative or SISO system, we start with the power consumed by the power amplifier, Ppa. As given in (Cui et. al., 2004; Nguyen et. al., 2007), Ppa is dependent on the transmit power Pt and can be approximated as:

$$P_{pa} = (1+\alpha)P_t \quad (1)$$

where α= Ξ /n-1 with Ξ denoting the drain efficiency of the Radio Frequency (RF) power amplifier and ηdenoting the Peak-to-Average Ratio (PAR) which depends on the modulation scheme and the associated constellation size. The total circuit power is given by:

$$Pc \approx (M \times Pct) + (N \times Pcr) \quad (2)$$

where Pcr = PLNA + Pmix + PIFA + Pfilr + PADC + Psyn and Pct = PDAC + Pmix + Pfilt + Psyn are values for the power consumption of the Digital-to-Analogue Converter (DAC), mixer, Low Noise Amplifier (LNA), Intermediate Frequency Amplifier (IFA), active filters at the transmitter and the receiver, Analogue-to-Digital Converter (ADC) and frequency synthesizer whose values and a detailed block diagram are given in (Cui et. al., 2004; Nguyen et. al., 2007). Therefore, the total energy consumption per bit system can be obtained as:

$$E_{bt} = \frac{\left(P_{pa} + P_c\right)}{R_b} \tag{3}$$

when M = N = 1. Equations (1) and (2) can be used to model the cooperative BF, STBC and SM systems with an arbitrary number of M and N. For the traditional Carrier Sense Multiple Access with Collision Avoidance (CSMA-CA) protocol, the energy consumed for an unsuccessful transmission attempt is given as:

$$Eu\_siso = Erts + Ects + Edata\_siso \tag{4}$$

and that for a successful attempt is given as:

$$Es\_siso = Erts + Ects + Edata\_siso + Eack \tag{5}$$

where Erts , Ects , Edata _ siso , Eack are the energy consumed while sending Ready-to-Send (RTS), Clear-to-Send (CTS), SISO data and Acknowledgment (ACK). Given the size of each packet as Nrts, Ncts, Ndata_siso and Nack, Equations (4) and (5) can be rewritten as:

$$E_{u\_siso} - E_{bt}\left(N_{rts} + N_{cts} + N_{data\_siso}\right) \tag{6}$$

$$E_{s\_siso} = E_{bt}\left(N_{rts} + N_{cts} + N_{data\_siso} + N_{ack}\right). \tag{7}$$

The expected total energy consumption is given as:

$$E_{siso} = \left(\frac{P_{psiso}}{1 - P_{psiso}}\right) E_{u\_siso} + E_{s\_siso} \tag{8}$$

where P*psiso* is the packet error probability of the SISO system which can be obtained in (Ahmad et. al., 2008)

3.2 Cooperative MIMO System

In this sub-section, we consider two scenarios where the first scenario involves transmission from M cooperating transmitting nodes to 1 destination node with a local exchange of information at the transmitting side. This scenario applies to the cooperative MISO BF and STBC schemes. The second scenario deals with transmissions from M cooperating transmitting nodes to N receiving nodes with local exchanges at both the transmitting and receiving sides. This scenario applies to the cooperative MIMO SM scheme.

To model transmission energy for the first scenario, we start with the power consumed by the power amplifier, PpaBs during a local exchange between the source node and its cooperating neighbours. PpaBs is dependent on the local exchange transmitted power Ptm and can be approximated as:

$$PpaBs = (1 + \alpha)Ptm . \tag{9}$$

The total circuit power for the local exchange is given by:

$$PcBs \approx Pct + (M - 1)\times Pcr . \tag{10}$$

Therefore the total energy consumption per bit EbtBs for the local exchange can be obtained as:

$$E_{btBs} = \frac{\left(P_{paBs} + P_{cBs}\right)}{R_b} . \tag{11}$$

The energy consumed for an unsuccessful BF and STBC transmissions attempt is given as:

$$Eu\_sM = Erts + Ects + EBs + M . Edata\_sM \tag{12}$$

and that for a successful attempt is given as:

$$Es\_M = Eu\_M + Eack \tag{13}$$

where EBs and Edata _ M are the amounts of energy consumed during packet broadcasting from the source node to its neighbours and the energy consumed for Cooperative BF or STBC data transmission. Given the size of each packet as Nrts, Ncts, NBs, Ndata_M and Nack,, Equations (12) and (13) can be rewritten as:

$$E_{u\_M} = E_{bt}\left(N_{rts} + N_{cts}\right) + E_{bt\,Bs} N_{Bs} + M \cdot E_{bt\,data\_M} N_{data\_M} \tag{14}$$

$$E_{s\_M} = E_{u\_M} + E_{bt} \times N_{ack} . \tag{15}$$

The expected total energy consumption is given as:

$$E_M = \left(\frac{P_{pM}}{1 - P_{pM}}\right) E_{u\_M} + E_{s\_M} \tag{16}$$

where PpM is the packet error probability for BF or STBC which can be obtained in (Ahmad et. al., 2008). To model transmission energy for the second scenario, we start with the power consumed by the power amplifier, PpaBr from the destination node to its cooperating receiving nodes and PpaCol from N-1 receiving nodes to the destination node. PpaBr and PpaCol are dependent on the local exchange transmit power Ptm and can be approximated as:

$$PpaBr = (1 + \alpha)Ptm \tag{17}$$

$$PpaCol = (1 + \alpha)Ptm\,(N - 1) . \tag{18}$$

The total circuit power for the former case is given by:

$$PcBr \approx Pct + (N - 1) \times Pcr \quad (19)$$

and the total circuit power for the latter case is given by:

$$PcCol \approx (N - 1) \times Pct + Pcr . \quad (20)$$

Therefore the total energy consumption per bit EbtBr and EbtCol for both cases can be obtained as:

$$E_{btBr} = \frac{\left(P_{paBr} + P_{cBr}\right)}{R_b} \quad (21)$$

$$E_{btCol} = \frac{\left(P_{paCol} + P_{cCol}\right)}{R_b}. \quad (22)$$

The energy consumed for an unsuccessful SM transmission attempt is given as:

$$Eu\_SM = Erts + EBr + Ects + EBs + M . Edata\_SM + (N - 1). ECol \quad (23)$$

and that for a successful attempt is given as:

$$Es\_SM = Eu\_SM + Eack \quad (24)$$

where

EBr , ECol and Edata _ SM are the energy consumed during packet broadcasting from the destination node to its neighbours, the energy consumed by N-1 cooperating receiving nodes to the destination node and the energy consumed for the cooperative SM data transmission. Given the size of each packet as Nrts, Ncts, NBs, Ndata_SM and Nack, Equations (23) and (24) can be rewritten as:

$$E_{u\_SM} = E_{bt}\left(N_{rts} + N_{cts}\right) + E_{btBr}N_{Br} + E_{btBs}N_{Bs} + M \cdot E_{btdata\_SM}N_{data\_SM} + (N-1)E_{btCol}N_{Col} \quad (25)$$

$$E_{s\_SM} = E_{u\_SM} + \left(E_{bt} \times N_{ack}\right). \quad (26)$$

The expected total energy consumption is given as:

$$E_{SM} = \left(\frac{P_{pSM}}{1 - P_{pSM}}\right)E_{u\_SM} + E_{s\_SM} \quad (27)$$

where PpSM is the packet error probability of cooperative MIMO with spatial multiplexing which can be obtained in (Yang et. al., 2007). The values of the system parameters used in Figures 4 to 7 are listed in Table 1 (Cui et. al., 2004; Yang et. al., 2007).

Table 1. system parameter for energy consumption modeling

Symbol	Quantity
Nrts	65 bits
Ncts	55 bits
Nack	54 bits
NBs	1300 bits
NBr	120 bits
Ndata = NCol	1024 bits
Pmix	30.3mW
Psyn	50mW
Pfilt = Pfilr	2.5mW
PADC	9.85mW
PDAC	15.48mW
PLNA	20mW
PIFA	3mW

4. PACKET LATENCY PERFORMANCE ANALYSIS

As we noted earlier, each packet transmission in cooperative transmission requires more steps which introduces more overhead. These steps may increase packet delays. However, the reduction of PER as the diversity gain increases from the cooperative MIMO exploitation can reduce the retransmissions rates which in turn can reduce packet latency. Sub-section models packet latency performance for the non-cooperative SISO system. Comparison is then made with the models developed for the cooperative MIMO systems in Sub-section 4.2. The performance results are discussed in Section 5.

4.1 SISO System

For SISO communication, Trts, Tcts, Tdata and Tack are the transmission periods for the RTS, CTS, DATA and ACK packets. The period with a successful transmission attempt is given as:

$$Ts\_siso = Trts + Tcts + Tdata + Tack \tag{28}$$

and the period with an unsuccessful transmission attempt is given as:

$$Tu\_siso = Trts + Tcts + Tdata + Twait \tag{29}$$

where Twait is the duration for which the sender waits for an ACK packet. The packet transmission delay is then given as:

$$T_{d\_SISO} = \left(\frac{P_{psiso}}{1-P_{psiso}}\right)T_{u\_siso} + T_{s\_siso}. \tag{30}$$

4.2 Cooperative MIMO System

In addition to the delay incurred as calculated in the previous section, the broadcast packet transmission from the source node to its neighbours introduces a broadcast transmission period, TBs in cooperative BF, STBC and SM transmissions. The transmission period of cooperative BF, STBC and SM data packets is the same as that for the SISO system due to the fact that the packet size and the modulation scheme are the same. The duration of a successful transmission attempt is given as:

$$Ts\_M = Trts + Tcts + TBs + Tdata + Tack \tag{31}$$

and the period with an unsuccessful transmission attempt is given as:

$$Tu\_M = Trts + Tcts + TBs + Tdata + Twait\,. \tag{32}$$

The expected packet transmission delay is then given by:

$$T_{d\_M} = \left(\frac{P_{pM}}{1-P_{pM}}\right)T_{u\_M} + T_{s\_M}\,. \tag{33}$$

For the case of cooperative MIMO SM, we introduce the delay for the broadcast transmission time of a recruitment message sent by the destination node, TBr and the delay for the time required by the cooperating receiving nodes (N-1) to send the data to the destination, Tcol . The duration of a successful transmission attempt is given as:

$$Ts\_SM = Ts\_M + TBr + Tcol \tag{34}$$

and the period with an unsuccessful transmission attempt is given as:

$$Tu\_SM = Ts\_SM\ Twait - Tack\,. \tag{35}$$

The expected packet transmission delay is then given by:

$$T_{d\_SM} = \left(\frac{P_{pSM}}{1-P_{pSM}}\right)T_{u\_SM} + T_{s\_SM}\,. \tag{36}$$

The values of the system parameters used in Figures 8 to 11 are as follows: Trts = 0.52ms, Tcts = 0.44ms, Tack = 0.432ms, TBs = 10.4ms, TBr = 0.96ms, Tdata = 8.192ms, Tcol = 22.3ms (Nguyen et. al., 2007), and Twait = 70ms (Yang et. al., 2007).

5. PERFORMANCE RESULTS AND DISCUSSIONS

As shown in Figure 4, SISO is more energy efficient than the cooperative schemes at transmission powers above 100mW with any number of M and N nodes. The cooperative SM scheme suffers more in terms of energy efficiency because the total energy consumption is increasing as the diversity gain and the number of nodes M increases. The cooperative BF and STBC schemes suffer only with the increasing of the diversity gain.

As we noted earlier the cooperative schemes are more energy efficient when the transmission power is below 100mW. We can see in Figure 5, that the cooperative BF and STBC schemes outperform the cooperative SM scheme and that the cooperative BF scheme is more energy efficient than the cooperative STBC scheme with two transmitting nodes.

For imperfect synchronisation scenarios, as shown in Figure 6, in the case of equal diversity gain for all the schemes, the cooperative BF scheme is more energy efficient than the other schemes. However, as the diversity gain of the cooperative SM scheme is increased, as shown in Figure 7, cooperative SM outperforms the other schemes in terms of energy efficiency at and above 0.8Tb in the region of operating transmission power for WSNs (common operating transmission power is between 20mW to 60mW (Polastre et. al., 2004; Kohvakka et. Al., 2006; Kuorilehto et. al., 2007). These results indicate that if we allow some delays to occur within a particular range during transmission, the cooperative SM scheme can achieve a significant energy saving. However, by relaxing the synchronisation algorithm with 0.4Tb jitters tolerance, the cooperative BF scheme can achieve the highest energy saving among the other schemes.

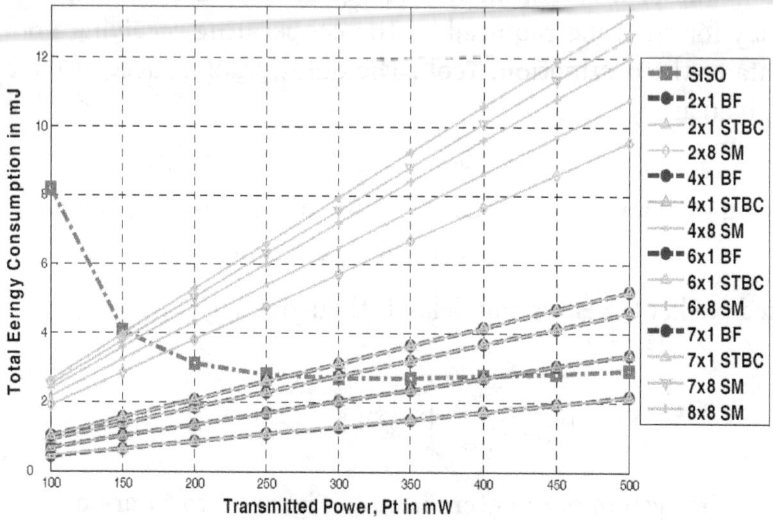

Fig. 4. Total energy consumption vs. transmission power for various schemes with M = 2, 4, 6, 7, 8 and N = 1 (Cooperative BF and STBC) and N = 8 (Cooperative SM).

As shown in Figures 8 and 9, the SISO scheme outperforms the cooperative schemes at the transmission power region above 800mW. At the lower transmission power region, the three cooperative schemes outperform the SISO scheme. The cooperative SM scheme enjoys a lower transmission delay when the diversity gain is increasing with any arbitrary number of transmitting nodes with one condition that the number of cooperative SM receiving N nodes must be greater than the number of M nodes in cooperative BF and STBC. It also important to note that cooperative BF outperforms cooperative STBC when M = 2.

For imperfect synchronisation scenarios, as shown in Figures 10 and 11, at the lower transmission power region, the three cooperative schemes outperform the SISO scheme. The cooperative BF scheme enjoys lower packet latency and outperforms the other schemes even when the diversity gain of the cooperative SM scheme is increased.

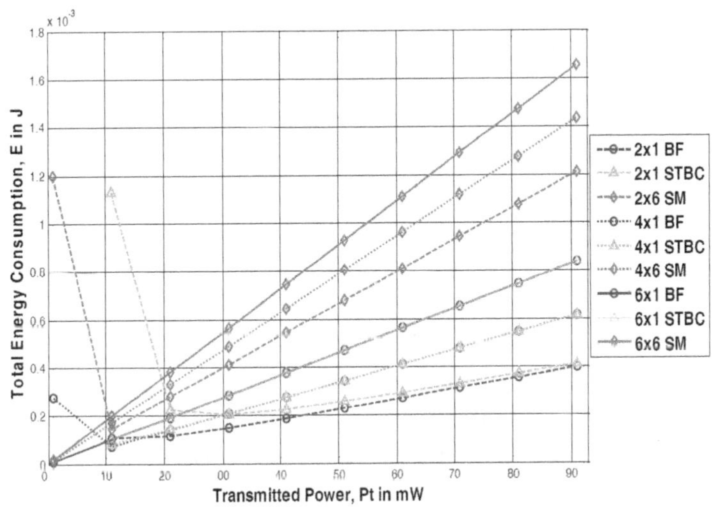

Fig. 5. Total energy consumption vs. transmission power for various schemes with M = 2, 4, 6 and N = 1 (Cooperative BF and STBC) and N = 6 (Cooperative SM).

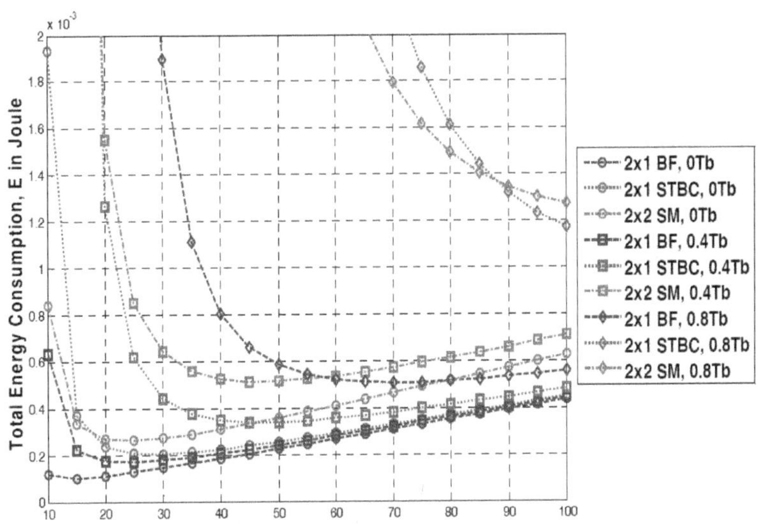

Fig. 6. Total energy consumption vs. transmission power (lower region) for various imperfect synchronisation schemes with M = 2 and N = 1 (Cooperative BF and STBC) and N = 2 (Cooperative SM).

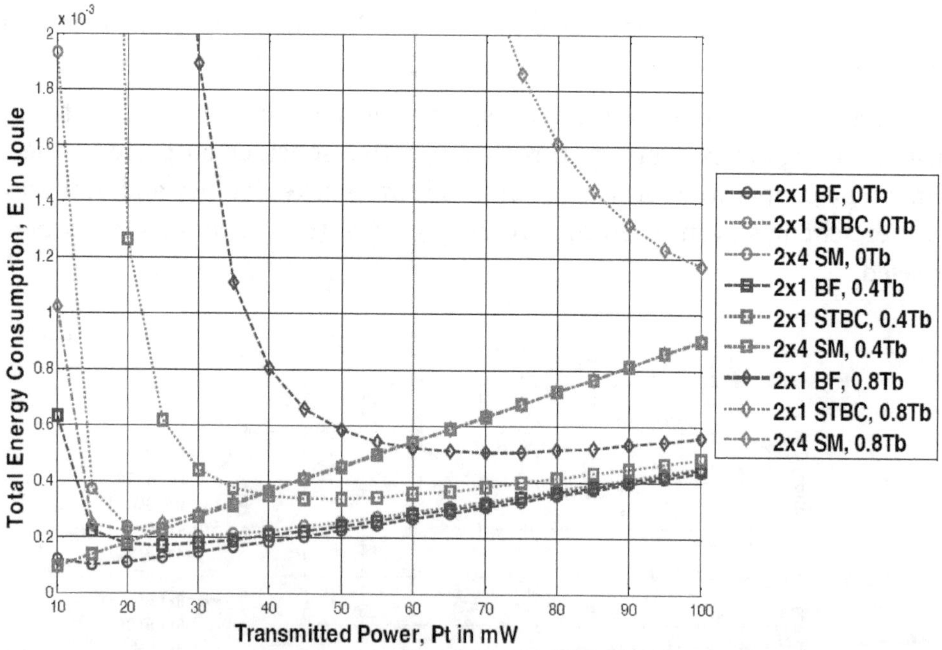

Fig. 7. Total energy consumption vs. transmission power (lower region) for various imperfect synchronisation schemes with M = 2 and N = 1 (Cooperative BF and STBC) and N = 4 (Cooperative SM).

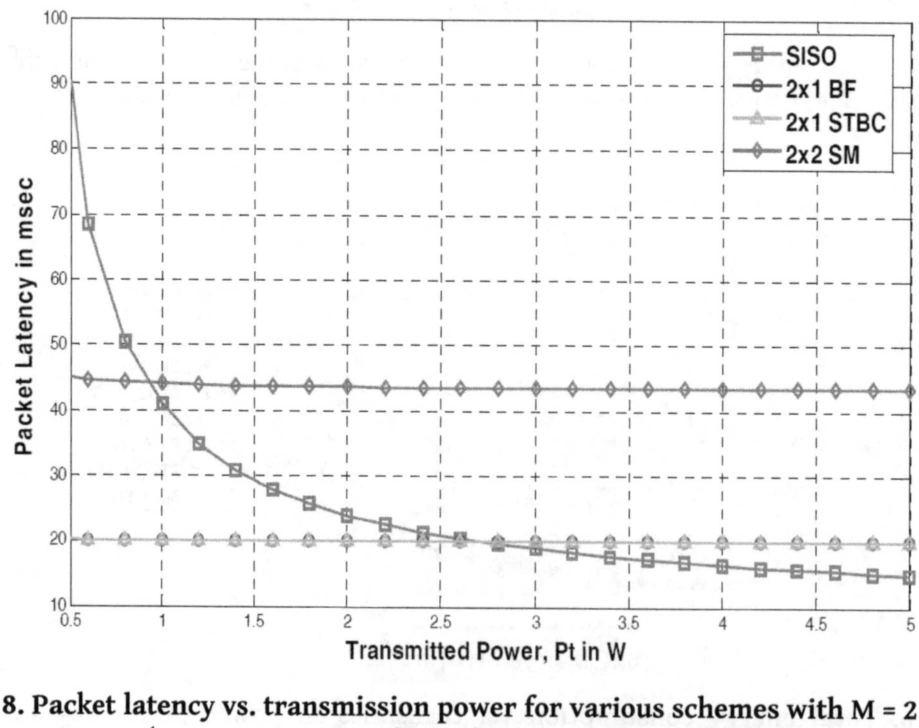

Fig. 8. Packet latency vs. transmission power for various schemes with M = 2 and N = 1 (Cooperative BF and STBC) and N = 2 (Cooperative SM).

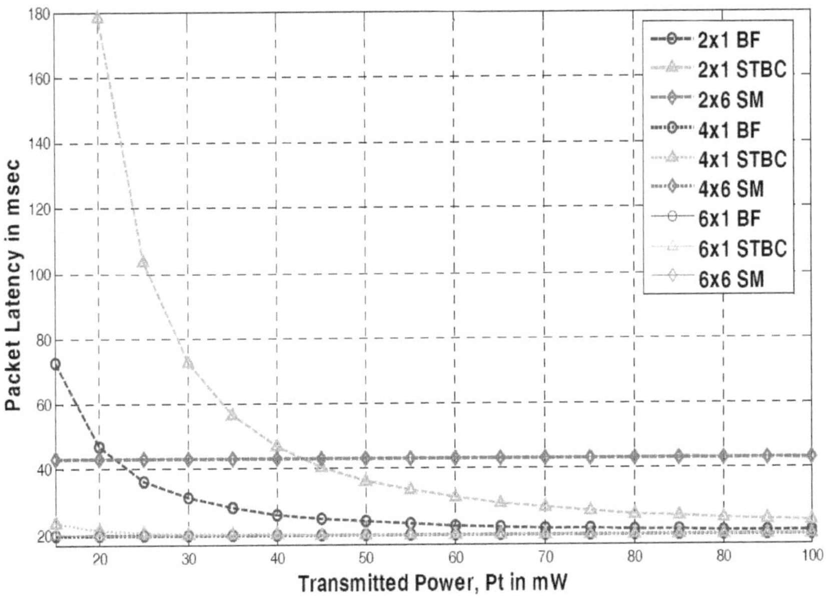

Fig. 9. Packet latency vs. transmission power for various schemes with M = 2, 4, and 6 and N = 1 (Cooperative BF and STBC) and N = 6 (Cooperative SM).

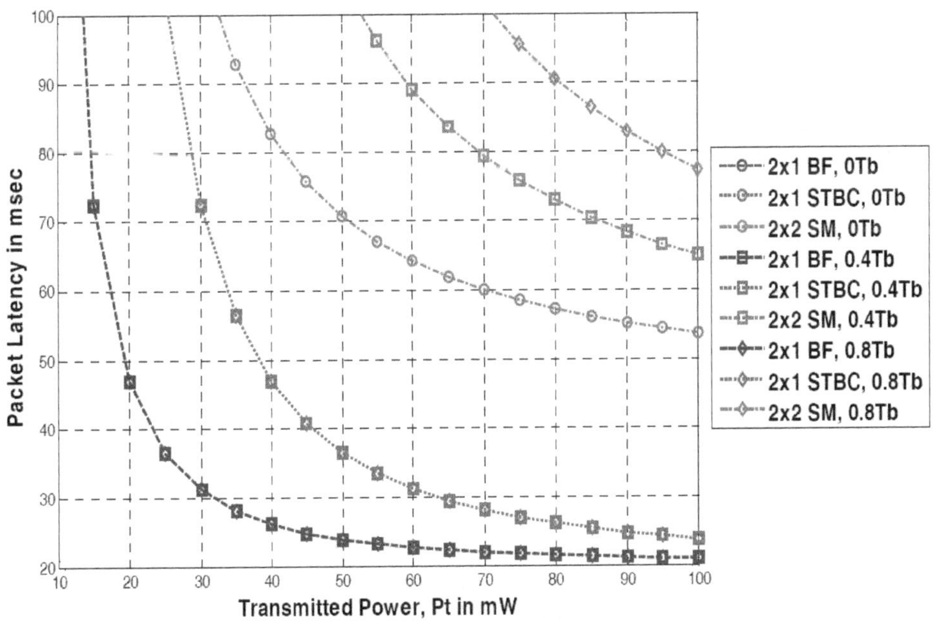

Fig. 10. Packet latency vs. transmission power (lower region) for various imperfect synchronisation schemes with M = 2 and N = 1 (Cooperative BF and STBC) and N = 2 (Cooperative SM).

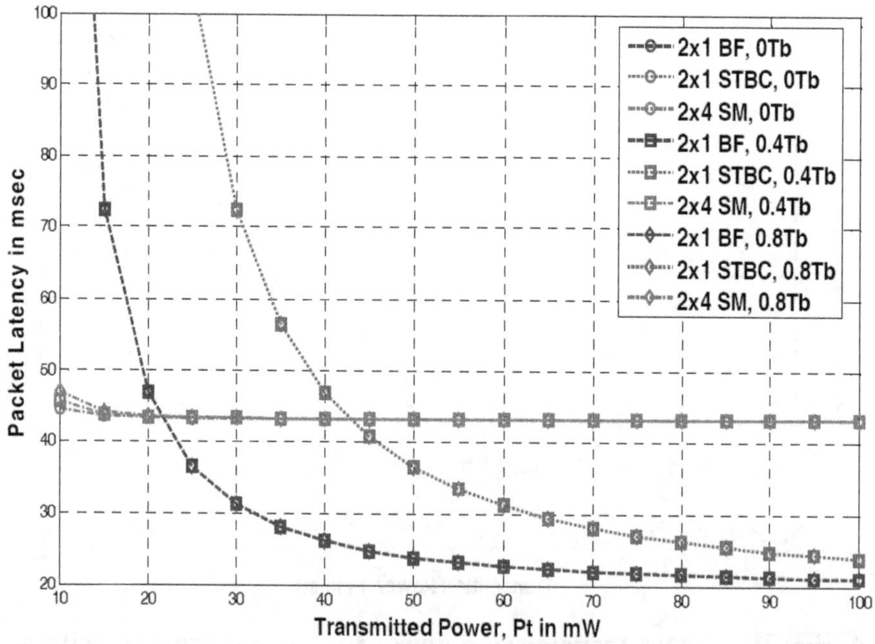

Fig. 11. Packet latency vs. transmission power (lower region) for various imperfect synchronisation schemes with M = 2 and N = 1 (Cooperative BF and STBC) and N = 4 (Cooperative SM).

6. CONCISE SUMMARY

This chapter provides a comparative analysis of three cooperative MIMO methods in wireless sensor networks (WSNs). We have constructed analytical models for Bit Error Rate (BER) and Packet Error Rate (PER) to predict retransmission rates based on PER, as referenced in Ahmad et al. (2008). These models are employed to assess the overall energy consumption and packet delay of the cooperative systems discussed in this chapter. The SISO method has superior energy efficiency and reduced delay at elevated transmission power levels, whereas the three cooperative MIMO schemes exhibit greater energy efficiency and surpass the SISO scheme at lower power levels. In the higher transmission power range, the SISO scheme exhibits reduced transceiver circuit energy consumption and incurs no energy expenditure for constructing a cooperative mechanism, in contrast to cooperative MIMO systems. These results impose a limitation on the ideal transmission power, or correspondingly, the optimal distance to be utilized in the implementation of cooperative MIMO transmission in wireless sensor networks.

The analysis indicates that in the lower transmission power range, the cooperative optimal BF scheme surpasses both the cooperative SM and STBC schemes regarding energy efficiency and packet latency, applicable to both perfect and imperfect synchronization conditions. We see that the cooperative BF scheme with M = 2 nodes constitutes an efficient cooperative system. Subsequent efforts will focus on the creation of MAC protocols optimized for cooperative transmission schemes, with the objective of establishing an optimal cooperative transmission mechanism for application in distributed WSNs.

REFERENCES

1. Ahmad, M.R.; Dutkiewicz, E.; & Huang, X. (2008). Performance Analysis of Cooperative MIMO Transmission Schemes in WSN, to be presented at the IEEE International Symposium on Personal, Indoor and Mobile Radio Communications (PIMRC), Cannes, France.
2. Cui, S.; Goldsmith, A.J.; & Bahai, A. (2004). Energy-efficient of MIMO and Cooperative MIMO Techniques in Sensor Networks, IEEE Journal on Selected Areas in Communications, vol. 22, issue 6, pp. 1089-1098.
3. Kohvakka, M.; Kuorilehto, M.; Hannikainen, M. & Hamalainen, T.D. (2006). Performance Analysis of IEEE 802.15.4 and Zigbee for Large-scale Wireless Sensor Network Applications, Proceedings of ACM International Workshop on Performance Evaluation of Wireless Ad hoc, Sensor, and Ubiquitous Networks,, pp. 1-6, Malaga, Spain.
4. Kuorilehto, M.; Kohvakka, M.; Suhonen, J.; Hamalainen, P.; Hannikainen, M. & Hamalainen, T.D. (2007). MAC Protocols, In: Ultra-Low Energy Wireless Sensor Networks in Practice, pp. 73-88, John Wiley & Sons, 978-0-470-05786-5, West Sussex, England.
5. Nguyen, T.D.; Berder, O.; & Sentieys, O. (2007). Cooperative MIMO Schemes Optimal Selection for Wireless Sensor Networks, presented at IEEE Vehicular Technology Conference (VTC2007), Baltimore, MD, USA.
6. Polastre, J.; Hill, J.; & Culler, D. (2004). Versatile Low Power Media Access for Wireless Sensor Networks, presented at The ACM Conference on Embedded Networked Sensor Systems (Sensys), Baltimore, Maryland, USA.
7. Yang, H.; Shen, H.-Y. & Sikdar, B. (2007). A MAC Protocol for Cooperative MIMO Transmissions in Sensor Networks, Proceedings of IEEE Global Telecommunications Conference (GLOBECOM), pp. 636-640, Washington, USA

9 Chapter | DIFFERENTIAL CAPACITY OF SINGLE/MULTI-USER MIMO

1. INTRODUCTION: AN OVERVIEW

This chapter will be organized around two contributions by the authors, (Castanheira & Gameiro 2008) and (Castanheira & Gameiro 2009).

The availability of broadband services to all is regarded as a fundamental element for facilitating the information society. It is generally agreed that achieving the high data rates projected by IMT-2000 (I. R. R. M. M1645 2003) of approximately 1 Gbit/s for pedestrians and 100 Mbit/s for high mobility necessitates the implementation of multiple antennas at the transceivers to leverage the scattering characteristics of the wireless medium. However, the physical size constraints of the transceivers restrict the number of antennas and limit the spacing between them, indicating that the level of channel independence attained is inadequate to reach the anticipated high capacity in most cases. A potential way to address this issue is to enable the mobile devices to concurrently communicate with a network of geographically dispersed antennas that exhibit optimal cooperation. The essential factor for attaining optimal cooperation is the transparent transmission and reception of radio signals to and from a central unit (CU), where all signal processing occurs (FUTON 2008). Given the substantial capacities anticipated, optical fiber, characterized by its minimal attenuation and vast bandwidth, is the evident technology of choice for constructing these transparent linkages. The collective processing of a collection of antennas and the remote transmission of their signals to the Central Unit will necessitate increased processing power and incur additional costs to the overall network. According to the law of diminishing returns, it is anticipated that as additional antennas are collectively processed, the enhancement in throughput will not rise linearly with the increased complexity. Consequently, a compromise must be established between the costs/complexity and the quantity of antennas utilized. A potential solution to mitigate the complexity issue is the implementation of low complexity/sub-optimal techniques, such as Zero-Forcing (ZF) (Caire & Shamai 2003) or Block-Diagonalization (BD) (Seijoon Shim et al. 2008) at the Central Unit (CU). In accordance with this reasoning, Jindal (2005) and Juyul Lee & Jindal (2007) examine the incurred losses, regarding power/rate offsets, between Zero-Forcing/Block Diagonal (ZF/BD) and the best method, recognized as Dirty Paper Coding (DPC). The authors determine that losses increase when the quantity of send antennas approaches the total number of receive antennas. The subsequent analysis of the benefits derived from connecting system users to additional transmit antennas is crucial, either for estimating a "reasonable" number of antennas for joint processing, for assessing whether it is advantageous to provide an extra connection to mobile devices in a distributed antenna system (DAS), for offering guidelines for the deployment of distributed antennas, or for comparing sub-optimal schemes with the optimal configuration. In this context, we define Differential CAPacity (DCAP) as the augmentation in ergodic sum-capacity resulting from the addition of one transmit antenna to the system users, in order to quantify the benefits conferred by the processing of an extra transmit antenna at the Central Unit and to examine its performance.This chapter is organized as follows: section 2 presents the channel model; section 3 describes the single-user and multi-user channel capacities. In section 4 and 5 the DCAP, for the single-user and multi-user scenarios, is studied. In section 6 numerical results are provided and finally in section 7 some conclusions are drawn.

2. CHANNEL MODEL

Throughout this chapter a Distributed Multiple-Input Multiple-Output (MIMO) Broadcast channel with K users, each with N receive antennas, and M transmit antennas is considered. A broadcast channel (BC) is a communication channel in which there is one sender and two or more receivers (Cover 1972). For a broadcast channel, the user k received signal, $\mathbf{y}_k(\in \mathbb{C}^{N\times 1})$ can be modeled by:

$$\mathbf{y}_k = \mathbf{H}_k\mathbf{x} + \mathbf{n}_k, \quad k = 1, \ldots, K \tag{1}$$

where $\mathbf{H}_k(\in \mathbb{C}^{N\times M})$ is the user channel matrix, $\mathbf{x}(\in \mathbb{C}^{M\times 1})$is the transmitted signal vector with power constraint $\mathbb{E}[\mathbf{x}\mathbf{x}^H] \leq P$ and $\mathbf{n}_k(\in \mathbb{C}^{N\times 1})$ is complex white Gaussian noise with zero mean and unit variance per vector component $(\tilde{\mathcal{N}}_N(\mathbf{0}, \mathbf{I}))$. $\mathbf{H}^H = [\mathbf{H}_1^H, \ldots, \mathbf{H}_K^H]$ denotes the concatenation of all channels and is matrix-variate complex Gaussian distributed (Shin & Lee 2003), with zero mean and covariance $\mathbf{\Sigma}(\in \mathbb{C}^{KNM\times KNM})$. Through the chapter it is assumed that the receiver has perfect knowledge of its own channel and the transmitter has perfect knowledge of all channels, for each channel realization. Since a DAS is considered all channel gains are independent $\mathbf{\Sigma}$(is diagonal).

Notations: Boldface letter denote matrix-vector quantities. The operation $tr(.)$, $(.)^H$ and $|.|$ represents the trace, the Hermitian transpose and the determinant of a matrix, respectively. By $\mathbf{A} > 0$ and $\mathbf{\Gamma}$ we denote that is positive $\mathbf{A}$ definite and an $n \times n$ identity matrix. The notation $\mathbf{a} \sim \tilde{\mathcal{N}}_p(0, \mathbf{\Sigma})$ and $\mathbf{B} \sim \tilde{\mathcal{W}}_p(n, \mathbf{\Gamma})$ is used to denote that the column vector is distributed as p-variate complex Gaussian, with zero mean and covariance $\Sigma \in \mathbb{C}^{p\times p}$, and to denote that matrix $\mathbf{B} \in \mathbb{C}^{p\times p}$ is complex Wishart distributed, with degrees of freedom and with$\mathbf{a}$ mean . The notation $\mathbf{A} \sim \mathbf{B}$ denotes that matrix$\mathbf{A}$ and $\mathbf{B}$ are identically distributed.

3. SINGLE/MULTI-USER SUM-CAPACITY

3.1 Single-User case

For the single-user case, if only one receive antenna is considered, the system reduces to the classical multiple input single output (MISO) system. As a consequence, the resulting capacity expression are much simpler to analyze than for the general case of a multi-user system. Thus for this case, the system capacity and the corresponding DCAP is described in more detail, either to introduce the reader to the topic, either to provide some baseline work to be used in the multi-user case.

According to (Liu & Li 2005a) and (Goldsmith 2005), if only one user with one receive antenna is considered ($K = N = 1$), the ergodic channel capacity can be expressed by:1

$$C = \mathrm{E}_H \left[log \left| \mathrm{I}_1 + \frac{\mathbf{hQh}^H}{\sigma^2} \right| \right] \tag{2}$$

xC where $\mathbf{h} = [h_1, h_2, \ldots, h_M]$ is the channel matrix, $\mathbf{Q}$ is the transmit signal covariance matrix and σ^2 is the noise variance. Subject to a power constrain P, $\mathrm{Tr}(\mathbf{Q}) = P$, must be circularly symmetric complex Gaussian (Telatar 1999) and its correlation matrix, Q, must be diagonal2 (Visotsky & Madhow 2001), which is equivalent to independent transmit signals, for the ergodic channel capacity, C, to be maximal.

P;Taking into account that $\mathbf{Q}$ must be a diagonal matrix, $\mathbf{Q} = diag([P_1, P_2, \ldots, P_M])$, where P is the signal x mean transmit power, and knowing that a single antenna user is considered, N=1, the ergodic capacity formula reduce to:

$$C_M = \mathrm{E}_H \left[log \left(1 + \sum_{i=1}^{M} \frac{|h_i|^2 P_i}{\sigma^2} \right) \right] \tag{3}$$

From the previous expression it is easy to identify $\frac{|h_i|^2 P_i}{\sigma^2}$ as the link *i* SNR (γ_i), then the capacity expression can be put into the following equivalent format:3

$$C_M = \mathrm{E}_{\Gamma_M}[log(1+\gamma)] = \int_0^{\infty} log(1+\gamma) f_{\Gamma_M}(\gamma) d\gamma \tag{4}$$

where Γ_M is a random variable (RV) corresponding to the sum M of exponential distributed RVs with mean λ_i^{-1} each, which follow the pdf:

$$f_{\Gamma_M}(\gamma) = \sum_{i=1}^{L} \sum_{n=1}^{K_i} \frac{a_{in}}{(n-1)!} \gamma^{n-1} e^{-\lambda_i \gamma} \tag{5}$$

La_{in} where L is the number of different mean SNR's, λ_i^{-1} is the mean SNR of link *i*, *ki* is the number of antennas with SNR λ_i^{-1}, *ain* are constants related to the partial fraction expansion (Ghosh 2005) of the product of Erlang distribution characteristic functions (Gubner 2006) and $M = \sum_{i=1}^{L} K_i$. Finally, after the integral evaluation,

(Dohler et al. 2006) or (Gradshteyn & Ryzhik 1994), the ergodic channel capacity is given by:

$$C_M = \sum_{i=1}^{L}\sum_{n=1}^{K_i}\sum_{k=0}^{n-1}\frac{a_{in}}{\lambda_i^n}C_i(\lambda_i,k) \tag{6}$$

where

$$C_i(\lambda_i,k) = \frac{(-\lambda_i)^k}{k!}\left[C_0(\lambda_i) + u(k-1)\sum_{p=1}^{k}\frac{(p-1)!}{(-\lambda_i)^p}\right]$$
$$C_0(\lambda_i) = e^{\lambda_i}E_1(\lambda_i)$$

$C_0(\lambda_i)$ is equal to the capacity of the link associated with a single transmit antenna with SNR λ_i^{-1} and is also equal to $C_i(\lambda_i, 0)$. $E_1(x)$ denotes the exponential integral function, given by $E_1(x) = \int_x^{\infty} e^t/t\, dt$ and $u(n)$ is the unit step function.

3.2 Multi-User case

In this section we briefly describe the broadcast channel sum-capacity and an affine approximation to this sum-capacity, in the high SNR regime. This approximation will be used in the following sections to analyze the DCAP for the multi-user case.

The broadcast channel capacity was over a large number of years an active area of research, which has culminated with an article by Weingarten et al., (Weingarten et al. 2006), where the authors have shown that the DPC rate region is the capacity region of the Gaussian MIMO BC. For the multi-user case the capacity expression is not as easy to analyze as the one for the single-user case, due to some additional constraints in the transmit covariance matrix and from the fact that there is no known closed form solution for this matrix that maximizes the channel capacity (Jindal et al. 2005).

From the MIMO BC-MAC duality, (Vishwanath et al. 2003), (Viswanath & Tse 2003), (Wei Yu & Cioffi 2004), the DPC sum rate with a total power constraint P, $(\sum_k tr(\mathbf{Q}_k) \leq P)$, can be expressed, by:

$$\mathbf{C}_{DPC}^{(M,K,N)} = \max_{\sum_k tr(\mathbf{Q}_k)\leq P} log\left|\mathbf{I}_M + \sum_{k=1}^{K}\mathbf{H}_k^H\mathbf{Q}_k\mathbf{H}_k\right| = \max_{tr(\mathbf{Q})\leq P} log|\mathbf{I}_M + \mathbf{H}^H\mathbf{Q}\mathbf{H}| \tag{7}$$

where $\mathbf{Q}_k (\in \mathbb{C}^{N\times N})$ is the transmit covariance matrix in the dual MAC channel and $\mathbf{Q} = diag(\mathbf{Q}_1, \ldots, \mathbf{Q}_K)$ is a block-diagonal matrix. In the high SNR regime and for $KN < M$, equal power allocation, $\mathbf{Q}_k = \frac{P}{KN}\mathbf{I}_N$, is asymptotically optimal (Juyul Lee & Jindal 2007). As a byproduct of that, the following affine approximation to the sum-capacity can be made (Juyul Lee & Jindal 2007), (Shamai & Verdu 2001):

$$\mathbf{C}_{DPC}^{(M,K,N)} \approx KNlog\, P - KNlog\, KN + log|\mathbf{H}\mathbf{H}^H| \tag{8}$$

From this affine approximation it is easy to see that the sum-capacity scales linearly with the number of aggregate receive antennas and that this scaling factor is not dependent on the individual values of K or N , in the high SNR regime. However, for the case of more aggregate receive than transmit antennas, $KN > M$, equal power allocation ceases to be asymptotic optimal, since even for the standard degraded BC $(M = 1)$ the throughput is maximized by transmitting only to the best user (Caire & Shamai 2003).

4. SINGLE-USER DCAP

4.1 Exact Expression

In this sub-section we obtain an exact expression for the DCAP considering the the single- user scenario. During our analysis of the DCAP behavior it will be observed that the DCAP tends to have a small decay relatively to the previous DCAP value, when the new added antenna has the same mean SNR of a previously connected antenna. In that context we also derive an expression for the DCAP that contains explicitly the value of the previous DCAP to, latter on, do an analysis of the sensitivity of the DCAP values versus the mean SNR of the new connected antenna, as more and more antennas are connected to the system.

From the definition of the Γ_M RV it is possible to prove that:

$$f_{\Gamma_M}(\gamma) = \lambda_M\, e^{-\lambda_M \gamma} \int_0^{\gamma} f_{\Gamma_{M-1}}(x)\, e^{\lambda_M x}\, dx \tag{9}$$

$a_{in}$with which a recursive algorithm for the calculation of the coefficients, which are central to the calculation of the capacity values, equation (6), can be obtained, and the following formula can be derived:

$$-\frac{df_{\Gamma_M}(\gamma)}{d\gamma} = \lambda_M [f_{\Gamma_M}(\gamma) - f_{\Gamma_{M-1}}(\gamma)] \tag{10}$$

From equation (10), after multiplying by $log(1+\gamma)$ and integrating from zero to plus infinity the variable, at both sides of the equation, the DCAP can be expressed by:

$$\begin{aligned}\Delta C_{M-1}^{M} = C_M - C_{M-1} &= -\lambda_M^{-1} \int_0^{\infty} \frac{df_{\Gamma_M}(\gamma)}{d\gamma}\, log(1+\gamma)\, d\gamma \\ &= \lambda_M^{-1} \int_0^{\infty} \frac{f_{\Gamma_M}(\gamma)}{1+\gamma}\, d\gamma = \lambda_M^{-1} \sum_{i=1}^{L} \sum_{n=1}^{K_i} \frac{a_{in}}{\lambda_i^{n-1}}\, C_i(\lambda_i, n-1)\end{aligned} \tag{11}$$

With some more mathematical manipulations, the differential capacity can also be equivalently expressed by:

$$\begin{aligned}\Delta C_{M-1}^{M} &= \frac{\lambda_{M-1}}{\lambda_M} \Delta C_{M-2}^{M-1} \\ &+ \frac{1}{\lambda_M^2} \left[C_0(\lambda_M) f_{\Gamma_M}(0) - \int_0^{\infty} \frac{f_{\Gamma_M}(\gamma)}{(1+\gamma)^2}\, d\gamma \right]\end{aligned} \tag{12}$$

$M = 1$where $f_{\Gamma_M}(0)$ is equal to n for M>1 and equal to λ_1 for M=1. This expression will be used in the following sections to analyze the DCAP sensitivity with the number of transmit antennas and the mean SNR's of the new connected antennas.

4.2 DCAP Bounds

Even if the previous expressions obtained for the DCAP, namely equation (11) and (12), are exact they are not easy to analyze, mostly because of the a_{in} presence of the coefficients. Therefore the derivation of some simple upper/lower bounds to the DCAP is an important step to analyze its behavior. For doing that, we will rely mostly on the second integral definition of the DCAP, from equation (11). From that expression one can easily see that if some bounds for equation $g(\gamma) = 1/(1+\gamma)$ are available, they can be easily used to bound also the DCAP. One simple bound for equation $g(\gamma)$ is $g(\gamma) \leq 1$, for all y in $[0, \infty[$. As a consequence the DCAP can be upper bounded by:

$$\Delta C_{M-1}^{M} \leq \frac{1}{\lambda_M} \int_0^{\infty} f_{\Gamma_M}(\gamma)\, d\gamma = \lambda_M^{-1} \quad (13)$$

and the channel capacity can be upper bounded by:

$$C_M \leq \sum_{k=1}^{M} \lambda_k^{-1} = \sum_{i=1}^{L} K_i\, \lambda_i^{-1} \quad (14)$$

xAnother possible bound for equation $g(\gamma)$ can be obtained from $1 + x \leq e^x$, for all x in $[0, \infty[$ by the Taylor series expansion of the exponential function around zero. Thus $g(\gamma) \leq e^{-\gamma}\gamma$, for all yin $[0, \infty[$, with a maximum difference of ($M_d \approx 0.204$)4, so:

$$e^{-\gamma} \leq g(\gamma) \leq e^{-\gamma} + M_d \quad (15)$$

and as a byproduct:

$$\frac{\varphi_{\Gamma_M}(-1)}{\lambda_M} \leq \Delta C_{M-1}^{M} \leq \frac{\varphi_{\Gamma_M}(-1)}{\lambda_M} + \frac{M_d}{\lambda_M} \quad (16)$$

where $\varphi_{\Gamma_M}(s)$ is the Γ_M RV moment generating function.

From bound (13) and (16) follows that in the low SNR regime the DCAP can be approximated by λ_M^{-1} and the channel capacity by:

$$C_M \approx \sum_{i=1}^{L} K_i\, \lambda_i^{-1} \quad (17)$$

The previous bounds although simple can provide some interesting information on the behavior of the DCAP, as will be seen in section 6.1. However they do not give any idea on the SNR vector that attain the maximum of the DCAP. This vector can give information on how the distributed antennas should be geographically positioned to attain most of the gains provided by the connection of additional antennas to the system. In the following paragraphs we answer this question, and prove that the SNR vector that attains the highest DCAP value is the SNR vector where all elements are equal. In other words the highest DCAP is obtained when all transmit antennas are co-located, have the same link SNR

From equation (11) one can see that $d\Delta C_{M-1}^{M}/d\lambda_i \geq 0$ for $M > 1$ and $i \neq M$. Therefore if we assume that the new connected antenna is always the one with the highest mean SNR, the DCAP will be upper bounded by the one where all mean SNRs are equal to the mean SNR of the new connected antenna:

$$\Delta C_{M-1}^{M}(\lambda_1, \ldots, \lambda_M) \leq \Delta C_{M-1}^{M}(\lambda_M, \ldots, \lambda_M) \quad (18)$$
$$\lambda_M \geq \lambda_n, \forall n \in [1, 2, \ldots, M-1]$$

When the mean SNR tends to infinity the maximum of the DCAP is obtained and is equal to:

$$\lim_{\lambda_M \to 0} \Delta C_{M-1}^{M}(\lambda_M, \ldots, \lambda_M) = \frac{1}{M-1} \quad (19)$$

Thus the DCAP in general is upper bounded by the co-located transmit antennas case and its maximal value is only dependent on the number of transmit antennas and not on the actual values of the mean SNR of the links. However this limit is not attainable in practice. But, how far is it from a real scenario? It can be shown that for a moderate SNR of 17 dB, for all links, the difference is lower than 0.1 bps/Hz when we pass from one connected antenna to two and even lower for the other connected antennas.

Since the previous bound is a limit bound it can be not very tight. However a tighter bound can be developed considering only a slight higher degree of information:

$$\Delta C_{M-1}^{M} \leq \frac{1}{\lambda_M + M - 1} \leq \frac{1}{M-1} \quad (20)$$

JFrom the previous expression one can also upper bound the capacity increase by the connection of new antennas, considering that the user is actually only connected to one antenna and that antenna has the greatest SNR of all of them, by:

$$\Delta C_1^{J+1} < \sum_{n=2}^{J+1} \frac{1}{n-1} = \sum_{n=1}^{J} \frac{1}{n} \approx \gamma + log(J + \beta) \quad (21)$$

where y is the Euler constant (0.5772156667) and $\beta = e^{1-\gamma} - 1$. Consequently as the number of connected antennas increase the DCAP decreases. However, if the number of antennas grows to infinity so does the capacity, but of course, in practice, one can only have a limited number of antennas. Thus a tradeoff between the cost and capacity gains must be made when we choose the number of antennas to be deployed in a real system.

5. MULTI-USER DCAP

In the previous section we have analyzed the DCAP for the single-user case and have provided an exact closed form expression for it, that is valid for all mean SNR's. We have started with the single user case due to its simplicity and also because the analysis of that simpler case can give some insight for the analysis of the more difficult case of a multi-user system. However for the more general case of a multi-user system the analysis of the DCAP over all mean SNR's is intractable. Thus, for this case, we consider only the DCAP in the high SNR regime. In this section we first define the DCAP and after derive a closed form expression for it, for the co-located antenna case and for $M > KN$. For $KN > M$ the DCAP is analyzed numerically.

According to equation (8), for $M > KN$, the DCAP can be expressed by:

$$\begin{aligned} \Delta C_{M,K,N}^{M+1,K,N} &= \mathbb{E}[\mathbf{C}_{DPC}^{(M+1,K,N)} - \mathbf{C}_{DPC}^{(M,K,N)}] \\ &= \mathbb{E}[log|\overline{\mathbf{H}}_{M+1}\overline{\mathbf{H}}_{M+1}^{H}|] - \mathbb{E}[log|\overline{\mathbf{H}}_{M}\overline{\mathbf{H}}_{M}^{H}|] \end{aligned} \tag{22}$$

$\mathrm{H}KN > M$where $\overline{\mathbf{H}}_i$, $(i = M, M+1)$ is the channel matrix for transmit antennas. Thus for the multiuser scenario the DCAP is only dependent on the matrix distribution. On the other hand, for , tho DCAP can be expressed by:

$$\begin{aligned} \Delta C_{M,K,N}^{M+1,K,N} &= \mathbb{E}[\mathbf{C}_{DPC}^{(M+1,K,N)} - \mathbf{C}_{DPC}^{(M,K,N)}] \\ &= \mathbb{E}[\mathbf{C}_{DPC}^{(M+1,M+1,1)} + \Delta C_{M+1,M+1,1}^{M+1,K,N} - (\mathbf{C}_{DPC}^{(M,M,1)} + \Delta C_{M,M,1}^{M,K,N})] \\ &= \Delta C_{M,M,1}^{M+1,M+1,1} + \Delta C_{M+1,M+1,1}^{M+1,K,N} - \Delta C_{M,M,1}^{M,K,N} \\ &= log(P) + \Delta \end{aligned} \tag{23}$$

From which we can see that the connection of the system users to a new transmit antenna is equal to $log(P)$ multiplexing gain, plus a $\Delta C_{M+1,M+1,1}^{M+1,K,N} - \Delta C_{M,M,1}^{M,K,N}$ factor, that is equal to plus the power offset gain provided when we pass from M to $M+1$ transmit antennas and users5, which can be closely approximated by $-log(e)$, for any number of transmit antennas. Hence, the significance of the factor versus the multiplexing gain must be analyzed to have a clear picture of the full obtained gain, please refer to section 5.2 and 6.2.

5.1 DCAP for M>KN

In this sub-section the DCAP for the optimal scheme, DPC, and for two sub-optimal schemes, namely ZF and BD is analyzed. A closed form expression and an approximation for it are also derived. Unfortunately, the general case of a distributed antenna system is difficult to analyze mathematically, thus for this case we will relie on numerical analysis, which are provided in section 6.2. In the analysis, contained in this sub-section, we consider that all transmit antennas are co-located.

For DPC, as shown in appendix (sub-section 9.1), the DCAP when we pass from M to M+1 transmit antennas is given by:

$$\Delta C_{M,K,N}^{M+1,K,N} = \sum_{n=M-KN+1}^{M} \frac{1}{n} - \sum_{n=M-KN+1}^{M} \Delta C_{n,1,1}^{n+1,1,1} \approx log\left(1+\frac{KN}{M-KN+\beta}\right) \tag{24}$$

where $\beta = e^{1-\gamma} - 1$ and $\gamma = 0.577215665$ is the Euler constant. For the linear precoding schemes a similar expression can be obtained, by noting that for BD the DCAP is equal to k times the DPC one, for a $(M-(K-1)N) \times N$ channel, from the BC equivalent point to point MIMO interpretation, in the high SNR regime (Juyul Lee & Jindal 2007). For that reason, the DCAP for ZF/BD can be show to be equal to:

$$\overline{\Delta C}_{M,K,N}^{M+1,K,N} \approx Klog\left(1+\frac{N}{M-KN+\beta}\right) \tag{25}$$

From the previous expression one can see that asymptotically in the number of transmit antennas,M, the DCAP behaves like $log_2(e)KN/(M-KN+\beta)$, for both DPC and ZF/BD, implying that the difference between the gains of the optimal scheme and the sub-optimal schemes is very small, when a high number of transmit antennas is considered. Nevertheless for a finite number of transmit antennas the DCAP gains provided by DPC are lower and the difference increases with K, as can be seen by equations (24) and (25). But how it scales with K, the number of users? It can be seen that for *M-KN* a constant the DCAP increases logarithmically with *K* for DPC and linearly with *K* for ZF/BD. Thus one can conclude that even if the optimal scheme has a higher complexity, it will need a much lower number of transmit antennas than the sub-optimal schemes, which require a lower complexity, for the same target capacity. Thus the number of antennas to be jointly processed must be carefully chosen, taking into account the tradeoff between complexity, network costs and obtained benefits.

5.2 DCAP for KV>M

In this sub-section the DCAP is analyzed for the case of more aggregate receive than transmit antennas. For this case, since equal power allocation stop to be asymptotically optimal and no closed form solution exists for the power allocation problem (Jindal et al. 2005), a mathematical study to attain a closed form expression for the DCAP is not possible. Nevertheless an approximation for this DCAP can be obtained. But how? It is know that for the case of only one transmit antenna, M=1 , it is optimal to transmit only to the best user (Caire & Shamai 2003) and as proven in the appendix (sub-section 9.2), for this case the maximum increase in capacity, when one additional user is connected to the system, is attained when all users are co-located i.e. when they have equal mean link SNR's. For M = 1 and N = 1 and for the high SNR regime this maximum is equal to, see appendix (sub-section 9.2):

$$\Delta C_{1,K,1}^{1,K+1,1} = \sum_{n=0}^{K} \binom{K}{n} (-1)^{K+1} log(K+1) \tag{26}$$

At this point we have only obtained an expression for the capacity increase by the connection of one additional system user, for the case of only one transmit antenna. But to obtain an approximation for the DCAP, for *KN* > M, we need also to know that for M > 1, see equation (23). For M > 1 the increase in capacity obtained by the connection of a new user to the system, can be approximated taking into account the DCAP expression for the case, equation (24) line , and making an extrapolation of equation (26). From those assumptions the capacity increase by the connection of one additional user to the system can be approximated by:

$$\Delta C_{M,K,1}^{M,K+1,1} \approx \sum_{n=K-M+1}^{K} \Delta C_{1,n,1}^{1,n+1,1} \tag{27}$$

and as can be confirmed in sub-section 6.2 (Fig. 3(a)), this approximation is close to the values obtained by numerical simulations and is better for a high number of users.

6. NUMERICAL RESULTS

6.1 Single-User DCAP analysis

In this sub-section, the DCAP, for a grid antenna placement, as show in Fig. 3 (a), is analyzed. First the exact DCAP values are compared to the obtained bounds, to access their tightness. Next we analyze the sensitivity of the DCAP to the variation of the mean SNR and finally we perform a DCAP analysis of a representative area covered by the antennas.

In all numerical analysis presented in this chapter we consider that the mean SNR is only dependent on the signal path loss (Simplified Path Loss Model, (Goldsmith 2005)), that6 $P_t K d_0^\gamma/\sigma_n^2 = 1$ and that $\gamma = 3$. It is also considered that the new connected antenna is always the one with highest mean SNR from the group of unconnected antennas and that $\Delta d_x = \Delta d_y = \Delta d$. By circular ring we mean the group of antennas with the same SNR.

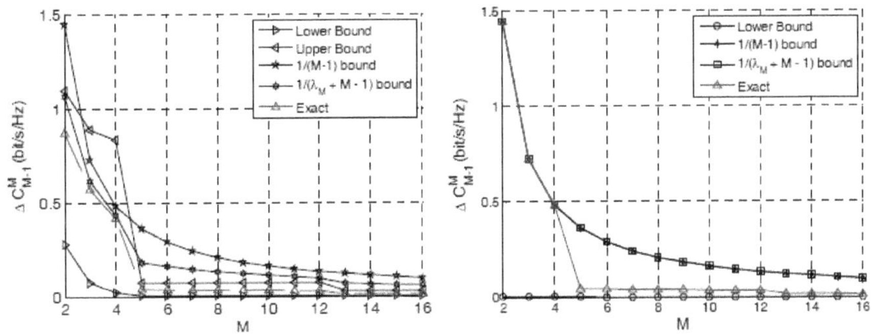

(a) Central Point $\Delta d = 1$.   (b) Central Point $\Delta d = 0.1$.

Fig. 1. Differential capacity by the connection to one more antenna, exact, upper and lower bounds.

In Fig. 1 we plot the exact DCAP values and respective bounds for the central point of the grid antenna placement and do that for two different inter-antenna distances, namely $\Delta d = 1$ and $\Delta d = 0.1$. From this figure one can see that if the new connected antenna is in the same circular ring as a previously connected antenna then its DCAP value, ΔC_M^{M-1}, will be approximately the same as the previous one, ΔC_{M-2}^{M-1}. On the other hand if the new connected antenna is far away from the circular ring of a previously connected antenna then the DCAP value decreases a lot. This approximation is better when a high number of transmit antennas is considered. Thus one can conclude intuitively that if all antennas are in the same circular ring, have the same mean SNR, their DCAP values will be maximum. Indeed this is true as shown in section 4.2. This behavior can be explained by the fact that ΔC_{M-1}^{M} is dependent on ΔC_{M-2}^{M-1} by a factor of λ_{M-1}/λ_M, an approximation that due to its importance will be analyzed in the following paragraphs. It can also be explained by the fact that in equation (16), $\varphi_{r_M}(-1)$ tends to zero as we connect to more antennas and as a consequence the bound becomes independent off all SNR's except the new one, which for a circular ring is constant. Thus, since the central point in the grid antenna placement is the one with highest symmetry we can say that if a target increase in capacity is pre-established then the user will be connected to or or or or or antennas, depending on the target increase in capacity defined.

Concerning the bounds tightness we can see from that figure that for low SNR's the upper bound provided by equation (16) is the better one, but for high SNR's the bound from equation (20) is more accurate. Although, the user will only connect to a small number of antennas in a real system, due to the diminishing returns expected as the number of antennas increase. Thus, taking into account this fact, the most important bounds will be the ones that are tighter for a low number of transmit antennas, and in this case the winner is the bound from equation (20).

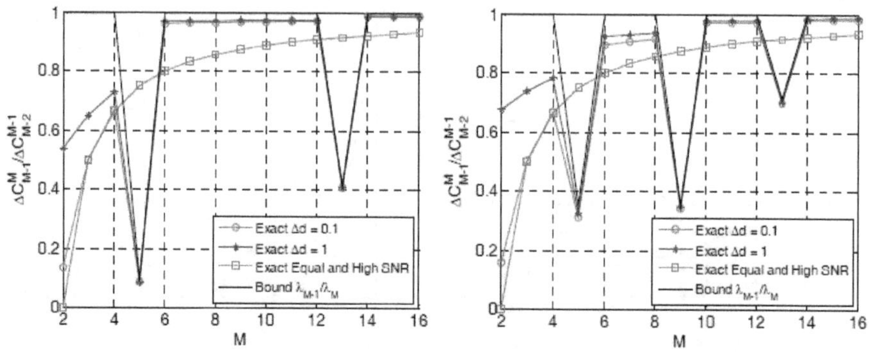

(a) Central Point. (b) $(0.5\Delta d_x, 0.5\Delta d_y)$ Point.

Fig. 2. Differential capacity sensitivity with respect to M and for different inter-antenna distances.

From Fig. 1 (a) and Fig. 1 (b) one can also see that the exact values of the DCAP, the dashed and solid blue lines, converge to the same value, for a high number of transmit antennas in the case of SNR vectors that are multiple among themselves. This fact can be easily proven together with the fact that as the SNR's get higher this convergence occurs at a smaller M value. In the case of high SNR's the DCAP cannot be higher than a given value, having as critical value 1/(M-1) , in the case of equal SNR's. As a consequence, if all transmit antennas are put closer to the user terminal, by a given factor, the only antennas for which the DCAP increases are the ones near the terminal.

As previously verified the DCAP in a circular ring tends to be constant. But how close to the previous value and when this approximation can be made? In the following paragraphs we propose to analyze this fact using a bound for the ratio $\Delta C^{M}_{M-1}/\Delta C^{M-1}_{M-2}$. If the ratio is close to one then the ΔC^{M}_{M-1} value will be close to ΔC^{M-1}_{M-2}. In Fig. 2 (a) and Fig. 2 (b) we plot this ratio for two different points in the grid antenna placement, namely for the central point and for $(0.5\Delta d_x, 0.5\Delta d_y)$.. In each figure the exact ratio value for two inter-antenna distances (d = 1 and d = 0.1), the bound from equation (12) and the exact value for equal and high SNR's are plotted. From those results one can view that as the number of connected transmit antennas increase the ratio sensitivity to the SNR vector variation decreases and that its exact value becomes closer to the bound. One can also see that when the new connected antenna is not from the same ring as the previously connected antenna, the bound is indeed very close to the actual value of the respective ratio and the ratio value as a step decrease that is lower as more connected antennas are considered. As a consequence the DCAP tends to be constant in a circular ring, as previously observed, and the approximation is better when a high number of transmit antennas is considered.

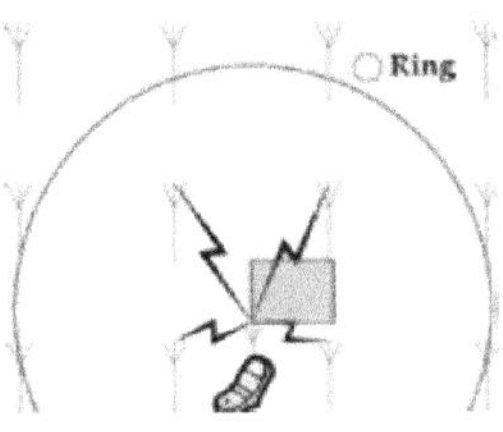

(a) Geographical antenna placement.

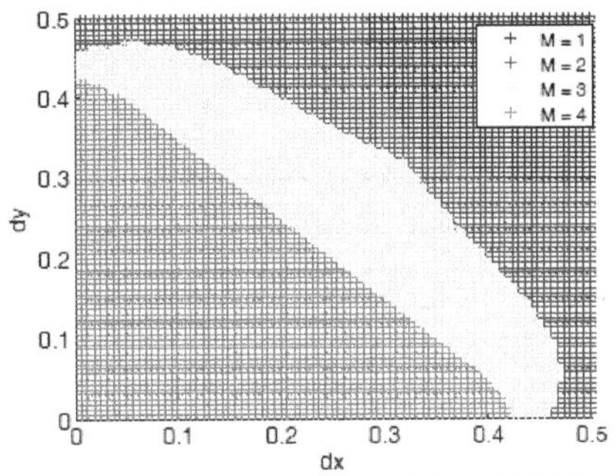

(b) Number of antennas where DCAP is higher than 0.1 bps/Hz.

Fig. 3. Single-User differential capacity analysis, for a regular antenna placement.

Thus far, we have only analyzed the DCAP values for a single point, but how it will behave if we consider a given area. The analysis of the DCAP values for a given area cannot be easily visualized in a two dimensional plot, thus we have relied on a different measure to analyze its behavior. The metric considered was the maximum number of transmit antennas that achieve a target DCAP value or more. In this study we have considered a target DCAP value of 0.1 bps/Hz. The geographical area considered was the one shown in figure Fig. 3 (a) in light blue, and we have also considered $\Delta d_x = \Delta d_y = 1$. The results of this study are presented on figure Fig. 3 (b). To explain the information contained into this figure it is easier to give an example. Thus, let's assume, for example, the point (0.4, 0.4). For this point $M = 4$ thus when we connect the second, third and fourth antennas the DCAP value is higher than the target, but departing from that number of transmit antennas, 4, the DCAP will be lower than the target.

For the considered scenario and for a target DCAP of 0.1bps/Hz only the first four antennas will be connected to the user, or equivalent the antennas presented in the first ring. This figure also shows a circular pattern in the number of necessary antennas. This is related to the fact that at a given distance the link mean SNR is only dependent on the distance from the user to the considered transmit antenna.

6.2 Multi-User DCAP analysis

In this sub-section the DCAP of DPC is compared to the one of ZF/BD, for the co-located antennas scenario. For the DAS, as stated before, we rely on numerical simulations to access the capacity gains provided by the connection of additional transmit antennas. For this numerical analysis we consider a scenario with 4 transmit antennas and 2 users, each with only one receive antenna. Finally for $KN > M$ we analyze the DCAP for the equal mean SNR's case. But to do that we first analyze the capacity gain provided by the connection of an additional user to the system and after that we investigate the gain provided by in comparison to $log(P)$ see equation (23).

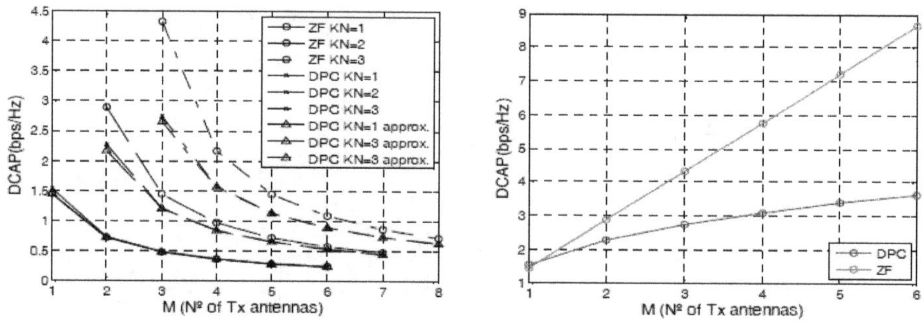

(a) DPC versus ZF. (b) DCAP for $M = KN$.

Fig. 4. Differential capacity for different number of user's and receive antennas.

As can be seen in Fig. 4 (a), were we present a plot of the DPC and ZF DCAP versus the number of connected transmit antennas, for the co-located scenario, the logarithm approximation although simple is very tight. Concerning the benefits of the connection of new transmit antennas, ZF has higher gains than DPC and the difference increase with KN . To see how this difference scales with we plot in Fig. 4 (b) the DCAP values versus M for $M = KN$. From this figure one can view that the DCAP scales logarithmically with the number of users for DPC and linearly for ZF, as already seen from equations (24) and (25). Thus even if the implementation complexity of DPC is much higher than the one for ZF, the sub-optimal scheme, ZF, will need a higher number of transmit antennas than the optimal KNscheme for a target system capacity.

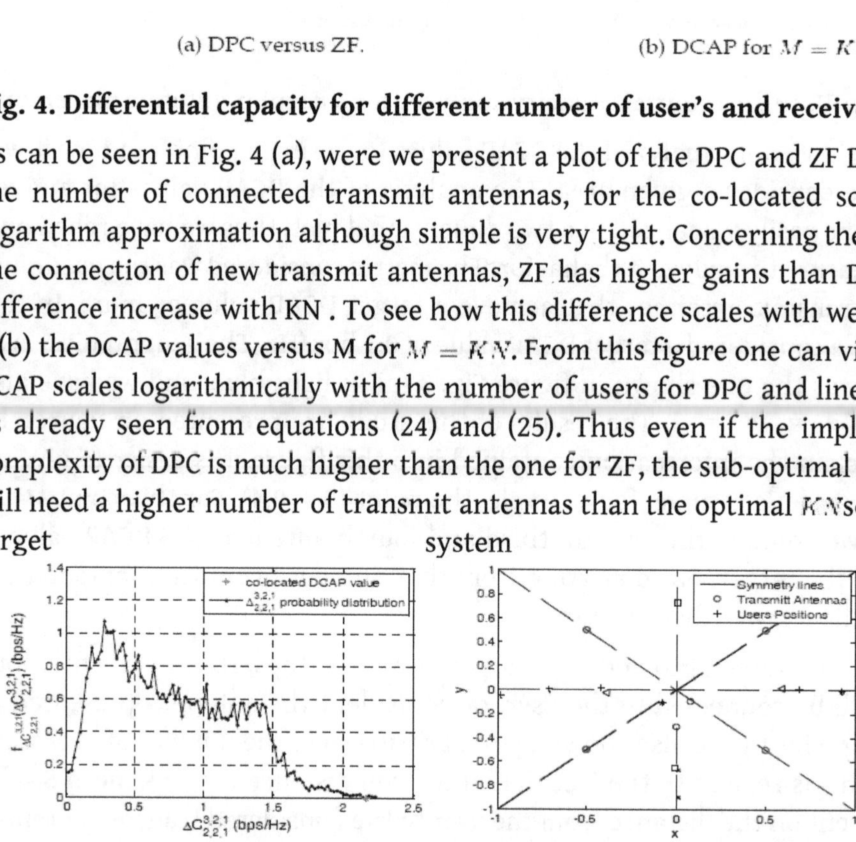

(a) DCAP distribution for $M = 2$. (b) User's position, where distributed DCAP is higher than co-located DCAP.

Fig. 5. Differential capacity distribution for a uniform user distribution and user's positions where the distributed DCAP is higher than the co-located DCAP. Each pair of equal black markers represent the positions of each user.

Thus a tradeoff must be made between the cost of additional processing power and the cost of additional physical resources, namely transmit antennas and respective connection to the central unit. As a result of this analysis, as a scheme approaches the optimal one, the gains obtained by the connection of additional antennas at the transmitter side decrease. But, remember that the optimal scheme will have always a higher sum-capacity. As seen before, from equations (24) and (25), the DCAP for the two precoding schemes converge to the same value for a high number of transmit antennas and the convergence point increases with KN .

For the DAS we will only analyze the DCAP for DPC and that analysis will rely on numerical simulations. For this simulation a scenario with 4 transmit antennas and two users, each with only one receive antenna, is considered. To model the channel we have considered the Simplified Path Loss Model again, (Goldsmith 2005), with a path loss exponent equal to 3, and have considered Rayleigh multipath fading. The transmit antennas were positioned as shown in Fig. 5 (b) and the user positions were randomly generated with an uniform distribution in $[-1,1]\times[-1,1]$. Ten thousand user's positions were generated and the DCAP was averaged over 10000 trials. The new connected antennas were always chosen to be the one that will imply the highest DCAP from the group of unconnected antennas. As a result of this simulation, we have Fig. 5, where the co-located DCAP, equation (24), value is represented by a red star. From that figure we see that most of the user's positions have a smaller DCAP than the co-located case. However for a small elite of users, 7 in this specific case, the DCAP is higher than the one obtained by the co-located scenario. Thus one can conclude that even if the DCAP for a DAS can be higher than the one for the co-located case the difference will not be high and the number of user positions in that condition will be low. To have a better understanding of the positions that attain the maximum DCAP gains for a DAS, in Fig. 5 (b), we show the 7 positions that have a higher DCAP than the co-located case. From that figure it is possible to infer that these positions are all very close to the system symmetry lines defined by the four transmit antennas and in that way, as in the co-located case, the new connected antenna will have the same distribution as a previous one. Thus system symmetry plays an important role in obtaining most of the DCAP gains, either for the single-user either for the multi-user cases.

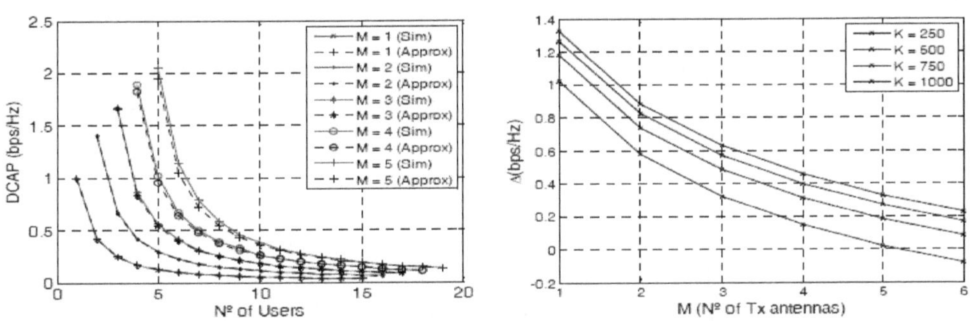

(a) Capacity increase by the connection of a new user (N = 1).

(b) Δ factor value (N=1).

Fig. 6. Capacity increase by the connection of one more transmit antenna to the system, for *KN* > *M*.

$\Delta N = \mathbb{H}\Delta 1000 K\Delta$When more aggregate receive than transmit antennas are considered it is important to analyze the Δ factor in equation (23), to see if it has some significance in relation to $log_2(P)$. Thus, we must evaluate the capacity increase obtained by the connection of an additional user to the system. To do that, we have relied on numerical simulations, considering that and that each column of is $\tilde{N}_{KN}(0, \mathbf{I})$ distributed. Since for this case no closed form expression exists for the power allocation we have relied on the algorithm presented in (Jindal et al. 2005) to optimally allocate power among users. As a result Fig. 6 (a) the ergodic capacity increase, when a new user is connected to the system, was obtained... In Fig. 6 (a)it is also shown the equation (27) approximation, which is very close to the obtained numerical results. Taking into account that approximation in our analysis, in Fig. 6 (b), we plot the Δ factor values for different number of users. From those values one can see that even for 1000 users this factor is small, not higher than 1.4 bps/Hz. Thus it has no significance in relation to $log(P)$, since we are considering the high SNR regime. From that figure we can also confirm that Δ increases fewer as K increases. Consequently, to obtain a value with the same order of magnitude of $log(P)$ a very high number of users should be jointly processed, which will result in a very high processing complexity at the CU, which must be avoided.

7. CONCISE SUMMARY

This chapter examines the advantages of integrating supplementary transmit antennas for the users of a broadcast channel. The single-user scenario has been examined in greater depth throughout all signal-to-noise ratios, while the multi-user scenario has been investigated solely in the high signal-to-noise ratio regime. For the single user case we have obtained a closed-form expression for DCAP that is valid for all SNR's and have analyzed its variation/sensitivity with respect to M. From that analysis we have seen that symmetry is the most important system property to obtain most of the gains provided by the connection of additional transmit antennas. It was also shown that the maximum increase in capacity is obtained when all links have the same mean SNR's and not when they are different. Thus showing that the DCAP maximum is obtained when all antennas are co-located and not distributed.

For the multi-user case a closed form expression for the co-located transmit antennas DCAP, for $M \geq KN$, has been obtained. In the general situation of a Distributed Antenna System (DAS), the Distributed Channel Access Protocol (DCAP) was examined numerically, focusing on a scenario including four broadcast antennas and two users, each equipped with a single receive antenna. In this instance, although the DCAP may exceed that of the co-located scenario, the difference is minimal, and the majority of user positions will exhibit a lower DCAP compared to the co-located situation. Positions that achieve a greater DCAP than the co-located scenario are situated near the system's symmetry lines, defined by the transmit antennas, hence underscoring the significance of symmetry in the multi-user context. In scenarios where the number of receive antennas exceeds that of transmit antennas, we have confirmed that the DCAP will be contingent upon power and will be determined by the multiplexing gain in addition to a supplementary factor. Nevertheless, this factor is much inferior than the multiplexing gain, even with one thousand users.. Thus for this case the most significant gain is the multiplexing gain, $log(P)$.

FOOTNOTES

1. We consider for now on that the capacity units are nats/s/Hz, when omitted.
2. The covariance matrix of the channel gains is diagonal, because the channel gains are independent. So their unitary singular value decomposition matrices are equal to the identity matrix.
3. According to (Goldsmith 2005) the $|h_i|^2$ random variable is exponential distributed and consequently γ_i
4. Obtained numerically, and knowing that this maximum is global.
5. $$\begin{aligned}\Delta C_{M,M,1}^{M+1,M+1,1} &\approx log(P) + log(M+\beta) + MlogM - (M+1)log(M+1) \\ &\approx log(P) - log(e)\end{aligned}$$
6. K is a unit less constant which depends on the antenna characteristics and on the average channel attenuation, do is a reference distance for the antenna far-field, is the path loss exponent and P1is the transmitted power at a distance do
7. The P term cancel out from the expression since it appears in $\overline{C}_{DPC}^{1,K+1,1}$ and $\overline{C}_{DPC}^{1,K,1}$.

REFERENCES

1. Caire, G. & Shamai, S., 2003. On the achievable throughput of a multiantenna Gaussian broadcast channel. Information Theory, IEEE Transactions on, 49(7), 1691-1706.
2. Castanheira, D. & Gameiro, A., 2008. Distributed MISO system capacity over Rayleigh flat fading channels'. In Personal, Indoor and Mobile Radio Communications, 2008. PIMRC 2008. IEEE 19th International Symposium on. pp. 1-5.
3. Castanheira, D. & Gameiro, A., 2009. High SNR Broadcast Channel Differential Capacity. In ICT-MobileSummit 2009. Santander, Spain, pp. 1-5.
4. Cover, T., 1972. Broadcast channels. Information Theory, IEEE Transactions on, 18(1), 2-14.

5. Dohler, M., Gkelias, A. & Aghvami, A., 2006. Capacity of distributed PHY-layer sensor networks. Vehicular Technology, IEEE Transactions on, 55(2), 622-639.
6. FUTON, 2008. FUTON - Fibre-Optic Networks for Distributed Extendible Heterogeneous Radio Architectures and Service Provisioning. Available at: http://www.ict- futon.eu/.
7. Ghosh, S., 2005. Network Theory, PHI Learning Pvt. Ltd.
8. Goldsmith, A., 2005. Wireless communications, Cambridge University Press.
9. Gradshteyn, I.S. & Ryzhik, I.M., 1994. Table of Integrals, Series, and Products 5th ed., Academic Press.
10. Gubner, J.A., 2006. Probability and Random Processes for Electrical and Computer Engineers 1st ed., Cambridge University Press.
11. I. R. R. M. M1645, 2003. M.1645 : Framework and overall objectives of the future development of IMT-2000 and systems beyond IMT-2000. Available at: http://www.itu.int/rec/R-REC-M.1645/e.
12. Jindal, N., 2005. High SNR analysis of MIMO broadcast channels. In Information Theory, 2005. ISIT 2005. Proceedings. International Symposium on. pp. 2310-2314.
13. Jindal, N. et al., 2005. Sum power iterative water-filling for multi-antenna Gaussian broadcast channels. Information Theory, IEEE Transactions on, 51(4), 1570-1580.
14. Juyul Lee & Jindal, N., 2007. High SNR Analysis for MIMO Broadcast Channels: Dirty Paper Coding Versus Linear Precoding. Information Theory, IEEE Transactions on, 53(12), 4787-4792
15. Liu, H. & Li, G., 2005a. OFDM-Based Broadband Wireless Networks: Design and Optimization, Wiley-Interscience.
16. Liu, H. & Li, G., 2005b. OFDM-Based Broadband Wireless Networks: Design and Optimization, Wiley-Interscience.
17. Seijoon Shim et al., 2008. Block diagonalization for multi-user MIMO with other-cell interference. Wireless Communications, IEEE Transactions on, 7(7), 2671-2681.
18. Shamai, S. & Verdu, S., 2001. The impact of frequency-flat fading on the spectral efficiency of CDMA. Information Theory, IEEE Transactions on, 47(4), 1302-1327.
19. Shin, H. & Lee, J.H., 2003. Capacity of multiple-antenna fading channels: spatial fading correlation, double scattering, and keyhole. Information Theory, IEEE Transactions on, 49(10), 2636-2647.

20. Telatar, I.E., 1999. Capacity of multi-antenna Gaussian channels. Available at: http://eprints.kfupm.edu.sa/29242/.

21. Vishwanath, S., Jindal, N. & Goldsmith, A., 2003. Duality, achievable rates, and sum-rate capacity of Gaussian MIMO broadcast channels. Information Theory, IEEE Transactions on, 49(10), 2658-2668.

22. Visotsky, E. & Madhow, U., 2001. Space-time transmit precoding with imperfect feedback. Information Theory, IEEE Transactions on, 47(6), 2632-2639.

23. Viswanath, P. & Tse, D., 2003. Sum capacity of the vector Gaussian broadcast channel and uplink-downlink duality. Information Theory, IEEE Transactions on, 49(8), 1912-1921.

24. Wei Yu & Cioffi, J., 2004. Sum capacity of Gaussian vector broadcast channels. Information Theory, IEEE Transactions on, 50(9), 1875-1892.

25. Weingarten, H., Steinberg, Y. & Shamai, S., 2006. The Capacity Region of the Gaussian Multiple-Input Multiple-Output Broadcast Channel. Information Theory, IEEE Transactions on, 52(9), 3936-3964.

APPENDIX

DCAP derivation

$\mathbf{A}_i$For the co-located transmit antennas case $\overline{\mathbf{H}}_i\overline{\mathbf{H}}_i^H,\ (i = M, M+1)$ is $\tilde{W}_{KN}(i, \Xi)$ distributed. But since $\overline{\mathbf{H}}_i\overline{\mathbf{H}}_i^H \sim \Xi^{1/2}\mathbf{A}_i\Xi^{1/2}$, where is $\tilde{W}_{KN}(i, \mathbf{I}_{KN})$ distributed, the DCAP can be expressed by:

$$\begin{aligned}
\Delta C_{M,K,N}^{M+1,K,N} &= \mathbb{E}[log|\overline{\mathbf{H}}_{M+1}\overline{\mathbf{H}}_{M+1}^H|] - \mathbb{E}[log|\overline{\mathbf{H}}_M\overline{\mathbf{H}}_M^H|] \\
&= \mathbb{E}[log|\mathbf{A}_{M+1}|] - \mathbb{E}[log|\mathbf{A}_M|] \\
&= \sum_{l=0}^{KN-1}\Psi(M+1-l) + \sum_{l=0}^{KN-1}\Psi(M-l) \\
&= \sum_{n=M-KN+1}^{M}\frac{1}{n} \approx \log\left(1+\frac{KN}{M-KN+\beta}\right)
\end{aligned} \tag{28}$$

where $\Psi(l) = -\gamma + \sum_{n=1}^{l-1}$, is the Euler's digamma function. The result from the second line comes from the determinant property $(|\mathbf{AB}| = |\mathbf{A}||\mathbf{B}|)$ and the result from the third line from lemma 1 of (Juyul Lee & Jindal 2007) $(\mathbb{E}[log|\mathbf{A}_i|] = \sum_{l=0}^{i-1}\Psi(i-l))$. To obtain an approximation to the partial sum of the harmonic series we have used $\sum_{n=1}^{M} 1/n = \gamma + log(M+\beta)$ which has a maximum error of 4.1×10^{-3}.

Capacity Increase by the connection of one more user, for N = 1and M = 1

For N = 1and M = 1 the broadcast channel ergodic sum-capacity, equation (7), in the high SNR regime, simplifies to:

$$\overline{C}_{DPC}^{1,K,1} = \mathbb{E}\left[log\left(P \max_{k=1...K}(\xi_k^{1/2} h_k^H h_k \xi_k^{1/2})\right)\right] = \mathbb{E}[log(Px)] \tag{29}$$

where ξ_k is the average SNR of user , $h_k \sim \tilde{N}(0,1)$ and $x = \max_k(\xi_k h_k^H h_k)$. It is easy to show that $d\Delta C_{1,K,1}^{1,K+1,1}/d\xi_k \leq 0$ for $k \neq K+1$ and that the opposite happens for $k = K+1$. Thus the maximum of $\Delta C_{1,K,1}^{1,K+1,1}$ is obtained when $\xi_k = \xi$ for all users, if the new connected

ξ_{x1}user is always the one which implies the highest increase in the ergodic sum-capacity. It can also be proven that the same value for $\Delta C_{1,K,1}^{1,K+1,1}$ is obtained for any . Hence, for simplicity we consider that $\xi = 1$. Thus has cumulative distribution function $F_X(x,K) = F_Y(y)^K$, (Liu & Li 2005b), where $y \sim \xi_k h_k^H h_k$ is exponential distributed with mean . Thus the capacity increase by the connection of an additional user to the system can be expressed by7:

$$\Delta C_{1,K,1}^{1,K+1,1} = \int_0^\infty log(x)\, dF_X(x, K+1) - \int_0^\infty log(x)\, dF_X(x, K) \tag{30}$$

which after the integral evaluation gives the result shown in equation (26).

Chapter 10 LOW-DIMENSIONAL MIMO SYSTEMS WITH FINITE-SIZED CONSTELLATION INPUTS

1. INTRODUCTION: AN OVERVIEW

The foundational studies by Foschini and Gans (1998) and Telatar (1999) on multiple antenna elements at both the transmitter and receiver demonstrate a significant enhancement in the throughput of this point-to-point channel, commonly known as a multiple input multiple output (MIMO) system. The encouraging outcomes of elevated spectral efficiency and improved dependability redirected research towards multi-antenna communications and prompted the incorporation of numerous antenna elements in forthcoming communication systems. Researchers continue to seek space-time codes (STC) with less decoding complexity. These codes consider both the spatial and temporal aspects of the MIMO channel. Orthogonal Space-Time Block Codes (OSTBCs) (Larsson & Stoica, 2003) are extensively utilized due to their simplicity in encoding and decoding processes. In the scenario involving two transmit antennas, the OSTBC is referred to as the Alamouti code (Alamouti, 1998). OSTBCs are repetition codes that just offer diversity gain. To reach the capacity limit, they must be utilized in conjunction with an outside code. Significant coding improvements can be achieved by utilizing a capacity-achieving temporal encoder, such as turbo or Low-Density Parity Check (LDPC) codes, in conjunction with a Space-Time Code (STC) (Gonzalez-Lopez et al., 2006). Recent findings indicate that for ergodic channels, the intricate combination of space-time codes (STC) and outer codes can be substituted by temporally coded and spatially multiplexed streams (coded spatial streams) to approach capacity (Ghaffar & Knopp, 2008a). Each spatial stream may be independently encoded with temporal encoders such as convolutional, turbo, or LDPC codes, while typical commercial decoders are employed at the receiver following demodulation. MIMO OFDM is the suitable approach to address the frequency selectivity of MIMO wireless channels while maintaining low complexity equalization at the receivers. To address the intrinsic degradation of MIMO OFDM wireless channels, enhanced code diversity of bit interleaved coded modulation (BICM) for fading channels is establishing it as the preferable choice. Therefore, future wireless systems will be predicated on BICM MIMO OFDM architectures. Nonetheless, the requisite antenna spacing, along with the complexity limitations at the reception, constrains future MIMO-based communication systems to a maximum of four spatial streams, while in most circumstances, it is limited to two spatial streams. The current and upcoming standards, such as IEEE 802.11n (2006), IEEE 802.16m (2007), and Third Generation Partnership Project Long Term Evolution (3GPP LTE) (2006), support this assertion.

This chapter concentrates on low-dimensional spatially multiplexed time-coded BICM MIMO OFDM systems, with the first section dedicated to transmission strategies and corresponding receiver architectures in a broadcast context, while the second section examines interference mitigation in cellular environments. This chapter specifically considers finite-sized constellation inputs and deviates from the conventional idealized Gaussian assumption for the codewords. Each section is supplemented with pertinent information-theoretic analysis and simulation results based on forthcoming wireless standards..

2. MIMO BROADCAST SCENARIO

This part deliberates on the broadcast scenario of BICM MIMO OFDM system though the dis- cussion also remains valid for the point-to-point MIMO systems. We consider the transmis- sion strategy in which each spatial stream is independently encoded and modulated. We focus on the case of uniform power and nonuniform rate spatial streams (Ghaffar & Knopp, 2008a) and the case of uniform rate and nonuniform power distribution (Ghaffar & Knopp, 2008b) between these spatial streams. In such a broadcast scenario, receiver consequently views a multiple access channel (MAC). Shamai (Shamai & Steiner, 2003) termed the approach of sin- gle code layer at each transmit antenna as MAC-outage approach. The reception is consequently based on successive interference cancellation (SIC) i.e. sequential decoding and subtraction (stripping) of spatial streams which introduces unequal error protection (UEP). This can be coarsely regarded as MMSE DFE as described in (Varanasi & Guess, 1997). The idea of mul- tiple data streams with UEP adds flexibility to the system which can be exploited for having prioritized users or advanced services in MIMO broadcast systems and in multimedia broad- cast multicast services (MBMS). For instance it can be the broadcast of multimedia streams with different rates (quality) of the same data and the users decoding the stream depending on the received SNR. It can also be the broadcast of low and high rate streams (as audio and video) with prioritized or high SNR users decoding both audio and video streams while low SNR users decoding only the low rate audio stream. It is also applicable to high-definition TV (HDTV) scenario where low priority/quality users are able to receive standard-definition TV (SDTV) transmission while high priority/quality users access HDTV. This idea has limited similarity to superposition codes (Liu et al., 2002) whose signal space has a cloud/ satellite topology. Cloud centers because of relatively higher distance amongst them carry information for low quality receivers whereas better receivers having larger noise tolerance can resolve up to the actual transmitted satellite symbol within the cloud.

For coded spatial streams (also for the STC), the well-known data model after appropriate filtering and sampling is y = Hx + z (to be made precise in the subsequent sections) where y is the received data, H is the channel matrix, x is the symbol vector with the elements from finite constellations and z is the noise. The problem is then to detect some or all elements of x from y. Essentially the same problem occurs in multiuser detection for CDMA (Verdu, 1998) and for single-carrier transmission over channels that induce intersymbol interference. In these cases, the matrix H usually has a specific structure.

The problem of detection of x from y has stimulated a large body of research (Verdu, 1998) and references therein. One can easily show that if the noise z is Gaussian then obtaining the maximum-likelihood (ML) solution for some or all elements of x is equivalent to mini- mizing the Euclidean distance || y — Hx ||2 with respect to x over the finite set spanned by all possible combinations of constellation points that can constitute the vector x. For ML soft MIMO detection, the demodulator calculates the log-likelihood ratios (LLRs) for all bits that constitute the desired elements of x by summing the Euclidean distances for the values of x for which that particular bit of the desired element of x is one and zero thereby amounting to 2log(M1)+···+log(Mnr) terms where Mk is the modulation alphabet of the k-th spatial stream and nr is the total number of spatial streams (Larsson & Jalden, 2008). In many cases of practical interest, one resorts to the approximation of replacing the sums with the largest term which is equivalent to minimizing the Euclidean distance and is termed as max log MAP approach. Unfortunately this problem is NP-hard for general H and y (Verdu, 1989) which implies that there are no known efficient (i.e. polynomial-time) solutions. Many sophisticated methods as lattice reduction and sphere decoding (Hochwald & Brink, 2003) exist which find the ML so- lution with high probability, but these methods are in general still computationally complex. This is true also in an average sense if H is random (i.e. for a fading channel). The popular "sphere decoding" method is much more efficient than a brute-force search, but it still admits an average complexity that is exponential in the dimension of x.

Naive solutions, like neglecting the integer constraint coupled with the Gaussian assumption for the alphabets and then subsequently projecting the so-obtained solution onto the finite set of permissible x [linear receivers as LMMSE and zero forcing ZF)], in general work poorly especially at lower SNRs. Standard linear detection approaches are further based on ignoring the spatial color at the output of linear detectors which results in the decoupling of spatial streams thereby fundamentally reducing the complexity of detection. These disregards proliferate the suboptimality of linear receivers which exhibit degraded performance especially at lower SNRs.

Standard receiver solutions for spatially multiplexed broadcast schemes including V-BLAST (Wolniansky et al., 1998) (Golden et al., 1999) use stripping decoders which incorporate sub- optimal linear minimum mean square error (MMSE) filters (Medvedev et al., 2006) against the yet undecoded streams at each successive cancellation stage. MMSE because of its relative improved performance in the family of linear detectors is the preferred choice. Its optimal- ity for power constrained Gaussian alphabets is well known but it is suboptimal for finite size constellations. Gaussian assumption of the post detection interference is open to discus- sion. Its behavior is close to Gaussian under various asymptotic conditions which include large SNRs and large number of transmit and receive antennas (Poor & Verdu, 1997). But the fidelity of Gaussian assumption in a low dimensional system at moderate SNRs is question- able. Degradation of the performance due to the suboptimality combined with the complexity in the calculation of linear equalizers at each frequency tone (in OFDM based system) renders their real-time implementation debatable especially in fast fading wideband environments.

2.1 System Model

Before deliberating further on these receiver structures, we discuss the system model. As the overall system is based on BICM MIMO OFDM, it is imperative to first understand the significance and the implication of using BICM.

2.1.1 BICM SISO System

BICM because of its improved code diversity for fading channels and its flexibility to vari- able transmission rates, is a likely choice for future wireless systems as IEEE 802.11n (802.11n, 2006), IEEE 802.16m (802.16m, 2007) and 3GPP LTE (LTE, 2006). The landmark paper of Caire (Caire et al., 1998) on BICM showed that on some channels, the separation of demodulation and decoding is beneficial, provided that the encoder output is interleaved bit wise and a suitable soft decision metric is used in the Viterbi decoder. Code diversity, and therefore the reliability of coded modulation over a Rayleigh channel, can be improved this way. The code diversity in this case is equal to the smallest number of distinct bits along any error event. This leads to a better coding gain over a fading channel when compared to other coded modulation schemes as Trellis Coded Modulation (TCM). BICM increases considerably Hamming distance while reducing (often marginally) Euclidean distance so BICM outperforms TCM over Rayleigh fading channel while suffering a moderate loss of performance over AWGN channel. If the channel model is nonstationary, in the sense that the propagation environment changes during transmission, then BICM provides a robust coding scheme.

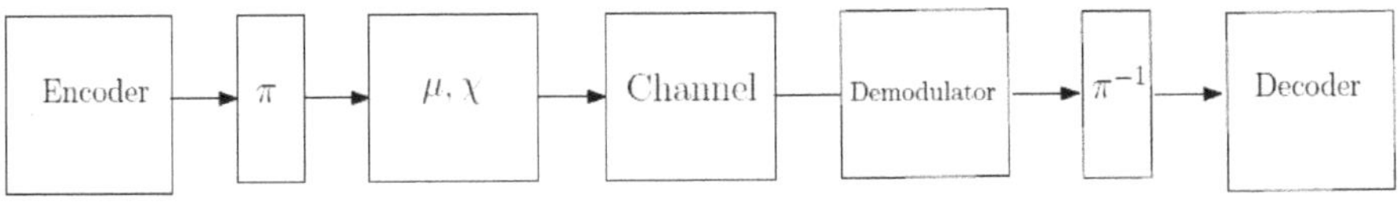

Fig. 1. Block Diagram of BICM system. π denotes denotes a bit interleaver.

The main idea of BICM is therefore to transform the channel generated by the multilevel con- stellation χ into parallel and independent binary channels. For transmission of complex mod- ulation, channel is not binary but after bit interleaving, any transmission of a multilevel signal from χ with |χ | = 2m, can actually be thought of as taking place over m parallel channels, each carrying one binary symbol from the signal label. However, these channels are generally not independent, due to the constellation structure. To make them independent, binary sym- bols are interleaved over infinite length before being used as signal labels. The maximum-likelihood decoding (MLD) of BICM requires combined demodulation/decoding, which is often too complicated to implement. As a result, MLD is separated at the receiver, concatenat- ing soft-metrics computation, deinterleaving and decoding. BICM block diagram is shown in fig. 1 which is the concatenation of an encoder for a code C with an interleaver π followed by a modulator (μ, χ). In the decoder, the metrics reflect the fact of bits separation. Suppose that the code word to be transmitted is c. After interleaving and modulation, we transmit the codeword x = (x1, x2,, xn) and we receive y at the output of a stationary memoryless channel. With symbol interleaving, we decode by maximizing the metricwith respect to x.

$$\log p(\mathbf{y}|\mathbf{x}) = \sum_{k=1}^{n} \log p(y_k|x_k) \tag{1}$$

The bit interleaver can be seen as a one-to-one correspondence π : kt → (k, i), where kt de- notes the original ordering of the coded bits ckt , k denotes the time ordering of the signals xk transmitted, and i indicates the position of the bit ckt in the symbol xk . Let χbi denote the subset of all signals x ∈χ whose label has the value b ∈ {0, 1} in position i. Then the ML bit metric is given as

$$\lambda^i(y_k, c_{k'}) = \log \sum_{x \in \chi^i_{c_{k'}}} p(y_k|x) \quad \text{where} \quad c_{k'} \in [0,1] \quad \text{and} \quad i = 1, 2, ..., log\,|\chi| \tag{2}$$

So in case of BICM, it is the summation of bit metrics Λi (yk , ckt) instead of the symbol metrics log p (yk|xk) for decoding. i.e.

$$\underline{\hat{c}} = \arg\max_{\underline{c} \in C} \sum_{k'} \lambda^i(y_k, c_{k'}) \tag{3}$$

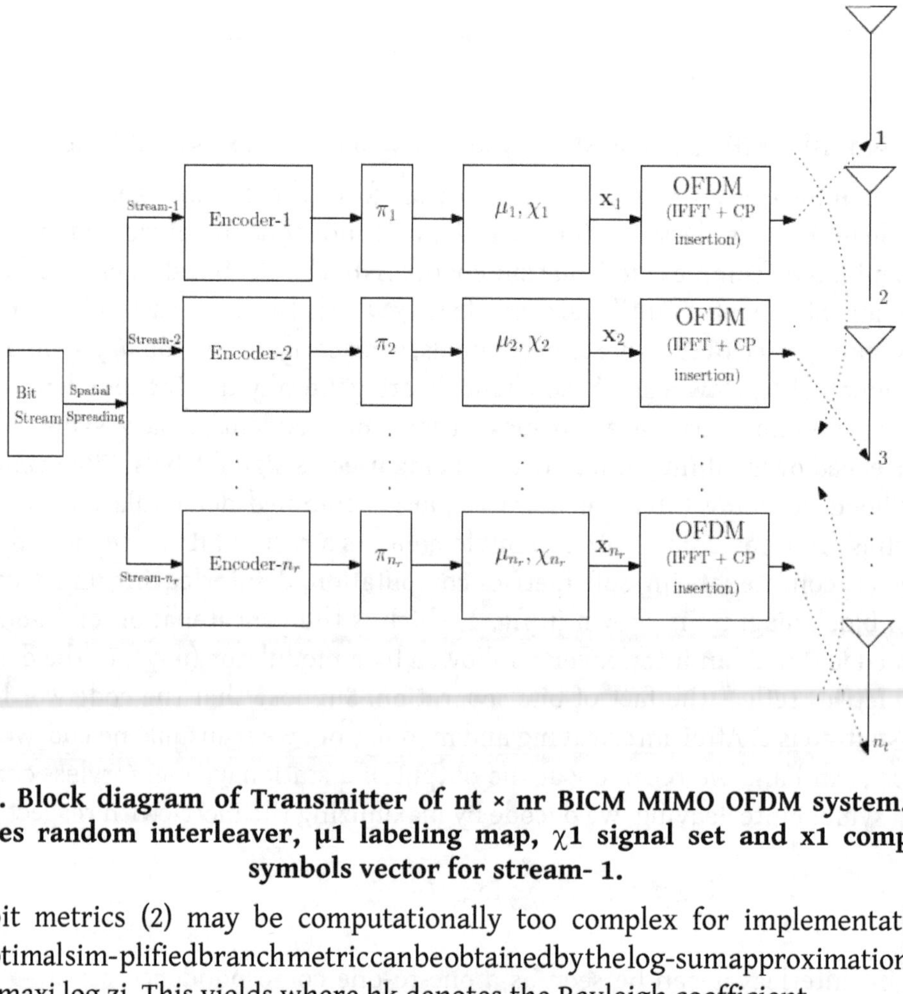

Fig. 2. Block diagram of Transmitter of nt × nr BICM MIMO OFDM system. π1 denotes random interleaver, μ1 labeling map, χ1 signal set and x1 complex symbols vector for stream- 1.

The bit metrics (2) may be computationally too complex for implementation. Suboptimalsim-plifiedbranchmetriccanbeobtainedbythelog-sumapproximationlog Σjzj ≈ maxj log zj. This yields where hk denotes the Rayleigh coefficient.

$$\lambda^{i}\left(y_k, c_{k'}\right) = \max_{x\in\chi^{i}_{c_{k'}}} \log p\left(y_k|x\right) = \min_{x\in\chi^{i}_{c_{k'}}} \left|y_k - h_k x\right|^2 \tag{4}$$

2.1.2 BICM MIMO OFDM System

We consider a MIMO broadcast system (without CSIT) which is a nt × nr (nt ≥ nr) BICM MIMO OFDM system with nr spatial streams as shown in figs. 2 and 3. We effectively reduce this to nr × nr system by antenna cycling at the transmitter (Foschini & Gans, 1998) with each stream being transmitted by one antenna in any dimension. The antenna used by a particular stream is randomly assigned per dimension so that each stream sees all degrees of freedom of the channel. Let the spatial streams be x1, ·· , xnr . xl is the symbol of xl over a signal set χl ⊆ C with a Gray labeling mapμl : {0, 1}log2 |χl | → χl . During the transmission of l-th spatial stream, the code sequence cl is interleaved by πl and then is mapped onto the signal sequence xl ∈ χl . Bit interleaver for the l-th stream can be modeled as πl : k' → (k, i) where k denotes the original ordering of the coded bits ck of the l-th stream, k denotes the time ordering of the signal xl,k and i indicates the position of the bit ck in the symbol xl,k . We assume that the frequency reuse factor is one and cyclic prefix (CP) of appropriate length is added to the OFDM symbols. Cascading IFFT at the transmitter and FFT at the receiver

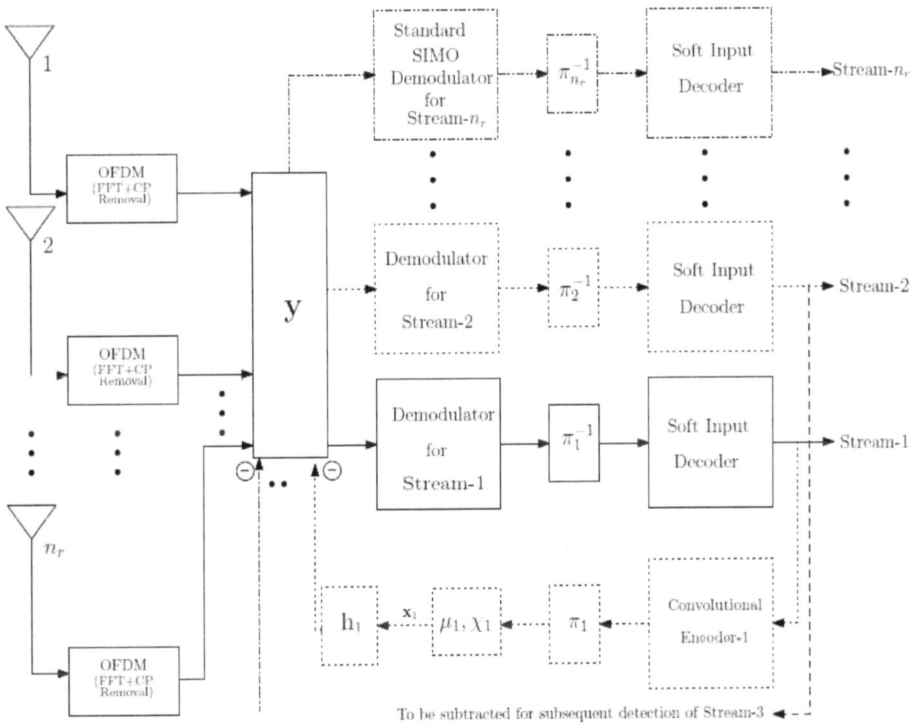

Fig. 3. Block diagram of SIC Receiver of BICM MIMO OFDM system. π1-1 denotes deinter- leaver and h1 denotes the channel seen by stream-1.

with CP extension, transmission at the k-th frequency tone can be expressed as:-

$$yk = h1,kx1 + h2,kx2 + \cdots + hnr,kxnr + zk, \qquad k = 1, 2, \cdots, T \qquad (5)$$
$$= Hk\, xk + zk$$

where $\mathbf{H}_k = [\mathbf{h}_{1,k} \cdots \mathbf{h}_{n_r,k}]$ i.e. the channel at the k-th frequency tone, $\mathbf{x}_k = [x_{1,k}, \cdots, x_{n_r,k}]^T$ and $(.)^T$ indicates the transpose operation. Each subcarrier corresponds to a symbol $\mathbf{x}$ from a constellation map $\chi_1, \cdots \chi_{n_r}$. $\mathbf{y}_k, \mathbf{z}_k \in \mathbb{C}^{n_r}$ are the vectors of received symbols and circularly symmetric complex white Gaussian noise of double-sided power spectral density $N_0/2$ at the n_r receive antennas. $\mathbf{h}_{l,k} \in \mathbb{C}^{n_r}$ is the vector characterizing flat fading channel response from l-th transmitting antenna to n_r receive antennas at k-th subcarrier. This vector has complex-valued multivariate Gaussian distribution with $E[\mathbf{h}_{l,k}] = 0$ and $E[\mathbf{h}_{l,k}\mathbf{h}_{l,k}^{\dagger}] = \mathbf{I}$. The antennas at the transmitter are also assumed to be sufficiently spaced and therefore are uncorrelated. The complex symbols $x_{1,k}, \cdots, x_{n_r,k}$ of the spatial streams are assumed to be independent with variances $\sigma_1^2, \cdots, \sigma_{n_r}^2$ respectively. The channels at different subcarriers are also assumed to be independent. Bit metric for the bit $c_{k'}$ at the i-th location of the symbol $x_{l,k}$ is given as

$$\lambda_l^i\left(\mathbf{y}_k, c_{k'}\right) = \log \sum_{x_1 \in \chi_1} \cdots \sum_{x_l \in \chi_{l,c_{k'}}^i} \cdots \sum_{x_{n_r} \in \chi_{n_r}} \exp\left[-\frac{1}{N_0}\|\mathbf{y}_k - \mathbf{H}_k\mathbf{x}\|^2\right]$$

Applying log-sum approximation we have:-

$$\lambda_l^i\left(\mathbf{y}_k, c_{k'}\right) \approx \min_{x_1 \in \chi_1 \cdots x_l \in \chi_{l,c_{k'}}^i \cdots x_{n_r} \in \chi_{n_r}} \left[\|\mathbf{y}_k - \mathbf{H}_k\mathbf{x}\|^2\right] \tag{6}$$

2.2 Information Theoretic View

We now calculate the mutual information of this system for the cases of Gaussian and finite sized constellation inputs.

2.2.1 Gaussian Inputs

The system equation ignoring the frequency index takes the form:-

$$y = h1\ x1 + h2\ x2 + \cdots + hnr\ xnr + z \tag{7}$$

Since the receiver knows the realization of H, the channel output is the pair (y; H) = (Hx + z; H). The mutual information between input and output is then Telatar (1999)

$$I(x; (y, H)) = I(x; H) + I(x; y|H)$$
$$= I(x; y|H)$$
$$= EH\ I(x; y|H = H)$$

For the Gaussian inputs, we consider the following two cases:-

1. Spatial streams of uniform power and non-uniform rate.
2. Spatial streams of uniform rate and non-uniform power.

For Gaussian inputs, channel capacity of the system as per the chain rule (Foschini & Gans, 1998) is

$$I(x1, x2 \cdots xnr; y) = I(x1; y) + I(x2; y|x1) + \cdots + I(xnr; y|x1, x2 \cdots xnr-1)$$

The terms in the summation represent the channel capacities of each spatial stream once they are detected in the successive subtractive cancellation way. Conditioned on the channel, these terms can be written as:-

$$I(x_1; \mathbf{y}|\mathbf{H}) = \log_2\left[\det\left\{\mathbf{I} + \sigma_1^2\mathbf{h}_1\mathbf{h}_1^\dagger\left(N_0\mathbf{I} + \sigma_2^2\mathbf{h}_2\mathbf{h}_2^\dagger + \cdots + \sigma_{n_r}^2\mathbf{h}_{n_r}\mathbf{h}_{n_r}^\dagger\right)^{-1}\right\}\right]$$

$$I(x_2; \mathbf{y}|\mathbf{H}, x_1) = \log_2\left[\det\left\{\mathbf{I} + \sigma_2^2\mathbf{h}_2\mathbf{h}_2^\dagger\left(N_0\mathbf{I} + \sigma_3^2\mathbf{h}_3\mathbf{h}_3^\dagger + \cdots + \sigma_{n_r}^2\mathbf{h}_{n_r}\mathbf{h}_{n_r}^\dagger\right)^{-1}\right\}\right]$$

and

$$I(x_{n_r}; \mathbf{y}|\mathbf{H}, x_1, x_2 \cdots, x_{n_r - 1}) = \log_2\left(1 + \frac{\sigma_{n_r}^2}{N_0}\|\mathbf{h}_{n_r}\|^2\right)$$

where H = [h1h2 ... hnr] is the channel matrix. Fig. 4 shows the ergodic capacity for the case of 2×2 system with spatial streams of uniform power and nonuniform rate. Note is the received SNR per antenna i.e. SNR = $\frac{\sigma_1^2+\sigma_2^2}{N_0}$. It is evident that the stream to be detected first has lower capacity as compared to the stream to be detected last which enjoys higher diversity.

Fig. 5 compares two cases of spatial streams with uniform power and nonuniform rate and spatial streams with uniform rate and nonuniform power for 2 ×2, 3 ×3 and 4 ×4 systems. Key to the optimality of stripping is the use of Gaussian inputs as long as the stripping de- coders incorporate MMSE filters against yet undecoded streams at each successive cancella- tion stage. Successive stripping requires that each stream must be transmitted at a different rate with uniform power. We investigate a slightly suboptimal solution where we guarantee equal rate with nonuniform powers on each stream. Numerical optimization revealed that uniform rate and nonuniform power distribution leads to negligible suboptimality as shown in fig. 5.

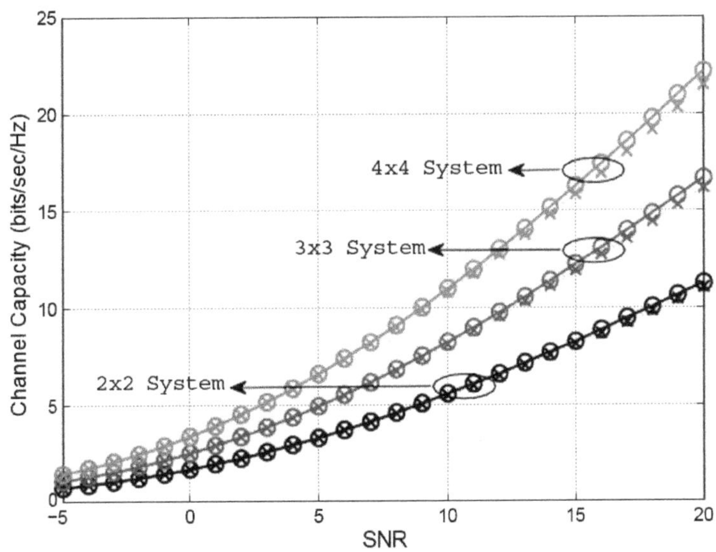

Fig. 4. Capacity of 2 × 2 system for Gaussian alphabets for the case of uniform power and nonuniform rate spatial streams.

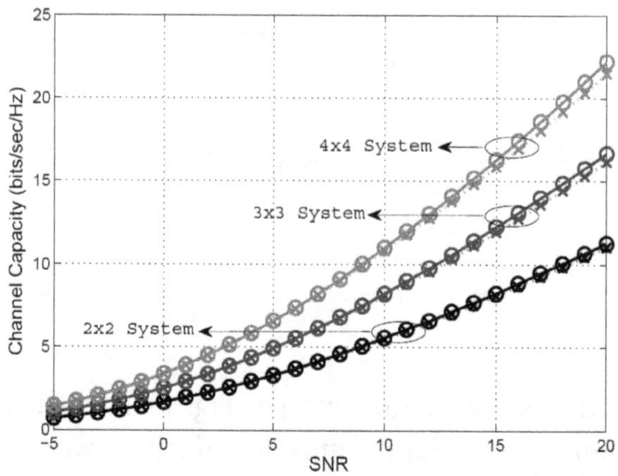

Fig. 5. Capacity of 2 × 2, 3 × 3 and 4 × 4 systems for Gaussian alphabets for the cases of spatial streams of uniform power and nonuniform rate and the spatial streams of uniform rate and nonuniform power. Note that the circles indicate the case of uniform power and nonuniform rate spatial streams while crosses indicate the case of uniform rate and nonuniform power spatial streams.

2.2.2 Finite Sized Constellation Inputs

To reduce the complexity and enhance the understanding of mutual information for finite sized constellation inputs, we restrict to the case of dual stream transmission. The system equation ignoring the frequency index takes the form:-

$$y = h1\ x1 + h2\ x2 + z \tag{8}$$

Mutual information expression for the dual streams from the chain rule (Foschini & Gans, 1998) is given as

$$I\ (y;\ x1, x2) = I\ (y;\ x1) + I\ (y;\ x2\ |x1) \tag{9}$$

For equal power distribution, I(y;x1)<I(y;x2|x1) dictating rate of first stream being less than rate of second stream (R1<R2). For finite size QAM constellation with x1 ∈ M1 and x2∈ M2, the mutual information expression conditioned on the channel takes the form (Ghaffar & Knopp, 2008a)

$$I\ (y;\ x1\ |H) = H\ (x1\ |H) - H\ (x1\ |y, H) = \log M1 - H\ (x1\ |y, H) \tag{10}$$

where H (.) = -E log p (.) is the entropy function. Second term of eq. (10) is given as:-

$$\begin{aligned}\mathcal{H}\left(x_1|\mathbf{y},\mathbf{H}\right) &= \frac{1}{M_1M_2N_zN_H}\sum_{x_1}\sum_{x_2}\sum_{\mathbf{H}}^{N_H}\sum_{\mathbf{z}}^{N_z}\log\frac{\sum_{x_1'}\sum_{x_2'}\exp\left[-\frac{1}{N_0}\left\|\mathbf{y}-\mathbf{h}_1x_1'-\mathbf{h}_2x_2'\right\|^2\right]}{\sum_{x_2'}\exp\left[-\frac{1}{N_0}\left\|\mathbf{y}-\mathbf{h}_1x_1-\mathbf{h}_2x_2'\right\|^2\right]}\\ &= \frac{1}{M_1M_2N_zN_H}\sum_{x_1}\sum_{x_2}\sum_{\mathbf{H}}^{N_H}\sum_{\mathbf{z}}^{N_z}\log\frac{\sum_{x_1'}\sum_{x_2'}\exp\left[-\frac{1}{N_0}\left\|\mathbf{h}_1x_1+\mathbf{h}_2x_2+\mathbf{z}-\mathbf{h}_1x_1'-\mathbf{h}_2x_2'\right\|^2\right]}{\sum_{x_2'}\exp\left[-\frac{1}{N_0}\left\|\mathbf{h}_2x_2+\mathbf{z}-\mathbf{h}_2x_2'\right\|^2\right]}\end{aligned} \tag{12}$$

For our purposes, it suffices to note that for each choice of x1 and x2, there are two sources of randomness in the choices of channel and noise. The above quantities can be easily approxi- mated numerically using sampling (Monte-Carlo) methods with Nz realizations of noise and NH realizations of the channel i.e.

Similarly the mutual information of second stream conditioned on the channel when first stream has been detected is given by:-

$$
\begin{aligned}
I(\mathbf{y}; x_2|x_1, \mathbf{H}) &= \mathcal{H}(x_2|x_1, \mathbf{H}) - \mathcal{H}(x_2|\mathbf{y}, x_1, \mathbf{H}) \\
&= \log M_2 - \sum_{x_1}\sum_{x_2}\int_{\mathbf{y}}\int_{\mathbf{H}} p(x_1, x_2, \mathbf{y}, \mathbf{H}) \log \frac{1}{p(x_2|\mathbf{y}, x_1, \mathbf{H})} d\mathbf{y} d\mathbf{H} \\
&= \log M_2 - \sum_{x_1}\sum_{x_2}\int_{\mathbf{y}}\int_{\mathbf{H}} p(x_1, x_2, \mathbf{y}, \mathbf{H}) \log \frac{p(\mathbf{y}, x_1, \mathbf{H})}{p(x_1, x_2, \mathbf{y}, \mathbf{H})} d\mathbf{y} d\mathbf{H} \\
&= \log M_2 - \sum_{x_1}\sum_{x_2}\int_{\mathbf{y}}\int_{\mathbf{H}} p(x_1, x_2, \mathbf{y}, \mathbf{H}) \log \frac{\sum_{x_2'} p\left(\mathbf{y}|x_1, x_2', \mathbf{H}\right)}{p(\mathbf{y}|x_1, x_2, \mathbf{H})} d\mathbf{y} d\mathbf{H} \qquad (13)
\end{aligned}
$$

Estimation of this quantity using Monte-Carlo simulation

$$
\begin{aligned}
I(\mathbf{y}; x_2|x_1, \mathbf{H}) &= \log M_2 - \frac{1}{M_1 M_2 N_{\mathbf{z}} N_{\mathbf{H}}} \sum_{x_1}\sum_{x_2}\sum_{\mathbf{H}}^{N_{\mathbf{H}}}\sum_{\mathbf{z}}^{N_{\mathbf{z}}} \log \frac{\sum_{x_2'} \exp\left[-\frac{1}{N_0}\left\|\mathbf{y} - \mathbf{h}_1 x_1 - \mathbf{h}_2 x_2'\right\|^2\right]}{\exp\left[-\frac{1}{N_0}\left\|\mathbf{y} - \mathbf{h}_1 x_1 - \mathbf{h}_2 x_2\right\|^2\right]} \\
&= \log M_2 - \frac{1}{M_1 M_2 N_{\mathbf{z}} N_{\mathbf{H}}} \sum_{x_1}\sum_{x_2}\sum_{\mathbf{H}}^{N_{\mathbf{H}}}\sum_{\mathbf{z}}^{N_{\mathbf{z}}} \log \frac{\sum_{x_2'} \exp\left[-\frac{1}{N_0}\left\|\mathbf{h}_2 x_2 + \mathbf{z} - \mathbf{h}_2 x_2'\right\|^2\right]}{\exp\left[-\frac{1}{N_0}\left\|\mathbf{z}\right\|^2\right]}
\end{aligned}
\qquad (14)
$$

Fig. 6 shows the capacity of first stream once second stream is not yet decoded for different combinations of finite constellation alphabets. For moderate values of SNR, the capacity of first stream is a function of the yet undetected second stream and this capacity decreases as the rate (constellation size) of second stream increases. This degradation is not observed at low and high values of SNR as at low SNR, two streams are orthogonal while at high SNR, second stream can be perfectly stripped off leading to detection of first stream. Rate of first stream being a function of the rate of second stream leads to nonuniform rates in uniform power dual stream scenario and this leads to the following proposed broadcast strategy.

2.3 Broadcast Strategy

We restrict to dual stream scenario for the broadcast case. The broadcast approach in dual stream scenario based on UEP (MAC-outage (Shamai & Steiner, 2003)) is motivated by the capacity of a Gaussian broadcast channel with two users i.e.

$$C = I(x1; y1) + I(x2; y2 \,|x1) \qquad (15)$$

where user 2 sees a better channel and so is able to decode and strip off the interference.

The broadcast strategy (Ghaffar & Knopp, 2008a) incorporates the transmission of two spatial streams of uniform power and nonuniform rate and incorporates two levels of performance. The reliably decoded information rate depends on the state of the channel which is determined by monitoring the received SNR being above or below a certain threshold. Transmitter is operating at a constant power and data rate but the limited adaptability of the system helps receivers to gear up to a higher data rate as the channel conditions improve.

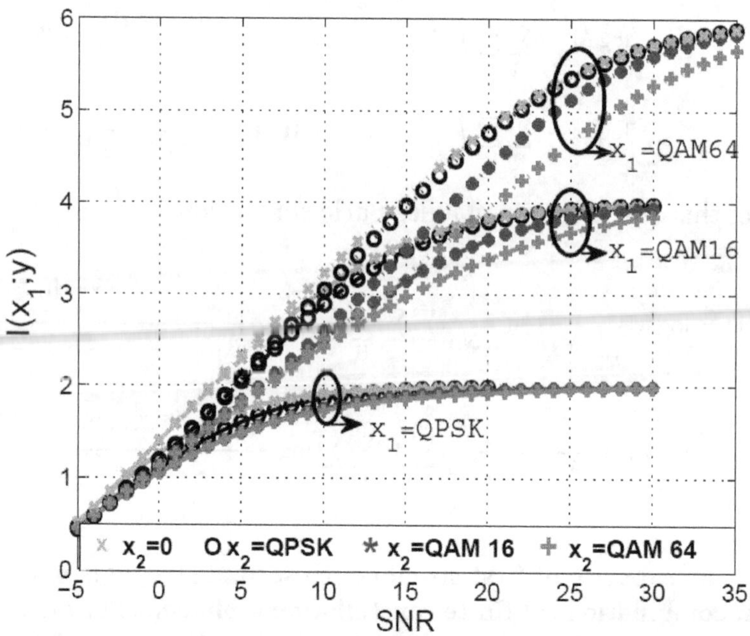

Fig. 6. Capacity of first stream in dual-stream broadcast approach for finite size alphabets once second stream is not known. Both streams have equal power. x2 = 0 indicates the special case when second stream has been decoded and stripped off. Note that SNR includes power of both streams.

Low priority/quality users are able to decode low rate stream x1 while high priority/quality users are able to decode both low and high rate streams i.e. x1 and x2 by successive stripping. The rates of two streams are

$$R1 \leq I\,(y; x1) \tag{16}$$

and

$$R2 \leq I\,(y; x2\,|x1) \tag{17}$$

The notion of priority/quality is typically the received SNR and/or stream decoupling. The users are divided into two groups i.e. near-in users and far-out users based on their received SNR. The lower rate stream x1 is designed for a lower value of SNR1 i.e. SNwhile the higher rate stream x2 is designed for higher value of SNR i.e. SNR2. The received SNR of a particular user dictates two decoding options.

1. If SNR2 >SNR≥SNR1, the user decodes x1.
2. If SNR SNR2, the user decodes both streams i.e. x1 and x2. The user first decodes low rate stream x1 strips it out and then decodes high rate stream x2.

This leads us to SIC detection based MIMO broadcast scenario with uniform power and nonuniform rate spatial streams. We now discuss the detectors for such broadcast scenario.

2.4 Detectors

The detectors discussed in this section are valid not only for spatially multiplexed MIMO systems but may be extended to other types of STC systems. We discuss two types of detectors as MMSE detector and low complexity max log MAP detector (Ghaffar & Knopp, 2009b).

2.4.1 MMSE

The frequency domain MMSE filter for x1,k is given as

$$\mathbf{h}_{1,k}^{MMSE} = \left(\mathbf{h}_{1,k}^{\dagger}\mathbf{R}_{1,k}^{-1}\mathbf{h}_{1,k} + \sigma_1^{-2}\right)^{-1}\mathbf{h}_{1,k}^{\dagger}\mathbf{R}_{1,k}^{-1} \tag{18}$$

where R1,k = σ2h2,k h† + σ2h3,k h† + ⋯ + σ2 hn ,k h† + N0I. After the application of MMSE filter we get

$$yk = \alpha kx1,k + z \tag{19}$$

where zk is assumed to be zero mean complex Gaussian random variable with variance Nk = h1MMSE, R1kh1 = h1,k MMSE† and α MMSE 1,k 1,k . Gaussianity has been assumed for post detection interference which increases the suboptimality of MMSE in the case of less number of interferers. Bit metric for the bit ckt on first stream is given as:-

$$\lambda_1^i\left(y_k, c_{k'}\right) \approx \min_{x_1 \in \chi_{1,c_{k'}}^i}\left[\frac{1}{N_k}\left|y_k - \alpha_k x_1\right|^2\right] \tag{20}$$

where χi 1,ckt denotes the subset of the signalset x ∈ χ1 whose labels have the value ckt ∈ {0, 1} in the position i. This metric has computational complexity O (|χ1|).

2.4.2 Low complexity max log MAP Detector

The max log MAP bit metric as per (6) is given as

$$\lambda_1^i\left(\mathbf{y}_k, c_{k'}\right) \approx \min_{x_1\in\mathcal{X}^i_{1,c_{k'}}, x_2\in\mathcal{X}_2,\cdots,x_{n_r}\in\mathcal{X}_{n_r}} \left\|\mathbf{y}_k - \mathbf{h}_{1,k}x_1 - \cdots - \mathbf{h}_{n_r,k}x_{n_r}\right\|^2 \tag{21}$$

which has computational complexity o (|χ1|). ··· (|χnr|).).. For brevity we drop the frequency index k and the bit position index k' i.e.

$$\begin{aligned}
\lambda_1^i(\mathbf{y},c) &\approx \min_{x_1\in\mathcal{X}^i_{1,c},x_2\in\mathcal{X}_2,\cdots,x_{n_r}\in\mathcal{X}_{n_r}} \|\mathbf{y}-\mathbf{h}_1x_1-\cdots-\mathbf{h}_{n_r}x_{n_r}\|^2\\
&= \min_{x_1\in\mathcal{X}^i_{1,c},x_2\in\mathcal{X}_2,\cdots,x_{n_r}\in\mathcal{X}_{n_r}} \left\{\|\mathbf{y}\|^2+\sum_{j=1}^{n_r}\left\|\mathbf{h}_jx_j\right\|^2+2\Re\sum_{j=1}^{n_r-1}\sum_{l=j+1}^{n_r}\left(\mathbf{h}_jx_j\right)^{\dagger}(\mathbf{h}_lx_l)-2\Re\sum_{j=1}^{n_r}\left(\mathbf{h}_j^{\dagger}\mathbf{y}\right)x_j^*\right\}\\
&= \min_{x_1\in\mathcal{X}^i_{1,c},x_2\in\mathcal{X}_2,\cdots,x_{n_r}\in\mathcal{X}_{n_r}} \left\{\|\mathbf{y}\|^2+\sum_{j=1}^{n_r-1}\left\|\mathbf{h}_jx_j\right\|^2+2\Re\sum_{j=1}^{n_r-1}\sum_{l=j+1}^{n_r-1}p_{jl}x_j^*x_l-2\Re\sum_{j=1}^{n_r-1}y_jx_j^*\right.\\
&\qquad\left.+2\Re\sum_{j=1}^{n_r-1}p_{jn_r}x_j^*x_{n_r}-2\Re y_{n_r}x_{n_r}^*+\|\mathbf{h}_{n_r}x_{n_r}\|^2\right\}
\end{aligned}\tag{22}$$

where yk = h†y be the matched filter (MF) output for k-th stream and pkm = h†hm be the cross correlation between k-th and m-th channel. Breaking some of the terms in their real and imaginary parts with subscripts (.)R and (.)I indicating real and imaginary parts of a complex number, we have

$$\begin{aligned}
\lambda_1^i(\mathbf{y},c) = \min_{x_1\in\mathcal{X}^i_{1,c}\cdots x_{n_r}\in\mathcal{X}_{n_r}} &\left\{\sum_{j=1}^{n_r-1}\left\|\mathbf{h}_jx_j\right\|^2+2\Re\sum_{j=1}^{n_r-1}\sum_{l=j+1}^{n_r-1}p_{jl}x_j^*x_l-2\Re\sum_{j=1}^{n_r-1}y_jx_j^*\right.\\
&+\left(2\sum_{j=1}^{n_r-1}\left(p_{jn_r,R}x_{j,R}+p_{jn_r,I}x_{j,I}\right)-2y_{n_r,R}\right)x_{n_r,R}+\|\mathbf{h}_{n_r}\|^2x_{n_r,R}^2\\
&\left.+\left(2\sum_{j=1}^{n_r-1}\left(p_{jn_r,R}x_{j,I}-p_{jn_r,I}x_{j,R}\right)-2y_{n_r,I}\right)x_{n_r,I}+\|\mathbf{h}_{n_r}\|^2x_{n_r,I}^2\right\}
\end{aligned}\tag{23}$$

This equation reduces one complex dimension of the system. For xnr belonging to equal en- ergy alphabets, the bit metric is written as

$$\begin{aligned}
\lambda_1^i(\mathbf{y},c) = \min_{x_1\in\mathcal{X}^i_{1,c}\cdots x_{n_r-1}\in\mathcal{X}_{n_r-1}} &\left\{\sum_{j=1}^{n_r-1}\left\|\mathbf{h}_jx_j\right\|^2+2\Re\sum_{j=1}^{n_r-1}\sum_{l=j+1}^{n_r-1}p_{jl}x_j^*x_l-2\Re\sum_{j=1}^{n_r-1}y_jx_j^*\right.\\
&\left.-\left|2\sum_{j=1}^{n_r-1}\left(p_{jn_r,R}x_{j,R}+p_{jn_r,I}x_{j,I}\right)-2y_{n_r,R}\right||x_{n_r,R}|-\left|2\sum_{j=1}^{n_r-1}\left(p_{jn_r,R}x_{j,I}-p_{jn_r,I}x_{j,R}\right)-2y_{n_r,I}\right||x_{n_r,I}|\right\}
\end{aligned}$$

For xnr belonging to non-equal energy alphabets, it's real and imaginary part which minimizes (23) are given as

$$x_{n_r,R} \rightarrow -\frac{\sum_{j=1}^{n_r-1}\left(p_{jn_r,R}x_{j,R} + p_{jn_r,I}x_{j,I}\right) - y_{n_r,R}}{\|\mathbf{h}_{n_r}\|^2}$$

$$x_{n_r,I} \rightarrow -\frac{\sum_{j=1}^{n_r-1}\left(p_{jn_r,R}x_{j,I} - p_{jn_r,I}x_{j,R}\right) - y_{n_r,I}}{\|\mathbf{h}_{n_r}\|^2} \quad (24)$$

where indicates the quantization process in which amongst the finite available points, the point closest to the calculated continuous value is selected.

This bit metric implies reduction in the complexity to O (|χ1|··· | χnr−1|). Reduction of one complex dimension without any additional processing is a fundamental result of significant importance for lower dimensional systems. Additionally this bit metric is based on MF out-puts and channel correlations and is therefore simpler for fixed point implementations. The intricacy in the practical implementation of a higher dimensional MIMO system due to space (requisite antenna spacing) and technology constraints underlines the significance of complex- ity reduction algorithms for lower dimensional systems. MMSE based demodulators involve computationally complex operations of matrix inversions which are very hard for fixed point implementations. Moreover MMSE demodulator additionally needs the knowledge of noise variance.

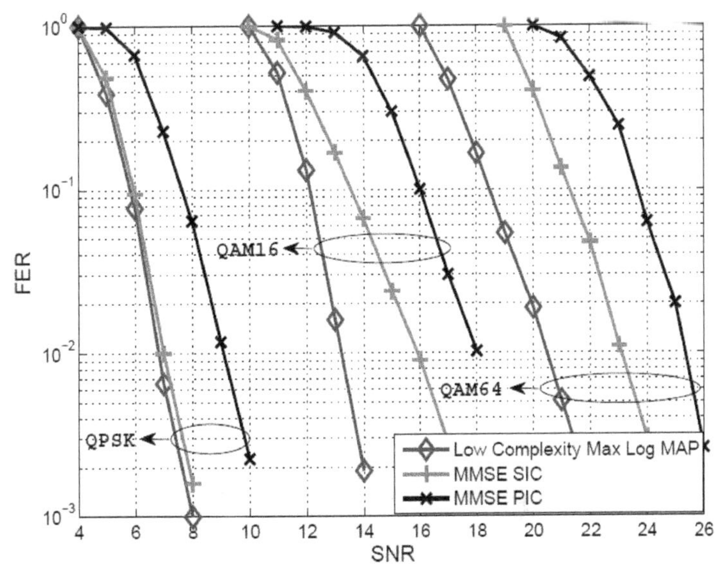

Fig. 7. 2 × 2 system with uniform rate and nonuniform power spatial streams. For QPSK 2 = 0.63PT , σ2 = 0.37PT , for QAM 16 σ2 = 0.67PT , σ2 = 0.33PT while for QAM64 σ2 = 0.70PT , σ2 = 0.30PT .

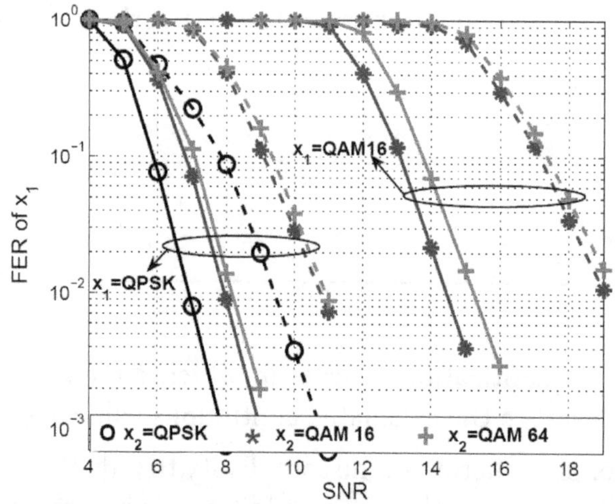

Fig. 8. Performance of lower rate stream in 2 2 BICM MIMO OFDM system using 802.11n convolutional code. Continuous lines indicate low complexity max log MAP detector while dashed lines indicate MMSE detector.

2.5 Simulations

We consider a 2 × 2 BICM MIMO OFDM system using the de facto standard, 64 state rate-1/2 convolutional encoder of 802.11n standard (802.11n, 2006) and rate-1/2 punctured turbo code proposed for 3GPP LTE (LTE, 2006) 1. MIMO channel has iid Gaussian matrix entries with unit variance. The channel is independently generated for each time instant and perfect CSI at the receiver is assumed. Furthermore, all mappings of coded bits to QAM symbols use Gray encoding. We consider MMSE and low complexity max log MAP detector. There are two scenarios.

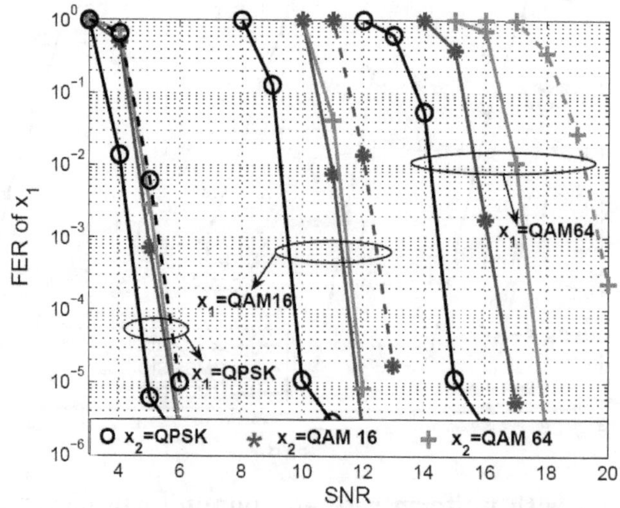

Fig. 9. Performance of lower rate stream in 2 × 2 BICM MIMO OFDM system using 3GPP LTE turbo code. Continuous lines indicate low complexity max log MAP

detector while dashed lines indicate MMSE detector. Block length of the lower rate stream is 1296 bits while number of decoding iterations are 5.

In first scenario, spatial streams of uniform rate and nonuniform power are transmitted in 2 × 2 MIMO broadcast system. The upcoming WLAN standard 802.11n (802.11n, 2006) supports the codeword sizes of 648, 1296, and 1944 bits. For our purposes, we selected the codeword size of 1296 bits and coding scheme of convolutional coding. We focus on the frame error rates (FER) of the system. We consider the low complexity max log MAP and MMSE SIC approach in which the higher power stream is detected first and is subsequently stripped off leading to the detection of lower power stream. With PT being the total power available, the power distribution between two streams is optimized to equate their rates in the desired SNR region where SNR is defined as the received SNR per antenna i.e. $\frac{P_T}{N_0}$. As a reference, MMSE parallel interference cancellation (PIC) has also been simulated in which two streams are independently detected using MMSE filters and two streams have equal power. Fig. 7 shows the improved performance of low complexity max log MAP approach with respect to both MMSE SIC and MMSE PIC approach. The gap widens as the constellation proliferates i.e QAM 16 and QAM64 which is attributed to the higher suboptimality of MMSE for larger sized constellations.

In second scenario, spatial streams of uniform power and nonuniform rate are transmitted in 2 × 2 MIMO broadcast system. We focus on the FER of first stream (lower rate) as subsequent to stripping, the detection of second stream (higher rate) is trivial (using SIMO detectors). The frame length of first stream is fixed to 1296 information bits as per 802.11n (802.11n, 2006). Figs. 8 and 9 compare the performance of low complexity max log MAP detector with MMSE detector. The max log MAP detector performs significantly better than the MMSE detector. Degradation of the performance for first stream as the rate (constellation size) of second stream increases confirms the earlier result of sec. 2.2.2 that rate of first stream is a function of the rate of second stream.

3. INTERFERENCE SUPPRESSION FOR FUTURE WIRELESS SYSTEMS

To cope with the ever-increasing demands on the higher spectral efficiency, appendage of spatial dimension (MIMO) needs to be coupled with a tight frequency reuse as is advocated in the future wireless communication systems as 3GPP LTE (LTE, 2006) and LTE-Advanced (LTE-A, 2008). Adaptive modulation and coding schemes will be supported in the next gener- ation wireless systems which combined with the diversified data services will lead to variable transmission rate streams. These system characteristics will overall lead to an interference- limited system. Most state-of-the-art wireless systems deal with the interference either by orthogonalizing the communication links in time or frequency (Gesbert et al., 2007) or allow the communication links to share the same degrees of freedom but model the interference as additive Gaussian random process (Russell & Stuber, 1995). Both of these approaches may be suboptimal as first approach entails an a priori loss of the degrees of freedom in both links, in- dependent of the interference strength while second approach treats the interference as pure noise while it actually carries information and has the structure that can be potentially ex- ploited in mitigating its effect.

3GPP LTE (LTE, 2006) has chosen orthogonal frequency division multiple access (OFDMA) technology for the downlink in order to provide multiple access and eliminate the intracell interference. However frequency reuse factor being 1 will lead to intercell interference impair- ments among neighboring cells. Intercell interference coordination techniques (Gesbert et al., 2007) are studied to minimize the interference level while spatial interference cancellation fil- ters are the focus of attention to cancel the interferers which will be 1 in most cases (near cell boundaries) and 2 in rare cases (near cell corners). Different spatial interference cancellation techniques involving equalization and subtractive cancellation (Bladsjö et al., 1999) (Debbah et al., 2000) have been proposed in the literature. Amongst them, MMSE linear detectors are being considered as likely candidates for 3GPP LTE (Dahlman et al., 2006). The suboptimality of MMSE for non Gaussian alphabets in low dimensional systems (less number of interfer- ers) has already been discussed and simulated in the previous sections and moreover MMSE detection being based on interference attenuation is void of exploiting the interference struc- ture in mitigating its effect. Though not optimal, but their low complexity still makes them attractive for practical systems.

Optimal strategy for treating the interference in the regime of very strong (Carleial, 1975) and very weak interference is well known however if the interference is in the moderate region, no optimal strategy is known but partial decoding of interference can significantly improve per- formance (Han & Kobayashi, 1981). This part of the chapter discusses a low complexity spatial interference cancellation algorithm for single frequency reuse synchronized cellular networks in the presence of one strong interferer. This algorithm is based on the low complexity max log MAP detector and benefits from its ability to exploit interference structure in mitigating its effect. The algorithm encompasses two strategies for interference mitigation i.e. interfer- ence suppression and interference cancellation and their selection in the receiver is dictated by the relative strength and the rate of interfering stream. In the scenario of interfering stream being weak or of higher rate relative to the desired stream, thereby making it unfeasible to be decoded, the mobile station (MS) resorts to the strategy of interference suppression. It can be interpreted as partial decoding of the interference which is the recommended strategy in the regime of moderate interference (Han & Kobayashi, 1981). When the interfering stream is relatively stronger or is of lower rate thereby making it feasible to be decoded, MS adopts interference cancellation strategy (subtractive cancellation) which is the optimal strategy in the case of strong interference (Carleial, 1975).

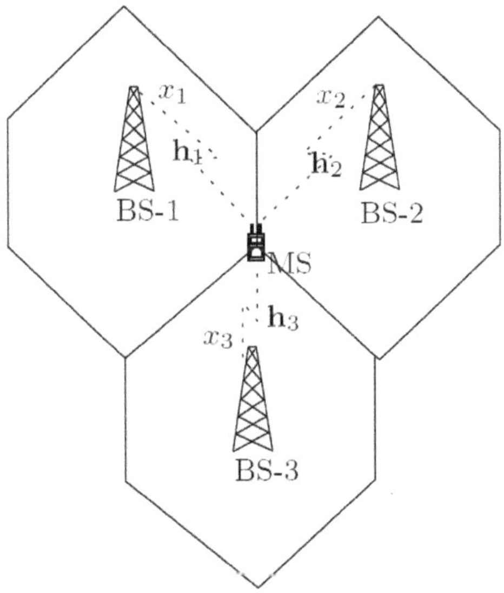

Fig. 10. Interference cancellation in single frequency cellular network. x1 is the desired signal while x2 and x3 are the interference signals.

3.1 System Model

The system model as shown in fig. 10 remains same as described in the sec.2.1.2 with 3 spatial streams. However these streams arriving at the receiver (MS) are now from three different base stations (BS) thereby ensuring independent channels. The MS has receive diversity with nr receive antennas. All the BSs are assumed to be synchronous.

3.2 Information Theoretic view

For better understanding of the effect of strength and rate (alphabet size) of interference, the case of one strong interference is considered in this section. The focus is on the mutual in- formation of the desired stream in the presence of one strong interferer (Ghaffar & Knopp, 2009b).

$$I(\mathbf{y}; x_1) = \log M_1 - \frac{1}{M_1} \sum_{x_1} \int_{\mathbf{y}} p(\mathbf{y}|x_1) \log \frac{\sum_{x_1} p(\mathbf{y}|x_1)}{p(\mathbf{y}|x_1)} d\mathbf{y} \tag{25}$$

Fig. 11 shows the mutual information of the desired stream in the presence of the interference stream. We define the term α =σ22/ σ12. Mutual information of the desired stream is a function of the rate as well as the strength of the interference stream. For moderate values of α and when the interference has a lower rate (smaller constellation size) relative to the desired stream, as the interference strength increases, the mutual information of the desired stream increases. However when the interference stream has a higher rate as compared to the rate of the desired stream, this behavior is observed for higher values of α. This can be interpreted as the decoding capability of the MS of the interference in the presence of the desired stream. Once the interference strength and its rate relative to the strength and the rate of the desired stream permits the decoding of the interference, we observe an increase in the mutual infor- mation of the desired stream with the increase of α. Fig. 11 also authenticates the well known result of Gaussian being the worst case interference however the gap decreases as the rate of the interference stream increases. This diminution of gap may be related to the proximity of the behavior of large size constellations to Gaussianity as both are characterized by high peak to average power ratios.

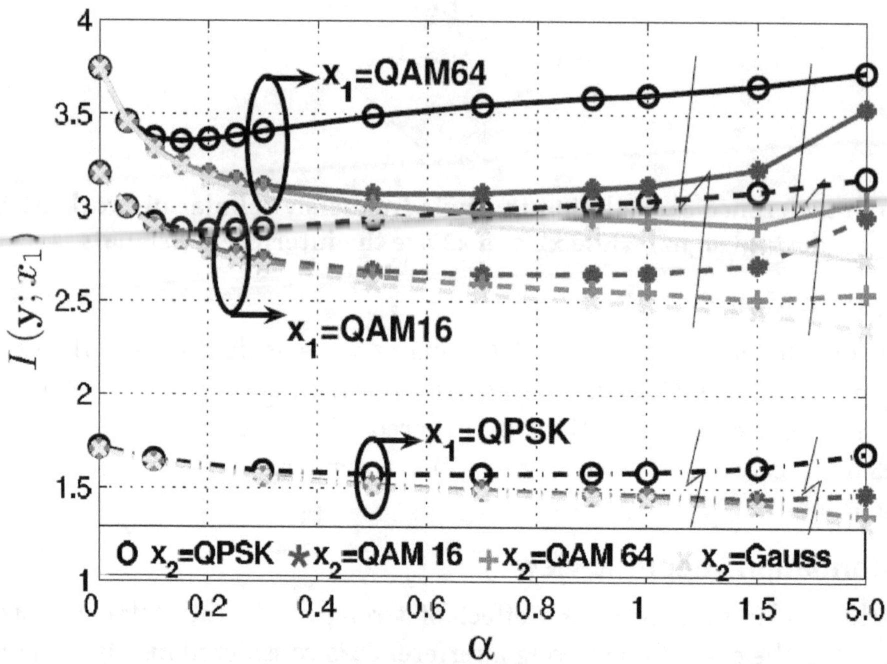

Fig. 11. Mutual information of the desired stream x1 in the presence of the interference stream x2 for different constellations. SNR is 4.5 dB for x1=QPSK, 11 dB for x1 = QAM16 and 13 dB for x1 = QAM64. Note that the flash sign indicates a discontinuity of abscissa

3.3 Interference Mitigation Strategies

Based on the low complexity max log MAP detector, an interference mitigation strategy (Ghaf- far & Knopp, 2009a) is discussed which is based on the partial decoding of the interference in the regime when interference because of its relative rate or strength is undecodable and subtractive cancellation when the interference is quite strong and is decodable. This strategy is based on exploiting the structure of the interference in mitigating its effect once subtractive cancellation is not possible and resorting to subtractive cancellation otherwise. So there are two options for interference mitigation.

1. In the regime when interference has higher rate or is weaker in strength relative to the desired stream thereby rendering the absolute decoding of interference unfeasible, tar- get stream is decoded using the low complexity max log MAP detector which takes into account the effect of interference and can be termed as the partial decoding of interfer- ence or partial joint decoding. This approach is termed as interference suppression.
2. In the regime when interference has lower rate or is stronger in strength relative to the desired stream thereby rendering the absolute decoding of the interference feasible, the interference stream is decoded using low complexity max log MAP detector, stripping it off and then decoding the desired stream. This approach is termed as interference cancellation.

The factors that will decide the strategy to be adopted will be the relative rate and the strength of the interference stream comparative to the desired stream. The requisites for this algorithm are the knowledge of interference channel and the modulation and coding scheme (MCS) of interfering stream. The BSs need to be synchronous with pilot signals from the adjacent BSs to be orthogonal to meet these requisites.

3.4 Performance Analysis

This section deliberates on the performance analysis of two detectors for detecting the desired stream in the presence of interfering stream (Ghaffar & Knopp, 2009c).

3.4.1 PEP Analysis - Max Log MAP Detector

The conditional PEP i.e. $P(\underline{c}_1 \rightarrow \hat{\underline{c}}_1|\mathbf{H})$ of max log MAP detector is given as

$$P(\underline{c}_1 \rightarrow \hat{\underline{c}}_1|\mathbf{H}) = P\left(\sum_{k'} \min_{x_1 \in \chi^i_{1,c_{k'}}, x_2 \in \chi_2} \frac{1}{N_0}\left\|\mathbf{y}_k - \mathbf{h}_{1,k}x_1 - \mathbf{h}_{2,k}x_2\right\|^2 \geq \right.$$
$$\left. \sum_{k'} \min_{x_1 \in \chi^i_{1,\hat{c}_{k'}}, x_2 \in \chi_2} \frac{1}{N_0}\left\|\mathbf{y}_k - \mathbf{h}_{1,k}x_1 - \mathbf{h}_{2,k}x_2\right\|^2\right) \tag{26}$$

where H = [H1 ·· ·]HK] i.e. the complete channel for the transmission of the codeword c1 and$\mathrm{H}_k = \mathrm{h}_{1,k}\ \mathrm{h}_{2,k}$ i.e. the channel at k-th frequency tone. For the worst case scenario once d (c¹ - c¹) = d f ree, the inequality on the right hand side of (26) shares the same terms on all but d f ree summation points for which $c^k = c^k$ where (¯.) denotes the binary complement. Let

$$\tilde{x}_{1,k}, \tilde{x}_{2,k} = \arg \min_{x_1 \in \mathcal{X}^i_{1,c_{k'}}, x_2 \in \mathcal{X}_2} \frac{1}{N_0} \left\| \mathbf{y}_k - \mathbf{h}_{1,k} x_1 - \mathbf{h}_{2,k} x_2 \right\|^2$$

$$\hat{x}_{1,k}, \hat{x}_{2,k} = \arg \min_{x_1 \in \mathcal{X}^i_{1,\hat{c}_{k'}}, x_2 \in \mathcal{X}_2} \frac{1}{N_0} \left\| \mathbf{y}_k - \mathbf{h}_{1,k} x_1 - \mathbf{h}_{2,k} x_2 \right\|^2 \quad (27)$$

As $x_{1,k}$ and $x_{2,k}$ are the transmitted symbols so $\left\| \mathbf{y}_k - \mathbf{h}_{1,k} x_{1,k} - \mathbf{h}_{2,k} x_{2,k} \right\|^2 \geq \left\| \mathbf{y}_k - \mathbf{h}_{1,k} \tilde{x}_{1,k} - \mathbf{h}_{2,k} \tilde{x}_{2,k} \right\|^2$. The conditional PEP is given as

$$\begin{aligned} P\left(\underline{c}_1 \to \hat{\underline{c}}_1 | \mathbf{H}\right) \leq & P\left(\sum_{k,d_{free}} \frac{1}{N_0} \left\| \mathbf{y}_k - \mathbf{h}_{1,k} x_{1,k} - \mathbf{h}_{2,k} x_{2,k} \right\|^2 \geq \sum_{k,d_{free}} \frac{1}{N_0} \left\| \mathbf{y}_k - \mathbf{h}_{1,k} \hat{x}_{1,k} - \mathbf{h}_{2,k} \hat{x}_{2,k} \right\|^2 \right) \\ = & Q\left(\sqrt{ \sum_{k,d_{free}} \frac{1}{2N_0} \left\| \mathbf{H}_k \left(\hat{\mathbf{x}}_k - \mathbf{x}_k \right) \right\|^2 } \right) \\ = & Q\left(\sqrt{ \frac{1}{2N_0} \mathrm{vec}\left(\overline{\mathbf{H}}^{\dagger} \right)^{\dagger} \mathbf{\Delta} \mathrm{vec}\left(\overline{\mathbf{H}}^{\dagger} \right) } \right) \end{aligned} \quad (28)$$

where $\overline{\mathbf{H}} = \left[\mathbf{H}_1 \cdots \mathbf{H}_{k,d_{free}} \right]$, $\hat{\mathbf{x}}_k = \left[\hat{x}_{1,k}\ \hat{x}_{2,k} \right]^T$ and $\mathbf{\Delta} = \mathbf{I}_{n_r} \otimes \mathbf{D}\mathbf{D}^{\dagger}$ while $\mathbf{D} = \mathrm{diag}\left\{ \hat{\mathbf{x}}_1 - \mathbf{x}_1, \hat{\mathbf{x}}_2 - \mathbf{x}_2, \cdots, \hat{\mathbf{x}}_{k,d_{free}} - \mathbf{x}_{k,d_{free}} \right\}$. Q is the Gaussian Q-function i.e. $Q(y) = \frac{1}{\sqrt{2\pi}} \int_y^{\infty} e^{-x^2/2} dx$ and vec indicates vectorization of a matrix. For a Hermitian quadratic form in complex Gaussian random variable $q = \mathbf{m}^{\dagger} \mathbf{A} \mathbf{m}$ where $\mathbf{A}$ is a Hermitian matrix and column vector $\mathbf{m}$ is a circularly symmetric complex Gaussian vector i.e. $\mathbf{m} \sim \mathcal{NC}(\boldsymbol{\mu}, \boldsymbol{\Sigma})$ with $\boldsymbol{\mu} = E[\mathbf{m}]$ and $\boldsymbol{\Sigma} = E\left[\mathbf{m}\mathbf{m}^{\dagger}\right] - \boldsymbol{\mu}\boldsymbol{\mu}^{\dagger}$, the moment generating function (MGF) is

$$E\left[\exp\left(-t \mathbf{m}^{\dagger} \mathbf{A} \mathbf{m} \right) \right] = \frac{ \exp\left[-t \boldsymbol{\mu}^{\dagger} \mathbf{A} \left(\mathbf{I} + t \boldsymbol{\Sigma} \mathbf{A} \right)^{-1} \boldsymbol{\mu} \right] }{ \det\left(\mathbf{I} + t \boldsymbol{\Sigma} \mathbf{A} \right) } \quad (29)$$

Using Chernoff bound $Q(x) \leq \frac{1}{2} \exp\left(\frac{-x^2}{2} \right)$ and the MGF, PEP is upper bounded as

$$\begin{aligned} P\left(\underline{c}_1 \to \hat{\underline{c}}_1\right) \leq & \frac{1}{2 \det\left(\mathbf{I} + \frac{1}{4N_0} \mathbf{I} \mathbf{\Delta} \right)} \\ = & \frac{1}{2 \prod_{k=1}^{d_{free}} \left(1 + \frac{1}{4N_0} \left\| \hat{\mathbf{x}}_k - \mathbf{x}_k \right\|^2 \right)^{n_r}} \end{aligned} \quad (30)$$

$\left\| \hat{\mathbf{x}}_k - \mathbf{x}_k \right\|^2 \geq d_{1,\min}^2 + d_{2,\min}^2$ if $\hat{x}_{2,k} \neq x_{2,k}$ and $\left\| \hat{\mathbf{x}}_k - \mathbf{x}_k \right\|^2 \geq d_{1,\min}^2$ if $\hat{x}_{2,k} = x_{2,k}$. There exists $2^{d_{free}}$ possible vectors of $\left[\hat{x}_{2,1}, \cdots, \hat{x}_{2,d_{free}} \right]^T$ basing on the binary criteria that $\hat{x}_{2,k}$ is equal or not equal to $x_{2,k}$. Taking into account all these cases combined with their corresponding probabilities, the PEP is upper bounded as

$$P\left(\underline{c}_1 \rightarrow \hat{\underline{c}}_1|\mathrm{H}\right) \leq \frac{1}{2}\left(\frac{4N_0}{\sigma_1^2 d_{1,\min}^2}\right)^{n_r d_{free}} \left(\sum_{j=0}^{d_{free}} C_j^{d_{free}} \frac{\left(P\left(\hat{x}_{2,k} \neq x_{2,k}\right)\right)^j \left(1 - P\left(\hat{x}_{2,k} \neq x_{2,k}\right)\right)^{d_{free}-j}}{\left(1 + \frac{\sigma_2^2 d_{2,\min}^2}{\sigma_1^2 d_{1,\min}^2}\right)^{j n_r}}\right) \tag{31}$$

where $d_{j,\min}^2 = \sigma_j^2 \check{d}_{j,\min}^2$ with $\check{d}_{j,\min}^2$ being the normalized minimum distance of the constellation χ_j for $j = \{1, 2\}$ and $C_j^{d_{free}}$ is the binomial coefficient. $P\left(\hat{x}_{2,k} \neq x_{2,k}\right)$ has been derived in the following section.

3.4.2 $P\left(\hat{x}_{2,k} \neq x_{2,k}\right)$

Considering (27), $P\left(\hat{x}_{2,k} \neq x_{2,k}|\mathbf{h}_{1,k}, \mathbf{h}_{2,k}, x_{1,k}\right)$ is

$$\begin{aligned}
&P\left(\hat{x}_{2,k} \neq x_{2,k}|\mathbf{h}_{1,k}, \mathbf{h}_{2,k}, x_{1,k}\right) \\
&= P\left(-2\Re\left(\left(\mathbf{h}_{1,k}\left(x_{1,k} - x_1\right) + \mathbf{z}_k\right)^{\dagger} \mathbf{h}_{2,k}\left(x_{2,k} - x_2\right)\right) \geq \left\|\mathbf{h}_{2,k}\left(x_{2,k} - x_2\right)\right\|^2 |\mathbf{H}_k, x_{1,k}\right) \\
&= Q\left(\sqrt{\frac{\left\|\mathbf{h}_{2,k}\left(x_{2,k} - x_2\right)\right\|^2}{2N_0}} + \sqrt{\frac{2}{N_0}}\Re\left(\frac{\left(\mathbf{h}_{1,k}\left(x_{1,k} - x_1\right)\right)^{\dagger} \mathbf{h}_{2,k}\left(x_{2,k} - x_2\right)}{\sqrt{\left\|\mathbf{h}_{2,k}\left(x_{2,k} - x_2\right)\right\|^2}}\right)\right)
\end{aligned}$$

Using the relation Q (a + b) ≤ Q (amin - |bmax|) and $\Re\left(a^{\dagger}\hat{b}\right) \leq \|a\|$ where b^ is the unit vector we get

$$P\left(\hat{x}_{2,k} \neq x_{2,k}|\mathbf{h}_{1,k}, \mathbf{h}_{2,k}\right) \leq \frac{1}{2}\exp\left(-\frac{\left\|\mathbf{h}_{2,k}\right\|^2 d_{2,\min}^2}{4N_0} - \frac{\left\|\mathbf{h}_{1,k}\right\|^2 d_{1,\max}^2}{N_0} + \frac{\left\|\mathbf{h}_{2,k}\right\|\left\|\mathbf{h}_{1,k}\right\| d_{2,\min} d_{1,\mathrm{ma}}}{N_0}\right. \tag{32}$$

Conditioned on the norm of $\mathbf{h}_{1,k}$ we make two non-overlapping regions as $\left(\left\|\mathbf{h}_{2,k}\right\| \geq \left\|\mathbf{h}_{1,k}\right\| |\mathbf{h}_{1,k}\right)$ and $\left(\left\|\mathbf{h}_{2,k}\right\| < \left\|\mathbf{h}_{1,k}\right\| |\mathbf{h}_{1,k}\right)$ with the corresponding probabilities as $\mathcal{P}_{\mathbf{h}_1}^{<}$ and $\mathcal{P}_{\mathbf{h}_1}^{>}$. Note that in first region $\left\|\mathbf{h}_{2,k}\right\|\left\|\mathbf{h}_{1,k}\right\| \leq \left\|\mathbf{h}_{2,k}\right\|^2$ while for second region $\left\|\mathbf{h}_{2,k}\right\|\left\|\mathbf{h}_{1,k}\right\| < \left\|\mathbf{h}_{1,k}\right\|^2$. So

$$\begin{aligned}
P\left(\hat{x}_{2,k} \neq x_{2,k}\right) &\leq \frac{1}{2}E_{\mathbf{h}_1}\left[\left(\frac{4N_0}{d_{2,\min}^2 - 4d_{2,\min}d_{1,\max}}\right)^{n_r} \exp\left(-\frac{\left\|\mathbf{h}_{1,k}\right\|^2 d_{1,\max}^2}{N_0}\right) E_{\mathbf{h}_2|\mathbf{h}_1}\left(\mathcal{P}_{\mathbf{h}_1}^{<}\right)\right. \\
&\quad \left. + \left(\frac{4N_0}{d_{2,\min}^2}\right)^{n_r} \exp\left(-\left\|\mathbf{h}_{1,k}\right\|^2 \frac{d_{1,\max}^2 - d_{2,\min}d_{1,\max}}{N_0}\right) E_{\mathbf{h}_2|\mathbf{h}_1}\left(\mathcal{P}_{\mathbf{h}_1}^{>}\right)\right] \\
&\leq \frac{1}{2}\left(\frac{4N_0}{\sigma_2^2 d_{2,\min}^2}\right)^{n_r}\left(\frac{N_0}{\sigma_1^2 d_{1,\max}^2}\right)^{n_r}\left(\frac{1}{\left(1 - \frac{4\sigma_1 \check{d}_{1,\max}}{\sigma_2 \check{d}_{2,\min}}\right)^{n_r}} + \frac{1}{\left(1 - \frac{\sigma_2 \check{d}_{2,\min}}{\sigma_1 \check{d}_{1,\max}}\right)^{n_r}}\right)
\end{aligned} \tag{33}$$

where we upper bound $E_{\mathbf{h}_2|\mathbf{h}_1}\left(\mathcal{P}_{\mathbf{h}_1}^{<}\right)$ and $E_{\mathbf{h}_2|\mathbf{h}_1}\left(\mathcal{P}_{\mathbf{h}_1}^{>}\right)$ by 1.

$P\left(\hat{x}_{2,k} \neq x_{2,k}\right) \to 0$ as $\sigma_2^2 \to \infty$ while $P\left(\hat{x}_{2,k} \neq x_{2,k}\right)$increasesasσ22increases.Eq.(31)demonstrates strates a significant result of achieving full diversity by the low complexity max log MAP detector and converging to the performance of single stream using maximum ratio combin- ing in the case of very weak and strong interference. In the moderate region, as the strength of interference increases, P x^2,k = x2,k reduces and there is a coding gain for the detection of desired stream contrary to the case of MMSE where there is a coding loss as the interference gets stronger (shown in the next section).

3.4.3 PEP Analysis - MMSE Detector

3.5 Gaussian Assumption

Conditional PEP for MMSE basing on Gaussian assumption of post detection interference (20) is given as

$$P\left(\underline{c}_1 \to \hat{\underline{c}}_1 | \mathbf{H}\right) = P\left(\sum_{k'} \min_{x_1 \in \mathcal{X}^i_{1,c_{k'}}} \frac{\left|y_k - \alpha_k x_1\right|^2}{N_k} \geq \sum_{k'} \min_{x_1 \in \mathcal{X}^i_{1,\hat{c}_{k'}}} \frac{\left|y_k - \alpha_k x_1\right|^2}{N_k}\right) \tag{34}$$

Let

$$\tilde{x}_{1,k} = \arg \min_{x_1 \in \mathcal{X}^i_{1,c_{k'}}} \frac{\left|y_k - \alpha_k x_1\right|^2}{N_k}, \quad \hat{x}_{1,k} = \arg \min_{x_1 \in \mathcal{X}^i_{1,\hat{c}_{k'}}} \frac{\left|y_k - \alpha_k x_1\right|^2}{N_k}$$

Considering the worst case scenario $d\left(\underline{c}_1 - \hat{\underline{c}}_1\right) = d_{free}$ and using the fact that $\frac{1}{N_k}\left|y_k - \alpha_k x_{1,k}\right|^2 \geq \frac{1}{N_k}\left|y_k - \alpha_k \hat{x}_{1,k}\right|^2$, the conditional PEP is upper bounded as

$$P\left(\underline{c}_1 \to \hat{\underline{c}}_1 | \mathbf{H}\right) \leq Q\left(\sqrt{\sum_{k,d_{free}} \frac{\alpha_k^2}{2N_k}\left|\hat{x}_{1,k} - x_{1,k}\right|^2}\right) \tag{35}$$

Bounding $\left|\hat{x}_{1,k} - x_{1,k}\right|^2 \geq d^2_{1,\min}$ and using the Chernoff bound

$$P\left(\underline{c}_1 \to \hat{\underline{c}}_1 | \mathbf{H}\right) \leq \frac{1}{2}\exp\left(-\frac{d^2_{1,\min}}{4}\sum_{k,d_{free}} \mathbf{h}^{\dagger}_{1,k}\mathbf{R}^{-1}_{2,k}\mathbf{h}_{1,k}\right) \tag{36}$$

where the summation in (36) can be written as

$$\sum_{k,d_{free}} \mathbf{h}^{\dagger}_{1,k}\mathbf{R}^{-1}_{2,k}\mathbf{h}_{1,k} = \left[\mathbf{h}^{\dagger}_{1,1}, \cdots, \mathbf{h}^{\dagger}_{1,d_{free}}\right] \operatorname{diag}\left[\mathbf{R}^{-1}_{2,1}, \cdots, \mathbf{R}^{-1}_{2,d_{free}}\right] \left[\mathbf{h}^{T}_{1,1}, \cdots, \mathbf{h}^{T}_{1,d_{free}}\right]^T$$

The eigenvalues of $\mathbf{R}^{-1}_{2,k}$ are

$$\lambda_l = \begin{cases} \left(\sigma_2^2 \left\|\mathbf{h}_{2,k}\right\|^2 + N_0\right)^{-1}, & l = 1 \\ N_0^{-1}, & l = 2, \cdots, n_r \end{cases} \tag{37}$$

Using the MGF (29), PEP conditioned on $\overline{\mathbf{h}}_2 = \left[\mathbf{h}_{2,1}, \cdots, \mathbf{h}_{2,d_{free}}\right]$ is upper bounded as

$$P\left(\underline{c}_1 \rightarrow \hat{\underline{c}}_1 | \overline{\mathbf{h}}_2\right) \leq \frac{1}{2}\left(\frac{4N_0}{d^2_{1,\min}}\right)^{d_{free}(n_r-1)} \left(\frac{4}{d^2_{1,\min}}\right)^{d_{free}} \prod_{l=1}^{d_{free}} \left(\sigma_2^2 \left\|\mathbf{h}_{2,l}\right\|^2 + N_0\right)$$

Channel independence at each subcarrier yields

$$P\left(\underline{c}_1 \rightarrow \hat{\underline{c}}_1\right) \leq \frac{1}{2}\left(\frac{4N_0}{\sigma_1^2 d^2_{1,\min}}\right)^{d_{free}(n_r-1)} \left(\frac{4}{\sigma_1^2 d^2_{1,\min}}\right)^{d_{free}} \left(n_r \sigma_2^2 + N_0\right)^{d_{free}} \quad (38)$$

which not only demonstrates the well known result of the loss of one diversity order in MMSE in the presence of one interferer (Winters, 1984) but also exhibits a coding loss as interference gets stronger.

3.6 Simulation Results

Moderate and high SNR regime in the interference-limited scenario demands more attention as when the noise is small, interference will have a significant impact on the performance. Low SNR regime is less interesting since here the performance is noise-limited and interference is not having a significant effect. For simulations, we have restricted ourselves to the case of one strong interference. These simulations have been performed in moderate and high SNR region while the interference strength is being varied.

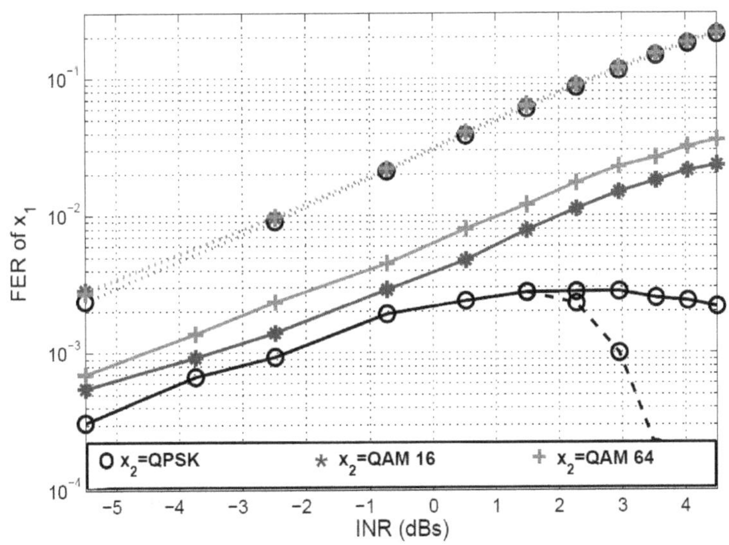

Fig. 12. Desired stream x1 is QPSK while interference stream x2 is from QPSK, QAM16 and QAM64. SNR is 4.5 dB. Continuous lines indicate interference suppression while dashed lines indicate interference cancellation. Dotted lines indicates detection of x1 by MMSE detector. 64—state, rate 1/2 Convolutional Code is used. Note that SNR is with respect to the desired stream

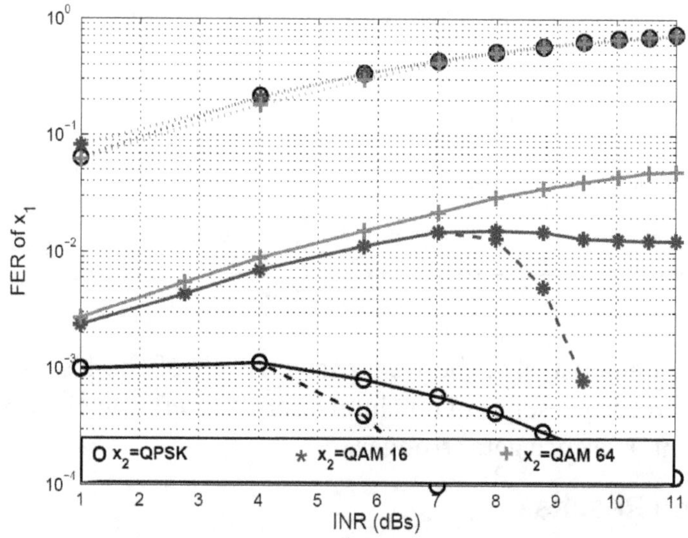

Fig. 13. Desired stream x1 is QAM 16 while interference stream x2 is from QPSK, QAM16 and QAM64. SNR is 11 dB. Continuous lines indicate interference suppression while dashed lines indicate interference cancellation. Dotted lines indicates detection of x1 by MMSE detector. 64-state, rate 1/2 Convolutional Code is used.

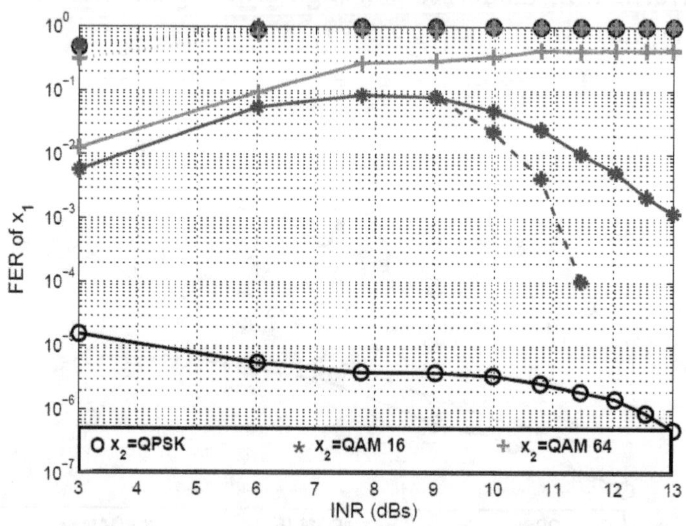

Fig. 14. Desired stream x1 is QAM 64 while interference stream x2 is from QPSK, QAM16 and QAM64. SNR is 13 dB. Continuous lines indicate interference suppression while dashed lines indicate interference cancellation. Dotted lines indicates detection of x1 by MMSE detector. Punctured rate 1/2 3GPP turbo code is used with 5 decoding iterations.

We consider 2 BSs each using BICM OFDM system for downlink transmission using the de facto standard, 64 state (133, 171) rate-1/2 convolutional encoder of 802.11n standard (802.11n, 2006) and the punctured rate 1/2 turbo code of 3GPP LTE (LTE, 2006)2. Each BS has multiple antennas and employs antenna cycling. MS has two antennas. We consider an ideal OFDM based system (no ISI) and analyze the system in frequency domain. Due to bit interleaving followed by OFDM, this can be termed as frequency interleaving. Therefore SIMO channel at each sub carrier from BS to MS has iid Gaussian matrix entries with unit variance. Perfect CSI is assumed at the receiver. Furthermore, all mappings of coded bits to QAM symbols use Gray encoding. We consider interference suppression and interference cancellation approaches us- ing low complexity max log MAP detector. For comparison we also consider interference suppression using MMSE detector.

Figs. 12, 13 and 14 show the FERs of target stream in the presence of one interference stream. The simulation findings indicate that the performance of MMSE detection is hardly affected by the rate of the interference stream, while its dependence on interference strength is considerable. This can be understood as a result of the reduction in interference strength at the output of the MMSE filter and the ensuing assumption of Gaussian behavior. The low complexity max log MAP detector exhibits a notable enhancement in performance when the interference stream rate diminishes, aligning with previous mutual information analysis findings (fig. 11). It is noted that, for a specific amount of interference, performance often deteriorates as the rate (constellation size) of the interfering stream escalates. The performance disparity relative to MMSE diminishes as the desired and interference streams increase in constellation size, attributable to the convergence towards Gaussianity of these larger constellations, owing to their elevated peak-to-average power ratio and the optimality of MMSE for Gaussian alphabets.

FOOTNOTES

1. LTE turbo decoder design was performed using the coded modulation library www.iterativesolutions.com
2. The LTE turbo decoder design was performed using the coded modulation library www.iterativesolutions.com

REFERENCES

1. 802.11n (2006). Enhancements for Higher Throughput, IEEE 802.11 WG. IEEE 802.11n/D1.0 Draft Amendment.
2. 802.16m (2007). Draft IEEE 802.16m Evaluation Methodology, IEEE 802.16m-07/037r1.
3. Alamouti, S. (1998). A simple transmit diversity technique for wireless communications, IEEE Journal on Selected Areas in Communications Vol. 16(No. 8): 1451–1458.

4. Bladsjö, D., Furuskär, A., Jäverbring, S. & Larsson, E. (1999). Interference cancellation using antenna diversity for EDGE - Enhanced data rates in GSM and TDMA/136, IEEE Vehicular Technology Conference Proceedings, 1999. VTC 1999-Fall, Vol. 4, pp. 1956–1960.
5. Caire, G., Taricco, G. & Biglieri, E. (1998). Bit-interleaved coded modulation, Vol. 44(No. 3): 927–946.
6. Carleial, A. (1975). A case where Interference does not reduce Capacity, IEEE Transactions on Information Theory Vol. 21(No. 5): 569–570.
7. Dahlman, E., Ekstrom, H., Furuskar, A., Jading, Y., Karlsson, J., Lundevall, M. & Parkvall, S. (2006). The 3G long-term evolution - radio interface concepts and performance evaluation, IEEE 63rd Vehicular Technology Conference VTC-Spring, Vol. 1, pp. 137–141. Debbah, M., Muquet, B., de Courville, M., Muck, M., Simoens, S. & Loubaton, P. (2000).
8. A MMSE successive interference cancellation scheme for a new adjustable hybrid spread OFDM system, IEEE 51st Vehicular Technology Conference Proceedings, 2000. VTC 2000-Spring Tokyo., Vol. 2, pp. 745–749 vol.2.
9. Foschini, G. J. & Gans, M. J. (1998). On limits of wireless communication in a fading envi- ronment when using multiple antennas, Wireless Personal Communications. Vol. 6(No. 3): 311–335.
10. Gesbert, D., Kiani, S., Gjendemsj, A. & Oien, G. (2007). Adaptation, coordination, and dis- tributed resource allocation in interference-limited wireless networks, Proceedings of the IEEE Vol. 95(No. 12): 2393–2409.
11. Ghaffar, R. & Knopp, R. (2008a). Dual-antenna BICM reception with applications to MIMO broadcast and single frequency cellular system, IEEE 19-th International Symposium on Personal, Indoor and Mobile Radio Communications (PIMRC 2008), Cannes.
12. Ghaffar, R. & Knopp, R. (2008b). Low complexity BICM demodulation for MIMO transmis- sion, 9th IEEE Workshop on Signal Processing Advances for Wireless Communications, SPAWC 2008, Recife.
13. Ghaffar, R. & Knopp, R. (2009a). Interference Suppression for Next Generation Wireless Sys- tems, IEEE 69-th Vehicular Technology Conference VTC-Spring 2009, Barcelona.
14. Ghaffar, R. & Knopp, R. (2009b). Spatial Interference Cancellation Algorithm, Proc. IEEE Wire- less Communications and Networking Conference WCNC 2009, Budapest, Budapest, Hun- gary.
15. Ghaffar, R. & Knopp, R. (2009c). Spatial Interference Cancellation and Pairwise Error Proba- bility Analysis, IEEE International Conference on Communications, ICC 2009.

16. Golden, G., Foschini, C., Valenzuela, R. & Wolniansky, P. (1999). Detection algorithm and initial laboratory results using v-blast space-time communication architecture, Elec- tronics Letters Vol. 35(No. 1): 14–16.

17. Gonzalez-Lopez, M., Vazquez-Araujo, F., Castedo, L. & Garcia-Frias, J. (2006). Optimized serially-concatenated LDGM and Alamouti codes for approaching MIMO Capacity, IEEE 17th International Symposium on Personal, Indoor and Mobile Radio Communica- tions, PIMRC 2006, pp. 1–5.

18. Han, T. & Kobayashi, K. (1981). A new achievable rate region for the interference channel, IEEE Transactions on Information Theory Vol. 27(No. 1): 49–60.

19. Hochwald, B. & Brink, S. T. (2003). Achieving near-capacity on a multiple-antenna channel, IEEE Transactions on Communications, Vol. 51(No. 3): 389–399.

20. Larsson, E. G. & Stoica, P. (2003). Space-Time Block Coding for Wireless Communications, Cam- bridge University Press, Cambridge, U.K.

21. Larsson, E. & Jalden, J. (2008). Fixed-complexity soft MIMO detection via partial marginaliza- tion, IEEE Transactions on Signal Processing, Vol. 56(No. 8): 3397–3407.

22. Liu, Y., Lau, K., Takeshita, O. & Fitz, M. (2002). Optimal rate allocation for superposition coding in quasi static fading channels, IEEE International Symposium on Information Theory, ISIT 2002, pp. 111–.

23. LTE (2006). Requirements for Evolved UTRA (E-UTRA) and Evolved UTRAN (E-UTRAN), 3GPP TR 25.913 v.7.3.0,.

24. LTE-A (2008). Requirements for Further Advancements for EUTRA, 3GPP TR 36.913,. Medvedev, I., Bjerke, B., Walton, R., Ketchum, J., Wallace, M. & Howard, S. (2006). A comparison of MIMO receiver structures for 802.11N WLAN - Performance and complexity, IEEE 17th International Symposium on Personal Indoor and Mobile Radio Communica- tions,, pp. 1–5.

25. Poor, H. & Verdu, S. (1997). Probability of error in MMSE multiuser detection, IEEE Transac- tions on Information Theory Vol. 43(No. 3): 858–871.

26. Russell, M. & Stuber, G. (1995). Interchannel interference analysis of OFDM in a mobile environment, IEEE 45th Vehicular Technology Conference, Vol. 2, pp. 820–824.

27. Shamai, S. & Steiner, A. (2003). A broadcast approach for a single-user slowly fading MIMO channel, IEEE Transactions on Information Theory Vol. 49(No. 10): 2617–2635.

28. Telatar, I. E. (1999). Capacity of multi-antenna Gaussian channels, European Transactions on Telecommunications Vol. 10(No. 6): 585–595.

29. Varanasi, M. K. & Guess, T. (1997). Optimum decision feedback multiuser equalization with successive decoding achieves the total capacity of the Gaussian MAC channel, Asilomar Conference on Signals, Systems and Computers.
30. Verdu, S. (1989). Computational complexity of multiuser detection, Algorithmica,, Vol. 4, pp. 303–312.
31. Verdu, S. (1998). Multiuser Detection., Cambridge University Press, Cambridge, U.K.
32. Winters, J. (1984). Optimum combining in digital mobile radio with cochannel interference, IEEE Journal on Selected Areas in Communications Vol. 2(No. 4): 528–539.
33. Wolniansky, P., Foschini, G., Golden, G. & Valenzuela, R. (1998). V-blast: an architecture for realizing very high data rates over the rich-scattering wireless channel, International Symposium on Signals, Systems, and Electronics, 1998. ISSSE 98., pp. 295–300.

11 Chapter

ADVANCED HYBRID AUTOMATIC REPEAT REQUEST RECEIVERS FOR BROADBAND MULTIPLE INPUT MULTIPLE OUTPUT COMMUNICATIONS

1. INTRODUCTION: AN OVERVIEW

Multiple Input Multiple Output (MIMO) and hybrid Automatic Repeat reQuest (ARQ) mechanisms are crucial in advancing contemporary wireless communication systems towards high data rate wireless packet access. MIMO approaches utilize the spatial dimension of the MIMO channel by employing multiple antennas at both the transmitter and receiver ends. This results in enhanced spectral efficiency and/or improved link quality (Wolniansky et al., 1998). Hybrid–ARQ methods offer a significant source of temporal variability by integrating channel coding with Automatic Repeat reQuest (ARQ). This is executed using packet combining techniques, wherein erroneous data packets are retained at the receiver to facilitate the detection and decoding of retransmitted frames.

In broadband MIMO communications, the MIMO wireless link experiences intersymbol interference (ISI) due to multipath propagation. This impact can be alleviated with channel equalization and/or Hybrid-ARQ. This chapter addresses the concurrent design of the packet combiner and the channel equalization for MIMO ARQ transmission across the broadband wireless channel. This chapter commences with an examination of the several methodologies for joint packet combining and equalization. We provide the examined broadband MIMO ARQ transmission system. Subsequently, we derive the configuration of the optimal maximum a posteriori (MAP) turbo packet combiner and examine its outage performance. We provide a novel category of low-complexity minimum mean square error (MMSE)-based turbo packet combiners and examine their implementation prerequisites and block error rate (BLER) performance.

2. ADVANCED RECEIVERS FOR MIMO ARQ

In the last few years, a special interest has been paid to the design of advanced MIMO ARQ receivers where packet combining and signal processing, i.e., detection/

equalization, are jointly performed. The concept of integrated equalization (IEQ) has been proposed in the framework of MIMO systems with flat fading for joint multiple antenna interference (MAI) suppression and packet combining (see for instance Onggosanusi et al. (2003) and Samra & Ding (2006)). Turbo coded ARQ schemes with iterative MMSE frequency domain equalization (FDE) for MIMO code division multiple access (CDMA) has been proposed in Garg & Adachi (2006). Recently, we have introduced a new family of packet combining techniques for broadband MIMO ARQ systems, where the decoding of a data packet is performed with the aid of an iterative (turbo) processing between the soft combiner, i.e., joint packet combining and equalization unit, and the soft input soft output (SISO) decoder (see Ait-Idir & Saoudi (2009)). The following sections of this chapter focus on this new class of broadband MIMO ARQ tech- niques. Our notation is introduced in the next section followed by the communication model of the considered MIMO ARQ system.

3. NOTATION

In this chapter, scalars are denoted by small-case letters, vectors by small-case boldface letters, and matrices by upper-case boldface letters. Superscripts T and H denote the transpose and transpose conjugate, respectively. IN is the N × N identity matrix, and 0N×M is the N × M zeros matrix. ⊗ is the Kronecker product, and Pr {.} denotes the probability of a given event.

4. BROADBAND MIMO ARQ TRANSCEIVER SCHEME

4.1 MIMO ARQ Transmission

Let us consider a broadband multi-antenna, i.e., multiple input multiple output (MIMO), system operating over a frequency selective fading channel and using an ARQ protocol at the upper layer. The transmitter and the receiver are equipped with NT transmit (index t = 1,..., NT) and NR receive (index r = 1,..., NR) antennas, respectively. The MIMO channel suffers from intersymbol interference (ISI) and is composed of L symbol-spaced taps (index l = 0,..., L − 1). Each data stream is first encoded with the aid of a ρ-rate chan- nel encoder, interleaved using a semi-random interleaver Π, then modulated and space–time multiplexed over the NT transmit antennas. This transmission scheme corresponds to the so-called space–time bit interleaved coded modulation (STBICM). Let S denote the constel- lation set, andM = log2{S} its cardinality. A sequence of M coded and interleaved bits b1,t,i , ... , bM,t,i available on antenna t is transmitted at discrete-time instant i = 0, · ·· , T - 1 over symbol st,i ∈ S according to the mapping function Ψ : {0, 1}M . The symbol vector to be transmitted at time i is denoted

$$\mathbf{s}_i \triangleq \left[s_{1,i}, \cdots, s_{N_T,i}\right]^{\top} \in \mathcal{S}^{N_T}. \tag{1}$$

The rate of this transmission scheme is therefore R = ρMNT . The transmit symbol energy is normalized to one. Assuming infinitely deep space–time interleaving we get, E[sisiH] = INT . At the receiver side, a positive/negative acknowledgment ACK/NACK message is sent back to the transmitter upon the decoding of the information block. When the transmitter receives a NACK message due to an erroneously decoded packet, subsequent transmission rounds occur until the packet is correctly received or a preset maximum number of rounds K (index k = 1,..., K) is reached. Parameter K is called the ARQ delay. Reception of a ACK message indicates a successful decoding and the transmitter moves on to the next packet. We assume an error-free feedback channel (the signaling channel carrying the ACK/NACK message), and perfect packet error detection (using a cyclic redundancy check –CRC code). We focus on Chase-type ARQ, i.e., the entire information block is retransmitted using the same STBICM code. To prevent inter-block interference (IBI), we use either zero padding (ZP) or cyclic prefix (CP)-aided transmission.

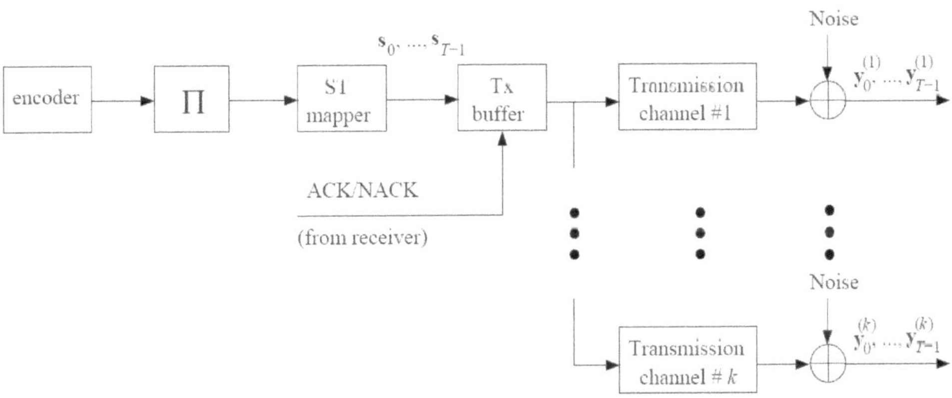

Fig. 1. STBICM ARQ Transmission over a short-term quasi-static MIMO channel

The MIMO-ISI channel is assumed to be short-term quasi-static block fading, i.e., constant during one ARQ round and independently changes from round to round. The long-term dynamic corresponds to the case when the channel is constant during all ARQ rounds cor- responding to the transmission of the same information packet (see El Gamal et al. (2006)). The short-term assumption is justified by the fact ARQ protocols are mainly used to improve the link quality in the case of delay-tolerant applications where the processing delay is not a major constraint. Let H(k) denote the NR × NT complex matrix of the lth tap connecting the transmitter and the receiver at ARQ round k. The elements of H(k) are zero-mean circularly symmetric Gaussian random variables, i.e., h(k) ~ CN 0, σ2 , where h(k) denotes the (r, t) th

element of matrix $H_l^{(k)}$ and σ_l^2 is the energy of tap l. The total channel energy is normalized as $\sum_{l=0}^{L-1} \sigma_l^2 = 1$. The discrete baseband signal received by antenna r at ARQ round k and time instant i is given by

$$y_{r,i}^{(k)} = \sum_{l=0}^{L-1} \sum_{t=1}^{N_T} h_{r,t,l}^{(k)} s_{t,i-l} + n_{r,i}^{(k)}, \tag{2}$$

$$\mathbf{n}_i^{(k)} \triangleq \left[n_{1,i}^{(k)}, \cdots, n_{N_R,i}^{(k)}\right]^{\top}$$

where ni(k) $\sim\mathcal{CN}(0_{N_R\times 1}, \sigma^2 \mathbf{I}_{N_R})$ is the thermal noise at the NR receive antennas. The STBICM ARQ transmission scheme over a short-term MIMO channel, i.e., k distinct MIMO channels, is depicted in Fig. 1.

4.2 MIMO ARQ Turbo Receiver

In Ait-Idir & Saoudi (2009), turbo packet combining has been introduced as an efficient tech- nique for combining multiple transmissions in the case of broadband MIMO ARQ systems. In turbo packet combining, the decoding of a data packet is performed in an iterative (turbo) fashion through the exchange of soft (extrinsic) information between the SISO packet com- biner and the SISO decoder. The soft combiner exploits signals received at multiple ARQ rounds to compute extrinsic log-likelihood ratios (LLR)s. Note that in conventional LLR-level combining techniques, the soft outputs obtained at different transmissions are simply added togother before channel decoding.

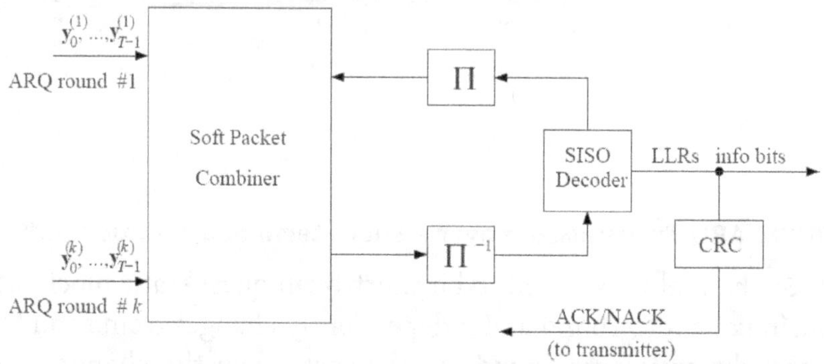

Fig. 2. Block diagram of the turbo packet combing-aided MIMO ARQ receiver

The general block diagram of the turbo packet combining-aided MIMO ARQ receiver is depicted in Fig. 2. Let

$$\boldsymbol{\phi}_{t,i}^{a} \triangleq \left[\phi_{1,t,i}^{a}, \cdots, \phi_{M,t,i}^{a}\right]^{\top} \tag{3}$$

denote the M × 1 real vector of a priori LLRs corresponding to coded and interleaved bits b1,t,i , · ·· , bM,t,i , and available at the input of the soft combiner at a certain iteration of ARQ round k. Using a priori information Φ a a NT,T-1 and signals received at rounds 1, · ·· , k, the soft packet combiner computes extrinsic LLR vectors

$$\boldsymbol{\phi}^{e}_{t,i} \triangleq \left[\phi^{e}_{1,t,i}, \cdots, \phi^{e}_{M,t,i}\right]^{\top}, \tag{4}$$

which are de-interleaved and sent to the SISO decoder to obtain a posteriori LLRs about useful bits and extrinsic information about coded bits. The generated extrinsic LLR values are then interleaved and fed back to the soft combiner to help compute soft information during the next turbo iteration of the same ARQ round. After a preset number of iterations, the decision about the data packet is performed, and the ACK/NACK message is sent back to the transmitter accordingly. Note that during the first iteration, a priori information corresponds to the soft information available from the last iteration of previous ARQ round k - 1.

5. INFORMATION-THEORETIC ISSUES

In this section, we derive the optimal maximum a posteriori (MAP) turbo packet combining receiver for broadband MIMO ARQ transmission, and investigate its outage performance. We first show that optimal turbo packet combining can be formulated as a MIMO-ISI turbo equalization problem. We then obtain the outage probability of the broadband MIMO ARQ channel, and analyze the impact of the ARQ delay, i.e., maximum number of ARQ rounds K, on the outage performance.

5.1 Optimal Turbo Packet Combining

To derive the optimal maximum a posteriori (MAP) turbo packet combiner at ARQ round k, let us consider the following signal vector that groups signals corresponding to all ARQ rounds 1, · ·· , k, is the vector of received signals at ARQ round u = 1, , k and time instant i.

$$\mathbf{y}^{(k)} \triangleq \left[\mathbf{y}^{(1)^{\top}}_{T-1}, \cdots, \mathbf{y}^{(k)^{\top}}_{T-1}, \cdots, \mathbf{y}^{(1)^{\top}}_{0}, \cdots, \mathbf{y}^{(k)^{\top}}_{0}\right]^{\top} \in \mathbb{C}^{kN_R T}, \tag{5}$$

where

$$\mathbf{y}^{(u)}_{i} \triangleq \left[y^{(u)}_{1,i}, \cdots, y^{(u)}_{N_R,i}\right]^{\top} \in \mathbb{C}^{N_R} \tag{6}$$

The formulation in (5) is of a great importance because it allows us to view each ARQ round as a set of virtual NR receive antennas. Note that in this section we assume that all signals and channel matrices corresponding to previous ARQ rounds are available at the receiver side at round k. In Section 6, we will present an optimized turbo packet combining technique that makes use of all signals and channel matrices without being required to be explicitly stored in the receiver. With respect to (2) and (5) and assuming a ZP-aided transmission strategy, the signal vector y(k) corresponding to the transmission of the entire symbol frame over k MIMO-ISI channels can be expressed as,

$$y(k) = H(k)\, s + n(k), \tag{7}$$

where H(k) is a block Toeplitz matrix given as

$$\mathbf{H}^{(k)} \triangleq \begin{bmatrix} \boxed{\begin{matrix} \mathbf{H}_0^{(1)} \\ \vdots \\ \mathbf{H}_0^{(k)} \end{matrix}} & \cdots & \boxed{\begin{matrix} \mathbf{H}_{L-1}^{(1)} \\ \vdots \\ \mathbf{H}_{L-1}^{(k)} \end{matrix}} & & \\ & \ddots & & \ddots & \\ & & \boxed{\begin{matrix} \mathbf{H}_0^{(1)} \\ \vdots \\ \mathbf{H}_0^{(k)} \end{matrix}} & \cdots & \boxed{\begin{matrix} \mathbf{H}_{L-1}^{(1)} \\ \vdots \\ \mathbf{H}_{L-1}^{(k)} \end{matrix}} \end{bmatrix}_{kN_R T \times N_T T}, \tag{8}$$

and vectors s and n(k) are defined as,

$$\mathbf{s} \triangleq \left[\mathbf{s}_{T-1}^{\top}, \cdots, \mathbf{s}_0^{\top}\right]^{\top} \in \mathcal{S}^{N_T T}, \tag{9}$$

$$\mathbf{n}^{(k)} \triangleq \left[\mathbf{n}_{T-1}^{(1)\top}, \cdots, \mathbf{n}_{T-1}^{(k)\top}, \cdots, \mathbf{n}_0^{(1)\top}, \cdots, \mathbf{n}_0^{(k)\top}\right]^{\top} \in \mathbb{C}^{kN_R T}. \tag{10}$$

The communication model (7) corresponds to a MIMO ISI equalization problem with NT transmit and kNR virtual receive antennas. It allows for jointly (over all ARQ rounds) can- celing both multiple antenna interference (MAI) and ISI, while exploiting all the diversities available in the MIMO-ISI ARQ channel. Using the MAP criterion and given a priori LLRs, the extrinsic information about coded and interleaved bit bm,t,i can be expressed as,

$$\phi_{m,t,i}^{e} = \log \frac{\Pr\left\{\mathbf{y}^{(k)} \mid b_{m,t,i} = 1; \mathbf{H}_0^{(1)}, \cdots, \mathbf{H}_{L-1}^{(k)}, \textit{a priori} \text{ LLRs}\right\}}{\Pr\left\{\mathbf{y}^{(k)} \mid b_{m,t,i} = 0; \mathbf{H}_0^{(1)}, \cdots, \mathbf{H}_{L-1}^{(k)}, \textit{a priori} \text{ LLRs}\right\}}. \tag{11}$$

Then, by invoking the multi-round communication model (7)$\phi_{m,t,i}^{e}$, can be obtained as,

$$\phi_{m,t,i}^{e} = \log \frac{\sum_{\mathbf{s} \in \mathcal{S}_{m,t,i}^{1}} \exp\left\{-\frac{1}{2\sigma^2}\left\|\mathbf{y}^{(k)} - \mathbf{H}^{(k)}\mathbf{s}\right\|^2 + \sum_{(m',t',i') \neq (m,t,i)} \Upsilon_{m'}^{-1}\left(s_{t',i'}\right)\phi_{m',t',i'}^{a}\right\}}{\sum_{\mathbf{s} \in \mathcal{S}_{m,t,i}^{0}} \exp\left\{-\frac{1}{2\sigma^2}\left\|\mathbf{y}^{(k)} - \mathbf{H}^{(k)}\mathbf{s}\right\|^2 + \sum_{(m',t',i') \neq (m,t,i)} \Upsilon_{m'}^{-1}\left(s_{t',i'}\right)\phi_{m',t',i'}^{a}\right\}}, \tag{12}$$

where the subset $\mathcal{S}_{m,t,i}^{b}$ is defined as $\mathcal{S}_{m,t,i}^{b} \triangleq \left\{\mathbf{s} \in \mathcal{S}^{N_T T} \mid \Upsilon_m^{-1}\left(s_{t,i}\right) = b\right\}, \; b = 0, 1.$

5.2 Outage Performance Analysis

Outage probability is a useful tool that allows to analyze the performance of non-ergodic channels, i.e., quasi-static channels. It provides a lower bound on the

BLER, and is generally defined as the probability that the mutual information, as a function of the channel realization and the average signal to noise ratio (SNR) Γ per receive antenna, is below the transmission rate R Tse & Viswanath (2005).

The outage probability of an ARQ protocol can be derived using the renewal theory (see Wolff (1989)) as in Caire & Tuninetti (2001) and El Gamal et al. (2006). In the case of a broadband MIMO system with Chase-type ARQ, perfect packet error detection, and error-free ACK/ NACK feedback, the outage probability can be derived using the multi-round communication model (7) and the renewal theory (see Ait-Idir & Saoudi (2009)) as

$$P_{out}^{R}(\gamma) = \Pr\left\{\frac{1}{K} I\left(\mathbf{s}; \mathbf{y}^{(K)} \mid \mathbf{H}^{(K)}, \gamma\right) < R, \bar{A}_1, \cdots, \bar{A}_{K-1}\right\}, \tag{13}$$

where K is the ARQ delay, and Ak denotes the event that an ACK message is fed back at round k, i.e., the data packet is positively acknowledged at ARQ round k. The quantity $\frac{1}{K}$ I (s; y(K) | H(K), Γ) denotes the mutual information rate at the last ARQ round K, and is expressed in the case of a MIMO broadband channel with Gaussian inputs as

$$\frac{1}{K} I\left(\mathbf{s}; \mathbf{y}^{(K)} \mid \mathbf{H}^{(K)}, \gamma\right) = \frac{1}{KT} \sum_{i=0}^{T-1} \log_2\left(\det\left(\mathbf{I}_{KN_R} + \frac{\gamma}{N_T} \boldsymbol{\Lambda}_i^{(K)} \boldsymbol{\Lambda}_i^{(K)^H}\right)\right), \tag{14}$$

where Λ(K) is the discrete Fourier transform (DFT) of the KNR x NT virtual MIMO-ISI channel at round K and frequency bin i, i.e.,

$$\boldsymbol{\Lambda}_i^{(K)} \triangleq \sum_{l=0}^{L-1} \begin{bmatrix} \mathbf{H}_l^{(1)} \\ \vdots \\ \mathbf{H}_l^{(K)} \end{bmatrix} \exp\left\{-j\frac{2\pi}{T} il\right\}. \tag{15}$$

Note that the factor $\frac{1}{K}$ appearing in the outage probability (13) is due to the fact that a transmission scheme with Chase-type ARQ, and an ARQ delay K is equivalent to a repetition coding scheme where K parallel sub-channels are used to transmit the same symbol frame.

In the following, we investigate the impact of the ARQ delay K on the outage performance. We consider a MIMO-ISI channel with L = 2 taps having equal powers, i.e., $\sigma_0^2 = \sigma_1^2 = \frac{1}{2}$.

At each ARQ round k, the mutual information rate of the MIMO $\frac{1}{k} I\left(\mathbf{s}; \mathbf{y}^{(k)} \mid \mathbf{H}_0^{(k)}, \mathbf{H}_1^{(k)}, \gamma\right)$ ARQ system after k rounds is evaluated similarly to (14). If the target rate R is not reached and k < K, the system moves on to the next round k + 1. An ARQ process is stopped and an another is started, either because of system outage, i.e., the mutual rate after K rounds is below R, or the rate R is achieved at a certain round k ≤ K. In all scenarios, we take T = 256 discrete time instants.

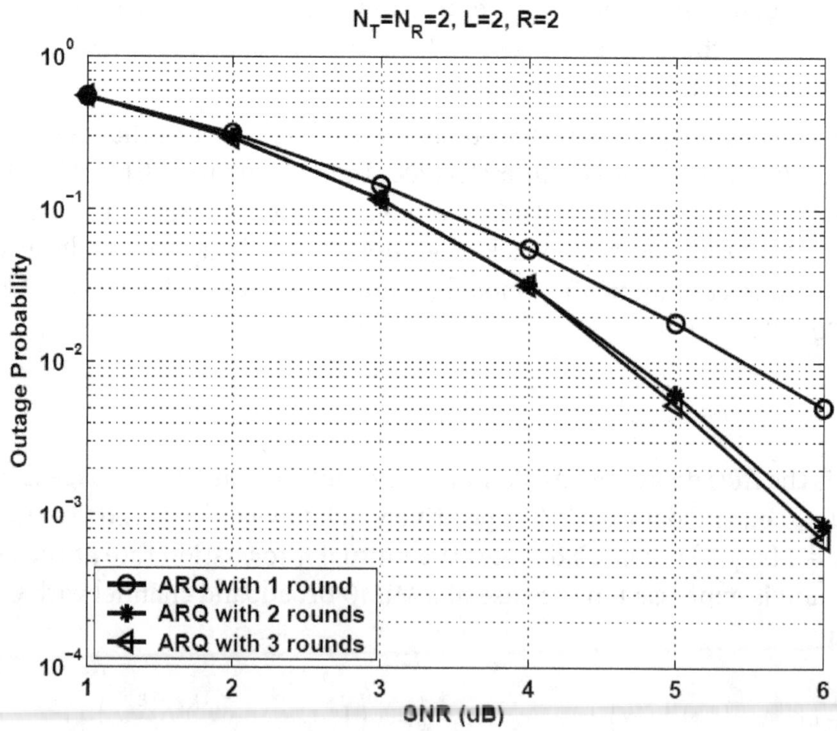

Fig. 3. Outage probability performance for two transmit and two receive antennas

In Fig. 3, we plot the outage probability performance for the NT = NR = 2 antenna configura- tion, with a target rate R = 2. We observe that the ARQ diversity gain, due to the short-term static channel dynamic, clearly appears when the ARQ delay is set to K = 2. It offers a signif- icant SNR gain compared with the non-ARQ case (K = 1). When, the ARQ delay is increased to K = 3, the outage performance is similar to that of K = 2. This means that if the system is in outage in the second ARQ round, then it will almost be in outage in the third round. In Fig. 4, we investigate the outage performance when the number of transmit antennas is increased to NT = 4, while NR = 2. The target rate is set to R = 4. As in the previous configuration, both ARQ delays K = 2 and K = 3 provide almost the same outage performance, while the overall diversity gain is more important than that corresponding to NT = NR = 2. This can be seen from the steeper slopes of outage curves. Note that the ARQ diversity due to multiple trans- missions does not completely translate into a receive diversity gain (related to the NR virtual receive antennas at each ARQ round). This is due to the fact that the target rate R has to be maintained, as it can be seen from the expression of the outage probability (13). This means that the diversity gain does not linearly increase with increase of the ARQ delay K. This issue has been addressed by El Gamal et al. (2006) in the case of flat fading MIMO ARQ systems.

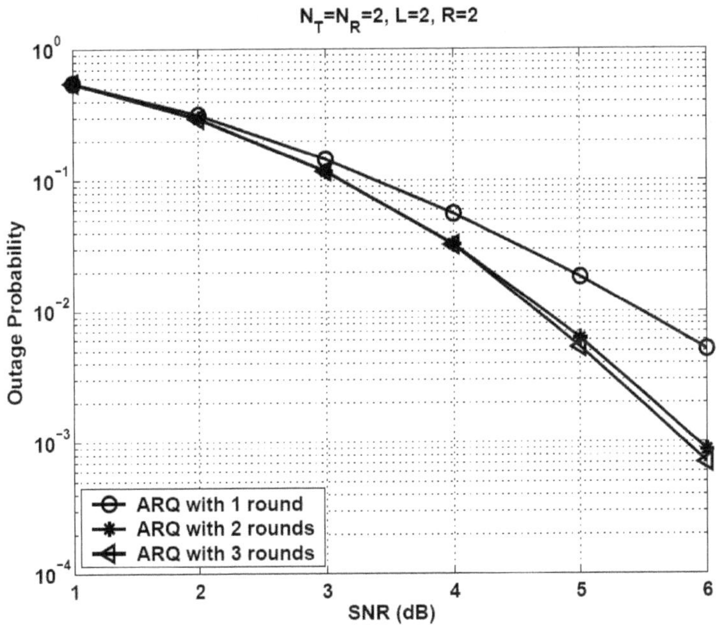

Fig. 4. Outage probability performance for four transmit and two receive antennas

6. MMSE-BASED TURBO PACKET COMBINING

The optimal MAP turbo packet combining algorithm we have presented so far in Subsection 5.1 has a computational complexity that exponentially increases with the increase in the num- ber of ARQ rounds. In addition, all signals and channel matrices have to be stored in the receiver to perform combining at each ARQ round. In this section, we present alternative MMSE-based sub-optimal techniques (see Ait-Idir & Saoudi (2009)) that allow for performing turbo packet combining with reduced computational complexity and memory requirements. We first introduce the so-called signal-level turbo combining technique where packet combining is performed at the signal level similarly to MAP combining but based on MMSE processing. Then, we present the symbol-level turbo combining algorithm where packets are combined at the input of the soft demapper after performing MMSE channel equalization separately for each transmission. We also provide a brief presentation of the conventional LLR-level combining technique. For all combining schemes, we assume a ZP-aided block transmission. The multiround block communication model is therefore described by a block Toeplitz channel matrix as in (7).

6.1 Signal-Level Turbo Combining

The signal-level turbo packet technique is a low-complexity MMSE-based combining algo- rithm that performs packet combining jointly with MAI and ISI cancellation using a block length equal to ε = ε1 + ε2 + 1 T, where ε1 and ε2 are the lengths of the forward and backward filters, respectively. Packet combining at ARQ round k is therefore performed with respect to the following ε-length block communication model and H(k) is a block Toeplitz matrix which is defined similarly to (8) but using ε block rows and (ε + L – 1) block columns.

$$\underline{\underline{\mathbf{y}}}_i^{(k)} = \underline{\underline{\mathbf{H}}}^{(k)} \underline{\mathbf{s}}_i + \underline{\underline{\mathbf{n}}}_i^{(k)}, \tag{16}$$

where

$$\underline{\underline{\mathbf{y}}}_i^{(k)} \triangleq \left[\mathbf{y}_{i+\varepsilon_1}^{(1)^\top}, \cdots, \mathbf{y}_{i+\varepsilon_1}^{(k)^\top}, \cdots, \mathbf{y}_{i-\varepsilon_2}^{(1)^\top}, \cdots, \mathbf{y}_{i-\varepsilon_2}^{(k)^\top} \right]^\top \in \mathbb{C}^{kN_R\varepsilon}, \tag{17}$$

$$\underline{\underline{\mathbf{n}}}_i^{(k)} \triangleq \left[\mathbf{n}_{i+\varepsilon_1}^{(1)^\top}, \cdots, \mathbf{n}_{i+\varepsilon_1}^{(k)^\top}, \cdots, \mathbf{n}_{i-\varepsilon_2}^{(1)^\top}, \cdots, \mathbf{n}_{i-\varepsilon_2}^{(k)^\top} \right]^\top \in \mathbb{C}^{kN_R\varepsilon}, \tag{18}$$

$$\underline{\mathbf{s}}_i \triangleq \left[\mathbf{s}_{i+\varepsilon_1}^\top, \cdots, \mathbf{s}_{i-\varepsilon_2-L+1}^\top \right]^\top \in \mathcal{S}^{N_T(\varepsilon+L-1)}, \tag{19}$$

First of all, the soft packet combiner computes conditional means and variances of transmitted symbols using a priori information vectors Φat,i , where t ∈ {1, ·· · , NT}, and i ∈ {0, ·· · , T 1}, available from the previous iteration. Note that, as it has been mentioned before, the soft information generated by the SISO decoder during the last iteration of ARQ round k 1 serves as a priori information at the first iteration of round k. Conditional symbol expectations, also called soft symbols, serve for regenerating soft interference caused by multiple antenna transmission and multipath propagation, i.e., MAI plus ISI. Conditional symbol variances and channel matrices corresponding to ARQ rounds 1, , k are used for computing the multiround MMSE filter that serves for performing signal combining. At each iteration of ARQ round k, the signal-level turbo packet combiner exploits the communication model (16) to cancel soft MAI plus ISI (estimated at the current iteration of round k) from all signals received at rounds 1, , k. Then, it combines the resulting soft interference-free signals to generate soft decisions about transmitted symbols.

Let $\tilde{s}_{t,i} \triangleq \mathbb{E}\left[s_{t,i} \mid \boldsymbol{\phi}_{t,i}^a\right]$ and $\tilde{\sigma}_{t,i}^2 \triangleq \mathbb{E}\left[|s_{t,i} - \tilde{s}_{t,i}|^2 \mid \boldsymbol{\phi}_{t,i}^a\right]$ denote the conditional mean and variance of symbol st,i. By invoking the special block Toeplitz structure of matrix H(k), and the structure of the multi-round signal vector (17), the signal-level turbo packet combiner computes, at a particular iteration of ARQ round k, soft decision χt,i(k) about symbol st,i using the following forward–backward filtering structure,

$$\zeta_{t,i}^{(k)} = \mathbf{F}_t^{(k)} \underline{\mathbf{z}}_i^{(k)} | \mathbf{B}_t^{(k)} \underline{\tilde{\mathbf{s}}}_{i|t}, \tag{20}$$

where s˜i|t is the NT (ε + L - 1)-length soft symbol vector corresponding to (19) with zero at the (ε1 NT + t)th position corresponding to soft symbol s˜t,i . F(k) and

B(k) are the forward and backward filters related to antenna t. z(k) is a vector that contains properly weighed and combined copies of signals received at rounds 1,..., k. It does not change in the course of turbo iterations corresponding to the same ARQ round, and is produced at round k according to the following recursion

$$\begin{cases} \underline{\mathbf{z}}_i^{(k)} & = \underline{\mathbf{z}}_i^{(k-1)} + \underline{\mathbf{H}}^{(k)^H} \underline{\mathbf{y}}_i^{(k)}, \\ \underline{\mathbf{z}}_i^{(0)} & = \mathbf{0}_{N_T(\varepsilon+L-1)\times 1}. \end{cases} \tag{21}$$

The signal vector y(k) and the channel matrix H(k) correspond to the ε-length block communication model of ARQ round k, and are given as,

$$\underline{\mathbf{H}}^{(k)} \triangleq \begin{bmatrix} \mathbf{H}_0^{(k)} & \cdots & \mathbf{H}_{L-1}^{(k)} & & \\ & \ddots & & \ddots & \\ & & \mathbf{H}_0^{(k)} & \cdots & \mathbf{H}_{L-1}^{(k)} \end{bmatrix}_{N_R\varepsilon \times N_T(\varepsilon+L-1)}, \tag{22}$$

$$\underline{\mathbf{y}}_i^{(k)} \triangleq \left[\mathbf{y}_{i+\varepsilon_1}^{(k)^\top}, \cdots, \mathbf{y}_{i-\varepsilon_2}^{(k)^\top} \right]^\top \in \mathbb{C}^{N_R\varepsilon}. \tag{23}$$

Filters Ft(k) and Bt(k) are iteration-dependent, and are computed as

$$\mathbf{F}_t^{(k)} = \left(\sigma^2 + \left(1 - \tilde{\sigma}_t^2\right) \mathbf{e}_t^\top \mathbf{\Lambda}^{(k)} \mathbf{Y}^{(k)} \mathbf{e}_t\right)^{-1} \mathbf{e}_t^\top \mathbf{\Lambda}^{(k)}, \tag{24}$$

$$\mathbf{B}_t^{(k)} = \mathbf{F}_t^{(k)} \mathbf{Y}^{(k)}. \tag{25}$$

where et is a NT (ε + L - 1)-length vector of zeros with one at the (ε1 NT + t)th position, i.e.,

$$\mathbf{e}_t \triangleq [\underbrace{0, \cdots, 0}_{\varepsilon_1 N_T + t - 1}, 1, \underbrace{0, \cdots, 0}_{(\varepsilon_2 + L) N_T - t}]^\top. \tag{26}$$

$\tilde{\sigma}_t^2$ is the unconditional variance of symbols transmitted over antenna t, and is computed as the time average of conditional variances $\tilde{\sigma}_{t,0}^2, \cdots, \tilde{\sigma}_{t,T-1}^2$, i.e., $\tilde{\sigma}_t^2 = \frac{1}{T}\sum_{i=0}^{T-1} \tilde{\sigma}_{t,i}^2$. The square matrix $\mathbf{\Lambda}^{(k)}$ is updated at each turbo iteration according to,

$$\mathbf{\Lambda}^{(k)} = \mathbf{I}_{N_T(\varepsilon+L-1)} - \mathbf{Y}^{(k)} \left(\mathbf{Y}^{(k)} + \sigma^2 \Xi^{-1}\right)^{-1}, \tag{27}$$

where

$$\Xi = \mathbf{I}_{\varepsilon+L-1} \otimes \begin{bmatrix} \tilde{\sigma}_1^2 & & \\ & \ddots & \\ & & \tilde{\sigma}_{N_T}^2 \end{bmatrix} \in \mathbb{C}^{N_T(\varepsilon+L-1)\times N_T(\varepsilon+L-1)}, \tag{28}$$

and Y(k) is recursively computed as,

$$\begin{cases} \mathbf{Y}^{(k)} & = \mathbf{Y}^{(k-1)} + \underline{\mathbf{H}}^{(k)^H}\underline{\mathbf{H}}^{(k)}, \\ \mathbf{Y}^{(0)} & = \mathbf{0}_{N_T(\varepsilon+L-1)\times N_T(\varepsilon+L-1)}. \end{cases} \tag{29}$$

Details regarding the derivation of the forward–backward filtering structure (20) can be found in Ait-Idir & Saoudi (2009) and the set Sb is defined as 1.

Extrinsic information Φe m,t,i about coded and interleaved bit bm,t,i , m = 1,· ·· , M, can be obtained using the decision statistic Ξ(k) of (20) as,

$$\phi^{e}_{m,t,i} = \log \frac{\sum_{s\in\mathcal{S}^1_m} \exp\left\{-\frac{1}{2\delta_t^{(k)^2}}\left|\xi^{(k)}_{t,i} - \alpha^{(k)}_t s\right|^2 + \sum_{m'\neq m}\Psi^{-1}_{m'}(s)\phi^{a}_{m',t,i}\right\}}{\sum_{s\in\mathcal{S}^0_m} \exp\left\{-\frac{1}{2\delta_t^{(k)^2}}\left|\xi^{(k)}_{t,i} - \alpha^{(k)}_t s\right|^2 + \sum_{m'\neq m}\Psi^{-1}_{m'}(s)\phi^{a}_{m',t,i}\right\}}, \tag{30}$$

where it is assumed that conditional soft demapper input $\xi^{(k)}_{t,i} \mid s_{t,i}$ is Gaussian with mean $\alpha^{(k)}_t$ and variance $\delta^{(k)^2}_t$, and are given by,

$$\begin{cases} \alpha^{(k)}_t & = \mathbf{B}^{(k)}_t \mathbf{e}_t \\ \delta^{(k)^2}_t & = \left(1 - \alpha^{(k)}_t\right)\alpha^{(k)}_t, \end{cases} \tag{31}$$

and the set $\mathcal{S}^b_m$ is defined as $\mathcal{S}^b_m \triangleq \{s \in \mathcal{S} \mid \Psi^{-1}_m(s) = b\}$ for $b = 0, 1$.

6.2 Symbol-Level Turbo Combining

In symbol-level turbo packet combining, MMSE turbo equalization is separately performed for each ARQ round k based on the ε-length block communication model of round k,

$$\underline{\mathbf{y}}^{(k)}_i = \underline{\mathbf{H}}^{(k)}\underline{\mathbf{s}}_i + \underline{\mathbf{n}}^{(k)}_i, \tag{32}$$

where $\underline{\mathbf{s}}_i$, $\underline{\mathbf{H}}^{(k)}$, and $\underline{\mathbf{y}}^{(k)}_i$ are given by (19), (22), and (33), respectively, and

$$\underline{\mathbf{n}}^{(k)}_i \triangleq \left[\mathbf{n}^{(k)^\top}_{i+\varepsilon_1}, \cdots, \mathbf{n}^{(k)^\top}_{i-\varepsilon_2}\right]^\top \in \mathbb{C}^{N_R\varepsilon} \tag{33}$$

is the spatially and temporally white Gaussian noise at the input of the equalizer at ARQ round k, i.e., $\underline{\mathbf{n}}^{(k)}_i \sim \mathcal{CN}(\mathbf{0}_{N_R\varepsilon\times 1}, \sigma^2\mathbf{I}_{N_R\varepsilon})$. Soft combining is iteratively performed at the level of unconditional MMSE filter outputs by combining the output at each iteration of ARQ round k with those obtained at the last iteration of previous rounds 1, ..., k - 1.

The forward and backward filters $\mathbf{F}_t^{(k)}$ and $\mathbf{B}_t^{(k)}$ in the case of symbol-level turbo packet combining can easily be derived using the equations provided in the previous subsection with $k = 1$. Now, let $\breve{\xi}_{t,i}^{(k)}$ denote the MMSE filter output corresponding to symbol $s_{t,i}$ at a specific turbo iteration of round k. The conditional decision statistic $\breve{\xi}_{t,i}^{(k)} \mid s_{t,i}$ is Gaussian, with mean $\breve{\alpha}_t^{(k)}$ and variance $\breve{\delta}_t^{(k)^2}$ given similarly to (31). For ARQ rounds $u = 1, \cdots, k-1$, $\breve{\xi}_{t,i}^{(u)}$ denotes the decision statistic obtained at the last iteration of round u. Therefore, the soft combiner provides extrinsic information $\phi_{m,t,i}^{e}$ about coded and interleaved bit $b_{m,t,i}$ as

$$\phi_{m,t,i}^{e} = \log \frac{\sum_{s \in \mathcal{S}_m^1} \exp\left\{-\frac{1}{2}\left(\breve{\boldsymbol{\xi}}_{t,i}^{(k)} - s\breve{\boldsymbol{\alpha}}_t^{(k)}\right)^H \boldsymbol{\Delta}_t^{(k)^{-1}} \left(\breve{\boldsymbol{\xi}}_{t,i}^{(k)} - s\breve{\boldsymbol{\alpha}}_t^{(k)}\right) + \sum_{m' \neq m} \Upsilon_{m'}^{-1}(s)\phi_{m',t,i}^{a}\right\}}{\sum_{s \in \mathcal{S}_m^0} \exp\left\{-\frac{1}{2}\left(\breve{\boldsymbol{\xi}}_{t,i}^{(k)} - s\breve{\boldsymbol{\alpha}}_t^{(k)}\right)^H \boldsymbol{\Delta}_t^{(k)^{-1}} \left(\breve{\boldsymbol{\xi}}_{t,i}^{(k)} - s\breve{\boldsymbol{\alpha}}_t^{(k)}\right) + \sum_{m' \neq m} \Upsilon_{m'}^{-1}(s)\phi_{m',t,i}^{a}\right\}}, \tag{34}$$

where vector

$$\breve{\boldsymbol{\xi}}_{t,i}^{(k)} \triangleq \left[\breve{\xi}_{t,i}^{(1)}, \cdots, \breve{\xi}_{t,i}^{(k)}\right]^T \in \mathbb{C}^k \tag{35}$$

gathers MMSE filter soft outputs corresponding to all rounds $1, \cdots, k$. $\breve{\boldsymbol{\alpha}}_t^{(k)}$ and $\boldsymbol{\Delta}_t^{(k)}$ are the mean and covariance of the conditional Gaussian vector $\breve{\boldsymbol{\xi}}_{t,i}^{(k)} \mid s_{t,i}$, and are given by,

$$\breve{\boldsymbol{\alpha}}_t^{(k)} \triangleq \left[\breve{\alpha}_t^{(1)}, \cdots, \breve{\alpha}_t^{(k)}\right]^T \in \mathbb{C}^k, \tag{36}$$

6.3 LLR-Level Turbo Combining

In conventional LLR-level combining, LLR values of transmitted bits obtained at multiple ARQ rounds are stored in the receiver and simply added together to update the LLRs at each ARQ round. In our framework, LLR-level turbo combining is carried out by separately per- forming MMSE turbo equalization for multiple transmissions using the the ε-length block communication model (32). Extrinsic LLRs Φm,t,ie corresponding to coded and interleaved bits bm,t,i ∀ m, t, i are then computed at each iteration of ARQ round k using only decision statistics Ξ˘(k) introduced in the previous subsection. LLR values obtained at multiple ARQ rounds are then added together to produce the soft LLR outputs

$$\mathrm{LLR}_{m,t,i}^{(k)} = \sum_{u=1}^{k} \phi_{m,t,i}^{e(u)}, \quad \forall m,\ t,\ i, \tag{38}$$

which are de-interleaved and fed back to the SISO decoder. Note that in (38), Φe m,t,i denotes the extrinsic LLR at the last iteration of ARQ round u = 1,· ·· , k.

6.4 Implementation Issues

In signal-level turbo combining, the computation of the forward and backward filters Ft(k) and B(k)t involves, at each turbo iteration of ARQ round k, one inversion of the NT (ε + L – 1) × NT (ε + L – 1) matrix Y(k) + σ2 Ξ−1. The cost of computing F(k) t and B(k)t is therefore in the order of complex operations. This indicates that the computational complexity of the signal-level combining scheme is less sensitive to k. The number of ARQ rounds only influences the number of additions required for performing recursions (21) and (29), which is in the order of N2T(ε + L – 1) × NR εT complex additions. Note that the operations of computing are also required in the case of symbol-level combining. Therefore, the computational cost of forward and backward filters is almost the same for both signal and symbol-level turbo combining schemes. The LLR-level turbo combining algorithm approximately involves the same amount of operations as symbol-level combining.

In the case of signal-level combining, memory requirements are determined by (21) and (29), where two NT (ε + L – 1) × NT (ε + L – 1) and NT (ε + L – 1) × T complex matrices are required to accumulate channel matrices $\underline{z}_0^{(k)},\cdots,\underline{z}_{T-1}^{(k)}$, and $\underline{H}^{(k)^H}\underline{H}^{(k)}$ signal vectors respectively.

Note that the two recursions (21) and (29) play a key role in signal-level turbo combining since they avoid the storage of all signals and channel matrices as in MAP turbo combining.

In symbol-level combining, only NT complex matrices of size K×T and two K× NT complex matrices are required to store filter outputs and their corresponding parameters given by (35), (36), and (37). Therefore, signal-level combining requires slightly more memory than its symbol-level counterpart. Finally, in LLR-level turbo combining, a real vector of size NTMT is required to combine extrinsic values. Therefore, the three combining strategies have similar implementation requirements. They slightly differ in the number of additions and storage memory.

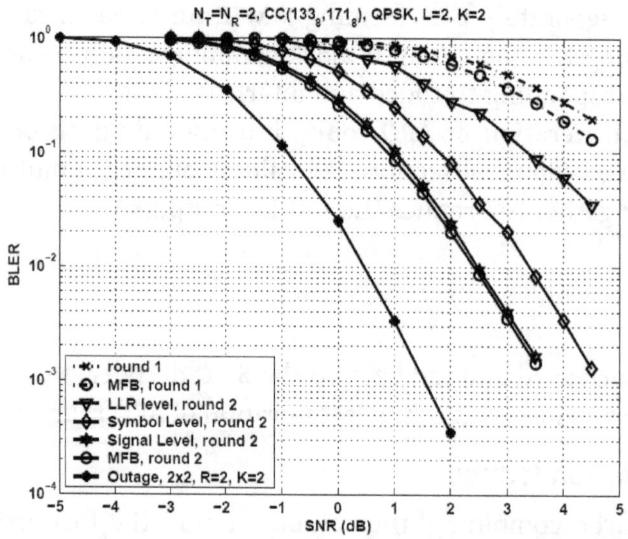

Fig. 5. BLER performance comparison for NT = NR = 2 and QPSK.

6.5 BLER Performance

In this subsection, we provide simulated BLER performance for the packet combining strategies studied in the previous subsections. The main focus of the analysis we provide is to show that signal-level turbo combining has better ISI cancellation capability and diversity gain com- pared with the other combining schemes.

We consider an STBICM transmitter with a 64-1/2state -rate convolutional code whose polynomial generators are (1338, 1718). The length of the code frame is 1800 bits. The modulation scheme is quadrature phase shift keying (QPSK). The MIMO-ISI channel has the same profile as in Subsection 5.2, i.e., two equal power taps. The ARQ delay is chosen K = 2 according to the theoretic analysis in Subsection 5.2. In all figures, the BLER is per ARQ round, and the SNR is per symbol per receive antenna.

We compare the resulting BLER performance with the outage probability and the matched filter bound (MFB). Note that for the purpose of fair comparison, the computation of the outage probability does not take into account the rate distortion as in (14). The MFB curves are obtained for each transmission assuming perfect ISI cancellation and maximum ratio combining (MRC) of all time, space, multipath, and delay diversity branches.

In Fig. 5, we consider an STBICM code with NT = NR = 2 transmit and receive antennas. This corresponds to a rate R = 2. The filter length is chosen equal to ε = 9 (ε1 = ε2 = 4)for all combining schemes. A quick inspection of Fig. 5, shows that both signal and symbol-level turbo combining offer a significant performance improvement after the second ARQ round compared with LLR-level combining. The signal-level scheme has better ISI cancellation capability compared with symbol-level combining. It almost achieves the MFB, while the symbol-level scheme presents a gap of approximately 1dB compared with the MFB. Also, note that both signal and symbol-level combining achieve the asymptotic slope of the outage probability.

In Fig. 6, we evaluate the BLER performance of a ST-BICM code with NT = 4. This cor- responds to a rate R = 4. The number of receive antennas is NR = 2. Note that this type of unbalanced MIMO configurations where the transmitter is equipped with more antennas than the receiver is suitable for the forward link. The filter length is increased to ε = 13 (ε1 = ε2 = 6) for all combining schemes. The signal-level combining technique is shown to achieve BLER performance close to the MFB with a gap less than 0.5dB, while both the LLR-level and the symbol-level techniques have degraded BLER performance. The signal- level combining manifests itself in almost achieving the diversity gain of the MIMO-ISI ARQ channel, while it is shown that symbol-level combining fails to do so. This is because in the second

ARQ round, the signal-level scheme constructs a 4 × 4 virtual MIMO-ISI channel for ISI cancellation and symbol detection, while the MIMO configuration remains unbalanced in the case of symbol and LLR-level combining.

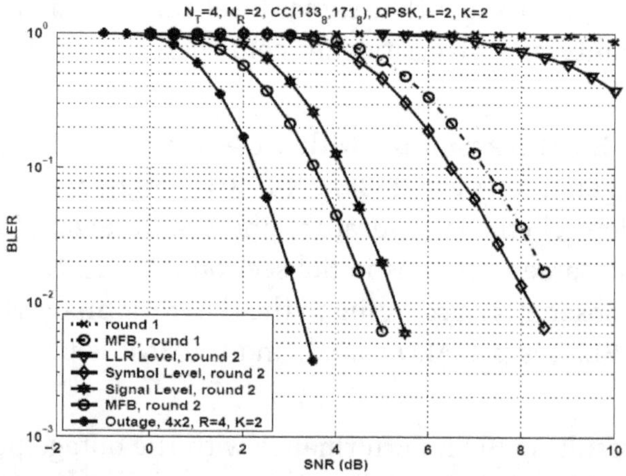

Fig. 6. BLER performance comparison for NT = 4, NR = 2 and QPSK.

7. CONCISE SUMMARY

This chapter examines the construction of efficient iterative turbo packet combining algorithms for broadband MIMO systems with Chase-type ARQ. We developed the framework of the optimal MAP turbo packet combining technique that utilizes all possible diversities in the MIMO-ISI ARQ channel for packet combining and examined its outage probability. Due to the significant computational expense and memory demands of optimal MAP turbo packet combining, we proposed a novel category of low-complexity MMSE-based turbo packet combining algorithms. In MMSE-based signal-level combining, each ARQ round is seen as a collection of virtual receive antennas, and packet combining is executed in conjunction with ISI cancellation at the signal level. In MMSE-based symbol-level combining, several transmissions are individually turbo equalized, and the combination occurs at the filter output level. The simulation findings presented in this chapter demonstrate that signal-level combining yields superior BLER performance compared to symbol-level and traditional LLR-level combining.

REFERENCES

1. Ait-Idir, T. & Saoudi, S. (2009) Turbo packet combining strategies for the MIMO-ISI ARQ chan- nel, IEEE Transactions on Communications vol. 57, no. 12, December 2009, 3782-3793
2. Caire, G. & Tuninetti, D. (2001). ARQ protocols for the Gaussian collision channel, IEEE Trans- actions on Information Theory, Vol.47, No.4, July -2001, 1971–1988

3. El Gamal, H.; Caire, G. & Damen, M. O. (2006) The MIMO ARQ channel diversity-multiplexing-delay tradeoff, IEEE Transactions on Information Theory, Vol.52, No.8, August -2006, 3601–3621
4. Garg, D. & Adachi, F. (2006) Packet access using DS-CDMA with frequency-domain equaliza- tion IEEE Journal of Selected Areas in Communications, vol. 24, no. 1, Jan. 2006
5. Onggosanusi, E. N.; Dabak, A. G.; Hui, Y. & Jeong, G. (2003) Hybrid ARQ transmission and combining for MIMO systems, Proceedings of IEEE International Conference on Commu- nications, pp. 3205-3209, ISBN 0-7803-7802-4, Anchorage, May 2003
6. Samra, H. & Ding, Z. (2006) New MIMO ARQ protocols and joint detection via sphere decod- ing, IEEE Transactions on Signal Processing, vol. 54, no. 2, pp. 473-482, Feb. 2006
7. Tse, D. & Viswanath, P. (2005). Fundamentals of Wireless Communication, Cambridge University Press, ISBN 978-0-521-84527-4
8. Wolff, R. (1989). Stochastic Modeling and the Theory of Queues, Upper Saddle River, NJ: Prentice- Hall, 1989
9. Wolniansky, P. W.; Foschini, G. J. & Valenzuela, R. A. (1998). V-BLAST: an architecture for realizing very high data rates over the rich scattering wireless channel, in Proc. Int. Symp. Signals, Systems, Electron., Pisa, Italy, Sep. 1998

12 Chapter COOPERATIVE ARQ: A PERSPECTIVE FROM THE MEDIUM ACCESS CONTROL (MAC) LAYER

1. INTRODUCTION: AN OVERVIEW

Cooperative Automatic Retransmission reQuest (C-ARQ) methods have emerged as a prominent area of research in recent years. C-ARQ schemes are an effective method for facilitating cooperation in wireless networks with pre-existing equipment. C-ARQ schemes utilize feedback from the receiver, so cooperation occurs solely when necessary, and are hence often termed on-demand cooperative schemes.

The concept of C-ARQ is to leverage the broadcast characteristic of the wireless channel, whereby any signal can be received by all stations within the transmitter's range. What has historically been regarded as interference is utilized in C-ARQ techniques to achieve spatial variety. In the event of a transmission error, a retransmission may be solicited from any or part of the stations that received the initial message, which can function as spontaneous relays. The outcome is that the recipient of a packet may obtain many copies of identical information transmitted along statistically independent pathways, known as space diversity.

C-ARQ systems have been extensively examined in the literature from a theoretical perspective, and it is unequivocal that, under certain situations, they can significantly enhance the performance of wireless communications in comparison to traditional ARQ, where retransmissions occur solely from the source. Involving multiple users in a communication link necessitates cooperation. Consequently, effective Medium Access Control (MAC) protocols are essential to achieve optimal communication efficiency. This chapter highlights the significant function of the MAC layer within the framework of C-ARQ.

2. COOPERATIVE ARQ (C-ARQ)

2.1 Background and Motivation

Traditionally, ARQ schemes have been used in communication networks to guarantee the reliable delivery of data packets. Upon the reception of a packet with errors, retransmissions are requested from the source (and along the same channel) until either the packet can be properly decoded or it is discarded for the benefit of the backlogged data.

Several variations of ARQ schemes have been proposed in the past to improve the performance of communications. These schemes perform well in wired networks where there is no correlation between consecutive packet error probabilities, i.e., packet errors are random and sparse. However, their performance in wireless networks is compromised by phenomena such as the shadowing and fading of the radio channel. In wireless channels, packet errors might come into bursts, and thus if a packet is received with errors, the immediate retransmissions will be also received with errors with high probability if they are performed through the same channel (Zorzi et al., 1997).

C-ARQ schemes constitute a practical solution to combat this fading nature of the wireless channel. Their operation is described in the following section.

2.2 Description of C-ARQ

Consider a wireless network formed by an arbitrary number of stations equipped with half- duplex radio frequency transceivers. In order to be able to execute a C-ARQ scheme, all the stations must listen to (overhear) every ongoing transmission in order to be able to cooperate if required. In addition, they should keep a copy of any received data packet (regardless of its destination address) until it is acknowledged (positively or negatively) by the destination. This packet is discarded whenever the destination successfully decodes the original packet.

It is assumed that, although both error detection and Forward Error Correction (FEC) bits are attached to all the transmitted data packets, errors can still occur due to the severe wireless channel impairments. Whenever a destination receives a data packet with unrecoverable errors, it broadcasts a retransmission request in the form of a control packet. This packet is referred to as the Call for Cooperation (CFC) packet. A cooperation phase is then initiated.

A subset of the stations which overheard both the original transmission from the source and the CFC from the destination, become active relays or helpers. As it will be further discussed later, some relay selection criteria can be attached to the CFC in order to activate the most appropriate subset of stations to act as helpers. Orthogonally in time (TDMA), frequency (FDMA or OFDMA), or code (CDMA), these active relays attempt to retransmit a copy of the original packet to assist in the failed transmission. For the sake of clarity in the explanation and without loss of generality, the data packets retransmitted by the relays will be referred to as cooperative packets.

Eventually, the destination might either receive a correct copy of the original packet from a relay or may be able to properly combine the different retransmissions from the relays to successfully decode the original packet. Otherwise, if the destination is not able to recover the data packet after some predefined time (cooperation time-out), it discards it. In any of the two cases, the cooperation phase is finished.

Although slight different variations to this general operation can be found in the literature, most of the proposed C-ARQ schemes follow this description. It is worth mentioning that the CFC has sometimes received the name of Negative ACK (NACK) in the literature (Dianati et al. 2006). However, this name falls short in describing the real function of the CFC. Besides informing the Negative ACK, it also calls for cooperation and, indeed, it could attach some relay selection criteria, among other control information required for the execution of a cooperative technique.

An example of operation of a C-ARQ mechanism is illustrated in Fig. 1. Therein, the communication between a source and a destination stations is assisted by an arbitrary number (N) of relays. In this particular example, the relays retransmit data orthogonally in time until the destination station can send the ACK.

The performance of a C-ARQ scheme might be mainly influenced by the following four parameters:

1. *The relay selection criteria;* as it could be expected, the number of potential helpers and the "quality" of those helpers will have a direct impact on the efficiency of the C-ARQ scheme. For this reason, there are several works focused on the design of efficient techniques to select either the best or a subset of the best potential helpers to act as relays (Gómez et al., 2007; Biswas & Morris, 2005).
2. *The PHY forwarding technique executed by the relays* (Nosratinia et al., 2004):
   a. Amplify and forward techniques, when the relays transmit an amplified version of the original received signal, without demodulating or decoding it.
   b. Compress and forward techniques, when the relays transmit a compressed version of the original transmitted signal, without decoding it.
   c. Decode and forward techniques, when the relays transmit recoded copies of the original message. Note that using decode and forward, the recoding process can be done on the basis of repeating the original codification, recoding the original data (or only a relevant part of it), or using more sophisticated Space-Time Codes (STC) (Fitzek & Katz, 2006).
3. The number of required retransmissions necessary to decode a packet which can mainly depend on:

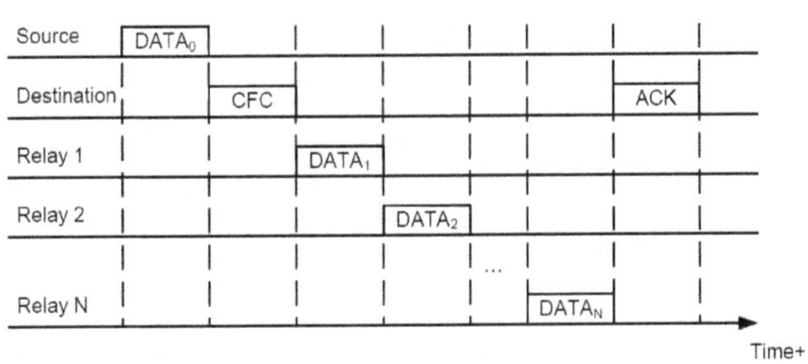

Fig. 1. C-ARQ Scheme with Time-Orthogonal Relays

a. The channel conditions between the source and the destination, the source and the relays, and the relays and the destination (Gómez & Pérez-Neira, 2006; Pfletschinger & Navarro, 2008).
b. The transmission scheme, which includes the forwarding technique executed by the relays and the combination technique executed by the destination station to combine the different retransmissions received from independent paths. The approach of combining different erroneous copies of a same packet to decode the original packet has been tackled in the past (Charaborty et al., 2005; Morillo-Pozo & García-Vidal, 2007).

4. The MAC protocol which is necessary to tackle with the contention among the relays. Just as an example, the ideal scheduling among the relays represented in Fig. 1 is impossible to attain in fully distributed networks without a central coordinator. Therefore, the set of active relays should contend for the channel in order to retransmit the packets. Efficient MAC protocols are necessary to execute a C-ARQ scheme in order to exploit the benefits of cooperation in wireless networks.

2.3 Motivation and Contributions of the Chapter

C-ARQ schemes have been so far analyzed from a fundamental point of view and mainly with emphasis on the PHY layer (Dianati et al. 2006; Zimmermann et al., 2004; Zimmermann et al., 2005; Gupta et al., 2004; Cerruti et al., 2008; Morillo-Pozo et al., 2005). These previous works put in evidence that C-ARQ schemes can yield an improvement in performance, lower energy consumption, and interference, as well as an extended coverage area by allowing communication at low Signal to Noise Ratios (SNRs). However, all of these contributions assume simplified topologies (with one or very few relays) and perfect scheduling among the relays at the MAC level. This scheduling might be difficult to attain in the fully decentralized scenario represented by the cloud of relays without infrastructure. Therefore, both the design of efficient MAC protocols and the evaluation of the actual performance of C-ARQ techniques considering the MAC overhead are mandatory if C-ARQ schemes are to find real application. Indeed, this is the main motivation for this chapter.

The focus in this chapter is on time-orthogonal C-ARQ schemes, which might be the easiest approach to implement with already existing off-the-shelf equipment. By slightly modifying the wireless controller (or driver), existing wireless cards could implement a C-ARQ scheme. The emphasis is on the design and analysis of a novel MAC protocol to deal with the unique characteristics of the contention process that takes place among the active relays within a cooperation phase. Note that in the considered C-ARQ schemes, upon the initialization of the cooperation phase, the network has the three following unique characteristics:

1. The spontaneous "sub-network" formed by the active relays is ad hoc and thus there is no infrastructure responsible for managing the access to the channel.

2. This sub-network formed by the active relays surrounding the node calling for cooperation is suddenly (sharply) set into saturation conditions whenever the cooperation phase is initiated. Upon the transmission of a CFC packet, all the active relays have a data packet ready to transmit in order to assist the failed transmission. Therefore, heavy contention takes place in a previously idle network.
3. Opposite to general communications systems, now fairness is not a major issue to achieve. Indeed, the main goal is to attempt to assist the failed transmission as fast and reliable as possible, minimizing the use of the radio resources.

These three characteristics determine the way MAC protocols should be designed within the context of C-ARQ schemes in wireless networks. Considering the aforementioned characteristics, we present in this chapter the design and performance evaluation of a novel high-performance MAC protocol for C-ARQ schemes, named DQCOOP.

It is worth mentioning at this point that, in the literature, there exists a family of cooperative MAC protocols which have not been designed for the execution of C-ARQ schemes in wireless networks, but they are aimed at solving other kind of interesting cooperative issues. For completeness, they are overviewed in the following section.

2.4 Related Work: Cooperative MAC Protocols

Some MAC protocols for cooperative communications have been proposed in the literature. Most of them have been designed to achieve a throughput enhancement, but actually none of them takes into account all of the unique characteristics of the on-demand C-ARQ schemes. It has to be mentioned that all these MAC protocols have been designed more as routing protocols with a cross-layer design that takes into account the transmission rates to decide the shortest route to a destination than as MAC protocols themselves. In what follows, a summary of the most relevant contributions is summarized.

In (Liu et al. 2007) two versions of the CoopMAC protocol are designed in the context of 802.11b WLANs in order to solve the performance anomaly induced by the multi-rate capability of the Distributed Coordination Function (DCF) of the standard (IEEE 802.11 Standard, 2007). Users with low transmission rate occupy the channel for long periods of time, reducing the overall throughput of the system and reducing the throughput seen by stations with higher transmission rates. The main idea of CoopMAC protocols is that stations transmit first to intermediate stations at a higher rate and then those intermediate stations transmit to the access point, reducing the total transmission delay. In the first version of CoopMAC, referred to as CoopMAC I, any station keeps updated a table with those stations that could potentially help in a transmission. Before transmitting any packet, a station calculates the shorter transmission path, either using direct communication with the intended destination or through any of the potential helpers with an entry in the table. In the case of using a relay, a previous handshake is done between the source station and the selected relay in order to ensure the validity of the route. The main drawback of CoopMAC I is that it requires the addition of three new fields in the Request To Send (RTS) frame and the addition of a new control frame named Helper ready To Send (HTS). As an alternative, CoopMAC II is proposed to overcome this problem. This second version of CoopMAC uses available empty fields in regular IEEE 802.11 control frames and eliminates the handshake between destination and helpers. Although the implementation is simpler, version II is more vulnerable to a change in the availability of a helping station caused by mobility. Computer simulations in (Liu et al., 2007) demonstrate the improved performance achieved with either CoopMAC I or II. Moreover, Korakis et al. implemented the protocol in actual WLAN cards, as reported in (Korakis et al., 2006). The main contribution of their work is the description of the overall implementation process and the limitations found when attempting to actually implement the protocol. These limitations were mainly due to the constraints imposed by the time sensitive tasks performed by the firmware of the wireless cards. In addition, the CoopMAC has been also adapted to wireless networks using directional antennas in (Tau et al., 2007).

On the other hand, both the Cooperative-MAC (CMAC) and FEC CMAC (FCMAC) protocols were presented in (Shankar et al., 2005) within the context of 802.11e networks to improve the overall performance and to ensure a certain QoS. In CMAC, a station detecting an erroneous packet transmission between any other pair of source-destination stations decides to cooperate by retransmitting a copy of the overheard transmission as long as the received packet has no errors. A random backoff mechanism with a constant backoff window is applied to avoid collisions among different helpers. The size of the contention window of the helpers has to be very small in comparison to the contention window of the source in order to ensure that helpers retransmit their copy before the original source retransmits on its own the failed packet. Each helper transmits the copy of the packet at most once, to ensure that all available helpers cooperate and thus the benefits of diversity are obtained. On the other hand, FCMAC extends the operation of CMAC by fragmenting data packets into smaller blocks. Each block contains its own inner FEC field and the whole packet contains an outer FEC. Upon error detection of a whole packet, only a predefined number of randomly selected blocks among those received without errors are retransmitted. If the retransmitted blocks are those that were received with errors at destination, then the performance is improved.

Otherwise, the increased overhead becomes useless. A possible solution consists in adding a negative acknowledgement (NACK) sent out by the destination upon error detection, indicating which are the blocks received with errors. However, the use of NACK in CMAC would imply higher overhead and again, it would require hardware modifications, thus breaking with the claimed backwards compatibility. The main limitation of CMAC and FCMAC is that they rely on the fact that helpers can learn whether other transmissions between any pair of source and destination are successful or not only by overhearing the radio channel.

In (Wang & Yang, 2005), the Cooperative Diversity Medium Access with Collision Avoidance (CD-MACA) protocol is proposed within the context of wireless ad hoc networks operating over the CSMA/CA protocol. Whenever a source terminal fails to receive the CTS packet, all those stations that had properly received it, take the place of the source terminal and retransmit the data packet. An analytical model based on Markov chain theory is proposed to obtain the achievable throughput of the system considering cooperation. Although the general idea of CD-MACA is rather interesting, the definition in (Wang & Yang, 2005) is quite general and several implementation details are not considered.

From an energy-efficient perspective, another cooperative MAC protocol is also presented within the context of ad hoc networks in (Azing et al., 2005). This proposal integrates cooperative diversity into two different wireless routing protocols by embedding a distributed cooperative MAC. The initial path establishment performed by the routing protocol can be done either considering cooperation or not. Cooperation is then achieved by forcing all the stations to act as a distributed virtual antenna, through which simultaneous transmissions are separated with CDMA.

In (Sadek et al., 2006) a cooperative MAC protocol was presented within the context of a mesh network formed by an access point, a number of regular stations, and one fixed wireless router (relay). A fixed TDMA scheme is applied and empty slots are used for cooperative relaying. The relay station keeps a copy of all those packets that are not properly received by the Access Point (AP). At the beginning of each time slot, the relay listens to the channel. If the channel is idle, it retransmits the packet at the head of its queue. Based on this main idea, two specific algorithms are proposed to exploit the benefits of cross-layer design between the PHY and MAC layers.

All these MAC protocols have been designed to achieve an improvement in the network performance by transmitting through faster multi-hop routes. However, none of them takes into account the unique characteristics of the C-ARQ schemes for their implementation in on-demand cooperative schemes. DQCOOP is presented in the next section as a novel MAC protocol that has been tailored to meet the requirements of the C-ARQ scenario. It constitutes the adaptation of the high-performance DQMAN protocol (Alonso-Zárate et al., 2008a) to this kind of scenarios.

3. DQMAN FOR C-ARQ: DQCOOP

The aim of this section is to present DQCOOP as an extension and adaptation of the high- performance DQMAN (Alonso-Zárate et al., 2008a) to match the unique requirements posed by the C-ARQ schemes. DQMAN, in its turn, is the extension of the infrastructure-based DQCA protocol (Alonso-Zárate et al., 2008b) for wireless ad hoc networks. The new resultant protocol is called DQCOOP. The rules of DQMAN and DQCA will not be described into detail in this chapter as they can be found in (Alonso-Zárate et al., 2008a) and (Alonso-Zárate et al., 2008b), respectively.

In short, the basic idea of DQMAN is that any idle station with data to transmit listens to the channel for a randomized period of time before establishing its cluster. This Clear Channel Assessment (CCA) period gets the name of Master Selection Phase (MSP). If the channel is idle for the whole MSP, then a cluster is established. The station becomes master and starts broadcasting a periodical clustering beacon (CB) that allows neighbor stations to get synchronized and become slaves. The master operates as such for as long as there is data activity within its cluster. Therefore, the cluster structure changes along time as a function of the aggregate traffic load of the network. Once the cluster is established, the master station transmits its own data and it acts as the AP of a WLAN wherein DQCA can be executed. For completeness, we review the basic protocol rules of DQCA in the next section.

3.1 DQCA Overview

The purpose of this section is to highlight the basic features of DQCA. As demonstrated in (Alonso-Zárate et al., 2008b), DQCA outperforms the widely commercially spread Distributed Coordination Function (DCF) of the IEEE 802.11 Standard and remains stable even when the traffic load occasionally exceeds the channel capacity.

DQCA is a MAC protocol designed to manage the access to the channel in the uplink of an infrastructure WLAN. Time is divided into MAC frames, and each frame is divided in three parts separated by a Short Inter Frame Space (SIFS) necessary to tolerate propagation delays, turnaround times, and processing delays. The three parts, depicted in Fig. 2, are:

1. A Contention Window (CW) further divided into m access minislots wherein the nodes can send a short chip sequence named Access Request Sequence (ARS) to request access to the channel. An ARS is a short chip sequence that contains no explicit information but has a specific and predefined pattern that allows the AP to distinguish between an idle minislot, the presence of just one ARS, or the occurrence of a collision between two or more simultaneous ARS.

2. A data slot reserved for the transmission of data packets.
3. A feedback part wherein the AP broadcasts a Feedback Packet (FBP) that contains the data acknowledgment, the state of the each of the minislots of the CW for contention resolution algorithm, and a 'final message bit' that is enabled (set to one) by the AP to identify the last data packet (fragment) of a message. Of course, nodes must also include a 'final message bit' in their data packet transmissions in order to advertise the transmission of the final fragment of each message.

All the nodes execute three sets of simple rules at the end of each MAC frame. By simply using the feedback information attached to the FBP, they can update the state of two distributed queues (explained below) to execute the access algorithm. According to the protocol rules, DQCA operates as a random access protocol when the traffic load is low (an immediate access rule of the protocol allows a station to get access to the channel immediately if the distributed queues are empty), and it switches smoothly and automatically to a reservation protocol as the traffic load increases. Therefore, it attains the better of the access methods.

The protocol operation is based on two concatenated distributed queues, the Collision Resolution Queue (CRQ) and the Data Transmission Queue (DTQ). The CRQ is responsible for the resolution of collisions among ARS and the DTQ handles the transmission of data. The number of occupied positions (or elements) in each queue is represented by an integer counter (RQ and TQ for the CRQ and the DTQ, respectively). Both counters have the same value for all the nodes in the system and are updated according to a set of rules at the end of each frame. Each node must also maintain and update another set of counters that reveal its position in the queue (pRQ and pTQ for the CRQ and the DTQ, respectively). By the term "position" it is meant the relative order of arrival (or age) of the node in the respective queue. In the CRQ, each position (or element) is occupied by a set of nodes that suffered an ARS collision (i.e. attempted an ARS transmission in the same access minislot of the same CW). The DTQ contains the nodes that successfully reserved the channel through an ARS and therefore each queue element corresponds to exactly one node.

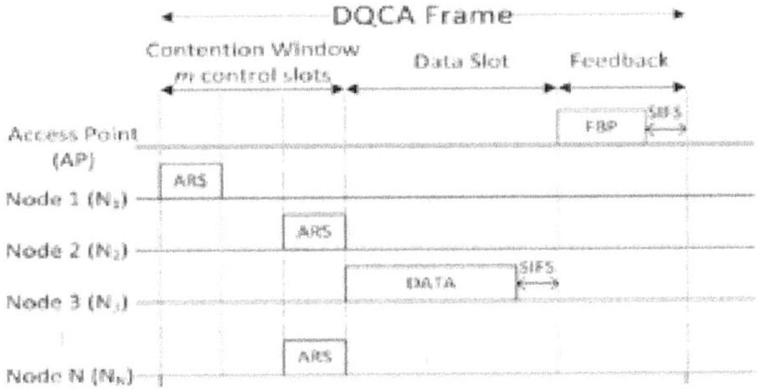

Fig. 2. DQCA Frame Structure

3.2 Motivation and Problem Statement

The intuitive idea behind DQCOOP is that the destination asking for cooperation gets the role of master and coordinates the retransmissions from the relays, which become slaves, as in DQMAN. Then, a temporary cluster is established around the destination and a variation of DQCA can be executed. This is represented in Fig. 3.

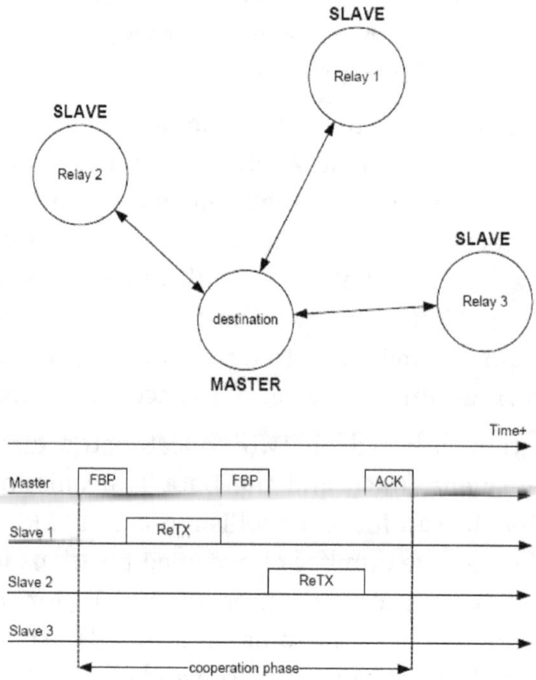

Fig. 3. Master-Slave Architecture of DQCOOP (simplified example)

The master, i.e., the destination, initiates the periodic broadcast of the FBP and creates a temporary cluster. A cooperation phase is initiated. The slaves, i.e., the relays, request access to the channel to retransmit their cooperative packet (retransmissions of the original source transmissions) by executing a variation of the DQCA rules. It is assumed that the relays attempt to retransmit persistently until the cooperation phase is finished. Whenever the cooperation phase is finished either an ACK or a NACK packet is transmitted, indicating either the successful or unsuccessful recovery of the data packet originally received with errors, respectively.

However, DQMAN, as defined in (Alonso-Zárate et al., 2008a), would be inefficient in managing the access to the channel in a C-ARQ scheme. This is mainly due to the fact that upon cooperation request (broadcast by the destination), the group of active relays forms an ad hoc network wherein all the active stations suddenly have a data packet ready to be transmitted. This turns temporarily the network from idle to saturation conditions. This idle-to-saturation sharp transition would cause DQMAN to spend a non-negligible start-up time before attaining its high performance, mainly due to:

1. The simultaneous channel access requests from the active relays in the first frame immediately after the transmission of the CFC would have a high probability of collision. Therefore, some empty frames would be needed until the first collision could be solved and data retransmissions could actually start.
2. Upon the transmission of the first FBP, all the active relays (slaves) would retransmit in the following frame by executing the immediate access rule of DQCA (Slotted ALOHA access for low traffic loads). All these transmissions would collide, causing a waste of resources for the duration of a complete MAC frame.
3. Even with the immediate access rule disabled, an empty frame would be present when the collision resolution process starts due to the MAC frame structure with the feedback broadcast at the end of the frame.

Therefore, it is necessary to expand and adapt the DQMAN operation to take into consideration the aforementioned issues that may potentially degrade its performance in C- ARQ schemes. DQCOOP is presented in the next section with the goal of attaining the near- optimum performance of DQMAN within the context of the considered C-ARQ scheme.

3.3 Protocol Description

The core operation of DQCOOP is highly based on DQMAN. However, the clustering algorithm and the MAC protocol (frame structure and protocol rules) are modified to meet the requirements of the C-ARQ scheme. Their descriptions are presented in the next two sections.

3.3.1 Clustering Algorithm

In DQCOOP, the clustering algorithm of DQMAN is modified as it follows:

1. The destination, and not the transmitter as in DQMAN, takes the master role when a cooperation phase is initiated with the transmission of a CFC packet. Some of the relays which received the original data packet (received with errors by the destination to trigger a cooperation phase) and also receive the CFC transmitted by the destination become active relays. These active relays get the role of slaves. A cluster is then established. The master periodically broadcasts a FBP, in the same way as in DQMAN, to provide the slaves with the minimum feedback information necessary to execute the protocol rules at the end of each frame.

2. There is no CCA prior to the establishment of the cluster. This means that the destination station does not have to contend with other users to get access to the channel. Therefore the contention within the MSP associated with DQMAN is avoided with DQCOOP. This can be actually performed as the CFC is transmitted instead of the ACK when receiving a packet with errors. ACK packets are usually given priority over all kind of traffic (in wireless networks), and thus there is no need for contention in this case.
3. The cluster is broken up whenever the master either manages to decode the original packet or discards the packet. The cooperation phase is ended with the transmission of the ACK packet. Otherwise, if a maximum time-out expires and the original packet cannot be decoded, a NACK packet is transmitted and the cluster is broken up as well. That is, in fact all the stations become idle upon the transmission of either the ACK or the NACK by the master.

3.3.2 The MAC Protocol: Frame Structure and Protocol Rules

When a cooperation phase is initiated, time is divided into five parts as represented in Fig. 4. Upon the transmission/reception of each FBP, all the stations execute the protocol rules of DQCA. The five parts of a cooperation phase within the context of DQCOOP are:

1. A CFC transmission. The cooperation phase is initiated when a CFC is broadcast by the destination station upon the reception of a data packet with errors. This CFC takes the form of a special FBP and indicates that immediate access is forbidden.
2. An initial contention window composed of m0 minislots follows the CFC transmission wherein every active relay station randomly selects (with equal probability) one out of the m0 minislots where to send an Access Request Sequence (ARS).
3. A FBP transmission. A FBP is broadcast by the master station with the feedback information regarding the state of each of the m0 previous minislots. As in DQMAN, for each minislot, this information can have one out of three values. It can be empty (E), i.e., no ARS transmitted, success (S), i.e., exactly one ARS transmitted, or collision (C), i.e., more than one ARS transmitted in the same minislot (no matter how many).
4. A number of regular DQMAN consecutive MAC frames follow this first FBP until the cooperation phase is ended. The rules of DQMAN, with the exception of the immediate access rule, are executed to manage the data retransmissions and the resolution of the collisions. The contention window of these frames has m minislots, where in general m<m0, although this is not a mandatory condition.

5. An ACK or NACK transmission. Whenever the destination is able to successfully decode the original packet, it broadcasts an ACK packet indicating the end of the cooperation phase. A NACK is transmitted if the packet cannot be decoded at some point in time.

Short Inter Frame Spaces (SIFS) are left between each of the parts of the cooperation phase to compensate for non-negligible propagation and data processing delays and turnaround times to switch the radio transceiver from receiving to transmitting mode.

It is worth mentioning that the value of m0 must be tuned according to the expected number of active relays. The higher the number of active relays, the higher the value of m0 in order to reduce the probability that all the access requests collide in the first frame. However, a high value for m0 has a cost in terms of control overhead. On the other hand, as long as at least one access request is successful, the data transmission process can be initiated from the first MAC frame, avoiding thus the loss of resources.

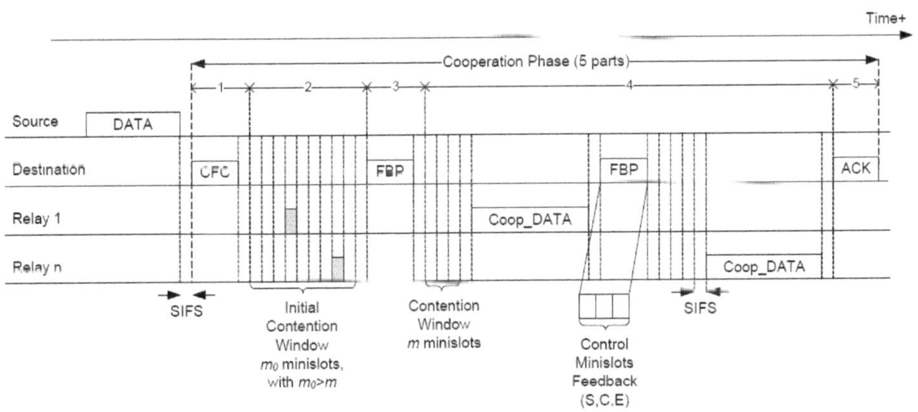

Fig. 4. DQCOOP MAC Frame Structure

3.3.3 Operational Example

A simple network layout with six stations is considered, all of them in the transmission range of each other. A source station (S) transmits to a destination station (D) with the support of relays R1, R2, R3, and R4. TQ and RQ represent the size of the DTQ and the CRQ, respectively, and pTQi and pCRi represent the position of the ith user in the DTQ and CRQ, respectively.

The cooperation phase is represented in Fig. 5 and explained as follows:

1. Upon the reception of the data packet with errors, D initiates a cooperation phase by broadcasting a CFC. This packet sets the start of frame 0.
2. Frame 0 contains 5 access minislots (m0=5). The set of relays {R1, R2, R3, R4} select the set of minislots {3, 1, 5, 5}.

3. At the end of frame 0, D broadcasts the FBP with the following feedback information regarding the state of the minislots, i.e., {Success, Empty, Success, Empty, Collision}.
4. Upon the execution of the protocol rules, R2 gets the first position of DTQ, R1 gets the second position of DTQ, and both R3 and R4 get the first position of CRQ. In terms of the four integer number representing the queues, this can be written as {pTQ1, pTQ2, pTQ3, pTQ4}={2,1,0,0} and {pRQ1, pRQ2, pRQ3, pRQ4}={0, 0, 1, 1}. On the other hand, TQ=2 and RQ=1.
5. During frame 1, both the data transmission and the collision resolution work in parallel. At the beginning of the frame, containing 2 access minislots (m=2), R3 and R4 attempt to solve their collision. They reselect an access minislot where to send an ARS. In this case, they select minislots 1 and 2 respectively, and thus they successfully solve their collision.
6. On the other hand, R2, which is at the first position of DTQ, transmits data (a retransmission of the original packet).
7. At the end of frame 1, the FBP broadcast by D indicates that a transmission has been successful and the next station in DTQ should transmit in the following frame. In addition, the feedback information on the state of the minislots allows R3 and R4 to queue, orderly in time, in DTQ.

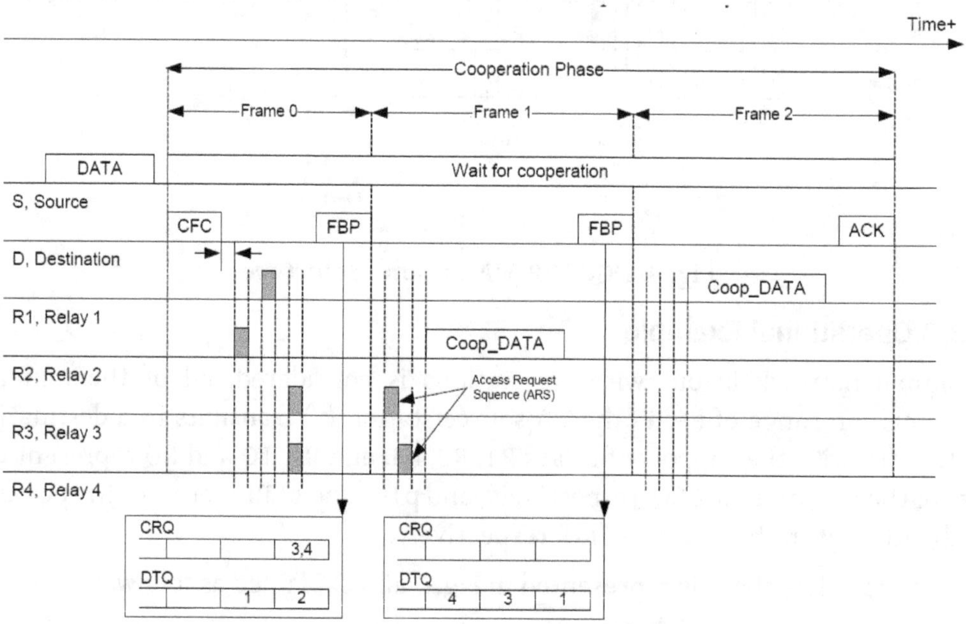

Fig. 5. DQCOOP Example of Operation

8. In frame 2, there are no collisions to be solved and thus the minislots are empty. R1 transmits data.

9. Upon the reception of the retransmission from R1, D is able to successfully decode the original packet. Therefore, it transmits an ACK packet indicating the end of the cooperation phase. All the relays discard the buffered cooperative packet.

3.4 Performance Evaluation

The performance of DQCOOP is evaluated in this section through a C++ custom-made simulator. In order to focus on the evaluation of the cooperation phases, a single-hop network wherein all the data transmissions from a fixed source to a fixed destination are received with errors is considered. That is, the destination always broadcasts a CFC packet upon the reception of every original data packet received from the source station. Moreover, the source has always a packet ready to be transmitted to the destination.

In this performance evaluation, we will measure the average packet transmission delay defined as the period of time elapsed from the moment that a packet is first transmitted from the source until it can be decoded at destination after receiving K retransmissions. For all the experiments, we assume that a constant number of relays are activated within each cooperation phase. Furthermore, and without loss of generality, the destination is considered to require a constant number K of retransmissions from the relay set to decode the original packet.

The simulation parameters are summarized in Table 1.

Table 1. Simulation Parameters

Parameter	Value	Parameter	Value
Control Rate	6 Mbps	MAC header	34 bytes
Data Rate (Source)	24 Mbps	PHY preamble	96 μs
Data Rate (Relays)	54 Mbps	ACK, CFC, FBP length	14 bytes
Packet Length	1500 bytes	SlotTime	10 μs
ARS	10 μs	SIFS	10 μs

3.4.1 Number of Minislots in the Cooperation Phase

The average packet transmission delay as a function of the number of active relays in a cooperative phase is represented in Fig. 6 when K=3 and for different values of m0 and m, which in addition accomplish that m0=m. Each curve represents the results obtained with different number of access minislots (m).

For low values of m, the average packet transmission delay gets lower as the value of m increases thanks to the faster collision resolution process. However, increasing the number of access minislots also increases the MAC overhead. The addition of an extra minislot entails an extension of the frame duration (devoted to overhead) and also enlarges the size of the FBP that contains the state of each one of the minislots. Therefore, as it can be seen in the figure, for high values of m, e.g., m=10, the fact that the collision resolution becomes shorter in time does not pay off the increase in the protocol overhead when the number of active relays is low and thus the average packet transmission delay gets higher. This can be better appreciated in Fig. 7 where the average packet transmission delay for the scenario with 5 relays is plotted as a function of the number of access minislots m=m0. In this curve it is easier to see that, for low number of access minislots, an increase in the number of minislots leads to lower average packet transmission delays. However, over a given threshold, the faster resolution of collisions due to the longer contention window does not compensate for the MAC overhead and the average packet transmission delay increases with the number of access minislots. For this reason, it is necessary to find a good compromise between the faster collision resolution and the protocol overhead. This tradeoff will be further discussed later in the next section.

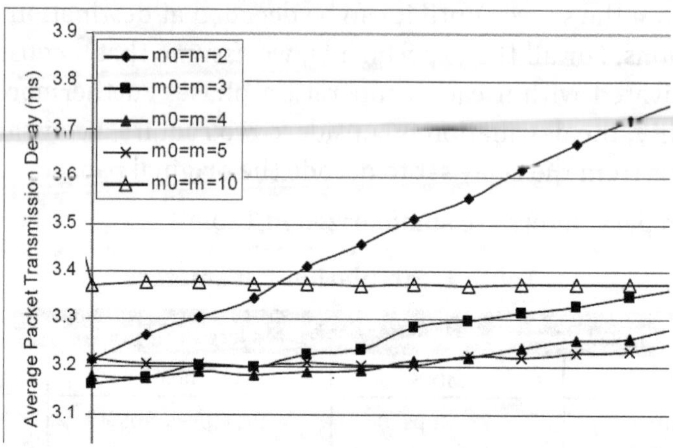

Fig. 6. Average Packet Transmission Delays for Different Values of m0=m

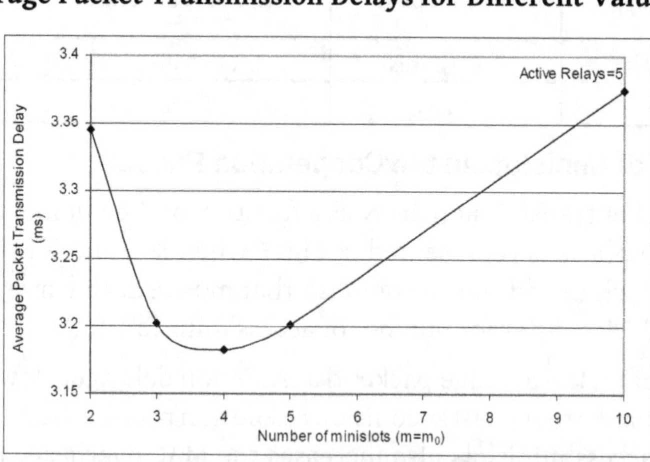

Fig. 7. Average Packet Transmission Delay for Different Values of m0=m

Getting back to the results in Fig. 6, they show that the average packet transmission delay drops remarkably when the number of access minislots is at least equal to 3. Higher values of m do not result in any substantial reduction of this time. Therefore, as it happens with the DQCA protocol (Alonso-Zárate et al., 2008b), a good operational point for DQCOOP is to set m=3.

It is interesting to evaluate whether this discussion is still valid for any arbitrary number of required retransmissions (K). The average packet transmission delay is plotted in Fig. 8 as a function of the value of K and for different values of m0=m when the number of active relays is 15. In all cases, there is a considerable reduction of the average packet transmission delay when shifting from 2 to 3 minislots. However, there is no much interest in increasing the number of access minislots to higher values than 3, at least in terms of packet transmission delay. Therefore, it is important to reinforce the already known argument that the number of access minislots should be set to 3 in any DQCA-like protocol.

However, it seems reasonable to think that the value of m0 (the number of access minislots within the very first frame after the transmission of the CFC) could be set to a higher value than m in order to absorb the first multiple access request arrival from all the active relays. Note that the first frame is the one that receives the maximum number of simultaneous access requests. In subsequent frames, the requests are split into smaller groups according to the m-ary tree-splitting collision resolution operation of DQMAN.

In the next section, m is set to 3 and the performance of the protocol is evaluated for different values of m0. The aim is to evaluate the reduction of the average packet transmission delay for m0>m.

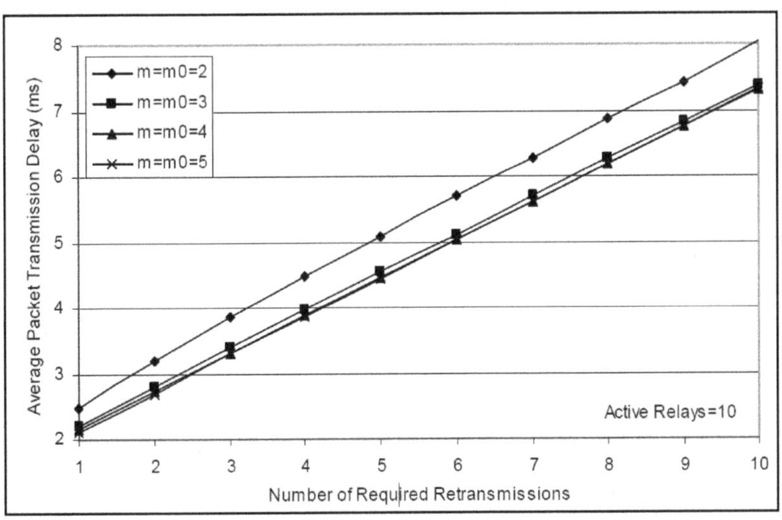

Fig. 8. Average Packet Transmission Times for Different Values of K

3.4.2 Number of Minislots in the Start-up Phase (m0)

The performance of DQCOOP for different values of m0 is evaluated in this section. As discussed before, an increase in the number of minislots of the first frame reduces the probability of collision in the first access requests upon initialization of a cooperation phase and, therefore, it should yield a lower average packet transmission delay. However, it also entails an increase of the protocol overhead (frame length and amount of required feedback information).

In order to quantify this tradeoff, first note that the duration of a cooperation phase can be decomposed as the sum of time devoted to the transmission of data and the overhead due to the necessary MAC protocol. This overhead time includes silent intervals as well as the time devoted to the transmission of control packets. Considering this, the relative overhead is defined as the ratio between the overhead time in the cases that m0>1 and the overhead time when m0=1 (this latter case is the worst case in terms of overhead since all the relays collide in the first access request with probability one). This definition allows plotting the curves with different values of K in the same vertical axis and also makes the results independent of the absolute values of the transmission rates used for the simulation and the numerical evaluation.

The relative overhead is plotted in Fig. 9 as a function of the value of m0, for different number of required retransmissions (K), and considering a total number of 5 active relays. The first observation is that there is a close relationship between the overhead of the protocol and the value of m0. The value of the relative overhead is very sensitive to the value of m0 if the number of required retransmissions is low. This means that if the value of K is low, the accurate tuning of the value of m0 has a remarkable effect on the performance of the C-ARQ scheme. All the curves show a local minimum of the relative overhead for any pair of values of m0 and K. However, on the other hand, the higher the values of K, the more flat the curves become. This means that if the number of required retransmission is high, the value of m0 becomes a non-critical parameter on the performance of DQCOOP.

The main reason for this behavior is that when the number of required retransmissions is high and thus the duration of the cooperation phase is long, the impact of the overhead of the first frame on the performance of DQCOOP is low. Note that if K retransmissions are needed, at least K frames are necessary.

On the other hand, it seems reasonable to believe that the selection of the value of m0 should depend on the number of active relays (which request access simultaneously in the first frame). In order to evaluate this relationship, the average packet transmission delay is plotted in Fig. 10 for K=3. Different curves are plotted for different number of active relays and as a function of the value of m0.

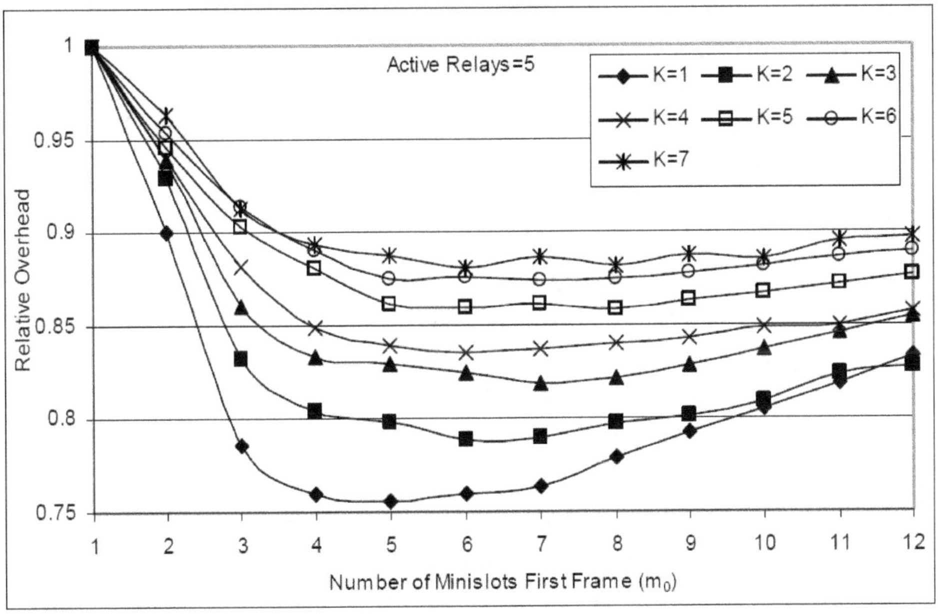

Fig. 9. Protocol Relative Overhead (DQCOOP)

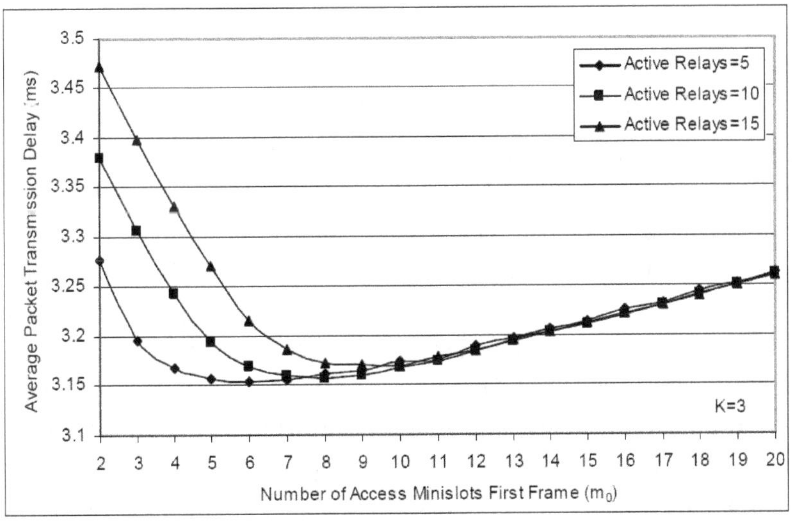

Fig. 10. Average Packet Transmission Delay as a Function of m0

It is worth noting that when m0 ≥ 10 the three curves almost overlap. This means that, if this condition is fulfilled, the average packet transmission delay is almost equal and independent of the number of active relays. In addition, the value of the average packet transmission delay at m0=10 is not substantially bigger than the one at the respective minimum values that can be found for m0=6 (for 5 active relays), m0=7 (for 10 active relays), and m0=10 (for 15 active relays). This constitutes a worthwhile design guideline since by setting m0=10 the average packet transmission delay for any value of K can be predicted with reliable accuracy regardless of the number of active relays in each cooperation phase (considering a practical situation with no more than 15 active relays). In addition, this fact relaxes the configuration requirements of the network, which is of remarkable interest when operating in fully decentralized and spontaneous networks.

4. CONCISE SUMMARY

This chapter emphasizes the significant significance of the MAC layer in the efficacy of C-ARQ schemes. Such schemes have often been assessed from foundational perspectives, presuming optimal scheduling among the relays. We have demonstrated that efficient MAC protocols are essential to meet the special demands of C-ARQ schemes and to maximize their potential in enhancing wireless communication efficiency.

Furthermore, we have introduced the DQCOOP protocol as an enhancement and modification of DQMAN to effectively manage the contention among relays in a C-ARQ framework. The initialization phase of a DQMAN cluster has been redesigned to effectively manage the transition from idle to sharp traffic during the transmission of a CFC. Due to the simultaneous assistance of active relays, the initial contention window of DQMAN must be adjusted. Furthermore, the protocol frame structure and the protocol regulations have been amended to enhance the performance of DQMAN within the framework of C-ARQ schemes.

The protocol's performance has been assessed through computer simulations. The results indicate that the performance of DQCOOP can remain unaffected by the quantity of active relays and the number of access minislots. This is a sought-after attribute in entirely decentralized networks, such as ad hoc networks, where prior knowledge of the network architecture and configuration may be absent. The results indicate that this independence can be achieved by configuring the number of access minislots to three, facilitating a more rapid resolution of collisions than data transmission, and appropriately sizing the number of access minislots in the initial frame, which is also adjusted to prevent an inevitable empty data field. This final update seeks to accommodate the initial simultaneous access request from all active relays. Results indicate that the quantity of access minislots in the initial frame can be excessively allocated with minimal expense, rendering the performance of DQCOOP independent of the number of relays. The expense of augmenting the number of access minislots by one unit, in terms of overhead, is justified by the diminished likelihood of collision during the initial access request.

REFERENCES

1. Alonso-Zárate J., Gómez J., Verikoukis C., Alonso L., & Pérez-Neira A. (2006). Performance Evaluation of a Cooperative Scheme for Wireless Networks,

Proceedings of the IEEE PIMRC, pp. 1-5, ISBN 1-4244-0329-4, Helsinki, Finland, September 2006

2. Alonso-Zárate J., Kartsakli E., Skianis C., Verikoukis C., & Alonso L. (2008a), Saturation Throughput Analysis of a Cluster-based Medium Access Control Protocol for Single-hop Ad Hoc Wireless Networks, Simulation: Transactions of the Society for Modeling and Simulation International, Vol. 84, No. 12, 619-633, ISSN 0037-5497

3. Alonso-Zárate J., Kartsakli E., Cateura A., Verikoukis C., & Alonso L. (2008b). A Near- Optimum Cross-Layered Distributed Queueing Protocol for Wireless LAN, IEEE Wireless Communications Magazine, Special Issue on MAC protocols for WLAN, Vol. 15, No. 2, (February 2008) 48-55, ISSN 1536-1284

4. Azgin A., Altunbasak Y., & AlRebig G. (2005). Cooperative MAC and Routing Protocols for Wireless Ad Hoc Networks, Proceedings of the IEEE GLOBECOM 2005, ISBN: 0-7803- 9414-3, December 2005

5. Biswas S. & Morris R. (2005). ExOR: Opportunistic Multi-hop Routing for Wireless Networks, Proceedings of the SIGCOMM '05, pp. 133-144, ISBN 1-59593-009-4 , New York, NY, USA, 2005.

6. Campbell G. et al. (2002), Method and apparatus for detecting collisions and controlling access to a communications channel, US Patent no. US6408009 B1, June 2002.

7. Cerruti I., Fumagalli A., & Gupta P. (2008). Delay Model of Single-Relay Cooperative ARQ Protocols in Slotted Radio Networks Poisson Frames Arrivals, IEEE/ACM Trans. on Networking, Vol. 16, No. 2, (April 2008) 371-382, ISSN 1063-6692

8. Chakraborty S. S., Liinaharja M., & Ruttik K. (2005). Diversity and packet combining in Rayleigh fading channels, IEE Proceedings-Communications, Vol. 152, No. 3, (June 2005) 353 – 356, ISSN 1350-2425

9. Dianati, M., Ling X., Naik K., & Shen X. (2006). A Node-Cooperative ARQ Scheme for Wireless Ad Hoc Networks, IEEE Trans. on Vehicular Technology, Vol. 55, No. 3, (May 2006) 1032-1044, ISSN 00189545

10. Fitzek F. H. P. & Katz M. D. (2006). Cooperation in Wireless Networks: Principles and Applications, Ed. Springer, ISBN 978-1-4020-4710-7, The Netherlands

11. García-Vidal J., Guerrero-Zapata M., Morillo J., & Fusté D. (2007). A Protocol Stack for Cooperative Wireless Networks, In: Wireless Systems and Mobility in Next Generation Internet, in Lecture Notes in Computer Science (LNCS), 62-73, Springer, ISBN: 978-3- 540-70968-8, Springer, (2007)

12. Goldsmith A. (2005). Wireless Communications, Cambridge University Press, ISBN 0521837162

13. Gómez J. & Pérez-Neira A. (2006). Average Rate Behavior for Cooperative Diversity in Wireless Networks, Proceedings of the IEEE International Symposium on Circuits and Systems (ISCAS), pp. 5309-5402, ISBN 0-7803-9389-9, Kos, Greece, May 2006

14. Gómez J., Alonso-Zárate J., Verikoukis C., Pérez-Neira A., & Alonso L. (2007). Cooperation On Demand Protocols for Wireless Networks, Proceedings of the IEEE PIMRC, pp. 5, ISBN: 978-1-4244-1144-3, Athens, Greece, September 2007

15. Gupta P., Cerruti I., & Fumagalli A. (2004). Three Transmission Scheduling Policies for a Cooperative ARQ Protocol in Radio Networks, Proceedings of the WNCG Conference, Austin, October 2004

16. IEEE 802.11 Standard, Part 11: Wireless LAN Medium Access Control (MAC) and Physical Layer (PHY) Specifications, IEEE Std. 802.-11-99, Revision 2007

17. Korakis T., Natayanan S., Bagri A., & Panwar S. (2006). Implementing a Cooperative MAC Protocol for Wireless LAN, Proceedings of the IEEE International Conference on Communications (ICC'06), pp. 4805-4810, ISBN: 1-4244-0355-3, June 2006

18. Liu P., Tao Z., Lin Z., Erkip E., & Panwar S. (2006), Cooperative Wireless Communications: A Cross-Layer Approach, IEEE Wireless Communications Magazine, Special Issue on Advances in Smart Antennas, Vol. 13, No. 4, (August 2006) 84-92, , ISSN 1536-1284

19. Liu P., Tao Z., & Panwar S. (2007). CoopMAC: A Cooperative MAC for Wireless LANs, IEEE Journal on Selected Areas on Communications, Vol. 25, No.2, (February 2007) 340-354, ISSN 0733-8716

20. Morillo-Pozo J., García-Vidal J., & Pérez-Neira A. I. (2005). Collaborative ARQ in Wireless Energy-Constrained Networks, Proceedings of the 2005 Joint Workshop on Foundations of Mobile Computing 2005 (DIAL-POM'05), ISBN 1-59593-092-2

21. Morillo-Pozo J. D., & García-Vidal J. (2007). A Low Coordination Overhead C-ARQ Protocol with Frame Combining, Proceedings of the IEEE PIMRC, pp. 1-5, ISBN 978-1-4244- 1144-3, Athens, Greece, September 2007

22. Nosratinia, A., Hunter, T. E., & Hedayat A. (2004). Cooperative Communications in Wireless Networks, IEEE Communications Magazine, Vol. 42, No. 10, (October 2004) 74-80, ISSN 0163-6804

23. Pfletschinger S. & Navarro M. (2008). Link Adaptation with Retransmissions for Partial Channel State Information, Proceedings of the IEEE GLOBECOM 2008, pp. 1-6, ISBN 978-1-4244-2324-8, New Orleans, Louisiana, USA, November 2008

24. Tao Z., Korakis T., Slutskiy Y., Panwar S., & Tassiulas L. (2007). Cooperation and Directionality: A Co-opdirectional MAC for Wireless Ad Hoc Networks, Proceedings of the WiOpt 2007, pp. 1-8, ISBN: 978-1-4244-0960-0, April 2007

25. Shankar S., Chou C., & Ghosh M. (2005). Cooperative Communication MAC (CMAC) – A new MAC protocol for Next Generation Wireless LANs, Proceedings of the IEEE International Conference on Wireless Networks, Communications, and Mobile Computing 2005, pp. 1-6, ISBN: 0-7803-9305-8, June 2005

26. Sadek B., Ray Liu K. J., & Ephremides A. (2006). Collaborative Multiple-Access Protocols for Wireless Networks, Proceedings of the IEEE International Conference on Communications (ICC'06), pp. 4495-4500, ISBN: 1-4244-0355-3, June 2006

27. Wang X. & Yang C. (2005). A MAC Protocol Supporting Cooperative Diversity for Distributed Wireless Ad Hoc Networks, Proceedings of the IEEE PIMRC, pp. 1396- 1400, ISBN: 9783800729098, Berlin, Germany, September 2005

28. Zimmermann M. D., Herhold P., & Fettweis G. (2004). The Impact of Cooperation on Diversity-Exploiting Protocols, Proceedings of the 59th IEEE Vehicular Technology Conference, pp. 410-414, ISBN 0-7803-8255-2, Milan (Italy), May 2004

29. Zimmermann E., Herhold P., & Fettweis G. (2005). On the Performance of Cooperative Relaying Protocols in Wireless Networks, European Trans. on Telecommunications, Vol. 16, No. 1, (January 2005) 5-16, ISSN 1541-8251

30. Zorzi M., Rao R. R., & Milstein L.B. (1997). ARQ error control for fading mobile radio channels, IEEE Trans. on Vehicular Technology, vol. 46, no. 2, (May 1997) 445-455, ISSN 00189545

13

Chapter

A HYBRID FEEDBACK MECHANISM FOR LEVERAGING MULTIUSER DIVERSITY IN WIRELESS NETWORKS

1. INTRODUCTION: AN OVERVIEW

The emergence of new multimedia applications, coupled with the substantial demand and growth for these applications, necessitates the provision of high-speed, high-rate transmission systems. A approach that can facilitate such applications is multiuser diversity (MUDiv), which leverages channel fading (1). Assume that a substantial number of users are concurrently transmitting and receiving packets within a certain cell, each experiencing independent, time-varying fading circumstances. Opportunistic scheduling (OS) can optimally optimize wireless resources by broadcasting data solely to the instantaneous "on-peak" user, thereby significantly enhancing overall system throughput (2), (3). To optimize user scheduling based on channel quality, each user assesses their instantaneous signal-to-noise ratio (SNR) and communicates this information to the network scheduler. Presently, Qualcomm's high data rate (HDR) system necessitates a comparable strategy (4). As the number of active users increases, resources are squandered on managing this volume of feedback, resulting in wasteful spectrum utilization. This issue prompted academics to propose novel approaches to diminish the feedback load when utilizing MUDiv.

Numerous studies have been undertaken to use multiuser diversity while minimizing overhead. The influence of the quantization level of SNR measurements on the throughput of constant rate transmission was examined in (5). It was demonstrated that decreasing the feedback rate (fewer quantization levels) results in superior performance relative to unquantized feedback. In single carrier systems, (6) introduced a discrete rate switch-based multiuser diversity (DSMUDiv) algorithm that diminished the feedback load and feedback rate while maintaining the performance of OS. The scheduling algorithm utilized a probing approach. A limitation of this approach is that when the average SNR diminishes, the requirement for comprehensive probing escalates, resulting in a substantial feedback load at low average SNR levels. The research was expanded to multi-carrier systems in (7), demonstrating additional reduction in the feedback burden. In (8), users evaluate their sum-rate across all sub-carriers against a specified threshold value. In (9), the threshold value was modified to achieve a designated outage probability. Users with channel quality exceeding the threshold are permitted to provide comment on their SNR measurements, while all others remain mute. In the absence of feedback, a random user is chosen, resulting in a reduction in capacity. The feedback values are unquantized (analog), resulting in an elevated feedback rate. In (10), the study was expanded, wherein the scheduler solicits comprehensive feedback if none of the users' channel qualities exceed the threshold. Despite the capacity loss being offset by complete feedback instead of (9), the feedback load was elevated. In (11), various feedback thresholds are employed to diminish the feedback burden and leverage multiuser diversity. The feedback load was diminished at the cost of a scheduling delay. Furthermore, a collection of switched-based multiuser access techniques was presented in (12) to mitigate the feedback load. In (13) and (14), the feedback rate was diminished to one bit per user. The scheduler utilizes these feedback bits to categorize all users into two groups and allocates the channel to one user from the group with advantageous channel circumstances. This decreases the feedback burden and feedback rate; however, some loss is anticipated due to the low resolution of the quantized feedback (one bit). Other studies have examined multi-carrier systems; for instance, in (15), a clustering technique was proposed to diminish the feedback load while marginally compromising performance. Each user provides a figure-of-merit enumerating its most robust clusters of subcarriers. In (16), a predetermined quantity of subcarriers for each user is relayed rather than comprehensive feedback. The subcarriers are either the optimal K out of M subcarriers or K specified subcarriers. All previously referenced studies examined polling threshold-based scheduling techniques to mitigate feedback load.

Other research examined random access methods to use multiuser diversity while minimizing overhead. A distributed multiaccess system was proposed in (17). Users report the top m channels that exceed a specified channel quality threshold. Optimization was conducted to determine the optimal threshold and m values to enhance system capacity. A random access threshold-based feedback technique was proposed in (18) to use diversity gain while minimizing feedback load. Parameter optimization is conducted to permit only users with elevated channel gains to provide feedback, hence maximizing system capacity. In (19), a medium access control system was developed utilizing splitting algorithms to resolve collisions across a series of minislots and identify the user with the optimal channel. Contention resolution algorithms that leverage diversity gain were proposed in (20). Ultimately, algorithms with lower feedback overhead were examined in (21). Static splitting was evaluated for the optimal effort traffic scenario. In the traffic mixture scenario, a combination of contention and polling-based feedback was employed to uphold quality of service.

Polling-based algorithms, such as DSMUDiv, provide optimal user selection but are hindered by scheduling delays. Conversely, while contention-based algorithms diminish overhead more than centralized scheduling, they experience a reduction in capacity. This chapter presents an opportunistic scheduling method that is a joint polling and contention-based feedback (JPCF) algorithm, rather than solely a polling-based feedback algorithm as described in (6). During the guard period, segmented into minislots, users provide input on their channel characteristics, relative to a predefined channel threshold, either in a polling-based feedback minislot (p-minislot) or a contention-based feedback minislot (c-minislot). Data transmission commences upon the identification of the optimal user. The scheduling algorithm is examined under the assumption of gradual Rayleigh fading, and closed-form formulas for both the feedback load and system capacity are found. We examine the impact of the delay on throughput, from which we derive the system's throughput. The scheduling method is evaluated against the DSMUDiv (6) and the optimal (full feedback) selective diversity scheduling algorithms.

2. SYSTEM MODEL

We consider a single free interference cell in a wireless network with K active users commu- nicating with a base station (BS). We assume downlink scheduling, where only one user is allowed to receive data transmission in each time slot. The communication is based on time division duplex (TDD), where downlink and uplink channels are reciprocal.

2.1 Downlink Transmission Model

Let,

$$yi\ (T)= hi\ (T) \cdot x(T)+ ni\ (T);\ i = 1, 2, 3, \ldots.., K \tag{1}$$

be the baseband channel model, where x(T) ∈C is the transmitted signal in time slot T and yi (T) ∈C is the received signal of user i in time slot T. The noise processes ni (T) are independent and identical distributed (i.i.d.) sequences of zero mean complex Gaussian noise with variance σn2. The fading channel gain from the BS to the ith user in time slot T is hi (T). We adopt a quasi-static fading channel model where hi (T) is i.i.d. from burst to burst but remains constant over each burst. We consider a flat Rayleigh fading model, assuming the fading coefficients of all users are i.i.d. Therefore, hi (T) is a zero-mean complex Gaussian random variable. The amplitude of hi (T), αi (T)= hi (T) is Rayleigh distributed with the probability density function (PDF) given by, where Ωi = E[αi2] is the average fading power of the ith user.

$$f_{\alpha_i}(\alpha_i) = \frac{2\alpha_i}{\Omega_i} \exp(-\frac{\alpha_i^2}{\Omega_i}) \tag{2}$$

2.2 Quantized Feedback

In this work we assume that users adapt their modulation level based on the instantaneous channel condition. Using this transmission strategy, which is called adaptive modulation (AM), if the channel is strong at a given time, the transmission can occur with a higher con- stellation size. Otherwise, a lower constellation size has to be used. Note that the switching thresholds of the adaptive transmission modes are functions of the modulation scheme and target error performance. We consider adaptive multilevel quadrature amplitude modulation (M-QAM) scheme (22). Specifically, we consider a transmission scheme employing uncoded adaptive discrete rate M-QAM schemes with constellation sizes M = {Mn : Mn < Mn+1,0 ≤ n ≤ N} , where M0 = 1 is the user outage (deep fade), and MN is the highest modulation level. We assume perfect channel estimation and negligible time delay between channel estimation and signal set adaptation, and as such, the rate adaptation can happen instantaneously. We also assume error free feedback channels. If we denote the target average bit error probability (BEP) by BEPo , thresholds or switching thresholds can be obtained according to (22, eq.(30)): where erfc-1( ) denotes the inverse complementary error function.

$$\begin{aligned} \gamma_{th}^{(1)} &= [\mathrm{erfc}^{-1}(2 \cdot \mathrm{BEP}_o)]^2, \\ \gamma_{th}^{(n)} &= -\frac{2}{3}(2^n - 1)\ln(5 \cdot \mathrm{BEP}_o);\ n = 2, 3, \ldots\ldots, N, \\ \gamma_{th}^{(N+1)} &= +\infty, \end{aligned} \tag{3}$$

Similar to (6), with the assumption of discrete rates, a user estimates his SNR and instead of feeding back the analog value it is mapped to a quantized value that represent the modulation level, which can be supported, and then this quantized value is fed back.

Define the set of quantized values (binary bits) Q = {q(n) : q(n) < q(n+1), 0 ≤ n ≤ N} that represents the modulation levels, (q(n) →map Mn). If we assume n modulation levels, then each quantized value q(m),0 ≤ m ≤ n, will be log2 n bits in length. To illustrate the idea of the SNR mapping, assume Γi is the estimated SNR of the ith user, then the quantized value is,

$$q_i = \begin{cases} q^{(0)} & \text{if } \gamma_i < \gamma_{th}^{(1)} \text{ (outage)}, \\ q^{(n)} & \text{if } \gamma_{th}^{(n)} \leq \gamma_i < \gamma_{th}^{(n+1)} \\ q^{(N)} & \text{if } \gamma_i \geq \gamma_{th}^{(N)}. \end{cases} \tag{4}$$

2.3 Uplink Feedback Structure

Fig. 1 shows the feedback channel structure, which consists of minislots. The number of minislots constructing the feedback channel can vary from 1 minislot, in the case the first user is granted the channel access, to 2K – 1 minislots, where K is the total number of users, in the case all users feed back their channel qualities. This variation in length assumes that data transmission can begin at different time periods. Such assumption can be possible if dynamic spectrum access is implemented. The JPCF scheduling algorithm assumes that the feedback is polling-based or contention-based. The feedback channel is divided into polling-based feedback minislots (p-minislot) and contention-based feedback minislots (c-minislot), where each p-minislot is followed by a c-minislot, except the last p-minislot. The contention protocol is based on a modified slotted ALOHA protocol (23). As any random multiple access protocol one out of three possible outcomes will occur: no access, one access, and a collision. Multiple users feeding back the requested information will cause signals to interfere at the receiver which we consider as a collision. When a collision occurs no resolution is consider and the information is discarded.

3. SCHEDULING ALGORITHM

In this section, we will introduce our proposed algorithm, the JPCF scheduling algorithm. Similar to the optimal selective scheduling algorithm, the JPCF algorithm always guarantees that the best user is granted the channel access. The difference between the two is in the se- lection process. In the JPCF algorithm decisions on whom to schedule are based on threshold test. In simple terms, the BS compares the channel quality of a user to a predetermined thresh- old value and selects the user if his channel quality exceeds the threshold. In case no user is found with channel quality exceeding the threshold, then the user with the highest channel quality among all is selected.

Let us define the following:

- $L = (D(i), l) : 1 \leq l \leq K$ is the probing order , and D(i) is the ID of user i . The set is generated randomly each time slot.
- The predetermined threshold value is set to $\Gamma(N)$. According to (3), $\Gamma(N)$ is the SNR threshold of the highest modulation level and q(N) is the quantized threshold value.
- The probability of contention in the c-minislot is ρ.

The feedback mechanism of the JPCF algorithm is based on both polling period and contention period. Each period is a minislot during. Fig. 1 shows the feedback channel structure, which consists of p-minislots and c-minislots. The following describes the scheduling algorithm (Fig. 2 shows the flowchart):

1. Through the broadcast channel all users know their polling order (L).
2. The feedback channel always begins with a p-minislot.

3. During the p-minislot the BS polls the channel state information of the user (his SNR) who is in order.
4. The feedback channel is terminated and the data transmission begins if the polled user has ql = q(N). By knowing (Γl) and according to (4) ql is determined.
5. If ql ≠ q(N), then his information is stored and the feedback channel continues with ac-minislot following the previous p-minislot and step (vi) is performed.
6. During the c-minislot, which is a contention based minislot, users feedback their SNRs, with probability ρ, if it satisfy q = q(N). Otherwise, they keep silent.
7. If the contention is successful, then the feedback channel is terminated and the data transmission begins for that successful user. Otherwise, the feedback channel continues with a p-minislot following the previous c-minislot and step (iii) is performed.
8. In case all users are polled, the BS picks the user with the highest channel quality among them and the data transmission begins for that user.
9. In case a tie occurs, a random pick is performed.

4. PERFORMANCE ANALYSIS

The performance of the JPCF algorithm is evaluated in this section. Basically, we concentrate on the feedback load, the system capacity, and the scheduling delay. Closed form expressions for all three performance measures are also derived.

4.1 Feedback Load

We define the average feedback load (AFL) as the average number of responses until a user is scheduled. The feedback response includes the response on the p-minislot, and the response on the c-minislot. In the c-minislot, a contention resulting a success or a collision is counted as one response, and zero response is considered in case no contention occurs.

Consider two consecutive minislots (p-minislot and c-minislot) and denote the discrete ran- dom variable η [1, 2] by the total number of feedback during them. Let U be the set of events where a successful search occurs during the two minislots. Note that a successful search occurs when a user with q = q(N) is found. Therefore, the occurrence of a successful search is associ- ated with one of the following events: (i) The polled user during the p-minislot has q = q(N), or (ii) The polled user during the p-minislot has q < q(N) and a successful contention occurs in the following c-minislot.

The probability of U given l probes is:

$$\Gamma^{U}(l,\rho) = \left[1 - F_{\gamma}(\gamma_{th}^{(N)})\right] + \left[F_{\gamma}(\gamma_{th}^{(N)})\left\{\sum_{i=1}^{K-l}\binom{K-l}{i}\left(1 - F_{\gamma}(\gamma_{th}^{(N)})\right)^{i}\left(F_{\gamma}(\gamma_{th}^{(N)})\right)^{K-l-i} \times \left(i\rho(1-\rho)^{i-1}\right)\right\}\right], \tag{5}$$

where

$$F_{\gamma}(\zeta) = P[\gamma < \zeta] = (1 - e^{\frac{-\zeta}{\bar{\gamma}}}), \tag{6}$$

is the cumulative distribution function (CDF) of the SNR (Γ). The first part of the right hand side of (5) refers to the success in the p-minislot and the second part refers in the success in the c-minislot.

let X represent the set of events where no feedback occurs on the c-minislot and Y to be the set of events where a feedback occurs on the c-minislot. Conditioning on l, the probability of X and the probability of Y, respectively, are:

$$\Gamma^{X}(l,\rho) = \left[1 - F_{\gamma}(\gamma_{th}^{(N)})\right] + \left[F_{\gamma}(\gamma_{th}^{(N)})\left\{\sum_{i=0}^{K-l}\binom{K-l}{i}\left(1 - F_{\gamma}(\gamma_{th}^{(N)})\right)^{i}\left(F_{\gamma}(\gamma_{th}^{(N)})\right)^{K-l-i} \times \left((1-\rho)^{i}\right)\right\}\right], \tag{7}$$

and

$$\Gamma^{Y}(l,\rho) = F_{\gamma}(\gamma_{th}^{(N)})\left\{\sum_{i=0}^{K-l}\binom{K-l}{i}\left(1 - F_{\gamma}(\gamma_{th}^{(N)})\right)^{i}\left(F_{\gamma}(\gamma_{th}^{(N)})\right)^{K-l-i}\left(1-(1-\rho)^{i}\right)\right\}. \tag{8}$$

The conditioned expected value of η is:

$$\overline{\eta}(l,\rho) = 1\cdot\Gamma^{X}(l,\rho) + 2\cdot\Gamma^{Y}(l,\rho). \tag{9}$$

Therefore, the AFL is:

$$\mathrm{AFL}(\rho) = \sum_{l=1}^{K-1}\left(\sum_{i=1}^{l}\overline{\eta}(i,\rho)\right)\prod_{i=1}^{l-1}\left(1 - \Gamma^{U}(i,\rho)\right)\Gamma^{U}(l,\rho) + \left[\left(\sum_{l=1}^{K-1}\overline{\eta}(l,\rho)\right) + 1\right]\prod_{l=1}^{K-1}\left(1 - \Gamma^{U}(l,\rho)\right). \tag{10}$$

4.2 System Capacity

The average spectral efficiency (ASE) is defined as the average transmitted data rate per unit bandwidth in bits/sec/Hz for specified power and target error performance. In this work we are considering discrete rates and using quantized

SNR values (q). For example: if two users with Γ1 ∈ [Γ(i), Γ(i+1)), Γ2 ∈ [Γ(i), Γ(i+1)), and Γ1 = Γ2, then according to (4) both users feedback q(i). Therefore, scheduling either one will result a transmission rate of log2 Mi bps/Hz.

Based on the algorithm's description in Section 3, it is clearly seen that both the DSMUDiv scheduling algorithm proposed in (6) and the JPCF scheduling algorithm will always select the best user. Therefore, resulting a similar performance in terms of spectral efficiency.

It has been shown in (6) that with i users in the system, scheduling the best user yields the following average spectral efficiency:

$$
\begin{aligned}
\mathrm{R}(i) = {} & b_o\left([F_\gamma(\gamma_{th}^{(1)})]^i \right) \\
& + \sum_{n=1}^{N-1} b_n \left([F_\gamma(\gamma_{th}^{(n+1)})]^i - [F_\gamma(\gamma_{th}^{(n)})]^i \right) \\
& + b_N \left(1 - [F_\gamma(\gamma_{th}^{(N)})]^i \right)
\end{aligned}
\tag{11}
$$

where bn = log2 Mn is the number of bits per constellation. Therefore, the ASE of the JPCF algorithm is:

$$\mathrm{ASE} = \mathrm{R}(\mathrm{K}). \tag{12}$$

In the above expression (12) it is assumed that the guard time duration is negligible, meaning that the feedback rate will not degrade the total system spectral efficiency. Practically, this is not valid. Therefore, the amount of bits transmitted as feedback has to be counted and at the end it will influence the performance of the system. To look into this issue, which is spectral efficiency degradation caused by the feedback traffic, we define a the system capacity as [bits/channel use]. Assuming N modulation levels, then we need log2 N bits to represent them. Therefore, the system capacity is:

$$\mathrm{C}_{sys} = \mathrm{R}(K) - \frac{\mathrm{AFL} \cdot \log_2 N}{S}, \tag{13}$$

where S is the number of symbols transmitted in the data transmission time slot.

In (13), the last term takes into account the amount of bits transmitted as feedback. Also, in the same expression the time delay is not taken into account, which is the guard time duration. The only consideration is the feedback rate, or the amount of bits transmitted as feedback. In the next section we investigate the effect of delay on the system performance.

4.3 Scheduling Delay

In this section we investigate the scheduling delay and its effect on the system performance. This time delay is part of the system resources and it is important to identify the amount of resources consumed when performing the JPCF algorithm.

4.3.1 Guard time

The scheduling process will take place during the gaud time (Tg), which is between bursts. The delay resulted from this scheduling process is measured as the time needed to schedule a user, which is simply the time duration of the minislots used (idle minislots are counted) until data transmission is allowed. By looking at Fig. 1, we can see that $Tf \leq Tg \leq (2K-1)Tf$. For simplicity, we assume that both p-minislot and c-minislot have the same time length (Tf).

Assuming a successful search at the lth p-minislot, then the guard time is:

$$Tg(l) = Tf(2l-1), \tag{14}$$

with probability:

$$P^{(p)}(l) = \left[\prod_{i=1}^{l-1}\left(1-\Gamma^{U}(i,\rho)\right)\right]\cdot\left[1-F_{\gamma}(\gamma_{th}^{(N)})\right]. \tag{15}$$

On the other hand, if the successful search occurs at the lth c-minislot, then the guard time is:

$$Tg(l) = 2lTf, \tag{16}$$

with probability:

$$P^{(c)}(l) = \left[\prod_{i=1}^{l-1}\left(1-\Gamma^{U}(i,\rho)\right)\right]\cdot\left[\Gamma^{U}(l,\rho)-\left(1-F_{\gamma}(\gamma_{th}^{(N)})\right)\right]. \tag{17}$$

Therefore, the average guard time is:

$$\begin{aligned}\overline{\tau} = &\sum_{l=1}^{K-1}\left[\tau_f(2l-1)P^{(p)}(l)+2l\tau_f P^{(c)}(l)\right]\\ &+\left((2K-1)\tau_f\right)\cdot\left[\prod_{i=1}^{K-1}\left(1-\Gamma^{U}(i,\rho)\right)\right].\end{aligned} \tag{18}$$

4.3.2 System throughput

The system throughput (STH) is the amount of data bits transmitted per time, where this time includes the data transmission time (Td) and the guard time (Tg). In (12), we looked at the amount of bits per data transmission time, where the effect of the scheduling delay was not included. To have a better insight, we derive the average system throughput (ASTH) by taking into account the effect of the guard time duration.

The average system throughput is:

$$\begin{aligned}\mathrm{ASTH} = \sum_{l=1}^{K-1}\left[\left(\frac{T_d - \tau_f(2l-1)}{T_d}\right)P^{(p)}(l) + \left(\frac{T_d - 2l\tau_f}{T_d}\right)P^{(c)}(l)\right]\cdot \mathrm{R}(K) \\ + \left(\frac{T_d - (2K-1)\tau_f}{T_d}\right)\cdot \mathrm{R}(K)\cdot\left[\prod_{i=1}^{K-1}\left(1-\Gamma^{\mathrm{U}}(i,\rho)\right)\right].\end{aligned} \tag{19}$$

4.4 Parameters Optimizations

The algorithm's objective is to strictly schedule the best user, therefore the search process will last until a user with q = q(N) is found, which depends on Γth(N) and ρ. In this section we investigate the optimization of ρ with the objective to minimize the feedback load:

$$\begin{aligned}\{\rho\} = &\arg\min_{\{\rho\}} \mathrm{AFL}(\gamma_{th}^{(N)},\rho,K), \\ &\text{subject to } 0 \le \rho \le 1.\end{aligned} \tag{20}$$

Similarly, the optimization solution is well defined by the equation:

$$\begin{cases}\dfrac{\partial \mathrm{AFL}(\rho,K)}{\partial \rho} = 0, \\ 0 \le \rho \le 1.\end{cases} \tag{21}$$

Note that the optimization may not be convex. The derivation of (10) is involved so we apply an exhaustive search method to find an optimal value. Table 3 shows the optimal values with different K given the parameters in Section 5. It is clearly seen from Table 3 that for a given K, ρ has two optimal values at the two average SNR regions. This is due to the collision. At low average SNR values, the value of ρ is increased to encourage good users to compete, whereas, at higher average SNR values the value of ρ is decreased to lower the possibility of collision.

5. NUMERICAL RESULTS

In this section we elaborate on the the performance of the JPCF algorithm by presenting some numerical examples. We compare its performance with both the DSMUDiv and the optimal selective diversity scheduling schemes. Parameters values are found in Tables 1 and 2. Fig. 3 shows the normalized average feedback load (i.e., the average feedback load divided by the number of users K) of the JPCF algorithm for different values of ρ, which is the probability of contention. As the value of the average SNR changes from low to high, the optimal value of ρ, at which the feedback is minimized, changes from ρ = 1 to ρ = 0.13, for a given value of K. Table 3 shows the optimal values of ρ for different values of K. The reason for the change of the optimal value is the threshold value. For a given threshold value, the percent of users with channel quality exceeding it increases as the average SNR increases, which leads to higher probability of collision. As more users contend the feedback load increases, which forces the value of ρ to change to maintain the minimization in (20). The point at which this change happens depend on the value of Γth (N) and the BEPo .

The comparison of the JPCF algorithm with both the DSMUDiv and the optimal selective diversity scheduling algorithms is presented in Fig. 4. In the figure, although the DSMUDiv algorithm has decreased the feedback load compared to the optimal algorithm, the JPCF al- gorithm has decreased the feedback load even more. This extra reduction comes from the introduction of the contention-based feedback (c-minislot), where not all users need to be polled as opposed to the DSMUDiv algorithm, which is a pure polling-based feedback algo- rithm. In terms of spectral efficiency, as shown in Section 4.2, both the JPCF algorithm and the DSMUDiv algorithm have the same spectral efficiency (here the feedback rate is not included). In (6), it has been proven that the DSMUDiv algorithm maintain the performance of the full feedback algorithm in terms of spectral efficiency, which means that the JPCF algorithm also maintain the same performance. The difference will come when you include the feedback rate (log2 N), which is defined as [bits/channel use]. From (13), we can see that as the feedback load increases the system capacity decreases, therefore, we deduce that the JPCF algorithm has the highest system capacity compared to the other two algorithms, which can be seen in Fig. 5 and 6. As a benchmark we include the average spectral efficiency (ASE) that does not include the feedback rate. The gap between the system capacity and the ASE shrinks with the increase of number of symbols transmitted in the data transmission time slot.

Although the number of minislots of the JPCF algorithm varies from 1 to 2K – 1, which is much greater than the DSMUDiv algorithm, where the minislots varies from 1 to K, the aver- age guard time of the JPCF algorithm is much smaller than the guard time of the DSMUDiv algorithm as depicted in Fig. 7. Such advantage occurs at medium to high average SNR. As the average SNR decreases this advantage diminishes as seen in Fig. 8. The reason is that the JPCF algorithm has contention minislots which creates an additional delay on top of the delay created by the polling minislots. This delay increase as the probability of finding a user with channel gain exceeding the threshold value decreases, which is the case for low average SNR values. Fig. 9 shows the effect of different data transmission time durations on the system throughput. Obviously, higher values give better performance.

6. CONCISE SUMMARY

This chapter presents a scheduling approach designed to optimize spectral efficiency while minimizing feedback load. The joint polling and contention-based feedback (JPCF) algorithm gathers channel quality information from users through either polling or contention methods. In comparison to the optimal (full feedback) approach, the JPCF algorithm exhibits comparable spectral efficiency and enhanced system capacity, factoring in the influence of the feedback rate. The JPCF algorithm demonstrates a greater reduction in feedback load than the DSMUDiv method. A disadvantage of the JPCF algorithm is the increased latency relative to the DSMUDiv method when the average SNR diminishes, hence impacting performance. As the average SNR rises, the latency associated with the JPCF method decreases below that of the DSMUDiv algorithm, hence enhancing system performance. This study presents an analysis of the JPCF algorithm under the premise of gradual Rayleigh fading. This chapter also presents closed-form formulas for the feedback load, system capacity, and scheduling delay.

Table 1. A List of Selected Modulation Levels (BEPo = 10-2)

Modulation Level	Switching Threshold (dB)
BPSK	$\gamma_{th}^{(1)} = 4.8$
4-QAM	$\gamma_{th}^{(2)} = 7.8$
16-QAM	$\gamma_{th}^{(3)} = 15$
64-QAM	$\gamma_{th}^{(4)} = 20$

Table 2. A List of Parameters

Parameter	Value
N	4 modulations
K	30 users
Tf	154 μsec (based on reference (24))
Td	5 msec (based on reference (24)) Table 2. A List of Parameters

Table 3. The Parameters Optimizations

K=5	K=30	K=50	K=100
$\rho = 0.2, \Gamma > 19$dB	$\rho = 0.13, \Gamma > 15$dB	$\rho = 0.12, \Gamma > 15$dB	$\rho = 0.1, \Gamma > 14$dB
$\rho = 1, \Gamma \leq 19$dB	$\rho = 1, \Gamma \leq 15$dB	$\rho = 1, \Gamma \leq 15$dB	$\rho = 1, \Gamma \leq 14$dB

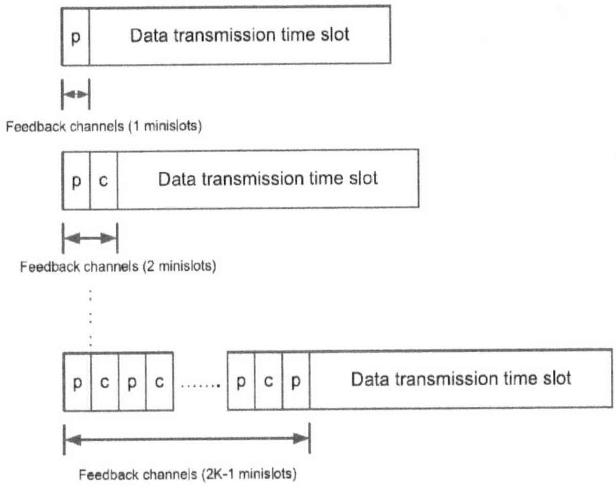

Fig. 1. The framing structure of a TDD system. Each polling-based feedback minislot (p-minislot) is followed by a contention-based feedback minislot (c-minislot), where they carry the feedback information.

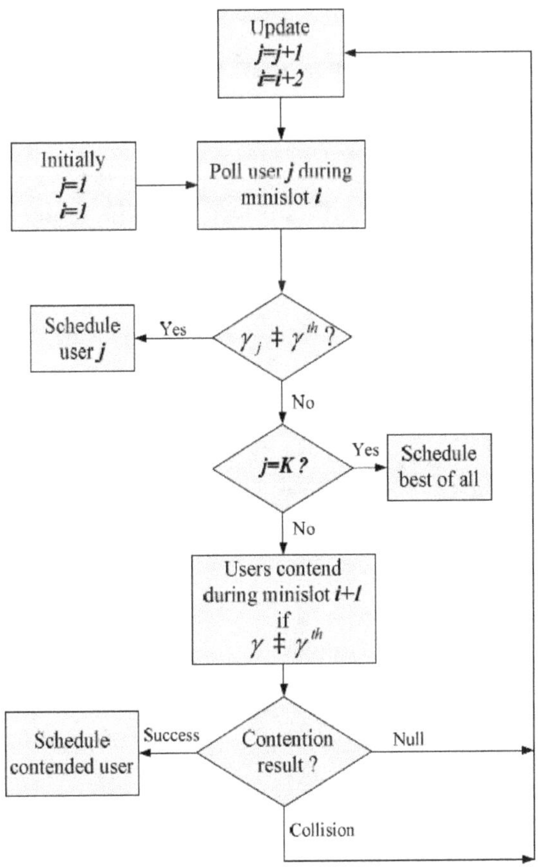

Fig. 2. A flowchart of the JPCF algorithm.

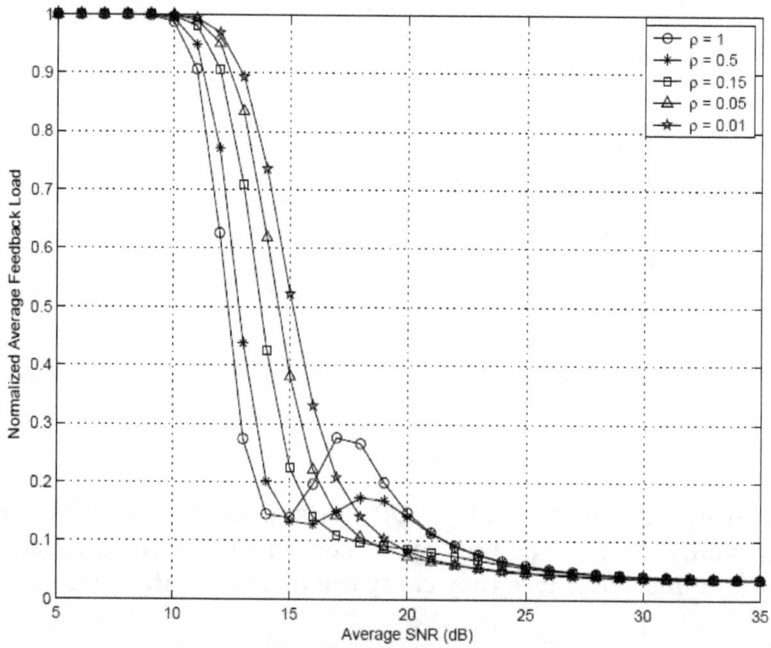

Fig. 3. Normalized average feedback load of the JPCF scheduling algorithm with different values of ρ.

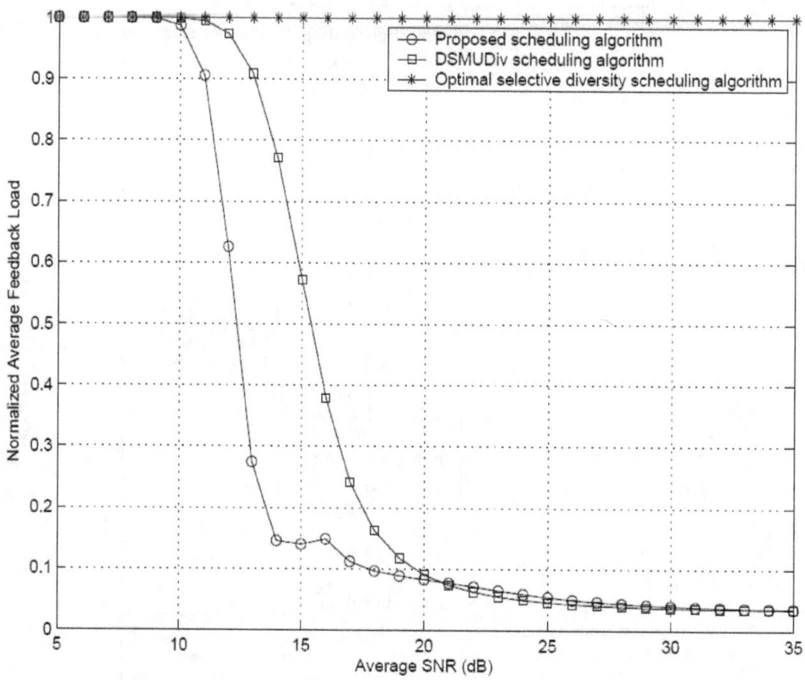

Fig. 4. Comparison of the normalized average feedback load of: (i) the proposed (JPCF) scheduling algo- rithm, (ii) the DSMUDiv scheduling algorithm, and (iii) the optimal (full feedback) scheduling algorithm.

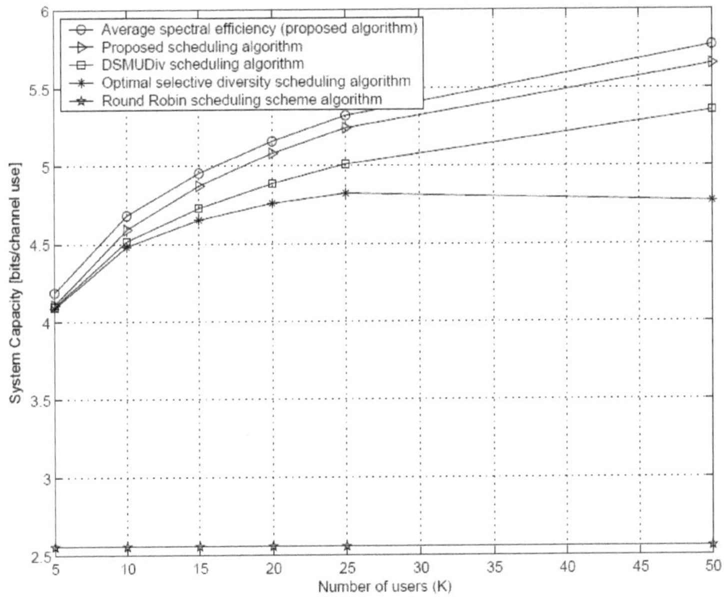

Fig. 5. System capacity of: (i) the proposed (JPCF) scheduling algorithm, (ii) the DSMUDiv scheduling algorithm, and (iii) the optimal (full feedback) scheduling algorithm. Setting ρ = 1, 100 symbols are transmitted, and Γ = 15dB.

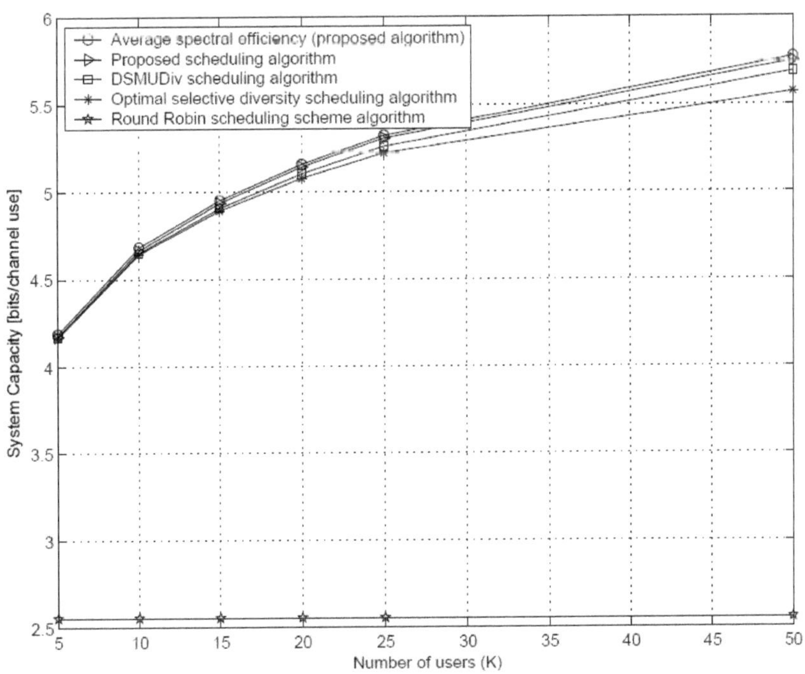

Fig. 6. System capacity of: (i) the proposed (JPCF) scheduling algorithm, (ii) the DSMUDiv scheduling algorithm, and (iii) the optimal (full feedback) scheduling algorithm. Setting ρ = 1, 500 symbols are transmitted, and Γ = 15dB.

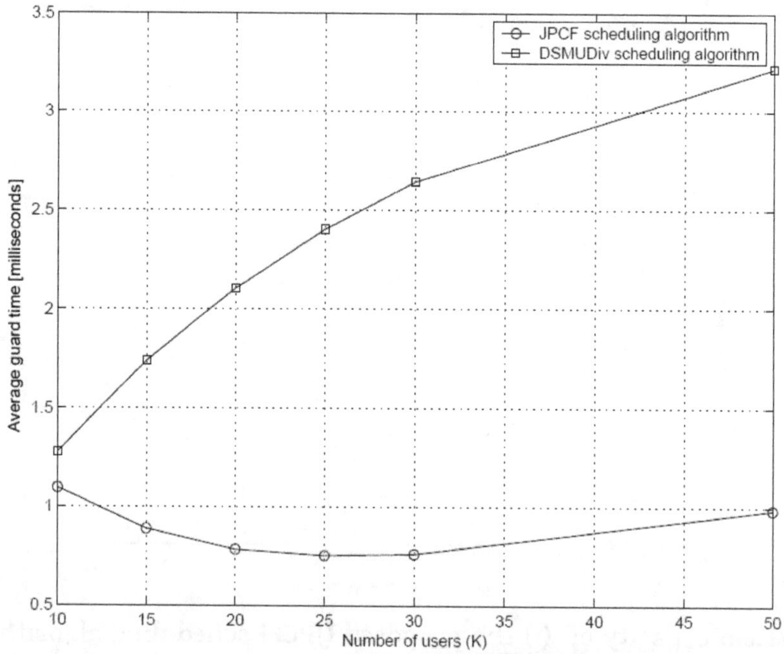

Fig. 7. Average guard time of: (i) the JPCF scheduling algorithm, and (ii) the DSMUDiv scheduling algorithm. Setting Γ = 15dB.

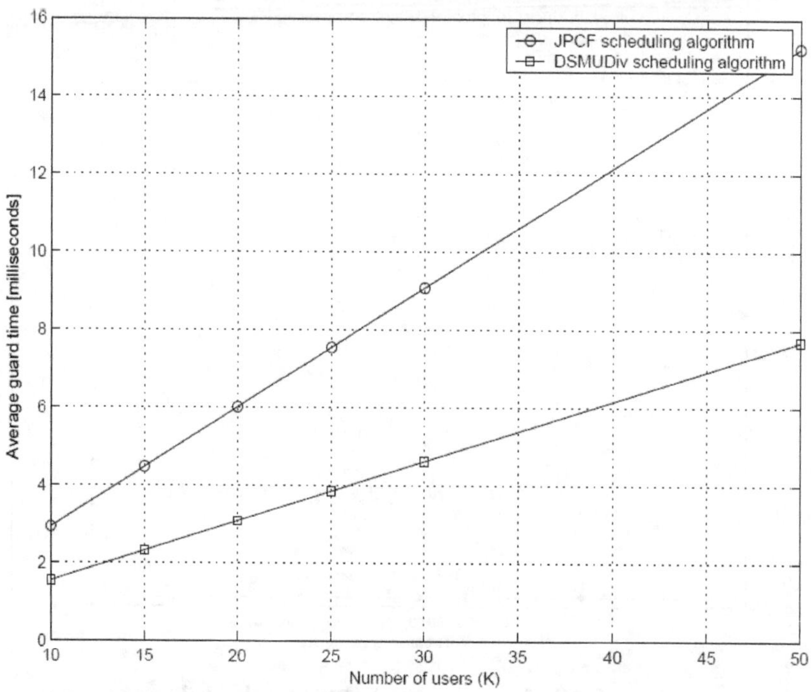

Fig. 8. Average guard time of: (i) the JPCF scheduling algorithm, and (ii) the DSMUDiv scheduling algorithm. Setting Γ = 5dB.

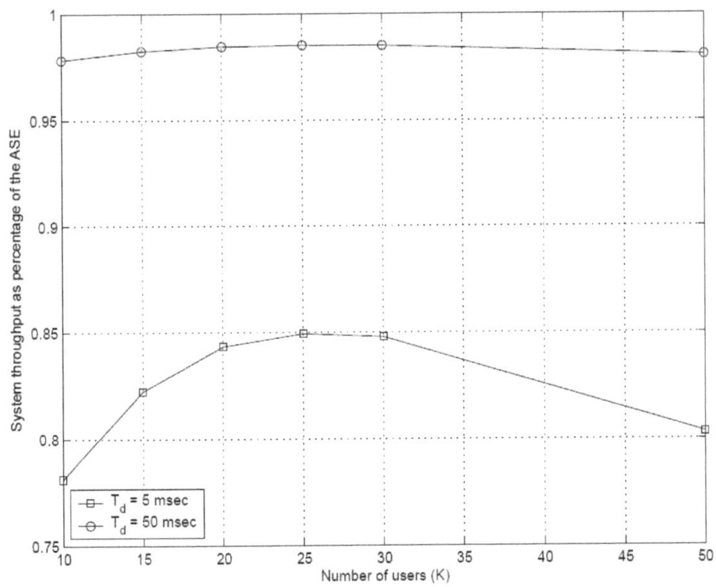

Fig. 9. System throughput as percentage of the average spectral efficiency of the JPCF scheduling algo- rithm. Setting Γ = 15dB, and 1 symbol is transmitted.

REFERENCES

1. P. Viswanath, D. N. C. Tse, and R. Laroia, "Opportunistic beamforming using dumb antenna," IEEE Transactions on Information Theory, vol. 48, no. 6, pp. 1277–1294, June 2002.
2. R. Knopp and P. Humblet, "Information capacity and power control in single-cell mul- tiuser communications," in Proc. IEEE International Communication Conference (ICC'95), Paris, France, June 1995, pp. 331–335.
3. D. N. C. Tse, "Optimal power allocation over parallel Gaussian broadcast channels," in Proc. IEEE International Symposium Information Theory (ISIT'97), Ulm, Germany, June 1997, p. 27.
4. P. Bender, P. Black, M. Grob, R. Padovani, N. Sindhushyana, and S. Viterbi, "CDMA/HDR: A bandwidth efficient high speed wireless data service for nomadic users," IEEE Communication Magazine, vol. 38, no. 7, pp. 70–77, July 2000.
5. F. Floren, O. Edfors, and B. A Molin, "The effect of feedback quantization on the through- put of a multiuser diversity scheme," in Proc. IEEE Global Telecommunication Conference (GLOBECOM'03), San Francisco, California, December 2003, pp. 497–501.
6. Y. S. Al-Harthi, A. Tewfik, and M. S. Alouini, "Multiuser diversity with quantized feed- back," IEEE Transactions on Wireless Communication, vol. 6, no. 1, pp. 330–337, January 2007.

7. Y. Al-Harthi, A. Tewfik, and M. S. Alouini, "Multiuser diversity-enhanced equal access with quantized feedback in multicarrier OFDM systems," in Proc. IEEE Vehicular Technol- ogy Conference (VTC-Fall'05), Dallas, TX, September 2005, pp. 568–572.

8. M. A. Regaeig, N. Hamdi, and M. S. Alouini, "Switched-based reduced feedback OFDM multi-user opportunistic scheduling," in Proc. IEEE International Symposium on Personal and Indoor and Mobile Radio Communication (PIMRC '05), Berlin, Germany, September 2005, pp. 2495–2499.

9. D. Gesbert and M. S. Alouini, "How much feedback is multi-user diversity really worth?," in Proc. IEEE International Communication Conference (ICC'04), Paris, France, June 2004, pp. 234–238.

10. V. Hassel, M. S. Alouini, G. E. Øien, and D. Gesbert, "Rate-optimal multiuser scheduling with reduced feedback load and analysis of delay effects," EURASIP Journal on Wireless Communications and Networking, vol. 2006, no. 36424, pp. 7, 2006.

11. V. Hassel, M.-S Alouini, D. Gesbert, and G. E. Øien, "Exploiting multiuser diversity using multiple feedback thresholds," in Proc. IEEE Vehicular Technology Conference (VTC- Spring'05), Stockholm, Sweden, 30 May-1 June 2005, pp. 1302–1306.

12. B. Holter, M. S. Alouini, G. E. Øien, and H-C. Yang, "Multiuser switched diversity trans- mission," in Proc. IEEE Vehicular Technology Conference (VTC-Fall'04), Los Angeles, CA, September 2004, pp. 2038–2043.

13. Y. Xue and T. Kaiser, "Exploiting multiuser diversity with imperfect one-bit channel state feedback," IEEE Transactions on Vehicular Technology, vol. 56, no. 1, pp. 183–193, January 2007.

14. S. Sanayei and A. Nosratinia, "Exploiting multiuser diversity with only 1-bit feedback," in Proc. IEEE Wireless Communications and Networking Conference (WCNC'05), New Or- leans, LA, March 2005, pp. 978–983.

15. P. Svedman, S. K. Wilson, Jr. L. J. Cimini, and B. Ottersten, "A simplified opportunistic feedback and scheduling scheme for OFDM," in Proc. IEEE Vehicular Technology Confer- ence (VTC-Spring'04), Milan, Italy, May 2004, pp. 1878–1882.

16. Z. H. Han and Y. H. Lee, "Opportunistic scheduling with partial channel information in OFDMA/FDD systems," in Proc. IEEE Vehicular Technology Conference (VTC-Fall'04), Los Angeles, CA, September 2004, pp. 511–514.

17. K. Bai and Junshan Zhang, "Opportunistic multichannel Aloha: distributed multiaccess control scheme for OFDMA wireless networks," IEEE Transactions on Vehicular Technol- ogy, vol. 55, no. 3, pp. 848–855, May 2006.

18. T. Tang and R. W. Heath, "Opportunistic feedback for downlink multiuser diversity," IEEE Communications Letters, vol. 9, no. 10, pp. 948–950, October 2005.

19. X. Qin and R. Berry, "Opportunistic splitting algorithms for wireless networks.," in Proc. IEEE Conference on Computer Communications (INFOCOM'04), Hong Kong, China, March 2004, pp. 1662–1672.

20. H. Koubaa, V. Hassel, and G. E. Øien, "Contention-less feedback for multiuser diver- sity scheduling," in Proc. IEEE Vehicular Technology Conference (VTC-Fall'05), Dallas, TX, September 2005, vol. 3, pp. 1574–1578.

21. S. Patil and G. de Veciana, "Reducing feedback for opportunistic scheduling in wireless systems," IEEE Transactions on Wireless Communications, vol. 6, no. 12, pp. 4227–4232, December 2007.

22. M. S. Alouini and A. J. Goldsmith, "Adaptive modulation over Nakagami fading chan- nels," Kluwer Journal on Wireless Communications, vol. 13, pp. 119–143, May 2000.

23. D. Bertsekas and R. Gallager, Data Networks, Prentice Hall, 1992.

24. IEEE Standards Department, "IEEE Std 802.11. part 11: Wireless LAN medium access control (MAC) and physical layer (PHY) specifications," Technical Report, IEEE, NJ, September 1999.

14 Chapter

OPPORTUNISTIC ACCESS STRATEGIES FOR MULTIUSER OFDM WIRELESS NETWORKS

1. INTRODUCTION: AN OVERVIEW

Bandwidth distribution in next-generation broadband wireless networks (4G systems) presents a significant challenge. The schedule will ensure mobile multimedia transmission services with sufficient quality of service (QoS). The new multimedia services with stringent QoS limits necessitate enhanced system capacity alongside elevated fairness. Recent decades have seen rigorous research endeavors in wireless communications. Unlike wired communications, wireless transmissions encounter numerous channel obstacles, including path loss, shadowing, and multipath fading. These phenomena significantly impair transmission capacities, thus impacting the Quality of Service (QoS) experienced by applications, particularly regarding data integrity and the additional delays or packet losses that occur when the effective bit rate at the physical layer is diminished.

Among all conceivable transmission systems for broadband communication, Orthogonal Frequency Division Multiplexing (OFDM) has emerged as the most viable physical layer method due to its ability to effectively mitigate the detrimental impacts of multipath fading. This approach is extensively utilized in contemporary wireless systems like as 802.11a/g and 802.16. The fundamental premise of OFDM in combating the effects of multipath propagation is to partition the available channel bandwidth into sub-frequency bands with widths less than the coherence bandwidth of the channel (the inverse of the delay spread). The transmission of a high-speed signal across a broadband frequency-selective channel is replaced by the transmission of many subcarriers carrying low-speed signals that exhibit significant resistance to intersymbol interference and are susceptible to flat fading. The partitioning of total bandwidth into numerous channels offers frequency diversity, which, when combined with time and multiuser diversity, can yield a very spectrally efficient system, contingent upon effective scheduling.

2. RESOURCE ALLOCATION IN A MULTIUSER OFDM WIRELESS ACCESS NETWORK

In this chapter, we focus on the proper allocation of radio resources among the set of mobiles situated in the coverage zone of a wireless access point in a centralized approach (Fig. 1). The packets originating from the backhaul network are buffered in the access point which schedules the downlink transmissions. In the uplink, the mobiles signal their traffic backlog to the access point which builds the uplink resource mapping.

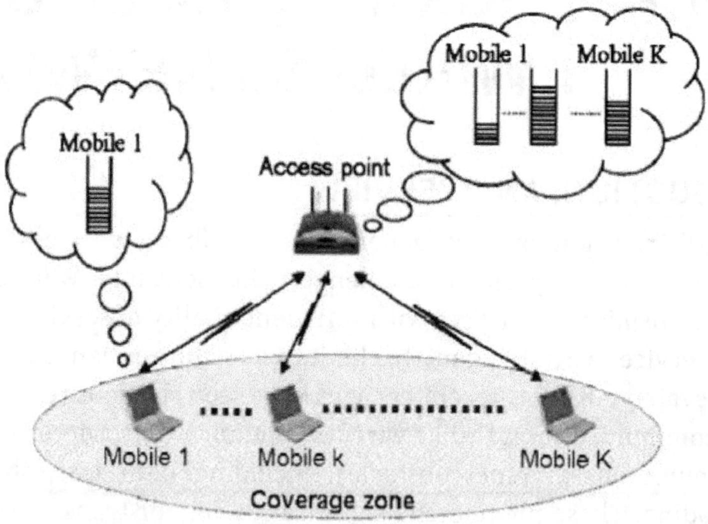

Fig. 1. Allocation of radio resources among the set of mobiles situated in the coverage zone of an access point.

The physical layer is operated using the frame structure described in Fig. 2. This structure is typical of OFDM wireless access networks like the OFDM mode of the IEEE 802.16-2004 (Hoymann, 2005). The total available bandwidth is divided in sub-frequency bands or subcarriers. The radio resource is further divided in the time domain in frames. Each frame is itself divided in time slots of constant duration. The time slot duration is an integer multiple of the OFDM symbol duration. The number of subcarriers is chosen so that the width of each sub-frequency band is inferior to the coherence bandwidth of the channel. Moreover, the frame duration is fixed to a value much smaller than the coherence time (inverse of the Doppler spread) of the channel. With these assumptions, the transmission on each subcarrier is subject to flat fading with a channel state that can be considered static during each frame.

The elementary resource unit (RU) is defined as any (subcarrier, time slot) pair. Each of these RUs may be allocated to any mobile with a specific modulation order. Transmissions performed on different RUs by different mobiles have independent channel state variations (Andrews et al., 2001). On each RU, the modulation scheme is QAM with a modulation order adapted to the channel state between the access point and the mobile to which it is allocated. This provides the flexible resource allocation framework required for opportunistic scheduling.

The system is operated using time division duplexing with four subframes: the downlink feedback subframe, the downlink data subframe, the uplink contention subframe and the uplink data subframe. The uplink and downlink data subframes are used for transmission of user data. In the downlink feedback subframe, the access point sends control information towards its mobiles. This control information is used for signalling to each mobile which RU(s) it has been allocated in the next uplink and downlink data subframes, the modulation order selected for each of these RUs and the recommended emission power in the uplink. In the uplink contention subframe, the active mobiles send their current traffic backlog and information elements such as QoS measures and transmit power. The uplink contention subframe is also used by the mobiles for establishing their connections. This frame structure supposes a perfect time and frequency synchronization between the mobiles and the access point as described in (Van de Beek et al., 1999). Therefore, each frame starts with a long preamble used for synchronisation purposes. Additional preambles may also be used in the frame.

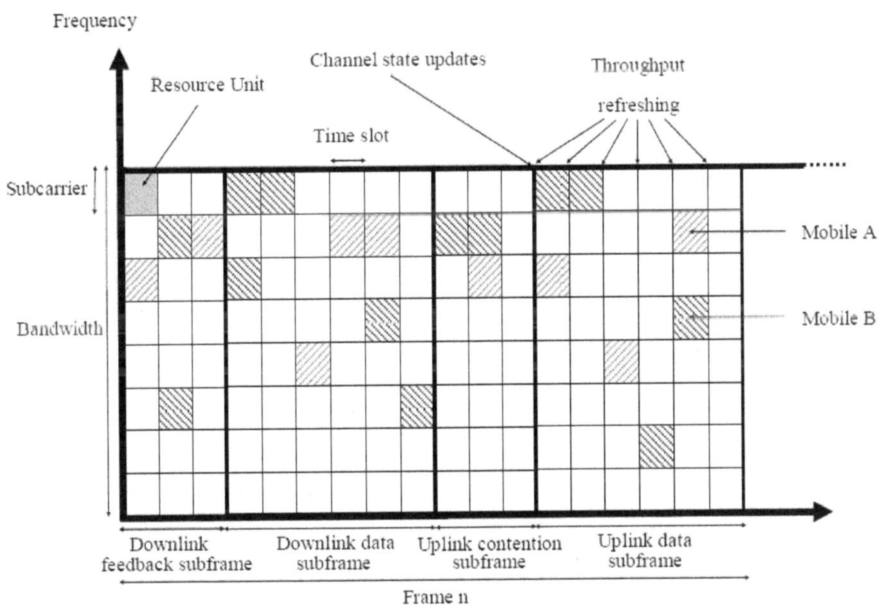

Fig. 2. Frame structure in TDD mode.

3. SCHEDULING TECHNIQUES IN OFDM WIRELESS NETWORKS

The MAC protocols currently used in wireless local area networks were originally and primarily designed in the wired local area network context. These conventional access methods like Round Robin (RR) and Random Access (RA) are not well adapted to the wireless environment and provide poor throughput. More recently intensive research efforts have been given in order to propose efficient schedulers for OFDM based networks and especially opportunistic schedulers which preferably allocate the resources to the active mobile(s) with the most favourable channel conditions at a given time. These schedulers take benefit of multiuser and frequency diversity in order to maximize the system throughput. All these schemes strongly rely on diversity for offering their good performances. Three major scheduling techniques have emerged: Maximum Signal-to-Noise Ratio (MaxSNR), Proportional Fair (PF) and recently, the Weighted Fair Opportunistic (WFO).

Note that for these schedulers, knowledge of the channel state is supposed to be available at the receiver (Li et al., 1999). The current channel attenuation on each subcarrier and for each mobile is estimated by the access node based on the SNR of the signal sent by each mobile during the uplink contention subframe. Assuming that the channel state is stable on a scale of 50 ms (Truman & Brodersen, 1997), and using a frame duration of 2 ms, the mobiles shall transmit their control information alternatively on each subcarrier so that the access node may refresh the channel state information once every 25 frames.

3.1 Maximum Signal-to-Noise Ratio

Many schemes are derived from the Maximum Signal-to-Noise Ratio (MaxSNR) technique (also known as Maximum Carrier to Interference ratio (MaxC/I)). In MaxSNR, priority is given at every scheduling event to the mobiles which have the greatest signal-to-noise ratio (SNR). It allocates the resource at a given time to the active mobile with the greatest SNR (Knopp & Humblet, 1995; Wong et al., 1999; Wang & Xiang, 2006). Denoting mk,n the maximum number of bits that can be transmitted on a time slot of Resource Unit n if this RU is allocated to the mobile k, MaxSNR scheduling consists in allocating the RU n to the mobile j which has the greatest mk,n such as:

$$j = \text{argmax}k\ (mk\ ,n\ ),\ k = 1,\ldots,\ K\ , \qquad (1)$$

Taking profit of multiuser and frequency diversity, MaxSNR scheduling continuously allocates the radio resource to the mobile with the best spectral efficiency. Consequently MaxSNR strongly increases the system throughput. Dynamically adapting the modulation and coding allows one to always make the most efficient use of the radio resource and come closer to the Shannon limit. However MaxSNR assumes that the user with the most favourable transmission conditions has information to transmit at the considered time instant. It does not take into account the variability of the traffic and the queuing aspects. Additionally, a negative side effect of this strategy is that the closest mobiles to the access point have disproportionate priorities over mobiles more distant since their path loss attenuation is much smaller. This results in a severe lack of fairness.

3.2 Proportional Fair

Proportional Fair (PF) algorithms have recently been proposed to incorporate a certain level of fairness while keeping the benefits of multiuser diversity (Viswanath et al., 2002; Kim et al., 2002; Anchun et al., 2003; Svedman et al., 2004; Kim et al., 2004). In PF based schemes, the basic principle is to allocate the bandwidth resources to a mobile j when its channel conditions are the most favourable with respect to its time average such as:

$$j = \arg\max_k \left(\frac{m_{k,n}}{M_{k,n}} \right), k = 1, \ldots, K, \tag{2}$$

where Mk,n is the time average of the mk,n values.

At a short time scale, path loss variations are negligible and channel state variations are mainly due to multipath fading, statistically similar for all mobiles. Thus, PF provides an equal sharing of the total available bandwidth among the mobiles as RR. Applying the opportunistic scheduling technique, system throughput maximization is also obtained as with MaxSNR. PF actually combines the advantages of the classical schemes and currently appears as the best bandwidth management scheme.

In PF-based schemes, fairness consists in guaranteeing an equal share of the total available bandwidth to each mobile, whatever its position or channel conditions. However, since the farther mobiles have a lower spectral efficiency than the closer ones due to pathloss, all mobiles do not all benefit of an equal average throughput despite they all obtain an equal share of bandwidth. This induces heterogeneous delays and unequal QoS. (Choi & Bahk, 2007; Gueguen & Baey (a), 2008; Holtzman, 2001) demonstrate that fairness issues persist in PF-based protocols when mobiles have unequal spatial positioning, different traffic types or different QoS targets. PF scheduling do not take into account the delay constraints and is not well adapted to multimedia services which introduce heterogeneous users, new traffic patterns with highly variable bit rates and stringent QoS requirements in terms of delay and packet loss.

3.3 Weighted Fair Opportunistic

More recently a new MAC scheduler, called “Weighted Fair Opportunistic (WFO)”, has been proposed for efficient support of multimedia services in multiuser OFDM wireless networks (Gueguen & Baey (b), 2008). Built in a higher layers/MAC/PHY cross-layer approach, this scheme is designed for best profiting of the multiuser diversity taking advantage of the dynamics of the multiplexed traffics. It takes into account both the transmission conditions and the higher layer constraints (traffic patterns, QoS constraints). In order to provide an efficient support of multimedia services, WFO dynamically favours the mobiles that go through a critical period with respect to their QoS requirements using dynamic priorities.

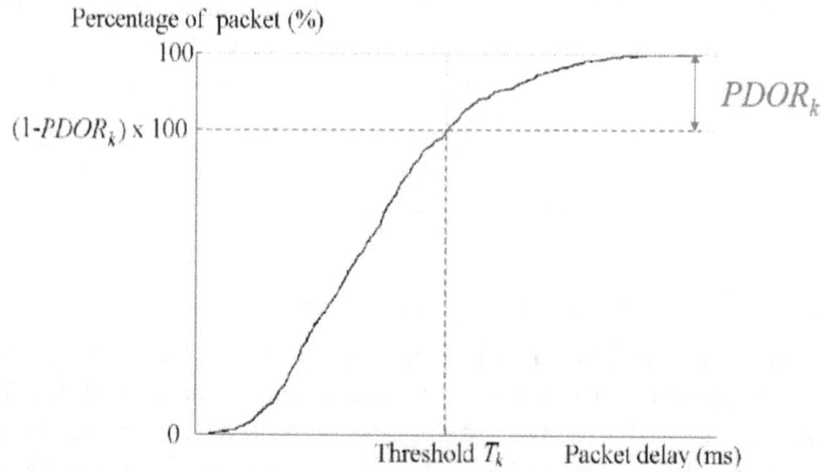

Fig. 3. Example packet delay CDF and experienced PDOR.

Evaluating if a mobile goes through a critical period should not only focus on the classical mean delay and jitter analysis. Indeed, a meaningful constraint regarding delay is the limitation of the occurrences of large values. Accordingly, (Gueguen & Baey (c), 2008) defines the concept of delay outage by analogy with the concept of outage used in system coverage planning. A mobile k is in delay outage (in critical period) when its packets experience a delay greater than a given threshold Tk defined by the mobile application requirements. The delay experienced by each mobile is tracked all along the lifetime of its connection. At each transmission of a packet of mobile k, the ratio of the total number of packets whose delay exceeded the threshold divided by the total number of packets transmitted since the beginning of the connection is computed. The result is called Packet Delay Outage Ratio (PDOR) of mobile k and is denoted PDORk. This measure is representative of the emergency for the mobile k to be served. Fig. 3 illustrates an example cumulative distribution of the packet delay of a mobile at a given time instant. A mobile can be considered as satisfied when, at the end of its connection, its delay constraint is met, i.e. its experienced PDOR is less than the application specific PDOR target.

In WFO scheduling, the required QoS, the experienced QoS and the transmission conditions are jointly considered in an extended cross-layer approach. The scheduling principle is to allocate a Resource Unit n to the mobile j which has the greatest WFO parameter value WFOk,n such as:

$$j = \arg\max_k (WFO_{k,n}), \; k = 1,\dots, K, \tag{3}$$

where WFOk,n is defined by:

$$WFO_{k,n} = m_{k,n} \times f(PDOR_k), \tag{4}$$

with f a strictly increasing polynomial function (Gueguen & Baey (d), 2008; Gueguen & Baey, 2009):

$$f(x) = 1 + \beta \times x\alpha, \quad (5)$$

The exponent parameter α allows being sensitive and reactive to PDOR fluctuations which guarantees fairness at a short time scale. β is a normalization parameter that ensures that f(PDORk) and mk,n are in the same order of magnitude.

With this scheduling, physical layer information (represented through the factor mk,n) are used in order to take advantage of the time, frequency and multiuser diversity and maximize the system capacity. Higher layer information (represented through the factor f(PDORk) are exploited in order to introduce dynamic priorities between flows for ensuring the same QoS level to all mobiles. With this original weighted system that introduces dynamic priorities between the flows, WFO keeps a maximum number of flows active across time but with relatively low traffic backlogs. This results in a well-balanced resource allocation. Preserving the multiuser diversity allows to continuously take a maximal benefit of opportunistic scheduling and thus maximize the bandwidth usage efficiency. When the frequency diversity is sufficient, WFO better conceals the system capacity maximization, QoS support and fairness objectives than PF and MaxSNR schemes.

4. PERFORMANCE EVALUATION

In this section we compare the most acknowledged schedulers, the Round Robin (RR), the MaxSNR and the PF schemes with the most promising, the Weighted Fair Opportunistic (WFO) scheduling. Each is implemented with subcarrier by subcarrier allocation. Performance evaluation results are obtained using OPNET discrete event simulations. We focus on the main scheduling problem: maximize the system capacity while ensuring high fairness between mobiles localised at heterogeneous spatial positions in the cell.

In the simulations we assume 128 subcarriers and 5 time slots in a frame. The channel gain model on each subcarrier considers free space path loss and multipath Rayleigh fading (Parsons, 1992). We introduce a reference distance dref for which the free space attenuation equals aref. As a result the channel gain is given by:

$$a_{k,n} = a_{ref} \times \left(\frac{d_{ref}}{d_k} \right)^{3.5} \times \alpha_{k,n}^2, \quad (6)$$

where dk is the distance to the access point of the mobile k and α2k,n represents the flat fading experienced by this mobile k if it transmits or receives on subcarrier n. In the following, α2k,n is Rayleigh distributed with an expectancy equal to unity.

The maximum transmit power satisfies:

$$10\log_{10}\left(\frac{P_{\max} \times T_s}{N_0} \times a_{ref} \right) = 31\, dB,$$

where Ts is the time duration of an OFDM symbol, Pmax is the maximum achievable transmit power and N0 is the single-sided power spectral density of noise. The BER target is taken equal to 10-3. With this setting, the value of mk,n for the mobiles situated at the reference distance is 6 bits when α2k,n equals unity.

We assume all mobiles run the same videoconference application. This demanding type of application generates a high volume of data with high sporadicity and requires tight delay constraints, which substantially complicate the task of the scheduler. Each mobile has only one service flow with traffic composed of an MPEG-4 video stream (Baey, 2004) and an AMR voice stream (Brady, 1969).

In these extended simulations, we analyzed the behaviour of the schedulers when mobiles occupy different geographical positions. The objective is to clearly exhibit the ability of the opportunistic schedulers to provide fairness whatever the respective position of the mobiles. We first study a general context that includes mobility. We constitute two groups of 7 mobiles that both move straight across the cell, following the pattern described in Fig. 4 and Fig. 5. Each mobile has a speed of 3 km/h and the cell radius is taken equal to 5 km (3 dref). When a group of mobiles comes closer to the access point, the other group simultaneously goes farther away. Additionally, the threshold time Tk is fixed to the value 80 ms in order to consider real time constraints and the PDOR target is 5 %.

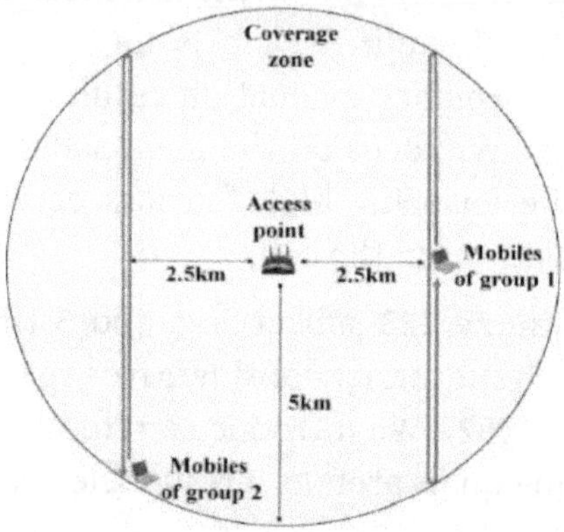

Fig. 4. Mobility pattern.

Considering the path loss, the Rayleigh fading and this mobility model, we have computed in Fig. 5 the evolution of the mean number of bits that may be transmitted per Resource Unit for each group of mobiles, averaging over all the Resource Units of a frame. This shows the impact of the mobile position on the mean mk,n values.

Regarding fairness, in wireless networks, it is well known that the closest mobiles to the access point generally obtain better QoS than mobiles more distant thanks to their higher spectral efficiency. Fig. 6 reports the mean PDOR experienced by each group of mobiles across the time. MaxSNR is highly unfair. Indeed, as soon as the mobiles move away from the access point, they experience high delays with a high number of packets in delay outage. PF offers better results. It brings more fairness and globally attenuates the delay peaks of the critical periods. However, we observe that WFO is the one that best smoothes these peaks. It adequately and continuously allocates the adequate priorities between the mobiles reacting to their relative movement across the cell. Providing a totally fair allocation of the bandwidth resources, the WFO scheduling smoothes the delay experienced by each mobile across time. Consequently, it further enhances the PF performances and the PDOR values are further decreased. WFO results in a very fair resource allocation that fully satisfies the delay constraints whatever the movement of the mobile.

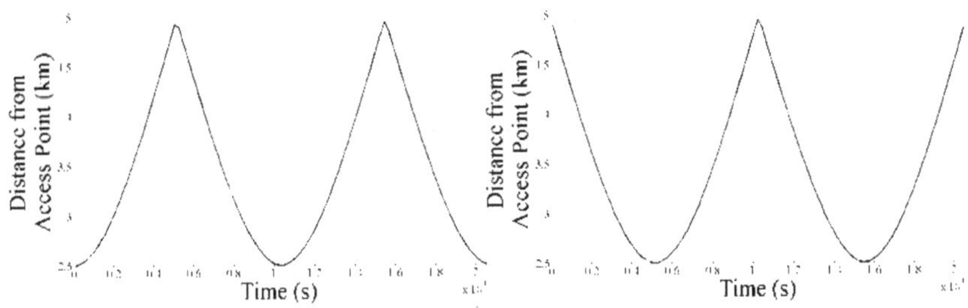

Fig. 5. Position of the mobiles across time (for mobiles of group 1 on the left and for mobiles of group 2 on the right).

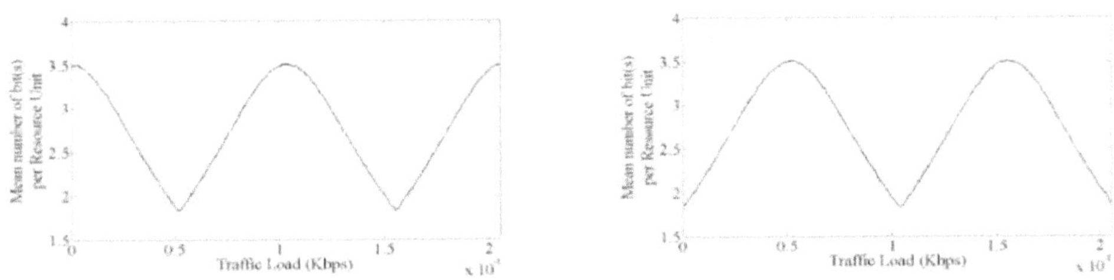

Fig. 6. Mean number of bit(s) per Resource Unit for each group of mobiles (for mobiles of group 1 on the left and for mobiles of group 2 on the right).

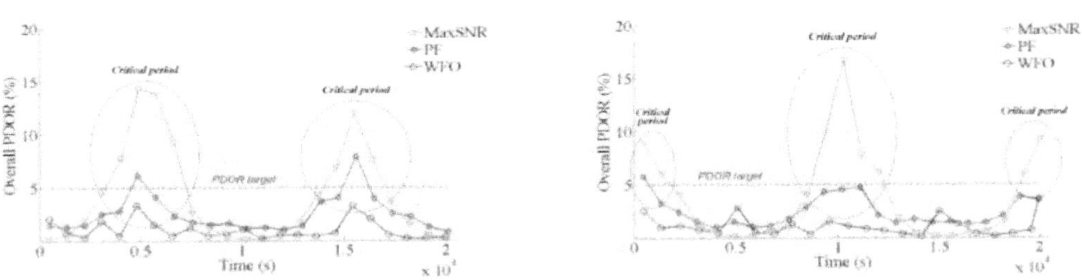

Fig. 7. PDOR fluctuation experienced by each group of mobiles (for mobiles of group 1 on the left and for mobiles of group 2 on the right).

In order to further underline the advantage of opportunistic schedulers compared to the classical Round Robin, we now study precisely the performance of the algorithms in a sub- scenario where all mobiles are static. A first half of mobiles are situated close to the access point and a second half 1.5 farther. The other parameters are identical for all the mobiles as described in Table 1. The total number of mobiles sets the traffic load.

Table 1. Scenario setup with static mobiles.

Group	Distance dk	Delay threshold Tk	Data rate
1	2 dref	80 ms	80 Kbps
2	3 dref	80 ms	80 Kbps

First we focus on the fairness provided by each scheduler. Fig. 7a, 7b, 7c and 7d display the overall PDOR for different traffic loads considering the influence of the distance on the scheduling.

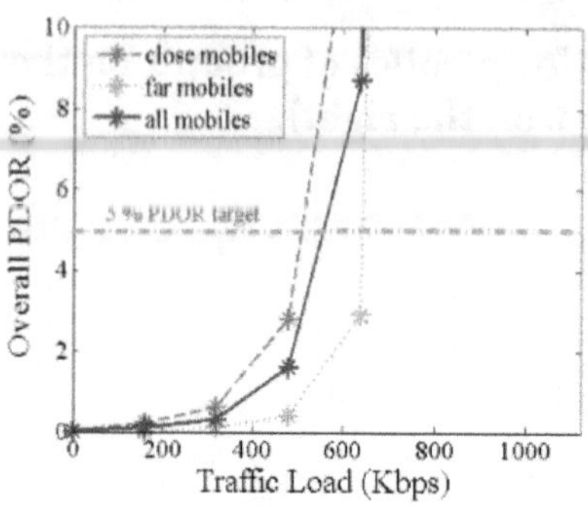

Fig. 8 a. With RR.

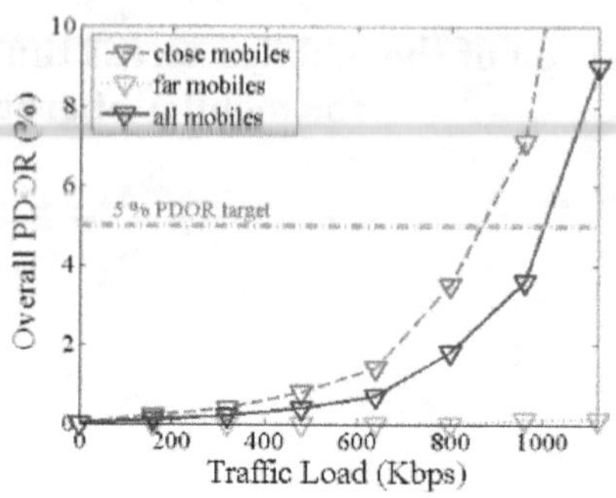

Fig. 8 b. With MaxSNR.

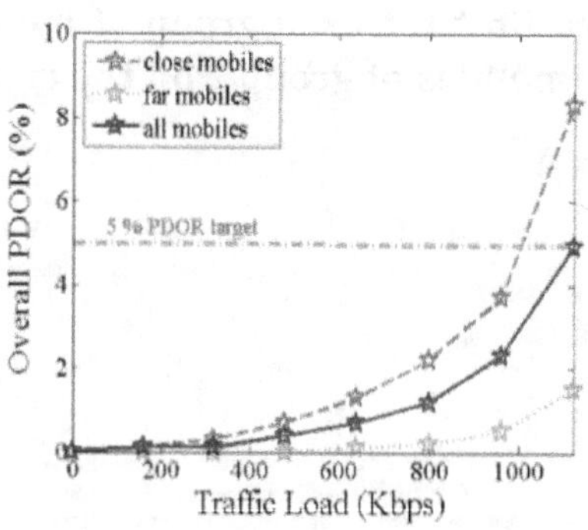

Fig. 8 c. With PF.

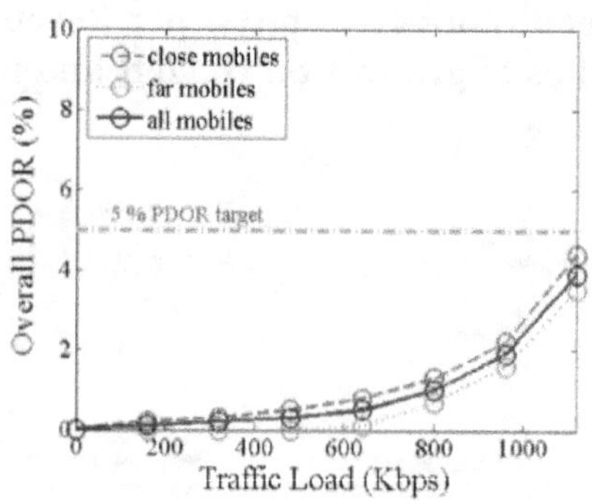

Fig. 8 d. With WFO.

Fig. 8. Measured QoS with respect to distance.

The classical RR fails to ensure the same PDOR to all mobiles. Actually, the RR fairly allocates the RUs to the mobiles without taking in consideration that far mobiles have a much lower spectral efficiency than closer ones. Moreover, the RR does not take benefit of multiuser diversity which results in a bad utilization of the bandwidth and in turn, poor system throughput. Consequently, an acceptable PDOR target of 5 % is exceeded even with relatively low traffic loads. Based on opportunistic scheduling, the three other schemes globally show better QoS performances supporting a higher traffic load. However, MaxSNR and PF still show severe fairness deficiencies. Close mobiles easily respect their delay requirement while far mobiles experience much higher delays and go past the 5 % PDOR target when the traffic load increases. In contrast, WFO provides the same QoS level to all mobiles whatever their respective position. WFO is the only one to guarantee a totally fair allocation. This allows reaching higher traffic loads with an acceptable PDOR for all mobiles. Additionally, looking at the overall PDOR for all mobiles at different traffic loads shows that, besides fairness, WFO provides a better overall QoS level as well.

Fig. 9 a. Mean buffer occupancy for close mobiles (solid lines) and far mobiles (dashed lines).

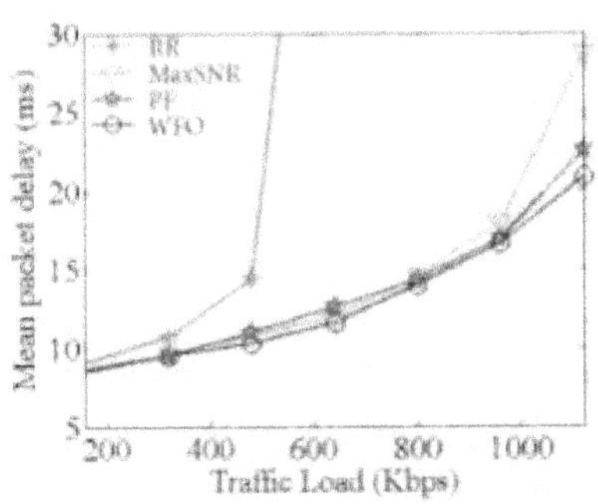

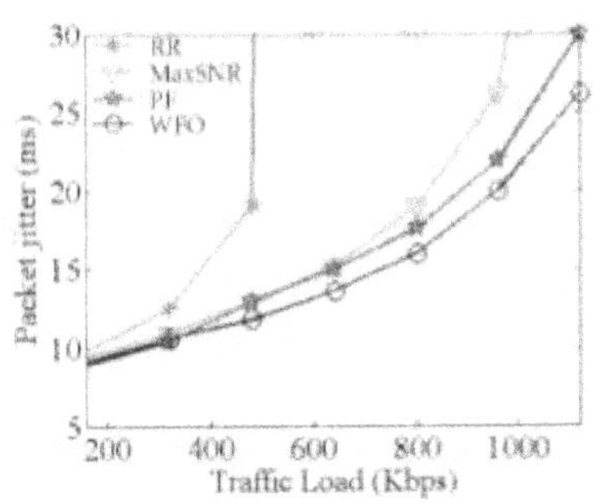

Fig. 9 b. Mean packet delay. Fig. 9 c. Packet jitter.

Fig. 9. Buffer occupancy, delay and jitter.

Observing the mean buffer occupancy in Fig. 8a, WFO clearly limits the buffer occupancy to a same and reasonable value whatever the position of the mobile. This allows staying under the PDOR target for any traffic load. With its system of weights, WFO dynamically adjusts the relative priority of the flows according to their experienced delay. With this approach, sparingly delaying the closer mobiles, WFO builds on the breathing space offered by the easy respect of the delay constraints of the closer mobiles (with better spectral efficiency) for helping the farther ones. The WFO interesting performance results are corroborated in Fig. 8b and 8c where the overall values of the mean packet delay and jitter obtained using WFO are smaller.

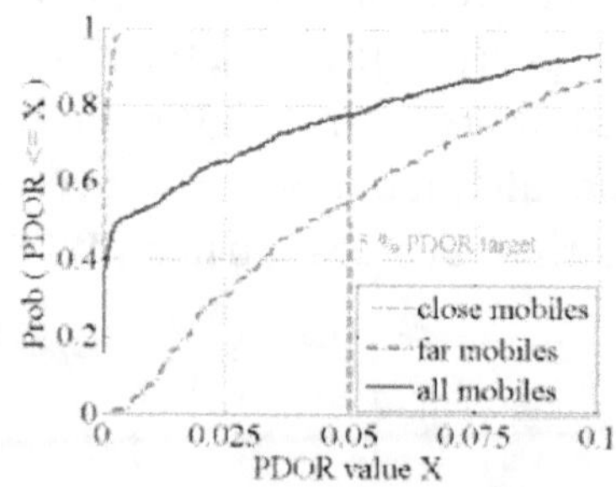

Fig. 10 a. CDF of end cycle PDOR with MaxSNR.

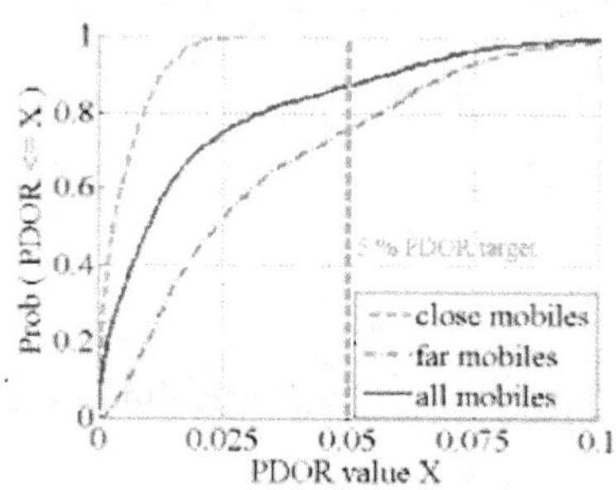

Fig. 10 b. CDF of end cycle PDOR with PF

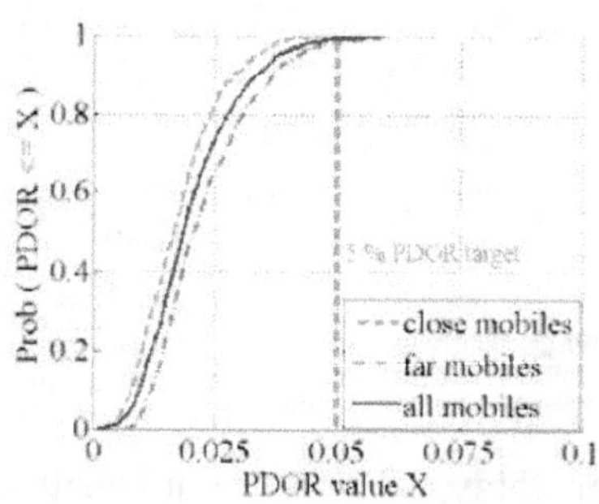

Fig. 10 c. CDF of end cycle PDOR with WFO

Fig. 10. Perceived QoS with different allocation schemes.

We then had a look at the QoS satisfaction level that each mobile perceives across the lifetime of a connection. We divided the connection of each mobile in cycles of five minutes and measured the PDOR at the end of each cycle. Fig. 9 shows the CDF of end cycle PDOR values for a traffic load of 960 Kbps, using respectively the MaxSNR, the PF and the WFO schemes (RR performances are not presented here since it is not able to support this high traffic load.). We also estimated the mobile dissatisfaction ratio. We checked if at the end of each cycle the delay constraint is met or not. We then computed the mobile dissatisfaction ratio defined as the number of times that the mobiles are not satisfied (experienced PDOR ≥ PDORtarget) divided by the total number of cycles (cf. Fig. 10).

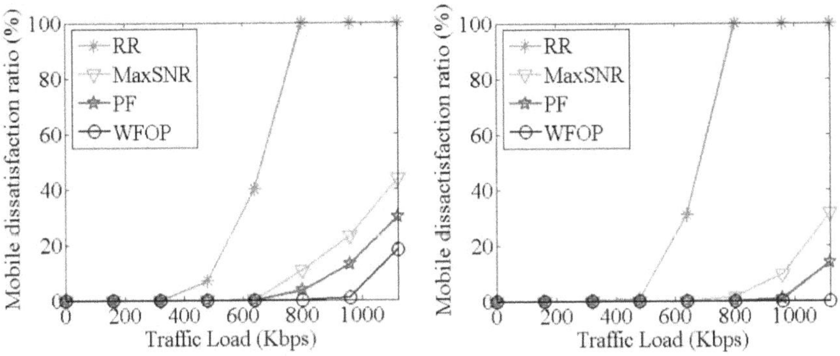

Fig. 11. Analysis of the respect of QoS constraints for different targeted QoS (Mobile dissatisfaction if PDORtarget = 5 % on the left, if PDORtarget = 10 % on the right).

Highly unfair, MaxSNR fully satisfies the required QoS of close mobiles at the expense of the satisfaction of far mobiles. Indeed, only 54.5 percents of these latter experience a final PDOR inferior to a PDOR target of 5 % (cf. Fig. 9a). Unnecessary priorities are given to close mobiles who easily respect their QoS constraints while more attention should be given to the farther. This inadequate priority management dramatically increases the global mobile dissatisfaction, which reaches 23 % as shown on Fig. 9a and Fig. 10 (on the left).

PF brings more fairness and allocates more priority to far mobiles. Compared to MaxSNR, PF offers a QoS support improvement with only 12.8 % of dissatisfied mobiles (cf. Fig. 9b and Fig. 10 (on the right)). Fairness is still not total since the farther mobiles have a lower spectral efficiency than the closer ones due to pathloss. All mobiles do not all benefit of an equal average throughput despite they all obtain an equal share of bandwidth. This induces heterogeneous delays and unequal QoS. This fairness improvement compared to MaxSNR indicates however that some flows can be slightly delayed to the benefit of others without significantly affecting their QoS.

WFO was built on this idea. The easy satisfaction of close mobiles (with better spectral efficiency) offers a degree of freedom which ideally should be exploited in order to help the farther ones. WFO allocates to each mobile the accurate share of bandwidth required for the satisfaction of its QoS constraints, whatever its position. With WFO, only 0.8 percents of the mobiles are dissatisfied (cf. Fig. 9c and Fig. 10 (on the left)). Additionally, compared to Fig. 9a and Fig. 9b, Fig. 9c exhibits superimposed curves, which prove the WFO high fairness, included at short term.

Fig. 10 shows that WFO brings the largest level of satisfaction. Indeed, for a tight PDOR target of 5 % (see on the left), the dissatisfaction ratio with a high traffic load of 1120 Kbps is equal to 18 % with WFO versus 29.7 % with PF, the best of the other scheduling schemes. If we set the PDOR target to 10 %, the dissatisfaction ratio with a high traffic load of 1120 Kbps is 0 % with WFO versus 13.8 % with the best of the other scheduling schemes (PF).

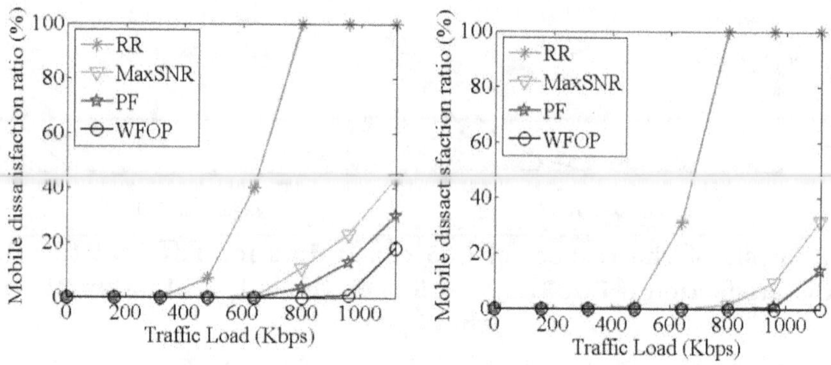

Fig. 12 a. Spectral efficiency. Fig. 12 b. Multiuser diversity Fig. 12. Bandwidth usage efficiency.

We finally studied the system capacity offered by the four scheduling algorithms. Fig. 11a shows the average number of bits carried on a used subcarrier by each tested scheduler under various traffic loads. As expected, the non opportunistic Round Robin scheduling provides a constant spectral efficiency, i.e. an equal bit rate per subcarrier whatever the traffic load since it does not take advantage of the multiuser diversity. The three other tested schedulers show better results. In contrast with RR, with the opportunistic schedulers (MaxSNR, PF, WFO), we observe an interesting inflection of the spectral efficiency curve when the traffic load increases. The join analysis of Fig. 11a and Fig. 11b shows that the spectral efficiency of opportunistic scheduling is an increasing function of the number of active mobiles, thanks to the exploitation of this supplementary multiuser diversity. Consequently MaxSNR, PF and WFO increase their spectral efficiency with the traffic load and the system capacity is highly extended compared to networks which use classical scheduling algorithms. With these three schedulers, all mobiles are served even at the highest traffic load of 1280 Kbps.

The performance of the four schedulers can be further qualified by computing the theoretical maximal system throughput. Considering the Rayleigh distribution, it can be noticed that α2k,n is greater or equal to 8 with a probability of only 0.002. In these ideal situations, close mobiles can transmit/receive 6 bits per RU while far mobiles may transmit/receive 4 bits per RU. If the scheduler always allocated the RUs to the mobiles in these ideal situations, an overall efficiency of 5 bits per RU would be obtained which yields a theoretical maximal system throughput of 1600 Kbps. Comparing this value to the highest traffic load in Fig. 11a (1280 Kbps) further demonstrates the good efficiency obtained with the opportunistic schedulers that nearly always serve the mobiles when their channel conditions are very good. This result also shows that the WFO scheduling has slightly better performances than the two other opportunistic schedulers. Keeping more mobiles active (cf. Fig.11b) but with a relatively lower traffic backlog (cf. Fig.8a), the WFO scheme preserves multiuser diversity and takes more advantage of it obtaining a slightly higher bit rate per subcarrier (cf. Fig. 11a).

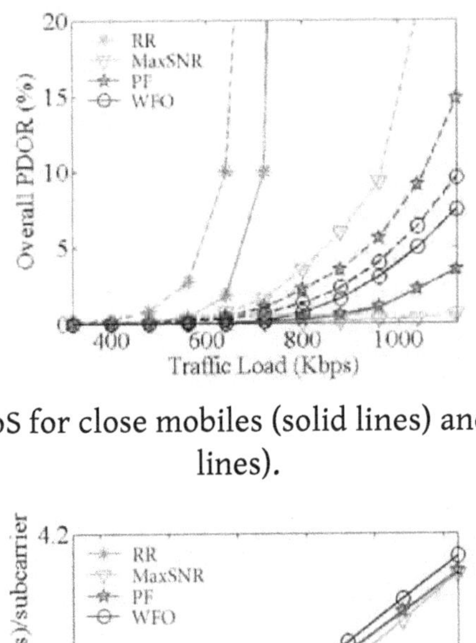

Fig. 13a. Measured QoS for close mobiles (solid lines) and far mobiles (dashed lines).

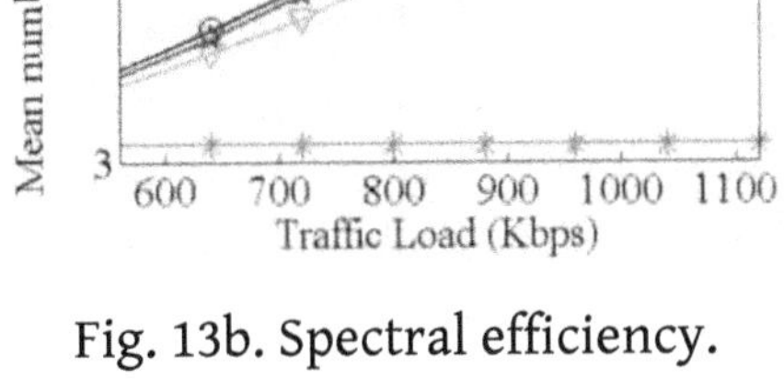

Fig. 13b. Spectral efficiency.

Fig. 13. Performances of schedulers with fixed multiuser diversity.

In the results described so far, the traffic load was varied by increasing or decreasing the number of mobiles in the system, which modified the multiuser diversity. This exhibited the opportunistic behaviour of the schedulers and especially their ability to take advantage of the multiuser diversity brought with the increase of the number of mobiles. We also studied the ability of each scheduler to take profit of the multiuser diversity brought by a given number of users. In Fig.12, we provide complementary results obtained in a context where the traffic load variation is done through just increasing the mobile bit rate requirement and keeping a constant number of users (10 mobiles). The results in Fig. 12a show that, as previously, WFO outperforms the other scheduling schemes. With its weighted algorithm, WFO dynamically adjusts the priorities of the mobiles and ensures a completely fair allocation. WFO is the only one which allows reaching higher traffic loads with an acceptable PDOR for all mobiles. Additionally, even if the traffic load increases without variation in the number of mobiles, WFO keeps more mobiles active across the time than the other schemes and takes better advantage of the multiuser diversity. The analysis of Fig. 12b confirms that WFO maximizes the average bit rate per subcarrier.

5. CONCISE SUMMARY

Opportunistic schedulers exploit multiuser and frequency variety. They preferentially distribute resources to the active mobile(s) exhibiting the most advantageous channel circumstances at any given moment. This optimizes the system throughput of OFDM wireless networks. Three principal algorithms have emerged: MaxSNR, PF, and more recently, WFO. Nonetheless, despite their superior capabilities in maximizing system throughput, both MaxSNR and PF exhibit significant fairness shortcomings due to the unequal spatial distribution of the mobile users. This issue is addressed by WFO, which seems to be the most effective opportunistic scheduler available at present. WFO concurrently evaluates the transmission conditions, the presently measured or experienced Quality of Service (QoS), and the QoS objectives of the mobile devices during the bandwidth allocation procedure. The original weighted method establishes dynamic priorities among the flows, favoring those traversing a vital period and consistently assigning appropriate priority to enhance Quality of Service (QoS) support. WFO is engineered to maintain a maximum number of active flows over time while minimizing traffic backlogs, hence optimizing the benefits of multi-user diversity and leveraging the dynamics of multiplexed traffic. By maintaining multiuser diversity, WFO optimally utilizes the opportunistic scheduling strategy to enhance system capacity. This also accomplishes a temporally consistent and equitable distribution of resource units to the flows, so maintaining short-term fairness. This elevated cross-layer strategy among layers, MAC, and PHY more effectively obscures the aims of system capacity maximization, fairness, and comprehensive support for multimedia services with sufficient QoS.

REFERENCES

1. Hoymann, C. (2005). Analysis and performance evaluation of the OFDM-based metropolitan area network IEEE 802.16. Computer Networks, Vol. 49, No. 3, pp. 341- 363, ISSN: 1389-1286
2. Andrews, M.; Kumaran, K.; Ramanan, K. Stolvar, A. & whiting P. (2001). Providing quality of service over a shared wireless link. IEEE Communications Magazine, Vol. 39, No.2, pp. 150-154, ISSN: 0163-6804
3. Van de Beek, J.-J. ; Borjesson, P.O. ; Boucheret, M.-J ; Landstrom, D. ; Arenas, J.-M. Odling, P.; Ostberg, C.; Wahlgvist, M. & Wilson, S.K. (1999). A time and frequency synchronization scheme for multiuser OFDM. IEEE J.Sel. Areas Commun, Vol.17, No.11, pp 1900-1914, ISSN: 0733-8716
4. Li, Y.G; Seshadri, N. & Ariyavisitakul, S. (1999). Channel estimation for ofdm systems with transmitter diversity in mobile wireless channels. IEEE J.Sel. Areas Commun, Vol.17, No.3, pp 461-471, ISSN: 0733-8716
5. Truman, T.E. & Brodersen, R.W (1997). A measurement-based characterization of the time variation of an indoor wireless channel, proceedings of Int. Universal Personal Communications Record (ICUPC), pp. 25-32, ISBN: 0-7803-3777-8, San Diego, CA, USA, October 1997
6. Knopp, R. & Humblet, P. (1995). Choi, J. (1996). Information capacity and power control in single-cell multiuser communications, proceedings of IEEE Conference on Communications (ICC), pp 331-335, ISBN: 0-7803-2486-2, Seattle, WA, USA, june 1995
7. Wong, C.Y.; Cheng, R.S.; Lataief, K.B. & Murch, R.D. (1999). Multiuser OFDM with adaptative subcarrier, bit and power allocation. IEEE J.Sel. Areas Commun, Vol.17, No.10, pp 1747-1758, ISSN: 0733-8716
8. Wang, X. & Xiang, Y. (2006). An OFDM-TDMA/SA MAC protocol with QoS constaints for broadband wireless LANs. ACM/Springer Wireless Networks, Vol. 12, No. 2, pp 159- 170, ISSN: 1022-0038
9. Viswanath, P.; Tse, D.N.C. & Laroia, R. (2002). Opportunistic beamforming using dumb antennas. IEEE Transactions on Information Theory, Vol. 48, No.6, pp. 1277–1294, ISSN: 0018-9448
10. Kim, H.; Kim, K.; Han, Y. & Lee, J. (2002). An efficient scheduling algorithm for QoS in wireless packet data transmission, proceedings of IEEE Int. Symposium on Personal, Indoor and Mobile Radio Communications (PIMRC), pp 2244-2248, ISBN: 0-7803-7589-0, Lisboa, Portugal, September 2002

11. Anchun, W.; Liang, X.; Xjiin, S.X. & Yan, Y. (2003). Dynamic resource management in the fourth generation wireless systems, proceedings of IEEE Int. Conference on Communication Technology (ICCT), pp 1095-1098, ISBN: 7-5635-0686-1, Beijing, China, April 2003
12. Svedman, P.; Wilson, K. & Ottersen, B. (2004). A QoS-aware proportional fair scheduler for opportunistic OFDM, proceedings of IEEE Int. Vehicular Technology Conference (VTC), pp 558-562, ISBN: 0-7803-8521-7, Los angeles, CA, USA, September 2004
13. Kim, H.; Kim, K.; Han, Y. & Yun, S. (2004). A proportional fair scheduling for multicarrier transmission systems, proceedings of IEEE Int. Vehicular Technology Conference (VTC), pp. 409-413, ISBN: 0-7803-8521-7, Los angeles, CA, USA, September 2004
14. Choi, J.-G. & Bahk, S. (2007). Cell-throughput analysis of the proportional fair scheduler in the single-cell environment. IEEE Transactions on Vehicular Technology, vol. 56, No.2, pp. 766-778, ISSN: 0018-9545
15. Gueguen, C. & Baey, S. (2008). Compensated proportional fair scheduling in multiuser OFDM wireless networks, proceedings of IEEE Wireless and Mobile Computing, Networking and Communications (WIMOB), pp119-125, ISBN: 978-0-7695-3393-3, Avignon, France, October 2008
16. Holtzman, J. (2001). Asymptotic analysis of proportional fair algorithm, proceedings of IEEE Int. Symposium on Personal, Indoor and Mobile Radio Communications (PIMRC), pp. 33- 37, ISBN: 0-7803-7244-1, San Diego, CA, USA, October 2001
17. Gueguen, C. & Baey, S. (2008). Weighted fair opportunistic scheduling for multimedia QoS support in multiuser OFDM wireless networks, proceedings of IEEE Int. Symposium on Personal, Indoor and Mobile Radio Communications (PIMRC), pp. 1-6, ISBN: 978-1- 4244-2643-0, Cannes, France, September 2008
18. Gueguen, C. & Baey, S. (2008). An efficient and fair scheduling scheme for multiuser OFDM wireless networks, proceedings of IEEE Int.Wireless Communications and Networking Conference (WCNC), pp. 1610-1615, ISBN: 978-1-4244-1997-5, Las Vegas, NV, USA, April 2008
19. Gueguen, C. & Baey, S. (2008). Scheduling in OFDM wireless networks without tradeoff between fairness and throughput, proceedings of IEEE Int. Vehicular Technology Conference (VTC), pp. 1-5, ISBN: 978-1-4244-1721-6, Calgary, Canada, September 2008
20. Gueguen, C. & Baey, S. (2009). A Fair Opportunistic Access Scheme for Multiuser OFDM Wireless Networks. EURASIP Journal on Wireless Communications and

Networking. Special issue on "Fairness in Radio Resource Management for Wireless Networks". Volume 2009 (2009), Article ID 726495, pp. 70-83

21. Parsons, J.D (1992). The Mobile Radio Propagation Channel, Wiley, ISBN: 978-0-471-98857-1 Baey, S. (2004). Modeling MPEG4 video traffic based on a customization of the DBMAP, proceedings of Int. Symposium on Performance Evaluation of Computer and Telecommunication Systems (SPECTS), pp. 705-714, ISBN: 1-56555-284-9, San Jose, California, USA, July 2004

22. Brady, P. (1969). A model for generating on-off speech patterns in two-conversation. Bell System Technical Journal, vol. 48, No.1, pp. 2445-2472

15 Chapter | BIDIRECTIONAL COOPERATIVE RELAYING

1. INTRODUCTION: AN OVERVIEW

Contemporary radio communication technologies seek to improve throughput and reliability in wireless networks with constrained resources. Wireless mobile communication via a radio channel is constrained by multipath propagation, fading, path loss, shadowing, and interference. Spatial diversity approaches are extensively utilized to mitigate fading and other channel degradations. Cooperative communications have recently been created to exploit spatial diversity even with single-antenna terminals. The scattered terminals collaborate by transmitting each other's messages to form a virtual antenna array and attain cooperative diversity. Cooperative relaying has emerged as a promising method for improving coverage, dependability, and throughput in wireless networks with strict spectrum and power limitations. Applications have been identified in wireless cellular networks, ad hoc/sensor networks, WiFi, and WiMAX, among others.

Dual-hop three-terminal channels, in which a relay terminal facilitates communication between source and destination terminals via a cooperative protocol, are of significant interest. Relaying can occur in either full-duplex or half-duplex mode. Full-duplex relaying enables radios to concurrently receive and broadcast on the same frequency channel, hence enhancing spectral efficiency. The significant disparity in power levels between the broadcast and receive signals (usually 100-150 dB) renders its implementation realistically challenging. In half-duplex mode, radio reception and transmission occur in orthogonal channels utilizing time, frequency, or code division. Half-duplex systems are thus practically viable. The primary disadvantage of half-duplex relaying is a significant reduction in spectral efficiency. This occurs because fifty percent of the channel resources are designated for the relay to facilitate cooperation, hence diminishing the overall data rate.

Although extensive research has concentrated on leveraging cooperative diversity, minimal attention has been devoted to enhancing spectral efficiency under half-duplex limitations. Rankov and Wittneben (2007) present a novel two-phase two-way relaying protocol that establishes a bidirectional connection between two terminals using a single half-duplex relay. Under this approach, two connections are established within the same physical channel, hence enhancing spectral efficiency. Known as the Two-Way Relay Channel (TWRC) in scholarly discourse, this pragmatic methodology has garnered significant attention in recent studies. An instance of a TWRC is the downlink and uplink in wireless mobile networks, where both the base station and the mobile station must communicate through an intermediary relay station due to the absence of a dependable direct connection. This is beneficial when the mobile device is significantly shaded or located near the cell edge. It is crucial to recognize that even when a high-quality direct link is accessible, it cannot be employed in two-phase TWRC, as both terminals would need to send and receive concurrently in the same phase.

The advent of network coding (Ahlswede et al., 2000) has transformed the design of communication networks. Network coding enables intermediary nodes to amalgamate and encode data from many sources to improve overall network throughput. Initially suggested for wired communication networks, there has recently been significant interest in implementing network coding in wireless relay networks (Hao et al., 2007). A coded bidirectional relaying technique with three transmission phases has been independently proposed in response to the spectral efficiency loss associated with half-duplex mode in (Wu et al., 2005) and (Larsson et al., 2006). The writers in Kim et al. (2008) studied and analyzed the efficacy of various half-duplex bidirectional relaying protocols. Network coding has been further utilized for bidirectional cooperation in the works of Hausl & Hagenauer (2006), Baik & Chung (2008), and Cui et al. (2008a, 2008b). Katti et al. (2007b) demonstrated that wireless two-way relaying combined with network coding attains superior data rates.

Bidirectional relaying is adaptable to accommodate several physical-layer transmission technologies. Extensive research is currently underway on subjects such as the TWRC capacity region or achievable rate region (Oechtering et al., 2008), channel estimation (Zhao et al., 2008; Gao et al., 2008), multi-hop relaying (Vaze & Heath Jr., 2008), resource allocation (Agustin et al., 2008), distributed space-time coding (Cui et al., 2008c), and distributed relay selection (Ding et al., 2009), employing various physical layer signaling techniques, including OFDM (Ho et al., 2008; Jitvanichphaibool et al., 2008). The bidirectional relaying technique has been expanded to encompass the multi-user scenario (Chen & Yener, 2008; Esli & Wittneben, 2008). Multiple-Input Multiple-Output (MIMO) bidirectional relaying (Unger & Klein, 2007; Gunduz et al., 2008) is a prominent study domain, frequently anticipated to enhance connection dependability and bidirectional throughput in wireless systems.

This chapter aims to comprehensively present the current advancements in bidirectional cooperative communication, elucidate recent analytical discoveries and their implications, substantiate them with diverse simulation outcomes, and explore prospective research avenues.

2. COOPERATIVE COMMUNICATIONS

Cooperative communication systems seek to enhance the link capacity and transmission reli- ability through cooperation between distributed radios. They exploit the broadcasting nature of the wireless medium and allow single-antenna terminals to cooperate through relaying. The conventional form of cooperation is multi-hopping, where a source communicates with a destination via a series of dedicated relays. It is mainly used to combat signal attenuation in long-range communication and it does not provide any diversity advantages. The key issue in cooperative communications is resource sharing among network nodes. A three-terminal net- work acts as a fundamental unit in cooperative communication and has been widely studied in the literature.

The three-terminal relay channel model, introduced in (Meulen, 1971), comprises a source T1, a destination T2, and a dedicated relay R (as shown in Figure 1). The relay aids in commu- nicating information from source to destination without actually being an information source or sink. It was assumed that all nodes operate in the full-duplex mode, so the system can be viewed as a Broadcast Channel (BC) at the source, and a Multiple Access Channel (MAC) at the destination. The upper and lower bounds on the capacity of the non-faded relay chan- nel, derived in (Meulen, 1971), were improved significantly in (Cover & Gamal, 1979). Later, models with multiple relays have been investigated in cooperation literature. However, the recent developments are motivated by the user cooperation (Sendonaris et al., 2003) and co- operative diversity (Laneman et al., 2004) in a fading channel. The authors in (Sendonaris et al., 2003) introduced user cooperation by allowing the relay to transmit its own independent information. Cooperative diversity introduced in (Laneman et al., 2004) is realized by relaying and user cooperation. They proposed different cooperative diversity protocols and analyzed their performance in terms of outage probability. The terms Amplify-&-Forward (AF) and Decode-&-Forward (DF) were introduced in their work.

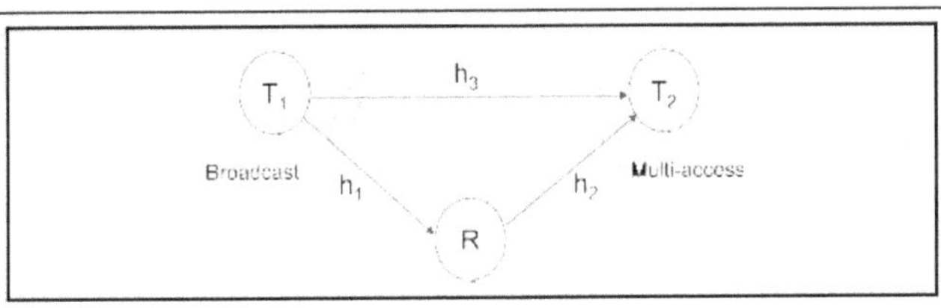

Fig. 1. The wireless relay channel.

2.1 Cooperative Relaying Protocols

Consider a three-terminal wireless network as shown in Figure 1 in which terminal T1 wants to transmit data to terminal T2 with the help of a relay terminal R. In view of cellular network, T1 and R might be mobile stations and T1 might be a base station. Under cooperative relaying strategy, T1 and a suitable R can share their resources, such as power and bandwidth, to transmit the information of T1. This cooperation might provide diversity because, even if the direct link between T1 and T2 is severely faded, the information might be successfully transmitted via R. It is assumed that the relay node operates in half-duplex mode and has no message of its own to transmit. Figure 2 illustrates the channel allocation for time-division approach with two orthogonal phases to ensure half-duplex operation. In phase 1, T1 sends information to its destination T2 and the information is also received by the relay R at the same time. In phase 2, the relay R can help the source T1 by forwarding or retransmitting the information to the destination. However, there is 50% loss in spectral efficiency because of transmission in two phases.

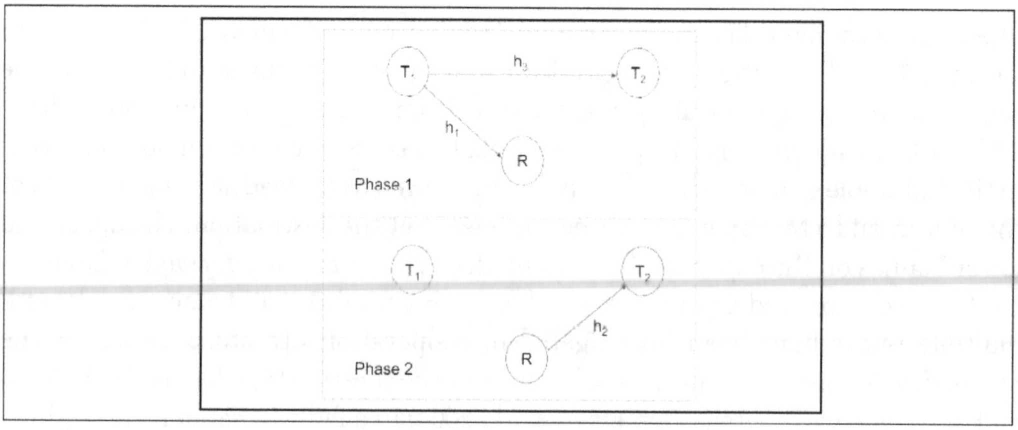

Fig. 2. Orthogonal relay transmission.

The source and relay nodes can share their resources on the basis of some cooperation strategies to achieve the highest throughput possible for any given coding scheme. Based on different signal processing schemes employed at the relays, the cooperative relaying methods are classified into fixed relaying and adaptive relaying (Laneman et al., 2004). For fixed re- laying, the relay can amplify its received signal subject to its power constraint, or decode, re-encode, and then retransmit the messages, referred to (respectively) as Amlify-&-Forward (AF) or Decode-&-Forward (DF). This scheme has the advantage of easy implementation, but the disadvantage of low spectral efficiency. This is because half of the channel resources are allocated to the relay for transmission. Adaptive relaying schemes build upon fixed relaying and adapt based upon Channel State Information (CSI) between cooperating terminals (selective relaying) or upon limited feedback from the destination (incremental relaying). Selective relaying allows transmitting terminals to select a suitable cooperative or non-cooperative action based on the measured SNR between them. If the received SNR at the relay exceeds a certain threshold, the relay performs DF operation on the message. Otherwise, if the channel between T1 and R has severe fading such that SNR falls below the threshold, the relay idles. Incremental relaying improves upon the spectral efficiency of both fixed and selective relaying by exploiting limited feedback from the destination and relaying only when direct link from source to destination has an SNR below a threshold.

2.2 Outage Analysis and Diversity Gain

When the channel is time-varying, the channel capacity has different notions depending on the different fading states. Ergodic (Shannon) capacity is an appropriate capacity metric for channels that vary quickly, or where the channel is ergodic over the time period of interest. It can be evaluated by averaging the mutual information over all possible channel realizations. An alternate outage capacity notion is suitable for applications where the data rate cannot depend on channel variations (except in outage states, where no data are transmitted). It is a measure of data rate that can be supported by a system with a certain error probability. To investigate the diversity gain, the performance of relaying protocols is characterised in terms of outage probability. Assume frequency flat slow fading channel with CSI knowledge at the receivers only. Perfect synchronization among the terminals is also assumed. Considering a baseband-equivalent discrete-time channel model, the transmissions in time slot k can be expressed as

$$y_r[k] = h_1[k]x_1[k] + n_1[k] \quad (1)$$

$$y_2[k] = h_3[k]x_1[k] + n_3[k] \quad (2)$$

where $x_1[k]$ is the transmitted signal from T1, $y_r[k]$ and $y_2[k]$ are the received signals at the relay and T2 respectively, h_i captures the effects of path-loss, shadowing and frequency nonse- lective fading, $n_i (0, \sigma^2)$ is the Additive White Gaussian Noise (AWGN) which captures the effects of receiver noise and other forms of interference in the system, where $i \in 1, 2, 3$. Throughout the chapter, we use $h_i[k]$ and h_i interchangeably for brevity. The relay processes $y_r[k]$ and relays the information by transmitting $x_r[k]$. The signal received at T2 in time slot k+1

$$y_2[k+1] = h_2[k+1]x_r[k] + n_2[k+1]. \quad (3)$$

As a function of the fading coefficients h_i (modeled as zero-mean, independent, circularly symmetric complex Gaussian random variables with variances σ_{hi}^2), the mutual information for a protocol is a random variable I. For a target rate R, $I < R$ denotes the outage event and $\Pr[I < R]$ denotes the outage probability (Laneman et al., 2004). The maximum average mutual information between input and output in direct transmission, achieved by independent identically distributed (i.i.d.) zero-mean, circularly symmetric complex Gaussian inputs, is given by

$$I_D = \log(1 + \Gamma|h_3|^2) \quad (4)$$

where Γ = P1/σ2 is defined as SNR without fading and P1 is the average transmit power of terminal T1. For Rayleigh fading, |h3|2 is exponentially distributed with parameter 1/σh32, the outage probability derived in (Laneman et al., 2004) is given as

$$\Pr[I_D < \mathcal{R}] = 1 - \exp\left(-\frac{2^{\mathcal{R}} - 1}{\gamma\sigma_{h3}^2}\right) \sim \frac{1}{\sigma_{h3}^2}\frac{2^{\mathcal{R}} - 1}{\gamma}. \tag{5}$$

The direct transmission does not achieve any diversity gain as is obvious from Γ-1 depen- dence of outage probability in Equation (5).

2.3 AF Relaying

In this protocol, the relay amplifies the received signal in the first time slot according to its available average transmit power and forwards a scaled signal in the second time slot to the destination terminal. To remain within its power constraint, an amplifying relay must use gain

$$g[k] \leq \sqrt{\frac{P_r}{P_1|h_1|^2 + \sigma^2}} \tag{6}$$

which is inversely proportional to the received power. Thus the relay transmits the signal xr [k + 1] = g[k]yr [k] with the power Pr in the second time slot. This scheme can be viewed as repetitive coding from two distributed transmitters T1 and R, except that the relay R amplifies the noise in its received signal. The destination T2 can decode its received signal y2 by suitably combining the signals from the two time slots. This protocol produces an equivalent one-input two-output complex Gaussian noise channel with different noise levels in the out- puts. The SNR received at the destination is the sum of the SNRs from T1 and R links. The maximum average mutual information between the input and the two outputs, achieved by i.i.d. complex Gaussian inputs, is given by

$$I_{AF} = \frac{1}{2}\log\left[1 + \gamma|h_3|^2 + \frac{\gamma|h_2 g h_1|^2}{(1 + |h_2 g|^2)}\right]. \tag{7}$$

Note that g is a function of h1. Notations g[k] and g are used interchangeably throughout for brevity. The outage probability can be approximated at high SNR (Laneman et al., 2004) as

$$\Pr[I_{AF} < \mathcal{R}] \sim \left(\frac{\sigma_{h1}^2 + \sigma_{h2}^2}{2\sigma_{h3}^2\left(\sigma_{h1}^2\sigma_{h2}^2\right)}\right)\left(\frac{2^{2\mathcal{R}} - 1}{\gamma}\right)^2. \tag{8}$$

The pre-log factor 1/2 in Equation (7) is due to half-duplex relaying which needs two channel uses to transmit the information from source to destination. The outage behavior decays as Γ-2, which indicates that fixed AF protocol offers diversity gain of 2.

2.4 DF Relaying

In this scheme the relay processes its received signal yr [k] in the first time slot to obtain an estimate x1 [k] of the source transmitted signal. Under a repetition-coded scheme, the relay transmits the signal xr [k + 1] = 1[k] in the second time slot. Although fixed DF relaying has the advantage over AF relaying in reducing the effects of additive noise at the relay, it entails the possibility of forwarding erroneously detected symbols to the destination. Therefore it is required that both the relay and destination decode the entire codeword without error. This leads to the expression of maximum average mutual information IDF between T1 and T2 as the minimum of the two maximum rates, one at which the relay R can reliably decode the source message, and the other at which the destination T2 can reliably decode the source message given repeated transmissions from the source and relay. This implies that

$$I_{DF} - \frac{1}{2}\min\left\{\log\left(1+\gamma|h_1|^2\right), \log\left(1+\gamma|h_3|^2+\gamma|h_2|^2\right)\right\}. \tag{9}$$

Hereitisobviousthattheperformanceofthissystemislimitedbytheworstlinkamongthe T1 - T2 and T2–R. The outage probability can be obtained for high SNR (Laneman et al., 2004) as

$$\Pr[I_{DF} < \mathcal{R}] \sim \frac{1}{\sigma_{h1}^2}\frac{2^{2\mathcal{R}}-1}{\gamma}. \tag{10}$$

The Γ-1 behavior in Equation (10) indicates that fixed DF protocol does not provide diversity gain for large SNR.

2.5 Numerical Results

We compare the outage analysis results of AF and DF relaying protocols with direct transmission. We consider the case of statistically symmetric networks in which the Rayleigh fading channel variances are identical i.e., σ2hi = 1. The noise variance σ2 is assumed to be unity. We realized 10000 random channels using Monte Carlo simulation. Figure 3 shows the outage probabilities versus SNR in dB for low spectral efficiency (roughly 2 bps/Hz). The diversity order of 2 achieved by AF protocol is clear from the steeper curve slope in Figure 3. Also the fixed DF relaying curve indicates no diversity gain and hence does not have any advantage over direct transmission. In Figure 4, the outage probabilities are depicted as functions of spectral efficiency R for a fixed SNR of 35 dB. It is clear from Figure 4 that the performance of fixed AF and DF protocols generally degrade with increasing rate R. It degrades faster for AF scheme because of the inherent loss in spectral efficiency. Again, fixed DF protocol does not have any diversity advantage over direct transmission. At sufficiently high rate , direct transmission becomes more efficient than cooperative relay communication. So we can conclude that half-duplex operation requires double channel resources compared to direct transmission for a given rate and hence leads to larger effective SNR losses for increasing rate. However the performance enhancements in low spectral efficiency regime can be translated into decreased transmit power for the same reliability.

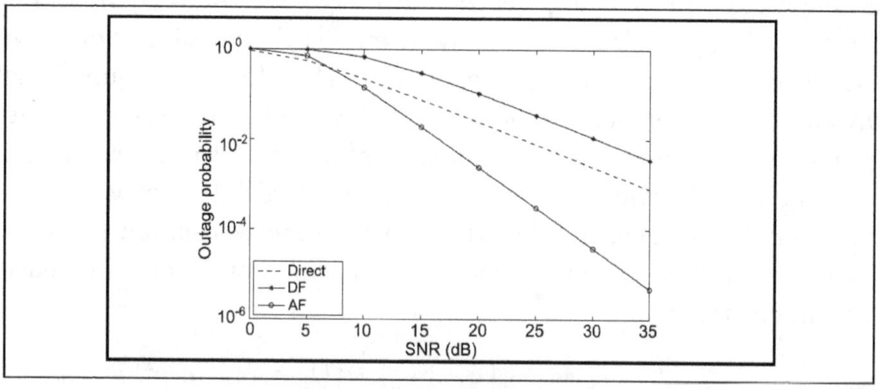

Fig. 3. Outage probabilities versus SNR in the low spectral efficiency regime.

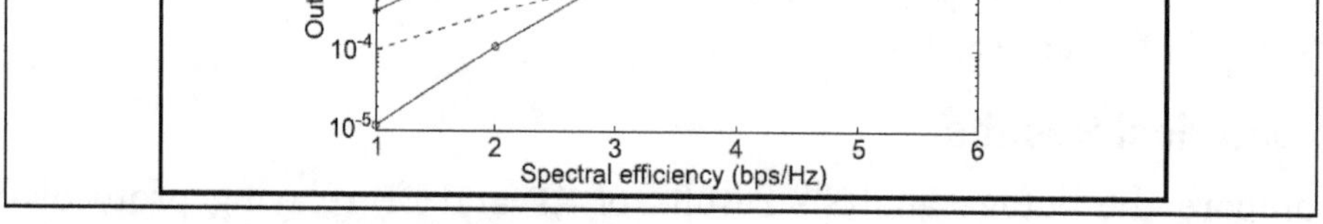

Fig. 4. Outage probabilities versus spectral efficiency for high SNR.

3. BIDIRECTIONAL RELAYING

Although unidirectional or one-way communication has been extensively considered in the literature, there is a lot of interest in recent years on bidirectional or two-way communication. In two-way communication, two terminals simultaneously transmit their messages to each other and the messages interfere with each other. The Two-Way Communication Channel (TWC) was first studied by Shannon, who derived inner and outer bounds on the capacity region (Shannon, 1961). He used a restricted two-way channel in which the encoders of both terminals do not cooperate, and the transmitted symbols at one terminal only depend on the message to be transmitted at that terminal (and not on the previously received symbols). He showed that the inner bound coincides with the capacity region of the restricted two-way channel. Later, the two-way communication problem was investigated for the full-duplex relay channel, and the achievable rate regions were derived in (Rankov & Wittneben, 2006), (Avestimehr et al., 2008), (Nam et al., 2008) and references therein. Further TWC has been exploited in (Rankov & Wittneben, 2007), as TWRC, in order to mitigate the spectral efficiency loss of cooperative protocols under half-duplex relaying. Recall that cooperative protocols can provide higher outage capacity but not ergodic capacity because of use of orthogonal time slots for relaying. Our goal here is to analyze spectrally efficient (measured in bits per channel use) transmission schemes for the half-duplex bidirectional relay channel. Presently the TWRC protocol has drawn much interest from both academic and industrial communities owing to its potential application in wireless networks.

3.1 One-Way Relay Channel (OWRC)

Consider a wireless channel in which two nodes T1 and T2 wish to exchange independent messages with the help of a relay node R. Once again, we assume that all terminals operate in half-duplex fashion. Therefore the relay terminal cannot receive and transmit simultaneously on the same channel resource; it receives a signal on a first hop, applies signal processing and retransmits the signal on a second hop. More importantly, there is no reliable direct link between T1 and T2 due to shadowing, large separation between them, or use of low power signaling. This is feasible in practice when the users are geographically separated, and the signals received from each other are very weak. This is the case when two distant land stations communicate with a satellite, or two mobile users located on opposite sides of a building communicate with the same base station on top of the building. When there is no direct connection between the two wireless terminals, relays are essential to enable communication.

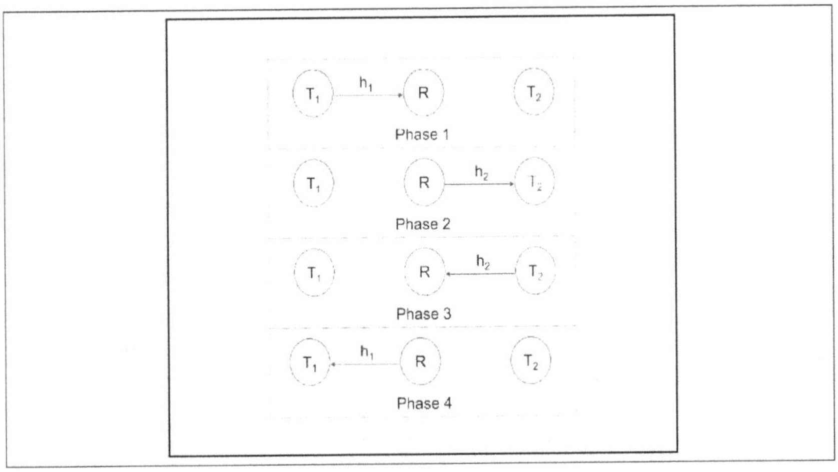

Fig. 5. Four-phase one-way relaying for bidirectional cooperation.

For a one-way relaying approach, two resources are required for the transmission from T1 to T2 via R and two resources are required for the transmission from T2 to T1 via R, leading to an overall requirement of four resources. This is a four phase protocol (Kim et al., 2008) whereby transmissions T1 → R, R → T2 , T2 → R, and R → T1 occur in four consecutive phases, as illustrated in Figure 5.

3.1.1 AF-OWRC

The source terminal T1 transmits in the first time slot an information symbol to the relay terminal R. The relay amplifies the received symbol (including noise) according to its available average transmit power and forwards a scaled signal in the second time slot to the destination terminal T2 (Rankov & Wittneben, 2007). In time slot k, the relay receives

$$yr\,[k] = h1[k]x1[k] + nr\,[k] \tag{11}$$

where h1 is the complex channel gain between source and relay (first hop), x1 ~ CN (0, P1) is the transmit symbol of the source, and nr ~ CN (0, σr2) is the AWGN at the relay. The relay scales yr [k] by

$$g[k] = \sqrt{\frac{P_r}{P_1|h_1[k]|^2 + \sigma_r^2}} \tag{12}$$

where Pr is the average transmit power of the relay. Depending on the amount of channel knowledge at the relay, different choices for the relay gain are possible. In time slot k+1, the destination receives

$$y2[k+1] = h2[k+1]g[k]h1[k]x1[k] + h2[k+1]g[k]nr\,[k] + n2[k+1] \tag{13}$$

where h2 is the complex channel gain between relay and destination (second hop) and n2 ~ CN (0, σr2) is the AWGN at the destination. The information rate of this scheme for i.i.d. fading channels h1[k] and h2[k] is given by (Rankov & Wittneben, 2007)

$$I_{AF} = \frac{1}{2}E\left\{\log\left(1 + \frac{P_1|h_2gh_1|^2}{\sigma_2^2 + \sigma_r^2|h_2g|^2}\right)\right\} \tag{14}$$

where E {·}denotes the expectation with respect to the channels h1 and h2. The pre-log factor 1/2 follows because of the two channel uses needed to transmit the information from T1 to T2 .

3.1.2 DF-OWRC

In this scheme, the relay decodes the message sent by the source, re-encodes it (by using the same or a different codebook), and forwards the message to the destination. In time slot k, the relay receives

$$yr\,[k] = h1[k]x1[k] + nr\,[k]. \tag{15}$$

After decoding and retransmission, the destination receives in time slot k+1

$$y2[k+1] = h2[k+1]xr[k+1] + n2[k+1] \quad (16)$$

where xr ~ CN (0, Pr) is the transmit symbol of the relay. The information rate of this scheme for i.i.d. fading channels h1[k] and h2[k] is given by (Rankov & Wittneben, 2007)

$$I_{DF} = \frac{1}{2}\min\left[E\left\{\log\left(1+\frac{P_1|h_1|^2}{\sigma_r^2}\right)\right\}, E\left\{\log\left(1+\frac{P_r|h_2|^2}{\sigma_2^2}\right)\right\}\right]. \quad (17)$$

This rate is exactly the ergodic capacity of the conventional half-duplex cooperative relay channel with no direct connection. Compared to a bidirectional communication between T1 and T2 without two-hop relaying, the number of required resources is doubled. Therefore this protocol is spectrally inefficient and does not take full advantage of the broadcast nature of the wireless channel.

3.2 Two-Way Relay Channel (TWRC)

The two-way relaying protocol (Rankov & Wittneben, 2007) is an effective means to increase the spectral efficiency of a half-duplex relay network. As illustrated in Figure 6, messages of nodes T1 and T2 are delivered to nodes T2 and T1 respectively in two phases, named the Multiple Access Channel (MAC) and Broadcast Channel (BC) phase. In the first (MAC) phase, T1 and T2 transmit their signals to the relay node at the same time. After receiving the signals, the relay node performs appropriate signal processing and broadcasts the resulting signal to both nodes T1 and T2 in the second (BC) phase. At each node, its symbols contribute self interference but can clearly be canceled (because they are known). The channels in the forward direction are assumed to be the same as in the backward direction i.e., channel reciprocity is assumed.

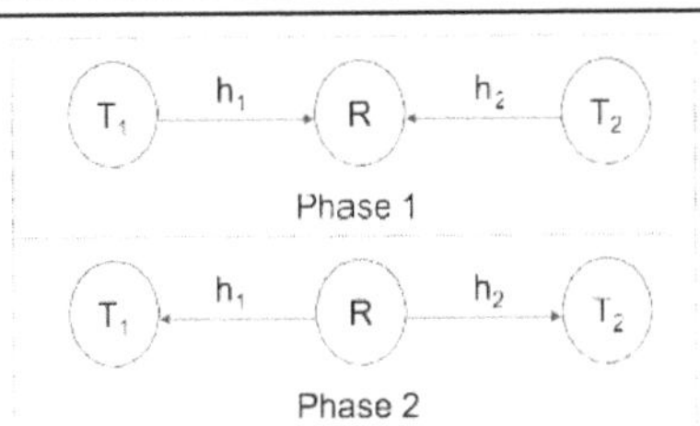

Fig. 6. Two-phase two-way relaying for bidirectional cooperation.

3.2.1 AF-TWRC

In this scheme, both terminals T1 and T2 transmit their symbols to relay R in the same time slot k using the same bandwidth. The relay then receives

$$yr[k] = h1[k]x1[k] + h2[k]x2[k] + nr[k] \quad (18)$$

where the symbols x1[k] ~ CN(0, P1) and x2[k] ~ (0, P2) are the i.i.d. transmit symbols of terminals T1 and T2 respectively. The relay scales the received signal by

$$g[k] = \sqrt{\frac{P_r}{P_1|h_1[k]|^2 + P_2|h_2[k]|^2 + \sigma_r^2}} \tag{19}$$

in order to meet its average transmit power constraint. It then broadcasts the signal in the next time slot to both terminals T1 and T2. The signals received at terminals T1 and T2 are

$$y_2[k+1] = h_2[k+1]g[k]h_1[k]x_1[k] + h_2[k+1]g[k]h_2[k]x_2[k] + h_2[k+1]g[k]n_r[k] + n_2[k+1] \tag{20}$$

$$y_1[k+1] = h_1[k+1]g[k]h_2[k]x_2[k] + h_1[k+1]g[k]h_1[k]x_1[k] + h_1[k+1]g[k]n_r[k] + n_1[k+1]. \tag{21}$$

Assuming channel reciprocity for h1 and h2. Unless mentioned otherwise, we assume that hi remains static at least over two time slots. Since nodes T1 and T2 know their own transmitted symbols, they can subtract the back-propagating self-interference prior to decoding, assum- ing perfect knowledge of the corresponding channel coefficients. The sum-rate is given by (Rankov & Wittneben, 2007)

$$I_{AF(sum)} = \frac{1}{2}E\left\{\log\left(1 + \frac{P_1|h_2 g h_1|^2}{\sigma_2^2 + \sigma_r^2|h_2 g|^2}\right)\right\} + \frac{1}{2}E\left\{\log\left(1 + \frac{P_2|h_2 g h_1|^2}{\sigma_1^2 + \sigma_r^2|h_1 g|^2}\right)\right\}. \tag{22}$$

The transmission in each direction suffers still from the pre-log factor 1/2. However, the half- duplex constraint can here be exploited to establish a bidirectional connection between two terminals and to increase the sum rate of the network.

3.2.2 DF-TWRC

Consider now a two-way communication between terminals T1 and T2 via a half-duplex DF relay R. In time slot k both terminals T1 and T2 transmit their symbols to relay R. In this MAC phase, the relay receives

$$y_r[k] = h_1[k]x_1[k] + h_2[k]x_2[k] + n_r[k], \tag{23}$$

decodes the symbols x1[k] and x2[k] and transmits xr [k + 1] = $\sqrt{1-\beta}x_2$ + $\sqrt{1-\beta}x_2$ [k] in the next time slot (BC phase). The received signals at T1 and T2 are

y2[k + 1]= h2[k + 1]xr [k + 1]+ n2[k + 1] (24)

y1[k + 1]= h1[k + 1]xr [k + 1]+ n1[k + 1]. (25)

The relay uses an average transmit power of βPr for the forward direction and (1 – β)Pr for the backward direction. Since T1 knows x1[k] and T2 knows x2[k], these symbols (back- propagating self-interference) can be subtracted at the respective terminals prior to decoding of the symbol transmitted by the partner terminal. We assume that the relay decodes x1[k] and x2[k] without errors. The sum-rate is given (Rankov & Wittneben, 2007) by

$$I_{DF(sum)} = \max_{\beta} \min(I_{MA}, I_1(\beta) + I_2(1-\beta)) \tag{26}$$

$$\text{where} \quad I_{MA} = \frac{1}{2} C\left(\frac{P_1|h_1|^2 + P_2|h_2|^2}{\sigma_r^2}\right)$$

$$I_1(\beta) = \frac{1}{2}\min\left\{C\left(\frac{P_1|h_1|^2}{\sigma_r^2}\right), C\left(\frac{\beta P_r|h_2|^2}{\sigma_2^2}\right)\right\}$$

$$I_2(1-\beta) = \frac{1}{2}\min\left\{C\left(\frac{P_2|h_2|^2}{\sigma_r^2}\right), C\left(\frac{(1-\beta)P_r|h_1|^2}{\sigma_1^2}\right)\right\}$$

$$\text{where} \quad C(x) = E\{\log(1+x)\}.$$

In the absence of CSI knowledge in the BC phase, $\beta = \frac{1}{2}$ is used by the relay. Note that in fast fading channels, the channel coefficients change from phase to phase, and reliable CSI may not be available. In other case β may be optimally chosen to maximize the sum rate. The choice of β will depend on the amount of channel knowledge available (CSI or its statistics), and applicable path losses in the links.

3.3 Simulation Results

We compute the achievable rates of the one-way and two-way relaying schemes by Monte Carlo simulations. We consider a fixed symmetric network in which the relay is equidistant from the two terminals. The Rayleigh fading channel gains are modeled as hi ~ CN(0, 1). The AWGN variances are chosen as σ12 = σ22 = σr2 = σ2 and the transmit powers P1 = P2 = P/2 is defined as the ratio P/σ2. Over 10000 random channels were used to average the rates in Figures 7 and 8.

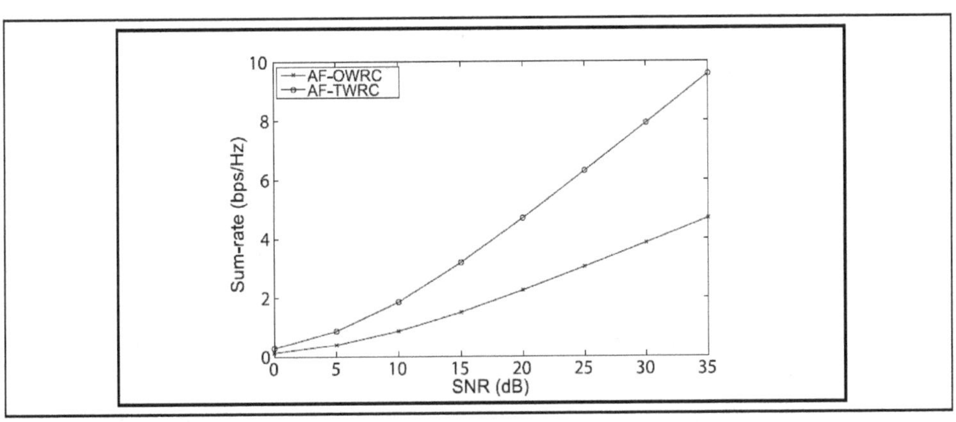

Fig. 7. Sum rate for two-way half-duplex AF relaying protocol.

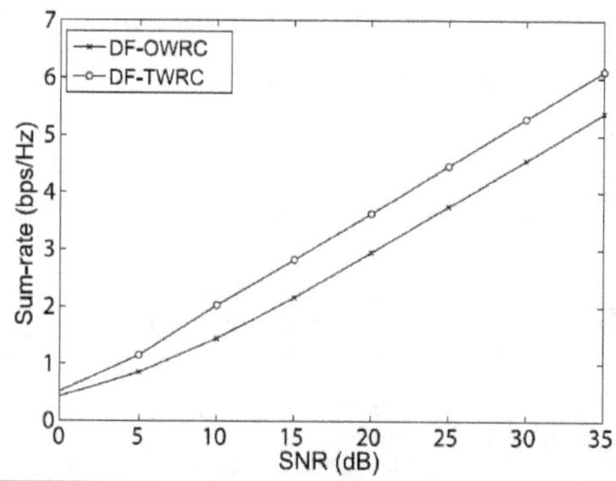

Fig. 8. Sum rate for two-way half-duplex DF relaying protocol.

We compare the sum rate of the two-way AF and two-way DF protocols with their one-way counterparts in Figures 7 and 8 respectively. We observe that both two-way protocols, AF and DF, achieve sum-rates that are larger than the rates of their one-way counterparts. Moreover, AF scheme has more pronounced improvement compared with DF. For the two-way sym- metric case considered here, the DF protocol is worse than AF protocol because the sum rate is dominated by the multiple-access sum rate. Intuitively we can say that for an asymmetric channel scenario, when the relay is in the vicinity of one terminal T1 or T2 (and thereby experi- ences a stronger channel gain than the other terminal), the DF scheme achieves the maximum sum rate which can be further improved by optimal choice of β.

4. RESOURCE ALLOCATION

The performance of wireless relay networks can be significantly improved by efficient man- agement of available radio resources. Mostly, resource management via power allocation is employed. We have discussed bidirectional relaying in the previous section, static resource allocation was assumed where all transmission phases are of same duration and all terminals have individual power constraints with balanced rates. Dynamic resource allocation has been investigated in (Agustin et al., 2008) in terms of phase durations, individual and sum-average power, and data rate. The system model employs a DF relay that applies superposition coding and takes into account the traffic asymmetry. It is assumed that the transmission is performed in frames of length υ with N channel uses and normalized bandwidth of unity. The duration of the two phases (MAC and BC) are denoted by v1 and v2 respectively. The two power constraints considered are maximum power and sum-average power (both denoted by P). The first constraint assumes that all terminals transmit with power P, whereas in second case the total average power used by the three terminals is considered to be P. The mutual information of different links assuming equal noise power at all terminals is given by

$$I_{1r}(P_1) = N\log\left(1+\frac{P_1|h_1|^2}{\sigma^2}\right) \tag{27}$$

$$I_{2r}(P_2) = N\log\left(1+\frac{P_2|h_2|^2}{\sigma^2}\right) \tag{28}$$

$$I_{MAC}(P_1,P_2) = N\log\left(1+\frac{P_1|h_1|^2}{\sigma^2}+\frac{P_2|h_2|^2}{\sigma^2}\right) \tag{29}$$

where I1r and I2r represent mutual information of T1 - R and T2 - RR links respectively, and IMAC is the mutual information at the relay when both terminals transmit simultaneously in the MAC phase. The signal received by the relay in MAC phase is given by

$$y_r[k] = \begin{cases} h_1[k]x_1[k]+h_2[k]x_2[k]+n_r[k] & \text{for} \quad 0\le k\le \upsilon_1 N \\ 0 & \text{for} \quad \upsilon_1 N\le k\le N. \end{cases} \tag{30}$$

Under superposition coding, the DF relay forwards one signal xr [k] intended to each destina- tion by distributing the total power between them as

$$x_r = \sqrt{\frac{\beta_1 P_r}{P_1}}x_1+\sqrt{\frac{\beta_2 P_r}{P_2}}x_2 \tag{31}$$

where β1 and β2 indicate the fraction of power allocated to each signal. The signal received by each destination in second phase is given by

$$y_1[k] = \begin{cases} 0 & \text{for} \quad 0\le k\le \upsilon_1 N \\ h_1[k]x_r[k]+n_1[k] & \text{for} \quad \upsilon_1 N\le k\le N \end{cases} \tag{32}$$

$$y_2[k] = \begin{cases} 0 & \text{for} \quad 0\le k\le \upsilon_1 N \\ h_2[k]x_r[k]+n_2[k] & \text{for} \quad \upsilon_1 N\le k\le N. \end{cases} \tag{33}$$

The optimal selection of phase duration, data rate of each terminal are found as the maximization of the following problem (Agustin et al., 2008):

$$arg \max_{\upsilon,R_1,R_2,P_1,P_2,P_r} \vartheta_1 R_1+\vartheta_2 R_2 \quad \text{s.t.} \begin{cases} (R_1,R_2)\in\rho(\upsilon) & \text{for} \quad 0\le \ell(\upsilon)\le 1 \\ \varphi(P_1,P_2,P_r)\le P & \text{for} \quad \zeta(R_1,R_2)=\kappa \end{cases} \tag{34}$$

where R1, R2 represents the rate transmitted by terminal T1, T2 respectively, v is a vector that contains the duration of different phases, function .(v) defines the linear connection between duration of phases, ρ(v) denotes the achievable rate region for a given v, function Φ(P1, P2, Pr) represents a combination of the transmitted power by the terminals considering the power constraints, function ζ(R1, R2) indicates a linear dependence between data rates R1 and R2. The achievable rate region boundary can be attained with optimum phase and rate selection (by adjusting the parameters θ1 and θ2).

The achievable rate region ρ(υ) for the two-way DF protocol, described under MAC (Cover & Thomas, 1991), is given by

$$\rho(v_1, v_2) = \begin{cases} R_1 \le \min\{v_1 I_{1r}(P_1), v_2 I_{2r}(\beta_1 P_r)\} \\ R_2 \le \min\{v_1 I_{2r}(P_2), v_2 I_{1r}(\beta_2 P_r)\} \\ R_1 + R_2 \le v_1 I_{MAC}(P_1, P_2) \end{cases} \tag{35}$$

with • (v1, v2) = v1 + v2. For terminals transmitting with their maximum power P, the maxi- mum power constraint can be expressed as

$$\Phi max\ (P1, P2, Pr\ )= \{P1 = P, P2 = P, Pr = P\}\ . \tag{36}$$

The power distribution at the relay satisfies 0 ≤ β1 + β2 ≤ 1. Hence the power allocation can be optimized at the relay only. For sum-average power constraint, each terminal uses a fraction of total power P which is controlled by variables δ and β as follows

$$\varphi_{avg}(P_1, P_2, P_r) = \left\{ P_1 = \frac{\delta_1 P}{v_1}, P_2 = \frac{\delta_2 P}{v_1}, P_r = \frac{P}{v_2} \right\}. \tag{37}$$

It has been shown in (Agustin et al., 2008) that the sum-average power constraint must satisfy

$$P1\ \upsilon 1 + P2\ \upsilon 1 + \sigma Pr\upsilon 2 = P \tag{38}$$

where σ = β1 + β2 so that δ1 + δ2 + β1 + β2 = 1. The data rates achieved on each link are connected through

$$\zeta(R1, R2)= R1 - \kappa R2 \le 0 \tag{39}$$

where κ is a positive real number accounts for the traffic asymmetry.

Under the sum-average power constraint the optimization problem for resource allocation is convex and has a unique solution. However for maximum power constraint, the problem has to be transformed into a convex one by introducing some auxiliary variables [see (Agustin et al., 2008) and references therein].

5. CODED BIDIRECTIONAL RELAYING

So far we have discussed the TWRC from cooperative communication perspectives with a major objective being compensation to make up for for the half-duplex loss. In a separate but significant development, the authors in (Ahlswede et al., 2000) have proposed the concept of network coding in which intermediate network nodes are allowed not only to route but also to mix and code the incoming data from multiple links. This reduces the amount of data transmissions in the network (thus improving the overall network throughput). Originally, the network coding concept was proposed for wired communication networks. Later it was applied to wireless communication networks by exploiting the broadcasting nature of wireless medium [it was used for relay networks for the first time in (Hao et al., 2007)]. Network coding has been proven to be a very effective solution to overcome the interuser interference in wireless networks because of its ability to combining the different signals instead of separating them from a traditional viewpoint.

Traditionally simultaneous transmission from T1 and T2 was avoided in order to simplify the medium access control, and to avoid the interference at the relay R. Thereby four phases were required to perform one round of information exchange between T1 and T2 through R. However, by applying the idea of network coding, the authors in (Wu et al., 2005) proposed a scheme to reduce the number of required phases from four to three as illustrated in Figure 9. In this scheme, T1 first transmits during first phase the message x1 to R consisting of bits b1(1), ..., b1(N) with N denoting the message length in bits, which are decoded. During the second phase, T2 transmits to R the message x2 consisting of bits b2(1), ..., b2(N), which R decodes. In the third phase, R broadcasts to T1 and T2 a new message xr consisting of bits br (n)'s, n = 1, ..., N, obtained by bit-wise exclusive-or (XOR) operation over b1(n)'s and b2(n)'s i.e., br(n)= b1(n) $\oplus$ b2(n), $\forall$n. Since T1 knows b1(n)'s, T1 can recover its desired message x2 by first decoding br(n) and then obtaining b2(n)'s of x2 as b1(n) br (n), $\forall$n. Similarly, T2 can recover x1. The same type of three-phase coded bidirectional relaying scheme was proposed independently in (Larsson et al., 2006). The resulting pre-log factor with respect to the sum-rate of this three-phase coded scheme is thus 2/3 compared to 1/2 for conventional half-duplex scheme. In this protocol, if a reliable direct link is possible, then the scheme may gain in additional diversity and often better coverage as discussed in (Kim et al., 2008).

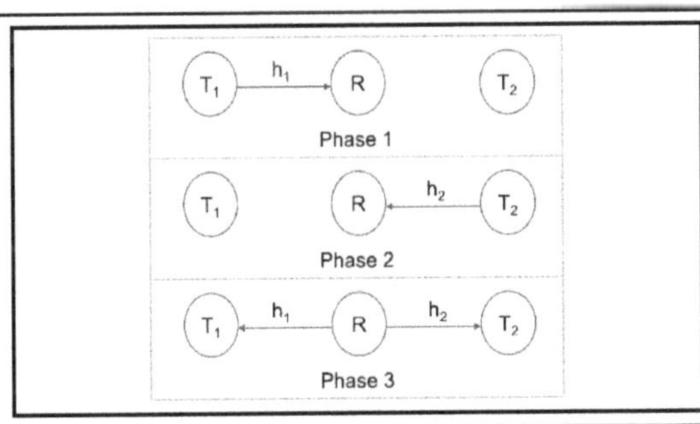

Fig. 9. Three-phase two-way relaying.

In (Popovski & Yomo, 2006); (Popovski & Yomo, 2007a); (Popovski & Yomo, 2007b), the authors reduce the number of required phases from three to two by allowing T1 and T2 to transmit simultaneously to R during the first phase, thereby eliminating the need for the second phase. This corresponds to the MAC phase of DF-TWRC (Rankov & Wittneben, 2007). The scheme proposed in (Katti et al., 2007a) is named as Analog Network Coding (ANC), while that in (Zhang et al., 2006) is referred to as Physical-layer Network Coding (PNC). These schemes differ in their relay operations, which are Amplify-and-Forward (AF) and Estimate- and-Forward (EF), respectively. In ANC, R simply amplifies the mixed signal received simultaneously from T1 and T2 and then broadcasts it to both. By subtracting the back-propagating self-interference, both T1 and T2 are able to receive their intended messages. Thus ANC scheme is similar to the AF-TWRC (Rankov & Wittneben, 2007). Compared to ANC, PNC (Zhang et al., 2006) performs more sophisticated operations than AF at R. Instead of decoding messages x1 from T1 and x2 from T2 separately in two different phases like in (Wu et al., 2005), the EF method estimates at R the bitwise XORs between b1(n)'s and b2(n)'s from the mixed signal received, and re-encodes the decoded bits into a new broadcasting message xr . Each of T1 and T2 then recovers the others message by the same decoding method discussed in (Wu et al., 2005).

Although the schemes proposed in these works are similar to AF- and DF-TWRC, they are inspired by network coding. The principle of network coding has been further investigated for the TWRC in (Hausl & Hagenauer, 2006); (Baik & Chung, 2008); (Cui et al., 2008a); (Cui et al., 2008b). It has been shown in (Katti et al., 2007b) that joint relaying and network coding achieves higher data rates as compared to routing at the relay. In (Kim et al., 2008), the authors compared the different half-duplex bidirectional DF relaying protocols and derived their performance bounds. Note that two-phase TWRC does not exploit spatial diversity advantage like conventional approach. Including the direct link would provide diversity gain but at the cost of spectral efficiency. Even more recently, the authors in (Li et al., 2009) analyze the outage performance of two-phase AF- and DF-TWRC under half-duplex constraint. They derived the exact closed-form expressions for the outage probabilities by considering network coding at the relay for DF case. Furthermore, they propose an adaptive bidirectional relaying protocol which switches between AF and DF to minimize the outage probability of the system. TWRC coupled with network coding is thus developing as a promising technology to combat interference and to improve throughput in wireless networks.

6. MIMO BIDIRECTIONAL RELAYING

It is well known that Multiple-Input Multiple-Output (MIMO) communication systems have the ability to enhance the channel capacity and link reliability without requiring an increase in power or bandwidth. In (Unger & Klein, 2007) it is proposed to extend two-way relaying to terminals with multiple antennas (leading to MIMO-TWRC). They investigate the average performance of MIMO-TWRC by using multiple antennas at the ralay terminal only. The proposed scheme exploits the fact that the relay R is a receiver as well as a transmitter in the dual-hop case, and hence assumes CSI at the R is not unreasonable. Like in a Time Division Duplex (TDD) system, CSI for receive and transmit processing can be obtained by directly estimating the channel from T1 to the R and from T1 to the R in the first phase, and then exploiting channel reciprocity in the second phase. Thereafter, the relay can perform spatial filtering to its receive and transmit signal. In (Han et al., 2008) the average sum rate improvement of two-way relaying is analyzed by deriving an upper and a lower bound for average sum rate of two-way relaying which was not derived in (Rankov & Wittneben, 2007). They also extend the work to the case when the source terminal and the destination terminal have two anten- nas each and the relay has only one antenna (in order to implement Alamouti's scheme). The proposed scheme achieves higher average sum rate compared to the single antenna case, and furthermore both the source and destination terminals achieve diversity of order two. The au- thors in (Zhang et al., 2009) analyze the capacity region for of the ANC/AF-based TWRC with linear processing (beamforming) at the relay with multiple antennas. They have also shown that the ANC/AF-based TWRC have a capacity gain over the DF-based TWRC for sufficiently large channel correlations and equal MAC and BC phase-durations.

In (Hammerstrom et al., 2007) the authors further extend the two-way relaying scheme of (Rankov & Wittneben, 2007) to the case when multiple antennas are used at all terminals (assuming the knowledge of transmit CSI at the DF relay). Figure 10 shows a set up for MIMO two-way relaying where all the terminals are equipped with M > 1 antennas.

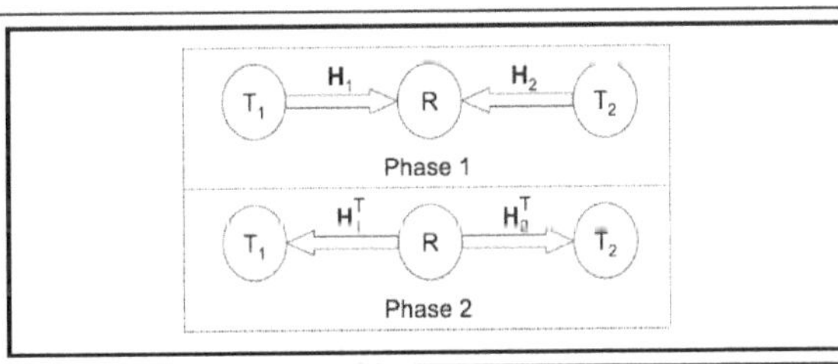

Fig. 10. MIMO two-way relay channel.

It is assumed that both T1 and T2 perfectly know (H1, H2, H1T and H2T) in the receiving mode, but not in the transmit mode. The relay R on the other hand has knowledge of both receive and transmit CSI. This is a reasonable assumption since the relay has to estimate the channels (H1 and H2) for decoding in the first phase and exploting channel reciprocity in the second phase (like in TDD system). Terminal T1 transmits vector x1 to T2 whereas T2 transmits vector x2 to T1 respectively in two phases. Frequency flat slow fading and perfect synchronization is assumed between all terminals. The signal received at the relay in the first phase is given by

$$yr = H1x1 + H2x2 + nr \qquad (40)$$

where H1 and H2 are the M M channel matrices (with each element being i.i.d. complex Gaussian with zero mean and unit variance) that remain constant during the block transmission, x1 and x2 are M × 1 symbol vectors with power P1 and P2 respectively, and nr ~ (0, σ2IM) is the M × 1 complex AWGN vector.

During first phase, the relay decodes the messages from both terminals T1 and T2. Using a Gaussian codebook, the achievable rates of both terminals are theoretically described by the MIMO-MAC (Cover & Thomas, 1991), which imposes constraints on the individual first- phase rates R1,I and R2,I , as well as the first-phase sum rate R1,I + R2,I for successful decoding at the destination terminal:

$$R_{1,I} \le I_{1,I} = \log \left| \mathbf{I} + \frac{P_1}{M\sigma_r^2} \mathbf{H}_1 \mathbf{H}_1^H \right| \tag{41}$$

$$R_{2,I} \le I_{2,I} = \log \left| \mathbf{I} + \frac{P_2}{M\sigma_r^2} \mathbf{H}_2 \mathbf{H}_2^H \right| \tag{42}$$

$$R_{1,I} + R_{2,I} \le I_I = \log \left| \mathbf{I} + \frac{\frac{P_1}{M}\mathbf{H}_1\mathbf{H}_1^H + \frac{P_2}{M}\mathbf{H}_2\mathbf{H}_2^H}{\sigma_r^2} \right| . \tag{43}$$

In the second phase, the relay applies bit-level XOR precoding on decoded messages. The relay therefore broadcasts the vector xr with power Pr . The received signals at T1 and T2 are given by

y1 = HT xr + n1 (44)

y2 = HT xr + n2 (45)

where n1 ~ CN (0, σ,2IM) and nr ~ CN (0, σ2IM) are the complex AWGN M × 1 vectors at T1 and T2 respectively. Since both destinations have to be able to decode xr , the maximum data rate in the second phase is given by

$$I_{II} = \min \{ I_{1,II}, I_{2,II} \} \tag{46}$$

where

$$I_{1,II} = \log \left| \mathbf{I} + \frac{1}{\sigma_1^2} \mathbf{H}_1^T \Lambda_r \mathbf{H}_1^* \right| \tag{47}$$

$$I_{2,II} = \log \left| \mathbf{I} + \frac{1}{\sigma_2^2} \mathbf{H}_2^T \Lambda_r \mathbf{H}_2^* \right| \tag{48}$$

{where Λ_r ={xixr^H} and trace$(\Lambda_r) = P_r$. The maximum sum-rate of this MIMO two-way relaying scheme is given by (Hammerstrom et al., 2007)

Rsum = 1 min {II , min {I1,I , I2,II} + min {I2,I , I1,II}} . (49)

The above rate expression can be optimized by exploiting CSI knowledge at the relay subject to the relay transmit power constraint. This is achieved by maximizing the data rate in the second phase as follows

III,opt = max min {I1,II , I2,II} (50)

s.t. trace (Λr) = Pr .

This optimization problem is independent of first phase data rates and can be solved by semidefinite programming method by assuming Λr to be positive semidefinite [see (Ham- merstrom et al., 2007) and references therein].

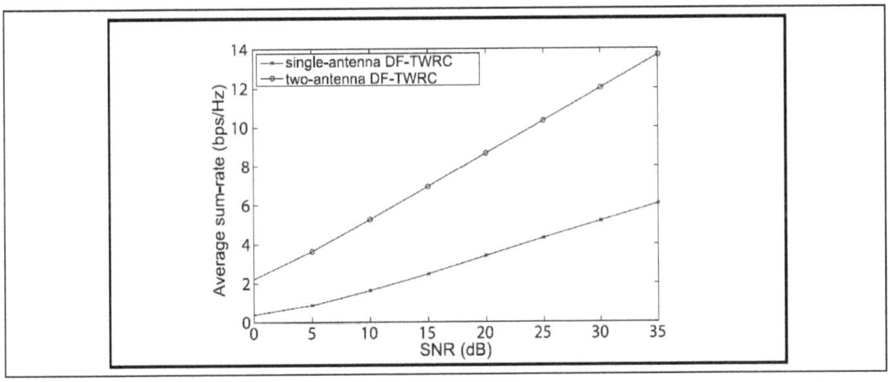

Fig. 11. Average sum-rate of two-antenna DF-TWRC with XOR precoding compared to one- antenna case.

Figure 11 compares the average sum-rate obtained (assuming Gaussian codebook) for DF- TWRC using XOR precoding with one and two antennas at the terminals T1 and T2. Rayleigh fading is assumed, and the elements of the channel matrices H1 and H2 are zero mean and unit variance complex Gaussian random variables. All nodes use the same transmit power P1 = P2 = Pr = P and are assumed to have the same noise variance σ12 = σ22 = σr2 = σ2. The SNR is defined as P/ σ2. We simulated 10000 random channels for each value in Figure 11. We observe that there is considerable improvement in sum-rate by using two antennas at each node compared to the single antenna case.

Further, the authors in (Hammerstrom et al., 2007) compared two approaches of combining the messages in the second phase at the relay (the superposition coding and the XOR pre- coding) and showed that MIMO-TWRC achieves substantial improvement in spectral effi- ciency compared to conventional relaying with or without transmit CSI at the relay. They also showed that the difference in sum-rate compared to the case where no CSIT is used increases with increasing ratio between number of relay antennas and number of node antennas. Also XOR precoding always achieves higher minimum user rates than superposition coding if CSIT is used. In (Oechtering & Boche, 2007) the authors propose transmit strategies in a MIMO two-way DF relaying scenario with individual power constraints. The optimal relay transmit strategy is given by two point-to-point water-filling solutions which are coupled by the re- lay power distribution. The diversity-multiplexing trade-off analysis for the MIMO-TWRC is dealt in (Gunduz et al., 2008). In (Yang & Chun, 2008), the transmission rate is improved by using the generalized Schur decomposition-based MIMO-TWRC.

7. BIDIRECTIONAL RELAYING WITH MULTIPLE RELAYS

This section extends the theory of single-relay two-way communication to one level up in the network hierarchy by employing multiple relays. In two-way multiple relay channel two terminals T1 and T2 exchange information with the help of M relay terminals in two phases. Dedicated multiple relays can be utilized to relay copies of the transmitted information to the destination such that each copy experiences independent channel fading, hence providing diversity gain to the system. Such communication strategy is best suited for applications in wireless ad-hoc networks, cellular scenarios, and wireless backhaul interconnections.

7.1 Distributed Space-Time Coding

The idea of space-time coding devised for MIMO systems can be applied to a wireless relay network [see (Jing & Hassibi, 2006)] by having the relays that cooperate distributively. The concept of distributed space-time coding (Jing & Hassibi, 2006) is investigated for two-way multiple relay channel in (Cui et al., 2008c). The authors in (Cui et al., 2008c) propose a new type of relaying scheme called partial DF for distributed TWRC where each relay removes part of the noise beore relaying information in the broadcast phase. They suggest two-way relaying protocols using Linear Dispersion (LD) codes that operate over two time slots. In this scheme, two terminals T1 and T2 communicate through multiple relays Ri , i = 1, ..., M. Each half-duplex terminal is equipped with a single antenna. Terminal Tj, j ∈ [1, 2], transmits the signal vector sj = [sj1, ..., sjT]T where sjt ∈ Am, t = 1, ..., T, Am is a finite constellation with average power of unity, and T is the length of each time slot. Hence, E {sjH sj} = T. The average power of terminal Tj is Pj and each relay has the equal power Pr /M so that the total power of all the relays is Pr . The noise variance is assumed to be unity at every node.

During the first phase, both terminals T1 and T2 transmit their message to the relays. The signal received by the ith relay is given by

$$\mathbf{y}_{ri} = \sqrt{2P_1}h_{1i}\mathbf{s}_1 + \sqrt{2P_2}h_{2i}\mathbf{s}_2 + \mathbf{n}_{ri} \tag{51}$$

where hji ~ CN (0, 1) represents the channel gain between terminal Tj and relay Ri , nri is the T × 1 vector representing the AWGN at the ith relay. The source transmit power is assumed to be $\sqrt{2P_j}$ because each source terminal transmits every two time slots. During second time slot, the ith relay processes yri and transmits sri scaled by g to maintain average power Pr . The signal received by jth terminal is given as

$$\mathbf{y}_j = \sum_{i=1}^{M} g h_{ji}\mathbf{s}_{ri} + \mathbf{n}_j, \quad j = 1, 2, \tag{52}$$

where nj is the AWGN vector at the jth terminal.

7.1.1 2-AF

In this scheme $\mathbf{s}_{ri}$ is obtained by precoding $\mathbf{y}_{ri}$ with a unitary matrix $\mathbf{W}_{ri}$ and then scaled by $g = \sqrt{\frac{2P_r}{M(2P_1+2P_2+1)}}$. The signal received at terminal T_2 is given by

$$\mathbf{y}_2 = g\left(\sqrt{2P_1}\mathbf{S}_1\mathbf{h}_1^{'} + \sqrt{2P_2}\mathbf{S}_2\mathbf{h}_2^{'}\right) + \mathbf{z}_2 = g\left(\sqrt{2P_1}\mathbf{H}_1\mathbf{s}_1 + \sqrt{2P_2}\mathbf{H}_2\mathbf{s}_2\right) + \mathbf{z}_2 \tag{53}$$

where $\mathbf{S}_j = [\mathbf{W}_{ri}\mathbf{s}_j, ..., \mathbf{W}_{rM}\mathbf{s}_j]$, $\mathbf{h}_1^{'} = [h_{11}h_{21}, ..., h_{1M}h_{2M}]^T$, $\mathbf{h}_2^{'} = [h_{21}^2, ..., h_{2M}^2]^T$, $\mathbf{z}_2 = g\sum_{i=1}^{M} h_{2i}\mathbf{W}_{ri}\mathbf{n}_{ri} + \mathbf{n}_2$, $\mathbf{H}_1 = g\sum_{i=1}^{M} h_{1i}h_{2i}\mathbf{W}_{ri}$, $\mathbf{H}_2 = g\sum_{i=1}^{M} h_{2i}^2\mathbf{W}_{ri}$.

Since terminal T_2 knows the back propagating signal $\mathbf{s}_2$, the maximum-likelihood (ML) decoding of $\mathbf{s}_1$ is obtained as (Cui et al., 2008c)

$$\hat{\mathbf{s}}_1 = arg \min_{\tilde{\mathbf{s}}_1 \in \mathcal{A}_1^M} \left\| \mathbf{y}_2 - g\left(\sqrt{2P_1}\mathbf{H}_1\tilde{\mathbf{s}}_1 + \sqrt{2P_2}\mathbf{H}_2\mathbf{s}_2\right)\right\|^2. \tag{54}$$

Similarly, ML decoding of s2 is performed at terminal T1. The disadvantage of this scheme is that it amplifies the relay noise.

7.1.2 Partial DF I

This protocol overcomes the drawback of 2-AF scheme (Cui et al., 2008c) by allowing each relay Ri to first decode s1 and s2 via the ML decoder

$$\{\hat{\mathbf{s}}_{1i}, \hat{\mathbf{s}}_{2i}\} = arg \min_{\tilde{\mathbf{s}}_1 \in \mathcal{A}_1^M, \tilde{\mathbf{s}}_2 \in \mathcal{A}_2^M} \left\| \mathbf{y}_{ri} - \sqrt{2P_1}h_{1i}\mathbf{W}_{ri}\tilde{\mathbf{s}}_1 - \sqrt{2P_2}h_{2i}\mathbf{W}_{ri}\tilde{\mathbf{s}}_2 \right\|^2. \tag{55}$$

The number of unknowns in the above equation is twice the number of equations, this making the error probability high. For this reason it has been suggested in (Cui et al., 2008c) that instead of sending $\hat{\mathbf{s}}_{1i}$ and $\hat{\mathbf{s}}_{2i}$ directly, each relay transmits

$$\mathbf{s}_{ri} = \mathbf{W}_{ri}\left(\sqrt{2P_1}h_{1i}\hat{\mathbf{s}}_{1i} + \sqrt{2P_2}h_{2i}\hat{\mathbf{s}}_{2i}\right) \tag{56}$$

scaled by $g = \sqrt{\frac{P_r}{M(P_1+P_2)}}$. Thus the relays remove noise from the received signal without dealing with the channel effects. If $Pr(\Delta\mathbf{s}_{1i}, \Delta\mathbf{s}_{2i})$ represents the pairwise error probability at the ith relay, where $\Delta\mathbf{s}_{1i} = \mathbf{s}_1 - \hat{\mathbf{s}}_{1i}$ and $\Delta\mathbf{s}_{2i} = \mathbf{s}_2 - \hat{\mathbf{s}}_{2i}$, then the ML decoding at T_2 is given as (Cui et al., 2008c)

$$\hat{\mathbf{s}}_1 = arg \max_{\tilde{\mathbf{s}}_1 \in \mathcal{A}_1^M} \sum_{\Delta\mathbf{s}_{1i}, \Delta\mathbf{s}_{2i}} \prod_{i=1}^{M} Pr(\Delta\mathbf{s}_{1i}, \Delta\mathbf{s}_{2i}) \exp\left\{-\left\|\mathbf{y}_2 + \mathbf{y}' - \mathbf{y}''\right\|^2\right\} \tag{57}$$

where $\mathbf{y}' = g\sum_{i=1}^{M} \mathbf{W}_{ri}\left(\sqrt{2P_1}h_{1i}\Delta\mathbf{s}_{1i} + \sqrt{2P_2}h_{2i}\Delta\mathbf{s}_{2i}\right)$ and $\mathbf{y}'' = g\left(\sqrt{2P_1}\mathbf{H}_1\tilde{\mathbf{s}}_1 + \sqrt{2P_2}\mathbf{H}_2\mathbf{s}_2\right)$.

It is difficult to implement the above decoder directly when either number M or constellation size is large. At high SNR, $\prod_{i=1}^{M} Pr(\Delta\mathbf{s}_{1i}, \Delta\mathbf{s}_{2i})$ is dominated by $\Delta\mathbf{s}_{1i} = \mathbf{0}, \Delta\mathbf{s}_{2i} = \mathbf{0}$. Therefore the ML decoding at terminal T_2 can be approximated as follows

$$\hat{\mathbf{s}}_1 = arg \min_{\tilde{\mathbf{s}}_1 \in \mathcal{A}_1^M} \left\| \mathbf{y}_2 - g\left(\sqrt{2P_1}\mathbf{H}_1\tilde{\mathbf{s}}_1 + \sqrt{2P_2}\mathbf{H}_2\mathbf{s}_2\right)\right\|^2. \tag{58}$$

Similarly, ML decoding at terminal T1 can be approximated (Cui et al., 2008c).

7.1.3 Partial DF II

In both AF and *partial* DF I schemes, a weighted sum of symbols is transmitted from two terminals. This causes wastage of power since each destination knows the back-propagating signal. In *partial* DF II (Cui et al., 2008c), components are superimposed via modular arithmetic. Let the size of constellation $\mathcal{A}_j$ be Z_j with $\mathcal{A}_j(q)$ representing the qth element of $\mathcal{A}_j$, where $j = 1, 2$ and $q = 0, \ldots, Z_j - 1$. Consider $\mathbf{u}_1$ and $\mathbf{u}_2$ such that $\mathcal{A}_1(\mathbf{u}_1) = \mathbf{s}_1$ and $\mathcal{A}_2(\mathbf{u}_2) = \mathbf{s}_2$. With the setting $Z = \max\{Z_1, Z_2\}$, it can be assume that $Z_1 \geq Z_2$ without loss of generality. Under this protocol, each relay obtains $\hat{\mathbf{s}}_{1i}, \hat{\mathbf{s}}_{2i}$ from Equation (55) as in *partial* DF I. If $\mathcal{A}_1(\hat{\mathbf{u}}_{1i}) = \hat{\mathbf{s}}_{1i}$ and $\mathcal{A}_2(\hat{\mathbf{u}}_{2i}) = \hat{\mathbf{s}}_{2i}$ then each relay transmits

$$\mathbf{s}_{ri} = \mathbf{W}_{ri}\mathcal{A}_1\left(mod\left(\hat{\mathbf{u}}_{1i} + \hat{\mathbf{u}}_{2i}, Z\right)\right) \tag{59}$$

where "*mod*" stand for the componentwise modular operation and $g = g_i = \sqrt{\frac{2P_r}{M}}$. Since fading channels are considered, the probability that there exists a pair of vectors $\{\mathbf{u}_1, \mathbf{u}_2\}$ and $\{\hat{\mathbf{u}}_1, \hat{\mathbf{u}}_2\}$ such that $\sqrt{2P_1}h_{1i}\mathcal{A}_1(\mathbf{u}_1) + \sqrt{2P_2}h_{2i}\mathcal{A}_2(\mathbf{u}_2) = \sqrt{2P_1}h_{1i}\mathcal{A}_1(\hat{\mathbf{u}}_1) + \sqrt{2P_2}h_{2i}\mathcal{A}_2(\hat{\mathbf{u}}_2)$ is very small. It has been shown in (Cui et al., 2008) that the AF protocol achieves the diversity order $min\{M, T\}\left(1 - \frac{\log\log P}{\log P}\right)$, where P is the total power of the network whereas the *partial* DF II protocol achieves a diversity order M when $T \geq M$.

7.2 Distributed Relay Selection Scheme

A distributed relay selection strategy is proposed in (Ding et al., 2009) that selects the best suited relay for realizing PNC in a dense relays network. In this transmission scheme, both T1 and T2 broadcast their information to all M relays simultaneously during first phase. The signal received at the ith relay Ri is given by

$$y_{ri} = \sqrt{P}h_{1i}s_1 + \sqrt{P}h_{2i}s_2 + n_{ri} \tag{60}$$

where P is the source transmission power, sj represents the unit-power signal transmitted by the jth source, and hji represents the channel gain between the jth source and the ith relay. The channel model for frequency flat Rayleigh fading is considered as

$$h_{ji} = \frac{\hbar_{ji}}{\sqrt{d_{ji}^{\alpha}}} \tag{61}$$

where h¯ji accounts for the channel fading characteristics due to the rich scattering environ- ment, dji represents the distance between the jth source and the ith relay, and α is the path loss exponent. It is reasonable to assume that each relay terminal has its local channel information under channel reciprocity condition. This local channel information can be exploited in realiz- ing a distributed strategy of relay selection to improve the system performance. For instance, consider that the relay Rb has been chosen as the best relay with corresponding channels h1b and h2b. In the second phase the best relay Rb performs AF operation and transmits the mixed signal given by

$$s_{rb} = \frac{\sqrt{P}h_{1b}s_1 + \sqrt{P}h_{2b}s_2 + n_{rb}}{\sqrt{P|h_{1b}|^2 + P|h_{2b}|^2 + \sigma^2}}\sqrt{P} \tag{62}$$

to the two destinations. After removing the back-propagating self interference, the signal received at jth terminal is given by

$$y_j = \frac{\sqrt{P}h_{jb}}{\sqrt{P|h_{1b}|^2 + P|h_{2b}|^2 + \sigma^2}}\left(\sqrt{P}h_{lb}s_l + n_{rb}\right) + n_j. \tag{63}$$

Therefore the mutual information between the lth source and jth destination is given by

$$I_{jl} = \log\left(1 + \frac{\gamma^2|h_{1b}|^2|h_{2b}|^2}{2\gamma|h_{jb}|^2 + \gamma|h_{lb}|^2 + 1}\right), \forall \quad j \neq l \quad \& \quad j, l \in [1, 2], \tag{64}$$

where Γ = P/σ2 represents the SNR. Relay selection (Ding et al., 2009) is performed in medium access layer. It has been claimed that the two destinations have different prefer- ences but they do not tend to contradict each other. The relay with channels yielding large I12 also has channels that give a large value for I21, if not exactly the maximum. The best relay is selected based on the following criterion

$$\frac{|h_{1b}|^2|h_{2b}|^2}{2\gamma|h_{1b}|^2 + \gamma|h_{2b}|^2 + 1} \tag{65}$$

that maximizes the value of I12. Then for this selected relay, the mutual information for second source, I21 is determined. The relay selected in such a way is suboptimal for the second source and hence some performance loss for the second source can be expected. The outage probability for this scheme (Ding et al., 2009) at high SNR is

$$Pr[I_{jl} < \mathcal{R}] = \frac{[(d_{jb}^{\alpha} + 2d_{lb}^{\alpha})(2^{\mathcal{R}} - 1)]^M}{\gamma^M}. \tag{66}$$

It is clear from Equation (66) that the proposed transmission scheme in (Ding et al., 2009) has the advantage of diversity of order M. While the authors in (Ding et al., 2009) dealt with the relay selection scheme for the specific case of PNC-based TWRC, the problem is relevent in all TWRC based links.

8. SUMMARY AND FUTURE DIRECTIONS

Cooperative relaying has evolved in recent years as a powerful tool to enhance the reliability and throughput of wireless radio networks. The basic research challenge is to design spec- trally efficient relaying schemes for better utilization of the available resources like power and spectrum. This chapter examines various half-duplex cooperative relaying protocols and related performance metrics. Two-way relaying is proposed as an effective strategy for conserving radio resources in wireless networks, allowing simultaneous transmission of both uplink and downlink over the same channel resources. Numerous unresolved questions persist concerning the channels examined to date. The research predominantly focuses on slow frequency flat fading scenarios; nevertheless, performance analysis for fast and frequency selective fading in two-way relay channels requires attention. The theoretical capacity limits or attainable rate regions of TWRC require further development for clustered and dispersed scenarios. The documented protocols continue to experience performance degradation relative to the predicted limits. Improved code architectures with manageable complexity must be urgently developed to address the aforementioned difficulty. MIMO bidirectional relaying systems have gained traction; nonetheless, techniques like as beamforming, distributed coding, and relay selection require further investigation. Achieving perfect synchronization among several radios is arguably the most challenging endeavor for bidirectional traffic in a cooperative network. Cooperative relaying techniques are anticipated to be integrated into future wireless networks, as established in the IEEE 802.16j (WiMAX) standard. Significant research endeavors are required to develop functional systems predicated on bidirectional collaboration for expansive wireless networks. Significant research interest is presently directed towards evaluating whether cooperative technology facilitates the deployment of cognitive radio..

REFERENCES

1. Agustin, A.; Vidal, J. & Munoz, O. (2008). Protocols and resource allocation for the two-way relay channel with half-duplex terminals. Submitted to IEEE Transactions on Wireless Communications, Paper-TW-Oct-08-1427, Oct. 2008.
2. Ahlswede, R.; Cai, N.; Li, S.Y.R. & Yeung, R.W. (2000). Network information flow. IEEE Trans- actions on Information Theory, Vol. 46, No. 4, July 2000, 1204-1216.
3. Avestimehr, A.S.; Sezgin, A. & Tse, D.N.C. (2008). Approximate capacity of the two- way relay channel: A deterministic approach. Available at http://arxiv.org/PS- cache/arxiv/pdf/0808/0808.3145v1.pdf, Aug. 2008.
4. Baik, I.J. & Chung, S.Y. (2008). Network coding for two-way relay channels using lattices. Proceedings of IEEE International Conference on Communications (ICC), 3898-3902, June 2008.
5. Chen, M. & Yener, A. (2008). Multiuser two-way relaying for interference limited systems. Proceedings of IEEE International Conference on Communications (ICC), 3883-3887, May 2008.

6. Cover, T.M. & Gamal, A.A.E. (1979). Capacity theorems for the relay channel. IEEE Transactions on Information Theory, Vol. 25, No. 5, Sep. 1979, 572-584.

7. Cover, T.M. & Thomas, J.A. (1991). Elements of Information Theory, ISBN 0-471-06259-6, New York: Wiley, 1991.

8. Cui, T.; Ho, T. & Kliewer, J. (2008a). Memoryless relay strategies for two-way relay channels: Performance analysis and optimization. Proceedings of IEEE International Conference on Communications (ICC), May 2008.

9. Cui, T.; Gao, F.F. & Tellambura, C. (2008b). Physical layer differential network coding for two-way relay channels. Proceedings of IEEE Global Communications Conference (GLOBE- COM), New Orleans, Nov. 2008, LA, USA.

10. Cui, T.; Gao, F.F.; Ho, T. & Nallanathan, A. (2008c). Distributed space-time coding for two-way wireless relay networks. Proceedings of IEEE International Conference on Communica- tions (ICC), Beijing, May 2008, China.

11. Ding, Z.; Leung, K.K.; Goeckel, D. & Towsley, D. (2009). On the study of network coding with diversity. IEEE Transactions on Wireless Communications, Vol. 8, No. 3, Mar. 2009, 1247-1259.

12. Esli, C. & Wittneben, A. (2008). One- and two-way decode-and-forward relaying for wire- less multiuser MIMO networks. Proceedings of IEEE Global Communications Conference (GLOBECOM), New Orleans, Nov. 2008, LA, USA.

13. Gao, F.; Zhang, R. & Liang, Y.C. (2008). On channel estimation for amplify-and-forward two- way relay networks. Proceedings of IEEE Global Communications Conference (GLOBE- COM), New Orleans, Nov. 2008, LA, USA.

14. Gunduz, D.; Goldsmith, A. & Vincent Poor, H. (2008). MIMO two-way relay chan- nel: diversity-multiplexing tradeoff analysis. Available at http://arxiv.org/PS- cache/arxiv/pdf/0812/0812.3642v1.pdf, Dec. 2008.

15. Hammerstrom,I.; Kuhn, M.; Esli, C.; Zhao, J. ; Wittneben, A. & Bauch, G. (2007). MIMO two- way relaying with transmit CSI at the relay. Proceedings of IEEE Workshop on Signal Processing Advances in Wireless Communications (SPAW), June 2007, Finland.

16. Han, Y.; Ting, S.H.; Ho, C.K. & Chin, W.H. (2008). High rate two-way amplify-and-forward half-duplex relaying with OSTBC. Proceedings of IEEE Vehicular Technology Conference (VTC), Marina Bay, 2426-2430, May 2008, Singapore.

17. Hao, Y.; Goeckel, D.; Ding, Z.; Towsley, D.& Leung, K.K. (2007). Achievable rates for network coding on the exchange channel. Proceedings of IEEE Military Communications Confer- ence (MILCOM), Orlando, 371-382, Oct. 2007, Florida.

18. Hausl, C. & Hagenauer, J. (2006). Iterative network and channel decoding for the two-way relay channel. Proceedings of IEEE International Conference on Communications (ICC), 1568-1573, June 2006.

19. Ho, C.K.; Zhang, R. & Liang, Y.C. (2008). Two-way relaying over OFDM: Optimized tone per- mutation and power allocation. Proceedings of IEEE International Conference on Com- munications (ICC), 3908-3912, May 2008.

20. Jing, Y. & Hassibi, B. (2006). Distributed space-time coding in wireless relay networks. IEEE Transactions on Wireless Communications, Vol. 5, No. 12, Dec. 2006, 3524-3536, ISSN 1536-1276.

21. Jitvanichphaibool, K. ; Zhang, R. & Liang, Y.C. (2008). Optimal resource allocation for two- way relay-assisted OFDMA. Proceedings of IEEE Global Communications Conference (GLOBECOM), New Orleans, Nov. 2008, LA, USA.

22. Katti, S.; Gollakota, S. & Katabi, D. (2007a). Embracing wireless interference: Analog network coding. Proceedings of Conference on Applications, Technologies, Architectures, and Proto- cols for Computer Communications, 397-408, ISBN 978-1-59593-713-1, Kyoto, Feb. 2007, Japan.

23. Katti, S.; Maric, I.; Goldsmith, A.; Katabi, D. & Medard, M. (2007b). Joint relaying and network coding in wireless networks. Proceedings of IEEE International Symposium on Informa- tion Theory, Nice, June 2007, France.

24. Kim, S.J.; Mitran, P. & Tarokh, V. (2008). Performance bounds for bi-directional coded coop- eration protocols. IEEE Transactions on Information Theory, Vol. 54, No. 11, Nov. 2008 , 5235-5241.

25. Laneman, J.N.; Wornell, G.W. & Tse, D.N.C. (2004). Cooperative diversity in wireless net- works: Efficient protocols and outage behavior. IEEE Transactions on Information The- ory, Vol. 50, No. 12, Dec. 2004, 3062-3080, ISSN 0018-9448.

26. Larsson, P.; Johansson, N. & Sunell, K.E. (2006). Coded bidirectional relaying. Proceedings of IEEE Vehicular Technology Conference (VTC), 851-855, ISBN 1-7803-9392-9, Melbourne, May 2006, Australia.

27. Li, Q.; Ting, S.H.; Pandharipande, A. & Han, Y. (2009). Adaptive two-way relaying and outage analysis. IEEE Transactions on Wireless Communications, Vol. 8, No. 6, June 2009.

28. Meulen, E.C. (1971). Three-terminal communication channels. Adv. Appl. Probab., Vol. 3, No. 1, 120-154, 1971.

29. Nam, W.; Chung, S.Y. & Yong H.L. (2008). Capacity bounds for two-way relay channels. Pro- ceedings of IEEE International Zurich Seminar on Communications, 2008.

30. Oechtering, T.J. & Boche, H. (2007). Optimal transmit strategies in multi-antenna bidirectional relaying. Proceedings of IEEE Intern. Conf. on Acoustics, Speech, and Signal Processing (ICASSP), Honolulu, Hawaii, Apr. 2007, USA.

31. Oechtering, T.J.; Schnurr, C.; Bjelakovic, I. & Boche, H. (2008). Broadcast capacity region of two-phase bidirectional relaying. IEEE Transactions on Information Theory, Vol. 54, No. 1, Jan. 2008, 454-458.
32. Popovski, P. & Yomo, H. (2006). Bi-directional amplification of throughput in a wireless multi- hop network. Proceedings of IEEE Vehicular Technology Conference (VTC), 588-593, ISBN 1-7803-9392-9, Melbourne, May 2006, Australia.
33. Popovski, P. & Yomo, H. (2007a). Wireless network coding by amplify-and-forward for bi- directional traffic flows. Proc. IEEE Communication Letters, Vol. 11, No. 1, Jan. 2007, 16-18, ISSN 1089-7798.
34. Popovski, P. & Yomo, H. (2007b). Physical network coding in two-way wireless relay channels. Proceedings of IEEE International Conference on Communications (ICC), 707-712, ISBN 1- 4244-0353-7, Glasgow, June 2007, Scotland.
35. Rankov, B. & Wittneben, A. (2006). Achievable rate regions for the two-way relay channel. Proceedings of IEEE International Symposium on Information Theory, Seattle, 2006, WA. Rankov, B. & Wittneben, A. (2007). Spectral efficient protocols for half-duplex relay channels. IEEE Journal on Selected Areas in Communications, Vol. 25, No. 2, Feb. 1979, 379-389, ISSN 0733-8716.
36. Sendonaris, A.; Erkip, E. & Aazhang, B.(2003). User cooperation diversity-Part I: System de- scription. IEEE Transactions on Communications, Vol. 51, No. 11, Nov. 2003, 1927-1938, ISSN 0090-6778.
37. Shannon, C.E. (1961). Two-way communication channels. Proc. 4th Berkeley Symp. Math. Stat. and Prob., Vol. 1, 1961, 611-644, UC Press, Berkeley.
38. Unger, T. & Klein, A. (2007). Linear transceive filters for relay stations with multiple antennas in the two-way relay channel. Proceedings of 16th IST Mobile and Wireless Communica- tions Summit, Budapest, July 2007, Hungary.
39. Vaze,R. & Heath Jr., R.W. (2008). To code or not to code in multi-hop relay channels. available at http://arxiv.org/abs/0805.3164, May, 2008.
40. Wu, Y.; Chou, P. & Kung, S.Y. (2005). Information exchange in wireless networks with net- work coding and physical-layer broadcast. Proceedings of 39th Annual Conference on Information Sciences and Systems (CISS), Baltimore, Mar. 2005, MD.
41. Yang, H.J. & Chun,J. (2008). Generalized Schur decomposition-based two-way relaying for wireless MIMO systems. Proceedings of IEEE Global Communications Conference (GLOBECOM), New Orleans, Nov. 2008, LA, USA.

42. Zhang, S.; Liew, S.C. & Lam, P.P. (2006). Physical-layer network coding. Proceedings of the 12th Annual International Conference on Mobile Computing and Networking, 358-365, ISBN 1-59593-286-0, Los Angeles, CA, Sept. 2006, USA.

43. Zhang, R.; Liang, Y.C.; Chai, C.C. & Cui, S. (2009). Optimal beamforming for two-way multi- antenna relay channel with analogue network coding. IEEE Journal on Selected Areas in Communications, Vol. 27, No. 5, June 2009, 699-712.

44. Zhao, J.; Kuhn, M.; Wittneben, A. & Bauch, G. (2008). Self-interference aided channel estima- tion in two-way relaying systems. Proceedings of IEEE Global Communications Confer- ence (GLOBECOM), New Orleans, Nov. 2008, LA, USA.

16 Chapter

A NOVEL AMPLIFY-AND-FORWARD RELAY CHANNEL MODEL FOR MOBILE-TO-MOBILE FADING CHANNELS UNDER LINE-OF-SIGHT CONDITIONS

1. INTRODUCTION: AN OVERVIEW

M2M communications within cooperative networks have garnered significant attention among several new wireless technologies in recent years. The primary motivation for integrating M2M communications with cooperative networks is the potential to enhance link quality (diversity gain), extend network range, and augment overall system capacity. M2M cooperative wireless networks utilize the cooperation of single-antenna mobile stations to share their antennae, so creating a virtual multiple-input multiple-output (MIMO) system in a multi-user context (Dohler, 2003). In these networks, cooperative diversity (Laneman et al., 2004; Sendonaris et al., 2003a;b) is accomplished by relaying the signal from a mobile station to the ultimate destination through other mobile stations within the network. To address the challenges encountered in the creation of such systems, a comprehensive understanding of the fundamental properties of multipath fading channels is necessary.. Therefore, the aim of this chapter is to develop a flexible M2M fading channel model for relay-based cooperative networks and to analyze its statistical properties. This newly developed model would help communication system designers to investigate the overall performance of cooperative communication systems.

To date, M2M amplify-and-forward relay fading channels have been studied only for particular communication scenarios, either presuming NLOS or partial LOS propagation conditions. Research by Patel et al. (2006) demonstrates that in NLOS propagation conditions, the M2M amplify-and-forward relay fading channel can be characterized as a double Rayleigh fading channel (Erceg et al., 1997; Kovacs et al., 2002). Inspired by the research on double Rayleigh fading channels for keyhole channels (Almers et al., 2006), the double Nakagami-m fading channel model was subsequently introduced (Shin & Lee, 2004). Additionally, in amplify-and-forward relay scenarios, the M2M fading channel in line-of-sight conditions can be represented as a double Rice fading channel (Talha & Pätzold, 2007a) and/or as an SLDS fading channel (Talha & Pätzold, 2007b). Moreover, M2M fading channels in cooperative networks can be effectively represented by the multiple scattering idea (Andersen, 2002).

In situations characterized by multiple scattering in radio propagation, the received signal consists of a summation of single, double, or often multiple dispersed components. This chapter models the amplify-and-forward relay fading channel as a second-order scattering channel, comprising solely the single and double scattered components (Salo et al., 2006). This approach is novel as it expands the NLSS (Salo et al., 2006) and SLSS (Salo et al., 2006) channel models into an MLSS channel model (Talha & Pätzold, 2008b) by integrating multiple line-of-sight components across all transmission links, specifically in the direct link between the source mobile station and the destination mobile station, as well as in the link through the mobile relay. Additionally, a significant aspect of the proposed MLSS channel model for M2M fading channels is its incorporation of other established channel models as specific instances, such as the double Rayleigh model, the double Rice model, the SLDS model, the NLSS model, and the SLSS model. We derive an analytical equation for the probability density function (PDF) of the MLSS process, as well as the PDF of the associated phase process. The accuracy of all theoretical conclusions will be validated using a high-performance channel simulator. Moreover, all given results demonstrate that the statistics of MLSS fading channels are fundamentally distinct from the aforementioned special situations.

2. THE MLSS FADING CHANNEL

Under NLOS propagation conditions, the complex time-varying channel gain of the multiple scattering radio propagation channel proposed in (Andersen, 2002) can be written as

$$\chi(t) = \alpha 1\, \mu(1)(t) + \alpha 2\, \mu(2)(t)\, \mu(3)(t) + \alpha 3\, \mu(4)(t)\, \mu(5)(t)\, \mu(6)(t) + \cdots \quad (1)$$

where $\mu(i)(t)$ ($i = 1, 2, 3, \ldots$) is a zero-mean complex Gaussian process that represents the scattered component of the ith link and αi ($i = 1, 2, 3, \ldots$) is a real-valued constant that determines the contribution of ith scattered component. In (1), Gaussian processes $\mu(i)(t)$ are mutually independent. However, when the fading channel is modeled by taking into account only the first two terms of (1), the resulting channel is referred to as the NLSS channel (Salo et al., 2006). Here, we are presenting an extension of the NLSS channel to the MLSS channel by incorporating LOS components in a novel manner for M2M amplify-and-forward relay fading channels. The considered communication scenario determined by a source mobile station, a destination mobile station and mobile relay is shown in Fig. 1.

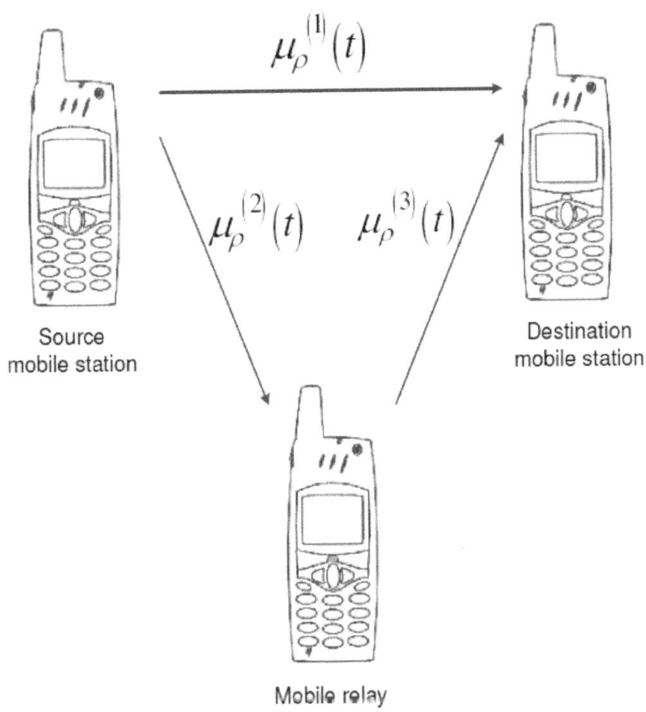

Fig. 1. The propagation scenario behind MLSS fading channels.

Starting from (1), ignoring μ(i) (t) ∀ i ≥ 4, and replacing μ(i) (t) by μp(i) (t) for i = 1, 2, 3, results in

$$\chi\rho\ (t) = \mu p(1)\ (t) + \text{AMR}\ \mu p(2)\ (t)\ \mu p(3)\ (t) \tag{2}$$

where $\alpha_1 = 1$ and $\alpha_2 = A_{\mathrm{MR}}$. The quantity A_{MR} in (2) is referred to as the relay gain. Since we have assumed fixed gain relays in our system, it follows that A_{MR} is a real constant. Furthermore, in (2), $\mu_\rho^{(1)}(t)$, $\mu_\rho^{(2)}(t)$, and $\mu_\rho^{(3)}(t)$ are statistically independent non-zero-mean complex Gaussian processes, which model the individual M2M fading channel in the source mobile station to the mobile relay, the mobile relay to the destination mobile station, and the source mobile station to the destination mobile station links (see Fig. 1). Each complex Gaussian process $\mu_\rho^{(i)}(t) = \mu_{\rho_1}^{(i)}(t) + j\mu_{\rho_2}^{(i)}(t)$ represents the sum of the scattered component $\mu^{(i)}(t)$ and the LOS component $m^{(i)}(t)$, i.e., $\mu_\rho^{(i)}(t) = \mu^{(i)}(t) + m^{(i)}(t)$. The scattered component $\mu^{(i)}(t)$ is still modeled by a zero-mean complex Gaussian process $\mu^{(i)}(t) = \mu_1^{(i)}(t) + j\mu_2^{(i)}(t)$ with variance $2\sigma_i^2$. The LOS component $m^{(i)}(t) = \rho_i e^{j(2\pi f_{\rho_i} t + \theta_{\rho_i})}$ assumes a fixed amplitude ρ_i, a constant Doppler frequency f_{ρ_i}, and a constant phase θ_{ρ_i} for $i = 1, 2, 3$. Furthermore, it is obvious that

the product term μ(2) (t) μ(3) (t) in (2) is a non-zero-mean complex double Gaussian process, i.e., μ(2) (t) μ(3) (t) = σρ (t) = σρ (t) + jσρ (t). Furthermore, σρ (t) models the overall fading in the source mobile station to the destination mobile station link via the mobile relay. It should also be noted here that the relay gain AMR would just scale the mean value and variance of the complex Gaussian process μ(3) (t), i.e., m(3) (t) = E{AMR μ(3) (t)} = ρ ej(2π fρ3 t+θρ3) where ρAMR = AMR ρ3, and 2σ2 = Var{AMR μ (t)} = 2 (AMR σ3) . Finally, the overall fading process consisting of the direct link between the source mobile station and the destination mobile station as well as the source mobile station to the destination mobile station link via the mobile relay results in the complex process χρ (t) = χρ1 (t) + jχρ2 (t) given in (2). The absolute value of χρ (t) defines the MLSS process, i.e., Ξ (t) = |χρ (t) |. Furthermore, the argument of χρ (t) introduces the phase process Θ (t), i.e., Θ (t) = arg{χρ (t)}.

3. STATISTICAL ANALYSIS OF THE MLSS FADING CHANNEL

In this section, we derive the analytical expressions for the statistical properties of MLSS fading channels introduced in Section 2. The starting point for the derivation of the an- alytical expression of the PDF of MLSS fading channels, as well as the PDF of the corre- sponding phase process is the computation of the joint PDF pχρ1 χρ2 χ˙ρ1 χ˙ρ2 (u1, u2, u˙1, u˙2; t) of the stochastic processes χρ1 (t), χρ2 (t), χ˙ρ1 (t), and χ˙ρ2 (t) at the same time t. Throughout this chapter, the overdot indicates the time derivative. Equation (2) shows that the joint PDF pχρ1 χρ2 χ˙ρ1 χ˙ρ2 (u1, u2, u˙1, u˙2; t) can be written in terms of a 4-dimensional (4D) convolution in- tegral as

$$p_{\chi_{\rho_1}\chi_{\rho_2}\dot{\chi}_{\rho_1}\dot{\chi}_{\rho_2}}(u_1,u_2,\dot{u}_1,\dot{u}_2;t)=\int_{-\infty}^{\infty}\int_{-\infty}^{\infty}\int_{-\infty}^{\infty}\int_{-\infty}^{\infty} p_{\mu_{\rho_1}^{(1)}\mu_{\rho_2}^{(1)}\dot{\mu}_{\rho_1}^{(1)}\dot{\mu}_{\rho_2}^{(1)}}(u_1-y_1,u_2-y_2,\dot{u}_1-\dot{y}_1,\dot{u}_2-\dot{y}_2;t)$$
$$p_{\varsigma_{\rho_1}\varsigma_{\rho_2}\dot{\varsigma}_{\rho_1}\dot{\varsigma}_{\rho_2}}(y_1,y_2,\dot{y}_1,\dot{y}_2;t)\,d\dot{y}_2\,d\dot{y}_1\,dy_2\,dy_1 \quad (3)$$

where $p_{\mu_{\rho_1}^{(1)}\mu_{\rho_2}^{(1)}\dot{\mu}_{\rho_1}^{(1)}\dot{\mu}_{\rho_2}^{(1)}}(u_1,u_2,\dot{u}_1,\dot{u}_2;t)$ is the joint PDF of the processes $\mu_{\rho_1}^{(1)}(t)$, $\mu_{\rho_2}^{(1)}(t)$, $\dot{\mu}_{\rho_1}^{(1)}(t)$, and $\dot{\mu}_{\rho_2}^{(1)}(t)$ at the same time t. Similarly, $p_{\varsigma_{\rho_1}\varsigma_{\rho_2}\dot{\varsigma}_{\rho_1}\dot{\varsigma}_{\rho_2}}(y_1,y_2,\dot{y}_1,\dot{y}_2;t)$ in (3), represents the joint PDF of the processes $\varsigma_{\rho_1}(t)$, $\varsigma_{\rho_2}(t)$, $\dot{\varsigma}_{\rho_1}(t)$, and $\dot{\varsigma}_{\rho_2}(t)$ at the same time t. It is worth mentioning here that the processes $\mu_{\rho_i}^{(1)}(t)$, $\dot{\mu}_{\rho_i}^{(1)}(t)$, $\varsigma_{\rho_i}(t)$, and $\dot{\varsigma}_{\rho_i}(t)$ $(i=1,2)$ are uncorrelated in pairs. Furthermore, the process pairs $\{\mu_{\rho_i}^{(1)}(t),\dot{\mu}_{\rho_i}^{(1)}(t)\}$ and $\{\varsigma_{\rho_i}(t),\dot{\varsigma}_{\rho_i}(t)\}$ $(i=1,2)$ are statistically independent, which allows us to express $p_{\varsigma_{\rho_1}\varsigma_{\rho_2}\dot{\varsigma}_{\rho_1}\dot{\varsigma}_{\rho_2}\mu_{\rho_1}^{(1)}\mu_{\rho_2}^{(1)}\dot{\mu}_{\rho_1}^{(1)}\dot{\mu}_{\rho_2}^{(1)}}(y_1,y_2,\dot{y}_1,\dot{y}_2,u_1,u_2,\dot{u}_1,\dot{u}_2;t)$ as given in (3). The joint PDF $p_{\mu_{\rho_1}^{(1)}\mu_{\rho_2}^{(1)}\dot{\mu}_{\rho_1}^{(1)}\dot{\mu}_{\rho_2}^{(1)}}(u_1,u_2,\dot{u}_1,\dot{u}_2;t)$ can be obtained using the multivariate Gaussian distribution (see, e.g., (Simon, 2002, Eq. (3.2))). The expression for the joint PDF $p_{\varsigma_{\rho_1}\varsigma_{\rho_2}\dot{\varsigma}_{\rho_1}\dot{\varsigma}_{\rho_2}}(y_1,y_2,\dot{y}_1,\dot{y}_2;t)$ is presented in (4), where the quantity β_i $(i=2,3)$ is the negative curvature of the autocorrelation function of the inphase and quadrature components of $\mu^{(i)}(t)$ $(i=2,3)$. Under isotropic scattering conditions, β_i $(i=2,3)$ can be expressed as (Akki, 1994; Pätzold, 2002)

$$
\begin{aligned}
&p_{\varsigma_{\rho_1}\varsigma_{\rho_2}\dot{\varsigma}_{\rho_1}\dot{\varsigma}_{\rho_2}}\left(y_1, y_2, \dot{y}_1, \dot{y}_2; t\right) = \\
&\int_{-\infty}^{\infty}\int_{-\infty}^{\infty} dz_2\, dz_1 \frac{e^{-\frac{\left(z_1-m_1^{(3)}(t)\right)^2+\left(z_2-m_2^{(3)}(t)\right)^2}{2\sigma_{A_{\mathrm{MR}}}^2}}\, e^{-\frac{\left(\dot{m}_1^{(3)}(t)\right)^2+\left(\dot{m}_2^{(3)}(t)\right)^2}{2\beta_3}}}{(2\pi)^3\,\sigma_2^2\sigma_{A_{\mathrm{MR}}}^2\left[\beta_3\left(y_1^2+y_2^2\right)+\beta_2\left(z_1^2+z_2^2\right)^2\right]}\, e^{\frac{\beta_2\left(z_1^2+z_2^2\right)^2\left\{\left(\dot{m}_1^{(3)}(t)\right)^2+\left(\dot{m}_2^{(3)}(t)\right)^2\right\}+\beta_3\left(y_1^2+y_2^2\right)\left(\dot{m}_1^{(2)}(t)+\dot{m}_2^{(2)}(t)\right)}{2\beta_2\left\{\beta_3\left(y_1^2+y_2^2\right)+\beta_2\left(z_1^2+z_2^2\right)^2\right\}}} \\
&\times e^{-\frac{y_1^2+y_2^2-2\left(y_2 m_2^{(2)}(t)+y_1 m_1^{(2)}(t)\right)z_1-2\left(y_2 m_1^{(2)}(t)-y_1 m_2^{(2)}(t)\right)z_2+\left\{\left(m_1^{(2)}(t)\right)^2+\left(m_2^{(2)}(t)\right)^2\right\}\left(z_1^2+z_2^2\right)}{2\sigma_2^2\left(z_1^2+z_2^2\right)}}\, e^{\frac{z_1\dot{m}_2^{(3)}(t)\left(-y_2\dot{y}_1+y_1\dot{y}_2-\dot{m}_2^{(2)}(t)y_1z_1+\dot{m}_1^{(2)}(t)y_2z_1\right)}{\beta_3\left(y_1^2+y_2^2\right)+\beta_2\left(z_1^2+z_2^2\right)^2}} \\
&\times e^{-\frac{\dot{y}_1^2+\dot{y}_2^2-2\left(\dot{y}_2\dot{m}_2^{(2)}(t)+\dot{y}_1\dot{m}_1^{(2)}(t)\right)z_1-2\left(\dot{y}_2\dot{m}_1^{(2)}(t)-\dot{y}_1\dot{m}_2^{(2)}(t)\right)z_2+\left\{\left(\dot{m}_1^{(2)}(t)\right)^2+\left(\dot{m}_2^{(2)}(t)\right)^2\right\}\left(z_1^2+z_2^2\right)}{2\beta_2\left(z_1^2+z_2^2\right)}}\, e^{\frac{z_1\dot{m}_1^{(3)}(t)\left(y_1\dot{y}_1+y_2\dot{y}_2-\dot{m}_1^{(2)}(t)y_1z_1+\dot{m}_2^{(2)}(t)y_2z_1\right)}{\beta_3\left(y_1^2+y_2^2\right)+\beta_2\left(z_1^2+z_2^2\right)^2}} \\
&\times e^{\frac{2\beta_2z_2\left(z_1^2+z_2^2\right)\left\{\dot{m}_1^{(3)}(t)\left(y_2\dot{y}_1-y_1\dot{y}_2+2\dot{m}_2^{(2)}(t)y_1z_1-2\dot{m}_1^{(2)}(t)y_2z_1\right)+\dot{m}_2^{(3)}(t)\left(y_1\dot{y}_1+y_2\dot{y}_2-2\dot{m}_1^{(2)}(t)y_1z_1-2\dot{m}_2^{(2)}(t)y_2z_1\right)\right\}+\beta_3\left(y_1^2+y_2^2\right)\left(\dot{y}_1^2+\dot{y}_2^2\right)}{2\beta_2\left(z_1^2+z_2^2\right)\left\{\beta_3\left(y_1^2+y_2^2\right)+\beta_2\left(z_1^2+z_2^2\right)^2\right\}}} \\
&\times e^{\frac{z_2^2\left\{\dot{m}_1^{(2)}(t)\dot{m}_1^{(3)}(t)y_1+\dot{m}_2^{(2)}(t)\dot{m}_2^{(3)}(t)y_1+\dot{m}_2^{(2)}(t)\dot{m}_1^{(3)}(t)y_2-\dot{m}_1^{(2)}(t)\dot{m}_2^{(3)}(t)y_2\right\}}{\beta_3\left(y_1^2+y_2^2\right)+\beta_2\left(z_1^2+z_2^2\right)^2}}\, e^{\frac{\beta_3\left(y_1^2+y_2^2\right)\left[-2\dot{y}_2\left(\dot{m}_2^{(2)}(t)z_1+\dot{m}_1^{(2)}(t)z_2\right)+2\dot{y}_1\left(-\dot{m}_1^{(2)}(t)z_1+\dot{m}_2^{(2)}(t)z_2\right)\right]}{2\beta_2\left(z_1^2+z_2^2\right)\left\{\beta_3\left(y_1^2+y_2^2\right)+\beta_2\left(z_1^2+z_2^2\right)^2\right\}}}\,.
\end{aligned}
$$

$$
\begin{aligned}
p_{\Xi\dot{\Xi}\Theta\dot{\Theta}}\left(x, \dot{x}, \theta, \dot{\theta}; t\right) &= \frac{x^2\, e^{-\frac{x^2}{2\sigma_1^2}}\, e^{-\frac{\left(\dot{m}_1^{(2)}(t)\right)^2+\left(\dot{m}_2^{(2)}(t)\right)^2}{2\beta_2}}\, e^{-\frac{\left(\dot{m}_1^{(3)}(t)\right)^2+\left(\dot{m}_2^{(3)}(t)\right)^2}{2\beta_3}}\, e^{-\frac{\left(\dot{m}_1^{(1)}(t)\right)^2+\left(\dot{m}_2^{(1)}(t)\right)^2}{2\beta_1}}}{(2\pi)^4\,\sigma_1^2\sigma_2^2\sigma_{A_{\mathrm{MR}}}^2} \\
&\int_{-\infty}^{\infty}\int_{-\infty}^{\infty}\int_{-\infty}^{\infty}\int_{-\infty}^{\infty} dz_2\, dz_1\, dy_2\, dy_1 \frac{e^{-\frac{\left(z_1-m_1^{(3)}(t)\right)^2+\left(z_2-m_2^{(3)}(t)\right)^2}{2\sigma_{A_{\mathrm{MR}}}^2}}\, e^{-\frac{\left(y_1+m_1^{(1)}(t)\right)^2+\left(y_2+m_2^{(1)}(t)\right)^2}{2\sigma_1^2}}}{\beta_1\left(z_1^2+z_2^2\right)+\beta_3\left(y_1^2+y_2^2\right)+\beta_2\left(z_1^2+z_2^2\right)^2}\, e^{\frac{x\left(y_1+m_1^{(1)}(t)\right)\cos\theta+x\left(y_2+m_2^{(1)}(t)\right)\sin\theta}{\sigma_1^2}} \\
&\times e^{-\frac{y_1^2+y_2^2-2\left(y_2m_2^{(2)}(t)+y_1m_1^{(2)}(t)\right)z_1-2\left(y_2m_1^{(2)}(t)-y_1m_2^{(2)}(t)\right)z_2+\left\{\left(m_1^{(2)}(t)\right)^2+\left(m_2^{(2)}(t)\right)^2\right\}\left(z_1^2+z_2^2\right)}{2\sigma_2^2\left(z_1^2+z_2^2\right)}}\, e^{\frac{\beta_3\left(y_1^2+y_2^2\right)\left\{\left(\dot{m}_1^{(1)}(t)\right)^2+\left(\dot{m}_2^{(1)}(t)\right)^2\right\}}{2\beta_1\left\{\beta_1\left(z_1^2+z_2^2\right)+\beta_3\left(y_1^2+y_2^2\right)+\beta_2\left(z_1^2+z_2^2\right)^2\right\}}} \\
&\times e^{\frac{\beta_2^2\left(z_1^2+z_2^2\right)^2\left[\beta_3\left\{\left(\dot{m}_1^{(1)}(t)\right)^2+\left(\dot{m}_2^{(1)}(t)\right)^2\right\}+\beta_1\left\{\left(\dot{m}_1^{(3)}(t)\right)^2+\left(\dot{m}_2^{(3)}(t)\right)^2\right\}\right]+\beta_3\beta_1\left\{\left(\dot{m}_1^{(2)}(t)\right)^2+\left(\dot{m}_2^{(2)}(t)\right)^2\right\}\left[\beta_3\left(y_1^2+y_2^2\right)+\beta_1\left(z_1^2+z_2^2\right)\right]}{2\beta_3\beta_2\beta_1\left\{\beta_1\left(z_1^2+z_2^2\right)+\beta_3\left(y_1^2+y_2^2\right)+\beta_2\left(z_1^2+z_2^2\right)^2\right\}}} \\
&\times e^{\frac{z_2^2\left\{\dot{m}_1^{(2)}(t)\dot{m}_1^{(3)}(t)y_1+\dot{m}_2^{(2)}(t)\dot{m}_2^{(3)}(t)y_1+\dot{m}_2^{(2)}(t)\dot{m}_1^{(3)}(t)y_2-\dot{m}_1^{(2)}(t)\dot{m}_2^{(3)}(t)y_2-z_1\left(\dot{m}_1^{(1)}(t)\dot{m}_1^{(2)}(t)+\dot{m}_2^{(1)}(t)\dot{m}_2^{(2)}(t)\right)-z_2\left(\dot{m}_2^{(1)}(t)\dot{m}_1^{(2)}(t)-\dot{m}_1^{(1)}(t)\dot{m}_2^{(2)}(t)\right)\right\}}{\beta_1\left(z_1^2+z_2^2\right)+\beta_3\left(y_1^2+y_2^2\right)+\beta_2\left(z_1^2+z_2^2\right)^2}} \\
&\times e^{\frac{z_2\left\{2z_1\left(\dot{m}_2^{(2)}(t)\dot{m}_1^{(3)}(t)y_1-\dot{m}_1^{(2)}(t)\dot{m}_2^{(3)}(t)y_1-\dot{m}_1^{(2)}(t)\dot{m}_1^{(3)}(t)y_2-\dot{m}_2^{(2)}(t)\dot{m}_2^{(3)}(t)y_2\right)-z_1^2\left(\dot{m}_2^{(1)}(t)\dot{m}_1^{(2)}(t)-\dot{m}_1^{(1)}(t)\dot{m}_2^{(2)}(t)\right)+\left(\dot{m}_2^{(1)}(t)\dot{m}_1^{(3)}(t)-\dot{m}_1^{(1)}(t)\dot{m}_2^{(3)}(t)\right)y_1\right\}}{\beta_1\left(z_1^2+z_2^2\right)+\beta_3\left(y_1^2+y_2^2\right)+\beta_2\left(z_1^2+z_2^2\right)^2}} \\
&\times e^{\frac{z_1^2\left(\dot{m}_1^{(2)}(t)\dot{m}_2^{(3)}(t)y_2-\dot{m}_1^{(2)}(t)\dot{m}_1^{(3)}(t)y_1-\dot{m}_2^{(2)}(t)\dot{m}_2^{(3)}(t)y_1-\dot{m}_2^{(2)}(t)\dot{m}_1^{(3)}(t)y_2\right)-z_1\left(\dot{m}_1^{(1)}(t)\dot{m}_1^{(3)}(t)y_1+\dot{m}_2^{(1)}(t)\dot{m}_2^{(3)}(t)y_1+\dot{m}_2^{(1)}(t)\dot{m}_1^{(3)}(t)y_2-\dot{m}_1^{(1)}(t)\dot{m}_2^{(3)}(t)y_2\right)}{\beta_1\left(z_1^2+z_2^2\right)+\beta_3\left(y_1^2+y_2^2\right)+\beta_2\left(z_1^2+z_2^2\right)^2}} \\
&\times e^{-\frac{z_1^3\left(\dot{m}_1^{(1)}(t)\dot{m}_1^{(2)}(t)+\dot{m}_2^{(1)}(t)\dot{m}_2^{(2)}(t)\right)+\left\{\dot{m}_1^{(3)}(t)\left(y_2z_1-y_1z_2\right)+\dot{m}_2^{(3)}(t)\left(y_1z_1+y_2z_2\right)+\left(\dot{m}_2^{(1)}(t)+\dot{m}_2^{(2)}(t)z_1+\dot{m}_1^{(2)}(t)z_2\right)\left(z_1^2+z_2^2\right)\right\}\left(x\dot{\theta}\cos\theta+\dot{x}\sin\theta\right)}{\beta_1\left(z_1^2+z_2^2\right)+\beta_3\left(y_1^2+y_2^2\right)+\beta_2\left(z_1^2+z_2^2\right)^2}} \\
&\times e^{\frac{\left\{\dot{m}_2^{(3)}(t)\left(y_1z_2-y_2z_1\right)+\dot{m}_1^{(3)}(t)\left(y_1z_1+y_2z_2\right)+\left(\dot{m}_1^{(1)}(t)+\dot{m}_1^{(2)}(t)z_1-\dot{m}_2^{(2)}(t)z_2\right)\left(z_1^2+z_2^2\right)\right\}\left(\dot{x}\cos\theta-x\dot{\theta}\sin\theta\right)-\left\{\dot{m}_2^{(1)}(t)\dot{m}_2^{(3)}(t)+\dot{m}_1^{(1)}(t)\dot{m}_1^{(3)}(t)\right\}y_2z_2}{\beta_1\left(z_1^2+z_2^2\right)+\beta_3\left(y_1^2+y_2^2\right)+\beta_2\left(z_1^2+z_2^2\right)^2}} \\
&\times e^{-\frac{\left(z_1^2+z_2^2\right)\left\{\dot{x}^2+\left(x\dot{\theta}\right)^2\right\}}{2\left\{\beta_1\left(z_1^2+z_2^2\right)+\beta_3\left(y_1^2+y_2^2\right)+\beta_2\left(z_1^2+z_2^2\right)^2\right\}}}\, e^{\frac{\beta_1\left(z_1^2+z_2^2\right)\left\{\left(\dot{m}_1^{(3)}(t)\right)^2+\left(\dot{m}_2^{(3)}(t)\right)^2\right\}}{2\beta_3\left\{\beta_1\left(z_1^2+z_2^2\right)+\beta_3\left(y_1^2+y_2^2\right)+\beta_2\left(z_1^2+z_2^2\right)^2\right\}}},\quad x\geq 0,\ |\dot{x}|<\infty,\ |\theta|\leq\pi,\ |\dot{\theta}|<\infty\,.
\end{aligned}
$$

$$\beta_2 = 2\left(\sigma_2\pi\right)^2\left(f_{\max_1}^2+f_{\max_2}^2\right) \tag{5a}$$

$$\beta_3 = 2\left(\sigma_{A_{\mathrm{MR}}}\pi\right)^2\left(f_{\max_2}^2+f_{\max_3}^2\right)\,. \tag{5b}$$

The symbols $f_{\max_1}$, $f_{\max_2}$, and $f_{\max_3}$ appearing in (5a) and (5b) denote the maximum Doppler frequency caused by the motion of the source mobile station, the mobile relay, and the destination mobile station, respectively. Substituting the joint PDF $p_{\mu_{\rho_1}^{(1)}\mu_{\rho_2}^{(1)}\dot{\mu}_{\rho_1}^{(1)}\dot{\mu}_{\rho_2}^{(1)}}(u_1, u_2, \dot{u}_1, \dot{u}_2)$ and (4) in (3), applying the concept of transformation of random variables (Papoulis & Pillai, 2002), and doing tedious algebraic manipulations, the joint PDF $p_{\Xi\dot{\Xi}\Theta\dot{\Theta}}(x, \dot{x}, \theta, \dot{\theta}; t)$ of the processes $\Xi(t)$, $\dot{\Xi}(t)$, $\Theta(t)$, and $\dot{\Theta}(t)$ can be derived. The resulting joint PDF $p_{\Xi\dot{\Xi}\Theta\dot{\Theta}}(x, \dot{x}, \theta, \dot{\theta}; t)$ is presented in (5), which is of fundamental importance, because it provides the basis for the computation of the PDF, the level-crossing rate (LCR), and the average duration of fades (ADF) of MLSS processes $\Xi(t)$ as well as the PDF of the phase process $\Theta(t)$. Using (5), the analytical expressions of the LCR and the ADF of the MLSS processes $\Xi(t)$ have been derived in (Talha & Pätzold, 2008a). In (5), the quantity β_1 is given by $\beta_1 = 2(\sigma_1\pi)^2(f_{\max_1}^2 + f_{\max_3}^2)$ (Akki, 1994; Pätzold, 2002).

3.1 PDF of the MLSS Process

The joint PDF $p_{\Xi\Theta}(x, \theta; t)$ of the MLSS process $\Xi(t)$ and the phase process $\Theta(t)$ can be obtained by solving the integrals over the joint PDF $p_{\Xi\dot{\Xi}\Theta\dot{\Theta}}(x, \dot{x}, \theta, \dot{\theta}; t)$ according to

$$p_{\Xi\Theta}(x, \theta; t) = \int_{-\infty}^{\infty}\int_{-\infty}^{\infty} p_{\Xi\dot{\Xi}\Theta\dot{\Theta}}(x, \dot{x}, \theta, \dot{\theta}; t)\, d\dot{\theta}\, d\dot{x} \tag{6}$$

for $x \geq 0$ and $|\theta| \leq \pi$. Solving (6) results in the following expression

$$p_{\Xi\Theta}(x, \theta; t) = \frac{x\, e^{\frac{x^2}{2\sigma_1^2}}}{(2\pi)^2 \sigma_1^2 \sigma_2^2 \sigma_{A_{\mathrm{MR}}}^2} \int_0^{\infty}\int_0^{\infty}\int_{-\pi}^{\pi} \frac{\omega}{\nu} e^{-\frac{(\omega/\nu)^2+\rho_2^2}{2\sigma_2^2}} e^{-\frac{\nu^2+\rho_{A_{\mathrm{MR}}}^2}{2\sigma_{A_{\mathrm{MR}}}^2}} e^{-\frac{g_1(\omega,\psi;t)}{2\sigma_1^2}} e^{-\frac{x g_3(\omega,\theta,\psi;t)}{\sigma_1}}$$
$$\times I_0\left(\sqrt{g_2(\omega,\nu,\psi;t)}\right) d\psi\, d\omega\, d\nu,\ x \geq 0,\ |\theta| \leq \pi \tag{7}$$

where

$$g_1(\omega, \psi; t) = \omega^2 + \rho_1^2 + 2\rho_1\omega\cos(\psi - 2\pi f_{\rho_1} t - \theta_{\rho_1}) \tag{8a}$$

$$g_2(\omega, \nu, \psi; t) = \left(\frac{\rho_2\omega}{\sigma_2^2\nu}\right)^2 + \left(\frac{\rho_{A_{\mathrm{MR}}}\nu}{\sigma_{A_{\mathrm{MR}}}^2}\right)^2 + \frac{2\rho_2\rho_{A_{\mathrm{MR}}}\omega}{\sigma_2^2\sigma_{A_{\mathrm{MR}}}^2}$$
$$\cos\left[\psi - 2\pi(f_{\rho_2} + f_{\rho_3})t - (\theta_{\rho_2} + \theta_{\rho_3})\right] \tag{8b}$$

$$g_3(\omega, \theta, \psi; t) = \frac{\rho_1\cos(\theta - 2\pi f_{\rho_1} t - \theta_{\rho_1}) + \omega\cos(\theta - \psi)}{\sigma_1}. \tag{8c}$$

In (7), I0 () is the zeroth-order modified Bessel function of the first kind (Gradshteyn & Ryzhik, 2000).

The PDF pΞ (x) of the MLSS fading process Ξ (t) can be obtained by integrating (7) over θ in the interval [-π, π]. Hence,

$$p_{\Xi}(x) = \frac{x e^{-\frac{x^2}{2\sigma_1^2}}}{2\pi\,\sigma_1^2\sigma_2^2\sigma_{A_{MR}}^2} \int_0^\infty\int_0^\infty d\nu\, d\omega\, \frac{\omega}{\nu} e^{-\frac{(\omega/\nu)^2+\rho_2^2}{2\sigma_2^2}} e^{-\frac{\nu^2+\rho_{A_{MR}}^2}{2\sigma_{A_{MR}}^2}} \int_{-\pi}^{\pi} d\psi\, e^{-\frac{g_4(\omega,\psi)}{2\sigma_1^2}} I_0\left(\frac{x}{\sigma_1^2}\sqrt{g_4(\omega,\psi)}\right) I_0\left(\sqrt{g_5(\omega,\nu,\psi)}\right),\ x \geq 0 \tag{9}$$

where

$$g_4(\omega,\psi) = \omega^2 + \rho_1^2 + 2\rho_1\omega\cos(\psi) \tag{10a}$$

$$g_5(\omega,\nu,\psi) = \left(\frac{\rho_2\omega}{\sigma_2^2\nu}\right)^2 + \left(\frac{\rho_{A_{MR}}\nu}{\sigma_{A_{MR}}^2}\right)^2 + \frac{2\rho_2\rho_{A_{MR}}\omega}{\sigma_2^2\sigma_{A_{MR}}^2}\cos(\psi). \tag{10b}$$

It is worth mentioning that the joint PDF pΞΘ (x, θ; t) in (6) is dependent on time t. Neverthe- less, the PDF pΞ(x) in (9) is independent of time t showing that MLSS processes Ξ (t) are first order stationary. From the PDF pΞ(x) of MLSS fading processes Ξ (t), the following special cases can be obtained.

Substituting AMR = 1, ρ1 = ρ2 = ρ3 = 0, and taking the limit σ2 → 0 in (9), reduces the PDF of MLSS processes to the PDF of double Rayleigh processes (see, e.g., (Kovacs et al., 2002; Patel et al., 2006))

$$p_{\Xi}(x)\Big|_{\substack{A_{MR}=1\\ \rho_1,\rho_2,\rho_3=0\\ \sigma_1^2\to 0}} = \frac{x}{\sigma_2^2\sigma_{A_{MR}}^2} K_0\left(\frac{x}{\sigma_2\sigma_{A_{MR}}}\right), \quad x \geq 0. \tag{11}$$

For the special case when $A_{MR} = 1$, $\rho_1 = 0$, and $\sigma_1^2 \to 0$, the PDF of MLSS processes given in (9) reduces to the PDF of double Rice processes (Talha & Pätzold, 2007a)

$$p_{\Xi}(x)\Big|_{\substack{A_{MR}=1\\ \rho_1=0\\ \sigma_1^2\to 0}} = \frac{x}{\sigma_2^2\sigma_{A_{MR}}^2} \int_0^\infty \frac{1}{\nu} e^{-\frac{(x/\nu)^2+\rho_2^2}{2\sigma_2^2}} e^{-\frac{\nu^2+\rho_{A_{MR}}^2}{2\sigma_{A_{MR}}^2}} I_0\left(\frac{x\rho_2}{\nu\sigma_2^2}\right) I_0\left(\frac{\nu\rho_{A_{MR}}}{\sigma_{A_{MR}}^2}\right) d\nu,\ x \geq 0. \tag{12}$$

Similarly, substituting $A_{MR} = 1$, $\rho_2 = \rho_3 = 0$, and $\sigma_1^2 \to 0$ in (9) allows us to write the PDF of SLDS processes in the form (Talha & Pätzold, 2007b)

$$p_{\Xi}(x)\Big|_{\substack{A_{MR}=1\\ \rho_2,\rho_3=0\\ \sigma_1^2\to 0}} = \begin{cases} \frac{x}{\sigma_2^2\sigma_{A_{MR}}^2} I_0\left(\frac{x}{\sigma_2\sigma_{A_{MR}}}\right) K_0\left(\frac{\rho_1}{\sigma_2\sigma_{A_{MR}}}\right), & x < \rho_1 \\ \frac{x}{\sigma_2^2\sigma_{A_{MR}}^2} K_0\left(\frac{x}{\sigma_2\sigma_{A_{MR}}}\right) I_0\left(\frac{\rho_1}{\sigma_2\sigma_{A_{MR}}}\right), & x \geq \rho_1. \end{cases} \tag{13}$$

The PDF of NLSS processes (see, e.g., (Salo et al., 2006)) can be derived from the PDF of MLSS processes by substituting ρ1 = ρ2 = ρ3 = 0 in (9), i.e.,

$$p_{\Xi}(x)\Big|_{\substack{A_{MR}=1\\ \rho_1,\rho_2,\rho_3=0}} = \frac{x\, e^{-\frac{x^2}{2\sigma_1^2}}}{\sigma_1^2\sigma_2^2\sigma_{A_{MR}}^2}\int_0^\infty \omega\, e^{-\frac{\omega^2}{2\sigma_1^2}} K_0\left(\frac{\omega}{\sigma_2\sigma_{A_{MR}}}\right) I_0\left(\frac{\omega}{\sigma_1^2}x\right) d\omega,\ x \geq 0. \quad (14)$$

Finally, solving (9) for $\rho_2 = \rho_3 = 0$, the PDF of SLSS processes (Salo et al., 2006) is obtained as

$$p_{\Xi}(x)\Big|_{\substack{A_{MR}=1\\ \rho_2,\rho_3=0}} = \frac{x}{2\pi\,\sigma_1^2\sigma_2^2\sigma_{A_{MR}}^2}\int_0^\infty\int_{-\pi}^{\pi} d\theta\, d\omega\, \omega\, e^{-\frac{\omega^2}{2\sigma_1^2}} e^{-\frac{g_5(x,\theta)}{2\sigma_1^2}} K_0\left(\frac{\omega}{\sigma_2\sigma_{A_{MR}}}\right) I_0\left(\frac{\omega}{\sigma_1^2}\sqrt{g_6(x,\theta)}\right),\ x \geq 0 \quad (15)$$

where

$$g_6(x,\theta) = x^2 + \rho_1^2 - 2x\rho_1\cos\theta\,. \quad (16)$$

3.2 PDF of the Phase Process

Integrating (7) over x in the interval $[0, \infty)$ results in the following expression for the PDF $p_\Theta(\theta; t)$ of the phase process $\Theta(t)$

$$p_\Theta(\theta;t) = \int_0^\infty\int_0^\infty\int_{-\pi}^{\pi} \frac{\omega}{\nu}\frac{e^{-\frac{(\omega/\nu)^2+\rho_2^2}{2\sigma_2^2}}\, e^{-\frac{\nu^2+\rho_{A_{MR}}^2}{2\sigma_{A_{MR}}^2}}}{(2\pi)^2\sigma_2^2\sigma_{A_{MR}}^2} e^{-\frac{g_1(\omega,\psi;t)}{2\sigma_1^2}} I_0\left(\sqrt{g_2(\omega,\nu,\psi;t)}\right)\left[1+\sqrt{\frac{\pi}{2}}g_3(\omega,\theta,\psi;t)\right.$$
$$\left.\times\, e^{\frac{1}{2}g_3^2(\omega,\theta,\psi;t)}\left\{1+\Phi\left(\frac{g_3(\omega,\theta,\psi;t)}{\sqrt{2}}\right)\right\}\right] d\psi\, d\omega\, d\nu,\ |\theta| \leq \pi \quad (17)$$

where $g_1(\cdot,\cdot;t)$, $g_2(\cdot,\cdot,\cdot;t)$, and $g_3(\cdot,\cdot,\cdot;t)$ are defined in (8a), (8b), and (8c), respectively. In (17), $\Phi(\cdot)$ represents the error function (Gradshteyn & Ryzhik, 2000, Eq. (8.250.1)). From (17), it is obvious that the phase process $\Theta(t)$ is not strict sense stationary because the density $p_\Theta(\theta; t)$ is a function of time t. This time dependency is due the Doppler frequency $f_{\rho i}$ of the LOS component $m^{(i)}(t)$ (i = 1, 2, 3). However, for the special case when $f_{\rho i} = 0$, $\rho_i \neq 0$ (i = 1, 2, 3), the phase process $\Theta(t)$ becomes first order stationary.

The PDF $p_\Theta(\theta; t)$ of the phase process $\Theta(t)$ given in (17) reduces to the PDF of the phase process corresponding to double Rayleigh (Talha & Pätzold, 2007a), double Rice (Talha & Pätzold, 2007a), SLDS (Talha & Pätzold, 2007b), NLSS, and SLSS processes by selecting ρ_1, ρ_2, ρ_3, and σ_1^2 in a similar fashion as described in Subsection 3.1.

4. NUMERICAL RESULTS

In this section, we will provide sufficient evidence to support the validity of the analytical expressions with the help of simulations. Furthermore, for the sake of completeness, a detailed comparison of the PDF $p_\Xi(x)$ of MLSS processes $\Xi(t)$ to that of the special cases mentioned above will be presented. Similarly, a comparison of the PDF $p_\Theta(\theta)$ of the phase process $\Theta(t)$ with other phase PDFs will also be presented. The concept of sum-of-sinusoids (Pätzold, 2002) was employed to simulate the underlying uncorrelated Gaussian noise processes of the overall MLSS process Ξ(t). The number of sinusoids required to simulate the inphase and quadrature components of Gaussian processes μ(i) (t) was selected to be 20 and 21, respectively. Furthermore, the simulation model parameters were computed using the generalized method of exact Doppler spread (GMEDS1) (Pätzold & Hogstad, 2006). The maximum Doppler frequencies, i.e., fmax1 , fmax2 , and fmax3 were set to 91 Hz, 75 Hz, and 110 Hz, respectively. Furthermore, for simplicity, the amplitudes of the three LOS components ρ1, ρ2, and ρ3 are assumed to be equal, i.e., ρ1 = ρ2 = ρ3 = ρ. The quantities σ12, σ22, σ32, and the relay gain AMR are set to 1, unless stated otherwise.

The results presented in Figs. 2 and 3 show a good fitting between the analytical and simulation results. In Fig. 2, the PDF pΞ(x) of MLSS processes Ξ(t) is compared to that of classical Rayleigh, classical Rice, double Rayleigh, double Rice, SLDS, NLSS, and SLSS processes for ρ = 1, where fρ1 , fρ2 , and fρ3 , were set to 166 Hz, 185 Hz, and 201 Hz, respectively. It can be observed that the maximum value of the PDF pΞ(x) of MLSS processes Ξ(t) is lower than that of all the other processes under consideration for the same value of ρ. However, the PDF p (x) of MLSS processes (t) has a higher spread as compared to the spreads of the above mentioned processes for the same value of ρ. The same trend can be seen when different values of ρi (i = 1, 2, 3) are selected. Furthermore, increasing the value of the relay gain AMR causes a decrease in the maximum value and an increase in the spread of the PDF of MLSS processes Ξ (t).

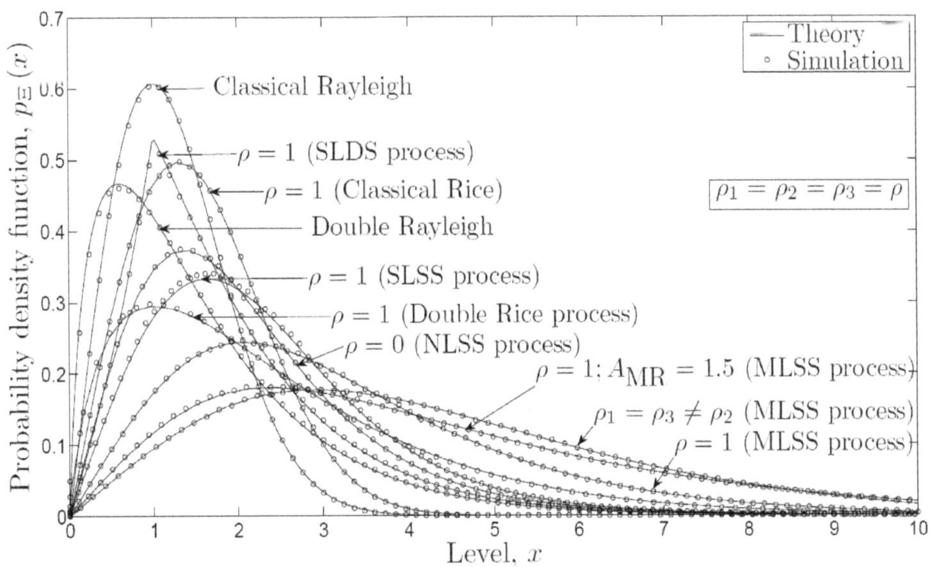

Fig. 2. A comparison of the PDF pΞ(x) of the MLSS process Ξ(t) with that of various other stochastic processes.

Figure 3 presents a comparison of the PDF pΘ(θ) of the phase process Θ(t) with that of the phase processes corresponding to the classical Rayleigh and double Rayleigh processes, the classical Rice and double Rice processes, the SLDS process, the NLSS process, and the SLSS process for ρ = 1. It should be noted that the results presented in Fig. 3 are valid for the case when fρi (i = 1, 2, 3) is set to zero. It can be observed that the PDF of the SLDS phase process has the highest peak. The PDF pΘ(θ) of the phase process Θ(t) follows the same trend in terms of the maximum value and the spread as that of the classical Rice process for the same value of ρ. Furthermore, it is interesting to note that for the phase process Θ(t) with ρi (i = 1, 2, 3) being selected as ρ1 = ρ3 = 0.5 and ρ2 = 1, the PDF pΘ(θ) is almost the same as that of the double Rice process for ρ = 1. Figure 3 also shows the impact of the relay gain AMR on the PDF pΘ(θ) of the phase process Θ(t).

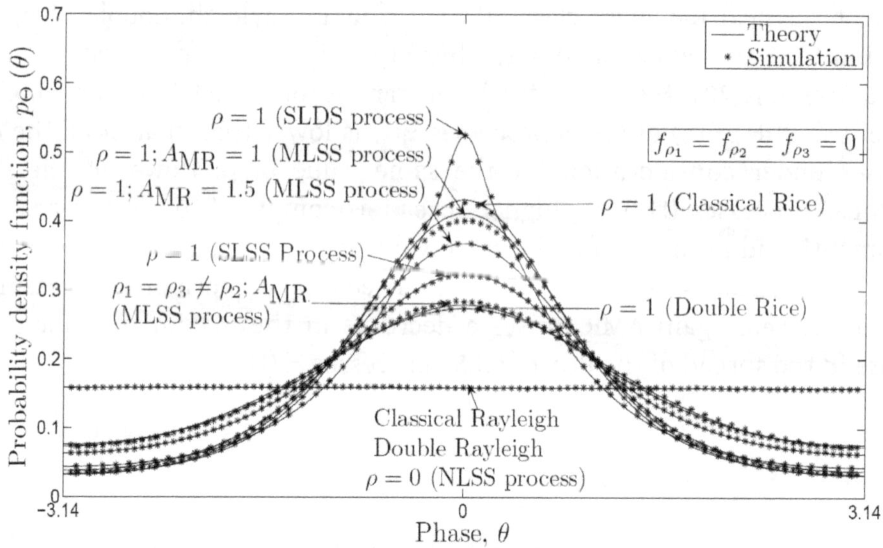

Fig. 3. A comparison of the PDF pΘ(θ) of the phase process Θ(t) with that of various other various processes.

5. CONCISE SUMMARY

This chapter introduces a novel flexible M2M amplify-and-forward relay fading channel model under line-of-sight propagation conditions. The innovation in the model lies in our consideration of the line-of-sight components in both transmission connections, specifically the direct link between the source mobile station and the destination mobile station, as well as the link through the mobile relay. Drawing parallels with multiple scattering radio propagation channels, we have formulated the MLSS fading channel as a second-order scattering channel, wherein the received signal consists of both single and double scattered components. The versatility of the MLSS fading channel model arises from its capacity to be simplified to double Rayleigh, double Rice, SLDS, NLSS, and SLSS channel models under specific assumptions.

This chapter also presents a deep analysis of the statistical properties of MLSS fading channels. The statistical properties studied, include the PDF of MLSS processes along with the PDF of the corresponding phase processes. Accurate analytical expressions have been derived for the above mentioned statistical quantities. The accuracy and validity of the analytical expressions are confirmed by simulations. The excellent fitting of the theoretical and simulation results verifies the correctness of the derived analytical expressions. The results indicate that the statistical characteristics of MLSS channels significantly differ from those of the processes incorporated in the MLSS channel model as specific instances. The exhibited findings clearly demonstrate that relay gain significantly influences the statistical features of MLSS channels. The characteristics of a fading channel determine the selection of transmitter and receiver techniques, encompassing detection, modulation, and coding schemes, among others. Consequently, the theoretical findings delineated in this chapter are highly beneficial for the designers of the physical layer in M2M cooperative wireless networks. The created M2M channel model may be utilized to assess the overall performance of M2M communication systems in both NLOS and LOS propagation circumstances..

FOOTNOTES

1. The material in this chapter was presented in part at the 19th IEEE International Symposium on Per- sonal, Indoor and Mobile Radio Communications, PIMRC 2008, Cannes, France, September 2008

REFERENCES

1. Akki, A. S. (1994). Statistical properties of mobile-to-mobile land communication channels, IEEE Trans. Veh. Technol. Vol. 43(No. 4): 826–831.
2. Almers, P., Tufvesson, F. & Molisch, A. F. (2006). Keyhole effect in MIMO wireless channels: measurements and theory, IEEE Trans. Wireless Commun. Vol. 5(No. 12): 3596–3604.
3. Andersen, J. B. (2002). Statistical distributions in mobile communications using multiple scat- tering, Proc. 27th URSI General Assembly, Maastricht, Netherlands.
4. Dohler, M. (2003). Virtual Antenna Arrays, Ph.D. dissertation, King's College, London, United Kingdom.
5. Erceg, V., Fortune, S. J., Ling, J., Rustako, Jr, A. J. & Valenzuela, R. A. (1997). Comparison of a computer-based propagation prediction tool with experimental data collected in urban microcelluar environment, IEEE J. Select. Areas Commun. Vol. 15(No. 4): 677– 684.

6. Gradshteyn, I. S. & Ryzhik, I. M. (2000). Table of Integrals, Series, and Products, 6th edn, New York: Academic Press.
7. Kovacs, I. Z., Eggers, P. C. F., Olesen, K. & Petersen, L. G. (2002). Investigations of outdoor-to- indoor mobile-to-mobile radio communication channels, Proc. IEEE 56th Veh. Technol. Conf., VTC'02-Fall, Vol. 1, Vancouver BC, Canada, pp. 430–434.
8. Laneman, J. N., Tse, D. N. C. & Wornell, G. W. (2004). Cooperative diversity in wireless net- works: efficient protocols and outage behavior, IEEE Trans. Inform. Theory Vol. 50(No. 12): 3062–3080.
9. Papoulis, A. & Pillai, S. U. (2002). Probability, Random Variables and Stochastic Processes, 4th edn, New York: McGraw-Hill.
10. Patel, C. S., Stüber, G. L. & Pratt, T. G. (2006). Statistical properties of amplify and forward relay fading channels, IEEE Trans. Veh. Technol. Vol. 55(No. 1): 1–9.
11. Pätzold, M. (2002). Mobile Fading Channels, Chichester: John Wiley & Sons.
12. Pätzold, M. & Hogstad, B. O. (2006). Two new methods for the generation of multiple un- correlated Rayleigh fading waveforms, Proc. IEEE 63rd Semiannual Veh. Tech. Conf., VTC'06-Spring, Vol. 6, Melbourne, Australia, pp. 2782–2786.
13. Salo, J., El-Sallabi, H. M. & Vainikainen, P. (2006). Statistical analysis of the multiple scattering radio channel, IEEE Trans. Antennas Propagat. Vol. 54(No. 11): 3114–3124.
14. Sendonaris, A., Erkip, E. & Aazhang, B. (2003a). User cooperation diversity — Part I: System description, IEEE Trans. Commun. Vol. 51(No. 11): 1927–1938.
15. Sendonaris, A., Erkip, E. & Aazhang, B. (2003b). User cooperation diversity — Part II: Im- plementation aspects and performance analysis, IEEE Trans. Commun. Vol. 51(No. 11): 1939–1948.
16. Shin, H. & Lee, J. H. (2004). Performance analysis of space-time block codes over keyhole Nakagami-m fading channels, IEEE Trans. Veh. Technol. Vol. 53(No. 2): 351–362.
17. Simon, M. K. (2002). Probability Distributions Involving Gaussian Random Variables: A Handbook for Engineers and Scientists, Dordrecht: Kluwer Academic Publishers.
18. Talha, B. & Pätzold, M. (2007a). On the statistical properties of double Rice channels, Proc. 10th International Symposium on Wireless Personal Multimedia Communications, WPMC 2007, Jaipur, India, pp. 517–522.

19. Talha, B. & Pätzold, M. (2007b). On the statistical properties of mobile-to-mobile fading chan- nels in cooperative networks under line-of-sight conditions, Proc. 10th International Symposium on Wireless Personal Multimedia Communications, WPMC 2007, Jaipur, In- dia, pp. 388–393.
20. Talha, B. & Pätzold, M. (2008a). Level-crossing rate and average duration of fades of the envelope of mobile-to-mobile fading channels in cooperative networks under line- of-sight conditions, Proc. 51st IEEE Globecom 2008, New Orleans, USA, pp. 1–6. DOI 10.1109/GLOCOM.2008.ECP.860.
21. Talha, B. & Pätzold, M. (2008b). A novel amplify-and-forward relay channel model for mobile- to-mobile fading channels under line-of-sight conditions, Proc. 19th IEEE Int. Symp. on Personal, Indoor and Mobile Radio Communications, PIMRC 2008, Cannes, France, pp. 1–6. DOI 10.1109/PIMRC.2008.4699733.

17 Chapter

RESOURCE MANAGEMENT WITH RESTRICTED CAPACITY OF FIXED RELAY STATIONS IN MULTI-HOP CELLULAR NETWORKS

1. INTRODUCTION: AN OVERVIEW

This chapter aims to create a resource management strategy for the efficient utilization of resources in multi-hop cellular networks. Multi-hop cellular networks have been suggested to improve throughput and broaden coverage (Cho & Haas, 2004). This improvement may generally be accomplished by implementing relay stations in traditional cellular networks. The benefit of multi-hop networks stems from the decreased total route loss attained by employing a relay station between a base station and a mobile station. Furthermore, heavily obstructed mobile stations might be facilitated by employing relay stations to circumvent barriers.

Despite the benefits of multi-hop transmission, it incurs a drawback: the requirement for supplementary resources to facilitate data transmission in a multi-hop configuration (for instance, in two-hop transmission, two time slots or frequency channels are necessary for the base station-relay station link and the relay station-mobile station link) (Lee et al., 2008). Consequently, this consequence of multi-hop transmission is characterized by 'worms' that consume resources (Ju et al., 2009).

The trade-offs inherent in multi-hop networks complicate the evaluation of their overall effectiveness. For mobile stations with guaranteed quality-of-service (QoS) requirements via single-hop transmission with limited resources, multi-hop transmission may result in unnecessary resource expenditure due to numerous hops, despite potentially offering greater end-to-end data speeds. A greater end-to-end data throughput does not ensure enhanced efficiency in resource consumption. Therefore, the resources necessary to ensure Quality of Service (QoS) must be taken into account while evaluating multi-hop transmission performance, which may vary based on the mobile station.

Furthermore, the infrastructure costs escalate approximately linearly with the equipment's capability (Johansson et al., 2004), and it is infeasible to adjust the capability of the installed equipment flexibly in response to changes in the required capability. Therefore, a relay station have a constrained and defined capacity. Owing to restricted capacity, certain mobile stations are unable to broadcast in multi-hop if the relay station's capabilities have been entirely allocated to other mobile stations. Consequently, resource management for allocating the restricted capacity to the mobile station, which can better utilize multi-hop transmission, is necessary..

2. MULTI-HOP CELLULAR NETWORKS

The network under consideration in this chapter is a downlink orthogonal frequency division multiple access (OFDMA) multi-hop cellular network. The multi-hop system adopted here is the two-hop relaying system, which is known to be the most efficient multi- hop system with respect to system capacity (Cho & Haas, 2004). In this system, data can be transmitted from a base station to a mobile station in one of two transmission modes: single- hop transmission or multi-hop transmission via a fixed relay station.

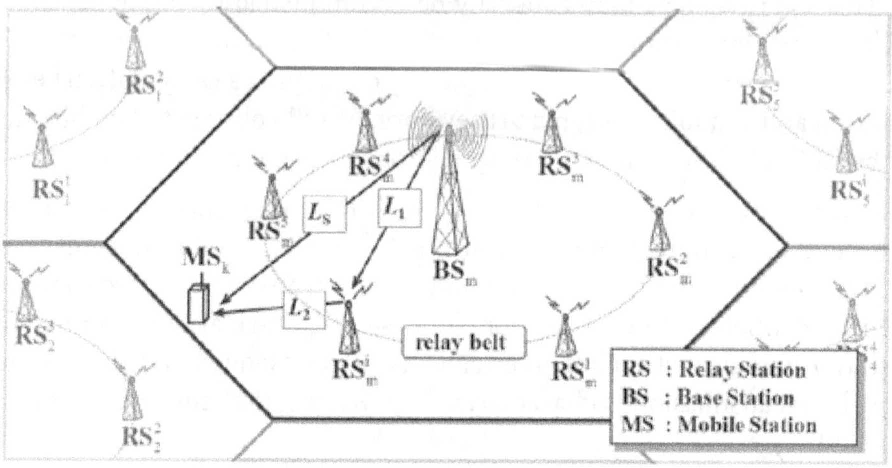

Fig. 1. Downlink multi-hop cellular networks

Fig. 1 shows an example of the connectivity for this system. In Fig. 1, the k th mobile station, MSk , is connected with the m th base station, BSm , and MSk uses the i th fixed relay station in the m th cell, RSi , for multi-hop transmission. A number of fixed relay stations are placed on the relay belt. All the fixed relay stations are regenerative relays, so they decode data received from the base station and then forward it to the target mobile stations. In this system, three kinds of links are formed. The base station-fixed relay station links and the fixed relay station-mobile station links occurring with two-hop transmission are denoted by the link for the first hop (L1) and the link for the second hop (L2), respectively. The link for single-hop transmission (LS) also denotes the base station-mobile station link. Generally, it is assumed that L1 has good channel condition for a line-of-sight (LOS) environment, and L2 and LS are in a non line-of-sight (NLOS) environment (Liu et al., 2006). The LOS assumption can be satisfied by deploying fixed relay stations at selected locations, such as on top of a blinding.

As QoS parameters which can be handled in the physical layer, the target data rate and the target bit-error-rate (BER) can be considered. In the regenerative relay, errors generated at each hop are propagated to the next hop. The sum of the target bit-error-rates for each hop in two-hop transmission should therefore be equal to or less than the target bit-error-rate in two-hop transmission, BT , as Σ i =1 BT ≤ BT where BT is the target bit-error-rate on the link of the i th hop (Boyer et al., 2004).

In addition, the end-to-end data rate from a base station to a mobile station is determined by the minimum data rate among the rates in each hop (Jing et al., 2005). Hence, the target data rate for each hop should be equal to or greater than the target data rate, RT , as R1iT ≥ R1iT where RT is the target data rate on the link of the i th hop.

In OFDMA systems, each subcarrier can obtain a different channel gain. So, the received signal to interference and noise ratio (SINR) on the n th subcarrier of the link L (L ∈{LS ,L1,L2}) can be defined as

$$\Gamma_L(n) = \frac{G_L(n) \cdot P_I}{\sum_{j \neq m} \alpha_j(n) \cdot G_{I_j}(n) \cdot P_I + \eta}, \quad \forall L, \tag{1}$$

where η is the additive Gaussian noise power and GL (n) is the channel gain of link L on the n th subcarrier. I j is the link between an interferer in the j th cell and the target node, and PI is the transmission power of the transmitter on that link.

If it is assumed that every link in a cell utilizes different resources and resources used for transmission on a link are also reused at the same link in other cells concurrently, then the link BSm - RSmi and the link BSj - RSj i (j ≠ m) use the same resources. Hence, in single-hop transmission, L is the link BSm - MSk , I j is the link BS j - MSk , and PI = PBS , where PBS is the transmission power of the base station in (1). In addition, in two-hop transmission, L is the link BS - RSi , I is the link BSm - RSmi , and P = P on the first hop. L is the link RSi - MS , I is the link RS i - MS , and P = P *FRS* on the second hop where P *FRS* is the I FRS FRStransmission power of the fixed relay station.

Some of subcarriers are not being used when the mobile stations do not require all of subcarriers in OFDMA systems. Hence, α j (n) in (1) is adopted to express the loading state of the n the subcarrier in the j th cell. α j (n)= 1 if the n th subcarrier is used to transfer data in the j th cell, while α j (n) = 0 otherwise. Therefore, the average loading state of the j th cell, ρ j , is defined as

$$\rho_j = \frac{1}{N}\sum_{n=1}^{N}\alpha_j(n), \tag{2}$$

where N is the total number of subcarriers in a cell. In addition, ρ j becomes one when there is full loading.

With adaptive modulation coding (AMC), the throughput on the link L is expressed as the function of ΓL(n) and BTL , as follows:

$$\begin{aligned} R_L(n) &= f(B_L^T, \Gamma_L(n)) \\ &= \frac{1}{T_s}\log_2\left(1+\frac{-1.5}{\ln(5\cdot B_L^T)}\cdot\Gamma_L(n)\right), \forall L, n, \end{aligned} \tag{3}$$

where Ts is the symbol duration (Qiu and Chawla, 1999). The number of subcarriers on link required to guarantee the QoS for MSk , Ck , L , is determined by R and RL (n) . For instance, when the channel gains of all subcarriers are equal and the average loading state for the other cells is one, then RL (1) = RL (2) =••• = RL , and Ck, L can be defined as

$$C_{kL} = \lceil RT / R \rceil \mid \forall\, k, L, \tag{4}$$

where $\lceil \chi \rceil$ is the least integer equal to or greater than χ . Hence, the total numbers of subcarriers of MSk required to transmit data with a QoS guarantee by single-hop transmission and multi-hop transmission, C_kSH and C_kMH , are respectively defined as

$$C_k^{SH} = C_{k,L_S}, \; C_k^{MH} = \sum_{i=1}^{2} C_{k,L_i}, \; \forall k. \tag{5}$$

A fixed relay station has a limited capability due to the cost, the limitation of power amplifier and so on. In this chapter, the number of supportable subcarriers is considered as the capability of the fixed relay station. It means that the i th fixed relay station can support up to Ni, RX subcarriers for receiving on L1 (the link between the base station and the relay station) and Ni,TX subcarriers for transmitting on L2 (the link between the relay station and the mobile station) in a time. Hence, the total number of required subcarriers of each link should be equal or fewer than the supportable number of subcarriers of a fixed relay station in each link as follows:

$$\sum_{k\in MU_i} C_{k,L_1} \le N_{i,RX}, \; \sum_{k\in MU_i} C_{k,L_2} \le N_{i,TX}, \tag{6}$$

where MUi is the set of mobile stations who want to use the i th fixed relay station in transmission. Fixed relay stations which have higher capabilities can generally support more subcarriers with higher total power.

3. TRANSMISSION MODEL SELECTION: MULTI-HOP VS. SINGLE-HOP

The multi-hop transmission needs for additional resources, but it achieves more reliable transmission than the single-hop transmission. Due to this trade-off, the multi-hop transmission cannot be better than the single-hop transmission for all users. Hence, the elements, which affect the performance of multi-hop transmission, are investigated and the transmission mode selection for more efficient resource utilization is discussed in this section.

3.1 Achievable Gain from Multi-hop Transmission

With respect to efficiency of resources, the gain associated with multi-hop transmission is achieved when subcarriers are saved by transmitting in multi-hop instead of in single-hop. Hence, the multi-hop gain, Sk , can be defined as the relative ratio of the amount of saved subcarriers to the number of required subcarriers in single-hop transmission as follows (Lee et al., 2008):

$$S_k = \frac{C_k^{SH} - C_k^{MH}}{C_k^{SH}}, \quad \forall k. \tag{7}$$

This approach shows the amount of gain or loss with multi-hop transmission. Thus, if Sk has a positive value, that means that the multi-hop transmission is saving subcarriers with guaranteeing the QoS requirements for the k th mobile station. On the other hand, if the value of Sk is negative, that implies that the multi-hop transmission is wasting subcarriers.

Fig. 2 presents the multi-hop gain in various environments with the assumption of the equal average loading states of other cells as ρ j = ρ,∀j ≠ m in (2). The distance between the k th mobile station and the base station is denoted by dk and the cell radius is dcell . System parameters in Table 1 are used for simulations. Fig. 2 and the formulas from (1) to (5) show that multi-hop gain is affected by three elements: loading state of other cells, location of the mobile station, and QoS requirements. Due to the long transmission distance in single-hop transmission, Ck ,L is generally greater than Ck ,L or Ck ,L . However, for the multi-hop transmission, subcarriers for multi-hops, the sum of Ck ,L and Ck ,L , should be used. By this relation, the multi-hop gain is affected by the loading states of other cells and the location of the mobile station. As the loading state of other cells increases or if the mobile station is located near the cell boundary, the SINRs of the three links decrease. At a lower SINR, the achievable data rate is more sensitive to variation of SINR due to the log function as in (3). This means that the farther the SINR falls, the faster the number of subcarriers required for guaranteeing QoS increases. Hence, in this environment, Ck ,L increases more rapidly than the sum of Ck ,L and Ck ,L , so that a bigger multi-hop gain can be achieved.

Table 1. System parameters (for simulations of Fig. 2, Fig. 3, Fig. 5 and Fig. 6)

System Parameters	Values
System bandwidth	5MHz
Number of subcarriers	1024
Path loss exponent (LOS/NLOS)	2.35 / 3.76
Standard deviation of shadowing (LOS/NLOS)	3.4 dB / 8 dB
Transmission power of base station /fixed relay station	43 dBm / 40 dBm
Cell radius /Radius of the relay belt	500 m / 250 m
Number of cells	7
Number of fixed relay stations per cell	6, Symmetrically located on the relay belt
Number of mobile stations per cell	200, Uniformly distributed
Modulation order	BPSK, QPSK, 16-,64-,128- QAM
Power control	Equal power allocation

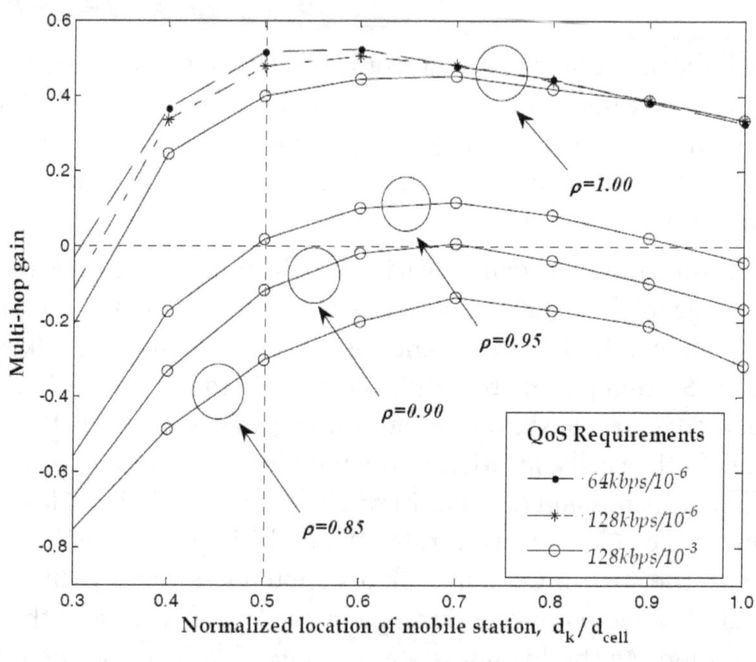

Fig. 2. Multi-hop gain based on QoS requirements (target data rate/target BER), loading state of other cells (ρ) and mobile station location (the mobile station's QoS parameters are 128kbps / 10-3 for all cases except for the case of ρ = 1.0.)

However, this increasing multi-hop gain begins to decrease when dk is above a certain value (e.g., dk / dcell ≥ 0.7 when ρ = 0.95 in Fig. 2). The reason for this is that Ck,L is also increasing rapidly due to larger interference as the mobile station moves to the cell edge, causing the difference between CSH and CMH to get smaller.

On the other hand, as the mobile station approaches the base station or the loading states of other cells decrease, the SINRs for all three links are increasing. When the SINR has increased enough, the required number of subcarriers becomes small and it is no longer sensitive to the variation in SINR. Hence, in this environment, all of Ck ,L , Ck ,L and Ck ,L are small, so that the multi-hop transmission would waste subcarriers because of the usage of subcarriers for two hops. For this reason, the multi-hop transmission does not have any gain as the loading states of other cells decrease or the mobile station approaches the base station (e.g., dk / dcell ≤ 0.5 when ρ = 0.95 in Fig. 2).

In addition, comparing the upper three lines in Fig. 2 shows that the multi-hop gain has different values depending on the target data rate and the target BER. Even the multi-hop gains for these three cases become similar when the mobile station approaches the cell boundary because of the large amount of interference, a lower target BER induces a higher multi-hop gain because the reliable transmission is more important to mobile stations requiring lower target BERs. The multi-hop gain also varies depending on the target data rate due to the subcarrier allocation process.

In this subsection, the affecting elements on the multi-hop gain, the loading state of other cells, the location of mobile station, and QoS requirement, have been discussed. Since the multi-hop transmission can save (or waste) resources according to those elements, the multi- hop transmission should be used selectively for efficient utilization of resources. Hence, transmission mode selection is required to determine the appropriate transmission mode for each mobile station: multi-hop transmission or single-hop transmission.

3.2 Mechanism for Transmission Mode Selection

The number of required subcarriers changes depending on the transmission mode, the QoS requirements, and the channel condition. To save subcarriers, whichever transmission mode requires fewer subcarriers should be the one selected. Hence, the subcarrier-based criterion, Λk ,S , is defined as follows (Lee et al., 2008):

$$\Lambda \qquad = CSH - CMH , \forall k. \tag{8}$$

If Λk ,S is greater than zero, then the selected transmission mode becomes the multi-hop transmission; otherwise, single-hop transmission mode is selected.

In the case where the SINRs for each subcarrier are different, CSH and CMH cannot be calculated before the transmission mode is determined because the frequency bands for single-hop and multi-hop transmission may be different. The subcarrier allocation which determines the number of required subcarriers should therefore be performed after determination of the transmission mode. In this case, the average number of required subcarriers $\overline{C_k^{\varphi}}$ can be used instead of C k Φ to calculate $\Lambda_{k,S}$ where $\varphi \in \{SH, MH\}$. $\overline{C_k^{SH}}$ and

$\overline{C_k^{MH}}$ are respectively defined as $\overline{C_k^{SH}} = \left\lceil R^T / \overline{R_{L_S}} \right\rceil$, and $\overline{C_k^{MH}} = \sum_{i=1}^{2} \left\lceil R^T / \overline{R_{L_i}} \right\rceil, \forall k$, where $\overline{R_L} = (1/N) \cdot \sum_{n=1}^{N} R_L(n)$.

As simpler way to select transmission mode, the distance based criterion can be used. As discussed in Section 3.1, the multi-hop gain changes depending on the locations of mobile stations. Positive gain could be obtained when a mobile station is located near the base station. Hence, the transmission mode can be determined using the following criterion (Lee et al., 2008):

$$\Lambda k, D = dk - dref, \forall k. \quad (9)$$

In (9), d_k is $\sqrt{(x_0 - x_k)^2 + (y_0 - y_k)^2}$ where (x_0, y_0) and (x_k, y_k) are the coordinates (x and y) of a base station's location and the mobile station's location obtained by a positioning system (e.g., global positioning system), respectively, and d_{ref} is the reference distance for the transmission mode selection. If d_k is greater than d_{ref}, $\Lambda_{k,D}$ has a positive value and the multi-hop transmission is selected. This means that the multi-hop transmission is applied for mobile stations located outside of the circle with radius d_{ref}.

The performance of the transmission mode selection can be expressed as blocking probability, which is the ratio of the number of unsupportable mobile stations, KU, to the total number of mobile stations which access the system, KT , or KU / KT as Fig. 3. In this figure, TMS-S and TMS-D represent the transmission mode selections using the subcarrier- based criterion (Λk ,S) and the distance-based criterion (Λk, D), respectively.

In Fig. 3, TMS-D and TMS-S demonstrate better performance, regardless of the loading states of other cells, than the cases where either single-hop transmission or the multi-hop transmission is applied without the selection process. This means that more mobile stations can be supported in a cell with lower blocking probability when the transmission mode selection is applied. Specifically, when the loading states of other cells are 1.0 and the blocking probability is 0.1, only 45 mobile stations and 95 mobile stations can be supported using conventional single-hop transmission and the multi-hop transmission, respectively. The number of supportable mobile stations increases to 150 with TMS-D and 250 with TMS-S.

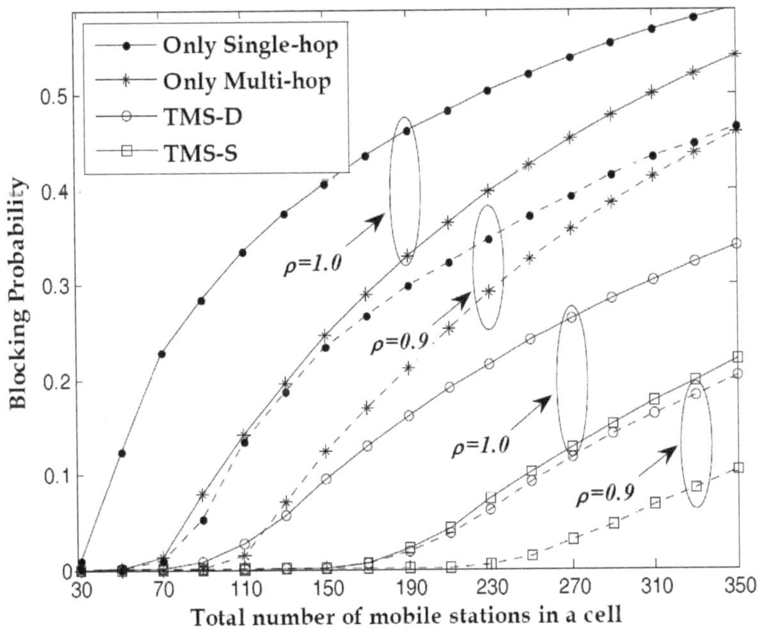

Fig. 3. Comparison of blocking probabilities based on total number of mobile stations in a cell

4. MULTI-HOP USER ADMISSION FOR RELAY STATIONS WITH LIMITED CAPABILITIES

Based on the transmission mode selection in Section 3.2, the multi-hop user and the single-hop user, which denote the mobile stations which select the multi-hop transmission and the single-hop transmission, respectively, are determined. Since all fixed relay stations have the limited capabilities, a fixed relay station may not be able to support all of multi-hop users. When the required subcarriers of multi-hop users are beyond the number of supportable subcarriers in (6), some multi-hop users cannot receive data in multi-hop. Hence, to utilize the limited capability of the fixed relay station efficiently, the multi-hop user admission is required to allow the multi-hop users, which achieve high multi-hop gain, to use a fixed relay station. Therefore, in this section, the problem of multi-hop user admission is discussed and the multi-hop user admission algorithms are presented.

4.1 Formulation of Multi-hop User Admission

The multi-hop user admission strategy is formulated to determine the admitted multi-hop users to use the fixed relay station among all multi-hop users for maximizing the total multi- hop gains which can be obtained from the admitted multi-hop users as follows:

$$
\begin{aligned}
\text{max} \quad & \sum_{i=1}^{F} \sum_{k \in MU_i} x_k \cdot S_k \\
\text{s.t} \quad & \Omega_{1,i} : \sum_{k \in MU_i} x_k \cdot C_{k,L_1} \leq N_{i,RX}, \ \forall i \\
& \Omega_{2,i} : \sum_{k \in MU_i} x_k \cdot C_{k,L_2} \leq N_{i,TX}, \ \forall i \\
& \Omega_3 : x_k \in \{0,1\}, \ \forall k,
\end{aligned} \tag{10}
$$

where F is the total number of fixed relay stations in a cell, and the xk is the indicator of admission. If MSk is admitted to transmit in multi-hop using the fixed relay station, then xk = 1 , otherwise xk = 0 and MSk should transmit in single-hop.

For each fixed relay station, there are two constraints from the limited capabilities: Ω1,i and Ω2,i based on the i th fixed relay station. The Lagrangian of multi-hop user admission problem, Lag (u, u′) , can be defined as follows:

$$
\begin{aligned}
Lag(u,u') &= \sum_{i=1}^{F} \left(\sum_{k \in MU_i} x_k \cdot S_k - u_i \sum_{k \in MU_i} \left(x_k \cdot C_{k,L_1} - N_{i,RX} \right) - u_i' \sum_{k \in MU_i} \left(x_k \cdot C_{k,L_2} - N_{i,TX} \right) \right) \\
&= \sum_{i=1}^{F} Lag(u_i, u_i')
\end{aligned} \tag{11}
$$

where u and u’ are Lagrangian multipliers. Hence, it is shown that the primal problem can be decomposed into sub-problems Z (ui ,ui’) where Z (ui ,ui’) = max Lag(ui ,ui’) . It means that the parallel multi-hop user admissions for each fixed relay station can work independently since the result of one fixed relay station’s multi-hop user admission does not affect the other fixed relay stations’ multi-hop user admission. Therefore, we can deal with the multi- hop user admission problem by decomposing into the independent multi-hop user admission problems for each fixed relay station, which can be formulated as follows:

$$
\begin{aligned}
\text{max} \quad & \sum_{k \in MU_i} x_k \cdot S_k \\
\text{s.t} \quad & \Omega_{1,i}, \Omega_{2,i}, \text{and}\, \Omega_3.
\end{aligned} \tag{12}
$$

The problem in (12) has the equivalent form with the two-dimensional knapsack problem (TDKP) which is a kind of multi-dimensional knapsack problem (MDKP) (Qiu & Chawla, 1999). The MDKP is a variant of the classical 0-1 knapsack problem (KP) with more than two knapsacks.

4.2 Algorithms for Multi-hop User Admission

As shown in Section 4.1, the multi-hop user admission strategy can be represented as the two-dimensional knapsack problem a kind of MDKP. The KP and the MDKP are proven to be NP-hard, so the optimal solutions of them cannot be obtained in a polynomial time (Akbar et al., 2005). Hence, a heuristic algorithm could be used for multi-hop user admission, and two multi-hop user admission algorithms are presented in this section.

4.2.1 Balanced Link Multi-hop User Admission (BL-MUA) Algorithm

In the multi-hop user admission, the balance between the used resources on L1 and those on L2 is important. The reason for this is that no additional multi-hop users can be admitted when at least one of Ni , RX on L1 and Ni,TX on L2 is fully occupied for other multi-hop users. Hence, the balanced link multi-hop user admission (BL-MUA) algorithm has been proposed in (Lee et al., 2007) considering the balance in admission by adopting the primal effective gradient method (PEGM) (Toyoda, 1975).

The PEGM determines the priority of admission using the new measurement of the aggregate resource. The aggregate resource is to penalize the multi-hop user which requires many subcarriers in the more loaded link. The *aggregate resource* in multi-hop user admission can be defined as $A_k = (C_{k,L_1} \cdot l_1 + C_{k,L_2} \cdot l_2) / \sqrt{l_1^2 + l_2^2}$ where l_1 and l_2 are the total numbers of used subcarriers on L_1 and L_2 by the currently admitted multi-hop users, respectively. The priority function of the BL-MUA algorithm, $U_{BL,k}$, is set by the multi-hop gain over the aggregate resources, S_k / A_k, as follows:

$$\mathrm{U}_{BL,k} = \frac{S_k \sqrt{l_1^2 + l_2^2}}{C_{k.L_1} \cdot l_1 + C_{k.L_2} \cdot l_2}. \tag{11}$$

If at least one of Ni,TX and Ni, RX is insufficient for supporting all multi-hop users in MUi , the multi-hop user with the lowest priority is rejected to use the fixed relay station one by one. The priority function helps to balance between the loading states of two links while rejecting the multi-hop user.

4.2.2 Focused Link Multi-hop User Admission (FL-MUA) Algorithm

The BL-MUA algorithm attaches importance to the balance of used resources in L1 and L2 . However, if fixed relay stations are located in a LOS environment with the base station and the environment of L2 is a NLOS (like a general assumption), then the number of required subcarriers to guarantee the same target data rate in L2 is much more than that in L1 , Ck ,L < Ck , L. This means that more multi-hop users could not be admitted in a fixed relay station generally due to the full loading of L2 , not that of L1 (the supportable subcarriers in L2 is exhausted quickly than that in L1).

Therefore, the multi-hop user admission considering both loading states of L1 and L2 can be simplified to that considering only that of L2 . In this case, the multi-hop user admission strategy becomes a simple knapsack problem, not the two-dimensional knapsack problem anymore. Hence, the focused link multi-hop user admission (FL-MUA) algorithm is proposed to focus only on the loading state of L2 (Lee et al., 2007). As the priority function in the FL-MUA algorithm, the multi-hop gain per the average number of required subcarriers in L2 is used as

UFL, k = Sk / Ck , L . (12)

When the supportable subcarriers of a fixed relay station are not sufficient, the multi-hop users are excluded in a low-priority order one by one.

4.2.3 Procedure of multi-hop user admission algorithms

The process of the multi-hop user admission algorithms progresses independently for each fixed relay station, and the overall procedure is shown by the flow chart in Fig. 4. If multi- hop users which want to use the i th fixed relay station exist, the total number of required subcarriers for supporting all multi-hop users in L and L, lo and lo , can be calculated as

$$l_1^o = \sum_{k \in \overline{MU}_i} C_{k,L_1}, \quad l_2^o = \sum_{k \in \overline{MU}_i} C_{k,L_2}. \qquad (13)$$

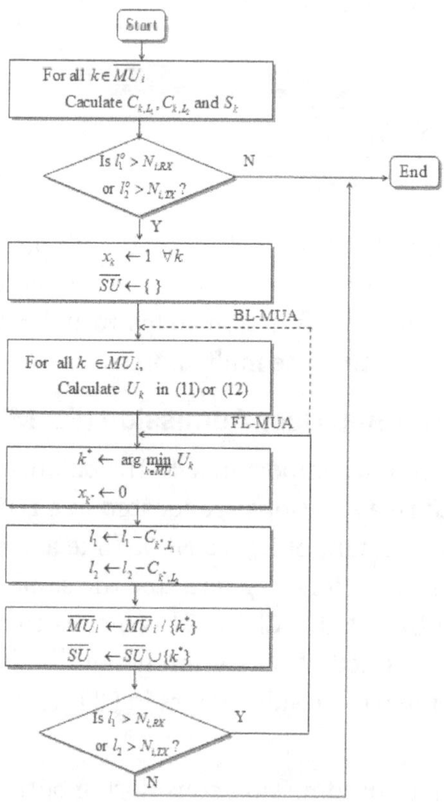

Fig. 4. Flow chart of the multi-hop user admission algorithms (BL-MUA algorithm and FL- MUA algorithm)

If l1o > N i, RX or lo > N i,TX, then the multi-hop user admission algorithm starts. First of all, the priority values of all multi-hop users are obtained based on the priority function in (11) or (12). After that, the multi-hop user with the lowest priority is selected and the indicator of admission is set to zero. The selected multi-hop user should do single-hop transmission, so the multi-hop user is excluded from the MUi and added to the set of single-hop users, SU .

If one or both of the capabilities in the first hop and the second hop, Ni, RX and Ni,TX , are still insufficient after one multi-hop user exclusion, the multi-hop user admission process progresses again. At this time, the used resources, l1 and l2, are changed due to the exclusion of a multi-hop user, so the priority function of the BL-MUA algorithm should be updated. On the other hand, in the FL-MUA algorithm, the updating process is not required and the algorithm just keeps using the previously determined priorities, so it is simpler than the BL-MUA algorithm. The process of the multi-hop user admission continuously works until both of Ni, RX and Ni,TX are sufficient for supporting all multi-hop users in MUi .

4.3 Performance of Multi-hop User Admission Algorithms

In this section, the performance of the BL-MUA algorithm and that of the FL-MUA algorithm are evaluated with the assumption that the deployed fixed relay stations have the same capabilities as NR and all capabilities for transmitting and receiving are equal as Ni, RX = Ni,TX = NR ,∀i . The performances of the multi-hop user algorithms are verified with two types of fixed relay stations: the fixed relay station with low capability (L-FRS) and that with high capability (H-FRS). The numbers of supportable subcarriers per fixed relay station are set to 16 for L-FRS and 64 for H-FRS, and the average loading state of other cells is set to one. The other system parameters are the same as Table 1. In addition, the performances of the multi-hop user admission algorithms are compared to the case where multi-hop users are randomly admitted without an admission algorithm (w/o MUA in Fig. 5).

In both multi-hop user admission algorithms, with the higher priority, the supportable subcarriers of a fixed relay station are used for the mobile stations which occupy fewer subcarriers with higher multi-hop gain. Hence, the number of admitted multi-hop users in a fixed relay station can be increased by the algorithms. Those are verified in Fig. 5.

Fig. 5 presents the number of admitted multi-hop users in a fixed relay station according to two types of fixed relay stations. More multi-hop users can be supported in a fixed relay station by the multi-hop user admission algorithms within the limited capability of fixed relay station compared to the case without multi-hop user admission algorithm.

Moreover, the performance difference between the multi-hop user admission algorithms and the case without the algorithm becomes more significant as the number of multi-hop users increases. When the number of multi-hop users is small, the capability of fixed relay station is generally sufficient for supporting all multi-hop users. Hence, the multi-hop user admission is not actually required and the performance of the multi-hop user admission algorithms is similar to the case without the algorithms. However, the multi-hop user admission becomes meaningful when the fixed relay station cannot support all multi-hop users because of the insufficient capability.

In addition, the performance of BL-MUA algorithm and that of FL-MUA algorithm are similar. The reason for this is from the physical characteristics of L1 and L2 . The number of required subcarriers in L2 is much more than that in L1 as Ck , L > Ck , L . In this case, the priority function of the BL-MUA algorithm in (11) can be approximated to the priority function of the FL-MUA algorithm in (12) as $U_{BL,k} = S_k$ (C k.L1· l + Ck.L2 · l) ≈ Sk/Ck,L2 = UFL,k. Thus, the similar priority functions are used in both algorithms, so the total numbers of admitted users of them do not have big difference. It implies that the FL-MUA algorithm could obtain similar performance to the BL-MUA algorithm with less complexity.

In addition, in the aspect of total capacity in a cell, more mobile stations can be supported with guaranteeing their QoS requirements regardless of single-hop or multi-hop transmissions using the multi-hop user admission algorithms. This can be verified by Fig. 6 which shows the blocking probability as the number of mobile stations per cell increases.

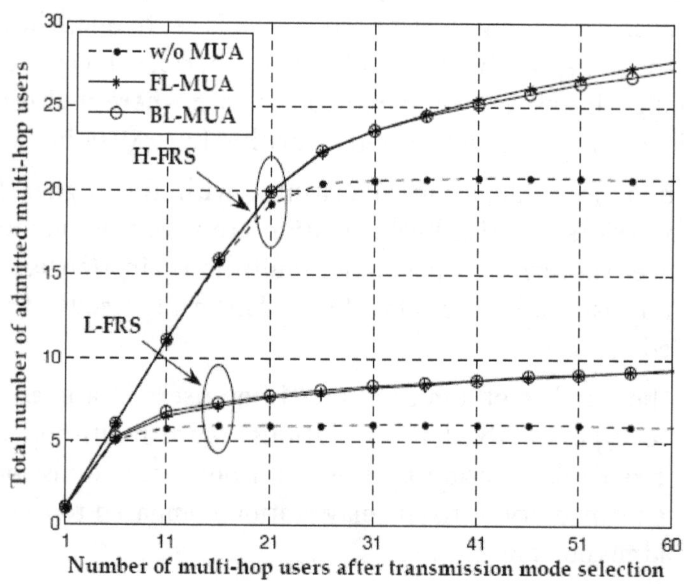

Fig. 5. The total multi-hop gain obtained from the admitted multi-hop users in a fixed relay station according to two types of fixed relay stations

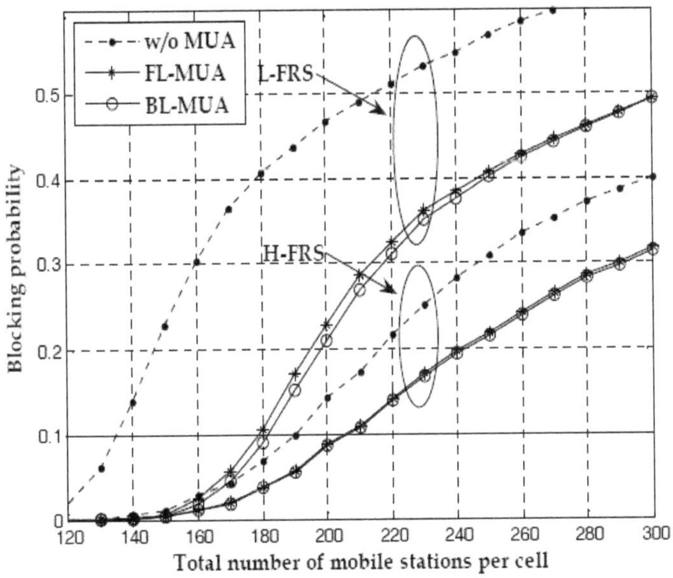

Fig. 6. The blocking probabilities according to two types of fixed relay stations

The blocking probabilities of the multi-hop user admission algorithms are smaller than that of the case without the algorithm over all range. Specifically, within 0.1 blocking probability, the case without the algorithm can support at most 135 mobile stations with L-FRSs and 185 mobile stations with H-FRSs. On the other hand, the numbers of supportable mobile stations are increased up to 180 mobile stations with L-FRSs and 223 mobile stations with H-FRSs by the multi-hop user admission algorithms. It implies that 33 % and 20 % of the supportable mobile stations in a cell are increased by the multi-hop user admission algorithms with L- FRSs and H-FRSs, respectively. Thus, more mobile stations can be supported in a cell with low blocking probability by the multi-hop user admission algorithms.

5. OVERALL STRUCTURE OF RESOURCE MANAGEMENT IN MULTI-HOP CELLULAR NETWORKS

In Section 3 and Section 4, the transmission mode selection and the multi-hop user admission have been discussed. The transmission mode determined through the transmission mode selection can be changed after the multi-hop user admission. The reason for this is that some mobile stations should transmit in single-hop due to the limitation of the fixed relay station's capability even though they select the multi-hop transmission in the transmission mode selection. Therefore, the final transmission mode determination and the resource allocation should be performed after the multi-hop user admission. The overall process of the resource management including the transmission mode selection and the multi-hop user admission is summarized as follows:

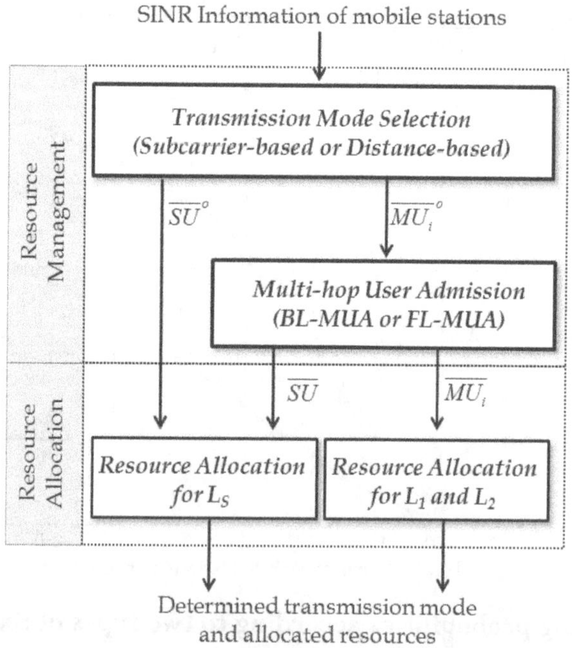

Fig. 7. The overall structure of resource management in multi-hop cellular networks

1. Once the mobile station set is defined and the required SINR information of the mobile stations are collected in a base station, the resource management process can start. The required SINR information is determined according to the criterion of the transmission mode selection and it could include the received SINRs of L1 , L2 and LS .
2. During the transmission mode selection with a specific criterion (subcarrier-based or distance-based criterion), the set of multi-hop users, MUi , and the set of single-hop users, o SU , are determined.
3. After determining the set of multi-hop users, the multi-hop user admission can be performed. Through a multi-hop user admission algorithm (BL-MUA or FL-MUA algorithm), the mobile stations who can finally receive data in multi-hop, MUi and the mobile stations who should receive data in single-hop, SU , due to the lack of the capability of the fixed relay station are determined.
4. The single-hop users in the sets of SU and SU are forwarded to the resource allocation process based on SINR information of LS , and the multi-hop users in the set of MUi undergoes the resource allocation process based on SINR information of L1 and L2 .

After all of those processes are progressed, the final transmission mode which can maximize the multi-hop gain within the limited capability can be obtained.

According to the transmission mode selection criterion and the multi-hop user admission algorithm, the complexity of this resource management could be changed. In the transmission mode selection, the complexity of the transmission mode selection with the subcarrier-based criterion is O(K N (log p) p2) where p is the required number of digits used in the operations such as square root and multiplication. It is higher than the complexity of transmission mode selection with the distance-based criterion, O(K p2) (Lee et al., 2008). Hence, the subcarrier-based selection criterion's complexity is higher than the distance-based selection criterion, but it achieves better performance since it consider more elements for determining an appropriate transmission mode as shown in Section 3.

In the multi-hop user admission, the FL-MUA algorithm is simpler than the BL-MUA algorithm while the BL-MUA algorithm could achieve better performance as shown in Section 4.

Therefore, designers can use appropriate selection criterion and multi-hop user admission algorithm based on what the acceptable complexity level for that system is.

6. CONCISE SUMMARY

This chapter presents resource management strategies for optimal resource use in multi-hop cellular networks. Resource management comprises two components: transmission mode selection and multi-hop user admission. The selection of transmission mode determines the right choice between multi-hop and single-hop transmission to conserve resources while ensuring the QoS needs of mobile stations are met. After examining the factors influencing multi-hop gains, including QoS requirements, the mobile station's location, and the loading conditions of nearby cells, two types of selection criteria are presented: subcarrier-based and distance-based criteria. Nevertheless, owing to the restricted capacity of a relay station, certain mobile stations are unable to send data in a multi-hop configuration, despite opting for the multi-hop transmission mode. Consequently, multi-hop user admission is implemented to allocate the restricted capacity of a relay station to mobile stations, thereby optimizing multi-hop gain. Since the multi-hop user admission strategy is a NP-hard problem, two heuristic algorithms are provided: the BL-MUA algorithm focused on the load balance between L1 and L2 and the FL-MUA algorithm focused only on the load state of L2 . Through the transmission mode selection and the multi-hop user admission, the resources can be used efficiently with supporting more mobile stations with lower blocking probability.

REFERENCES

1. Akbar, M. M.; Rahman, M. S.; Kaykobaad M. & Manning, E. G. (2005). Solving the Multidimensional Multiple-choice Knapsack Problem by Constructing

Convex Hulls. Computers & operations research, Vol. 33, No. 5, pp. 1259-1273, ISSN 0305-0548.

2. Boyer, J.; Falconer, D. D. & Yanikomeroglu, H. (2004). Multihop Diversity in Wireless Relaying Channels. IEEE Transactions on Communications, Vol. 52, No. 10, pp. 1820- 1830, ISSN 0090-6778.

3. Cho, J. & Haas, Z. J. (2004). On the Throughput Enhancement of the Downstream Channel in Cellular Radio Networks through Multihop Relaying. IEEE Journal on Selected Areas in Communications, Vol. 22, No. 7, pp. 1206-1219, ISSN 0733-8716.

4. Jing, S.; Zhao-yang, Z.; Pei-liang, Q. & Guan-ding, Y. (2005). Subcarrier and Power Allocation for OFDMA-Based Regenerative Multihop Links. International Conference on Wireless Communications, Networking and Mobile Computing, Vol. 1, pp. 207-210.

5. Johansson, K.; Furuskar, A.; Karlsson, P. & and Zander, J. (2004). Relation between Base Station Characteristics and Cost Structure in Cellular Systems. IEEE International Symposium on Personal, Indoor and Mobile Radio Communications.

6. Ju, H.; Oh, E. & Hong, D. (2009). Catching Resource-Devouring Worms in Next-Generation Wireless Relay Systems - Two-way Relay and Full-Duplex Relay. IEEE Communications Magazine, Vol. 47, No. 9, pp. 58-65, ISSN 0163-6804.

7. Lee, J.; Wang, H.; Lim, S. & Hong, D. (2007). A Multi-hop User Admission Algorithm for Fixed Relay Stations with Limited Capabilities in OFDMA Cellular Networks. IEEE 18th International Symposium on Personal, Indoor and Mobile Radio Communications, pp. 1-5, ISBN 978-1-4244-1144-3, Athens, Sept. 2007.

8. Lee, J.; Wang, H.; Seo, W. & Hong, D. (2008). QoS-guaranteed Transmission Mode Selection for Efficient Resource Utilization in Multi-hop Cellular Networks. IEEE Transactions on Wirelss Communications, Vol. 7, Issue 10, pp. 3697-3701, ISSN 1536-1276.

9. Liu, T. et al. (2006). Radio Resource Allocation in Two-hop Cellular Relaying Network, IEEE Vehicular Technology Conference, Vol. 1, pp. 91-95, ISBN 1-7803-9392-9, May 2006.

10. Qiu, X. & Chawla, K. (1999). On the Performance of Adaptive Modulation in Cellular Systems. IEEE Transactions on Communications, Vol. 47, No. 6, pp. 884-895, ISSN 0090-6778.

11. Toyoda, Y. (1975). A Simplified Algorithm for Obtaining Approximate Solution to Zero-one Programming Problems. Management Science, Vol. 21, No. 12, pp. 1417-1427, ISSN 0025-1909.

18 Chapter ON CROSS-LAYER ROUTING IN WIRELESS MULTI-HOP NETWORKS

1. INTRODUCTION: AN OVERVIEW

Wireless multi-hop networks signify a crucial advancement in the progression of wireless communications. Recent advancements have introduced various applications of these networks, including community wireless networks, last-mile access for individuals, instantaneous surveillance systems, backhaul services for extensive wireless sensor networks, local high-speed peer-to-peer networking, and connectivity to rural or remote locations previously constrained by cabling.

Wireless multi-hop networks comprise computers and devices (nodes) interconnected by wireless communication channels, referred to as links. Due to the restricted range of wireless communication, numerous node pairs cannot connect directly and must relay data through one or more collaborative intermediate nodes. In unicast routing, the source node sends its packets to a directly communicable nearby node. The next node subsequently relays the packets to one of its neighbors, continuing this process until the packets arrive at their ultimate destination. Each node that transmits packets is termed a hop, while the collection of links used for packet transfer is referred to as the route. A distributed routing mechanism in the network identifies several paths from any nodes to any destinations. Figure 1 illustrates a wireless mesh network where node S2 transmits data to destination D through the collaboration of intermediate nodes R1 and R2, while source node S1 directs its data traffic to the gateway via node A.

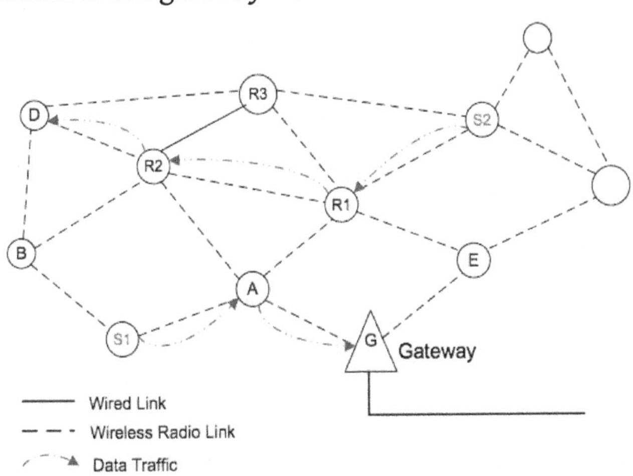

Fig. 1. An illustration of a Wireless Multi-Hop Network.

Wireless multi-hop networks are self-expanding systems; the network's connectivity relies solely on the presence of nodes, allowing for expansion or contraction via the addition or removal of a node. Conversely, cellular networks constitute a far more costly infrastructure, as they require a minimum of one base station to facilitate connectivity. Furthermore, the base station's capacity is constrained, preventing all nodes within the coverage area from connecting to the network. Consequently, wireless multi-hop networks represent a viable solution for network expansion, offering flexibility and rapid implementation at minimal expense.

The Challenges of Wireless Multi-hop Routing in a Time Varying Environment Routing is the fundamental issue for the multi-hop networks. A lot of routing protocols have been proposed for the wired networks and some of them have been widely used such as Routing Information Protocol (RIP) (Hedrick, 1998) and Open Shortest Path First (OSPF)(Moy, 1998). Characteristics of wireless links differ extremely from wired links. Thus, the existing routing protocols for wired networks can not work efficiently in the face of the vagaries of the radio channels and limited battery life and processing power of the devices. Moreover, the traditional routing metric of minimum-hop is not always the best solution for routing in wireless network. In the sequel, the wireless links characteristics and limitations of shortest path routing are described.

Wireless networks have intrinsic characteristics that affect intensely the performance of transport protocols. These peculiarities, which distinguish themselves from conventional wireline networks, can be summarized as follows:

- Wireless links have fundamentally low capacity. The upper band for the capacity of a wireless link follows the Shannon capacity bound.
- Signal propagation experiences large scale and small scale attenuations. Mobility of the nodes, path loss, shadowing and multi-path fading due to reflection, diffraction, scattering, absorption lead to slow and fast variations in channel quality even within the milliseconds scale (Proakis, 2004).
- The wireless medium is a broadcast medium. Therefore, in contrast to wired networks, the interference caused by other in-range traffic can unlimitedly disturb a transmission. This causes the wireless link capacity to depend also on the sensitivity of receivers in sensing the environment as well as other links status in terms of their transmission range and power.
- Packet reception reliability over a link depends on several parameters such as modulation, source/channel coding of that link, the sensitivity of the link and the length of the packets.

Radio channels have some additional features such as asymmetrical nature and non- isotropic connectivity (Ganesan et. al, 2002; Cerpa et. al, 2003; Zhou et. al,

2004). Asymmetry of the channels means connectivity from node A to node B might differ significantly from B to A and non-isotropic connectivity means nodes geographically far away from source may get better connectivity than nodes that are geographically closer.

As a result of these characteristics, the radio cell is neither binary nor static. From the perspective of a node, the set of other nodes it can hear and the loss probability to or from these nodes vary abruptly over time with a large magnitude. This has been widely confirmed in real platforms (Couto et al, 2002; Ganesan et. al, 2002; Cerpa et. al, 2003; Couto, 2004). These random variations induce much more complexity for wireless networks to guarantee performance to transmit real-time or even critical data.

1.2 Limitations of Shortest Path Routing

Most of the existing routing algorithms use the shortest-path metric to find one or more multi-hop paths between the node pairs (Perkins & Royer, 1994; Johnson & Maltz, 1994; Park & Corson, 1997; Perkins & Belding-Royer, 2003; De Couto et. al, 2005). The advantage of this metric is its simplicity and a low overhead to the network. Once the topology is known, it is easy to find a path with a minimum number of hops between a source and a destination without additional measurement and overhead. Recent researches show that choosing the path with the smallest number of hops between nodes often leads to poor performances (De Couto et. al, 2002; De Couto et. al, 2005; Yarvis et. al, 2002).

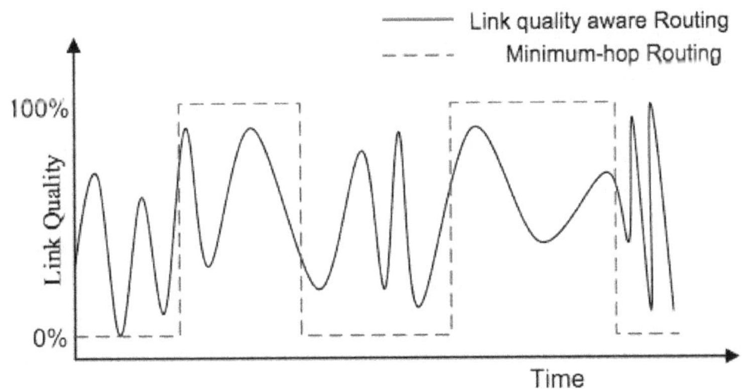

Fig. 2. Different assumptions for wireless link connectivity made by minimum-hop routing and link quality aware routing.

One of the limitations of shortest path routing is that it does not capture the variable nature of wireless links. Instead, it assumes that the links between nodes either work well or do not work at all. Figure 2 shows an illustration of the different assumptions made by minimum- hop routing and link quality aware routing on the wireless links. This shows that the arbitrary choice made by minimum hop-count is not likely to select the best path among the same minimum length with widely varying qualities. Moreover, one of the current trends in wireless communication is to enable devices to operate using many different transmission rates to deal with changes in connectivity due to mobility and interference. In multi-rate wireless networks, minimum-hop works even worse. Selecting the minimum-hop paths leads to maximizing the distance travelled by each hop, but longer links are not robust enough to operate at the higher rates. Therefore, shortest path routing results in selecting the paths with the lowest rates, which degrades dramatically the overall throughput of the network.

Furthermore, transmitting the flow over the low-rate links degrades the performance of other flows, which are transmitted over higher rate links. The main reason of this effect is that slow-speed links require larger amount of medium time to transmit a packet over the shared wireless medium and so block the other flows for a longer time. Heusse et al. denotes this problem as Performance Anomaly of 802.11b (Heusse et. al, 2003). They show analytically that a contending node with lower nominal bit rate degrades the throughput of faster contenders to even a lower bit-rate than the slowest sender. (Mahtre et. al, 2007; Razaϕındralambo et. al, 2008; Choi et. al, 2005) have evaluated and shown the same effect.

Another effect of multi-rate option for a minimum hop routing is that in multi-rate networks broadcast packets benefit from the longer range of low rate transmissions to reach farther nodes and so are always sent at the lowest transmission rate. Therefore, hearing the broadcast Hello messages from a node is not a good enough basis for determining that two nodes are well connected for transferring data packets at high rates. Lundgren et al. have referred to this effect as the gray-zone area (Lundgren et. al, 2002). A gray zone is the maximum area, which is covered by the broadcast messages at low rate, but not all the nodes in this area can forward the packets at high rates.

Choosing closer nodes with shorter-range links instead of minimum-hop routes can solve this problem. Consequently, minimum-hop metric has no flexibility in dealing with random quality fluctuations of the links. Link quality aware routing counters these limitations by using observation of miscellaneous parameters such as frame delivery or signal strength to select the good paths. In this approach, link quality metric is measured and observed in order to predict the near future quality of the links. This estimation is then used to determine the best route.

1.3 Cross Layer Interaction as a Solution

Typically, Open System Interconnection protocol stack (OSI) is divided into several layers which are designed independently. The interactions between adjacent layers are defined by some specific interfaces. Recently, in the quest of finding a link quality aware routing for wireless multi-hop networks, numerous link quality aware metrics have been proposed, which most of them are based on cross layer interactions between various layers of the protocol stack. Lately, there are many research efforts which show that transferring the status information between the layers can lead to a great improvement in network performance (Conti et. al, 2004; Shakkottai et. al, 2003; Goldsmith & Wicker, 1998). Recent activities of IEEE 802.11 task group in mesh networking have released IEEE 802.11s. It extends the IEEE 802.11 Medium Access Control (MAC) standard by defining an architecture and protocol that support both broadcast/multicast and unicast delivery using radio-aware metrics over self-configuring multi-hop topologies. This evolution pushes employing the cross layering technique in the real platforms in near future.

This chapter argues that the cross layering technique can be a promising solution in providing flexibility to the wireless network changes. Nevertheless evaluating the benefits of cross layer routing is often only based on the throughput, which is simplistic. Current studies generally do not consider the impact of other criteria such as response time or route flapping, which influence greatly applications performances in terms of throughput, but also mean delay, jitter and packet loss.

In the next section, a state-of-the-art of the main cross- layering metrics that have been proposed in the literature are presented. Then, the concept of reactivity for a link quality aware routing as a mean to analyse the true benefits of the cross-layer routing is introduced. Section 4 concludes this chapter.

2. LINK QUALITY AWARE ROUTING

Most of the primitive works in routing protocols for wireless multi-hop networks are inherited from existing routing protocols in wired networks. They devise mostly on coping with changing topology and mobile nodes (Perkins & Bhagwa, 1994; Perkins & Royer, 1999; Johnson & Maltz , 1994) and traditionally find the possible routes to any destination in the network with the minimum hop-count. As explained in Section 1.2, shortest path routing has sub-optimal performance, as they tend to include wireless links between distant nodes (De Couto et. al, 2002). A multitude of quality aware metrics have been proposed in the last decade which deal with the strict bandwidth and variable quality of wireless links and try to overcome the disadvantages of the minimum hop (MH) routing. Although most of them have been designed with the objective of increasing the transport capacity, each of them considers different QoS demands such as overall throughput, end-to-end delay, etc. Therefore, the proposed approaches for link quality aware routing can be categorized according to the aim of their design.

2.1 Wireless Network Capacity

The main purpose of efficient routing in mesh networks is improving the achieved capacity. The notion of capacity for wireless ad hoc network was defined as the maximum obtainable throughput from the network. It was first introduced by Gupta and Kumar in their seminal work (Gupta & Kumar, 2000). Network capacity for wireless multi-hop networks is generally unknown, except for some centralized scheduling-based MAC protocols like Time Division Multiple Access (TDMA) where the problem finds a mathematical formulation.

The main finding in (Gupta, 2000) is that per-node capacity of a random wireless network with n static nodes scales as $\Theta(\frac{1}{n \log n})$. They assume a threshold-based link layer model in which a packet transmission is successful if the received SNR at the receiver is greater than a fixed threshold. Instead of this ideal link layer model, Mhatre et al. considere a probabilistic lossy link model and show that the per-node throughput scales as only $\Theta(\frac{1}{n})$ instead of $\Theta(\frac{1}{n \log n})$ (Mahtre & Rosenberg, 2006).

These asymptotic bounds are calculated under assumptions such as node homogeneity and random communication patterns. Therefore, some researches try to relax some of these assumptions on network configuration. Jain et al. focus on interference status among the transmitters as one of the main limiting factors on routing performance (Jain et. al, 2003). They propose to represent interference among wireless links using a conflict graph. A conflict graph shows, which wireless links interfere with each other, such that each edge in the connectivity graph is represented by a vertex and there exists an edge between two vertices if the links interfere with each other. Thus, the throughput optimization problem is posed as a linear programming problem in which upper and lower bounds of the maximum throughput are obtained by finding the maximal clique and independent set in the conflict graph.

Karnik et al. extend the conflict graph idea to a conflict set (Karnik et. al, 2007). Their rational is that an interference model can not be binary since for a given link, generally there is a subset of links that at least one of them should be silent when the given link is transmitting. They propose a joint optimization of routing, scheduling and physical layer parameters to achieve the highest throughput. Both these proposals bring valuable achievement but as they investigate the highest capacity of a network, they have to assume TDMA instead of contention-based algorithm, which leads to probabilistic results. Hence, they implicitly assume that data transmissions are scheduled by a central entity. Therefore they may not be applied easily to more practical networks such as IEEE 802.11 with random access to the channel.

Computing the optimal throughput, despite of giving a good vision to the maximum achievable throughput in the network, may not be implementable in a real network. There are many complicated issues such as necessity of having a distributed routing/scheduling protocol, random quality for the wireless links, limited allowable overhead to the network, compatibility with MAC 802.11, etc., that motivate the researchers to find a practical solution to achieve a good performance.

2.2 Maximum Throughput Routing

Most of the work done in this area relies on the broadcasting of extra probe packets to estimate the channel quality (ex. Sivakumar et. al, 1999; De Couto et. al, 2005; Draves & Zill, 2004). However, since the quality of the wireless links depends significantly on physical settings (such as transmit rate and packet size), the probes may not reflect the actual quality of the links. The reason is that for preventing to throttle the entire channel capacity they have to use small-sized probes at low transmission rate. Therefore the quality experienced by larger data packets at variable transmission rate is not the same as probe packets.

De Couto et al proposes a simple and effective routing metric called the expected transmission count (ETX) for 802.11-based radios employing link-layer retransmissions to recover frame losses (De Couto et. al, 2005). ETX of a wireless link is defined as thc average number of transmissions necessary to transfer a packet successfully over a link. For estimating the expected number of transmission of the links, each node broadcasts periodically fixed-size probe packets. This enables every node to estimate the frame loss ratio pf to each of its neighbors over a window time, and obtain an estimate pr of the reverse direction from its neighbors. Then, assuming uniform distribution of error-rate over each link, the node can estimate the expected transmission count as $\frac{1}{(1-p_f)(1-p_r)}$ .The ETX of a path is obtaincd by summing up the ETX of its links. Therefore, each node picks the path that has the smallest ETX value from a set of choices. ETX has several drawbacks. First, its measurement scheme by using identical small-sized probe packets does not reflect the actual error-rate that the data packets experience over each link. The accuracy of the measurement scheme of a link quality metric has a great impact on its functionality (Karbaschi et al. 2008). Furthermore, ETX does not account the link layer abandon after a certain threshold of retransmissions. This may induce to select a path, which contains links with high loss rate. Koksal et al. introduce another version of ETX, called ENT (Effective Number of Transmissions), which deals with this problem (Koksal & Balakrishnan, 2006). ENT takes into account the probability that the number of transmissions exceeds a certain threshold and then calculates the effective transmission count based on an application requirement parameter, which limits this probability. Moreover, ETX by taking an inversion from the delivery rate to get the expected number of transmissions implicitly assumes uniform distribution for the bit error rate (BER) of the channel, which may not be correct.

The Expected Transmission Time (ETT), proposed by Draves et al. improves ETX by considering differences in link transmission rates and data packet sizes (Draves & Zill, 2004). The ETT of a link l is defined as the expected MAC layer latency to transfer successfully a packet over link l. The relation between ETT and ETX of a link l is expressed as:

$$ETT_l = ETX \frac{s_l}{r_l} \tag{1}$$

where rl is the transmission rate of link l and sl is the data packet size transmitted over that link. The weight of a path is simply the summation of the ETT's of the links of that path. The drawback of ETT is, as it is based on ETX, it may choose the paths, which contain the links with high loss rates. (Draves & Zill, 2004) proposes also another new metric based on ETT, which is called Weighted Cumulative Expected Transmission Time (WCETT). The purpose of this metric is finding the minimum weight path in a multi-radio network. The WCETT is motivated by observing that, enabling the nodes with multi-radio capability reduces the intra-flow interference. This interference is caused by the nodes of a path of a given flow competing with each other for channel bandwidth. For a path p, WCETT is defined as:

$$WCETT(p) = (1-\beta).\sum_{l \in P} ETT_l + \beta.\underset{1 \le j \le k}{Max}(X_j) \tag{2}$$

where X j is the number of times channel j is used along path p and β is an adjustable parameter for the moving average subject to $0 \le \beta \le 1$. (Yang et. al, 2005) shows that WCETT is not non-isotonic and thus it is not a loop-free metric.

One of the characteristics of wireless links that can be observed is the received signal strength. It is very attractive if link quality can be reliably inferred by simply measuring the received signal strength from each received packet. Theoretically, the BER is expected to have a direct correlation with the received signal-to-noise ratio (SNR) of the packet, and the packet error rate is a function of the BER and coding. Therefore, the SNR level of the received packets has been widely used as a predictor for the loss rate of the wireless links (ex. Goff et. al, 2001; Dube et. al, 1997). (Aguayo et. al, 2004; Woo, 2004) through collecting experimental data have shown that although SNR has an impact on the delivery probability, lower values of SNR has a weak correlation with the loss rate of the links. Thus, it can not predict the quality of the links easily. In addition, (Woo, 2004) illustrates that where traffic load interference happens, collisions can affect link quality even though the received signal is very strong. The main reason is that prediction of the link quality by observing the SNR samples of the packets, counts only on the packets which are received successfully. This leads to ignoring the congestion status of the links.

A number of proposed wireless routing algorithms collect per-link signal strength information and apply a threshold to avoid links with high loss ratios (Goff et. al, 2001; Yarvis et. al, 2002). In the case that there is only one lossy route to the destination, this approach may eliminate links that are necessary to maintain the network connectivity.

2.3 Minimum Delay Routing

Some existing link quality metrics focus on finding the best paths based on the end-to-end delay associated to each path. The rational for minimizing the paths latency is that in a fixed transmission power scenario, packets latency for reaching successfully to the other end of a link can provide an estimation of the quality of that link. The average round trip time (RTT) of the packets over each link is one of the delay based parameters representing the link quality. (Adya et. al, 2004) for instance proposes this metric. To calculate RTT, a node sends periodically a probe packet carrying its time stamp to each of its neighbors. Each neighbor immediately responds to the received probe with a probe acknowledgment which echoes its time stamp. This enables the sending node to calculate the RTT to each of its neighbors. Each node keeps an average of the measured RTT to each of its neighbors. If a probe or a response probe is lost, the average is increased to reflect this loss. A path with the least sum of RTTs is selected between any node pair.

The RTT reflects several factors, which have impact on the quality of a link. First, if a link between the nodes is lossy its average RTT is increased to give a higher weight to that link. Second, either if the sender or the neighbor is busy, the probe or its response is delayed due to queuing delay which leads to higher RTT. Third, if other nodes in the transmission range of the sender are busy, the probes experience higher delay to access the channel again resulting in higher RTT. Concisely, RTT measures the contention status and error rate of a link.

However, the small probe packets in comparison to larger data packets are rarely dropped over a lossy channel. This hides the actual bandwidth of the links. Moreover, (Draves et. al, 2004) shows that RTT can be very load-sensitive which leads to unnecessary route instability. Load-dependency of a metric is a well-known problem in wired networks (Khanna& Zinky, 1989). To suppress the queuing delay in the RTT, Keshav, 91, proposed the packet-pair technique to measure delay of a link. In this approach to calculate the per-hop delay, a node sends periodically two probe packets back to back to each of its neighbors such that the first probe is small and the next one is large. The neighbor upon receiving the probes calculates the delay between them and then reports this delay back to the sender. The sender keeps an average from the delay samples of each neighbor and paths with lower cumulated delay are selected. This technique, by using larger packet for the second probe, reflects more accurately the actual bandwidth of the links, although it has higher overhead than RTT. Draves et. al, 2004 discusses again that packet-pair measurement is not completely free of self interference between the neighbors, although less severe than RTT. Awerbuch et. al 2004 proposes the Medium Time Metric (MTM) which assigns a weight to each link proportional to the amount of medium time consumed by transmitting a packet on the link. It takes the inverse of the nominal rate of the links to estimate the medium time.

The variable rate of the links is determined by an auto-rate algorithm employed by the networks, such as ARF or RBAR. Existing shortest path protocols will then discover the path that minimizes the total transmission time. This metric only handles the transmission rate of the links and does not account the medium access contention and retransmission of packets at the MAC layer. Zhao et al. 2005 introduces a cross layer metric called PARMA, which aims to minimize end-to-end delay which includes the transmission delay, access delay and the queuing delay.

They consider a low saturated system with ignorable queuing delay. A passive estimation is used for the channel access delay and the transmission delay on each link is calculated as the ratio of packet length to the link speed. This metric has a good insight into estimating the total delay of each link but has simplified very much the problem of the delay calculation. For instance, it assumes that the links are error free and no packet retransmissions occur over them.

2.4 Load Balancing

In order to make routing efficiently and increase network utilization, some researchers have proposed congestion aware routing with the aim of load balancing in the network. One of the methods for spreading the traffic is using multiple non-overlapping channels. Kyasanur & Vaidya, 2006 propose a Multi-Channel Routing protocol (MCR) with the assumption that the number of interfaces per node is smaller than the number of channels. The purpose of their protocol is choosing paths with channel diversity in order to reduce the self interference between the node pairs. Moreover, they take into account the cost of interface switching latency. MCR is based on on-demand routing in a multi-channel network. While the on-demand route discovery provides strong resistance to mobility-caused link breaks, the long expected lifetimes of links in mesh networks make on-demand route discovery redundant and expensive in terms of control message overhead. Therefore, this protocol is not totally appropriate for mesh networks. Yang et al. focus more on mesh networks and propose another path weight function called Metric of Interference and Channel-switching (MIC). A routing scheme, called Load and Interference Balanced Routing Algorithm (LIBRA) is also presented to provide load balancing (Yang, 2005). MIC includes both interference and channel switching cost.

2.5 Routing with Controlling Transmission Power

Numerous works in efficient routing in multi-hop networks has focused on power control routing. The problem of power control has been investigated in two main research directions: energy-aware and interference-aware routing. In energy-aware routing approaches the objective is to find power values and routing strategy, which minimizes the consumption of power in order to maximize the battery lifetime of mobile devices. Therefore these works are suitable for sensor and ad hoc networks as in wireless mesh networks power is not a restricted constraint. Power control in interference-aware routing aims to find the optimal transmission power which gives the higher throughput or the lowest end-to-end delay. Therefore, transmission power of the nodes is controlled in order to reduce interference while preserving the connectivity. There are a lot of researches in this area. For instance Iannone et al. propose Mesh Routing Strategy (MRS) in which transmission rate, PER and interference of each link are taken into account (Iannone & Fdida, 2006). The interference is calculated based on the transmission power and number of reachable neighbors with that power level. The disadvantage of their approach is that they do not consider that links with different transmission rate have different sensibility for being disturbed by the neighbors' transmission. This effect has been taken into account in (Karnik et. al., 2008) where the authors propose a network configuration to have an optimal throughput.

The foreseen alternatives to minimum hop metric consist in establishing high quality paths, by tracking various link quality metrics in order to significantly improve the routing performances. Thus, the challenge lies in selecting good paths, based on a relevant link quality metric. However, the stability issue of link quality aware routing which can be extremely important specially in providing quality of service for jitter sensitive applications has not been addressed by the existing research efforts. In the next section, a quantitative tool to investigate the routing reactivity and its impact on applications performances is introduced.

3. REACTIVITY OF LINK QUALITY AWARE ROUTING

A more reactive routing responds faster to link quality changes. This leads to detect the lossy channel faster and so, to converge to the higher quality path in a shorter time. Meanwhile, fast reacting to channel variations may produce higher path flapping and consequently higher jitter level. Therefore, there is a trade-off between providing ensured stability in selecting the paths and obtaining a high possible throughput from the network. The frequency of link quality changes may be very different for distinct wireless links (due to some factors such as fast or slow fading, nodes mobility, etc.) (Koskal & Balakrishnan, 2006; Aguayo et. al, 2004). In order to track as much as possible all the link changes and always choose a high quality path, the routing should respond accurately and as fast as possible to these changes. Response time refers to the time required by the routing agent to take into account the new link quality status.

The reactivity of the routing depends on the updating frequency of the routing tables and the sensitivity degree of the routing metric to channel variations. The updating frequency of the routing tables defines the rate at which the shortest paths are recalculated based on the current value of the link quality metrics. Although the updating period of the routing is generally longer than the time-scale of link quality variations, a shorter update period is able to respond faster to link breakage or quality degradation and in turn will lead to a higher throughput. However, frequent changes of the selected route induce packet reordering and jitter issues. Moreover, reducing the updating period of the metric obviously produces a higher amount of routing overhead. This may overload the network and could severely degrade the network performance. The sensitivity degree of the routing metric to link quality variations is the other parameter which obviously has a great impact on the routing response time. The sensitivity degree depends on the way the set of measured parameters (frame loss, delay, SNR, ...) are mapped onto the metric. Sensitivity degree S of a link quality metric is defined as the norm of the gradient of the defined metric function with respect to the set of parameters that measures the link quality. Let q be the set of measured parameters and m(q) the calculated metric based on q. The sensitivity of the metric is:

$$S_m(q) = \left\| \vec{\Delta} m(q) \right\| \tag{3}$$

With a highly sensitive metric, the variations of link conditions are intensified. The path metric, which aggregates the link metrics along a path, fluctuates faster and the probability of changing the selected route increases. The possibly resulting route flapping may cause higher jitter which for some applications is harmful as reordered or delayed packets may be considered as lost ones. This section focuses on investigating the impact of a more sensitive metric on route flapping, control overhead and real-time application performances.

3.1 Impact of the Sensitivity of a Link Quality Metric

In (Karbaschi et. al, 2008) it is shown that measurement scheme and obviously the relevance of the measured parameters have a great impact on the measurement accuracy and thus on the final result. Numerous link quality routing have been proposed in the last decade. However, in order to compare the impact of the sensitivity of two link quality metrics on the routing performance, their measurement scheme and the parameters they measure for estimating the quality of the links should be the same. No such two link quality metrics with identical observed parameters and measurement scheme can be found in the literature.

Therefore, to conduct the study, two comparable and realistic link quality metrics are introduced in the following.

ARQ mechanism in 802.11b with retransmission of frames over lossy channels wastes bandwidth and causes higher end-to-end delay and interference to the other existing traffics. Therefore, the number of frame retransmissions at the MAC layer has been widely used as an estimator of the link quality (De Couto et. al, 2005; Koskal & Balakrishnan, 2006; Karbaschi et. al, 2008). Therefore, this section presents two comparable link quality metrics based on this retransmissions number.

The first link quality metric, called m1, is based on the FTE metric introduced in (Karbaschi et. al. 2005). Assuming that RTS/CTS is enabled for solving the hidden terminal problem, the quality and interference status of the adjacent links of a sender can be estimated by measuring the average number of required retransmissions of data and RTS frames at the MAC layer to transfer a unicast packet across a link. Therefore, each node measures the m1 by keeping the retransmissions count of RTS and data frames over the neighbor links as follows.

Let $k_{xy}(i)$ - respectively $l_{xy}(i)$ - be the number of transmissions (including retransmissions) of the ith data packet - respectively i^{th} RTS packet - over the x to y link. Thus the set of measured parameters (q) over this link will be defined as $q_{xy}(i) = \{k_{xy}(i), l_{xy}(i)\}$. The success rate in delivering two frames of data and RTS from x to y denoted by $m_1(q^i_{xy})$ is computed as:

$$m_1(q^i_{xy}) = \frac{2}{k_{xy}(i) + l_{xy}(i)} \tag{4}$$

Referring to Equation 4, increasing the number of retransmissions of RTS or data frames reduces the value of m1 and for a perfectly efficient link m (qi) is equal to unity. If the 1 xy number of retransmissions reaches a predefined threshold, the sender gives up sending the frame. In this case, m (qi) is set to zero which degrades the overall average link quality very much. m1 can be interpreted as an estimation of the success rate of transmissions over a link. Another metric, called m2 is defined based on the same measured parameters. Assuming that the failure in transmission of data and RTS frames are independent from each other, the success rate of transmission over the link x to y can be calculated by multiplying the success probability of sending RTS and data frames as follows:

$$m_2(q^i_{xy}) = \frac{1}{k_{xy}(i)} \times \frac{1}{l_{xy}(i)} \tag{5}$$

With the same argument, if the sender gives up sending RTS or data frames, m2 (qi xy) is set to zero. Figure 3 illustrates the calculated success rate returned by m1 and m2 as a function of the number of data and RTS retransmissions for each sent packet over a given link (Equation 4 and 5). As shown in this figure, an interesting property of both m1 and m2 is that their variations over the range of RTS and data retransmission numbers is not uniform. Indeed, both metrics are much more sensitive to a given variation of its arguments kxy and lxy when these parameters ranges between 1 and 4 than for values ranging between 6 to 10. In other words, the quality variations of a poor link are far less reflected in the metric than the variations of a high quality link. This is desirable since if a link does not work well and there is no alternate much higher quality link, it is not worth changing the selected path. In counterparts, quality variations of a good links have a much greater impact on the throughput of that link. As a result, good quality links should be more prone to changes.

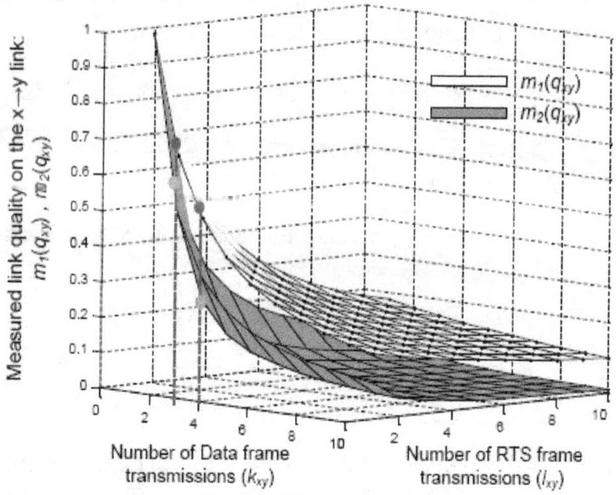

Fig. 3. Measured link quality using m1 and m2 function of the number of Data and RTS frames retransmissions.

From this point of view, the two metrics differ. Indeed, m2 differentiates better than m1 a small degradedness from a former high quality measured value. As clearly shown in Figure 3, both functions return 1 when no retransmission occurs which confirms the value of 100% success for the transmission while by lessening in link quality, m2 drops more sharply than m1 . For example, an increase in the number of data transmissions from 3 to 4 causes 32% decrease in m2 and about 15 % in m1 . Therefore, m2 is called as Faster FTE (FFTE).

The variations of the metric with respect to quality changes can be evaluated using the sensitivity degree (Equation 3). Figure 4 compares the sensitivity degree of m1 and m2 using the difference Sm1 (qxy) -Sm 2(qxy) . We see that for all the variations range of lxy (i) , Sm2 is larger or equal to Sm1 . kxy (i) and Consequently, m2 has an even greater sensitivity in detecting changes in the estimated link quality than m1 . m2 obliges the routing agent to be more reactive and changes the selected route more often than m1 .

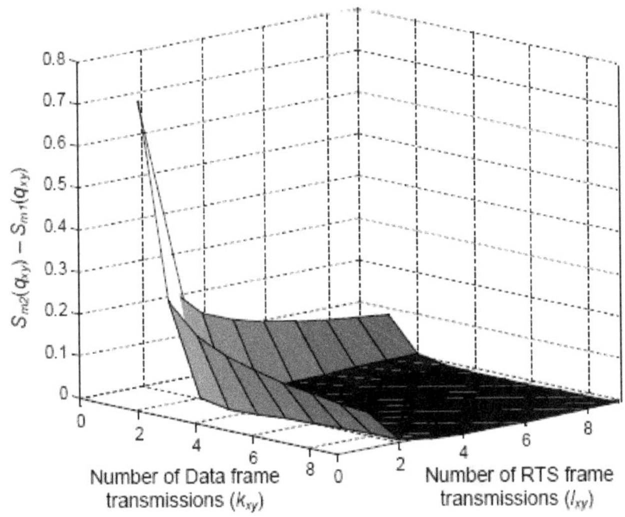

Fig. 4. Comparison of the sensitivity of the metrics m1 and m2 .

3.2 Simulation Study

This section presents simulation results to illustrate the performance of the link quality metrics compared to the Minimum Hop (MH) metric as the reference. Both m1 and m2 have been employed in DSDV (Perkins, 1994). The efficiency of the routes is estimated by multiplying the EWMA of m1 values (or m2) along the path towards the destination. This estimation of the link quality is piggy backed into the Hello messages that are sent in a periodic manner.

The simulations are performed under ns2.28 with the enriching the simulator in order to contain wireless channel fading effects, time variable link quality for wireless links, signal to interference and noise ratio, etc (cf. Karbaschi, 2008).

In order to show the impact of the link quality aware routing on the quality of service for a jitter-sensible flow, VoIP traffic of is modelled and multiple random connections are set in a 30-nodes random topology. VoIP is basically UDP packets encapsulating RTP packets which contain the voice data. For accurately modelling the bursty VoIP traffic, Pareto On/Off traffic is used (Dang et. al, 2004), with different transmission rates corresponding to the widely used ITU voice coders.

Firstly, the impact of the sensitivity of the metric on the performance of the DSDV is evaluated and then the resultant instability and the generated jitter are investigated. T (resp. T0) are used as the routing update period used in the case that m1 and m2 (resp. MH) are implemented.

In order to unify the impact of the update period on the reactivity of the routing, T and T0 are set to 15 s. The three metrics in terms of received throughput, defined as the average number of data bits received per second, are compared in Figure 5. The result of one connection confirms that both the link quality metrics are able to transfer more bits in comparison to the MH metric in a time duration of 2000 s. Figure 5 also shows that m2 outperforms the two other metrics. This confirms that m2, the more sensitive metric, is able to find a higher throughput path faster than m1 and so reduces the packet drops.

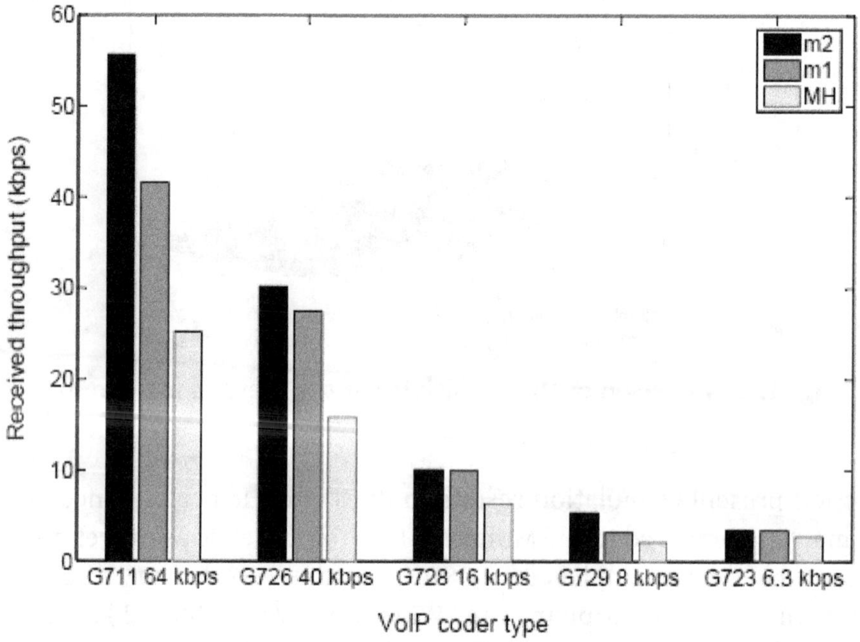

Fig. 5. Average received throughput with same routing update period (T = T0 = 15s)

Comparing in Figure 6 the number of times that one dedicated flow flaps per second reveals that a link quality metric leads the routing to change the selected path more frequently. This effect is even greater when the sensitivity of the metric increases (m2 compared to m1). To show the impact of the metrics on the routing overhead, the average bit rate of control messages for the three metrics are compared in Figure 7. This reveals that the overhead generated by m1 and m2 are nearly the same and both more than MH's overhead. The reason is that the higher sensitivity of m1 and m2 generates more paths changes than MH. This obliges the nodes to piggy back more neighbors entries into their broadcast message and makes it larger, thus raising the routing overhead. Another cause of overhead increase is that a link quality metric needs a larger field in the control message than a hop metric (32 bits compared 16 bits). This enlarges the overall size of the control messages.

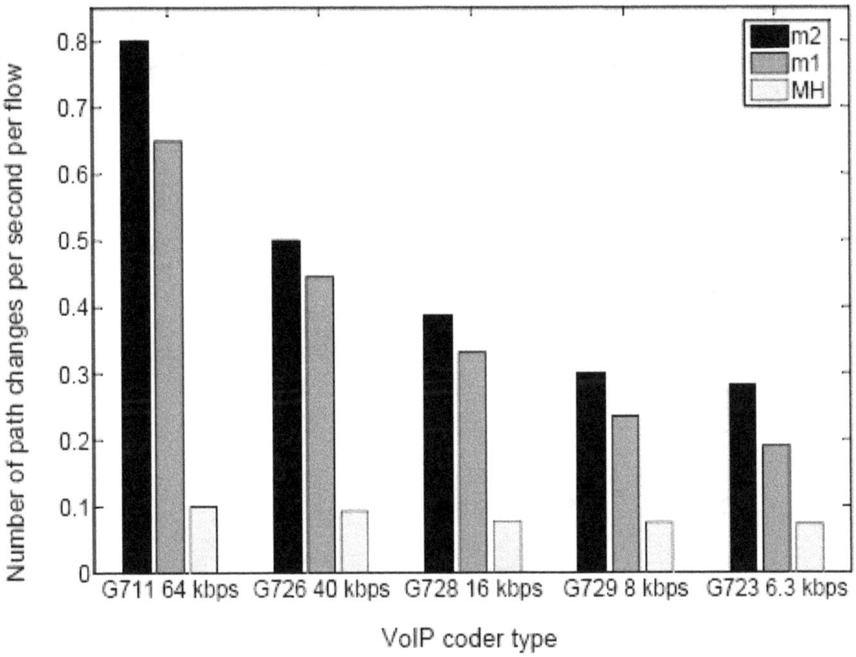

Fig. 6. Number of path changes per second per flow.

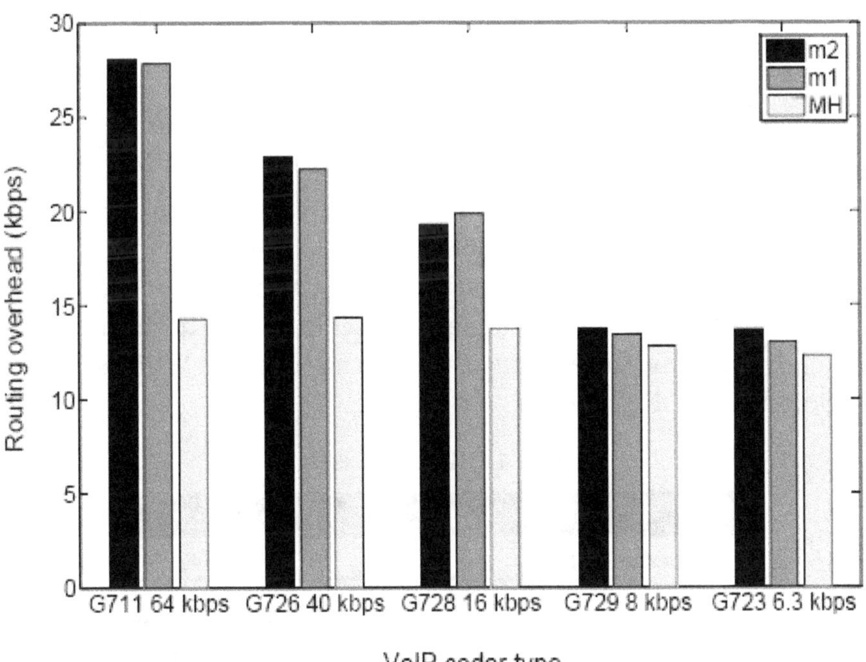

Fig. 7. Routing overhead for different VoIP coder types.

To see the efficiency of functionality of the link quality metrics, the evaluation is repeated by adjusting the amount of overhead to an identical value for the three metrics by tuning the value of T to 30 s. As explained in Section 3 this may reduce the throughput of m1 and m2 due to lower update rate of the metric. However, the average throughput comparison shows that m2 still brings a much higher throughput (Figure 8).

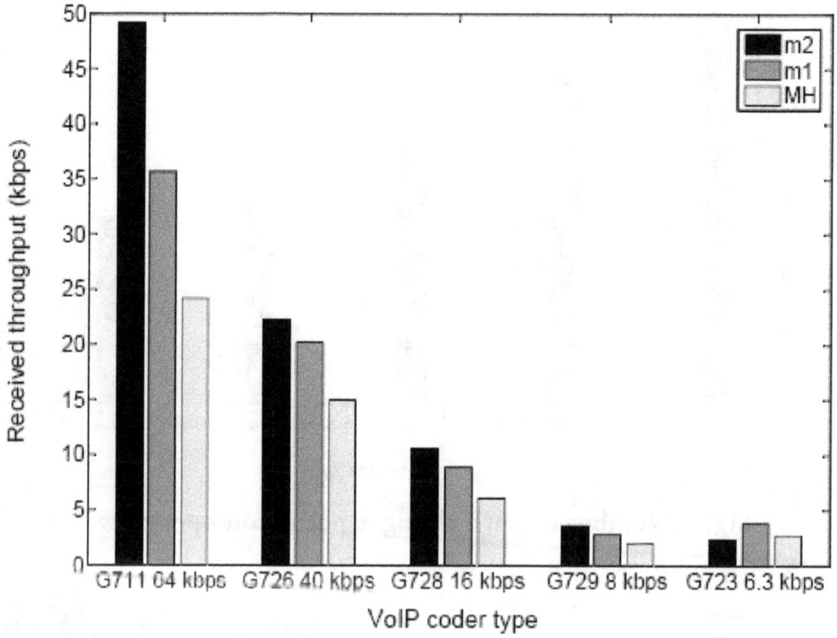

Fig. 8. Average received throughput with same overhead amount (T = 30 s, T0 = 15 s) for different VoIP coder types.

Flapping the selected route may cause the consecutive packets to be routed through different routes. The subsequent instability of the selected path may cause a higher jitter level. Figure 9 illustrates the measured jitter per packet for the three metrics during a sample interval of a VoIP connection. Table 1 gives the mean and standard deviation of the jitter measured using the three metrics, which gives an idea of the spreading of the jitter distribution.

Table 1. Jitter statistics

	MH	m1	m2
mean (ms)	9.5	9.6	9.43
std (ms)	20	25	30.2

The jitter experienced using m2 is much greater than the jitter observed with m1 and MH. High jitter levels can have a great impact on the perceived quality in a voice conversation and as a result, many service providers now account for maximum jitter levels.

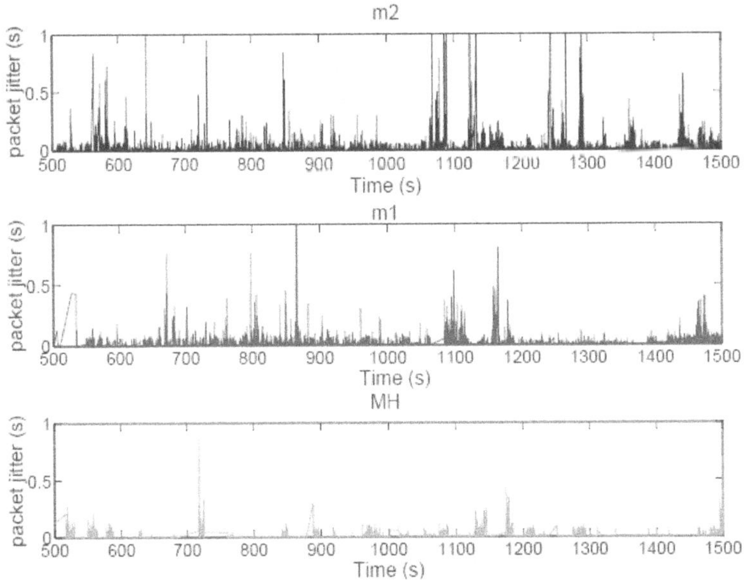

Fig. 9. Comparison of the jitter per received packet in a VoIP connection.

Most of the VoIP end-devices use a de-jitter buffer to compensate the jitter transforming the variable delay into a fixed delay (Khasnabish, 2003). Thus, high levels of jitter increase the network latency and cause a large number of packets to be discarded by the receiver. This may result in severe degradation in call quality. Therefore, real-time applications may not benefit from the higher throughput obtained with a more sensitive metric.

4. CONCISE SUMMARY

Wireless multi-hop networks represent a promising technology that offers flexibility and rapid implementation for linking users at a cheap cost. This chapter has analyzed the challenges of link quality-aware routing in wireless multi-hop networks. The quality of wireless communications is contingent upon numerous parameters, resulting in significant variability over time and with minor environmental alterations. The unique characteristics of wireless networks and significant variations in their quality provide obstacles in the design of wireless multi-hop routing systems. Consequently, the need for more efficient routing than that envisaged for wired networks has emerged. Conventional hop count shortest-path routing protocols are ineffective in ensuring reliability and good performance due to their insensitivity to the condition of underlying layers. This attracts significant research efforts to enhance routing performance by selecting optimal paths through the transmission of connection status information from underlying layers.

This chapter examined the stability concerns of link quality aware routing, which is crucial for ensuring quality of service in jitter-sensitive applications. It was contended that using reactive routing to address unpredictable fluctuations in wireless networks is crucial. A quantitative instrument for assessing the sensitivity of a link quality metric was introduced, demonstrating the extent to which the metric correlates with variations in quality. The sensitivity significantly influences routing adaptivity. To illustrate this, two comparable link quality metrics (FTE and FFTE) with different sensitivity were introduced and the routing performance observed with these metrics was compared by simulation. Research shown that employing a sensitive metric can enhance routing efficiency by facilitating the transfer of a greater volume of data packets across the network. Nevertheless, a consequent side consequence is increased oscillation in path selection. This results in elevated jitter levels that a sensitive application like VoIP may not withstand.

REFERENCES

1. Adya, A. ; Bahl, P. ; Padhye, J. ; Wolman, A. & Zhou, L (2004). A multi-radio uniϕιcation protocol for ieee 802.11wireless networks, First International Conference on Broadband Networks (BROADNETS'04), ISBN 0-7695-2221-1, pp. 344–354, October 2004, San Jose, California, USA, IEEE Computer Society, 2004.
2. Aguayo, D. ; Bicket, J. ; Biswas, S. ; Judd, G. & Morris, R. (2004). Link-level measurements from an 802.11b mesh network, Proceedings of ACM Sigcomm, Vol. 34, No. 4, pp. 121–132, Aug-Sept 2004, ACM, 1-58113 862-8/04/0008.
3. Awerbuch, B. ; Holmer, D. & Rubens, H. (2004). High throughput route selection in multi- rate ad hoc wireless networks, Kluwer Mobile Networks and Applications (MONET) Journal Special Issue on Internet Wireless Access: 802.11 and Beyond, Vol. 2928, pp. 253– 270, ISBN 3-540-20790-2, January 2004.
4. Cerpa, A. ; Busek, N. & Estrin, D. (2003). Scale: A tool for simple connectivity assessment in lossy environments, In CENS Technical Report 0021, September 2003, experimental evaluation of wireless links.
5. Conti, M. ; Maselli, G. ; Turi, G. & Giordano, S. (2004). Cross-Layering in Mobile Ad Hoc Network Design, Computer, Vol. 37, No. 2, pp. 48-51, Feb. 2004, doi:10.1109/MC.2004.1266295
6. Choi, S. ; Park, K. & Kim, C. (2005). On the performance characteristics of WLANs: Revisited. Proceedings of the 2005 ACM SIGMETRICS international conference on Measurement and modeling of computer systems, pp. 97-108, ISBN 1-59593-022-1, Banff, Alberta, Canada, ACM, New York, USA.
7. Dang, T. D. ; Sonkoly, B. & Molnar, S. (2004). Fractal analysis and modelling of VoIP traffic, In International Telecommunications Network Strategy and Planning Symposium, ISBN: 3-8007-2840-0, pp. 556–562, June 2004, DOI 10.1109/NETWKS.2004.1341826

8. De Couto, D. S. J. ; Aguayo, D. ; Chambers, B. A. & Morris, R. (2002). Performance of multihop wireless networks: Shortest path is not enough. Proceedings of the First Workshop on Hot Topics in Networks (HotNets-I). Princeton, New Jersey: ACM SIGCOMM, October 2002.

9. De Couto, S. J. D. (2004). High-throughput routing for multi-hop wireless networks. Ph.D. dissertation, Department of Electrical Engineering and Computer Science, Massachusetts Institute of Technology, June 2004.

10. De Couto, D. S. J., Aguayo, B ; Chambers, B. A. & Morris R. (2005). A high-throughput path metric for multi-hop wireless routing, Wireless Networks, Volume 11 , Issue 4, July 2005, pp 419 – 434, ISSN:1022-0038.

11. Draves, R. ; Padhye, J. & Zill B. (2004). Routing in multi-radio, multi-hop wireless mesh networks, Proceedings of the 10th annual international conference on Mobile computing and Networking, pp. 114–128, ISBN:1-58113-868-7, International Conference on Mobile Computing and Networking, Philadelphia, PA, USA, ACM, New York, NY, USA, 2004.

12. Dube, R. ; Rais, C. D. ; Wang, K.-Y. & Tripathi, S. K. (1997). Signal stability-based adaptive routing (ssa) for ad hoc mobile networks, IEEE Personal Communications, Vol 4, pp 36-45, February 1997, Digital Object Identifier 10.1109/98.575990

13. Ganesan, D. ; Krishnamachari, B. ; Woo, A. ; Culler, D. ; Estrin, D. & Wicker, S. (2002). Complex behavior at scale: An experimental study, UCLA Computer Science, Tech. Rep. TR 02-0013, 2002.

14. Goldsmith A. & Wicker S. (1998). Design challenges for energy-constrained ad hoc wireless networks, IEEE Wireless Communications, vol. 9, no. 4, pp. 8–27, 2002.

15. Goff, T. ; Abu-Ghazaleh, N. B. ; Phatak, D. S. & Kahvecioglu, R. (2001). Preemptive routing in ad hoc networks, Proceeding of ACM/IEEE MobiCom, pp. 43–52, ISBN 1-58113-422- 3, July 2001, ACM SIGMOBILE, Rome, Italy, 2001.

16. Gupta P. & Kumar P. R. (2000). The capacity of wireless networks, IEEE Transactions on Information Theory, March 2000, Vol. 46, No. 2, pp. 388–404, Digital Object Identifier 10.1109/18.825799.

17. Hedrick, C. (1998). Routing information protocol. Network working group, RFC 1058, The Internet Society, June 1988.

18. Heusse, M. ; Rousseau, F. ; Berger-Sabbatel, G. & Duda, A. (2003) . Performance anomaly of 802.11b, Proceedings of INFOCOM, Twenty-Second Annual Joint Conference of the IEEE Computer and Communications Societies. Vol. 2, pp. 836–843, 2003, ISBN: 0- 7803-7752-4, ISSN: 0743-166X.

19. Iannone, L.& Fdida, S. (2006). Evaluating a cross-layer approach for routing in wireless mesh networks, Telecommunication Systems Journal (Springer) Special issue: Next Generation Networks - Architectures, Protocols, Performance, vol. 31, no. 2–3, pp. 173– 193, March 2006.
20. Jain, K. ; Padhye, J. ; Padmanabhan, V. & Qiu L. (2006). Impact of interference on multi-hop wireless network performance, MobiCom '03: Proceedings of the 9th annual international conference on Mobile computing and networking, pp. 66--80, ACM Press, New York, NY, USA, 2003.
21. Johnson D. B. & Maltz, D. A. (1994). Dynamic source routing in ad-hoc wireless networks. Proceedings of the Workshop on Mobile Computing Systems and Application, pp. 158–163, December 1994.
22. Karbaschi, G. (2008). Link Quality Aware Routing in IEEE 802.11 Multi Hop Networks, PhD Thesis dissertation, University of Pierre et Marie Curie, April 2008.
23. Karbaschi, G. & Fladenmuller, A. (2005). A link-quality and congestion-aware cross layer metric for multi-hop wireless routing, Proceedings of IEEE Mobile Ad hoc and Sensor Systems (MASS), Nov. 2005.
24. Karbaschi, G. ; Fladenmuller, A. & Wolϕınger, B. E. (2008) Link-quality measurement enhancement for routing in wireless mesh networks, Proceedings of International Symposium on a World of Wireless, Mobile and Multimedia Networks, 2008 (WoWMoM 2008), ISBN: 978-1-4244-2099-5, pp. 1-9, Digital Object Identifier: 10.1109/WOWMOM.2008.4594842
25. Keshav, S. (1991). A control-theoretic approach to low control, ACM SIGCOMM Computer Communication Review, Vol. 21, no. 4, pp. 3–15, 1991, ISSN 0146-4833
26. Khanna, A. & Zinky, J. (1989). The revised arpanet routing metric, ACM SIGCOMM Computer Communication Review, Vol. 19, No. 4, pp. 45–56, ACM New York, NY, USA 1989, ISSN 0146-4833.
27. Karnik, A. ; Iyer A. & Rosenberg C. (2008). Throughput-optimal conϕıguration of wireless networks, IEEE/ACM Transaction in Networking, vol 16, Issue 5, Oct. 2008, pp 1161-1174, Digital Object Identifier 10.1109/TNET.2007.909717.
28. Khasnabish, B. (2003), Implementing Voice over IP, 1st edition, ISBN-10: 0471216666, ISBN- 13: 978-0471216667, Wiley-Interscience publisher, 2003.
29. Koksal C. E. & Balakrishnan H. (2006). Quality-aware routing metrics for time-varying wireless mesh networks, IEEE Journal on Selected Areas of Communication Special Issue on Multi- Hop Wireless Mesh Networks, vol. 24, no. 11, pp. 1984–1994, November 2006.

30. Kyasanur, P. & Vaidya, N. H. (2006). Routing and link-layer protocols for multi channel multi-interface ad hoc wireless networks, ACM SIGMOBILE Mobile Computing and Communications Review, vol. 10, no. 1, pp. 31 –43, ISSN:1559-1662, Jan. 2006.
31. Lundgren, H. ; Nordstrom, E. & Tschudin, C. (2002). Coping with communication grey zones in IEEE 802.11b based ad hoc networks. Proceedings of IEEE Intl Symposium on a World of Wireless, Mobile and Multimedia Networks (WoWMoM), pp. 49–55, Atlanta, Ga, USA, September 2002.
32. Mhatre, V. P. ; Lundgren, H. & Diot, C. (2007). Mac-aware routing in wireless mesh networks. Proceedings of the Fourth Annual Conference on Wireless on Demand Network Systems and Services (WONS'07), pp. 46–49, Jan. 2007, ISBN: 1-4244-0860-1, Digital Object Identifier 10.1109/WONS.2007.340461, 2007-04-02.
33. Mhatre V. & Rosenberg C. (2006). The impact of link layer model on the capacity of a random ad hoc network, Proceedings of IEEE International Symposium on Information Theory (ISIT), pp. 1688–1692, July 2006, Digital Object Identifier 10.1109/ISIT.2006.261642
34. Moy, J. (1998). OSPF version 2, network working group, RFC 2328, The Internet Society, April 1998.
35. Park V. D. & Corson M. S. (1997). A highly adaptive distributed routing algorithm for mobile wireless networks, Proceedings of IEEE Infocom, vol.3, pp.1405–1413, April 1997.
36. Perkins, C. E. & Bhagwa, P. (1994). Highly dynamic destination-sequenced distance-vector routing (dsdv) for mobile computers," ACM SIGCOMM Computer Communication Review, pp. 234–244, 1994, ACM, New York, NY, USA, ISSN 0146-4833
37. Perkins C. E. & Belding-Royer E. (1999). Ad-hoc on-demand distance vector routing, Proceedings of the 2nd IEEE Workshop on Mobile Computing Systems and Applications, pp. 90–100, New Orleans, LA, USA, Feb 1999.
38. Perkins C. E. & Belding-Royer E. (2003). Ad hoc On-demand Distance Vector (aodv) routing, Internet RFC 3561, The Internet Society, July 2003.
39. Perkins C. E. & Bhagwa, P. (1994). Highly dynamic destination-sequenced distance-vector routing (dsdv) for mobile computers. Association for Computing Machinery's Special Interest Group on Data Communication'94, Volume 24, Issue 4 October 1994, ISBN: 0- 89791-686-7, pp. 234–244, ACM, New York, NY, USA

40. Proakis, J. (2001). Digital Communications, McGraw-Hill, Fourth edition, ISBN 0-07-232111- 3, New York.
41. Razaϕındralambo, T. ; Guérin-Lassous, I. ; Iannone, L. & Fdida, S. (2008). Dynamic and distributed packet aggregation to solve the performance anomaly in 802.11 wireless networks. Elsevier Computer Networks journal, Special Issue: Wireless Network Performance, vol. 52, no. 1, pp. 77–95, 2008.
42. Shakkottai, S. ; Rappaport, T. S. & Karlsson, P. C. (2003). Cross-layer design for wireless networks, IEEE Communications Magazine, Oct 2003, Vol. 41, o. 10, pp. 74–80, ISSN: 0163-6804.
43. Sivakumar R. ; Sinha P. & Bharghavan V. (1999). Cedar: a core-extraction distributed ad hoc routing algorithm, Communication IEEE Journal, vol. 17, no. 8, Aug. 1999.
44. Woo A. (2004). A holistic approach to multihop routing in sensor networks, Ph.D. dissertation, University of California, Berkeley, 2004
45. Yang, Y. ; Wang, J. & Kravets, R. (2005). Interference-aware load balancing for multi-hop wireless networks, Tech Report UIUCDCS-R-2005-2526, Department of Computer Science, University of Illinois at Urbana-Champaign, 2005.
46. Yarvis, M. Conner, W. S. Krishnamurthy, L. Chhabra, J. Elliott, B. & MainWaring A. (2002). Real-world experiences with an interactive ad hoc sensor network, Proceedings of 31st International Conference on Parallel Processing Workshops (ICPP 2002 Workshops), pp. 143–151, ISBN 0-7695-1680-7,20-23 August 2002, Vancouver, BC, Canada, IEEE Computer Society, August 2002.
47. Zhao, S. ; Wu, Z. ; Acharya, A. & Raychaudhuri, D. (2005). PARMA: A Phy/Mac aware routing metric for ad-hoc wireless networks with multi-rate radios. Proceedings of IEEE International Symposium on a World of Wireless, Mobile and Multimedia Networks(WoWMoM), pp. 286 – 292, ISBN: 0-7695-2342-0, June 2005.
48. Zhou, G. ; He, T. ; Krishnamurthy, S. & Stankovic, J. A. (2004). Impact of radio irregularity on wireless sensor networks, Proceedings of the 2nd international conference on Mobile systems, applications, and services (MobiSys), pp. 125–138, June 6-9, 2004, Hyatt Harborside, Boston, Massachusetts, USA, USENIX, 2004.

19 Chapter INVESTIGATION OF MOBILE WIMAX PERFORMANCE

1. INTRODUCTION: AN OVERVIEW

The IEEE802.16-2004 Air Interface standard (IEEE Std 802.16-2004, 2004), foundational to WiMAX technology, represents the latest solution for delivering fixed broadband wireless services over extensive geographical areas and has demonstrated efficacy in the establishment of wireless metropolitan area networks (WirelessMAN).

In February 2006, the IEEE802.16e-2005 amendment (IEEE Std 802.16e-2005, 2006) to the IEEE802.16-2004 standard was released, introducing several characteristics designed to allow user mobility, hence establishing the Mobile-WiMAX profile. The IEEE802.16 Task Group and WiMAX Forum are presently designing the forthcoming Mobile-WiMAX, which will be delineated in the future IEEE802.16m standard.

Despite the deployment of Mobile-WiMAX technology throughout the United States, Europe, Japan, Korea, Taiwan, and the Middle East, questions regarding its potential continue. The Mobile-WiMAX profile is notably characterized by the extensive degrees of freedom afforded to manufacturers. The ultimate determination regarding numerous fundamental and critical elements, including but not limited to bandwidth, frame duration, duplexing technique, and up/downlink traffic imbalance, is delegated to the implementers. Consequently, the efficacy of this technique remains ambiguous, even to network operators.

This thought inspired our research, which aims to develop an analytical framework that, based on system factors and implementation decisions, enables the assessment of the performance level offered by this technology, meticulously considering all aspects of IEEE802.16e. The analysis commences with decisions at the physical layer, as permitted by the specification, and progresses through the protocol hierarchy to ultimately quantify the application layer throughput and the capacity for supporting voice over IP (VoIP) users, meticulously accounting for all attributes of the medium access control (MAC) layer, resource allocation strategies, introduced overhead, and inherent inefficiencies throughout the process.

The analytical framework outlined here serves not only to elucidate the performance of IEEE802.16e but, more importantly, to guide network operators in their system configuration decisions. This is especially pertinent as, in addition to the model derivation, we present criteria, equations, and algorithms to optimize decisions from the perspective of system efficiency.

2. IEEE802.16 OVERVIEW

Before starting our analysis let us introduce the most relevant characteristics of the IEEE802.16 technology, that are recalled hereafter.

The result of the IEEE802.16 TG/WiMAX Forum activity is a complete standard family (IEEE Std 802.16-2004, 2004; IEEE Std 802.16e-2005, 2006) that specifies the air interface for both fixed and mobile broadband wireless access systems, thus enabling the convergence of mobile and fixed broadband networks through a common wide area broadband radio access technology and a flexible network architecture.

The IEEE802.16 standard family supports four transmission schemes:

- WirelessMAN-SC, which has been mainly developed for back-hauling in line-of-sight (LOS) conditions and operates in the 10 GHz - 66 GHz frequency range adopting a single carrier modulation scheme;
- WirelessMAN-SCa, which has the same characteristics of WirelessMAN-SC but oper- ates even in non-LOS conditions in frequency bands below 11 GHz;
- WirelessMAN-OFDM, which has been developed for fixed wireless access in non-LOS conditions and adopts the orthogonal frequency division multiplexing (OFDM) modu- lation scheme in frequency bands below 11 GHz;
- WirelessMAN-OFDMA, which has been conceived for mobile access and adopts the orthogonal frequency division multiple access (OFDMA) scheme in the 2 GHz - 6 GHz frequency range.

Since we are interested in the mobility enhancement provided by the IEEE802.16e amend- ment, here we focus our attention on the WirelessMAN-OFDMA transmission scheme.

WirelessMAN-OFDMA is based on the OFDMA multiple-access/multiplexing technique which is, on its turn, based on an NFFT subcarriers OFDM modulation scheme (Cimini, 1985; Van Nee & Prasad, 2000) with NFFT equal to 128, 512, 1024 or 2048.

The NFFT subcarriers form an OFDM symbol and can be further divided into three main groups:

- data subcarriers, used for data transmission;
- pilot subcarriers, used for estimation and synchronization purposes;
- null subcarriers, not used for transmission: guard subcarriers and DC subcarrier.

Considering sequences of OFDM symbols, it is easy to understand that transmission resources are available both in the time domain, by means of groups of consecutive OFDM symbols, and in the frequency domain, by means of groups of subcarriers (subchannels); it follows that a given mobile station can be allocated one or more subchannels for a specified number of symbols.

Several different schemes (in the following, permutation schemes) for subcarriers grouping are provided by the specification, with different possibilities for the downlink and uplink phases: among them we can cite DL-FUSC (downlink full usage of subchannels), DL-PUSC (downlink partial usage of subchannels), DL-TUSC (downlink tile usage of subchannels), or UL-PUSC (uplink partial usage of subchannels) (see the first column of table 1 for a complete list).

The minimum OFDMA time-frequency resource that can be allocated is one OFDMA-slot, which corresponds to 48 data subcarriers that can be accommodated in one, two or three OFDMA symbols, depending on which kind of permutation scheme (DL-FUSC, DL-PUSC, UL-PUSC, ...) is adopted; in particular:

Table 1. Permutation schemes' parameters.

Permutation scheme	Available subchannels NCh				NGS
	NFFT 128	NFFT 512	NFFT 1024	NFFT 2048	
DOWNLINK					
DL-FUSC	2	8	16	32	1
DL-PUSC	3	15	30	60	2
DL-OptFUSC	2	8	16	32	1
DL-TUSC1	4	17	35	70	3
DL-TUSC2	4	17	35	70	3
UPLINK					
UL-PUSC	4	17	35	70	3
UL-OptPUSC	4	17	35	70	3

- with DL-FUSC a subchannel is constituted by 48 subcarriers in each OFDM symbol (hence, one OFDMA-slot covers one symbol);
- with DL-PUSC a subchannel is constituted by 24 subcarriers in each OFDM symbol (hence, one OFDMA-slot covers two symbols);
- with UL-PUSC a subchannel is constituted by 12 subcarriers in the first OFDM symbol, 24 subcarriers in the second OFDM symbol, 12 subcarriers in the third OFDM symbol and so on, according to the sequence 12-24-12-12-24-12. In this case one OFDMA-slot covers three symbols.

Since seven fixed combinations of modulation scheme and coding rate Rc, hereafter denoted as transmission modes, are provided by the IEEE802.16e physical layer, it follows that a single OFDMA-slot allows to transmit differently sized payloads (see table B in figure 1).

Both time division duplex (TDD) and frequency division duplex (FDD) are supported. How- ever, the initial release of Mobile-WiMAX certification profiles only includes TDD, since it makes resource allocation more flexible (the downlink/uplink ratio can be easily adjusted to support asymmetric DL/UL traffic); for this reason, here we only consider the TDD duplexing scheme.

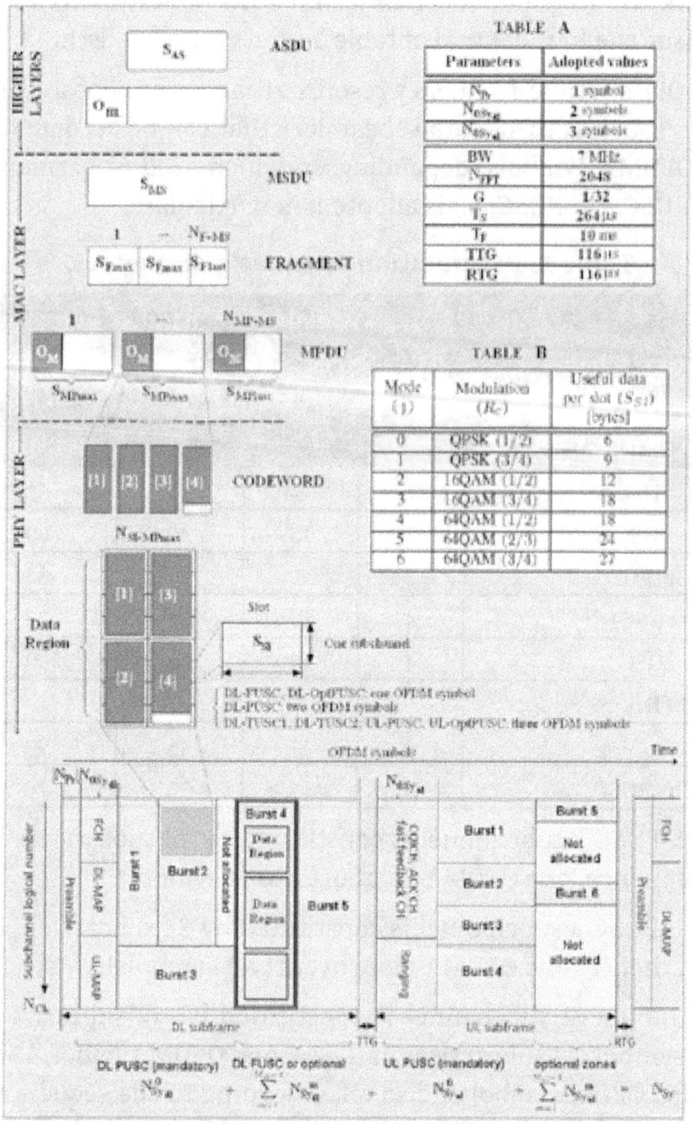

Fig. 1. IEEE802.16e WirelessMAN-OFDMA data processing and parameters setting.

The TDD frame structure is depicted in the bottommost part of figure 1. Each TDD frame is divided into downlink and uplink subframes, separated by transmit/ receive and receive/transmit transition gaps (TTG and RTG).

Each subframe may include "multiple zones", which means that the permutation method can be changed, thus moving, for instance, from DL-PUSC to DL-FUSC.

Focusing on the TDD frame, the first OFDM symbol of the DL subframe always carries a preamble, while a number of subsequent OFDM symbols are necessarily allocated to accomo- date MAC layer control messages (FCH, DL-MAP and UL-MAP) adopting the DL-PUSC per- mutation scheme; similarly, a number of OFDM symbols are necessarily allocated in the UL subframe to accomodate several common signalling channels (e.g. UL Ranging, UL CQICH, UL ACK CH) adopting the UL-PUSC permutation scheme (see figure 1).

Finally, in order to correctly manage each data flow giving an acceptable quality of service to the end user, IEEE802.16e-2005 provides five different scheduling services for traffic delivery:

- Unsolicited Grant Service (UGS),
- Real-Time Polling Service (rtPS),
- Extended Real-Time Polling Service (ertPS),
- Non-Real-Time Polling Service (nrtPS),
- Best Effort (BE)

Each scheduling service is associated with a set of quality of services (QoS) parameters: (a) maximum sustained rate, (b) minimum reserved rate, (c) maximum latency tolerance, (d) jitter tolerance and (e) traffic priority. These are the basic inputs for the service scheduler placed in the base station, which is aimed at fulfilling service specific QoS requirements. The main differences among these services are on the uplink resource allocation; resource allocation is, in fact, defined by the base station, which cannot have a perfect knowledge of all uplink buffers in any instant. The interested reader can find a detailed description of the scheduling services in (IEEE Std 802.16-2004, 2004) and (IEEE Std 802.16e-2005, 2006).

3. TRANSMISSION RESOURCES: OFDMA-SLOTS

In this section the amount of resources that are available for data transmission is evaluated as a function of all parameters that can be chosen by system implementers. In particular, the OFDMA-slot, which is the minimum resource available at the physical layer for data allo- cation, is focused and the amount of available OFDMA-slots is derived as a function of the physical layer configuration.

In order to ease the reader's task, the scheme reported in figure 2 summarizes the analytical framework outlined in this section, which lead to the assessment of the amount of available OFDMA-slots.

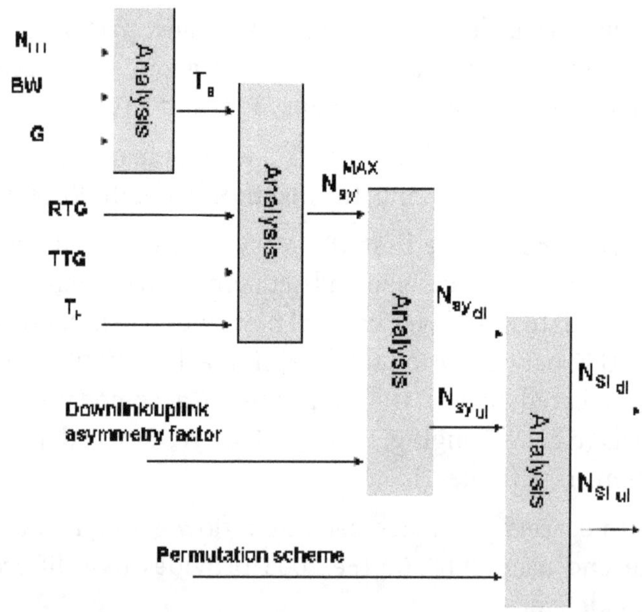

Fig. 2. Analytical framework for the derivation of the amount of OFDMA-slots per down- link/uplink subframe.

3.1 OFDM symbol duration

In order to assess the amount of resources available for data transmission at the physical layer, the OFDM symbol duration Ts must be obtained at first. Ts depends on the transmission bandwidth BW (it is typically a multiple of 1.75 MHz or 1.25 MHz), the number NFFT of OFDM subcarriers (equal to 128, 512, 1024 or 2048) and the normalized (to the useful symbol duration) guard interval G (equal to 1/4, 1/8, 1/16 or 1/32).

Given BW, the value of an auxiliary parameter n (called sampling factor), introduced by the specification, can be immediately derived: in particular, n = 28/25 if BW is a multiple of 1.25 MHz, 1.5 MHz, 2 MHz or 2.75 MHz, otherwise n = 8/7.

Once BW and n are known, we can derive the sampling frequency Fs, which is defined by the specification as follows:

$$F_s = \left\lfloor n \cdot \frac{BW}{8000} \right\rfloor \cdot 8000, \tag{1}$$

having denoted with [x]the highest integer not greater than x.

Given the number NFFT of OFDM subcarriers, the subcarriers spacing Δ f and the useful OFDM symbol duration Tu can be immediately derived from the knowledge of Fs:

$$\Delta f = \frac{F_s}{N_{FFT}}, \qquad T_u = \frac{1}{\Delta f}. \tag{2}$$

The guard time interval Tg and, finally, the OFDM symbol duration Ts follow:

$$Tg = G \cdot Tu, Ts = Tu + Tg. \tag{3}$$

3.2 Number of OFDM symbols per frame

Once TS has been obtained, the second step to derive the amount of OFDMA-slots available at the physical layer is to assess the number of useful OFDM symbols in a frame.

Since we are interested in the TDD version of IEEE802.16e WirelessMAN-OFDMA, we have to consider a frame structure consisting of two parts, that represent the downlink and uplink subframes, separated by the TTG and RTG time intervals (see figure 1).

In order to derive the number of useful OFDM symbols in a frame, let us recall that the first symbol of the frame is used to transmit the preamble (thus the number of preamble symbols is NPr = 1) and that both TTG and RTG cannot be smaller than 5 μs (RTGmin = TTGmin = 5 μs). Thus, once the frame duration TF has been chosen (possible values admitted by the specifi- cation are 2, 2.5, 4, 5, 8, 10, 12.5 and 20 ms), and given the previously derived value of Ts, the maximum number NsyMAX of OFDM symbols per frame (excluding the preamble) can be derived:

$$N_{Sy}^{MAX} = \left\lfloor \frac{T_F - TTG_{min} - RTG_{min}}{T_s} \right\rfloor - N_{Pr} , \tag{4}$$

as depicted in figure 2.

3.3 Number of OFDMA-slots per frame

Given the value of NSyMAX , it is now possible to assess the number of OFDMA-slots that can be allocated in the downlink and uplink subframes. Since OFDMA-slots extend both in the time and in the frequency domains, the derivation of their amount requires considerations on both domains.

As for the time domain, let us recall that, depending on the adopted permutation scheme (DL- FUSC, DL-PUSC, UL-PUSC, ...), an OFDMA-slot is spread over NGS = 1, 2 or 3 consecutive OFDM symbols, as reported in the last column of table 1, whereas, as far as the frequency domain is concerned, the amount of available subchannels NCh depends on the permutation scheme and the number NFFT of OFDM subcarriers (as reported in the second column of table 1).

Please note that different permutation schemes are provided for the downlink and uplink subframes and that more than one scheme can be used in a single subframe. Each permutation scheme (denoted in the following with the superscript m) requires the allocation of a multiple of an integer (1, 2 or 3, depending on the permutation scheme) number of OFDM symbols NmSy (NmSydl in the downlink and NmSyul in the uplink, respectively) and the sum NSy of uplink and downlink symbols allocated for each permutation scheme is bounded by the above assessed N Sy MAX:

$$\sum_{m=0}^{M_{dl}-1} N^{m}_{Sy_{dl}} + \sum_{m=0}^{M_{ul}-1} N^{m}_{Sy_{ul}} = N_{Sy} \leq N^{MAX}_{Sy}, \tag{5}$$

where Mdl (Mul) is the amount of permutation schemes adopted in the downlink (uplink) subframe.

As recalled in section 2, at least two OFDM symbols are allocated with DL-PUSC in the down- link subframe, in order to carry frame management messages, while three OFDM symbols are allocated with UL-PUSC in the uplink subframe, in order to carry signalling common chan- nels; here we assume that the entire first two OFDM symbols in downlink (with DL-PUSC) and the entire first three OFDM symbols in uplink (with UL-PUSC) are used for this scope, denoting the related overhead with NOSydl = 2 and NOSyul = 3.

Moreover, the rest of the sub-frame is supposed to be transmitted adopting only one permutation scheme. Thus, the superscript correspondent to the adopted permutation scheme will be omitted in the following and (5) is rearranged as follows:

$$\text{NOSydl} + \text{NSydl} + \text{NOSyul} + \text{NSyul} = \text{NSy} \leq \text{NMAX}, \tag{6}$$

where NSydl and NSyul now represent the amount of downlink/uplink symbols available for user data.

Let us observe that the choice of NSydl and NSyul is not only constrained to fulfill (6), but is also a consequence of the desired asymmetry between the downlink and uplink phases of the TDD frame, hereafter referred to as "desired asymmetry factor" and denoted as AFin.

Let's keep in mind, in this regard, that the minimum resource that can be allocated is the OFDMA-slot and that the number of slots in a subframe is related not only to the number of OFDM symbols within the frame, but also to the adopted permutation scheme; as an exam- ple, with NFFT = 2048 subcarriers two OFDM symbols adopting the DL-PUSC permutation scheme carry 60 slots while three OFDM symbols adopting UL-PUSC carry 70 slots (refer to (8) and table 1). Thus, defining AFSl as the asymmetry factor in terms of ratio between the amounts of downlink and uplink slots:

$$AF_{Sl} = \frac{N_{Sl_{dl}}}{N_{Sl_{ul}}}, \tag{7}$$

and deriving the amount of OFDMA-slots available for data transmission in the down- link/uplink subframe through the equation (where dl/ul denotes downlink or uplink as al- ternatives):

$$N_{Sl_{dl/ul}} = N_{Ch_{dl/ul}} \cdot \left\lfloor \frac{N_{Sy_{dl/ul}}}{N_{GS_{dl/ul}}} \right\rfloor, \tag{8}$$

the desired asymmetry AFin can be approached finding the values NSydl and NSyul that make AFSl as near as possible to AFin. In general, a perfect matching between AFin and AFSl will be not possible, due to the system constrains.

The detection of NSydl and NSyul in such a way to minimize the resource wasting (that is, OFDM symbols within the frame that are unused because unable to accomodate entire OFDMA-slots) for a given AFin can be carried out by means of the algorithm provided in appendix I.

Equation (8) represent the final outcome of this section since, jointly with the constraints given by the desired asymmetry factor and system choices (bandwidth, guard interval, number of subcarriers, frame duration,) accounted for by the previous equations, allows to derive the amount of OFDMA-slots available in each subframe for data transmissions.

Please refer to figure 2 for a pictorial representation of the whole methodology described in this section.

4. FROM APPLICATION LAYER PACKETS TO SUBCARRIERS ALLOCATION

In the previous section the amount NSldl and NSlul of OFDMA-slots available for data alloca- tion have been derived, taking into account all the physical and MAC layers parameters. The next step is to understand how packets to be transmitted, coming from the higher protocol layers, are mapped onto these resources. A brief overview on the packet processing is given hereafter, followed by an analytical evaluation of the number of OFDMA-slots that are finally needed to allocate each packet.

4.1 Packet processing overview

The data mapping process, starting from the application layer data unit down to the physical layer, is illustrated step by step hereafter. Please refer to figure 1, where each step is depicted, to better understand the whole process.

Let us denote as ASDU the application level data fragment of SAS bytes that is allocated into the payload of a TCP/IP packet. Each ASDU is firstly added with OHL bytes, where OHL represents the overhead added from the application to the network layer, and then mapped, at the MAC layer, onto a MAC service data unit

(MSDU) of SMS bytes. Each MSDU is then partitioned into fragments of SFmax bytes, whose value is negotiated during the connection setup phase; obviously the last fragment of each MSDU may be smaller (SFlast bytes). If the ARQ mechanism is active fragments are also called ARQ blocks.

One or more fragments are then allocated into a MAC protocol data unit (MPDU), with some overhead: in particular, a MAC header will be added plus either (a) one fragmentation sub- header if all fragments are contiguous and related to the same MSDU or (b) a packetization subheader per each group of contiguous fragments belonging to the same MSDU; a CRC (cyclic redundancy check) tail of 32 bits will be added at the end of the MPDU, in order to check its integrity at the receiver side.

At the physical layer, MPDUs are partitioned into groups of bytes that are subject to the for- ward error correction coding process, giving birth to a certain number of codewords. One or more OFDMA-slots can be combined in order to convey each codeword. Adjacent slots, both in the time and subchannels domain, are grouped into OFDMA data regions, which are two-dimensional (squared o rectangular) allocations of a group of contiguous subchannels in a group of contiguous OFDM symbols (see figure 1).

4.2 From application layer data to MPDUs

After the data processing overview provided above, in this subsection we analytically de- rive the amount of OFDMA-slots needed to deliver an ASDU. Having derived (section 3) the amount of OFDMA-slots available in the uplink/downlink subframes of a TDD Mobile- WiMAX system, this is the second step along the path that leads to the Mobile-WiMAX per- formance assessment.

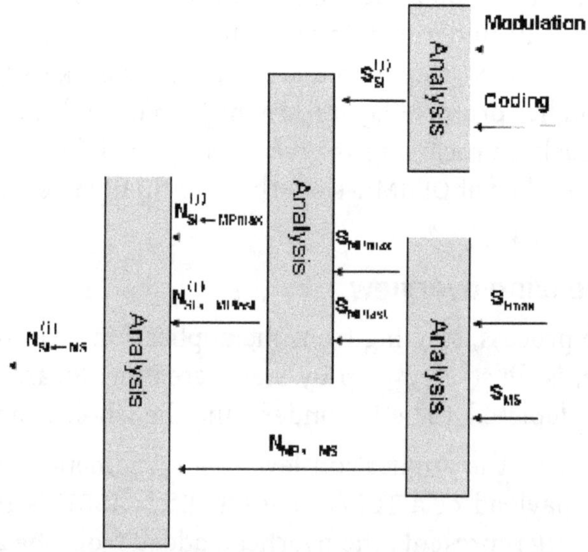

Fig. 3. Diagram of the calculation from the packet size to the number of OFDMA-slots that are needed to accomodate it.

Also in this case, in order to help the reader, the analytical framework outlined in the following has been summarized in a pictorial fashion, reported in figure 3.

Let us consider the aforementioned ASDUs of SAS bytes; as represented in figure 1 they even- tually arrive at the MAC layer with the addition of the higher layers overheads of OHL bytes, thus originating MAC layer service data units (MSDUs) of SMS bytes:

$$SMS = SAS + OHL. \quad (9)$$

The MSDUs are then fragmented into a fixed number NF←MS of fragments, each of them of size SFmax except, in case, the last one. This one has a size of SFlast ≤ SFmax bytes; thus:

$$N_{F\leftarrow MS} = \left\lceil \frac{S_{MS}}{S_{Fmax}} \right\rceil, \quad (10)$$

$$SFlast = SMS - [(NF\leftarrow MS - 1) \cdot SFmax] \quad (11)$$

where x indicates the lowest integer not less than x.

It follows that each MSDU is carried at the MAC layer by:

- (NF←MS - 1) fragments of size SFmax ,
- 1 fragment of size SFlast.

Of course, if SMS is a multiple of SFmax , then SFlast=SFmax .

Let us assume now, for the sake of simplicity, that no packetization is performed at the MAC layer; each fragment is therefore mapped onto one MPDU with the addition of the MAC layer overhead of OM bytes. It follows that the number NMP MS of MPDUs needed to carry a single MSDU is equal to NF MS. Since all but (in case) the last MPDU have the same size, we have:

- (NMP←MS - 1) MPDUs of size SMPmax ,
- 1 MPDU of size SMPlast,

where:

$$\begin{aligned} N_{MP\leftarrow MS} &= N_{F\leftarrow MS}, \\ S_{MPmax} &= S_{Fmax} + O_M, \\ S_{MPlast} &= S_{Flast} + O_M. \end{aligned} \quad (12)$$

Of course, if NMP←MS = 1, each MPDU carries a complete MSDU and its size is SMPlast.

4.3 MPDUs into OFDMA-slots

Starting from the results obtained in subsection 4.2, we can now derive the number of OFDMA-slots needed to carry any MPDU and, as a consequence, any MSDU.

Let us recall that every transmission mode j can convey a different amount SSl(j) of data bytes into a single OFDMA-slot (see table B in figure 1); since there are two possible sizes for MPDUs (SMPmax and SMPlast), we can derive, for every transmission mode j, the minimum number of slots needed to carry each of them:

$$N^{(j)}_{Sl \leftarrow MPmax} = \left\lceil \frac{S_{MPmax}}{S^{(j)}_{Sl}} \right\rceil, \quad N^{(j)}_{Sl \leftarrow MPlast} = \left\lceil \frac{S_{MPlast}}{S^{(j)}_{Sl}} \right\rceil. \tag{13}$$

These equations show that when the MPDU size is not a multiple of the amount of bytes carried by a single OFDMA-slot, some padding bits have to be added in order to fill the last slot, wasting some resources.

Thus, a single MSDU is transmitted with the generic transmission mode j through:

- $(N_{MP \leftarrow MS} - 1)$ $MPDUs$ of size S_{MPmax}, accommodated into $(N_{MP \leftarrow MS} - 1) \cdot N^{(j)}_{Sl \leftarrow MPmax}$ slots,
- 1 $MPDU$ of size S_{MPlast}, accommodated into $N^{(j)}_{Sl \leftarrow MPlast}$ slots.

Assuming no resource wastage due to data regions' allocations [1], the number $N^{(j)}_{Sl \leftarrow MS}$ of OFDMA slots needed to carry a complete $MSDU$ adopting transmission mode j is given by:

$$N^{(j)}_{Sl \leftarrow MS} = ((N_{MP \leftarrow MS} - 1) \cdot N^{(j)}_{Sl \leftarrow MPmax}) + N^{(j)}_{Sl \leftarrow MPlast} \,. \tag{14}$$

Recalling that the scope of the analysis reported in this section was to derive the amount of OFDMA-slots needed to accomodate an ASDU, we can state that (14) is the final outcome of this section since, jointly with the equations reported in subsection 4.2, it achieves our end.

5.SYSTEMPERFORMANCE:THROUGHPUTOFATCPCONNECTION

Having derived the resources (that is, OFDMA-slots) available for data allocation at the phys- ical layer (in section 3) and the amount of resources needed to carry each ASDU (in section 4), we can now assess the performance level provided by IEEE802.16e for a given configuration.

In this section, in particular, a TCP connection is considered, requiring a best effort service. In order to evaluate the maximum end-to-end throughput at the application layer (hereafter simply denoted as throughput), a single connection is supposed to be active either in the down- link or in the uplink. Furthermore, the return link (the uplink when considering a downlink TCP flow and vice versa) is considered to be always sufficient for the transmission of TCP acknowledgments; this assumption implies that the analysis is focused on the direction of the data flow.

Since a single link (uplink or downlink) is here considered for throughput derivation, in the following the subscript dl or ul will be omitted. Similarly, since a single (generic) transmission mode is considered, the superscript j will also be omitted.

In section 3.3 we evaluated the number NSl of OFDMA-slots available in a given direction (uplink or downlink) and in section 4.3 we derived the number NSl←MS of OFDMA-slots needed to carry a complete MSDU, that is, a complete ASDU; it follows that the number NMS of complete MSDUs that can be allocated in the considered subframe will be, therefore:

$$N_{MS} = \left\lfloor \frac{N_{Sl}}{N_{Sl \leftarrow MS}} \right\rfloor . \qquad (15)$$

Since, in general, N_{Sl} is not a multiple of $N_{Sl \leftarrow MS}$, it follows that R_{Sl} slots will remain available for the allocation of *MPDUs* that do not form a complete *MSDU*, where $R_{Sl} = mod(N_{Sl}, N_{Sl \leftarrow MS})$, having denoted with $mod(A, B)$ the remainder of the division $\frac{A}{B}$.
In particular, the number of *MPDUs* of size S_{MPmax} (which occupy $N_{Sl \leftarrow MPmax}$ slots each) that can be accommodated in R_{Sl} free slots is given by:

$$N_{MPinR_{sl}} = \left\lfloor \frac{R_{Sl}}{N_{Sl \leftarrow MPmax}} \right\rfloor . \qquad (16)$$

In general, after the allocation of NMPinRsl MPDUs of size SMPmax , a residual amount RRSl of slots will remain available, with RRSl = mod(RSl , NSl←MPmax); of course, another MPDU of size SMPmax cannot be allocated, but it could be possible to accommodate an MPDU of size SMPlast occupying NSl←MPlast slots.

If we denote with NMSextra the fraction of MSDU that, in average, can be allocated in the residual region of size RSl , it results:

$$N_{MSextra} = \begin{cases} \frac{N_{MPinR_{sl}}}{N_{MP \leftarrow MS}} & if\ RR_{Sl} < N_{Sl \leftarrow MPlast} \\ \frac{N_{MPinR_{sl}}}{N_{MP \leftarrow MS} - 1} & else. \end{cases} \qquad (17)$$

Obviously, if NMPinRsl = 0 it results NMSextra = 0.

Let us recall that the amount of application layer data conveyed by a single MSDU is given by SAS bytes; it follows that the average amount of application layer data accommodated in a given subframe is:

$$S = (NMS + NMSextra) \cdot SAS, \qquad (18)$$

The application layer throughput can be thus immediately derived as:

$$Thr_A[bit/s] = \frac{8 \cdot S[bytes]}{T_F[s]}, \qquad (19)$$

where TF represents the frame duration (see section 3.2).

5.1 Numerical results

In this section some numerical results obtained through (19) are given. ASDUs of SAS = 1460 bytes were chosen, since this is the payload size of a typical TCP/IP packet. Considering 20 bytes for the IP overhead, 20 bytes for the TCP overhead and neglecting the overhead introduced by the upper layers, we assumed that each MSDU has a size of SMS = SAS + OHL = 1500 bytes.

A further overhead of OM = 10 bytes is introduced by the MAC layer, following the assump tion of no packetization.

The OFDM modulation parameters were set to NFFT = 2048, BW = 7 MHz, G = 1/32; moreover a frame duration of TF = 10 ms has been chosen and RTG = TTG = 116 µs were considered; all other physical layer parameters are consequently derived (e.g. TS = 264 µs). The impact of the remaining parameters affecting the throughput will be investigated in the following. In particular, different values of SFmax and all transmission modes and permuta- tions schemes will be considered.

In figure 4, a comparison between physical layer and application layer throughput is given varying the fragments maximum size SFmax . The physical layer throughput ThrP has been evaluated considering the total amount of bits carried over the medium by all available OFDMA-slots, as follows:

$$Thr_P[bit/s] = \frac{N_{SI} \cdot 8 \cdot S_{SI}[bytes]}{T_F[s]}, \qquad (20)$$

where the same notation introduced in section 4.2 has been adopted (please note that the pre- vious equation considers only those resources available for data transmission, thus excluding the preamble symbol and the subcarriers used for signalling and control messages).

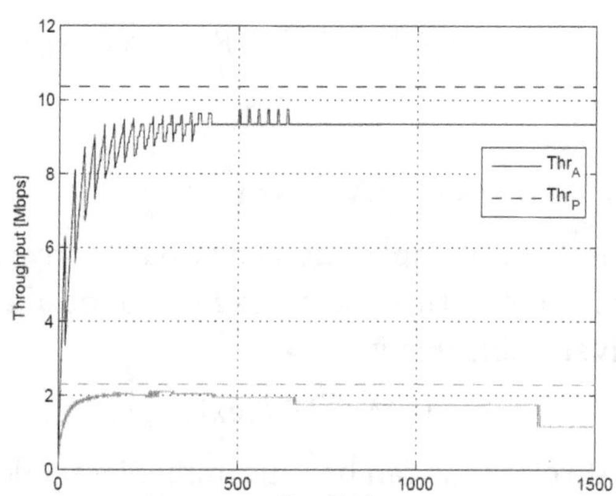

Fig. 4. Comparison between physical layer and application layer throughput (ThrP and ThrA) varying the fragment (ARQ block) maximum size SFmax . Transmission modes 0 and 6.

DL-PUSC has been considered in the downlink and UL-PUSC in the uplink, with AFin = 1 and AFSl = 1.37 (following the equations reported in section 3.3, we obtain NSydl = 16, NSyul = 15, NSldl = 480 and NSlul = 350). Transmission modes 0 and 6 are considered.

The comparison between the dashed and solid curves highlights the reduction of throughput due to both the allocation procedure of ASDUs and the overhead. As can be noted, small variations in the choice of SFmax may affect the system performance, due to the slot granularity in the physical resource allocation and the impossibility to further divide a fragment (i.e., an ARQ block).

These curves also show that a too small value of SFmax should not be chosen (this is mainly a consequence of the presence of the overheads OHL and OM). However, although considering error prone transmissions is out of the scope of the present work, it should be clear that a large value of SFmax should be avoided too, since each ARQ block must be entirely retransmitted if not correctly received.

Figure 5 deepens the previous results focusing the attention on the application layer through- put and considering all transmission modes.

A direct comparison of the throughput perceived adopting the different transmission modes as a function of SFmax shows that the choice of SFmax is a tricky task, since there is no optimal value providing the maximum throughput for all transmission modes.

As can be observed, a number of choices for SFmax are highlighted through vertical lines and the correspondent throughput values with circles. These values are somehow suboptimal and have been chosen according to the following steps:

1. for each value of SFmax in the range [1, 500 bytes] the throughput values achieved by each transmission mode normalized to the peak value for that mode were summed into SUMThr (SFmax);
2. the values of SFmax that brought to relative maximum of SUMThr (SFmax) were found, neglecting those values of SFmax that do not give an absolute value of SUMThr (SFmax) higher than the previous one.

The values of SFmax derived as previously described (SFmax = 98, 125, 134, 152, 206, 254, 422 bytes) allow to reduce resource wasting when a single fragment (ARQ block) is transmitted in a single MPDU.

In figure 6 the value of AFSl is compared to AFApp, which is defined as the ratio between the maximum application layer throughput in downlink and the one in uplink. The DL-PUSC and UL-PUSC permutation schemes have been considered in the downlink and in the uplink, respectively; AFin = 1, AFin = 2 and AFin = 3 have been assumed as desired asymmetry factors. Transmission mode 6 only.

As can be noted, a good match between AFSl and AFApp is achieved for all the considered AFin (avoiding to consider too large values for SFmax). On the contrary, it is quite hard to exactly respect the desired AFin with no wasting: note, in fact, that the cases AFin = 1 and AFin = 2 bring to the same result (that is, the need to minimize the resource wasting brings, in both cases, to the same choice of NSydl and NSyul).

In figure 7 the throughput is shown as a function of the number of OFDM symbols available for data transmission in the downlink subframe for all possible permutation schemes (refer to table 1). In this case, NSydl is set and the correspondent AFSl follows as a consequence (see section 3.3). Transmission mode 6 and SFmax = 206bytes have been considered. This figure also highlights that an increase (reduction) in NSydl has an effect only if it involves at least NGS symbols.

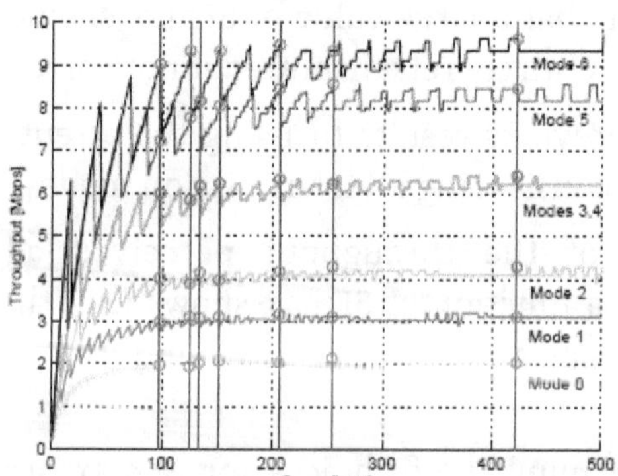

Fig. 5. Application layer throughput (ThrA) varying the fragments (ARQ blocks) maximum size SFmax for all transmission modes. The values of SFmax that allow to have a good occupa- tion adopting any possible transmission mode are marked with vertical lines and small circles (o); they correspond to SFmax = 98, 125, 134, 152, 206, 254, 422 bytes

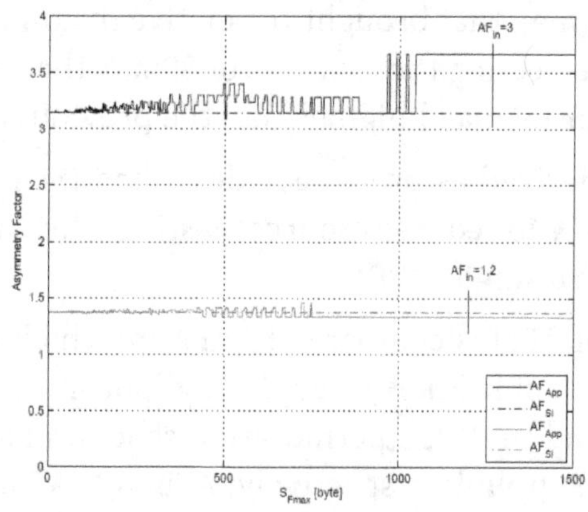

Fig. 6. Comparison between AFSl and AFApp, given AFin = 1, AFin = 2 and AFin = 3. Transmission mode 6.

6. SYSTEM PERFORMANCE: VOIP CAPACITY ON UGS OR ERTPS

In this section the maximum number of users performing a VoIP call that can be served by IEEE802.16e is evaluated, following the analysis described in sections 3 and 4.

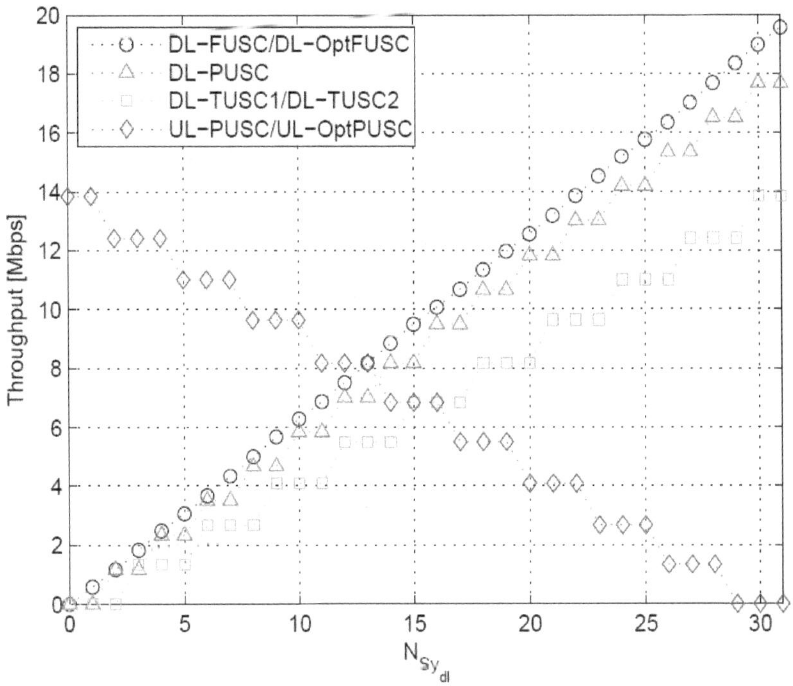

Fig. 7. Comparison of application layer throughput (ThrA) adopting the various permuta- tion schemes, varying the number of downlink useful symbols NSydl . Transmission mode 6. SFmax = 206 bytes.

A description of the considered VoIP codecs and scheduling services is given before entering into the details of the analytical model.

6.1 UGS and ertPS scheduling services

As already mentioned in section 2, five scheduling services are provided by the IEEE802.16e specification for traffic delivery. Since our attention is now focused on real-time VoIP traffic, UGS and ertPS are the only possible choices, due to latency constraints, and are therefore considered in the following:

- ***Unsolicited grant service (UGS)*** is designed to support real-time uplink service flows that generate transport fixed-size data packets on a periodic basis, such as T1/E1 and VoIP without silence suppression. The service offers fixed size grants on a real-time periodic basis, which eliminate the overhead and latency of user's requests and assure that grants are available to meet the flowŠs real-time needs.

- ***Extended real-time polling service (ertPS)*** (Lee et al., 2006) improves UGS when the application layer rate varies in time. The base station (BS) shall provide unicast grants in an unsolicited manner like in UGS, thus saving the latency of a bandwidth request. However, whereas UGS allocations are fixed in size, ertPS allocations are dynamic. The BS may provide periodic uplink allocations that may be used for requesting the band- width as well as for data transfer. By default, size of allocations corresponds to current value of maximum sustained traffic Rate at the connection. Users may request chang- ing the size of the uplink allocation by either using an extended piggyback request field of the grant management subheader or using BR field of the MAC signaling headers, or sending a specific codeword over the signalling channel CQICH. The BS shall not change the size of uplink allocations until receiving another bandwidth change request from the user.

6.2 VoIP codecs

The most important and mainly adopted voice codecs have been considered:

1. **ITU G.711** (ITU-T Rec. G.711, 1988), the well known constant bit rate PCM at 64 kbps; this is the codec used in PSTN networks, with no compression, neither during the speech nor during silences of a conversation;
2. **ITU G.729** (ITU-T Rec. G.729, 1996a), the most used codec for VoIP, at 8 kbps; when an active speech period is detected, it produces one packet of 80 bits every 10 ms, but more than one packet may be concatenated in order to reduce protocols overheads (Goode, 2002); obviously, this process enlarges the average delivery delay of packets. Hereafter, we will consider the concatenation of a couple of packets (Goode, 2002) and we will denote this codec as G.729. 160 bits packets are thus generated every 20 ms.
3. **AMR** (adaptive multi rate (3GPP TS 26.071, 2008)), standardized by 3GPP and used for voice in second and third generation cellular radio access; it generates one packet every 20 ms with a variable data rate, going from a minimum of 4.75 kbps (95 data bits plus 18 overhead bits for each packet) to a maximum of 12.2 kbps (244 data bits plus 18 over- head bits for each packet). The variation of the data rate is given in order to better select the appropriate tradeoff between resource usage and speech quality (obviously, a data rate reduction leads to a quality degradation). In order to investigate the capacity of the IEEE802.16e WirelessMAN-OFDMA system with the AMR codec, we will consider both the minimum data rate (4.75 kbps, denoted as AMR4.75) and the maximum data rate (12.2 kbps, denoted as AMR12.2).

ITU G.729 and AMR codecs have been designed, in particular, with the specific goal to reduce the resources occupation: when no voice activity is detected the silence suppression procedure is activated. As a consequence small and less frequent packets are transmitted, which convey the information for a "comfortable noise" generation at the receiver side.

In particular, adopting the AMR codec, the detection of a silence period (3GPP TS 26.092, 2008) gives rise to the following steps:

- eight full voice packets are normally transmitted in the first interval, called hangover period;
- then, a SID (silence insert descriptor) packet (36 data bits plus 18 overhead bits) is trans- mitted after 60 ms;
- further SID packets are transmitted every 160 ms until a new speech activity is detected. This process is depicted in the topmost part of figure 8.

As far as the G.729 codec is concerned, the silence suppression procedure is defined in the Annex B (Benyassine et al., 1997; ITU-T Rec. G.729, 1996b). In this case, each SID packet has a length of 15 bits. However, the time interval between two successive SID packets is not fixed: in fact, for a good quality at the receiver, a lower or a greater transmission rate may be needed depending on the specific background noise observed in each environment.

In order to allow the derivation of meaningful results, SID packets are here supposed to be generated with a fixed rate during silences, as with AMR. In particular, the rate of G.729 SID packets is assumed to be twice the one adopted by AMR, following the results provided in (Estepa et al., 2005).

In the following, the activity factor ν is defined as the ratio between the time during which full packets are generated and the total duration of the conversation. Thus, in particular, we will adopt $\nu = 1$ when no silence suppression is activated and $\nu < 1$ in the case of silence suppression.

Table 2. Codec parameters and analytical calculation of maximum number of allowed users. Multiple values refer to UGS/ertPS.

Codec	B[bits]	ρ [pack/s]	BSID [bits]	ρSID [pack/s]	ν	Maximum number of allowed users	
						Mode 0	Mode 6
G.711	1280	50	-	-	1	20 /	87 /
G.729	160	50	-	-	1	58 /	233 /
G.729ss	160	50	15	12.5	0.45	58 / 90	233 / 482
AMR4.75	113	50	-	-	1	63 /	233 /

AMR4.75ss	113	50	54	6.25	0.45	63 / 111	233 / 506
AMR12.2	262	50	-	-	1	50 /	175 /
AMR12.2ss	262	50	54	6.25	0.45	50 / 90	175 / 374

In the latter case, in order to derive a realistic value of ν, we simulated the dynamic of a con- versation according to a detailed model that takes into account also periods of simultaneous talks or silences of the two parties, and the short gaps through the speeches (Stern et al., 1996). This model gives a 33% of voice activity over the total conversation duration for each of the two parties. It must be noted, however, that since 8 full packets are still transmitted dur- ing the hangover period, the activity factor ν is approximately 0.45; please note that this value corresponds to both our simulations and the experimental results given in (Estepa et al., 2005). As for the less sophisticated G.711 codec, here it was considered only as a reference, and no silence suppression is introduced.

The parameters of all considered codecs, with and without silence suppression, are given in the first four columns of table 2. In particular: the first column indicates the considered codecs (the subscript ss indicates that silence suppression is considered); the second column defines the number of bits B of full packets and the number of full packets per second ρ that are transmitted when the voice is detected; similarly, the third column defines the number of bits BSID of SID packets and the number ρSID of SID packets per second that are transmitted when silences are detected; finally, the fourth column represents the activity factor ν; the rest of the table will be illustrated in the following.

6.3 Amount of supported VoIP users

In this section, the number of VoIP users that can be served will be evaluated as a function of the adopted codec x, the scheduling service k and the transmission mode j (all users are sup- posed to be served adopting the same mode). Also in this case we need to consider the whole packet processing from the application layer down to the transmission over the medium.

Before being transmitted, each packet generated by the codec must pass through the whole protocol pillar, thus increasing its size owing to the overheads introduced by each protocol layer. In particular, the RTP, UDP, IP and MAC layers overheads are added, which are, re- spectively, ORTP = 12 bytes, OUDP = 8 bytes, OIP = 20 bytes and OM = 10 bytes (thus,

OHL = ORTP + OUDP + OIP = 40 bytes). Assuming that no fragmentation is carried out from the application to the MAC layer, the size (in bytes) of full packets and SID packets generated by the codec x is given by:

$$S(x)ms = B(x)/8 + OHL + OM , \quad (21)$$

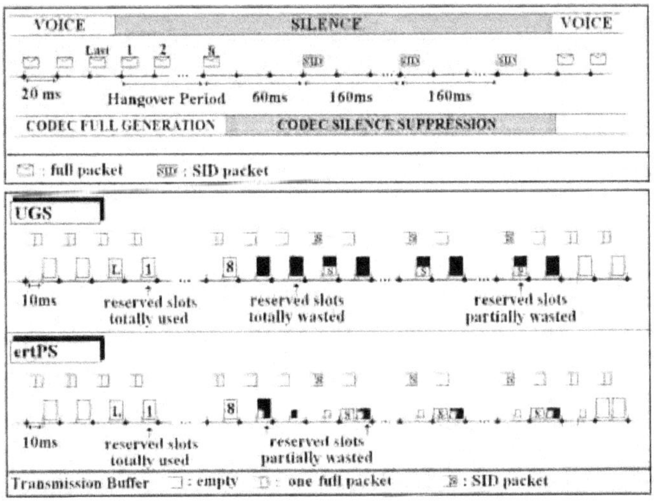

Fig. 8. Topmost part: AMR codec full packets and SID packets generation, with ρ = 50pack/s. Rest of the figure: buffer state and resource allocation of a generic uplink voice traffic flow with UGS and ertPS, following the packets generation depicted in the topmost part.

$$S^{(x)}_{MS_{SID}} = B^{(x)}_{SID}/8 + O_{HL} + O_{M} \;. \tag{22}$$

Of course, the ARQ mechanism is assumed inactive, since we are considering a real time service.

Let us recall (from section 6.2), now, that for a given codec x:

$$\nu^{(x)} = \frac{\textit{Time with full packets}}{\textit{Total conversation duration}} \tag{23}$$

is the activity factor, while

$$\rho^{(x)} = \frac{\textit{Number of full packets}}{\textit{Time with full packets}} \tag{24}$$

is the rate of transmission of full packets (of B(x)bits) during voice activity and

$$\rho^{(x)}_{SID} = \frac{\textit{Number of SID packets}}{\textit{Time without full packets}} \tag{25}$$

is the rate of transmission of SID packets (of BSID(x) bits) during silences, if silence suppression is considered.

As already recalled each packet to be transmitted is mapped onto OFDMA-slots, thus, in order to assess the maximum number of users that can be served, the number of slots that are needed for each packet must be firstly calculated, also considering that the number SSI(j) of bytes carried by one slot depends on the adopted mode j (see table B of figure 1).

In particular, for a given codec x and a given transmission mode j, the number $N^{(x,j)}_{SI\leftarrow MS}$ of slots needed to carry a full packet and the number $N^{(x,j)}_{SI\leftarrow MS_{SID}}$ of slots needed to carry a SID

packet are:

$$N^{(x,j)}_{SI\leftarrow MS} = \left\lceil \frac{S^{(x)}_{MS}}{S^{(j)}_{SI}} \right\rceil, \tag{26}$$

$$N^{(x,j)}_{SI\leftarrow MS_{SID}} = \left\lceil \frac{S^{(x)}_{MS_{SID}}}{S^{(j)}_{SI}} \right\rceil. \tag{27}$$

Depending on the considered scheduling service k and the specific VoIP codec x, the average number of slots required in a given (DL/UL) subframe by a single user adopting mode j, is given by:

$$M^{(x,k,j)}_{SI\leftarrow U} = f^{(x,k)}\left(N^{(x,j)}_{SI\leftarrow MS}, N^{(x,j)}_{SI\leftarrow MS_{SID}}\right), \tag{28}$$

where the analytical expression of f (x,k)( ) will be provided in the following for both the considered scheduling services.

As a general consideration, please note that all difficulties in resource allocation are on the uplink, since the base station has a perfect knowledge of all buffers in the downlink and no resource requests are needed. For this reason, and assuming that AFsl ≥ 1 (that is, we have more downlink slots than uplink slots), all evaluations will be done focusing on the uplink direction. Thus, given an amouvnt NSlul of available slots (in the uplink subframe), the maximum number NUMAX of users can finally be evaluated:

$$N^{(x,k,j)}_{U_{MAX}} = \left\lfloor \frac{N_{SI_{ul}}}{M^{(x,k,j)}_{SI\leftarrow U}} \right\rfloor. \tag{29}$$

Performance on UGS. Since UGS resources are statically allocated, as negotiated during con- nection setup, the silence suppression procedure does not provide any benefit in the uplink direction.

Denoting with TF the frame duration, (28) becomes:

$$M^{(x,UGS,j)}_{SI\leftarrow U} = T_F\left(\rho^{(x)} \cdot N^{(x,j)}_{SI\leftarrow MS}\right), \tag{30}$$

Please note that there is no dependence on the activity factor (some resources will be wasted if ν(x) < 1).

Combining (30) and (29) the maximum number N(x,UGS,j) of VoIP users supported by the UGS scheduling service can be easily derived.

Performance on ertPS. In the case of ertPS scheduling service, besides the adopted codec x and transmission mode j, also the activity factor v(x) must be considered in order to derive the amount of supported VoIP users. After the hangover period, in fact, the transmission rate is reduced and a single slot is allocated (NSl MH = 1) in order to allow the transmission of a stand-alone MAC signaling header for a quick modification of the resources request (see figure 8). Please note, by the way, that, although reduced, this allocation entails a resource wasting, since no transmission is performed in the most of cases. Resource wasting will occur also at any rate reduction (refer to figure 8): before a rate decreases, in fact, the request is sent in the uplink using an oversized resource.

Let us observe, furthermore, that following a rate increase request, the first (larger) resource is allocated in the subsequent frame, without respecting the normal rate of allocation, in order to reduce the latency.

In the case of ertPS scheduling service, therefore, in order to calculate $M_{SI\leftarrow U}^{(x,ertPS,j)}$ we must take into account:

- the slots needed for full packets, that are generated with rate $\rho^{(x)}$ during active voice periods: $R \cdot N_{SI\leftarrow MS}^{(x,j)}$ average slots per second, where $R = \nu^{(x)} \cdot \rho^{(x)}$ indicates the average number of full packets per second;
- the slots needed for SID packets, that are generated with rate $\rho_{SID}^{(x)}$ during silent periods: $R_{SID} \cdot N_{SI\leftarrow MS_{SID}}^{(x,j)}$ average slots per second, where $R_{SID} = (1-\nu^{(x)}) \cdot \rho_{SID}^{(x)}$ indicates the average number of SID packets per second,
- the slots needed for stand-alone MAC headers, allocated with rate $\rho^{(x)}$ when neither full packets nor SID packets are generated: $R_{MH} \cdot N_{SI\leftarrow MH}$ average slots per second, where $R_{MH} = 1 - R - R_{SID}$; indicates the average number of slots left for MAC headers per second, transmitted at the same rate;
- the slots that are wasted during variations from full packets allocation to stand-alone MAC headers allocations: $R_{CFG} \cdot N_{SI\leftarrow MS}^{(x,j)}$ average slots per second, where $R_{CFG} = \frac{1}{T_{CFG}^{av}+T_{CSS}^{av}}$ indicates the average number of uninterrupted periods of full packets per second, that depends on the average duration of a period of continuous full packets generation by the codec (T_{CFG}^{av}) and on the average duration of a period of silence suppression with SID packets generation (T_{CSS}^{av});
- the slots that are wasted during variations from SID packets to stand-alone MAC headers: $R_{SID} \cdot N_{SI\leftarrow MS_{SID}}^{(x,j)}$ average slots per second.

Thus, in this case, $M_{SI\leftarrow U}^{(x,ertPS,j)}$ is given by:

$$M_{SI\leftarrow U}^{(x,ertPS,j)} = T_F\left((R+R_{CFG}) \cdot N_{SI\leftarrow MS}^{(x,j)} + 2 \cdot R_{SID} \cdot N_{SI\leftarrow MS_{SID}}^{(x,j)} + R_{MH} \cdot N_{SI\leftarrow MH}\right), \quad (31)$$

Concerning the parameters Tav*CFG* and Tav*CSS*, please note that they are not only related to the adopted codec, but also to the characteristics of the specific conversation, also including, as an example, the language; in order to derive meaningful results, hereafter we adopted the values reported in (Stern et al., 1996) (Tav = 0.17s and Tav = 0.3428s), although they are related to the voice-silence intervals rather than to codec full generation-codec silence suppression (they do not consider the hangover periods); for this reason, a slight underestimation of the maximum number of VoIP users is expected in the numerical results.

Finally, combining (31) and (29), the maximum number N(x,ertPS,j) of VoIP users supported by the ertPS scheduling service can be easily derived.

6.4 Numerical results

For the numerical results derivation, the amount of OFDMA-slots available for data transmis- sion in the downlink subframe has been assumed equal to NSlul = 350; this value is a con- sequence of the same assumption reported in section 5.1: BW = 7 MHz, NFFT =2048 OFDM subcarriers, normalized OFDM guard interval G = 1/32, frame duration TF = 10 ms (which is the most suited value for VoIP traffic allocation); 15 of the 31 OFDM symbols of each frame are left for uplink data, adopting UL-PUSC (the rest of the symbols are used for the uplink common channels and the downlink subframe).

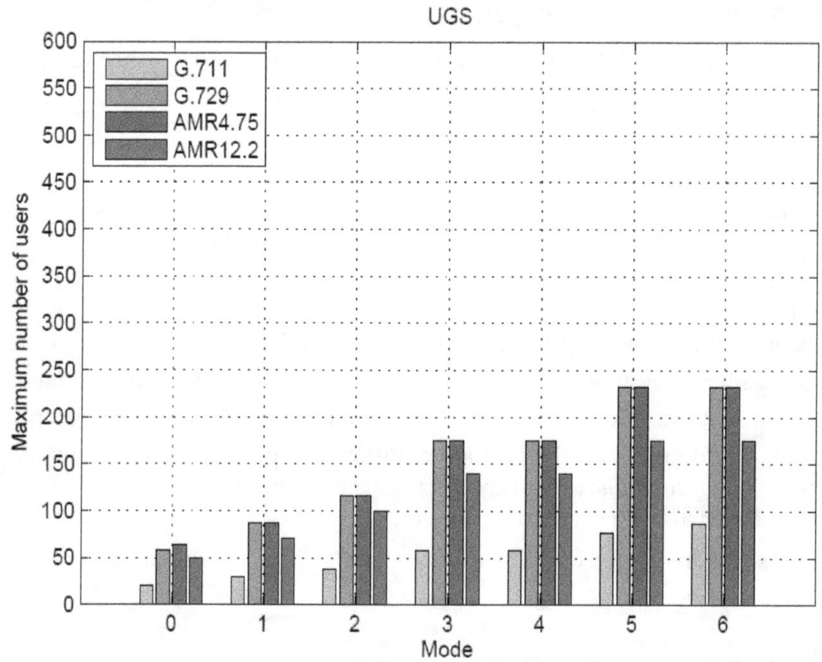

Fig. 9. Maximum number of users using UGS scheduling service. All modes. All VoIP codecs without silence suppression.

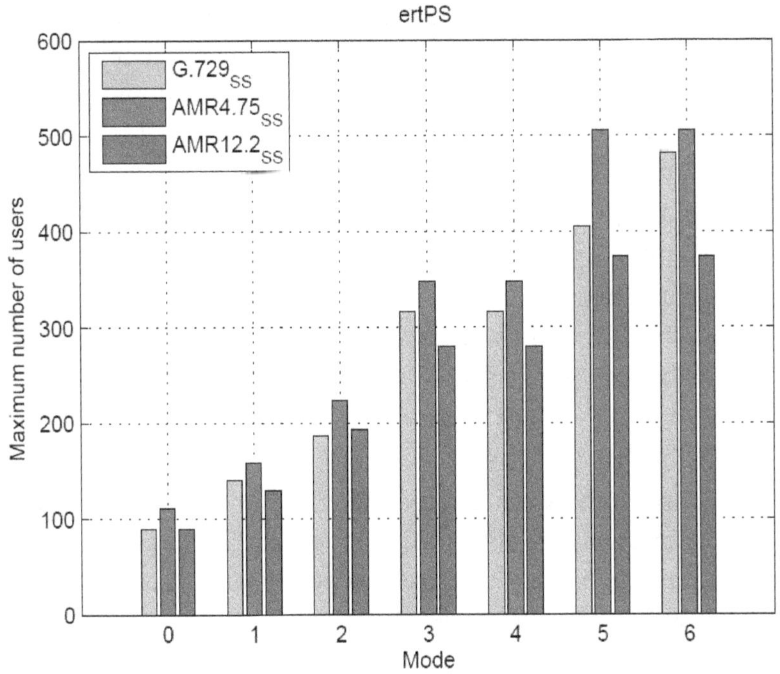

Fig. 10. Maximum number of users using ertPS scheduling services. All modes. All VoIP codecs with silence suppression.

In the last column of table 2 the maximum number of VoIP users that can be served with UGS and ertPS (separated by the symbol "/") are reported for each codec; modes 0 and 6 are considered. Two underscores are typed when the adoption of that scheduling service makes no sense with that codec (i.e., ertPS with no silence suppression).

The maximum amount of VoIP users that can be supported is shown for all modes in figures 9 and 10 focusing on UGS and ertPS, respectively. Obviously, the VoIP capacity adopting UGS with and without silence suppression is always the same; for this reason the results related to the case of silence suppression are not reported in figure 9.

It can be observed that, as expected, VoIP capacity is strictly related to the average data rate generated by the codec.

Comparing figures 9 and 10 we can also appreciate the significant benefit provided by the adoption of the ertPS instead of UGS.

7. CONCISE SUMMARY

The efficacy of IEEE802.16e WirelessMAN-OFDMA is contingent upon numerous system characteristics and implementation decisions, including, but not limited to, available bandwidth, frame duration, uplink/downlink traffic imbalance, and fragmentation policy.

In the preceding sections, we presented an analytical framework for assessing the throughput attainable with TCP/IP connections and the number of supported VoIP users, based on the most critical criteria defining this technology. In addition to the derivation of the analytical model, we have offered criteria, equations, and algorithms to optimize decisions from the perspective of system efficiency.

Additionally, certain numerical findings were presented, demonstrating the influence of particular parameters on system performance. Regarding TCP/IP connections, the challenging decision of the maximum size of ARQ blocks has been examined, along with the possible resource inefficiency resulting from an incorrect selection of the asymmetry factor between downlink and uplink subframes. The primary result of this analysis is a set of criteria designed to optimize the throughput delivered to the end user.

Regarding VoIP connections, we evaluated the maximum user capacity, meticulously considering the characteristics of the voice codec and the implemented scheduling service. The results of this study indicate the potential of this technology to serve as an alternative to other technologies, such as UMTS and LTE, for voice service providing.

In conclusion, the analytical approach presented in this chapter serves as a tool to assess the top limits of throughput and the maximum number of VoIP users that IEEE802.16e WirelessMAN-OFDMA can accommodate. To examine the actual performance of this complex technology in a specific scenario, accounting for degradation factors such as fading, shadowing, noise, and interference, the most viable approach is to utilize a simulation tool capable of meticulously replicating all facets of communication, particularly concerning the behavior of the physical layer.

This analysis has been conducted at WiLab (Italy) utilizing the SHINE simulation platform, which has been created in recent years to evaluate the performance of wireless networks in realistic circumstances. The inquisitive reader may consult (Andrisano et al., 2007; 2009; Bazzi et al., 2006).

APPENDIX I

Here we illustrate the algorithm that allows to maximize symbols usage starting from the number of useful symbols NUSy = NSy – NOSydl – NOSyul .

The following steps must be followed:

1. derive J = Resul = mod(NUSy, NGSul);
2. find, if possible:

$$a = \min_{a \in \left[0, \lfloor \frac{N_{USy}}{N_{GS_{ul}}} \rfloor\right]} \text{ so that } mod(J + a \cdot N_{GS_{ul}}, N_{GS_{dl}}) = 0. \quad (32)$$

3. if a was not found, then reduce J by one and return to step 2, else exit.

The obtained value a and the parameter J allow the derivation of the minimum value for NSydl ($N_{Sy_{dl}}^{MIN}$)that maximally reduces the symbols wasting:

$$N_{Sy_{dl}}^{MIN} = J + a \cdot N_{GS_{ul}}, \tag{33}$$

All possible solutions will be:

$$N_{Sy_{dl}}^{OPT}(b) = N_{Sy_{dl}}^{MIN} + b \cdot mcm(N_{GS_{ul}}, N_{GS_{dl}}), \tag{34}$$

where $b \in \left[0, \lfloor \frac{N_{USy} - N_{Sy_{dl}}^{MIN}}{N_{GS_{dl}}} \rfloor \right]$ and $mcm(x, y)$ is the minimum common multiplier of x and y.

It follows:

$$N_{Sy_{ul}}^{OPT}(b) = N_{USy} - (Res_{ul} - J) - N_{Sy_{dl}}^{OPT}(b). \tag{35}$$

and

$$AF_{SI}(b) = \frac{N_{SI_{dl}}^{OPT}(b)}{N_{SI_{ul}}^{OPT}(b)}. \tag{36}$$

Finally, we can choose the value of b that brings to the $AF_{SI}(b)$ nearer to AF_{in}.

FOOTNOTES

1. Data regions must be squared or rectangular.

REFERENCES

1. 3GPP TS 26.071 (2008). Mandatory speech codec speech processing functions; amr speech codec; general description.
2. 3GPP TS 26.092 (2008). Mandatory speech codec speech processing functions; adaptive multi- rate (amr) speech codec; comfort noise aspects.
3. Ahmadi, S. (2009). An overview of next-generation mobile wimax technology, IEEE Commu- nications Magazine Vol.47(n.6): pp.84–98.
4. Andrisano, O., Bazzi, A., Leonardi, G. & Pasolini, G. (2007). Ieee802.16e best effort perfor- mance investigation, Proceedings of IEEE International Conference on Communications, 2007 (ICC 2007), IEEE, Glasgow, Scotland, pp. 4837–4842.
5. Andrisano, O., Bazzi, A., Leonardi, G. & Pasolini, G. (2009). Ieee802.16e simulation issues, Proceedings of IEEE Mobile WiMAX Symposium 2009 (MWS 2009), IEEE, Napa Valley, California, pp. –.
6. Bazzi, A., Gambetti, C. & Pasolini, G. (2006). Shine: Simulation platform for heterogeneous in- terworking networks, Proceedings of IEEE International Conference on Communications, 2006 (ICC 2006), IEEE, Istanbul, Turkey, pp. 5534–5539.

7. Benyassine, A., Shlomot, E. & Su, H. (1997). Itu-t recommendation g.729 annex b: a silence compression scheme for use with g.729 optimized for v.70 digital simultaneous voice and data applications., IEEE Communications Magazine Vol.35(Issue 9): pp.64–73.
8. Cimini, J. (1985). Analysis and simulation of a digital mobile channel using orthogonal fre- quency division multiplexing., IEEE Trans. Comm. Vol.COM-33(n.7): pp.665–675.
9. Estepa, R., Vozmediano, J. & Estepa, A. (2005). Accurate prediction of voip traffic mean bit rate., ELECTRONICS LETTERS Vol.41(n.17): pp.985–987.
10. Goode, B. (2002). Voice over internet protocol (voip), Proceedings of the IEEE Vol.90(n.9): pp.1495–1517.
11. IEEE Std 802.16-2004 (2004). Ieee standard for local and metropolitan area networks part 16: Air interface for fixed broadband wireless access systems.
12. IEEE Std 802.16e-2005 (2006). Ieee std 802.16eZ′ -2005 and ieee std 802.16Z′ -2004/cor1-2005 ieee standard for local and metropolitan area networks part 16: Air interface for fixed and mobile broadband wireless access systems amendment 2: Physical and medium access control layers for combined fixed and mobile operation in licensed bands and corrigendum 1.
13. ITU-T Rec. G.711 (1988). Pulse code modulation (pcm) of voice frequencies.
14. ITU-T Rec. G.729 (1996a). Coding of speech at 8kbit/s using conjugate-structure algebraic- code-excited linear-predictive (cs-acelp)coding.
15. ITU-T Rec. G.729, A. (1996b). A silence compression scheme for g.729 optimized for terminals conforming to itu-t v.70.
16. Lee, H., Kwon, T., Cho, D., Lim, G. & Chang, Y. (2006). Performance analysis of scheduling algorithms for voip services in ieee 802.16e systems, Proceedings of IEEE Vehicular Technology Conference (VTC 2006-Spring)., IEEE, Melbourne, Australia, pp. 1231–1235.
17. Li, Q., Lin, X., Zhang, J. & Roh, W. (2009). Advancement of mimo technology in wimax: from ieee 802.16d/e/j to 802.16m, IEEE Communications Magazine Vol.47(n.6): pp.100–107.
18. Stern, H., Mahmoud, S. & Wong, K. (1996). A comprehensive model for voice activity in conversational speech-development and application to performance analysis of new- generation wireless communication systems, Wireless Networks Vol.2(n.4): pp.359– 367.
19. Van Nee, R. & Prasad, R. (2000). OFDM for Wireless Multimedia Communications, Artech House

www.ingramcontent.com/pod-product-compliance
Lightning Source LLC
LaVergne TN
LVHW081941200926
848484LV00009B/2491